P9-DXN-290

MASS LEISURE

MASS LEISURE

EDITED BY *Eric Larrabee*

AND *Rolf Meyersohn*

THE FREE PRESS

GLENCOE, ILLINOIS

PRINTED IN THE UNITED STATES OF AMERICA
DESIGNED BY SIDNEY SOLOMON
LIBRARY OF CONGRESS CATALOG CARD NO. 58-9397

CONTENTS

4. THE RUNAWAY WEEKEND—MASS LEISURE

Introduction

THIS BOOK is called *Mass Leisure,* not only to form a bond with its companion volume, *Mass Culture,* but to emphasize its aims and limits. We are primarily concerned with leisure as a social phenomenon in the modern world, especially in America—with, if you like, leisure as a "problem." There are many absurd aspects to this, not least of them that it provokes anxiety over a subject traditionally associated with ease and relaxation. This paradox is in fact one of our major themes.

There are many kinds of people, in the first place, for whom leisure as a social phenomenon simply does not exist. Even in our own leisure-conscious culture we continually encounter individuals who cannot play, whose every waking moment is for work, and whose life-span is barely enough to enclose their furious exertions. For most of humanity, moreover, caught in an iron round of toil and poverty, leisure has been either unavailable or indefinable as such. Where tradition rules, time empty of obligation is empty of everything else; there is literally nothing to do with it, and the peon sleeping in the sun is the perfect image of the man with free time but no leisure. And in the Orient, where men have made a virtue of transcending the human lot through inactivity, there least of all does leisure in our sense exist; the uses of time are exquisitely cultivated, yes, but in subordination to a contemplative, self-abnegating ideal which Westerners rarely share. Leisure, for perhaps the majority of men and women, is thus no "problem."

If, on the other hand, one considers leisure (as we do) to be deeply connected with the cultivation of the self, then here too there are absurdities. For those who were educated in this assumption, like ourselves, it will seem self-evident that the highest ends of mankind are advanced by the leisure activities commonly considered to make up "high culture"—music, literature, the arts, elegant food and conversation. This proposition, once stated, leaves little more to be said; it is a complete program in itself, and one with many advantages, such as open-endedness (no matter how long we saw away, we will never be Heifetz, and there are consolations in this). High culture, as many of our contributors aver, is what leisure is all about, but it is not what this book is about. We have therefore had to pay only scant attention to the very area in which a "solution" can be found, and less respect than we would have liked to those (quoting Stephen Botsford of the *New Yorker*) whose idea of happiness is eating *pate de foie gras* to the sound of trumpets.

Our subject is the leisure which has become available, on an increasing scale, to the populations of the modern, industrial West. Since these are societies mainly oriented to work, leisure is seen in contrast to it; and, since they are prosperous and productive, leisure is not only time free but time paid for. Something can be done with it. That is why "leisure" in the current meaning has taken on the complexities of choice, and become problematical. Not only is the individual confronted with choices, but there are so many of him that society's choice becomes even more exigent. What to do with Mass Leisure can become an agonizing question.

Yet it may not be taken seriously. The study of play has suffered from the notion that frivolity might rub off on it, or that frivolous behavior is inherently lacking in significance. This volume is an attempt to counter that impression. What we have tried to show are the possibilities open to serious consideration of leisure, and what we have tried to assemble are representative examples of material and technique. Much of the territory is still unexplored; there are enormous gaps that will be evident to the casual reader as well as to the student in search of unplowed fields. But we, as editors, are especially concerned that this sketchiness of plan should not be taken as lessening the size or importance of the area it covers. We share the most earnest conviction that on the uses and misuses of leisure will hinge much that is good and evil in coming years and, indeed, several of our authors raise dismal forebodings that we cannot wholly dispel.

Within those limits we have hoped to make this a cheerful book, or at least to give it some of the qualities of irreverence and folly that mass leisure, in practice, has presented. We have in some cases drawn on the literature of elite or aristocratic leisure where there have been useful anticipations, and we have given a place (perhaps, as noted above, too small a one) to the school of thought which treats leisure, if only for a minority, as a necessary condition of the civilized life. (Since the burden of consuming leisure for others may be more onerous than one expects, we have deliberately included examples of "Society" going wrong in that endeavor.) Limitations of space have been severe, and in one or two instances we have been prevailed upon to omit selections only because they could be found elsewhere so easily. For example, the third chapter of Veblen's *The Theory of the Leisure Class* most assuredly belongs here, but it is almost ubiquitously available in inexpensive reprint form.

For the preparation of the index we are indebted to Miss Alice M. Bettis. This is a publication of the Center for the Study of Leisure, established at the University of Chicago under a grant from the Behavioral Sciences Division of the Ford Foundation.

ERIC LARRABEE
ROLF MEYERSOHN

New York, N. Y.
Chicago, Illinois.
July 1958.

1 When Does Time Become Leisure?

What is leisure? The very meaning of the word has changed continually. At times it has referred to a state of freedom, an absence of obligations, a cluster of activities; at others, it has suggested a mood of contemplation. A full page from the Oxford English Dictionary illuminates the transformations of the term.

"Leisure" was once identifiable as a problem of the leisure class—as a product of individual *effort or exploitation (one's own or someone else's), as the definition of the Encyclopedia of the Social Sciences points out. Today's leisure, however, is rather a product of* social *change and may lead to a collective self-appraisal—rather than class-conscious criticisms. Margaret Mead provides one such appraisal, and throughout the book others are presented.*

The historical context of "leisure-" and "working-classes" has left an indelible imprint. Even current discussion of leisure revolves mainly around its relation to work. Here is a selection: Aldous Huxley shows that leisure is not simply non-work; Herbert Collins contends that sitting down must not be confused with taking it easy; Clive Bell assumes opposition of work and leisure to build his utopian scheme; and Clement Greenberg deplores the tendency to pit work against leisure.

Later in this section Richard D. Altick and Foster Rhea Dulles make explicit what the "historical context" of leisure is. Altick describes what may be considered the proper birthplace of mass leisure and show us how urban habits in nineteenth-century England, particularly, the growth of mass literacy, led to its development, and Dulles depicts the shrinking of rural entertainment in America.

"Leisure," According to the Oxford English Dictionary

a 1540 BARNES *Wks.* (1573) 358/2 If thou wilt leasurably lysten and beholde to the ende of the tragedye. 1658 SIR T. MAYERNE *Receipts Cookery* cxl. 90 Let it boyl leasurably. 1695 BP. ROCHESTER *Disc. Clergy* 13 Setting forth the public Prayers to all their due Advantage, by pronouncing them leasurably, fitly, warmly, decently. 1806 *Med. Jrnl.* XV. 172 Let him speak leisurably. 1889 *Longm. Mag.* June 164 He..pricked leisurably down the slope.

Leisure (le·ʒiŭɹ, lī·ʒiŭɹ). Forms: 4 **leisere, leysir,** *Sc.* **lasere,** 4–5 **leiser, leysere,** *Sc.* **lasair,** 4–6 **laiser, layser, leyser,** *Sc.* **laser, -are,** 5 **laisir, -our, -ure, laysar, -ir, leyzer, -soure, lesure,** 5–6 **leysar,** *Sc.* **lasar,** 6 **laisere, -ure, layso(u)r, -ure, leisar, -our, leaser, -our, leesar, leser, leysour(e, leys(s)or,** *Sc.* **laseir, lasar, lazar, laisar,** 5–7 **leysure,** 6–8 **leasure,** 7 **liesure, leizure,** 6– **leisure.** [a. OF. *leisir* (mod.F. *loisir*), subst. use of the infinitive *leisir*, repr. L. *licēre* to be permitted.

In Fr. the word has undergone much the same development of sense as in Eng.]

†**1.** Freedom or opportunity to do something specified or implied. *Obs.*

1303 R. BRUNNE *Handl. Synne* 28 Þe seruyng man þat serueþ yn þe ȝere Oweþ to come when he haþ leysere. *c* 1330 — *Chron.* (1810) 229 Whan þou sees leysere, þat he ne perceyue þi witte.. with þe knyfe him to smite. ?*a* 1366 CHAUCER *Rom. Rose* 462 No more was there..To clothe her with.. Gret leyser hadde she to quake. *c* 1386 — *Miller's T.* 107 She wol been at his comandement, Whan that she may hir leyser wel espie. *c* 1400 *Destr. Troy* 3119 Þai hade laisure at lust þere likyng to say. *c* 1440 *Promp. Parv.* 295/2 Leysere, *oportunitas*. *c* 1489 CAXTON *Blanchardyn* xliii. 169 Sadoyne folowed hym of so nyghe..that with grete peyne gaf them leyser to saue hem self. 1500–20 DUNBAR *Poems* ix. 8, I cry the mercy, and lasar to repent. 1513 DOUGLAS *Æneis* IV. x. 83 Quhy will thow nocht fle spedely be nycht, Quhen for to haist thow hes laisar and mycht? *a* 1533 LD. BERNERS *Huon* xci. 291 Huon mette with hym so hastly that he had no layser to stryke hym. 1640 BP. HALL *Chr. Moder.* I. viii. 75 The Jewes..hold, that after twenty yeares of age, who so finds (the lezer) in himselfe, is bound under paine of sin to marry.

†**b.** An opportunity. *Obs.*

c 1386 CHAUCER *Sqr.'s T.* 485 Whil þat I haue a leyser and a space Myn harm I wol confessen. 1390 GOWER *Conf.* II. 95 If so is, that I may hent Somtime amonge a good leiser. *Ibid.* II. 242 That she with him had [= might have] a leiser To speke and telle of her desir. 14.. *Epiph.* in *Tundale's Vis.* (1843) 116 They haue a leysar found To take hor leyve. 1412–20 LYDG. *Chron. Troy* I. v, Euer eft on him she cast an eye Whan that she founde a leyser opportune. 1430–40 — *Bochas* IX. xxxiii. (1554) 212 b, To their entent a leysure they did spie.

2. In narrower sense: Opportunity afforded by freedom from occupations.

c 1375 *Sc. Leg. Saints* iii. (*St. Andrew*) 999 Waitand bot lasare quhen he mycht purchess oportunitie. 1375 BARBOUR *Bruce* XX. 234 Gif God will me gif Laser and space so lange till liff. *c* 1400 MAUNDEV. (Roxb.) xxx. 137, I.. saw all þis ..and mykill mare þan I hafe layser for to tell. 1489 CAXTON *Faytes of A.* I. xxii. 70 Noo layser they had to putte hem self in ordynaunce. 1526 TINDALE *Mark* iii. 20 They had nott leesar so moche as to eate breed. 1553 T. WILSON *Rhet.* Ep. A ij, I traveyled so muche as my leasure myghte serve therunto. 1599 SHAKS. *Much Ado* III. ii. 84 If your leisure seru'd, I would speake with you. 1667 MILTON *P. L.* x. 510 He wonderd, but not long Had leasure, wondring at himself now more. 1712 ADDISON *Spect.* No. 418 ¶ 5 It does not give us Time or Leisure to reflect on ourselves. 1791 MRS. RADCLIFFE *Rom. Forest* ii, They had leisure to laugh at their late terrors. 1857 BUCKLE *Civiliz.* I. ii. 38 As long as every man is engaged in collecting the materials necessary for his own subsistence, there will be neither leisure nor taste for higher pursuits.

b. Duration of opportunity; time allowed before it is too late. Now *rare*.

1553 BALE *Vocacyon* 41 More than .xxvj. dayes of layser for the payment therof [of the ransom] might not be graunted. 1555 EDEN *Decades* 100 That Tumanama..myght haue no leasure to assemble an armye. 1603 KNOLLES *Hist. Turks* (1621) 1331 The Turkes had scarce leasure to leape to land, and to flie into the country. 1781 GIBBON *Decl. & F.* xxxi. III. 259 The unfortunate youth had scarcely leisure to deplore the elevation of his family. 1818 JAS. MILL *Brit. India* II. v. v. 547 The authority of the government of Batavia, for whose sanction there was no leisure to wait. 1828 SCOTT *F. M. Perth* xxix, He found himself unexpectedly in Eachin's close neighbourhood, with scarce leisure to avoid him. 1846 J. BAXTER *Libr. Pract. Agric.* (ed. 4) I. 383 The young blades in the field have leisure to expand and grow again before the scythe returns to cut them down a second time.

3. The state of having time at one's own disposal; time which one can spend as one pleases; free or unoccupied time.

13.. *K. Alis.* 234 Heo thougte heo wolde him y-here, Whan heo was of more leisere. 1479 in *Eng. Gilds* (1870) 413, I.. praye [them]..at theire ceasons of leysoure to rede ..this present boke. *c* 1540 GARDINER in Strype *Cranmer* II. (1694) 75 To spend some of my laysor to wryte..to your G[race] who hath lesse laysor. 1576 FLEMING *Panopl. Epist.* 255 To the perfourmance of such an enterprise, much leasure and labour is required. *c* 1600 SHAKS. *Sonn.* xxxix, Oh absence what a torment wouldst thou proue Were it not thy soure leisure gaue sweet leaue To entertaine the time with thoughts of loue. 1672 TEMPLE *Ess. Govt.* Wks. 1731 I. 97 Where Ambition and Avarice have made no Entrance, the Desire of Leisure is much more Natural, than of Business and Care. 1780 JOHNSON *Let. to Mrs. Thrale* 25 Aug., I am not grown, I am afraid, less idle; and of idleness I am now paying the fine by having no leisure. 1830 D'ISRAELI *Chas. I*, III. vi. 91 Charles commanded his Lordship to employ some of his leisure in a dramatic composition. 1887 RUSKIN *Præterita* II. 143 The first volume of 'Modern Painters' took the best of the winter's leisure.

personified. 1632 MILTON *Penseroso* 49 And adde to these retired Leasure, That in trim Gardens takes his pleasure.

b. In particularized sense: A period or spell of unoccupied time. Now *rare*.

c 1449 PECOCK *Repr.* II. xv. 236 That thei go in pilgrimage thanne or in sum other leiser which thei wolen to hem silf point. *a* 1535 FISHER *Wks.* (E. E. T. S.) 432 To spare a leysoure for hym to here the bottom of his mynde. 1597 MORLEY *Introd. Mus.* 115, I will then take my leaue of you for this time, till my next leisure. 1654 R. CODRINGTON tr. *Iustine* I. 2 In the leisures which in this City I enjoyed. 1856 EMERSON *Eng. Traits, Lit.* Wks. (Bohn) II. 110 It is because he [Bacon] had imagination, [and] the leisures of the spirit..that he is impressive to the imaginations of men. 1873 LOWELL *Among my Bks.* Ser. II. 181 In keeping with that sense of endless leisures which it is one chief merit of the poem to suggest.

c. *To tarry, attend or stay* (*upon*) *a person's leisure*: to wait until he is unoccupied; to wait his time. Also *fig. arch.*

1517 in Ellis *Orig. Lett.* Ser. I. II. 4 *note*, If ye be not contente to tary my Leysure, departe when ye wille. 1535 COVERDALE *Ps.* xxvi[i]. 14 [16] O tary thou yͤ Lordes leysure. 1595 SHAKS. *John* II. i. 58 The aduerse windes Whose leisure I haue staid, haue giuen him time To land his Legions all as soone as I. 1596 — *Merch. V.* I. i. 68 Wee'll make our leysures to attend on yours. 1605 — *Macb.* I. iii. 148 Worthy Macbeth, wee stay vpon your leysure. 1656 JEANES *Fuln. Christ* 91 Not contented to wait the Lords Leisure.

†**4.** Leisureliness, deliberation. *Obs.*

a 1300 *Cursor M.* 29370 Þe toþer [case] es of dorward or porter..þat clerk wit laiser smites oght. 1450–80 *Secreta Secret.* 25 Ete with leyser and good masticacioun. 1486 *Surtees Misc.* (1888) 55 Sex kinges..with certaine convenient laisour, avisedly shall commyt a ceptour unto Salamon. 1563–7 BUCHANAN *Reform. St. Andros* Wks. (1892) 8 Tellyng..to thayme the lettres..in sik lasar that the barnis may easely writ eftyr his pronunciation. 1664 POWER *Exp. Philos.* II. 123 Much leisure and accurateness were used in filling the Tube. 1677 MARVELL *Corr.* cccvi. Wks. 1872–5 II. 563, I having presented him your letter, he read it with great leisure.

5. Phrases. a. *At leisure*: with free or unoccupied time at one's disposal; without haste, with deliberation. Also with qualifying adjs., as *all, best, convenient, full, less, more.*

c 1340 *Cursor M.* 7239 (Trin.) Hir tyme she toke a leiser þere And whil he slepte kut his here. 1375 BARBOUR *Bruce* V. 390 He.. sat and ete at all lasare. *c* 1386 CHAUCER *Pars. T.* ¶ 761 Som folk stonden of hir owene wyl to eten at the lasse leyser. 1444 *Pol. Poems* (Rolls) II. 219 Whoo hath no dyneer, at leyser must abyde, To staunche his hungir abyde upon his ffood. *c* 1450 *Merlin* 7 Go youre wey, and anothir tyme, we shall speke more at leyser. 1522 SKELTON *Why nat to Courte?* 622 My lorde is nat at layser. 1590 SHAKS. *Com. Err.* IV. i. 100, I will debate this matter at more leisure. 1598 *Epulario* H iv, And so let it bake at leisure, strawing Sugar..vpon it. 1613 HEYWOOD *Silver Age* I. i. Wks. 1874 III. 92 The full circumstance I shall relate at leasure. 1655 FULLER *Ch. Hist.* I. v. § 17 We for the present are well at Leisure, we will present the Reader with the Description of their severall Principalities. 1687 CONGREVE *Old Bach.* V. i. (1693) 50 Marry'd in Haste, we may repent at leisure. 1823 BYRON *Juan* XIII. vi, Men love in haste, but they detest at leisure.

Const. *for*; also *inf.* or a clause introduced by *that*.

1603 KNOLLES *Hist. Turks* (1621) 1250 They were not at liesure now to send such great forces as they had before used, into Hungarie. 1669 CLARENDON *Ess.* Tracts (1727) 95 We complain..of those who are in place and authority.. that they are never at leisure that we may speak to them. 1732 BERKELEY *Alciphr.* VI. § 20, I am not at leisure to peruse the learned writings of divines. 1852 MRS. STOWE *Uncle Tom's C.* vii, The dinner being now fairly sent in, the whole kitchen was at leisure to gossip with her. 1875 JOWETT *Plato* (ed. 2) V. 334 The wardens..shall be men of ability, and at leisure to take care of the public interest.

b. *At one's leisure*: when one has unoccupied time at one's disposal; at one's ease or convenience. Also with adjs. as in a.

1481 CAXTON *Godfrey* Prol. 5 To whom I humbly beseche, at theyr leyzer and playsyr, to see & here redde this symple book. 1483 — *G. de la Tour* D iv, Wherfore atte his beste leyser he shewed her his deceyuable purpos. *c* 1592 SHAKS. *Ven. & Ad.* 518 A thousand kisses buyes my heart from me, And pay them at thy leisure, one by one. 1601 — *Jul. C.* III. i. 5 Trebonius doth desire you to ore-read (At your best leysure) this his humble suite. 1605 — *Macb.* II. i. 24 At your kind'st leysure. 1605 — *Lear* II. iv. 232 Mend when thou can'st, be better at thy leisure. 1636 SANDERSON *Serm.* (1681) II. 48 [They] think they can continue in their sins.. and then repent of them and forsake them at their leasure, whensoever they list. 1901 KIPLING *Kim* in *Cassell's Mag.* Jan. 176/2 He would go to Umballa at his leisure.

†**c.** *By leisure* (also *by good leisure*): with deliberation, in a leisurely manner; at one's leisure; in course of time, by degrees; slowly. Also (= Gr. σχολῇ), barely, not at all. *Obs.*

c 1386 CHAUCER *Melib.* ¶ 65 Thilke Iuge is wys that soone vnderstondeth a matiere and Iuggeth by leyser. 1430-40 LYDG. *Bochas* (1544) Prol. 34 From the trueth shall I not remoue But on the substance, by good leysar abyde. *c* 1483 CAXTON *Dialogues* viii. 46 William the brusshemaker Selleth the brusshes by leyzer. 1522 MORE *De quat. Noviss.* Wks. 99/1 By the stuffing of his paunch so ful, it bringeth in by leysour, the dropsy [etc.]. 1555 in Strype *Eccl. Mem.* III. App. xxxiii. 87 Let him tary, and..work by leysure. 1588 SHAKS. *Tit. A.* I. i. 301 Ile trust by Leisure him that mocks me once. 1589 R. HARVEY *Pl. Perc.* (1590) 20 Though it take fire quickly, yet it takes light by leisure. 1607 COLLINS *Serm.* (1608) 41 He gaue order to Salomon to see to the execution of them by leasure. 1633 BP. HALL *Hard Texts* 1 Not all together and at once, nor in this perfect form, at first. but by leisure and degrees. *c* 1700 *To Celia* in *Coll. Poems* 54, I must to lengthen on the Pleasure, Dwell on thy Lips, and Kiss by leisure.

†**d.** *In (good) leisure*: at leisure. *Obs.*

c 1315 SHOREHAM 61 Ine leyser other in haste. *c* 1375 *Sc. Leg. Saints* iii. (*St. Andrew*) 904 Þe bischope .. made hym chifte In gud lasere to here hyr schrift. *Ibid.* xxix. (*Placidas*) 34 He þat..penance to do here wil begyne & in gud lasare mend his syne.

6. *attrib.* often passing into *adj.* **a.** Of periods of time: = Free, unoccupied; *occas.* compared with *more* and *most.* †**b.** Leisurely (*obs.*). **c.** Leisured.

1669 STURMY *Mariner's Mag.* IV. 161 Some will expect.. other sort of Questions..For them, and their leisure-time, I have inserted these .. following. 1673 O. WALKER *Educ.* (1677) 112 The product of his leasure hours. 1681 DRYDEN *Abs. & Achit.* 612 If any Leisure time he had from Pow'r. 1694 ATTERBURY *Serm.* (1723) I. 90 It did not establish it self like other kingdoms in a slow and leisure manner. 1712 ARBUTHNOT *John Bull* III. vii, In his leisure minutes, he was posting his books. 1742 *Lond. & Country Brew.* I. (ed. 4) 34 By the leisure Putting over the Bowls of Water, the Goodness of the Malt is the more extracted and washed out .. than if the Wort was drawn out hastily. 1772 *Ann. Reg.* 198 This was the most leisure time of the year. 1785 BURNS *To Jas. Smith* iv, Hae ye a leisure-moment's time To hear what's comin? 1809 CAMPBELL *Gertr. Wyom.* II. xiii, His leisure pace. 1841 CATLIN *N. Amer. Ind.* (1844) I. xxiv. 194 A more leisure occasion. 1845 *Athenæum* 1 Feb. 110 That the leisure classes are not more misled and perverted than they are. 1850 H. MILLER *Footpr. Creat.* (1874) 325 They are in part the fruits of a leisure fortnight spent this autumn. 1859 SMILES *Self-Help* x. (1860) 258 This is an advantage which the working classes..certainly possess over the leisure classes. 1875 JOWETT *Plato* (ed. 2) III. 249 Let us pass a leisure hour in story telling.

Leisured (le·ʒiuɹd), *a.* [f. LEISURE + -ED [2].]

1. Of time, action: Characterized or accompanied by leisure.

1631 HEYWOOD *2nd Pt. Faire Maid of W.* Ded., Wks. 1874 II. 2 Please you at any of your more leisured hours to vouchsafe the perusal of these slight papers. 1647 BOYLE *Let. to Hartlib* 8 Apr., Wks. 1772 I. Life 39 The particulars .. do not only ask a profound knowledge .. but likewise a leisured and a great multiplicity of reading. 1899 *Allbutt's Syst. Med.* VI. 56 A leisured and level life, free from excitement, hurry and physical exertion or fatigue.

2. Of persons: Having ample leisure, esp. in *the leisured classes.*

1794 *Gentl. Mag.* II. 1132 Foliage op'ning to the day Courts the leisur'd mortal's stray. 1848 MILL *Pol. Econ.* II. ii. § 4 (1876) 140 The services which a nation having leisured classes is entitled to expect from them. 1877 MORLEY *Crit. Misc.* Ser. II. 347 The leisured student. 1891 A. CALDECOTT *Eng. Coloniz.* 101 The absorption of energy in the making of fortunes has prevented the formation of any such leisured class.

Leisureful (le·ʒiuɹful), *a.* [f. LEISURE + -FUL.] **a.** Having abundant leisure. **b.** Leisurely.

c 1449 PECOCK *Repr.* V. xi. 541 If this present argument be take .. into depe leiserful consideracioun. 1553 GRIMALDE *Cicero's Offices* III. (1558) 114 He was neuer more leasurelesse than when he was leasurefull and neuer less alone than when he was all alone. 1883 MRS. MACQUOID *About Yorksh.* 63 A large, leisureful handwriting. 1885 — *Louisa* I. xii. 226 It always cost his easy, leisureful nature an effort.

Lei·sureless, *a.* [-LESS.] Having no leisure.

1536 LD. BUTLER in *St. Papers Hen. VIII*, II. 358 Being as nowe leyserles, I omytt moche other mater. 1553 [see LEISUREFUL]. 1877 RUSKIN *Fors Clav.* VII. 337 Making all Time leisureless. [Plato *Legg.* 831 C πάντα χρόνον ἄσχολον ποιεῖν.] 1901 H. ROBERTS *Chron. Cornish Gard.* Ded., To the gardenless, the leisureless toilers of the world.

Lei·sureliness. [f. LEISURELY *a.* + -NESS.] The quality or condition of being leisurely.

1829 *Blackw. Mag.* XXVI. 147, I thought you might have a leisureliness at tea-time. 1863 J. BROWN *Horæ Subs.* (ed. 3) 144 There was a fine leisureliness and vague stare. 1879 FARRAR *St. Paul* (1883) 133 The habitual leisureliness of Eastern travelling.

Leisurely (le·ʒiuɹli), *a.* [f. LEISURE + -LY [1].]

1. Of persons: Having leisure or unoccupied time; proceeding without haste.

1613 PURCHAS *Pilgrimage* (1614) 515 With these and manifold other antiquities, Gillius can best acquaint the more leasurely Reader. 1816 COLERIDGE *Lay Serm.* 318 The men of leisurely minds. 1824-9 LANDOR *Imag. Conv.* Wks. 1846 II. 236 The leisurely and rich agriculturist, who goeth out a-field after dinner.

2. Of actions or agents: Performed or operating at leisure or without haste; deliberate.

1604 E. G[RIMSTONE] *D'Acosta's Hist. Indies* VII. ii. 500 They spent fourescore yeares in this manner of leisurely travell, the which they might have done in a moneth. 1711 ADDISON *Spect.* No. 159 ¶ 4 Upon a more leisurely Survey of it. 1746 BERKELEY *Sec. Let. Tar-water* § 10 Wks. 1871 III. 475 The same medicine .. is a leisurely alterative in chronical disorders. 1875 J. H. BENNET *Winter Medit.* II. xix. 614 A leisurely journey across the south of France.

Lei·surely, *adv.* [f. as prec. + -LY [2].] At leisure, without haste; with deliberate or leisurely motion or action.

1486 *Bk. St. Albans* B iv b, Than softe and layserly fall oppon yowre kneys. 1526 *Pilgr. Perf.* (W. de W. 1531) 161 b, That he synge or saye his duty distinctly and leyserly. 1598 *Epulario* G j, Let it broile very wel and leisurely. 1670 MILTON *Hist. Brit.* Wks. 1738 II. 2 After the Flood, and the dispersing of Nations, as they journey'd leisurely from the East. 1796 MRS. GLASSE *Cookery* v. 53 Let it do leisurely, keep it basting. 1807 WORDSW. *Misc. Sonn.* I. xiv, A flock of sheep that leisurely pass by One after one.

"Leisure," According to the Encyclopedia of the Social Sciences

By IDA CRAVEN

PHILOSOPHY and the common judgment of mankind are at one in holding leisure among the chief goods of life. Although in common parlance and in general practise leisure, the opportunity for disinterested activity, tends to become confused with amusement or recreation, one means of its utilization, yet in the high evaluation generally placed on leisure there lies a confused recognition of what in philosophy becomes more explicit: "Wisdom cometh by opportunity of leisure," said the ancient prophet. For Aristotle there were three kindred ideas expressing the end of human life: theoretical wisdom, happiness and leisure. Leisure was more than the condition for the attainment of the other two; it represented the satisfaction of the truly disinterested interest, the achievement of understanding, which is man's highest goal.

For purposes of social analysis the concept is usually narrowed—and widened—to mean simply freedom from activities centering around the making of a livelihood. It is indeed a rather bitter paradox that leisure has come to have a connotation of loose relaxation and that the term leisure class carries an accent of opprobrium. Earlier periods would have been far more ready than the present to see even in certain pursuits which result in the gaining of a livelihood exercises in leisure. The artist, the scientist, the scholar, work at their art or science or research for their living; in another sense theirs is the privilege of constant leisure to devote themselves to what are for them the highest pursuits. The methods by which the artist and scholar were supported in older societies emphasized the latter aspect of their position, as the commercial payment for their services emphasizes the former aspect. One might say that the more nearly ideal the organization of society, the more perfectly would every individual's work be adapted to his abilities and the greater would be the number of people who enjoyed similar qualitative leisure through rather than outside of their work.

The very concept of leisure as contrasted with work is largely foreign to primitive societies. To every member of the community falls his share of labor and of play, his opportunity for participation in the important rites and mysteries. The orientation of life is physiologically as well as socially toward long periods of leisurely work interspersed with occasional periods of intense expenditure of energy. The separation of a priestly class marks the first step toward the development of groups privileged through the possession of leisure. The fact that the priest's activities are regarded by the

Reprinted from *The Encyclopedia of the Social Sciences*, Volume V, pp. 402-5, by permission of the publishers. (Copyright 1933 by The Macmillan Company.)

community as in the highest degree necessary to its survival in no way negates this interpretation. The social implications of the development become clearer when the priestly class multiplies beyond a point consistent with its spiritual functions and engages in governmental and scholarly pursuits. Concurrently or somewhat later the emergence of a distinct warrior class and the recognition of a difference between the pursuits of men and those of women lay the basis for the growth of other leisure classes.

The full meaning of leisure is perhaps never apparent until one portion of society is deprived of all possibility of its enjoyment. Throughout antiquity slavery and slavery alone made possible to the higher classes emancipation from the necessity for constant attention to material needs. This indeed was its justification to the Greeks. Some such justification underlies all willing and thoughtful acceptance of a leisure class. The reverence and the privilege accorded the Chinese scholar are also the result of a conviction of his social indispensability. Something of the force of the concept of leisure as it developed in antiquity is indicated by the fact that the English word school is derived from the Greek word for leisure (*schole*). The philosophers were not unaware of the problem of the unprivileged, but their only solution was further insistence on freedom of the citizen from manual labor and labor for pay.

Even the artist and the sculptor were not regarded by Aristotle or Plato as leisured men, since the nature of their crafts tied them down to constant repetition of one kind of action and thus robbed them of the freeman's ability to choose his interests. The rigor of this conception has less appeal to the modern social philosopher; but it is grounded in a distinction which he too must recognize. Leisure is time at the disposal of the complete man; the man exhausted by fourteen hours of labor or eight hours under a speed up system and harassed by insecurity possesses no leisure but only time for recreation that will enable him to return again to toil.

The leisured members of society have been most often those with assured incomes not dependent on their personal efforts–landed proprietors, rentiers, holders of sinecures. Probably in every age there have been individuals who secured leisure by boldly claiming it as a necessity of existence and stripping themselves of all other requirements except those which can be supplied by a minimum of "making-a-living" activity. Certain occupations, more frequent in pre-industrial societies than today, in themselves afford considerable leisure. The shepherd and the small proprietor in rich country, if they have little opportunity for variety in the use of leisure, have long hours of freedom, out of which have come through the centuries folk songs, folklore and dancing. The craftsman of some skill who could travel about from country to country, as in the early period of the compagnonnage, had many of the perquisites of leisure. Under some conditions, although decreasingly in the modern world, the sailor has had leisure. The soldier of fortune often possessed it, but the leisure of the modern military man is of a different and spurious character. It should be remembered too that throughout antiquity and the Middle Ages the normal number of holidays during the year was about 115. Except in periods of unusual economic stress even slaves enjoyed such holidays, although their means of utilization of such time were limited. But the grouping of work around numerous holidays probably resulted in more effective leisure than the one day of rest out of seven in industrial society.

Throughout history where definite leisure classes have come into existence they have been based upon wealth—whether in the form of slaves, land, securities or the rights and goods of a corporate body, such as the church. In general such classes have been the inheritors of wealth, not in any dynamic sense its makers. In periods of rapid economic change the makers of fortunes have time for nothing but fortune making and luxury spending. A leisure class may fulfil certain productive or entrepreneurial functions, as did most of the English squires and many of the Roman landed proprietors living in the smaller villas scattered throughout Italy. A landed aristocracy which has not become too affected by absenteeism ordinarily combines leisure with such productive activity. On the other hand, a class endowed with the privilege of leisure may develop for itself a great number of time consuming ritualistic functions, such as those of a military caste or of the followers of a royal court or of the society woman of the contemporary middle and upper classes, which preclude the enjoyment of any real leisure. A leisure class is not essentially a wealth worshiping or a spendthrift class. Where the possession of wealth is so taken for granted that it loses all value as a sign of personal repute, other criteria come to the fore, among them those of individual worth and cultural fitness. But a leisure class may also take over the standards of other groups, and not infrequently through history leisure classes have been caught up in a whirl of luxury spending: the deposits of Asia, with their fabulous riches; the landed aristocracy of Egypt, with its nominal military duties and its days of hunting and nights of feasting; the luxurious urbanites of imperial Rome; the privileged of Renaissance Italy and the court of Louis XIV. If the display consisted in many cases of artistic appreciation and civilized enjoyments, it was nevertheless on a lavish scale and in contrast to a complete lack of opportunity for the masses.

Whatever complaints might be made against the luxury of the rich, however, the desirability of leisure itself was never really brought into question throughout antiquity or the Middle Ages. With the growth of capitalism there appeared a new and condemnatory attitude. The Puritan emphasis on the moral duty of continuous industry reflected the needs of a mercantilistic and later of an industrial economy. The further disparagements of arts and amusements represented the reaction of the vigorous rising bourgeois class to the luxury and display of the older aristocracy. The "economic man" appeared in the theory of political economy. The high point was reached with Carlyle's glorification of work. The economic and moral bases of the doctrine are contained in Carlyle's bitter observation that a man with an income of £200,000 a year consumes the whole fruit of 6666 men's labor and does nothing for it but "kill partridges." Ruskin and his followers went even farther and demanded that every individual spend some time each day in manual labor. This Puritan doctrine of work with its emphasis on the seriousness of life as a business took firmer hold in the United States than in Europe, where century-old traditions could not so easily be displaced. The doctrine was most effectively expressed for the United States by Benjamin Franklin in his *Advice to Young Tradesmen* and *Necessary Hints to Those That Would Be Rich.* Perhaps the effort of clearing a continent for settlement required some such emphasis on material things; but the gospel persisted past the period of its usefulness, intertwined with philosophies of activism, doctrines of progress and interest in the psychology of success.

It is one of the most striking commentaries on modern civilization that the machine, which offers the possibility of a measure of leisure for all, as slavery made possible leisure for a few, has thus far brought only unemployment on an increasing scale, idleness for many women of the middle class and, on the other hand, extended opportunities for education and leisure to the adolescents of the community. This failure of economic organization is perhaps partly to be traced to contemporary attitudes toward work and leisure. Certainly what the normal work span of the future is to be depends partly upon technological achievement, but it depends quite as much upon the balancing of choice between increased productivity and increased leisure. The reality of such choice is most obvious in a planned economy. The problem in Russia is still largely theoretical; the existing emphasis in that country on the provision of music, drama and art represents the influence of cultural traditions which regard such things as among the necessities even in war time; but if the Soviet system does not break down, the choice between shorter hours and increased productivity will sooner or later come up in acute form. Less visibly but quite as surely all of modern society is faced with a similar choice.

Certain changes of attitude are already apparent. When the eight-hour laws were under discussion in 1916 and 1917, the prospect of such accretions of free time led governments and social reformers to talk fearfully of the leisure "problem." Temperance societies prepared for increased drunkenness and attention was centered on the real evils of commercialized recreation as it prevailed in most large cities. Concurrently with the passage of the limitation of hours legislation a number of the European governments set up official commissions to study the problem of workers' leisure activities. In 1924 the International Labor Office devoted part of its sixth conference to a discussion of the problem; in 1930 the First International Congress on Workers' Spare Time met at Liége with 300 members from eighteen countries, the governments of fourteen of which were officially represented. In the discussions of this congress and previously in those of the International Labor Office the emphasis had completely shifted from repression of commercial recreation to provision of facilities for other ways of utilizing leisure, and the conception of leisure as a problem had given way to its recognition as an opportunity and a cultural necessity.

The gains involved in the eight-hour laws were largely lost through speeding up systems and through tacit abrogation of the legislation in a period of crisis. The achievement of real leisure for all is still a dream of the future. Nevertheless, the direction of recreational activities even under present conditions is of importance not only as indicating attitudes but because of the indirect influence on production. Without attempting to solve the problem of adequate housing for workers, the groups in Europe interested in workers' leisure increasingly insist that proper housing and city planning are essential prerequisites to socially or individually valuable utilization of leisure. Excessive urbanization and bad transportation facilities deprive the worker of much of his nominal free time; lack of space in his home throws him upon the streets and into commercialized amusements. The official leisure committees of the various European countries have encouraged and aided financially the allotment movement with its attempt to secure for every worker a small plot of ground on the outskirts of the city; they have aided the development of play fields and stadia and helped support the numerous athletic societies which have increased so rapidly since the war. They have either supported or set up choral and theatrical societies and organizations to promote folk dancing and public festivals. The great increase in free libraries since the World War has been largely due to their efforts and they have strengthened and supplemented the already existing adult education institutions. In addition the various trade union groups, the cooperative organizations and the socialist parties not only occupy a great deal of the leisure time of their members but themselves organize gymnastic societies, workers' classes and art exhibits, theatrical groups and similar projects.

In the United States the recreation movement is limited largely to adolescents, trade unionism is weak and, with a few notable exceptions, adult education is non-existent. The limited traditions of community living and the greater emphasis on the achievement of wealth as a goal have retarded the development of the idea of creative enjoyment of leisure. Nevertheless, here as well as in Europe, the automobile, the moving picture and the radio have provided the means for new forms of recreation which taste and economic change might transform into the basis of real leisure.

The tone of any society is largely determined by the quality of its leisure, whether that leisure be restricted to a few or spread widely. The definite leisure classes have played varying social parts, some purely wasteful, some creative. It may be questioned whether until very recent times the economic basis for art existed except in class inequalities. In the field of government a privileged leisure class may still have a function. The advantages of a group trained to an interest in public affairs, not in partisan affairs, cannot be lightly dismissed. The success of England in governing an empire and in making democracy work with a degree of satisfactoriness not achieved in any other country is in no small part due to the fact that it inherited from an earlier system a leisured class imbued with traditions of a statesmanship which, if it was conservative, was at least not corrupt.

If the leisure classes no longer need be the carriers and supporters of artists and scientists, they retain their more fundamental function of the carriers of tradition. Leisure is not only the germinating time of art and philosophy, the time in which the seer attains glimpses of the values and the realities behind ordinary appearance; it is also the opportunity for appreciation, the time in which such values get across into common experience. The quality of a civilization depends upon the effectiveness of the transmission of such values. The widespread enjoyment of leisure is thus a matter of greatest moment, culturally as well as economically. Modern mechanisms open up new possibilities of communication; it remains to be seen what traditions and standards will be spread.

The Pattern of Leisure in Contemporary American Culture

By MARGARET MEAD

WITHIN traditional American culture, leisure is something that has to be earned and re-earned, except for the very old. Seen as play for the child, recreation for the adult, and retirement for the old, both child and adult have to earn their rights–the child by growing and learning, the adult by working. Unearned leisure is something which will have to be paid for later. It comes under the heading of vice–where the pleasure comes first and the pain afterwards–instead of virtue, where the pain or work precedes the reward. In some cultures, the joyful consumption of the harvest is felt as part of a natural climax structure; in others, the slightest feasting must be paid for later, almost as if it had been taken out of one's flesh. Within American culture, however, there has been a rhythm of work, virtue, and leisure. Good works–to be distinguished from work because they yield no monetary rewards and yet are enjoined and not enjoyed–are classified with work, and the Sabbath comes into more and more of an ambiguous position.

The model year, with its model week units, is to be found in Australia, New Zealand, and English-speaking Canada, as well as the United States. It is a year made up of weeks in which Monday to Friday are characterized by work, meals–taken for sustenance before, during, and after work–and sleep which prepares one to work again. Meals are a duty on the part of the one who eats them "to keep his strength up," and sleep is something one must "get enough of." But regular meals and uninterrupted sleep cannot be claimed by people who are not "working." In many working-class homes this differentiates men who work from women who merely keep house.

Reprinted from *The Annals of the American Academy of Political and Social Science,* Volume 313 (September 1957), by permission of the author and the publisher. (Copyright 1957 by the American Academy of Political and Social Science.)

Likewise, of course, children need their food and their sleep—or how can you expect them to do their lessons. There are small shifts in rhythm for special groups such as nursemaids with a day out on Thursday afternoon and butchers whose shops close on Wednesdays. Except for these, the first five days of the week for the Christian and the first four days of the week for the Jew are exactly alike. When late parties during the working week result from unpreventable accidents such as birthdays or departures, they are expected to result in headaches and interfere with work the next day. Then comes Friday night—payday for the weekly wage earners, end of school for teachers and students, the Sabbath meal for the Jews. It is the night for dates, movies, later and more irregular eating, more consumption of alcohol, and, in some classes in some parts of the English-speaking world, weekly conjugal love-making, carefully avoided all week. Saturday falls between rhythms and is a day on which fun and recreation—getting fit so that one will be able to work some more—are almost prescriptive. There are preparations for Sunday; shopping for a traditional Sabbath meal or a picnic; chores in the morning and celebration, courtship, gaiety in the evening. Recovery requires several extra hours of sleep varying strongly between Catholics, church-attending Protestants, and nonchurchgoers. Sleep is needed to repair the effects of jollification least by the Catholics, most by the completely secular.

On Sunday morning there is a need for rest. This is either to make up for the fatigues of the week's work, the excesses of the weekend, or to "get ready for the hard week ahead." All three are argued by different age groups with different degrees of conviction. They argue as to whether "rest" is to be labeled as "good," because it keeps up one's strength, or "self-indulgent," the result of staying up too late on Saturday, or not caring enough about going to church. This calendrically regulated evaluation of eating, drinking, sleeping, love-making, foregathering with friends, theatergoing, newspaper reading, alarm clock setting, or turning over and going back to sleep, means that all of these various activities are seen in their relation to work. Some people may live for their weekends, a smaller number may endure the weekends in order to get back to school or work. Both states of mind are in the workweek context. The punctuations of Christmas and smaller holidays are bonuses—Sundays with less of the aura of religious duties, discharged or undischarged. It is not one's duty to sleep late or go to bed early on Washington's birthday so that one will be bright-eyed and fit on February 23. No one is to be as fit on February 23, nor on the late afternoon of February 21 either. But longer vacations such as a precious week taken in winter—with some apologies, for it is still felt that it is moral to escape the heat when people can't work so well anyway, but immoral to escape the bracing cold—or the two weeks to a month in summer are like extended weekends. They combine escape from routine and the right to relax with the duty to "get rested" and build up for the next year's work.

The Persistent Belief. Throughout this whole pattern—modified as it may seem to be by contemporary changes in custom, by the Californian's moral insistence on getting the most out of his climate at all times, by the young airplane workers who struck until they had satisfied their urge to go swimming, by the miners who used to time their strikes to the hunting season, by the recognition in some households that adolescents need more sleep, or that some small children do not need to be sent to bed as early as others —there runs a persistent belief that all leisure must be earned by work and good works. And second, while it is enjoyed it must be seen in a context of future work and good works. People who are called pleasure-loving simply accent one part of this interconnected rhythm more than the others. But the extremes, between those who are never weary of well-doing and those who neither work nor engage in good works, simply serve to point up the pervasive pattern.

The word *recreation* epitomizes this whole attitude of conditional joy in which the delights of both work and play are tied together in a tight sequence. Neither one may ever be considered by itself, but man must work, then weary and "take some recreation" so he may work again. The linkage effects both joy in leisure and joy in work. It is wrong to work too hard; to become deeply, obsessively interested in work, or good works; one *should* have some recreation. And the minute that it looks as if there would be more time in between work and good works than the amount needed for "healthy recreation," alarm spreads over the country. People are going to have too much leisure. . . . Seen in terms of "normal needs for recreation," this means more time than is needed to relax and get back to work again—unearned time, loose time, time which, without the holding effects of fatigue before and fatigue to come, might result in almost anything.

Unearned Gains. Experience of many different sorts has shown that the pessimists are right, that relaxations of this relationship between time spent in work and time spent in leisure do often result in boredom, apathy, frantic attempts to fill up the time, too much drinking, promiscuity, gambling, reckless driving, and so forth. Unearned gains are not moral gains, and so there is a tendency to spend them in ways which are labeled as immoral, or at least as idle luxury. In Elliot Jaques's study of an English factory,[1] he found that men who were making more than they believed, on a non-verbalized level, to be fair were spendthrift. This was characteristic of World War I war workers in the United States, whose position was felt to be twofold unfair—they were safe from the hazards of the trenches and were paid too much for their work, such earnings going into silk stockings and fur coats. And Jaques found that workers who were paid too little, within their deep evaluation of what their job was worth, became apathetic and wished to leave their jobs. The whole system is like a bowstring. If overstretched or slackened, pathological effects result.

The answer which the last hundred years have attempted to give to the problems of a discrepancy between the time and effort involved in work, the available patterns of good works, and the traditional amount of pleasure which could go with them without strain, has been the suggestion that people "take up something as a hobby"—that they should do something which is not serious, has no monetary value, and so will be of no use to anyone but oneself. It may, however, be "expensive," and so use up some discrepancy between earning and legitimate spending. It must be something which is somehow out of the value system, something neither good nor bad, neither quite work nor quite play, and which can therefore fall under the bridging concept of "recreation."

Pressures Toward a New Equilibrium. The period since World War II has seen a breakdown of this system of earned and re-earned limited pleasure. The depression brought a slackening of the whole system. When people did not have enough work, no money, and so no symbolic right to play, entertaining was curtailed, movie money was short, dates lacked gaiety, childbearing was postponed. Work when it came back would bring with it a renewed ability and right to get some joy out of life. But World War II introduced a mixed set of disturbances. These included war workers who made too much money; soldiers who had too little time on leave and who spent too much time in absolute dullness and boredom overseas; men and women who saw too little of each other; families who still had to postpone their little modicum of privacy and live with relatives. After the war, there came, understandably, a desire to recoup these quantitatively perceived losses, to get some joy out of life. This was, perhaps, less because joy was a goal than because of the desire to reattain an equilibrium which had been disturbed since the lush, disequilibrated days of the late twenties.

Somewhere in the last decade there has come a subtle shift in this picture. This is a shift characteristic of our culture throughout its life and characteristic of most peoples who have depended on long hard hours of work for the majority in order that they should simply survive.[2] Conditions which have contributed to this shift can only be sketched in very roughly. They include a rising standard of living; rising wages; creeping inflation; and ways in which the relationships between work done, money made, and what one can buy are continually threatened. They also include a lowered standard of work proficiency in almost all fields; high wages for adolescents, who often make more than their parents; easy installment buying, so that a car is fully used up by the time it is paid for, and the threat that this prosperity will not last. Furthermore, there is the fear that there will be an atomic war, or at least a devastating depression produced by automation. These are the terms in which individuals are experiencing the rapid shifts in our economy. There is our emphasis on the importance of mass markets to keep up production, on improved standards of living in other countries as helpful rather than threatening to our economy, on the unlimited possibilities inherent in automation on the one hand and free power on the other. There is a freeing of men from drudgery of all sorts so that their potentialities may be utilized. This is a thing which has only been experienced before in occasional small societies under conditions of extreme and usually temporary felicity. Such opportunities have never been experienced for the large majority of the people of a great civilization.

The Shifting Balance. The generation which has married since the war has responded to these conditions by shifting the balance from work and good works to the home. The home, in which one was once allowed a limited amount of recuperation and recreation in reward for working hard, has now become the reason for existence, which in turn justifies working at all. This does not mean that many young people are not working very hard. Husband and wife often both work, combining work, children, and going on getting an education. But the emphasis is different. Jobs are selected as they will bear on the home. In the familiar phrase of how a man will account to his Maker for his life on earth, having been a good husband and father heads the list. Good works in the form of community service within the social environment right around the home have been moved into home life, as has most of religious participation. "I had to join some church so my son could be a cub scout." Hours of work which permit a man to spend more time at home, length of vacation, amount of strain and overwork, all are valued as to how they will affect family life. As once it was wrong to play so hard that it might affect one's work, now it is wrong to work so hard that it may affect family life.

But has family life become leisure in this process of transformation? Reversing a proposition within the kind of moral book-balancing characteristic of our culture produces many complications. A great deal has been done to turn modern home life into a self-rewarding delight. It has become something that is neither work, something done in order to make a living, nor recreation, that is, something done to get you safely back to work again. The do-it-yourself movement, which parallels so neatly the shortage of skilled labor for home finishing and repairs, is not just a hobby. It is often a pleasant and meaningful contribution to family life. The newfound delight of young fathers in their babies is another intrinsically rewarding pattern which no large civilization has ever permitted its more privileged young men. The gay companionship of a large family, making do with a small house, one car, and two dogs, has many ways of fending off boredom and apathy and the demand for expensive entertainment. The car, the television set, the pets are seen as contributory to the home. Service on innumerable boards and committees in the community is also part of making the community safe for the children.

But there are hazards inherent in the old work-play rhythmic morality which lie just beneath the surface of these readjustments. If this home life really is to be classified as play, then it should be a good deal easier than it is. For our notions of play have been those of spectator sports and easy enjoyment for a long time. Do-it-yourself with five children, besides being delightful, is strenuous, time consuming, backbreaking, nerve-straining, and confining—most of the things once characteristic of a good job which a man enjoyed. The job outside the home, if not seen as recreation in the spiritual sense, is becoming recreation in the physical sense. It is a relief from the exactions of a close personal life at home, a chance for a little peace and quiet, a quiet smoke, time to collect one's thoughts. The insidious old rhythm between enjoying activity and permitted, brief, limited, relaxed behavior is reasserting itself. A girl goes to work until she marries, or after she marries, or after her children are in school, as a supplement to the home. It is unfair of her employer to ask much of her work hours–as it would once have been unfair for him to infringe on her day off. If a man is doing the best he can, getting up at night with his young babies, taking them off their mother's hands as soon as he gets home, or perhaps getting supper because she has a part-time job too, it is unfair to ask him to wear himself out at work. As home life and personal relations thus take the center of the stage, the old rhythm remains with the job–less and less often a career–becoming the subsidiary, determined part of the sequence.

It is obvious that the whole question of *recreation,* which gives merely instrumental value to joy, needs a type of revision. This must be a revision which will make the members of a society–where delight in high level proficiency should now replace dogged willingness to work long hours for very limited rewards–able to integrate the shorter hours of work and the new engrossing home rituals into some kind of a whole in which these outmoded sequences, heritage of an age of scarcity, can be overcome.

Notes

1. Elliot Jaques, "Psycho-Pathology in Industrial Life," *Twentieth Century,* Vol. 159, May 1956, pp. 493-500.
2. I have not discussed in this paper the conspicuous consumption of the rich. In the United States this is related to our ethical system by the larger, longer time balance between yachts and gifts to foundations, especially for medical research. It is related by the need for recreation of those whose political or business burdens are great, or, when it is a question of enormous salaries for television stars or baseball players, by putting it outside the system–like gambling gains, which should be used up in immediate conspicuous consumptions.

Accidie

By ALDOUS HUXLEY

THE COENOBITES of the Thebaid were subjected to the assaults of many demons. Most of these evil spirits came furtively with the coming of night. But there was one, a fiend of deadly subtlety, who was not afraid to walk

From *On the Margin; Notes and Essays,* by Aldous Huxley. Reprinted by permission of Chatto & Windus, Ltd., London, and Harper & Brothers, New York. (Copyright, 1923, 1951, by Aldous Huxley.)

by day. The holy men of the desert called him the *daemon meridianus*; for his favourite hour of visitation was in the heat of the day. He would lie in wait for monks grown weary with working in the oppressive heat, seizing a moment of weakness to force an entrance into their hearts. And once installed there, what havoc he wrought! For suddenly it would seem to the poor victim that the day was intolerably long and life desolatingly empty. He would go to the door of his cell and look up at the sun and ask himself if a new Joshua had arrested it midway up the heavens. Then he would go back into the shade and wonder what good he was doing in that cell or if there was any object in existence. Then he would look at the sun again and find it indubitably stationary, and the hour of the communal repast of the evening as remote as ever. And he would go back to his meditations, to sink, sink through disgust and lassitude into the black depths of despair and hopeless unbelief. When that happened the demon smiled and took his departure, conscious that he had done a good morning's work.

Throughout the Middle Ages this demon was known as Acedia, or, in English, Accidie. Monks were still his favourite victims, but he made many conquests among the laity also. Along with *gastrimargia, fornicatio, philargyria, tristitia, cenodoxia, ira* and *superbia, acedia* or *taedium cordis* is reckoned as one of the eight principal vices to which man is subject. Inaccurate psychologists of evil are wont to speak of accidie as though it were plain sloth. But sloth is only one of the numerous manifestations of the subtle and complicated vice of accidie. Chaucer's discourse on it in the "Parson's Tale" contains a very precise description of this disastrous vice of the spirit. "Accidie," he tells us, "makith a man hevy, thoghtful and wrawe." It paralyses human will, "it forsloweth and forsluggeth" a man whenever he attempts to act. From accidie comes dread to begin to work any good deeds, and finally wanhope, or despair. On its way to ultimate wanhope, accidie produces a whole crop of minor sins, such as idleness, tardiness, *lâchesse,* coldness, undevotion and "the synne of worldly sorrow, such as is cleped *tristitia,* that sleth man, as seith seint Poule." Those who have sinned by accidie find their everlasting home in the fifth circle of the Inferno. They are plunged in the same black bog with the Wrathful, and their sobs and words come bubbling up to the surface:

Fitti nel limo dicon: "Tristi fummo
nell' aer dolce che dal sol s' allegra,
portando dentro accidioso fummo;

Or ci attristiam nella belletta negra."
Quest' inno si gorgoglian nella strozza,
chè dir nol posson con parola integra.

Accidie did not disappear with the monasteries and the Middle Ages. The Renaissance was also subject to it. We find a copious description of the symptoms of acedia in Burton's *Anatomy of Melancholy*. The results of the midday demon's machinations are now known as the vapours or the spleen. To the spleen amiable Mr. Matthew Green, of the Custom House, devoted those eight hundred octosyllables which are his claim to immortality. For him it is a mere disease to be healed by temperate diet:

Hail! water gruel, healing power,
Of easy access to the poor;

by laughter, reading and the company of unaffected young ladies:

Mothers, and guardian aunts, forbear
Your impious pains to form the fair,
Nor lay out so much cost and art
But to deflower the virgin heart:

by the avoidance of party passion, drink, Dissenters and missionaries, especially missionaries: to whose undertakings Mr. Green always declined to subscribe:

I laugh off spleen and keep my pence
From spoiling Indian innocence;

by refraining from going to law, writing poetry and thinking about one's future state.

The Spleen was published in the 'thirties of the eighteenth century. Accidie was still, if not a sin, at least a disease. But a change was at hand. "The sin of worldly sorrow, such as is cleped *tristitia,*" became a literary virtue, a spiritual mode. The apostles of melancholy wound their faint horns, and the Men of Feeling wept. Then came the nineteenth century and romanticism; and with them the triumph of the meridian demon. Accidie in its most complicated and most deadly form, a mixture of boredom, sorrow and despair, was now an inspiration to the greatest poets and novelists, and it has remained so to this day. The Romantics called this horrible phenomenon the *mal du siècle*. But the name made no difference; the thing was still the same. The meridian demon had good cause to be satisfied during the nineteenth century, for it was then as Baudelaire puts it, that

L'Ennui, fruit de la morne incuriosité,
Prit les proportions de l'immortalité.

It is a very curious phenomenon, this progress of accidie from the position of being a deadly sin, deserving of damnation, to the position first of a disease and finally of an essentially lyrical emotion, fruitful in the inspiration of much of the most characteristic modern literature. The sense of universal futility, the feelings of boredom and despair, with the complementary desire to be "anywhere, anywhere out of the world," or at least out of the place in one happens at the moment to be, have been the inspiration of poetry and the novel for a century and more. It would have been inconceivable in Matthew Green's day to have written a serious poem about ennui. By

Baudelaire's time ennui was as suitable a subject for lyric poetry as love; and accidie is still with us as an inspiration, one of the most serious and poignant of literary themes. What is the significance of this fact? For clearly the progress of accidie is a spiritual event of considerable importance. How is it to be explained?

It is not as though the nineteenth century invented accidie. Boredom, hopelessness and despair have always existed, and have been felt as poignantly in the past as we feel them now. Something has happened to make these emotions respectable and avowable; they are no longer sinful, no longer regarded as the mere symptoms of disease. That something that has happened is surely simply history since 1789. The failure of the French Revolution and the more spectacular downfall of Napoleon planted accidie in the heart of every youth of the Romantic generation—and not in France alone, but all over Europe—who believed in liberty or whose adolescence had been intoxicated by the ideas of glory and genius. Then came industrial progress with its prodigious multiplication of filth, misery, and ill-gotten wealth; the defilement of nature by modern industry was in itself enough to sadden many sensitive minds. The discovery that political enfranchisement, so long and stubbornly fought for, was the merest futility and vanity so long as industrial servitude remained in force was another of the century's horrible disillusionments.

A more subtle cause of the prevalence of boredom was the disproportionate growth of the great towns. Habituated to the feverish existence of these few centres of activity, men found that life outside them was intolerably insipid. And at the same time they became so much exhausted by the restlessness of city life that they pined for the monotonous boredom of the provinces, for exotic islands, even for other worlds—any haven of rest. And finally, to crown this vast structure of failures and disillusionments, there came the appalling catastrophe of the War of 1914. Other epochs have witnessed disasters, have had to suffer disillusionment; but in no century have the disillusionments followed on one another's heels with such unintermitted rapidity as in the twentieth, for the good reason that in no century has change been so rapid and so profound. The *mal du siècle* was an inevitable evil; indeed, we can claim with a certain pride that we have a right to our accidie. With us it is not a sin or a disease of the hypochondries; it is a state of mind which fate has forced upon us.

The Sedentary Society

By HERBERT COLLINS

THE seated figure of the 20th century is unmatched by any conventional posture in the past. In all their relationships, modern men aspire to rationality, matter-of-factness, and objectivity. Their work requires reflection, observation, or hand manipulation of buttons and switches. In all these actions, chairs of one sort or another settle the worker into his sedentary occupation. With gigantic mechanisms, operated from a sitting position, the unwieldy phenomena of this world are manipulated. The derrick, bulldozer, and dredge perform tasks that far exceed ordinary human ability in any position other than sitting. There is even a diminishing resistance to the union of buttocks and machine in contemporary agriculture.

Whether sedentary workers supervise automatic machines, read dials and meters, or study molecular patterns, they are engaged in visual operations that require sitting. The extension and sensitization of vision create situations in which instrument-using individuals experience a new range of phenomena and extend their control over previously unfamiliar objects. Microscopists, radiologists, and meteorologists are characteristic products of the mechanization of vision. In order to achieve these results, modern men have had to adjust to stationary positions, retinal concentration, and a seated posture.

In airplanes or in tanks, the sedentary soldier extends the military campaign to unprecedented distances. The fixed individual of the sedentary society sits in sports stadiums and becomes the renowned spectator who is actually our seated figure at play. To communicate he sits down to telephone or to type a message. His thoughts then travel faster and farther than if he bodily moved himself. Instead of walking to his destination, he motors or takes a train. When he reserves passage on the next flight, the distance to his destination exceeds the possibility of body locomotion. In the pursuit of entertainment and recreation, multitudes of people view motion pictures from endless rows of seats. Or they remain at home to operate dials on recorders, radios, televisions, or turntables.

Not only is the chair the conspicuous container of modern men, but sitting is the symbolic posture of the age of science and technology. Since the earliest preliminaries of a quantitative, mechanical, and empirical approach to man, his environment, and his work, sedentary positions have been encouraged and sustained. Subsequently a stage in cultural development emerged in which man's characteristic act of bending himself and nature into a mutually harmonious relationship became assertive, and new outlets

Reprinted from *The Scientific Monthly*, Volume 79, Number 5 (November 1954), pp. 285-292, by permission of the author and the publisher.

occurred for reflection and inquiry concerning objects of different shape, judgments of value and conduct, as well as poses and postures. Yet modern men have acquiesced in the view of an impersonal universe in which each individual has a seated station as stubborn as the facts out of which scientific theories have been fashioned.

A whole philosophy lies concealed in the act of sitting. The Renaissance merchant-bankers painted by Quentin Matsys, Hans Holbein the Younger, and Petrus Christus sat in abstract positions of quantitative preoccupation signalizing a new idea and posture *(1)*. The symbols associated with the burghers were paper, writing instruments, books, coins, records, accounts, seals, scales, and secular possessions. These symbols of the external order of things show that the burghers thought the events and phenomena of this world were susceptible to measurement and human manipulation. The predecessors of the sedentary merchants were travelers, adventurers, sailors, itinerants, and craftsmen. When the techniques of business communication were perfected, with an array of ledgers and notations, mobility was outgrown and the sitting businessman was "born." Uppermost among his possessions were chairs, mirrors, and windows—the thrones, reflectors, and frames of a new social class. The orthodoxy of quantity that the merchants sponsored was appropriate to enumeration, analysis, standardization, (and accumulation. Such specialized modes of behavior were also conducive to sitting.

The scientists who inquired into the nature of the universe contemporaneously with the merchants had also outgrown the mobility of earlier empiricism based on travel, exploration, and field observation. A new crop of scientists, whose observations became restricted to contrived experiments that a sedentary but constant observer could attend, supplanted the earlier mobile explorers. Even when assisted "by exquisite instruments," Francis Bacon relegated the senses "to judge of the experiment" which itself "shall judge of the thing" *(2)*. Galileo, Huygens, Boyle, and Torricelli sat before their instruments of measurement and sight, created experimental situations, and altered man's view of the world without climbing Mount Ventoux. It was a field expedition to Cayenne with a simultaneous observation at Paris, in which Picard, Richer, and Cassini collaborated to secure a more accurate estimate of the earth's radius and the sun's mean distance from the earth, that enabled Isaac Newton to resume his researches on the inverse square law *(3)*. Out of his mathematizing, without his traveling to the equator, emerged the theory of universal gravitation.

The archetype of experimental perseverance in the 17th century occurred in the iatrophysicist, Sanctus Sanctorius. In his *Ars de statica medicina,* he tells us that during the greater part of 30 years his life was "in the balance." He had spent a considerable part of his time in a weighing chair, with a table nearby, carefully recording variations in his weight under all sorts of conditions. He was able to show that the loss of weight by perspiration was greater than all "the servile Evacuations together" *(4)*.

Other experimenters and philosophers, such as Harvey, Borelli, Descartes, and La Mettrie, contributed to the foundations of a mechanical view of the human organism. The method was derived from physics, the machine analogy was borrowed from mechanics, and the language echoed the matter-of-factness of mathematics. Descartes, for example, considered all the functions of the human body as proceeding "from the mere arrangement of its organs" as "do the movements of a clock, or other automaton, from that of its weights and wheels" *(5)*. The geometrization of human nature was announced by Spinoza when he wrote that he would "regard human actions and desires exactly as if I were dealing with lines, planes, and bodies" *(6)*.

Eventually physiological data, supported by clocks, tests, and efficiency ratings became useful in factory management. By 1914 the quantification of work and effort had attained some precision. Jules Amar reported in *The Human Motor (7)*:

> In the sitting position the base of support is much larger and the stability of the body is therefore considerably increased. Furthermore the muscles have but little to do. If we measure the relative consumption of oxygen by an adult, first standing in the easy attitude . . . and next sitting on a chair, leaning back with all the muscles of the legs relaxed, we shall find that the average economy of the consumption of oxygen is about 6% in favour of the sitting position.

Motivated by distinterested curiosity, employing a quantitative method of discovery, and in search of a new cosmic dramaturgy, the new scientists attained the same level of insight and expression as commercial men inspired by utility and expediency. The insights of both were governed by measurements and mathematical abstractions. According to Descartes *(8)*:

> Mathematics excels in utility and simplicity the sciences subordinate to it, by the fact that it can deal with all the objects of which they have cognizance and many more besides.

This much at least the businessmen and scientists had in common at the outset of the modern age of quantity: the search for a mathematical image of reality permanently recorded on a piece of paper and arrived at from a sitting position. Lucas Pacioli, one of the early expounders of commercial arithmetic, aphorized 2 years after the discovery of America that care be taken "of the things that go by number, of those which go by weight, and of those which go by measurement," and that "you give your daily attention to your affairs, chiefly holding the pen to paper and writing day by day that which you require" *(9)*. Here was a discipline compatible to business as well as to research.

The discipline of quantitative callings was not, however, without basis in European culture. The Benedictine ideal that work should be transfused with intellectual and moral vision linked knowledge and labor together. The Benedictine rule declared *(10)*:

Idleness is the enemy of the soul. And therefore, at fixed times, the brothers ought to be occupied in manual labor; and again, at fixed times, in sacred reading.

A portrayal of this ideal can be found in the medieval representation of the four Evangelists with their appropriate emblems prescriptively arranged around the Christ. Sometimes the Evangelists were separately chaired with book and writing instrument in hand, engrossed in divine labor. In order that nothing be omitted and all the symbols of communication, labor, and scholarship be seen, the masons included everything in the tympanum of the north portal of the Cathedral of Burgos: Christ enthroned and surrounded by angel, eagle, lion, and bull, and four desks and chairs with the Evangelists diligently bent over their work.

The Renaissance ideal did not, to be sure, center around the monastic laborer-scholar. Nevertheless, Arabic numerals, ledgers, weighing devices, clocks, and calipers arranged in a windowed room jointly symbolized the union of asceticism and worldliness. The appearance of portraiture, genre scenes, and lavishly seated Madonnas testified to the sedentary mannerism of a secular society. This is supported by the renditions of St. Jerome, the Christian scholar, translator, and bibliophile. When Lucas Cranach, Vittore Carpaccio, Domenico Ghirlandaio, and Albrecht Dürer, among others, portrayed the saint they did not take him literally: "Leave all, and come to the desert" *(11)*. They reenacted the solitude of the wilderness and the cave in a four-walled setting, richly treated with books, paneling, furniture, and an assortment of instruments and scholarly gadgets. Here is the learned, contemplative man who must have a silent room and a chair to sit on. The ideals of the emerging sedentary society are being sanctified with the virtues of monasticism *(12)*. These secular idealizations of the saint were matched by some of the depictions of the new science. In Dürer's "Melancholia" or Le Clerc's representation of the French Academy, geometric, mensural, and mechanical instruments and symbols were employed by seated or contemplative individuals on the verge of transforming knowledge and social life *(13)*.

An advanced admirer of the sedentary society was Francis Bacon. Whatever the appraisal of his social scheme, he was an ameliorator of mankind. In his *New Atlantis,* Bacon delineated not only a technologic society but a way of life founded on scientific research. Somewhere in the hierarchy of technicians and experts he planned to place a group assigned to draw out of experiments "things of use and practice for man's life and knowledge as well as . . . for plain demonstration of causes" *(14)*. Descartes also envisaged the time when, through science and its applications, men might be enabled "to enjoy without any trouble the fruits of the earth" *(15)*. For the first time, perhaps, the possibility occurred that science and technology might play into each other's hands. The myth maker met the artisan on common grounds, and scientific theories were used for practical ends. Under the auspices of scientists, processes of production were altered by phenomenal discoveries. A striking series of inventions, under the guidance of mechanicians, transformed production procedures. With the mingling of the two ways of knowing—on the one hand knowledge of what takes place and on the other hand knowledge of what had best be done—learning and stubborn facts became indistinguishable *(16)*.

What was novel about this arrangement was that it rapidly outmoded and even abandoned the traditional craftsman who had usually created something expressive of the potentialities of the union of hands, tools, and materials. The technology anticipated before the 19th century ignored the bodily motions of manualism. Instead, a quantitative approach to material resources in a setting of controlled research and dutiful matter-of-factness received approval. The manual operations of the workshop had been appropriated by the laboratory experimenter. As early as the 16th century, Andreas Vesalius, who was alert to the resources of the workshop, admonished anatomists to respect the practices of artisans *(17)*. The abundance of mechanical draftsmanship and inventions, which could never have been realized without the direct aid of a craftsman or the cultivation of his mentality, thrived on workshop conditions and made the laboratory and the factory possible.

The artisan had been free and independent, terribly personal and haphazard. He had learned to depend on past experience without any quantitative method for the appraisal of the validity of the ways in which he acquired experience or achieved workable results. But he was mobile. The discipline to which he was subjected was self-imposed or derived from his tools and materials. He would never have anticipated that higher predicament of freedom in which the machine process subordinates all human spontaneity and autonomy to the anonymous power of impersonal mechanism. Typing, calculating, machine assembly, sewing, visual inspection, and machine feeding—a partial list of services men perform from a sitting position—require skill and judgment. At the same time they are rationalized to conform to the performance of the machine.

The tests in use in personnel management, for all their value, signify subordination to the authority of impersonal numbers. Thomas A. Ryan claims in his book *Work and Effort (18)*:

> Until we have measures which indicate the performances of the individual in the more complex activities involving thinking, imagining, comprehension, and emotion, we are bound to miss many of the elements of cost of work when we use the techniques of fatigue tests.

The point is, however, as Herbert Marcuse observed *(19)*, that today

> . . . the apparatus to which the individual is to adjust and adapt is so rational that individual protest and liberation appear not only hopeless but as utterly irrational.

In this light Andrew Ure, the 19th century economist, no longer appears as a cruel exponent of the exploitation of the working class but as a pioneer observer of the realities of the mechanized society. Although Karl Marx had no patience with Ure and championed a different factory ideology, the 15th chapter in his *Capital* deserves attention *(20)*:

> In handicrafts and manufactures, the workman makes use of a tool; in the factory the machine makes use of him. . . . In the factory we have a lifeless mechanism independent of the workman, who becomes its mere living appendage.

By the end of the 19th century there was something quaint about the merchant-adventurer, the explorer-naturalist, and the manual craftsman. During the century a few approximate examples emerged in a last spurt of the upright stance. The captain of industry, versed in many phases of commerce and industry, brought to bear on his situation a capacity for activity and a range of interests that kept him away from the executive office. Alexander von Humboldt, Charles Darwin, and the field archeologists and ethnologists retained a degree of mobility at odds with the laboratory anchorage of other scientists. William Morris and other craftsmen attempted to remind an obviously mechanized society of the primacy of esthetic standards and personal workmanship in the fashioning of useful goods. At the same time, however, the cash register, the typewriter, and eventually the telephone curtailed the wanderlust of the merchant. The research laboratory and the lecture stage where Humphry Davy, John Tyndall, and Thomas H. Huxley so eloquently held forth to a seated audience obscured the men who with rations and ideas ranged the unexplored remnants of the planet. Industrial production, located in castellated factories, fed by new knowledge of materials and processes, incorporating the designs of mechanical engineers, and staffed by routinized workers, eventually superseded the older traditions of individual workmanship. The monastic virtue of work had so permeated society that the administrators of punishment enthusiastically instituted penitentiary work.

The stage was set. From the thinnest of beginnings and within 300 years, a social revolution has fanned out over the Western world and its provinces. In numerous areas of activity, mobility has succumbed to sitting. The man in demand is the sedentary, contemplative but worldly fellow, adept at figures, literate, and sitting apart from his neighbors. The table and desk have been mechanized. The chair acquires the standardized distinctions of the functions performed by the occupant. The merchant's desk has become an office of desks equipped with calculators, telephones, typewriters, and punch-card machines requiring seated operators. A hierarchy of seated workers replaces the mobile businessman ascending from the typist to the chairman of the board of directors. The scientist's desk has become an intricate laboratory with tubes, dials, and electronic equipment—a far cry from the alchemist's who also sat in the midst of a superabundance of paraphernalia. The artisan's table has become an automaton. The industrial plant has become the location for the rationalized flow of standardized production.

The concentration and attendance so consistently demanded by the machine have established the seated position as the postural model of the 20th century. "Everyone realizes the advantage, as a resting device, of anything upon which one can occasionally sit" *(21)*. Frank Gilbreth, a pioneer in advocating the seated posture in laboratory and factory, made that statement in 1916. Time, motion, and fatigue analysis have gone far since his innovations. Yet the seated manipulation of the control panels of the machine process continues to receive serious attention. A management engineer meticulously writes *(22)*:

> With 40 inches taken as the average elbow height of the female worker, and with the hand allowed to work 1 to 3 inches lower than the elbow, the average height of the working service should be 37 to 39 inches. The chair should be 25 to 31 inches, depending upon the proportions of the individual. With such table and chair heights the worker is permitted either to stand or sit at work, with the elbow and hand maintained at the same position relative to the work place.

Here we see how the quantitative method as applied to sedentary occupations has taken over even the act of sitting itself.

In this situation of transformation, a new diligence, a new attention to details, and a quantitative analysis of phenomena and men have triumphed. Never before have men known so much about the universe, have they produced with such abundance and precision, have they so rationally managed the components of social life. But never before have so many people sat so much of the time. Those who assume this posture, whatever their particular activities, are preoccupied with problems of concentration, assembly, repetition, restricted manual motions, visual attention, and relaxation. In these circumstances all men are equally situated. Their differences consist of degrees in intelligence, training, and posture.

The history of civilizations, although somewhat casually recapitulated in the construction and utilization of the chair, does not always record such equality in sitting. The chair is one of those objects man has made for human use by going beyond the human body. In doing this the materials employed have been molded into sympathy with the human body. All the efforts men have made to adapt themselves to the external world have required in one sense a departure from themselves. In another sense relatively formless materials have been sought which it has been the business of men to shape. Joseph Wood Krutch has indicated *(23)* how

> . . . man detaches himself from Nature, asserts the importance of himself as an individual, and proposes to himself ends and values which do not exist in her.

These projections of man, his body, and his personality into the physical universe are best realized and expressed by the implements and symbols that enhance his range of operations. The tools, clothing, utensils, shelters, furniture, and other modes of expression that characterize what it means to be human are all exemplary of a tendency to operate in what George

Santayana called "an environment in which everything is not already what man is presently to make it" *(24).*

There have been and are civilizations to which the idea of the chair has never occurred. The first appearance of detached seating furniture is seen in stools. Such circular, oval, oblong, curved, or hollowed-out seats served as buttocks props among pre-European South Americans, West Indians, and Africans. Not only did the earliest stools and joined chairs raise the body from the ground and provide outside support, but they served as adjuncts of social superiority, conveyed symbolic evidence of power, and were used as cult objects. In ancient Egypt, chair joinery became an organized craft. Mats sufficed in pre-Columbian Mexico for beds and seats. Many ancient civilizations produced thrones with legs and backs as honorific furniture. But not all sitting has been ceremonial. Leisure and comfort have sometimes been served by the furniture makers who have often produced sitting arrangements for the sheer object of turning out a decorative chair. Gothic choir stalls and lecterns, however, were straight, vertical, and narrow, built for ritual and never for comfort. The multitude either knelt or improvised seats.

In making the chair, the designer invents mechanical substitutes for the action of certain muscles to hold the body in a position other than supine. The solution of this problem dates from the use of furniture among sedentary people. No greater complexity faces the furniture designer than to construct a chair demanded by new habits of sitting and posture. The skeleton of the 18th century chair shows the designers' knowledge of lines of force, their insight into organic forms, and their mastery of wood. In the Bergere type, chair and posture became one. Siegfried Giedion has already displayed how this catering to the social conventions of sitting constituted one of the outstanding achievements of Rococo art *(25).* As the honorific associations of sitting waned, the chair speedily became the customary companion of whomsoever could afford to buy it. Almost at once the chair began to reflect the fashions of the hour, accommodating developments in clothes, hairdress, manners, and conversation. But the chair remained ostensibly a household article until industrial production asserted itself as a principle of social organization.

Although the 19th century became an upholsterer's holiday, producing mastodons with spring cushions and cylindrical arms, cushioned comfort was matched by maneuverability. Railroad, barber, typing, sewing, deck, invalid, surgical, and all manner of adjustable chairs were contrived to adjust the sitter to his tasks. Sitting was also rationalized in terms of engineering appraisals of the physiology of the seated posture. By constructing a shell as the container for a variously positionable body, a resilient mode of sitting was achieved. The chair became the inverse image of the body, and the postural model of the body was ingeniously served by an endless variety of mechanical counterparts. However, the adjustability of the body that characterized some furniture of the last decades of the century did not always successfully compete with the bulk, clutter, ornamentation, and archaism sponsored by the ruling taste.

Not until our own time have bent wood, molded plywood, laminated woods, and foam rubber been adapted to flexible sitting. We are also witnessing the incorporation of cantilever seats in all manner of automatic, adjustable, and convertible chairs. Since the late 1850's the free-hovering steel cantilever seat has been associated with agricultural implements that have extended the mobility of the farmer. This perforated sheet of steel stamped as the container for the buttocks stands resiliently as the symbol of standardized and serialized comfort. Durable and repeatable, it has grace, contour, utility, and is the mechanical counterpart of organic seatability. The underlying principles in each of these designs have been a direct attack on the problem of sitting, a rational use of materials, and a fusion of function and human use.

No man, except the cataleptic, ever learned to sit without having to come to terms with either the ruling taste or the material techniques of his time. The Rietveld, Thonet, Hardoy, Eames, Breuer, and Mathsson chairs are a discipline requiring the same finesse demanded in the rocker, hammock, or swivel chair. In each case a new mode of sitting emerges in which the body and the chair collaborate. Actually chair design affords insight into historically prevailing accommodations for the contour of the human frame. In this sense, the chair is a multiple document of technology, design, and physiological science at any time. But the chair cannot contend unopposed for the singular distinction of determining the posture that every century evolves as its own. William Robertson, an 18th century Scottish historian, remarked during a discourse on the habits of the American Indian that posture "is an emblem of the state of his mind" *(26)*. It might be added to his observation that posture is a visual record of the individual's body, his personality, the prevailing culture and the surrounding world. These are some of the primary experiences that constitute life and existence. Paul Schilder wrote *(27)*:

> It is clear that every emotion expresses itself in the postural model of the body, and that every expressive attitude is connected with characteristic changes in the postural model of the body. . . . We expand and contract; we take parts away and we add parts; we rebuild it; we melt the details in; we create new details; we do this with our body and with the expression of the body itself.

And when the body is not sufficient for either playful or destructive changes in the "body image," tailoring, cosmetics, jewelry, and furniture have been invented to perform the task. Each age, furthermore, sees the body differently. The reclining nudes of Cranach, Giorgione, Titian, Ingres, Matisse, and Modigliani have symbolized characteristically different attitudes and conceptions of the human body. In medieval iconography, nudity was reserved for Adam and Eve as well as for lost souls condemned to Hell. After the 15th century others may disrobe; and if they choose, they may sit down too.

But to come back to the chair. It often symbolizes, as well as instigates, rules of decorum by encouraging squatting, kneeling, lounging, or sleeping. The chair may be in sympathy with or in opposition to the ruling taste and morality of a time. A British designer recently observed *(28)*:

> Even though we no longer care to sit bolt upright, as our great-grandfathers did, and lounge a few inches nearer the floor than they would have thought consistent either with dignity or decency, we are no less concerned with posture (28).

During the last 100 years the chair has been severed from a restricted, honorific, ecclesiastical, academic, and domestic anchorage. It has invaded such fields as recreation, entertainment, war, travel, work, communication, and research. Today those are the very situations in which value transformations are under way. These changes in the circumstances of living impress themselves on the postural model of the human body, which is itself in a continuous process of construction, reconstruction, and dissolution.

But only as men depart from the chair in all its variations do they achieve perfect comfort. The reclining figure, completely relaxed, antedates psychoanalysis and is perhaps the postural antidote to sitting. A recent commentator, after surveying pictorially the profiles of 30 chairs in various uses during the day, observed *(29)* that

> . . . as the sitter approaches perfect comfort, the designer's problem disappears, for, perfectly relaxed, the sitter finally transfers herself to a mattress on which she can lie perfectly straight.

This would indicate the failure of all mechanical contrivances to obscure the distinction between lying and sitting. But the sedentary society is a specialized arrangement of men and activities. It was to be expected that this society would contrive mechanisms with finely varying distinctions for work and relaxation. But the emotional responses to the conditions of an industrial society have also produced a prolific variety of postural models, the most conspicuous of which has been sitting. Those who still stand must wait until the rationalizers of human posture provide them with the ubiquitous chair.

The age we inhabit has been shaped by science and the mechanical technology it breeds. It is no light responsibility that what men have been doing during the past 300 years will morally and intellectually influence many generations to come. For the sciences, however, no previous wisdom exists. They are no respecters of tradition, convention, or prescriptive canons of behavior. There is, nevertheless, nothing more devastating to thought and action than to drop with a minimum of discussion habitual concepts, attitudes, and beliefs. The revolution that science has been described as having ushered in actually was managed by those who refused to see themselves and their beliefs summarily dismissed. It must have been agonizing to dispute with opponents who possessed a standard of inquiry and truth that rested on heroic patience and refrained from

> . . . the din
> Of specious words, and tyranny of names. (30)

Yet the virtue of science is that it signalizes the first organizing and heuristic principle for the conduct of human affairs that willingly submits to the criticism of itself and the disturbances it provokes.

The early scientists fashioned a world-view at variance with traditional cosmologies, theories of man and nature, and modes of resources utilization. Moreover, they presided at the parturition of a new range of discourse, values, beliefs, manners, and social amenities. By becoming enmeshed in the social surroundings, the sciences have achieved the only kind of recognition that could have established their dominion. Together with other social activities, science constitutes one of the circumstances that make for history. And, like history, science remains inconclusive.

The cumulative and continuous character of science is impressive, but the response of the social surroundings interjects strong strains of noncumulativeness and discontinuity that impose some of the inconclusiveness and ambiguity of history on science. It is often suggested that art is noncumulative and science is cumulative. These concepts are correct so far as the recurrence of styles and taste in art prevail and criterions of beauty remain subjective and indeterminate. The self-corrective aspects of science also confirm this distinction. But science displays discontinuous elements whenever it influences fashions and manners, turns from one set of assumptions to another, or insists on holding pet theories without empirical verification. The customary explanation of the time lag between Spallanzani and Pasteur in the refutation of the theory of spontaneous generation tends to drain the irony and contradiction from scientific endeavors.

The claim that an esthetic experience accompanies the practice of research and scientific theorizing is another instance of the temporal and intermittent range of scientific accomplishments. The experience is private, and the record of it is period literature. Indeed, the differentiation of science has resulted not only in a new range of knowledge but in creative work and new temporal circumstances. The most prolonged social circumstance of such origin has been the sedentary society.

On the other hand, there are certain exceptions to the claim that art is noncumulative. The rules of composition, the mediums employed, the technique, the vision of the artist and what he knows of color, light, and sight, as well as the knowledge all artists have of the factual content of human experience and the surrounding world, are cumulative and corrective rather than capricious.

We are at the point where the social contingencies rule the direction of science, which otherwise is quite poised and consistent in its investigations. All the tragedy, irony, and contradiction that men have experienced under other historical circumstances are still with us. On the cumulative side, science builds up a body of rational, verifiable knowledge; on its discontinuous side, it encourages a society in which heteronomous behavior becomes the condition of specialization, efficiency, and routine. In the sedentary society, sitting is substituted for the upright gait; the foot is restricted to the operation of a pedal; the hand is relieved of tools and employed in the operation of buttons and levers; the eye concentrates on dials and gages that substitute for the other organs of perception; and the brain, which is the seat of men's capacity to associate, remember, imagine, reflect, abstract, and think, asserts itself. But the line between intelligence and instinct, between reflection and repetition, between choice and compliance, is so flimsy that the persuasive paradox of our time is that the sedentary society with all its conveniences resembles the termitary and the hive. As C. E. M. Joad has pointed out *(31),* the industrialized individual

> . . . is condemned by the conditions of his existence to perform with never varying efficiency operations of never varying monotony which conduce to no end except the continued performance of similar operations in the future.

This can scarcely be the social analog of science.

The scientists have dismissed most of the accumulated errors of men except their insights concerning themselves and their ways. Karl Mannheim once wrote *(32)*:

> Just as nature was unintelligible to primitive man and his deepest feelings of anxiety arose from the incalculability of the forces of nature, so for modern industrialized man the incalculability of the forces at work in the social system under which he lives, with its social crises, inflation, and so on, has become a source of equally pervading fears.

The sedentary society is racked by these fears. It is devoted to the application of science in ways at odds with the principles of science. In the sedentary society, the concepts and findings of science are transformed into the mannerisms and patois of routinized and reticent men. To paraphrase e. e. cummings, we are perpetually putting the secret of life in our pants and forgetting it is there and sitting down on it.

Notes

1. Q. Matsys, "The Banker and His Wife," in *Alinari Prints, a Thousand Paintings of Twenty Centuries* (International Art, Detroit, 1946), p. 135, pl. 1801; P. Christus, "St. Eloy," in *The Last Flowering of the Middle Ages,* J. Van der Elst (Doubleday, Garden City, 1945), pp. 68-69, pl. 26; H. Holbein, "The Merchant Giesze," in *Life's Picture History of Western Man* (Simon & Schuster, New York, 1951), p. 164. Also see L. C. Karpinski, *The History of Arithmetic* (Rand McNally, Chicago, 1925), pp. 34, 58, 59; D. E. Smith, *History of Mathematics* (Ginn, Boston, 1925), vol. 1, pp. 334; vol. 2, pp. 180, 182, 346.
2. E. A. Burtt, Ed., *The English Philosophers from Bacon to Mill* (Modern Library), p. 17.
3. A. Wolf, *A History of Science, Technology, and Philosophy in the 16th and 17th Centuries* (Allen & Unwin, London, 1950), pp. 175-176; H. Butterfield, *The Origins of Modern Science* (Bell, London, 1950), p. 140.
4. A. Wolf, *op. cit.,* pp. 433-434; J. F. Fulton, Ed., *Selected Readings in the History of Physiology* (Thomas, Springfield, Ill., 1930), pp. 140-145.
5. J. F. Fulton, Ed., *op. cit.,* pp. 238-240; R. Descartes, *A Discourse on Method* (Everyman), pp. 40, 44, 46.
6. B. Spinoza, *Ethics* (Everyman), p. 84.
7. J. Amar, *The Human Motor* (Routledge, London, 1920), p. 338.
8. "Rules for the direction of the mind," in *Great Books of the Western World,* R. M. Hutchins, Ed. (Encyclopaedia Britannica, Chicago, 1952), vol. 31, p. 7.
9. G. Bruun, *Europe in Evolution* (Houghton Mifflin, Boston, 1945), p. 103; Columbia University staff, *Introduction to Contemporary Civilization in the West, a Source Book* (Columbia University, Columbia Univ. Press, New York, 1947), vol. 1, p. 322; Karpinski, *op. cit.,* pp. 140-143; Smith, *op. cit.,* vol. 1, pp. 251-253.

10. *Introduction to Contemporary Civilization, op. cit.*, vol. 1, p. 139; A. N. Whitehead, *The Aims of Education* (Mentor), pp. 53-56.

11. H. O. Taylor, *The Medieval Mind* (Macmillan, London, 1938), vol. 1, p. 351, n. 1.

12. L. Cranach, "Cardinal Albrecht as St. Jerome," in *A Catalogue of Paintings in the John & Mable Ringling Museum of Art*, W. E. Suida, Ed. (Sarasota, Fla., 1949), p. 257; V. Carpaccio, "St. Jerome in His Study," in *The Italian Painters of the Renaissance*, B. Berenson (Phaidon, New York, 1953), pl. 10; A. Dürer, "St. Jerome in His Study," in *Albrecht Dürer*, E. Panofsky (Princeton Univ. Press, Princeton, 1943), vol. 2, pl. 208; D. Ghirlandaio, "St. Jerome," in *An Illustrated Handbook of Art History*, F. J. Roos (Macmillan, New York, 1944), p. 128g.

13. E. Panofsky, *op. cit.*, vol. 2, pl. 209; R. S. Stites, *The Arts and Man* (McGraw-Hill, New York, 1940), p. 641.

14. F. R. White, Ed., *Famous Utopias of the Renaissance* (Farrar, Straus, New York, 1948), p. 249.

15. R. Descartes, *op. cit.*, p. 49.

16. See T. Veblen, *The Place of Science in Modern Civilization and Other Essays* (Viking, New York, 1942), p. 18.

17. F. R. Moulton and J. J. Schifferes, Eds., *The Autobiography of Science* (Doubleday, Garden City, 1946), pp. 94-104.

18. T.A. Ryan, *Work and Effort, The Psychology of Production* (Ronald, New York, 1947), p. 153.

19. H. Marcuse, "Some social implications of modern technology," *Studies in Phil. and Social Sci.* 9 No. 3, 421, (1941).

20. K. Marx, *Capital, a Critique of Political Economy* (Modern Library), pp. 461-462.

21. F. B. Gilbreth, *Fatigue Study* (Macmillan, New York, 1919), p. 45.

22. R. M. Barnes, *Motion and Time Study* (Wiley, New York, 1949), p. 272. Also see the anthropometric study of railroad coach seating conducted by E. A. Hooton for the Haywood-Wakefield Co., *A Survey in Seating* (Gardner, Mass., 1954), *passim.*

23. J. W. Krutch, *The Modern Temper, a Study and a Confession* (Harcourt, Brace, New York, 1929), p. 36.

24. G. Santayana, *Life of Reason* (Scribner's, New York, 1923), vol. 4, p. 28.

25. S. Giedion, *Mechanization Takes Command* (Oxford Univ. Press, New York, 1948), pp. 309-319.

26. W. Robertson, *The History of the Discovery and Settlement of America* (Harper, New York, 1837), p. 188.

27. P. Schilder, *The Image and Appearance of the Human Body* (Kegan Paul, London, 1935), pp. 209, 210-211. Also see B. Rudofsky, *Are Clothes Modern? An Essay on Contemporary Apparel* (Paul Theobald, Chicago, 1947), *passim.*

28. J. Gloag, *Industrial Art Explained* (Allen & Unwin, London, 1946), pp. 183-184.

29. *Interiors and Industrial Design*, 108, 86 (1949).

30. J. Thomson (1700-48), "To the Memory of Sir Isaac Newton."

31. C. E. M. Joad, *Decadence, a Philosophical Inquiry* (Philosophical Library, New York, 1949), p. 390. The establishment of "uncontested knowledge" suggested to J. S. Mill the possibility of intellectual standardization for which he thought "negative philosophy" an antidote. Until people are pressed to examine the commonplaces of received opinion, "there will be few great thinkers . . . in any but the mathematical and physical branches of speculation." *On Liberty* (Everyman), pp. 103-105.

32. K. Mannheim, *Man and Society in an Age of Reconstruction* (Harcourt, Brace, New York, 1941), p. 59.

How to Make a Civilization

By CLIVE BELL

A CIVILIZED population, as distinct from that nucleus which gives it civility, will consist of men and women a fair proportion of whom adopt a slightly

---

critical attitude to life and possess a rudimentary taste for excellence. Clumsily but consciously it will try to train itself to make the most of such powers of thinking and feeling as it possesses. The Spartans discovered that a whole community, or rather the free part of it, could train itself for war: the Athenians were, so far as we know, the first to train themselves, deliberately, for the appreciation of life. This deliberate and self-conscious training is a peculiarity of civilization; the ensuing enjoyment, the good states of mind that come of it, is the end to which civilization is a means. '*A* means,' I say: for though civilization is the most fecund that we know of, it is not the only means to good. And this most likely means to good that human wit has yet devised is, as we have seen, nothing but the colour given to a community by a small but potent core of highly civilized individuals. If, therefore, society would civilize itself, it must first discover, then establish, conditions favourable to the production of civilizers.

No one can become highly civilized–and henceforth I use the term 'highly civilized' to distinguish the civilizers from the simply 'civilized' who take colour from them–no one, I say, can become highly civilized without a fair measure of material security. In fact, the *civitas,* or state, came into existence in consequence of a desire for material security. Do not run away, however, with the idea that material security alone can give the least tincture of civilization–think of the well-organized communities of the modern world. But to live a highly civilized life a man must be free from material cares: he must have food, warmth, shelter, elbow-room, leisure, and liberty. So here, at the outset, the eager philanthropist who, touched by my eloquence, has decided to devote his political abilities to the promotion of civilization, will be confronted by an urgent and awkward question: How are the civilizing few to be supplied with the necessary security and leisure save at the expense of the many?

The answer is that nohow else can they be supplied: their fellows must support them as they have always done. Civilization requires the existence of a leisured class, and a leisured class requires the existence of slaves–of people, I mean, who give some part of their surplus time and energy to the support of others. If you feel that such inequality is intolerable, have the courage to admit that you can dispense with civilization and that equality, not good, is what you want. Complete human equality is compatible only with complete savagery. But before plumping for barbarism let the philanthropist remember that there are such things as willing servants or, if he pleases, people content to make sacrifices for an ideal.

At any rate, to be completely civilized, to experience the most intense and exquisite states of mind, manifestly a man must have security and leisure. He must have enough to eat and drink, and the assurance of it, he must have warmth, shelter, and some elbow-room, all the necessaries and some of the superfluities of life. Also leisure is essential. He must have leisure to educate himself for the enjoyment of the best, and leisure to pursue it. Again he must have liberty: economic liberty which will put him above the soul-destroying dominion of circumstance and permit him to live how and where he will, and spiritual liberty—liberty to think, to feel, to express and to experiment. He must be free to cultivate his receptivity, and to be putting it always in the way of adventure. To get the best a man must live for the best.

Unluckily, material security, leisure, and liberty all cost money; and ultimately money is to be obtained only by productive labour. Now almost all kinds of money-making are detrimental to the subtler and more intense states of mind, because almost all tire the body and blunt the intellect. The case of artists, of whom the majority would cease altogether to create were they compelled to break stones or add up figures for six or seven hours a day, will serve to illustrate this truism. Further, a man who is to be educated to make a living cannot well be educated to make the most of life. To put a youth in the way of experiencing the best, a liberal and elaborate education to the age of twenty-four or twenty-five is essential; at the end of which the need for leisure remains as great as ever, seeing that only in free and spacious circumstances can delicate and highly-trained sensibilities survive. How many thousands of barristers, civil servants, and men of business, who left Oxford or Cambridge equipped to relish the best, have become, after thirty years of steady success, incapable of enjoying anything better than a little tipsy lust or sentimental friendship, cheap novels, cheaper pictures, vulgar music, the movies, golf, smoking-room stories, and laying down the law. As for physical labour; if anyone pretends that after a good day's digging or plumbing, hunting or shooting, he is in a mood to savour the subtler manifestations of the spirit, he is talking nonsense.

And there is more to be said. A combination of security, leisure, and liberty alone can give that sense of ease and that magnanimity lacking which life never attains its finest and fullest development. Generally speaking, those only who never had to earn money know how to spend it; they alone take it simply for what it is—a means to what they want. If freedom from wearing labour alone can preserve the fine edge of the mind, only independence will give a man courage to use it. Those who have never been obliged to please a master or conciliate a colleague alone retain the power of thinking and feeling with absolute honesty on all subjects. Only they know how to be perfectly disinterested and detached; how to pursue an idea without constantly looking to right and left for its practical implications; how to be remorseless in logic and in passion uncompromising. Will the most intellectual captain of industry be quite abstract in discussing political economy? Will the sublimest Platonist, should he happen also to be a paid teacher of Greek, judge the case for classical education wholly on its merits? Even socialists, when they happen also to be ill-paid wage-earners, fail to bring open minds to the very question we are discussing—Is economic equality compatible with the greatest good? Whereas socialism itself is the invention of leisured-class thinkers by whom mainly it was brought into practical politics.

As a means to good and a means to civility a leisured class is essential;

that is to say, the men and women who are to compose that nucleus from which radiates civilization must have security, leisure, economic freedom, and liberty to think, feel, and experiment. If the community wants civilization it must pay for it. It must support a leisured class as it supports schools and universities, museums and picture-galleries. This implies inequality—inequality as a means to good. On inequality all civilizations have stood. The Athenians had their slaves: the class that gave Florence her culture was maintained by a voteless proletariat: only the Eskimos and their like enjoy the blessings of social justice. Because few are born with ability to discover for themselves that world of thought and feeling whence come our choicest pleasures; because the abilities of these rot untended and run to seed in the open; because to be civilized society must be permeated and, what is more, continually nourished by the unconscious influence of this civilizing élite; a leisured class is indispensable. The majority must be told that the world of thought and feeling exists; must be shown, lying just behind the drab world of practical utility, a world of emotional significance. To point the road is the task of the few. Neither guides nor lecturers these, the highly civilized, will merely live their lives; and living will be seen to have pleasures and desires, standards and values, an attitude to life, a point of view, different from those of the busy multitude. By living passively they become the active promoters of good. For when it begins to appear that the few have discovered intense and satisfying delights which have escaped the notice of less inquisitive and less gifted pleasure-seekers, the many will begin to wonder. They will wonder whether there may not be pleasures better than their own. Can art and thought, the play of wit and fancy, and the subtler personal relations really mean more to these odd people than racing, yachting, hunting, football, cinemas, and whisky? One memorable day it will become unmistakably clear that they do; that there are people who could afford the latter and yet pursue the former. That makes one think. Here and there a barbarian grows inquisitive, grows suspicious of those easy, obvious pleasures the superiority of which he had always taken for granted. What if the more hardly won were the better worth having? As on a hot evening in late June the scent of hay will sometimes blow into a suburban slum, the faint fragrance of civility floats across his path. Dimly he surmises that here is good—better at any rate. As he passes across the public square that he has crossed a thousand times he is surprised by an inexplicable sense of well-being, and catches himself to his shameful amazement staring at a handsome fountain. Anything may happen. A sudden feeling of satisfaction may overcome him when he detects a contradiction in the newspaper which hitherto he had read with uncritical awe. The passionate denunciation, at a street corner, of some foreign government for doing what his own has failed to do may strike him as amusing rather than righteous. The fact that a bishop or a magistrate has declared something or other to be untrue or immoral may, on a sudden, be seen to prove nothing. One day, to his shocked delight, our barbarian will find himself laughing with Boccaccio at the monks.

That only a leisured class will produce a highly civilized and civilizing élite is an opinion supported by what seem to me incontrovertible arguments and borne out by history. In Athens, Florence, and eighteenth-century France the dirty work was done by a proletariat. Philanthropists seem to forget that Athenian culture was slave-supported: but he who would discover the conditions necessary to civilization must have a better memory, must remember that two-thirds–if not three-fourths of the inhabitants of Attica were slaves, without forgetting that Alcibiades was an exception. In Athens there were very few rich men. Civilization is not incompatible with socialism: a socialist state that wished to be civilized would support an idle class as a means to good just as it would support schools and laboratories. The only question would be how that class should be chosen. At present it is chosen by inheritance, a grossly extravagant system. There is no reason for supposing that the children of rich parents will be exceptionally intelligent and sensitive; and, in effect, the proportion of the existing leisured class which could be described as 'highly civilized' is absurdly small. Modern England maintains a multitude of idlers amongst whom are not enough highly civilized men and women to constitute a civilizing nucleus. Such a system is clearly uneconomical; and without undue optimism we may suppose that the future could devise some method which would exclude from the leisured class at least two thirds of those whose names now swell the peerage and whose portraits enliven 'the weeklies.' Without sacrificing anything more precious than Ascot and Cowes I think we might reduce considerably the cost of maintaining a leaven of idlers. Here it is none of my business to contrive the means: projects will be in the minds of all. There is something to be said for competitive examination. Each year the top boys and girls in the state schools might be promoted to the state-supported leisured class. Or, if you think it important–as I do rather–to begin the career of optimate at birth, choose by lot. Take every two-thousandth baby and make him or her a member, and you will get almost certainly a better result than you get from the present system. Remember, too, it is not necessary that all your idlers should be of the élite; it is necessary only that an adequate proportion should be. Some wasters you will get by any method. That does not matter. You will keep the number as low as you can without jeopardizing the essential, which is that there should be a class of men and women of whom nothing is required–not even to justify their existence; for, in the eyes of most of their contemporaries, many of the greatest benefactors of humanity, most of the great artists and thinkers, most, no doubt, of the nameless civilizers, have not justified theirs. Generally, their age could not appreciate their services; and only the existence of a leisured class, to which they belonged or in which they found patrons, made it possible for them to exist. Wherefore the existence of a leisured class, absolutely independent and without obligations, is the prime condition, not of civilization only, but of any sort of decent society. Not under compulsion, nor yet from a sense of duty, will the most valuable and difficult things be done. But create a class of which you ask nothing, and be sure that from it will come those who give most.

Do not mistake a crowd of big wage-earners for a leisured class. Men who earn several thousand pounds a year by their trade, profession, or calling are generally nothing better than overpaid helots. Of course there are exceptions; but by the nature of their lives these as a rule are rendered as incapable of becoming completely civilized as is any manual labourer by the nature of his: indeed, when he happens to be what is called 'a captain of industry,' or 'a great employer of labour,' the master is worse placed than the man. For the employer of labour, the great industrial, and the small, too, for that matter, tends to acquire a taste for power, a belief in success as the criterion of value, and a sense of the importance of his own undertakings, which unfits him peculiarly for clear thinking and fine feeling. It is a pretty comment on modern political thought that taxation should discriminate between earned and unearned income in favour of the former. The man who makes his money uses it generally as a means to more, as a means to power, consideration, ostentation, animal pleasures and barbarous amusements; it is amongst the receivers of unearned income that you must seek that leisured class which uses money as a means to good. The man who earns tends to grow hard, unsympathetic, narrow, impenetrable; he holds ferociously what he has and seeks ever to increase his store: it is from men of leisure have come most of our liberal, socialistic, and anarchical theories, to say nothing of that scepticism as to any individual's right to property or power which is nowadays a characteristic of culture almost. Seldom is earned income of much use to anyone but its owner—as mere capital it would be just as useful in the hands of the State; but of unearned income a fair part has ever been devoted to supporting those who by their unremunerative labours confer the highest benefits on mankind. That the basic principle of taxation should be the squeezing out of the leisured class for the benefit of great and small wage-earners is typical of a half-civilized age.

In a famous essay Renan points out with his usual persuasive reasonableness that the proper function of a leisured class is to stand aside from affairs and devote itself to maintaining standards by sacrificing the useful to the comely, and preserving in honour the fine and difficult things of life. A leisured class, bred to a tradition of independence, is in his opinion the *sine qua non* of civility. So far, naturally, I agree: where he seems to me to be on less sure ground is in his deduction, implied rather than stated, that the leisured class, if it is to exist, must rule. I see no necessity. On the contrary, it seems to me difficult, if not impossible, for anyone immediately and deeply concerned with the exercise of power to be completely civilized. Is not a ruling leisured class a contradiction in terms? What Renan had in mind was, I suspect, an aristocracy divided into two parts: a leisured class and a ruling, brought up in the same traditions and intermingling at every point. Certainly this is a possible way to civilization, providing as it does for a leisured class and a ruling class in sympathy with it; and on this system France was organized during the hundred and thirty years of her supreme civility–albeit Louis XIV drew the bulk of his administrators from a class that was not technically noble. An aristocracy may easily be divided into an active class (the *cracy*) and a contemplative. The latter will provide civilization; the former government; but it has yet to be proved–I express no opinion one way or the other–that active aristocrats make the best rulers. Clearly it is desirable that the civilizing élite should have no say whatever in the government, since the exercise of power, as we have seen, is likely to play havoc with a man's finer abilities. On the other hand, there is a danger, which Renan foresaw, that, unless the rulers have traditions, beliefs, sympathies, and material interests in common with the civilizers, human jealousy and stupidity, inflamed by a public and expensive recognition of human inequality, will, by refusing to maintain the leisured class, allow society to slip back into antisocratic savagery. The question does arise therefore–What form of government will be most favourable to civilization? It is a question almost impossible to answer.

Any form of government may be favourable provided it supply a sufficiency of children with the most thorough and liberal education wit can devise or money buy, provided it support these throughout life with an income adequate to their cultivated wants, provided above all it ask nothing of them. The notion that what are called 'free institutions' are necessary to civilization is contradicted by reason and history. To say nothing of the East–of China and Persia, of which we agreed to say nothing–we know that the civilization of the Renaissance was fostered and brought to flower in the age of the tyrants. For, as Burckhardt, writing of the Italian tyrants, sensibly observes, 'political impotence does not hinder the different tendencies and manifestations of private life from thriving in fullest vigour and variety.' But even after the government–whatever it may be–has decided to maintain a leisured class, still it will have to count and distribute the cost. On precisely what sum a man or woman can support his or her civility it is impossible to say, because the figure will vary with varying conditions. In present circumstances I do not think one could do with less than seven or eight hundred a year, the State, of course, making itself responsible for children. Likewise, it is impossible to say what proportion of the population must be highly civilized to civilize moderately the rest. All one knows is that in England the proportion is inadequate. This seems to require explanation: the amount of unearned income in the country is vast and the number of recipients considerable. One reason may be that a great many of those who draw unearned income and should therefore belong to the civilizing, leisured class prefer to increase their incomes by producing, and thus remain half-civilized at best; another, that too much unearned income is stuffed into a few pockets. Two obvious and practical measures for the promotion of British culture would be: a law to compel the rich to be idle; another to abolish that barbarous anomaly, the individual with more than three thousand a year.

This may be good political advice, it does not I fear bring us much nearer an answer to our question–What form of government would be most favourable to civilization? To answer that confidently we should have first to ask another, a psychological, question: Human envy and suspicion being what they are, is it conceivable that men should ever support freely, with eyes wide open, for their own spiritual good, but to their material detriment, a privileged group of apparently idle, happy, highly civilized people? Only politicians and police-court magistrates can tell for certain of what human nature is or is not capable; and to them I gladly leave the task. Only this I know: unless men are capable of such enlightened generosity, democracy and civilization are incompatible.

Work and Leisure under Industrialism

By CLEMENT GREENBERG

THERE has been much talk about how the new leisure created by the shortening of hours of work can be turned to the advantage of humanist culture by providing it with a broader social basis than ever before. Leisure is seen as not a matter merely of free, empty time, but as also determined by the material and social circumstances under which it is enjoyed. What is not realized, however, is the even greater degree to which it is determined by the kind of work, or necessary activity, that sets it off. Leisure–even for those who do not work–is down at bottom a function of work, flows from work, and changes as the nature of work changes.

Leisure in traditional society (the "peasant," feudal, semi-feudal, or merchant's society which was the most we knew until two hundred years ago) was–for most classes in theory, and for the upper classes that supported high culture, in practice–the *positive* aspect of life, and the condition for the realization of its highest values. Economically productive work lacked prestige, as we know, and was regarded as life's negative aspect. (However much the peasant or farmer has praised himself since time immemorial for doing such work, it was almost always with the resentful feeling that nobody in city or manor really agreed with him.) But even more fundamental was the fact that purposeful work was not separated from all that was not work as sharply and unequivocally in terms of time, effort, and attitude as it is now. For one thing, most work used to be work on the land, which is difficult to compartmentalize in terms of time; for another, traditional work was adulterated more or less by irrational practices–customs, rites, observances

Section V from "Work and Leisure under Industrialism," by Clement Greenberg, *Commentary*, Volume 16, Number 1 (July 1953), pp. 57-61. Reprinted by permission of the author and the publisher. (Copyright 1953 by the American Jewish Committee.)

—that, conceived of originally as means of helping work achieve its ends, then becoming ingrained as matters of propriety and custom, actually furnished occasions *inside* work for relief from the strain of its purposefulness. With the distinction between work and leisure blurred in this way, culture could preserve a certain place and role within the former—at the cost, to be sure, of its efficiency.

Whether work was rendered much less of an affliction thereby is debatable. But the easier or more "natural" rhythm and pace of traditional work did, it would appear, take a lighter toll of the nerves—and if the working classes of traditional society lived more brutish lives than ours, that may have been not so much because they toiled like beasts of burden, but because they had less material goods at their disposal as a result, precisely, of the fact that they did not work hard or rationally enough. The upper classes, at least—those whose members did not perform manual labor—were able to take fuller advantage of the orientation of traditional work towards leisure, and turn it to the benefit of high culture as well as of themselves, while escaping most of the consequences of its low productivity.

To the exact end of greater productivity, capitalism, Protestantism, and industrialism have brought about a separation of work from all that is not work which is infinitely sharper and more exclusive than ever in the past. And as work has become more concentratedly and actively work—that is, more strictly controlled by its purposes, more efficient—it has pushed leisure out of the foreground of life and turned it into the negative instead of positive complement of itself. Work may be less arduous physically than it used to be, but its present standards of efficiency require one to key oneself to a higher pitch of nervous and mental effort, if only for the sake of the self-control and self-denial required by any kind of sustained activity directed solely towards an end outside itself. Leisure, in compensation, has become much more emphatically the occasion for flight from all purposefulness, for rest, respite, and recuperation.[1] It is certainly no longer the sphere *par excellence* of realization, but a passive state, primarily, in which one's least passive need is for distraction and vicarious experience that will give those immediate satisfactions denied one during working hours by the constraint of efficiency. This in itself is a valid need, but when one's nerves insist that it be met with a minimum of mental exertion on one's own part only a base kind of culture can satisfy it, a kind of culture that has lost all efficacy as recreation (in the literal sense) and become entirely a matter of rudimentary entertainment and diversion—of the sort, exactly, that we see in lowbrow and much of middlebrow culture.

This new relation between work and leisure—which I have simplified and exaggerated in order to describe—would have less of an effect on culture, and particularly on high culture, were the rich still exempted from work. But as their monopoly on comfort has been broken by industrialism, so has the monopoly on economic work of those who are less than rich (as though industrialism could shorten working hours only by making work universal). The upper classes can no longer say to the rest of society: "Work–that's your fate, not ours." Status and prestige are not derived so implicitly as before from social origin, and are conferred more and more preponderantly on achievement, and sustained achievement at that. Old-fashioned, complete leisure is now felt by the rich, too, as idleness, as remoteness from reality, and therefore the way to demoralization, thus no longer presupposed as the natural and positive condition of the realization of the highest values–much less as the end for which one strives in youth as well as old age.[2]

In this point if no other, Puritanism has won a lasting victory. Work has now become the main business of life and the ground of reality for all classes of industrial society. And while the rich man may be far less "alienated" from his job than the poor, he is subject to the same "banausic" rule and pace of efficiency, which transform his leisure, too, into one without mental ease, a series of breathing spells, no matter how extended, in which it is difficult for him, too, to collect and recreate himself.[3]

The highest level that humanist culture seems to be able to attain under this new kind of leisure is the middlebrow. And according to the evidence we have so far, the quantitative increase and diffusion of such leisure do not promise of themselves to raise that level very much. Nor would the restriction of social movement, the further improvement of standards of living, or even the raising of standards of public education–not of themselves, not as long as leisure, and work, remain what they have latterly become for everyone.

Marx expected socialism, with a working day of four hours or less, to solve the problem of culture under modern industrialism (a problem to which he did not, for that matter, give a great deal of thought), but work, and efficiency in work, would still be necessary to the success of an integrally socialist as to any other kind of industrial order, and leisure, no matter how much enlarged, would still be dominated and enervated by work, and colored by the anxiety that the rule of efficiency seems to provoke wherever it is "internalized"–as it must be if industrialism is really to function.[4]

Nor is it likely that the presumably greater security of life under socialism would radically lessen that kind of anxiety and the demand for anodynes to relieve it. Thus not purely political or economic, not purely social or cultural measures appear to promise to solve the problem of authentic and high culture under industrialism–not as long as it goes unsolved in the sphere of work.

It is doubtful, moreover, whether that solution could be achieved merely by so changing work as to restore leisure as the theater of genuine culture while leaving work, as before, outside. This would require making leisure again the positive aspect of life and work the negative one. But this is impossible under full-fledged industrialism because it would mean relaxing efficiency. Industrialism, with all its burden, its work and routine, is accepted by and large because it opens up and begins to realize–for the first time–the prospect of a higher level of material well-being for all classes; to slacken efficiency would postpone that realization, and to this the mass of people in a country like ours, where the awareness of the relation between such causes and such effects has become almost universal, will not consent. If, therefore, the problem of achieving an authentic culture under industrialism has to be solved without reducing efficiency, or else not at all, then the only way out becomes the highly improbable one of making work itself the main sphere of culture—that is, of integrating it with culture *without* sacrifice of its efficiency. Which is also to say that work under industrialism, whether in factory or office, must be made the source of more immediate satisfactions for those who perform it.

The problem as stated looks so formidable, so unprecedented, that one's first impulse is to cast around for alternatives. May we not ask, with Sir Herbert Read, whether it won't be possible for authentic non-utilitarian culture to develop in industrial leisure on the basis of the kind of interest and activity that go into the hobby? May not leisure in that way be infused with some of the positive spirit of work and redeemed from its passivity? As it happens, the hobby is in its nature and history closely tied to industrialism. It has taken hold only during the last two centuries and, as distinct from the dilettante's or leisured man's avocation, can be defined as a homeopathic reaction from the purposefulness of serious and necessary work (or acquisition) that takes the form of work (or acquisition) itself. One works at the hobby for the sake of the pleasure in work, and is able to take pleasure in it because its end is not serious or necessary enough to subject its means to the rule of efficiency (though one can make a hobby of efficiency too). The hobby asserts the value of one's time and energy in terms of immediate rather than ultimate satisfactions, and relates the end of work directly to the particular person who performs it.

The hobby is play, and play, according to Jan Huizinga, is the mother of culture. But play as such, under industrialism, is no longer *serious* enough to open the way to the heart of things—is rather a detour or escape. Authentic culture must, by definition, not be that. It has, instead, to lie at the center, and from there irradiate the whole of life, the serious as well as the not serious. It is serious work that has become, as I have said, the center of all our lives. If serious work—not leisure—can be infused with something of the spirit of the hobby, with something of its unseriousness, well and good; but not the other way round—not as long as leisure remains peripheral, as it must, and the hobby finds its only existence there.

But looking again into the remoter past, we discover that the necessity of integrating non-material culture with economic work is not altogether novel. We have only to follow traditional society far enough back. In certain respects, as Marx saw, we have come full circle. Everyone, as a rule, had to work in primitive socities, as they do now in an advanced industrial one. This made the question of culture in early societies, too, coincide largely with that of work, for they likewise had no leisure class to carry on culture as something apart from work. But these societies solved the problem automatically: that is, it did not exist before its solution.

The remoter pre-urban, and archaic urban past shows us art, religion, and lore, not only as barely distinguishable from one another in practice, but also as hard to distinguish, in intention, from the technologies of production, war, and healing. Rite, myth, magic, decoration, image, music, dance, and poetry appear to have been art, religion, lore, defense, work, and healing at once, all of them parts of a single complex meant to safeguard mortal existence. Five thousand years of urban history have gradually separated these activities, with their implicit ends, and sealed them off from each other, so that we at last have art (or culture) for its own sake, religion for the sake of things knowable only outside life (or, like art to some degree, for the sake pure and simple of states of mind), and work for the sake of exclusively practical, "objective" aims. The problem now is to restore intimate relations between the three, or—with religion, as I think, ruling itself out as a social form—between the two. For if culture cannot be again closely related to work, it cannot be related closely enough to that reality which has again become fundamental for all of society.

Industrialism, imposing work on everyone—without, by that fact, doing away with exploitation—has confronted us more explicitly than ever before with work in its aspect as a limitation on human freedom—the aspect the author of Genesis must have had in mind when he described the fall of man (and beginning of history) as a fall into reproduction, work, and death. If man is to continue discovering and realizing his possibilities in history he will, at this point, have to broach the problem of culture and work—which is to say, of his mastery over work—more radically than he has so far.

It may be that industrial man will not be able even to begin to solve the problem;[5] it may be that the problem is permanently insoluble. But if so, then Eliot will have been right, and a revival of high, authentic urban culture must await the collapse or retreat of the industrial system, and the re-emergence of a leisured ruling class on the basis of a new form of the old order and of an economy of the old scarcity and squalor. . . . In the meantime, high culture, on its non-aesthetic side, may be able to survive as a set of special disciplines practiced during working hours by professionals—and to the extent necessary for the maintenance of the skills and knowledges required for the operation of the industrial system—but not as art, not as humanistic culture, not as something that informs, and is nurtured by, the presence of the mere well-educated citizen. And then high culture, as a department of industrial work—that is, as a thing worked at but not flowing from work—will impose the same strain as every other kind of industrial work, and the mandarins who work at it will have to devote their leisure to recuperation the way the rest of us do.

This is a speculation, not an assertion. The ingenuity shown by man in solving his social problems in the past—and especially in the pre-urban past—gives reason to hope that he will eventually solve this one too. The solution will not guarantee his happiness, but it will, if found, certainly make him more human.

Notes

1. The difference between modern and traditional work lies in this tension, and not as much as is commonly thought in the difference between the machine-tending "robot's" boredom and the solicitous interest and commitment of the craftsman who shapes the product of his work from beginning to end. It is forgotten that only a small proportion of traditional work was done by craftsmen; most of it was labor, drudgery, in town as well as country, and of a kind demanding even less use of the intelligence than does factory work.

2. See Aristotle in his *Politics,* VIII, 1337B and 1338A. With his customary psychological realism, he reports the common view, held from the dawn of urban civilization until a short while ago, of leisure as the highest condition of life for the young no less than the old: ". . . we should be able, not only to work well, but to use leisure *(schole)* well; for, as I must repeat once more, the first principle of all action is leisure. Both are required, but leisure is better than work and is its end; and therefore the question must be asked, what ought we do when at leisure? Clearly we ought not to be amusing ourselves, for then amusement would be the end of life . . . we should introduce amusements only at suitable times, and they should be our medicines, for the feeling that they create in the soul is a relaxation, and from the pleasure we get rest. But leisure *as such* (my italics) gives pleasure and happiness and enjoyment of life; these are experienced, not by the busy man, but by those who have leisure. . . . there are branches of learning and education which we must study merely with a view to leisure spent in intellectual activity, and these are to be valued for their own sake. . . ."

3. Also important is the difference between a leisure supported by servants and one in which you have to fend for yourself with the aid of "modern conveniences" and labor-saving appliances. A single housekeeper provides more ease than a thousand gadgets, as Schumpeter says.

4. Once efficiency becomes a matter of conscience, the failure to be completely efficient–or even to be able to imagine what the perfection of efficiency is–weighs like a sense of sin. For no one is ever efficient *enough.*

5. We do, I think, get a glimpse–if only that–of a part of such a solution in architecture, the healthiest of contemporary arts. The revival called the "international school" and–with less accuracy–"functionalism" is due in great measure to formal architecture's having, for practically the first time, been given the task of designing places of work. And in this task it has benefited from the growing realization on the part of industrial experts that cheerfulness and comfort can be as essential to efficiency as the more literally functional qualities of a building. That some number of people now get an immediate satisfaction from the décors in which they work such as they do not from the décors of their homes, and that this is provided by advanced, "highbrow" architecture, may be considered at least one gain for high culture under industrialism.

The Spread of Reading

By RICHARD D. ALTICK

Obviously, one cannot read without some leisure in which to do so. Leisure has never been equitably distributed in any civilized society, but in nineteenth-century England it was allotted with particular unevenness. In the middle class, even to some extent in its lower reaches, growing prosperity and the cheapness of labor enabled men and women to hire others for tasks

From Chapter 4 (originally titled "The Social Background") *The English Common Reader: A Social History of the Mass Reading Public 1800-1900,* by Richard D. Altick, published by The University of Chicago Press. (Copyright 1957 by The University of Chicago.) Reprinted by permission of the publishers.

they had hitherto done for themselves. The greater availability of cheap manufactured and processed goods—soap and candles, for instance, and food—gradually led people to give up producing such commodities for their own use, a practice that in any event was impossible for city-dwellers. Households in which repair work had formerly been done by father and sons now called in carpenters and masons. And most important of all, the menial chores which were traditionally the lot of wife and daughters could be transferred, at small expense, to domestic servants, one of whose regular duties, as often as not, was to exchange books at the circulating library or buy the new issue of *Eliza Cook's Journal* from the corner news agent. Hence to scores of thousands of families touched by the prosperity of the new age, relief from household duties provided a degree of leisure undreamed of in earlier generations.

But while leisure increased in the middle class, the ways it could be used were drastically limited, since this was the class most affected by the spread of evangelical principles. "For multitudes of the respectable population, outside entertainments, such as the theatre or the music-hall provided, were practically non-existent. Dancing was a snare of the devil. Even concerts, though Catalani might be singing and Paganini playing, were not encouraged by the unworldly; and it was not till the undeniable 'goodness' of Jenny Lind conquered the prejudice, that anything but oratorio was considered safe.[1] Nonconformists and Claphamites, therefore, on evenings not set aside for missionary meetings, shunned outside dangers, and spent the time in 'profitable' instruction and 'harmless' entertainment. Cards, of course, were forbidden, and, while a game of bagatelle might be allowed, billiards, even in the home, were never mentioned."[2] In so scrupulous an atmosphere, the reading habit flourished. The place of the evening reading circle in Victorian middle-class family life is so well known that it need be merely mentioned here. How widespread the institution was, and how deeply it influenced the tastes of the children who grew up in such homes, is attested in countless memoirs.

However, only the relatively well-to-do minority of the middle class, the merchants, bankers, professional men, manufacturers, and so on, could spend full evenings with their families and their books. In the lower levels of that class, most men spent long days at their work, small employers and overseers keeping as long hours as their workmen.[3] Retail tradespeople, a million and a quarter of them by the 1880's, were in their shops from seven or eight in the morning until ten at night, and on Saturdays until midnight. For skilled and unskilled laborers, the working day was so long during the first half of the century as to be a national scandal. Hundreds of thousands of miners and factory- and mill-hands crept to their employment before dawn and emerged after sunset. The fourteen-hour day was commonplace, and the sixteen-hour day was not rare. Only gradually were the hours reduced. London handicraft workers won a ten-hour day before the 1830's, and in 1847 a bitterly fought act of Parliament introduced it into the textile industry. Actually, however, the working day was longer than the bare figure suggests, for artisans and handicraftsmen frequently worked overtime, and in textile mills "ten hours" really meant 6:00 A.M. to 6:00 P.M. By the seventies, London artisans, after long agitation, achieved a fifty-four-hour week, while the textile trades worked two and a half hours longer. In the nineties the average work-week for such trades as shipbuilding, iron founding, cooperage, and building ranged from fifty to sixty hours, depending on the locality and, in outdoor trades, the season of the year. In the warehouses of the so-called "Manchester trade" the fourteen-hour day was still common.

On weekdays, therefore, few workers had time to read. Those in even the most favored trades came home no earlier than six or seven o'clock, and after the evening meal only an hour or two remained until fatigue and the prospect of rising before dawn the next day drove them to bed. Not until the sixties was the Saturday half-holiday generally introduced; and this involved only a modest curtailment of the working day—in the case of London building artisans, for instance, from eleven to seven hours. For shop assistants there was no relief at all. Saturday remained their longest day, a matter of sixteen hours behind the counter. Under such circumstances it was only natural that the workman confined most of his reading to Sundays. Hence the great popularity of the Sunday newspaper, and, beginning in the late forties, the weekly miscellany-*cum*-sensational-fiction paper which was issued on Saturday.

During the decades which witnessed the worst oppression of the wage-earning masses, the townsman with time to kill on Saturday night and Sunday had little choice of diversion. He could get drunk at a public house, or, to the accompaniment of song, at a concert room or a dancing saloon; he could visit a brothel, he could get into a fist fight or attend a bear-baiting, he could loaf in the streets—and not much else. The teeming cities had virtually no provision for decent public recreation: few theaters or music halls, no parks for strolling and picnicking, no museums or art galleries, no free libraries. In 1844 Preston was the only town in all of Lancashire with a public park. But shortly thereafter, local authorities were for the first time allowed to use public funds for recreational facilities, and parks and other places of resort appeared in most cities.[4] There remained, however, the somber pall of the English Sunday. While the working class as a whole was indifferent to Sabbatarianism, it nevertheless shared the consequences of the ban on Sunday recreation. In 1856 proposals to open the British Museum and the National Gallery after church services on Sunday and to hold Sunday band concerts in the London parks were shouted down from the pulpit, and not until forty more years had elapsed were London museums and art galleries opened on Sunday afternoons. Only in the seventies did the Midland workman have access to such institutions on his one day of relaxation.[5] Until well past mid-century, therefore, the man who was not content with aimless loafing or with grosser amusements had little alternative but to spend his Sunday leisure with a book or paper.

When the workweek was shortened and strict Sabbatarianism began to fade, the English worker found many ways of passing his leisure apart from reading. Railways ran special cheap trains to the country and the seaside; theaters and music halls multiplied; cricket, football, and other spectator sports became increasingly popular. Among the middle class, the partial emancipation of women encouraged the whole family to move outdoors for its pleasure, so that the domestic reading circle declined as an institution. The new fashion for participant sports—cycling, rowing, tennis, walking, croquet—offered powerful competition to the reading habit. Thus the spread of leisure both favored and discouraged the development of the reading public. There was more time to read, but eventually there were also many more things to do with one's spare time.

One major innovation, at least, resulted in an unquestionable increase in reading: the coming of railway travel. Cheap, swift, and more or less comfortable transportation was available to the ever greater number of men whose business required travel, as well as to those who wished to visit relatives or have a holiday in the Cotswolds or by the sea. A railway trip meant an hour or a day of enforced leisure; and to escape the boredom of staring out the window or listening to one's chance companions, one read. It was by no means accidental that from the 1850's onward a whole class of cheap books was known as "railway literature," and that a large portion of the retail book and periodical trade of England was conducted at railway terminals. Every passenger train of the hundreds that roared down the rails in the course of a single day carried a cargo of readers, their eyes fixed on *Lady Audley's Secret* or the *Times*. Perhaps no other single element in the evolving pattern of Victorian life was so responsible for the spread of reading. The effect was increased still further when, with the rise of dormitory suburbs around the great cities, commuting between home and business became a daily occupation of many thousands.

In the country, meanwhile, conditions of life among the masses offered little incentive or opportunity for reading. Education was hard to come by, and most children, if they went to school at all, did so for only a year or two and then were put to work in the fields, at crow-scaring if they were not yet strong enough for manual labor. Working hours for all laborers were long. Paul Tregarva, the studious gamekeeper in Kingsley's *Yeast,* observed: "As for reading, sir, it's all very well for me, who have been a keeper and dawdled about like a gentleman with a gun over my arm; but did you ever do a good day's farm-work in your life? If you had, man or boy, you wouldn't have been game for much reading when you got home; you'd do just what these poor fellows do,—tumble into bed at eight o'clock, hardly waiting to take your clothes off, knowing that you must turn up again at five o'clock the next morning to get a breakfast of bread, and, perhaps, a dab of the squire's dripping, and then back to work again; and so on, day after day, sir, week after week, year after year. . . ."[6]

While printed matter became more easily accessible in the towns and cities, with their coffeehouses and news vendors and free libraries, the humble countryman met few books or papers in his way through life. Hawkers came to his door occasionally with broadsides, tracts, and number-publications; but, with agricultural wages consistently the lowest in the nation, there was little money to buy them. In a certain Kentish farming parish in the 1830's, only four out of fifty-one families possessed any books besides the Bible, Testament, and prayer and hymn books, and only seven parents "ever opened a book after the labours of the day were closed."[7] Nor was this parish unusual. Again and again in the records of the time we find evidence of how little printed matter—perhaps no more than a copy or two of cheap magazine—regularly came to a country village. Not until the cheap periodical press made efficient use of railway transportation and local distributors, and rural education received much-needed aid under the Forster Act of 1870, did the majority of country-dwellers acquire much interest in reading.

Victorian writers and speakers never tired of reminding their audiences that the taste for reading has an almost unique advantage in that it can be indulged at any time and in any place. One must go from home to satisfy a love of nature or sports or the fine arts, and he must do so at certain hours or seasons; but one can read any time at one's own fireside—a great point in an age that venerated domesticity. Such a notion was not, however, very realistic. The typical nineteenth-century home was not a place where a man could read quietly and uninterruptedly during whatever free hours he had. For every household in which it was possible there were a hundred where it was out of the question.

This is not the place to rehearse the appalling story of housing conditions in the new industrial England, or, for that matter, in the countryside, where the sentimentally celebrated English cottage was, oftener than not, a ruinous hovel. It is enough to recall that town workers lived in bestial squalor, packed together in dark, stinking warrens in which privacy, quiet, and the most rudimentary comforts were alike unknown. To such people, as to the gamekeeper Tregarva, praise of books as a means of contenting one's self during a peaceful evening or a Sunday must have seemed a bitter jest. How, with a distraught, sickly wife complaining and a brood of ill-fed squalling children filling the room, and drunken neighbors brawling next door, could a reader, no matter how earnest, concentrate upon a book? It was even worse if, as was true of many working-class dwellings, some sort of handicraft was carried on on the premises. In 1849 a missionary to the handweavers of Spitalfields—once aristocrats of labor, with neat gardens beside their homes, and mutual-improvement societies—told a committee of Parliament, "I frequently find as many as seven or eight persons living all in one room; in that room, perhaps, there will be two looms at work, so that the noise and discomfort render it almost impossible that a working man, if he were ever so well inclined to read, could sit down and read quietly."[8] John Passmore Edwards, the son of a Cornish carpenter, recalled how as a child he read by the light of a single candle in the midst of a talkative and active family. "Hundreds and hundreds of times I pressed my thumbs firmly on my ears until they ached, in order to read with as little distraction as possible."[9]

To try to read in the midst of the domestic hurly-burly meant, too, that one would be subject to the ridicule, or at best the well-meant disapproval, of those who failed to share one's inclination. Thomas Burt, the future trade-union leader and M.P., grew up in a cottage that was virtually a neighborhood crossroads. "At it again, Thomas!" a constant visitor, who was a Methodist coal miner, would exclaim. 'What can thoo be aiming at? Thou won't join the church; thou won't preach or address temperance meetings. What's the meaning of all this poring over books, this plodding search for knowledge that thou won't use? Thou'll destroy thy health, and nobody will be the better for thy labours."[10] This was not the least of the difficulties which the pursuer of knowledge had to face.

It was not to be marveled at, then, that most workingmen, no matter how much they may have wished to read, sought relaxation outside the home. The street, the public house, the cheap theater if one was nearby, and later the park and the sports field were to be preferred to a fireside which was anything but peaceful. Nor was overcrowding confined to working-class tenements and cottages. It was found, to a scarcely smaller degree, in the homes of the lower-middle class. At no time in the century did residential building keep pace with the growth of the population, and in any case incomes were insufficient to rent quarters that were adequate according to the most modest standards of our own day. Taking the nation as a whole, the average number of persons to a living unit fell in the course of the century only from 5.67 to 5.2, and as late as the 1880's one-fifth of the entire population of London lived more than two to a room.[11]

Nor was this all. In the ordinary home, decent lighting was not to be found until late in the century. In the period 1808-23 the window tax, a relic dating from 1696, reached its highest level. Houses with six windows or less were taxed 6*s*.6*d*. to 8*s*. annually; seven-window houses, a pound; nine-window houses, two guineas, and so on up. Even an aperture only a foot square was considered a window. Although in 1823 the tax was halved, and in 1825 houses with less than eight windows were exempted, builders still were discouraged from putting any more openings in a house than were absolutely necessary, with the result that only one-seventh of all the houses in Britain fell under the tax.[12] Not without reason did Dickens remark that the window tax (abolished, finally, in 1851) was an even more formidable obstacle to the people's reading than the so-called "taxes on knowledge"—the duties on newspapers, advertisements, and paper.[13]

The average early nineteenth-century home was dark enough during the day; at night it was no brighter. In most houses at the beginning of the century tallow dips (rush lights) or candles were the only sources of illumination apart from the fireplace. During the thirties and forties colza-oil and whale-oil lamps were introduced into the households of the well-to-do, followed by paraffin lamps in the fifties and eventually by gas. It may well be that these improvements were hastened as much by the increased amount of reading being done in such homes as by the contrast between the brilliancy of gas lighting in streets and public places and the feeble illumination afforded by candles. In the dwellings of the working class, however, candles and rush lights remained the usual sources of light. They were not cheap. In the first half of the century a pound of candles (two dozen) cost about 7*d.* and in humble homes was made to last a week or longer. Each candle provided from two to three hours' light. When only one or two were used at a time, continuous reading was a trying experience. Rush lights, being cheaper, were used in the poorest households, but they gave an even feebler light. To the devoted reader, however, even they were precious; Kingsley's Alton Locke, for instance, recorded how, after putting out his candle for the night, he continued his studies by the glimmer of a rush light he had earned by bringing bits of work home from the tailor's sweatshop.[14]

Reading in such light could not help taxing the eyes. This was a powerful deterrent to the spread of the reading habit, especially in an age when print was villainously small (largely because the high paper duties requiring crowding as much as possible on a page). The eyestrain involved in many manufacturing operations, such as loom-tending, was great, and mills and factories were often wretchedly lighted. Furthermore, since the diet of the masses was not only scanty but ill balanced, poor nutrition must have affected the sight of countless thousands.

Spectacles were used, of course, but by no means everybody who needed them had them; in the country and slums especially they were something of a luxury. It was a remarkable event in the life of young Carlyle when he was able to send presents of two pairs of glasses to his parents from Edinburgh in 1821.[15] Not until the middle of the twentieth century, indeed, were spectacles freely available to all Englishmen. Without them, during the nineteenth century, a multitude of would-be readers, their eyes weakened by faulty diet or taxing occupation or simply by age, were barred irrevocably from the pleasures of print.

There was, finally, the element of sheer fatigue. A man's eyes might be perfect, but after working all day at some monotonous or strenuous task he was so tired that unless his will to read was very strong he was likely to fall asleep over his book or paper. Far preferable in his state of exhaustion was a refreshing visit to a public house (where, to be sure, he could glance over a paper if he were so disposed) or simply an hour or two spent loafing before his door. It would take a type of literature especially suited to men and women with dulled minds and tired bodies to turn manual workers into habitual readers.

It is hard, perhaps impossible, to recreate the spirit of so large and inarticulate a community as the English working classes in the nineteenth century. If we attempt to do so by examining only the immense body of sociological data assembled by parliamentary committees and statistical societies, we must believe that men and women were so brutalized out of any semblance to normal mortals that they were physical organisms and economic units alone, without any of the emotional life and the intellectual and spiritual aspirations which mark the man from the animal. But this is an incomplete view, springing from the limited nature of the age's humanitarianism. Reformers like Chadwick, Kay-Shuttleworth, and Shaftesbury were concerned simply with ameliorating the common man's physical existence, and parliamentary inquiries never showed the slightest curiosity, except where it was a question of religious observance or ordinary morality, about the inner lives of the workers—a subject which in any case hardly lends itself to investigative treatment.

One-sided though it is, the impression we receive of the worker and his family from the classic sources of early nineteenth-century social history is not wholly false. If there was ever a time when the English masses approached a state of downright bestiality, it was then. The great migration from village to city produced a crisis in popular culture. Though they were already deteriorating, there had still survived in the eighteenth century the rural institutions of holiday-making, pageantry, and fairs. There was still the lore of the countryside and the songs and stories that had been handed down in the cottage from generation to generation. Illiterate though the common countryman may have been, his participation in the popular cultural tradition saved him from being a stolid brute.

When the villager was transformed into the slum-dwelling factory laborer, however, this tradition was lost to him. In addition, whatever contact he had earlier with printed matter became more tenuous. Many cottages had had their little shelf of worn and precious books, family possessions passed down through a century or more—the Bible, *Robinson Crusoe, Pilgrim's Progress,* ballads, and chapbooks bought at a fair long ago or from a peddler at the door. But when the children moved to the cities, the books were left behind or soon were lost in the course of their owners' restless migration from one tenement to another, and there was little chance to replace them. The custom of reading by the fireside vanished, along with other homely habits, and books no longer were prized as symbols of a family's continuity.

Tragically, it was at this very time that the worker most needed the spiritual and emotional strength which reading might provide. He desperately needed some relief from the deadly monotony of factory work, which was, Friedrich Engels observed, "properly speaking, not work, but tedium, the most deadening, wearing process conceivable. The operative is condemned to let his physical and mental powers decay in this utter monotony, it is his mission to be bored every day and all day long from his eighth year."[16] It was no cause for surprise, as Engels went on to say, that drunkenness and sexual promiscuity—the only two solaces the worker had regularly available—reached such alarming proportions in the manufacturing towns.

Even more dreadful was the loss of personal individuality. Workers' lives were regulated by the ringing of the factory bell and regimented by a system of rules and penalties. They had no personal pride in their work, for the product of their labor was not theirs alone but that of many other workers. They had no sense of personal destiny, for their lives were totally at the mercy of conditions beyond their control, the fluctuations of trade, the whim of the employer, the invention of new labor-saving machinery.

And perhaps worst of all was the overwhelming loneliness the individual man and woman felt in the midst of the crowd. "The sons of farmers and agricultural laborers who congregated in newly created slums were natives of all four corners of England and Wales. They were foreign to each other, they even spoke different dialects and they were completely lost in that human flotsam and jetsam. The new rows of tenements had no parish church, no local vicar with his school, no cultural background or local tradition. In their native villages they were human personalities, although subordinate; here they became ciphers, an economic commodity which was bought and sold according to the market price of labour."[17] The only strong bond that held the victims of the industrial revolution together was a common misery of body and soul.

Torn away from the old cultural tradition, battered and adrift in a feelingless world, the millions of common people needed decent recreation more urgently than any generation before them. As Sir John Herschel, who was gifted with rare insight in this matter, observed in 1833, "The pleasant field-walk and the village-green are becoming rarer and rarer every year. Music and dancing (the more's the pity) have become so closely associated with ideas of riot and debauchery, among the less cultivated classes, that a taste for them for their own sakes can hardly be said to exist. . . . While hardly a foot of ground is left uncultivated, and unappropriated, there is positively not space left for many of the cheerful amusements of rural life. . . . It is physically impossible that the amusements of a condensed population should continue to be those of a scattered one."

Books, said Herschel, were the answer to the pressing problem of the workingman's amusement. Reading "calls for no bodily exertion, of which he has had enough, or too much. It relieves his home of its dulness and sameness, which, in nine cases out of ten, is what drives him out to the ale-house, to his own ruin and his family's. It transports him into a livelier, and gayer, and more diversified and interesting scene, and while he enjoys himself there, he may forget the evils of the present moment, fully as much as if he were ever so drunk." And most important of all, Herschel remarked, "Nothing unites people like companionship in intellectual enjoyment." With books, the dreary clouds of despair and loneliness could be driven away.[18]

With a few noteworthy exceptions like Herschel and Dickens, contemporary social critics and reformers failed to understand, or at least to sympathize with, this imperative need for escape on the part of the physically and spiritually imprisoned. The great majority of the missionaries of reading, who came bearing social soporifics put up by the church or by Brougham's Society for the Diffusion of Useful Knowledge, simply could not countenance this motive. The result was that their zeal to spread the taste for reading was seriously, almost fatally, misapplied. They preached true doctrine—the rewards that lie in the printed page—but for the wrong reasons. Had they recognized the deep-seated desire for imaginative and emotional release which disposes ordinary people to read, and not insisted upon their own well-meant but unrealistic program, their efforts would have borne far healthier fruit. Any man, observed Wilkie Collins, "can preach to them [the common people], lecture to them, and form them into classes; but where is the man who can get them to amuse themselves? Anybody may cram their poor heads; but who will lighten their grave faces?"[19]

The obstacles in the way of the spread of reading among the masses were varied and numerous, as the following chapters will show. But while the impediments were great, the need was greater. The hunger for diversion was only one of the incentives that sooner or later drew men to the printed page. Others were almost as powerful: the desire to keep up with the events of the fast-changing world; the spirit of self-improvement which permeated down to the masses from the prevalent individualistic philosophy of the age; and the seething social unrest which found expression and focus in the radical propaganda of the period from 1815 to 1850. The size of the audience that devoured the writings of Cobbett and the Chartists is perhaps the best proof that the working class had not been reduced to a completely bestial condition. "The very vileness of the life in the herded towns and the very misery and discontent," says A. S. Collins, "became creative forces. . . . For the harsh discipline of the factories and the ugly wretchedness of the houses that were often no better than hovels, led men naturally to a sphere where they might find some self-expression, and to dreams and theories which might feed hope in their starved spirits. . . . Those gloomy tenements were the forcing houses of intellectual discontent, and from them shot up a new class of uneducated readers."[20]

Whatever they read—escapist fiction, or recipes for improving their economic position through increased knowledge and application to their trade, or virulent diatribes against political and social injustice—the English common people of the nineteenth century were, like human beings in all ages, dreamers of dreams. However drab, weary, and monotonous their lives, somewhere in their oppressed souls persisted an unquenchable desire for a happier gift from life than unremitting toil and poverty. Of these millions of Englishmen, H. G. Wells's late Victorian Mr. Polly is as good a symbol as any. Deep in his being, despite the deadening influence of the elementary school and life as a draper's assistant, "deep in that darkness, like a creature which has been beaten about the head and left for dead but still lives, crawled a persuasion that over and above the things that are jolly and 'bits of all right,' there was beauty, there was delight, that somewhere—magically inaccessible perhaps, but still somewhere, were pure and easy and joyous states of body and mind."[21]

There were uncounted numbers of Mr. Pollys in nineteenth-century England. Few read as widely or as constantly as he did; but a great many found in the printed word at least something of the same excitement and imaginative release. Among them, whose forebears had lived on the outermost fringes of the literary tradition, if, indeed, they had touched it at all, the frustration produced by the birth-throes of a new society bred a wholly novel veneration for the printed word.

Notes

1. And there were plenty of people, among them George Eliot during her brief but fervent flirtation with Evangelical principles, who regarded even oratorio as dangerously sensuous.
2. E. E. Kellett, "The Press," *Early Victorian England,* ed. G. M. Young (1934), II, p. 49.
3. The ensuing discussion of working hours is based on Sidney Webb and Harold Cox, *The Eight Hours Day* (1891), *passim;* Pauline Gregg, *Social and Economic History of Britain* (1950), pp. 134-36. On the "Early Closing" movement, see E. S. Turner, *Roads to Ruin* (1950), chap. iii.
4. J. L. & B. Hammond, *The Age of the Chartists* (1930), pp. 29-30. The Hammonds' two chapters on "The Loss of Playgrounds" are a good summary of this topic.
5. Gregg, p. 349.
6. *Yeast,* chap. xiii.
7. *Central Society of Education Publications,* III (1839), 108.
8. Public Libraries Committee (1849), Q. 2751.
9. *A Few Footprints* (1905), p. 6. It was Edwards' recollection of this maddening experience which led him, as the millionaire proprietor of the London *Echo,* to found free libraries where people could read in comparative tranquillity.
10. Burt, *Autobiography* (1924), pp. 122-23.
11. J. H. Clapham, *Economic History of Modern Britain,* II, p. 490; Porter, *The Progress of the Nation* (1912 ed.), p. 91.
12. Hammond, pp. 84-85 n.; Cole and Postgate, *The Common People* (1938 ed.), p. 300.
13. Dickens, *Letters* (Nonesuch ed.), II, 205.
14. This material on household illumination is derived from Porter (1851 ed.), p. 582; Marjorie and C. H. B. Quennell, *A History of Everyday Things in England, 1733-1851* (1933), p. 181; *Early Victorian England,* ed. G. M. Young (1934), I, 81, 127, 129; Kingsley, *Alton Locke,* chap. iii.
15. *Early Letters of Thomas Carlyle,* ed. C. E. Norton (1886), II, 2-4.
16. *Condition of the Working Class in 1844* (1892), p. 177.
17. Nicholas Hans, *New Trends in English Education in the Eighteenth Century* (1951), p. 211.
18. *Essays from the Edinburgh and Quarterly Reviews* (1857), pp. 8-10.
19. *A Rogue's Life,* chap. vi.
20. *The Profession of Letters,* pp. 42-43.
21. *Mr. Polly,* chap. i.

Farm and Countryside

By FOSTER RHEA DULLES

CONTEMPORARY observers were generally well agreed upon the lack of amusements in the rural America of the late nineteenth century. Life on the farm varied greatly in different parts of the country, but it could not anywhere offer social or recreational opportunities comparable to those of town or city. A majority of all Americans—two out of every three people still lived in the country despite the increasing exodus to the cities—found themselves largely cut off from both the commercial amusements and the organized sports which had so transformed urban recreation.

In the Middle West, more typical of the agrarian scene than any other part of the country, the isolation which the telephone, the automobile, and the radio have now broken down was especially marked. The farmer was often miles from his nearest neighbor, and even farther away from the town. The incessant labor, the almost unbroken daily routine, and the dreary loneliness of the great farms being opened up on the prairies have been described again and again in sectional novel and autobiography. The lack of amusements played no small part in stirring up the discontent that led to agricultural revolt and to the Populist movement of the 1890's.

An even gloomier picture is sometimes drawn of rural life in the East with its equally back-breaking work and often less favorable rewards. "As for amusements and recreation," Nathaniel Egleston wrote in 1878, "there is next to none, at least that is worthy of the name. It has been said of the New England villagers particularly that their only recreations are their funeral occasions. . . . Life drags on with an almost unvarying round of toil. There is little to break up its monotony."[1]

There were several factors in the latter half of the century that tended to make the country scene duller than it had ever been before. "In town one can find the swimming school, the gymnasium, the dancing master, the shooting gallery, opera, theatre, and panorama," Emerson had written in mid-century. "In the country he can find solitude and reading, manly labor, cheap living, and his old shoes; moors for game, hills for geology, and groves for devotion."[2] But not all the world was a philosopher, and in the busy life of the 1890's the greater opportunities of the city were increasingly responsible for that drift to metropolis which had its obverse side in rural stagnation.

"Sloven farms alternate with vast areas of territory half forest, half pasturage," wrote one observant traveler in the New England of 1892; "farm

---

buildings, partly in ruins, testify at once to the former prosperity of agricultural industry and to its present collapse." Another traveler was struck by the number of abandoned churches, dismantled academies, and moribund lodges in sections where the greater number of inhabitants had fled "to the manufacturing villages, to the great cities, to the West."[3] The mute evidence of this depopulation still remains in stone fences running through land now completely overgrown, in the crumbling foundations of houses long since deserted. Every present-day resident of New England encounters them in cross-country rambles.

Under such circumstances the young people were oppressed by the growing contrast between their drab lives and the freedom of the city. With the loss of the more active and enterprising members of the community, the stay-at-homes often lacked the initiative to make the most of such opportunities as still remained to them. They resigned themselves to the limited and circumscribed life that the depleted countryside represented. Moreover, where conditions were more favorable, as has already been pointed out, there was no longer the diversity of occupations on the farm which had given so much variety to rural life in earlier days. Without any shortening of the long hours of labor from sunrise to sunset, the farmer had to work on day after day at the same routine jobs—planting and reaping, the endless weeding of crops, and a multitude of daily chores. Nor could he count, as he had in the past, upon many interruptions to this steady grind. There were still hunting and fishing. The latter remained in some parts of the country a favorite diversion, but the good old days were passing for hunting. The farmer had his rifle or shotgun, possibly a pack of dogs, but the growing scarcity of game, and restrictions on such shooting as still remained, greatly limited the scope of what had once been such universal sport.

Something was lost—and for settlers in the Middle West it was within their own experience—as the years rolled on and agriculture became more a demanding business and less a way of life. Fencing the land and driving out the game marked progress. So did improved farm machinery—reapers, self-binding harvesters, engines for threshing grain. They also spelled the end of an era.

Hamlin Garland has described how the West was affected by these changes. "Buoyant, vital, confident," he wrote of his family and their neighbors in their early years of pioneering, "these sons of the border bent to their work of breaking sod and building fences quite in the spirit of sportsmen. . . . With them reaping was a game, husking corn a test of endurance and skill, threshing a 'bee'. . . . My father's laughing descriptions of the barn-raisings, harvestings and rail-splittings of the valley filled my mind with vivid pictures of manly deeds." But as time went on there were fewer and fewer of "the changing works" which had served to bring people together. "We held no more quilting bees or barn raisings," he wrote of conditions a decade later. "Women visited less often. . . . The work on the farms was never ending, and all teams were in constant use during week days. The young people got together on one excuse or another, but their elders met only at public meetings."[4]

For all this evidence of the dreariness of rural life, a picture of the country painted in such somber colors would nevertheless not be wholly true. There were compensations for the passing of old sports and pastimes. The farmer still had an independence and freedom which the clerk and factory worker lacked; he still had the active outdoor life from which the city dweller was cut off. He was never wholly deprived of normal recreation. His opportunities were rare, spaced at long intervals, but for that very reason they meant a great deal to him. He enjoyed them with an intensity which his city cousin, often surfeited with a wealth of easy entertainment, seldom experienced. Frequency alone is no test for the value of amusements. The isolated farm family may well have got a greater sum of enjoyment from its occasional social gathering or informal entertainment than urbanites could possibly derive from all their passive commercialized amusements. The Grange meeting, a social at the local school-house, a country dance, the Fourth of July picnic, the annual county fair, the coming of the circus—here were events looked forward to for months with eager anticipation, and remembered for months afterwards with continuing pleasure.

The Grange had been founded, as the Patrons of Husbandry, in 1867. A secret fraternal order, somewhat along the lines of the Odd Fellows, its organizers hoped it could do something to aid the farmers through various coöperative activities. Its growth was amazing—as might be expected in a period which was to witness such a rapid multiplication of fraternal orders, women's clubs, and other comparable organizations. Within six years there were fifteen thousand local granges scattered throughout the country, most numerous in the Middle West and South, with a total membership of a million and a half. The Patrons of Husbandry were fully embarked on a broad program of agricultural education, cooperative buying and selling and political activity.[5]

The Grange meeting, whatever the business under discussion, soon became the principal social gathering of the farm community. And this aspect of it was emphasized by the presence of women, admitted from the first into full membership. They gave the Grange a vitality it could not otherwise have had. There were sometimes other farm organizations that promoted rural recreation. In Iowa an Anti-Horse Thief Association, having largely succeeded in its goal of affording protection for its members' live stock, concerned itself with the lighter side of life.[6] But the Grange was the social leader. It undertook to organize lectures and concerts, held young people's debates and spelling-bees, promoted singing-schools, and arranged evenings of general entertainment.

The latter were usually held at the school-house; it was the community center. The bleak little building might be bare and unadorned, but swinging oil lamps and the cheerful warmth of its large wood stove quickly transformed it into an attractive meeting-place. The wooden benches or desk seats, initialed by the jack-knives of countless school-boys, were rearranged for the audience, and the chairman or speaker took the proud eminence of the teacher's platform. The farm families would drive in from miles around, often bringing box suppers, and spend a long evening over the simplest amusements. The program would be very much like that of the social in a small town. Recitations were popular, and the singing of old songs. There were sometimes charades or tableaux. If there were refreshments, they were usually coffee and doughnuts.

Sometimes at these entertainments at the school-house, and once in a while at some farmer's house, there would be a country dance. They were family affairs, young and old taking part. Chairs and tables would be pushed back, the fiddler get out his precious instrument, and the company wait expectantly for the shouted signal "Ba-al-ance all" or "A-al-all dance."

"It was a joy to watch him 'start the set,'" reads a description of one country fiddler (also the butcher and horse-doctor) called upon for a farm-house dance. "With a fiddle under his chin he took his seat in a big chair on the kitchen table in order to command the floor. 'Farm on, farm on!' he called disgustedly. 'Lively now!' and then, when all the couples were in position, with one mighty No. 14 boot uplifted, with one bow laid to the strings he snarled, 'Already–*Gelang!*' and with a thundering crash his foot came down. 'Honors *tew* your pardners–right and left Four!' And the dance was on!"[7]

The tunes were "Money Musk," "Fisher's Hornpipe," "The Irish Washerwoman," "Cut the Pigeon Wing," "Turkey in the Straw"–all the old favorites. One very popular was the minstrel song "Old Dan Tucker." It gave rise to a dance, sometimes known as the "tag dance," which foreshadowed a modern custom. At one point the fiddler, or whoever was calling the numbers, shouted out, "Go in Tucker!" and any odd man was allowed to cut in on a temporarily unattached girl.[8]

In the New England village, a barn or shed was sometimes made over into a dance-hall where the young people from near-by farms met on Saturday nights. A description of one such hall relates that it was an unpainted one-story building with open sides–a kerosene lamp swinging from the ceiling, a few American flags as decorations, and a large sign, "Please do not spit on the floor." Buckboards and buggies were hitched to the horse-rails while the dance was on.[9]

There was a prejudice against playing the fiddle or other instrumental music in some rural communities that still did not go so far as to disapprove dancing. This did not greatly matter: the young people sang the dance tunes, and the party went on no less gaily. "Weevily Wheat" was one of the favorite singing tunes:

Oh, Charley, he's a fine young man,
Oh, Charley, he's a dandy;
Charley is a fine young man,
For he buys the girls some candy.

Another even more gay and lilting air was "Buffalo Gals," sung with many local variations:

> Oh, Buffalo gals, ain't you comin' out tonight,
> Ain't you comin' out to-night, ain't you comin' out to-night;
> Oh, Buffalo gals, ain't you comin' out to-night,
> To dance by the light of the moon?

Reminiscing of life in rural Indiana about 1880, Chase S. Osborn described such dances in a letter incorporated by Mark Sullivan in *Our Times.* "The violin (fiddle) was taboo, but we sang songs and danced to them and hugged the girls until they would often grunt as we swung them clean off the floor or ground, in the barn or house or on the green:

> Higher up the cherry trees the sweeter grows the cherry,
> The more ye hug and kiss the gals the sooner they will marry.

And 'Billy Boy'—'She's a young thing and cannot leave her mother!' It was the time of Captain Jinks of the Horse Marines, and 'Down in a Coal Mine'. . . . And ' 'Round and 'Round the Mulberry Bush.' "[10]

In the more thickly settled and prosperous areas the simplicity of these evening entertainments and country dances was already a thing of the past by the end of the century. Here recreation on the farm followed more nearly that of the town, and might be closely associated with it. But for a great part of the Middle West those twin phenomena, lack of opportunity and narrow religious views, had the restraining influence so often observed in earlier days. They upheld a prejudice against any departures from old customs which was intensified for the older generation by what they heard of urban amusements.

More exciting and colorful than the school-house socials was the annual Grange picnic. It did not bring together only friends and neighbors. From a radius of perhaps a hundred miles, as in earlier pioneer days, the farmers and their families gathered at the grove that had been selected for the meeting. A few of the more prosperious might drive in spring-board buggies, but farm wagons were far more common. Two families would double up, making a "bowery wagon" out of their wagon-box by means of a few planks, and hitch up four-horse or six-horse teams. Members of the different lodges formed in line as they drew near the grove, carrying gay banners on which the women had emblazoned the lodge mottoes. "Some of the columns had bands," reads a contemporary description, "and came preceded by far faint streams of music, with marshals in red sashes galloping to and fro in fine assumption of military command."[11]

There were invariably speeches. If the picnic was held on the Fourth of July, the fervid political oratory that the West loved so much might hold the audience of farmers and their wives for hours. Basket lunches of cold fried chicken—a Grange picnic involved wholesale slaughter in the hen-roosts of the community—were next on the program. The band played, the men talked politics, and the women gossiped. There were often sports in the afternoon, and this was the nearest approach to the old rural pastimes of colonial days:

races of all kinds, wrestling matches, and that most popular of rural diversions, pitching horseshoes. There was usually a baseball game. "Nothing more picturesque, more delightful, more helpful," Hamlin Garland has recalled, "has ever arisen out of American rural life. Each of these assemblies was a most grateful relief from the sordid loneliness of the farm."[12]

Sometimes the Fourth of July was celebrated by a gathering in the nearest town—however distant it might be. On July 1, 1890, the local paper of one small Illinois town printed its entire issue in red ink to draw the farmers' attention to the attractions it was planning for the Fourth. In response to such a glowing appeal, they came into town in greater numbers than on any previous holiday. A parade headed by a military band started the festivities, and this was followed by the usual patriotic address and an afternoon of sports. The townspeople had set up refreshment stands where the farmers supplemented their basket lunches. In the evening the firemen gave a ball at the city hall.[13]

The Fourth was always a tremendous day for men and women who day after day, week after week, seldom saw even their nearest neighbors. If they went to town, its life and movement, however small the place might actually be, held them enthralled. The games and sports were incidental. The crowd, the incessant activity of a large number of people, provided the real fun of the day at every Grange picnic or holiday celebration.

The annual state or county fair had its reason for being in the familiar exhibits of cows and pigs and chickens; pumpkins, corn, and tomatoes; jellies, pies, and fancywork. Farmers and their wives competed eagerly for the prized blue ribbons. But as time went on, the side-shows gradually overshadowed the main tent. "The people," sighed Josh Billings, "hanker fur pure agrikultural hosstrots."[14]

From colonial days America had enjoyed market fairs, and whether in New England or in the South, horse-races, prize contests, and the exhibitions of traveling showmen had been one of their distinctive features. When Elkanah Watson introduced the modern country fair early in the nineteenth century, he intended something quite different. The Berkshire Agricultural Society was concerned with rotation, use of fertilizer, careful seed selection, and intelligent animal-breeding. Its annual meetings were to teach a lesson the farmers could understand. The experiment was successful and quickly copied. In the period immediately following the Civil War there were over twelve hundred state, district, county, and township agricultural societies, and the greater number of them held annual fairs with an attendance from a few hundred to as many as ten thousand farmers.[15]

From the very first, plowing contests and speed trials had been necessary to show the advantages of careful breeding, and it was not long before the horse-race and the trotting match assumed an importance not entirely warranted on scientific grounds. Heavy milk-producers, mammoth sows, and prize pumpkins drew their crowds, but special stands had to be built at the track to hold the throngs that flocked to the harness races. We have seen what was happening in mid-century when even onetime Puritan New England produced crowds of thirty thousand for the trotting matches of the Boston Agricultural Club. After the Civil War the thousand-odd agricultural societies all had their races. A very reasonable economic motive furthered this development: the trotting matches drew so many people that they virtually supported the whole fair. Large purses consequently were put up to draw horses from all over the country and thereby attract still greater crowds. The fastest trotters, and a new professional class of drivers, made the rounds every fall. In the 1870's Goldsmith and American Maid were the bright stars of the Grand Trotting Circuit, and a few years later the famous Maud S lowered the mile record to 2:08¾ minutes. Adoption of the bicycle sulky and improvements in the tracks soon afterwards made the two-minute mile an almost everyday occurrence.[16]

Other commercial amusements now appeared. At first they were not officially permitted, but traveling showmen naturally took advantage of the crowds attracted by the fair. "On the outside of the grounds," stated the report of an Ohio fair in 1858, "there were any number *of outside shows;* learned pigs, fat women, snakes, monkeys, all jumbling together in Biblical confusion, while lager beer saloons and melon stands supplied those in quest of such delicacies."[17] It became obvious that if these amusements were to become associated with the fair, they might as well be within the grounds as without them, making their contribution to the running expenses of the often hard-pressed management.

"The same horse trots, ball-games, bicycle races, livestock exhibits, and trials of draught horses," a contemporary wrote of a New England fair in the 1890's, "the same side-shows, fakirs, freaks and uproarious fun that always go on such occasions."[18] Prizes were given for female equestrianism as well as for hooked rugs and samplers, for velocipedestrianism as well as for superior Guernseys. In 1888 a Rhode Island fair advertised "a grand tournament of bicyclers, a balloon ascension . . . polo games, steeple chasing, football match, and racing by wheelbarrows, greased poles, sacks and horses."[19]

On the day of the fair the town would be crowded, the grounds densely packed with medicine shows and itinerant peddlers adding to the confusion and excitement. Hamlin Garland has described the tremendous impression made upon him as a small boy by one of these fakirs. He was a tall, lean man with long black hair, wearing a large white hat, and had as his assistants a little fat man and a sad-eyed girl with a guitar. Dr. Lightner's spiel on his magic coil entranced the boy, but the girl was romance incarnate. As they sang

> O Mary had a little lamb,
> Its fleece was black as jet,

"her voice, a childish soprano, mingled with the robust baritone of the doctor and the shouting tenor of the fat man, like a thread of silver in a skein of brass."[20]

After the Chicago World's Fair one exhibition could be counted upon as certainly as a prize sow or a trotting race. "The lady on my right, who I now interduce," the barker might be heard announcing at every fair throughout the country, "is the world-famed Little Egypt." At other tents on hundreds of midways were dancing-girls, lady boxers, baby shows, and graphic reproductions of the Streets of Cairo—a camel, a donkey, and a few ragged Chicago Arabs.[21] There were always freak exhibitions—the three-legged calf and two-headed chicken; candy booths and soft-drink stalls; shooting-galleries and merry-go-rounds. Where the fair was not big enough to support professional trotting races, farmers drove or rode their own horses. A popular feature was the boys' race—a mad, helter-skelter run on ponies or plow-horses.

Again the farmers would bring their basket lunches of cold chicken and stay the entire day, not spending very much but seeing everything. And again what they enjoyed most were the crowds which gave them a fleeting taste of town life.

In the 1850's Barnum was touring the country with his Grand Colossal Museum and Menagerie. It had greatly expanded since those days; it reached its highest peak in the last quarter of the century. At least forty large shows were on tour, and many more smaller ones. They played cities, towns, and hamlets, pitching the big top wherever they could hope to draw a crowd. Popular everywhere, the circus meant for the farmer the one taste of theatrical entertainment that he might ever have a chance to enjoy. The circus had a glamour about it which nothing else in rural life could equal.

Barnum's name was still one to conjure with in the circus world. Historians point out that it was really William C. Coup who was the prime mover in establishing the Greatest Show on Earth and that James A. Bailey was the real circus king of the 1890's.[22] But it was Barnum's reputation that packed the main tent. Joining forces with Coup in 1871, he had brought together, with an immense fanfare of ballyhoo, the largest collection of wild animals, curiosities, acrobats, equestrian performers, and clowns ever assembled. There were giraffes from Africa and cannibals from the Fiji Islands; Admiral Dot (successor to General Tom Thumb) and Esau the Bearded Boy; more elephants than ever before; and, wonder of wonders, a hippopotamus—"blood-sweating Behemoth of Holy Writ." The big top was the largest tent area the world had ever known; it covered two rings, and then three rings. The entire company, animals and all, toured by rail in sixty-one special cars.[23]

With its accommodations for ten thousand and then twenty thousand people, this circus naturally played only the larger towns. But the farmers somehow got there. The railroads ran special half-rate excursion trains, and they camped out on the circus grounds. It was more than the event of a year; it seemed the event of a lifetime. Each season this popular show (it was already firing a man from the mouth of a cannon as one of its great attractions) took in anywhere from one to two million dollars in gross receipts.[24]

When his circus was almost totally destroyed by fire in 1880, Barnum made another merger. Barnum and Bailey's was born—a still bigger and better Greatest Show on Earth. The fire from whose ashes he had, Phoenix-like, arisen in still greater splendor, the irrepressible showman announced, had only served to illuminate his path of duty as the American people's champion amusement provider. Nor had he forgotten his earlier technique. Barnum still lectured on temperance; he still took care to enlist church support. He was not in this circus business merely to make money, he told the country. It was his mission to "provide clean, moral and healthful recreation for the public."[25]

A sensation almost comparable to those he had achieved in mid-century with his famous mermaid, General Tom Thumb, and Jenny Lind awaited him. His purchase of Jumbo, the world's largest elephant, from the Royal Zoölogical Gardens in London created an international furor in 1882 which brought the Greatest Show on Earth an avalanche of publicity. Englishmen were incensed. They were afraid that the loss of Jumbo would be followed by that of Shakespeare's grave or the Tower of London. All possible means were exhausted to prevent the famous pachyderm's departure. Barnum was adamant. Whatever the difficulty or expense, Jumbo was to be brought to America.

On the fateful day set for his removal, the elephant lay down in the middle of a London street. All England cheered. Barnum's agent cabled frantically for instructions. "Let him lie there a week if he wants to," came the quick answer. "It's the best advertisement in the world." When he finally reached this country, Jumbo led a torch-light parade for the opening of the circus at Madison Square Garden, cheered by half a million people.[26] Little wonder that villagers and farmers would travel miles to see him whenever they had an opportunity.

Barnum and Bailey's had many rivals. The Ringling brothers had developed their Classic and Comic Concert Company into one of the world's great circuses; and the Sells Brothers Circus and Menagerie, merging with Hadj Tahara's Wild Moorish Caravan, boasted four rings and fifty-one animal cages. Then there were Forepaugh's Circus and Menagerie, Van Amburgh's, the Irwin Brothers, Whitney's, Williams'. . . .[27]

The smaller road shows copied these larger circuses in every particular, their grandiloquent advertisements making equally fantastic claims. Miles Orton's New York and New Orleans Circus, Menagerie and Wild West Show toured through Illinois making one-night stands, admission twenty-five cents. With fifty star performers and the marvelous racing elephant Lizzie, its posters shouted from a hundred barns that it was the greatest circus of all time.[28] In Nevada, Montgomery Queen's Caravan, Circus and Menagerie advertised its "grand centralization of genius, concentration of merit, monopoly of equestrian stars, avalanche of attractions."[29]

In rural areas and small towns the program for circus day followed time-honored custom.[30] While the small boys were out at dawn to herald its arrival, watching the elephants cautiously test the bridges wherever the approaching road crossed a stream, the farmers gathered from all directions. Every kind of vehicle would be drafted into use. There were great farm wagons, drawn perhaps by a pair of powerful Clydesdales, the grown-up members of the family sitting stiffly in their best Sunday clothes and the excited children sprawled in the straw behind them; buckboards and carry-alls; phaetons and mule teams. Occasionally the son of some rich farmer might whirl by in a side-bar buggy, his best girl beside him, scattering clouds of dust over the plodding wagons. Even before the morning parade officially opened the day's festivities, the town's quiet streets would be a whirl of excitement. Strolling mountebanks, candy and popcorn sellers, vendors of palm-leaf fans and toy balloons, three-card monte men and sly practitioners of the shell game. Everywhere rang out the shrill cry of the vendors of pink lemonade—"Lemo! Lemo! Ice-cole lemo! Five cents, a nickel, a half-a-dime; the twentieth-potofadollah! Lemo! Ice-cole lemo!"

The parade would burst upon these excited crowds with a blast of trumpets which rattled all the windows on Main Street. The band sweated and puffed at their instruments as they rode proudly by in the great circus wagon, with its twenty- or even forty-horse hitch; chariots driven by helmeted Romans rumbled along behind wagon cages between whose bars could be seen chattering monkeys, restless tigers; the equestrienne performers, dazzling visions of grace and loveliness, haughtily sat their plumed and prancing steeds; the elephants swung ponderously by with swaying howdahs; and the clown made his uproarious progress through the crowd in a flashing donkey cart. Above the crack of whips and rumble of wheels floated the steam calliope's shrill rendition of the popular circus songs:[31]

My love has joined the circus,
And I don't know what to do,
She feeds the elephants crackers and cheese,
And she plays with the kangaroo.

or the rollicking tune of Van Amburg:

He sticks his head in the lion's mouth,
And holds it there awhile,
And when he takes it out again
He greets you with a smile.

Even more familiar to later generations was another popular song to which the circus gave a nation-wide currency:

He flew through the air with the greatest of ease,
The daring young man on the flying trapeze;
His movements so graceful, all girls he could please
And my love he purloined away.

A midsummer sun might beat down relentlessly on all this tinseled display. The dust might swirl in great clouds about the ponderous elephants and rumbling chariots. But none could resist the excited cry, *The circus is coming!*

After basket lunches, the crowd flowed to the flagged and tented circus lot, and soon the familiar call, "Right this way to the big show" was packing them in close rows on the wooden benches which rose around the sides of the tent. The bands flared forth the signal for the grand opening march. Here it all was—the ring-master cracking his whip, the cry of the popcorn vendors, the white-faced clowns, the dizzying swings on the flying trapeze, the living statues, the pervasive smell of sawdust. . . .

Even after the equestrians had given their last exhibition of trick riding, the tumblers and tight-rope dancers performed their final stunts, the day was not quite over for those whose endurance could stand further excitement. There were still the freaks and wild animals, and the raucous voice of the announcer declared that the minstrel show, all the songs and dances of the big city, was just about to start. As the tired holiday-makers finally jogged homewards in the gathering dusk, the children asleep on the straw-covered floor, it is not surprising that they often felt they had had entertainment enough to last them for many months.

"Each year one came along from the east," Hamlin Garland has written in vivid portrayal of what the circus meant not only for the small boy but for the entire family on the western prairie, "trailing clouds of glorified dust and filling our minds with the color of romance. . . . It brought to our ears the latest band pieces and taught us the popular songs. It furnished us with jokes. It relieved our dullness. It gave us something to talk about."[32]

Notes

The quotations from Hamlin Garland, *The Son of the Middle Border* (*see* Reference Numbers 4, 7, 11, 12, 20, 32) are reprinted by permission of the publisher. (Copyright 1917 by the Macmillan Company.)

1. Nathaniel H. Egleston, *Villages and Village Life* (New York, 1878), 35, 42.
2. Quoted *ibid.*, 25.
3. See series of articles in the *Atlantic Monthly:* "The Problems of Rural New England," LXXIX (1897), 577-98, and "The Future of Rural New England," LXXIX (1897), 74-83.
4. Hamlin Garland, *A Son of the Middle Border* (New York, 1917), 21, 123, 209.
5. Allan Nevins, *The Emergence of Modern America (A History of American Life,* VIII) (New York, 1927), 169-71.
6. Everett Dick, *The Sod-House Frontier,* 1854-1890 (New York, 1937), 384.
7. Garland, *A Son of the Middle Border,* 94. See also Grant Showerman, *A Country Chronicle* (New York, 1916), 46-52.
8. Mark Sullivan, *Our Times* (New York, 1925-35), II, 166.
9. Philip Morgan, "The Problems of Rural New England," *Atlantic Monthly,* LXXIX (1897), 377-88.
10. Sullivan, *Our Times,* II, 210-11.
11. Garland, *A Son of the Middle Border,* 165-66.
12. *Ibid.*, 165-66.
13. Nauvoo (Illinois) *Rustler,* July 1, 1890.
14. Henry Wheeler Shaw, *Josh Billings on Ice and Other Things* (New York, 1868), quoted in Wayne Caldwell Neely, *The Agricultural Fair* (New York, 1935), 193.
15. Neely, *The Agricultural Fair,* 83, 89, 96. See also article on Elkanah Watson in *Dictionary of American Biography.*
16. John A. Krout, *Annals of American Sport (The Pageant of America,* XV) (New Haven, 1929), 51-53.
17. Quoted in Neely, *The Agricultural Fair,* 204.
18. Alvan F. Sanborn, *"The Problems of Rural New England," Atlantic Monthly,* LXXIX (1897), 595.
19. Neely, *The Agricultural Fair,* 107.

20. Garland, *A Son of the Middle Border,* 167-68.
21. Lloyd Nelson, "The County Fair," *Scribner's Magazine,* XXXIV (1903), 129-47.
22. Earl Chapin May, *The Circus from Rome to Ringling,* (New York, 1932), 113-14.
23. P. T. Barnum, *Struggles and Triumphs* (Buffalo, 1889), 284; M. R. Werner, *Barnum* (New York, 1927), 306-10; May, *The Circus,* 113-17.
24. Barnum, *Struggles and Triumphs,* 284, 331, 334.
25. *Ibid,* 356.
26. *Ibid.,* 332ff; Werner, *Barnum,* 333ff.
27. May, *The Circus,* 224ff; *New York Dramatic Mirror,* 1890, advertisements.
28. Nauvoo (Illinois) *Rustler,* June 17, 1890.
29. *Carson Appeal,* May 29, 1875, quoted in Wells Drury, *An Editor on the Comstock Lode* (New York, 1936), 303.
30. For two colorful contemporary descriptions of circus day see Booth Tarkington, *A Gentleman from Indiana* (New York, 1899), 177-43 *passim;* Hamlin Garland, *Boy Life on the Prairie* (New York, 1899), 231-51 *passim.*
31. Quoted in Sullivan, *Our Times,* II, 171.
32. Garland, *A Son of the Middle Border,* 135-37.

2

"Time on Our Hands"

What do people feel about leisure? We believe that the sensations of leisure are in their essence these three: play, the renouncement of work, solitude.

Play is perhaps the most important; Piaget brilliantly analyzes this element, pointing out that play is not *a form of behavior or activity but an attitude, an "orientation." Where Piaget speaks for the individual, Johan Huizinga examines the meaning of play for society as a whole. One component of play—fun—is taken up by Martha Wolfenstein who analyzes how our attitudes toward it have shifted over the years.*

The renouncement of work is also a matter of attitude. To taste leisure requires an uncommon absence of busyness. Both Bertrand Russell and Paul Lafargue (who was Karl Marx's son-in-law) inveigh against such busyness, and from two different perspectives shout the praises of idleness.

Finally, there is a mysterious world of leisure: the element of solitude which borders closely upon loneliness and boredom and whose borders themselves may be too elusive for our comfort. This utter privacy of leisure is better understood after reading Picard and Halmos.

Those who can't face this utter privacy face a dreadful alternative instead—boredom. Surprisingly, in the frontiers of our technological development, this has become a more urgent problem. Atomic submarine crews, for example, and, eventually, space ship engineers and travelers must learn how to keep from being bored. Heron describes the extreme condition: the reaction of human beings to a situation in which nothing *is happening.*

Criteria of Play

By JEAN PIAGET

AN EXAMINATION of the main criteria usually adopted to distinguish play from non-ludic activities shows clearly that play is not a behaviour *per se,* or one particular type of activity among others. It is determined by a certain orientation of the behaviour, or by a general "pole" of the activity, each particular action being characterised by its greater or less proximity to the pole and by the kind of equipibrium between the polarised tendencies. For instance, according to a well-known formula play is an end in itself, whereas work and other non-ludic behaviours involve an aim not contained in the activity as such. If this were so, play would be "disinterested," or as J. M. Baldwin says "autotelic." But this first criterion is at once seen to be lacking in precision. On the one hand, as P. Souriau has already emphasized in his *Esthétique du mouvement,* every game is in a sense profoundly "interested," since the player is certainly concerned with the result of his activity. In the case of practice games the result is materially identical with that of the corresponding "serious" activity. If, then, the distinction is between "autotelism" and "heterotelism," it can only be made in relation to the kind of equilibrium that exists between the specific behaviour and the set of other behaviours. In "heterotelic" activities the direction of the behaviours is outwards, in so far as there is subordination of the schemas to reality, whereas in "autotelic" activities the direction is inwards, in so far as the child, while using the same schemas, enjoys exercising his powers and being aware of himself as the cause of the activity. On the other hand, almost all the activities of the first year of life seem to be autotelic, and yet they are not always ludic. The true meaning of this first criterion is therefore to be found in the opposition between assimilation of objects to the child's activity and accommodation of the child's activity to objects. When assimilation and accommodation are not differentiated, as at the beginning of the first year, there seems to be autotelism without there being play in the strict sense, but as assimilation gains on accommodation play is divorced from the corresponding non-ludic activities. The too sharp theoretical distinction between autotelism and heterotelism thus becomes rather a difference of degree, with the whole series of transitions it involves between behaviours in which assimilation and accommodation are still in equilibrium and those in which assimilation predominates in varying degrees.

A second criterion frequently used is that of the spontaneity of play, as opposed to the compulsion of work and real adaptation. But are the primitive

---

From Chapter VI (pp. 147-50), *Play, Dreams and Imitation in Childhood,* by Jean Piaget.

intellectual investigations of the child, and even those of pure science, not equally "spontaneous"? If what is intended is a more precise distinction between the "superior" games, science and art, and games which are not "superior" but just games, all that can be done is once again to distinguish two poles, the one truly spontaneous, since it is uncontrolled, the other controlled by society or by reality. But viewed in this way, this second criterion amounts to the same as the first: play is assimilation of reality to the ego, as distinct from "serious" thought, in which the assimilating process is in equilibrium with accommodation to other persons and things.

A third criterion often applied is that of pleasure. Play is an activity "for pleasure," while serious activity is directed towards a useful result irrespective of its pleasurable character. This might be expressed as autotelism and heterotelism translated into affective terms. But it confuses the issue even more, for much "work" properly so-called has no other subjective end than satisfaction or pleasure and yet it is not play. Can we agree with Claparède that play is an immediate realisation of desires or needs while work is a mediate realisation? But it is more than a question of degree of complexity. The action of grasping for the sake of grasping may be a non-ludic exercise although there may be immediate satisfaction, and on the other hand a game may involve all kinds of complicated intermediaries. Freud has expressed the exact shade of difference, in similar terms, in contrasting the "Lustprinzip" and the "Realitätsprinzip": on one side immediate satisfaction by way of non-compliance with the laws of reality, and on the other adaptation to reality in which there is an element of satisfaction, which is, however, subordinated to a kind of compliance, or respect for objective data. But one difficulty still remains. Certain games (which we called symbolic games of liquidation) are symbolic reproductions of painful occurrences with the sole aim of digesting and assimilating them. In such games we have situations analogous to those described, on another plane, by Freud himself as being beyond the pleasure principle: "Jenseits des Lustprinzips." These cases show that mere assimilation, in the form of repetition of an experienced event, even when such experience was painful, is the primary factor in play and is more widespread than the pursuit of pleasure for its own sake. Once this is understood, the difficulty disappears, for it is clear that although play sometimes takes the form of repetition of painful states of mind, it does so not in order that the pain shall be preserved, but so that it may become bearable, and even pleasurable, through assimilation to the whole activity of the ego. In a word, it is possible to reduce play to pleasure-seeking, but with the proviso that the pursuit of pleasure is conceived as subordinated to the assimilation of reality to the ego. Ludic pleasure then becomes the affective expression of this assimilation.

A fourth criterion which is sometimes applied, particularly by American writers, is the relative lack of organisation in play. Play is considered to be devoid of organised structure and contrasted with serious thought, which is always ordered. Here, again, one of Freud's remarks has bearing on the criterion. In his view, symbolic thought (in the Freudian sense of unconscious symbolism) is not "directed," in contrast to logical thought which is systematically directed. But this criterion also can be reduced to that of assimilation. Why is it that a day-dream or a symbolic game is not "directed," unless because reality is being assimilated to the whims of the ego instead of being thought in accordance with rules?

A fifth criterion, which is of interest to us, is freedom from conflicts. Conflicts are foreign to play, or, if they do occur, it is so that the ego may be freed from them by compensation or liquidation, whereas serious activity has to grapple with conflicts which are inescapable. There is no doubt that this criterion is on the whole sound. The conflict between obedience and individual liberty is, for example, the affliction of childhood, and in real life the only solutions to this conflict are submission, revolt, or co-operation which involves some measure of compromise. In play, however, the conflicts are transposed in such a way that the ego is revenged, either by suppression of the problem or by giving it an acceptable solution. But what this criterion does is to stress only one aspect of ludic assimilation in general. It is an important aspect, but nevertheless it is only part of the whole picture. It is because the ego dominates the whole universe in play that it is freed from conflicts, and not the converse, unless when we speak of conflicts we mean any limitation of the ego by reality.

Finally, there is the interesting criterion suggested by Mrs. Curti: overmotivation. For instance, sweeping a floor is not a game, but the fact of describing a figure as one sweeps gives it a ludic character (*cf.* the child cutting his spinach into little squares as he eats it, or taking "one spoonful for mummy," "one for daddy," etc.). Judging by this criterion, play would begin when incentives not contained in the initial action are included, and additional incentives would be characteristic of all play. But it then becomes a question of determining the nature of these ludic incentives, for it cannot be asserted that every behaviour which has successive polyvalent incentives is thereby play. In each particular case, the incentives depend on the pleasure gained through unrestricted combinations, or through symbolic imagination. But since this is so, we come back once again to the fact that an activity becomes ludic merely through a process used by the ego to integrate a reality which was independent of it and which sometimes required painful accommodation. Overmotivation thus becomes merely another way of expressing the predominance of assimilation.

To sum up, it is clear that all the criteria suggested in order to define play in relationship to non-ludic activity result, not in making a clear distinction between the two, but rather in stressing the fact that the tonality of an activity is ludic in proportion as it has a certain orientation. This amounts to saying that play is distinguishable by a modification, varying in degree, of the conditions of equilibrium between reality and the ego. We can therefore say that if adapted activity and thought constitute an equilibrium between assimilation and accommodation, play begins as soon as there is predominance of assimilation. This criterion seems to be generally applicable, from the merely functional assimilation characteristic of practice games, to the varied forms of assimilation of reality to thought found in symbolic games. Since all thought involves assimilation, and ludic assimilation is only distinctive in that it subordinates accommodation instead of being in equilibrium with it, play is to be conceived as being both related to adapted thought by a continuous sequence of intermediaries, and bound up with thought as a whole, of which it is only one pole, more or less differentiated.

The Play-Element in Contemporary Civilization

By JOHAN HUIZINGA

LET US not waste time arguing about what is meant by "contemporary". It goes without saying that any time we speak of has already become an historical past, a past that seems to crumble away at the hinder end the further we recede from it. Phenomena which a younger generation is constantly relegating to "former days" are, for their elders, part of "our own day", not merely because their elders have a personal recollection of them but because their culture still participates in them. This different time-sense is not so much dependent on the generation to which one happens to belong as on the knowledge one has of things old and new. A mind historically focussed will embody in its idea of what is "modern" and "contemporary" a far larger section of the past than a mind living in the myopia of the moment. "Contemporary civilization" in our sense, therefore, goes deep into the 19th century.

The question to which we address ourselves is this: To what extent does the civilization we live in still develop in play-forms? How far does the play-spirit dominate the lives of those who share that civilization? The 19th century, we observed, had lost many of the play-elements so characteristic of former ages. Has this leeway been made up or has it increased?

It might seem at first sight that certain phenomena in modern social life have more than compensated for the loss of play-forms. Sport and athletics, as social functions, have steadily increased in scope and conquered ever fresh fields both nationally and internationally.

Contests in skill, strength and perseverance have, as we have shown,

---

Chapter 12 from *Homo Ludens: A Study of the Play Elements in Culture,* by Johan Huizinga, translated by R. F. C. Hull (after Huizinga's own translation).

always occupied an important place in every culture either in connection with ritual or simply for fun and festivity. Feudal society was only really interested in the tournament; the rest was just popular recreation and nothing more. Now the tournament, with its highly dramatic staging and aristocratic embellishments, can hardly be called a sport. It fulfilled one of the functions of the theatre. Only a numerically small upper class took active part in it. This one-sidedness of mediaeval sporting life was due in large measure to the influence of the Church. The Christian ideal left but little room for the organized practice of sport and the cultivation of bodily exercise, except insofar as the latter contributed to gentle education. Similarly, the Renaissance affords fairly numerous examples of body-training cultivated for the sake of perfection, but only on the part of individuals, never groups or classes. If anything, the emphasis laid by the Humanists on learning and erudition tended to perpetuate the older under-estimation of the body, likewise the moral zeal and severe intellectuality of the Reformation and Counter-Reformation. The recognition of games and bodily exercises as important cultural values was withheld right up to the end of the 18th century.

The basic forms of sportive competition are, of course, constant through the ages. In some the trial of strength and speed is the whole essence of the contest, as in running and skating matches, chariot and horse races, weight-lifting, swimming, diving, marksmanship, etc.[1] Though human beings have indulged in such activities since the dawn of time, these only take on the character of organized games to a very slight degree. Yet nobody, bearing in mind the agonistic principle which animates them, would hesitate to call them games in the sense of play—which, as we have seen, can be very serious indeed. There are, however, other forms of contest which develop of their own accord into "sports". These are the ball-games.

What we are concerned with here is the transition from occasional amusement to the system of organized clubs and matches. Dutch pictures of the 17th century show us burghers and peasants intent upon their game of *kolf*; but, so far as I know, nothing is heard of games being organized in clubs or played as matches. It is obvious that a fixed organization of this kind will most readily occur when two groups play against one another. The great ball-games in particular require the existence of permanent teams, and herein lies the starting-point of modern sport. The process arises quite spontaneously in the meeting of village against village, school against school, one part of a town against the rest, etc. That the process started in 19th-century England is understandable up to a point, though how far the specifically Anglo-Saxon bent of mind can be deemed an efficient cause is less certain. But it cannot be doubted that the structure of English social life had much to do with it. Local self-government encouraged the spirit of association and solidarity. The absence of obligatory military training favoured the occasion for, and the need of, physical exercise. The peculiar form of education tended to work in the same direction, and finally the geography of the country and the nature of the terrain, on the whole flat and, in the ubiquitous commons, offering the most perfect playing-fields that could be desired, were of the greatest importance. Thus England became the cradle and focus of modern sporting life.

Ever since the last quarter of the 19th century games, in the guise of sport,[2] have been taken more and more seriously. The rules have become increasingly strict and elaborate. Records are established at a higher, or faster, or longer level than was ever conceivable before. Everybody knows the delightful prints from the first half of the 19th century, showing the cricketers in top-hats. This speaks for itself.

Now, with the increasing systematization and regimentation of sport, something of the pure play-quality is inevitably lost. We see this very clearly in the official distinction between amateurs and professionals (or "gentlemen and players" as used pointedly to be said). It means that the play-group marks out those for whom playing is no longer play, ranking them inferior to the true players in standing but superior in capacity. The spirit of the professional is no longer the true play-spirit; it is lacking in spontaneity and carelessness.[3] This affects the amateur too, who begins to suffer from an inferiority complex. Between them they push sport further and further away from the play-sphere proper until it becomes a thing *sui generis*: neither play nor earnest. In modern social life sport occupies a place alongside and apart from the cultural process. The great competitions in archaic cultures had always formed part of the sacred festivals and were indispensable as health and happiness-bringing activities. This ritual tie has now been completely severed; sport has become profane, "unholy" in every way and has no organic connection whatever with the structure of society, least of all when prescribed by the government. The ability of modern social techniques to stage mass demonstrations with the maximum of outward show in the field of athletics does not alter the fact that neither the Olympiads nor the organized sports of American Universities nor the loudly trumpeted international contests have, in the smallest degree, raised sport to the level of a culture-creating activity. However important it may be for the players or spectators, it remains sterile. The old play-factor has undergone almost complete atrophy.

This view will probably run counter to the popular feeling of to-day, according to which sport is the apotheosis of the play-element in our civilization. Nevertheless popular feeling is wrong. By way of emphasizing the fatal shift towards over-seriousness we would point out that it has also infected the non-athletic games where calculation is everything, such as chess and some card-games.

A great many board-games have been known since the earliest times, some even in primitive society, which attached great importance to them largely on account of their chanceful character. Whether they are games of chance or skill they all contain an element of seriousness. The merry play-mood has little scope here, particularly where chance is at a minimum as in chess, draughts, backgammon, halma, etc. Even so all these games remain within the definition of play as given in our first chapter. Only recently has publicity seized on them and annexed them to athletics by means of public championships, world tournaments, registered records and press reportage in a literary style of its own, highly ridiculous to the innocent outsider.

Card-games differ from board-games in that they never succeed in eliminating chance completely. To the extent that chance predominates they fall into the category of gambling and, as such, are little suited to club life and public competition. The more intellectual card-games, on the other hand, leave plenty of room for associative tendencies. It is in this field that the shift towards seriousness and over-seriousness is so striking. From the days of *ombre* and *quadrille* to whist and bridge, card-games have undergone a process of increasing refinement, but only with bridge have the modern social techniques made themselves master of the game. The paraphernalia of handbooks and systems and professional training has made bridge a deadly earnest business. A recent newspaper article estimated the yearly winnings of the Culbertson couple at more than two hundred thousand dollars. An enormous amount of mental energy is expended in this universal craze for bridge with no more tangible result than the exchange of relatively unimportant sums of money. Society as a whole is neither benefited nor damaged by this futile activity. It seems difficult to speak of it as an elevating recreation in the sense of Aristotle's *diagoge*. Proficiency at bridge is a sterile excellence, sharpening the mental faculties very one-sidedly without enriching the soul in any way, fixing and consuming a quantity of intellectual energy that might have been better applied. The most we can say, I think, is that it might have been applied worse. The status of bridge in modern society would indicate, to all appearances, an immense increase in the play-element to-day. But appearances are deceptive. Really to play, a man must play like a child. Can we assert that this is so in the case of such an ingenious game as bridge? If not, the virtue has gone out of the game.

The attempt to assess the play-content in the confusion of modern life is bound to lead us to contradictory conclusions. In the case of sport we have an activity nominally known as play but raised to such a pitch of technical organization and scientific thoroughness that the real play-spirit is threatened with extinction. Over against this tendency to over-seriousness, however, there are other phenomena pointing in the opposite direction. Certain activities whose whole *raison d'être* lies in the field of material interest, and which had nothing of play about them in their initial stages, develop what we can only call play-forms as a secondary characteristic. Sport and athletics showed us play stiffening into seriousness but still being felt as play; now we come to serious business degenerating into play but still being called serious. The two phenomena are linked by the strong agonistic habit which still holds universal sway, though in other forms than before.

The impetus given to this agonistic principle which seems to be carrying the world back in the direction of play derives, in the main, from external factors independent of culture proper—in a word, communications, which have made intercourse of every sort so extraordinarily easy for mankind as a whole. Technology, publicity and propaganda everywhere promote the competitive spirit and afford means of satisfying it on an unprecedented scale. Commercial competition does not, of course, belong to the immemorial sacred play-forms. It only appears when trade begins to create fields of activity within which each must try to surpass and outwit his neighbour. Commercial rivalry soon makes limiting rules imperative, namely the trading customs. It remained primitive in essence until quite late, only becoming really intensive with the advent of modern communications, propaganda and statistics. Naturally a certain play-element had entered into business competition at an early stage. Statistics stimulated it with an idea that had originally arisen in sporting life, the idea, namely, of trading records. A record, as the word shows, was once simply a memorandum, a note which the inn-keeper scrawled on the walls of his inn to say that such and such a rider or traveller had been the first to arrive after covering so and so many miles. The statistics of trade and production could not fail to introduce a sporting element into economic life. In consequence, there is now a sporting side to almost every triumph of commerce or technology: the highest turnover, the biggest tonnage, the fastest crossing, the greatest altitude, etc. Here a purely ludic element has, for once, got the better of utilitarian considerations, since the experts inform us that smaller units–less monstrous steamers and aircraft, etc.–are more efficient in the long run. Business becomes play. This process goes so far that some of the great business concerns deliberately instil the play-spirit into their workers so as to step up production. The trend is now reversed: play becomes business. A captain of industry, on whom the Rotterdam Academy of Commerce had conferred an honorary degree, spoke as follows:

> "Ever since I first entered the business it has been a race between the technicians and the sales department. One tried to produce so much that the sales department would never be able to sell it, while the other tried to sell so much that the technicians would never be able to keep pace. This race has always continued: sometimes one is ahead, sometimes the other. Neither my brother nor myself has regarded the business as a task, but always as a game, the spirit of which it has been our constant endeavour to implant into the younger staff."

These words must, of course, be taken with a grain of salt. Nevertheless there are numerous instances of big concerns forming their own Sports Societies and even engaging workers with a view not so much to their professional capacities as to their fitness for the football eleven. Once more the wheel turns.

It is less simple to fix the play-element in contemporary art than in contemporary trade. As we tried to make clear in our tenth chapter, a certain playfulness is by no means lacking in the process of creating and "producing" a work of art. This was obvious enough in the arts of the Muses or "music" arts, where a strong play-element may be called fundamental, indeed, essential to them. In the plastic arts we found that a play-sense was bound up with all forms of decoration; in other words, that the play-function is especially operative where mind and hand move most freely. Over and above this it asserted itself in the master-piece or show-piece expressly commissioned, the *tour de force,* the wager in skill or ability. The question that now arises is whether the play-element in art has grown stronger or weaker since the end of the 18th century.

A gradual process extending over many centuries has succeeded in de-functionalizing art and making it more and more a free and independent occupation for individuals called artists. One of the landmarks of this emancipation was the victory of framed canvases over panels and murals, likewise of prints over miniatures and illuminations. A similar shift from the social to the individual took place when the Renaissance saw the main task of the architect no longer in the building of churches and palaces but of dwelling-houses; not in splendid galleries but in drawing-rooms and bed-rooms. Art became more intimate, but also more isolated; it became an affair of the individual and his taste. In the same way chamber music and songs expressly designed for the satisfaction of personal aestheticisms began to surpass the more public forms of art both in importance and often in intensity of expression.

Along with these changes in form there went another, even more profound, in the function and appreciation of art. More and more it was recognized as an independent and extremely high cultural value. Right into the 18th century art had occupied a subordinate place in the scale of such values. Art was a superior ornament in the lives of the privileged. Aesthetic enjoyment may have been as high as now, but it was interpreted in terms of religious exaltation or as a sort of curiosity whose purpose was to divert and distract. The artist was an artisan and in many cases a menial, whereas the scientist or scholar had the status at least of a member of the leisured classes.

The great shift began in the middle of the 18th century as a result of new aesthetic impulses which took both romantic and classical form, though the romantic current was the more powerful. Together they brought about an unparalleled rise in aesthetic enjoyment all the more fervent for having to act as a substitute for religion. This is one of the most important phases in the history of civilization. We must leap over the full story of this apotheosis of art and can only point out that the line of art-hierophants runs unbroken from Winckelmann to Ruskin and beyond. All the time, art-worship and connoisseurship remained the privilege of the few. Only towards the end of the 19th century did the appreciation of art, thanks largely to photographic reproduction, reach the broad mass of the simply educated. Art becomes public property, love of art *bon ton.* The idea of the artist as a superior species of being gains acceptance, and the public at large is washed by the mighty waves of snobbery. At the same time a convulsive craving for originality distorts the creative impulse. This constant striving after new and unheard-of forms impels art down the steep slope of Impressionism into the turgidities and excrescences of the 20th century. Art is far more susceptible to the deleterious influences of modern techniques of production than is science. Mechanization, advertising, sensation-mongering have a much greater hold upon art because as a rule it works directly for a market and has a free choice of all the techniques available.

None of these conditions entitles us to speak of a play-element in contemporary art. Since the 18th century art, precisely because recognized as a cultural factor, has to all appearances lost rather than gained in playfulness. But is the net result a gain or a loss? One is tempted to feel, as we felt about music, that it was a blessing for art to be largely unconscious of its high purport and the beauty it creates. When art becomes self-conscious, that is, conscious of its own grace, it is apt to lose something of its eternal child-like innocence.

From another angle, of course, we might say that the play-element in art has been fortified by the very fact that the artist is held to be above the common run of mortals. As a superior being he claims a certain amount of veneration for his due. In order to savour his superiority to the full he will require a reverential public or a circle of kindred spirits, who will pour forth the requisite veneration more understandingly than the public at large with its empty phrases. A certain esotericism is as necessary for art to-day as it was of old. Now all esoterics presuppose a convention: we, the initiates, agree to take such and such a thing thus and thus, so we will understand it, so admire it. In other words, esoterics requires a play-community which shall steep itself in its own mystery. Wherever there is a catch-word ending in *-ism* we are hot on the tracks of a play-community. The modern apparatus of publicity with its puffy art-criticism, exhibitions and lectures is calculated to heighten the play-character of art.

It is a very different thing to try to determine the play-content of modern science, for it brings us up against a fundamental difficulty. In the case of art we took play as a primary datum of experience, a generally accepted quantity; but when it comes to science we are constantly being driven back on our definition of that quantity and having to question it afresh. If we apply to science our definition of play as an activity occurring within certain limits of space, time and meaning, according to fixed rules, we might arrive at the amazing and horrifying conclusion that all the branches of science and learning are so many forms of play because each of them is isolated within its own field and bounded by the strict rules of its methodology. But if we stick to the full terms of our definition we can see at once that, for an activity to be called play, more is needed than limitations and rules. A game is time-bound, we said; it has no contact with any reality outside itself, and its performance is its own end. Further, it is sustained by the consciousness of being a pleasurable, even mirthful, relaxation from the strains of ordinary life. None of this is applicable to science. Science is not only perpetually seeking contact with reality by its usefulness, i.e. in the sense that it is *applied,* it is perpetually trying to establish a universally valid pattern of reality, i.e. as *pure* science. Its rules, unlike those of play, are not unchallengeable for all time. They are constantly being belied by experience and undergoing modification, whereas the rules of a game cannot be altered without spoiling the game itself.

The conclusion, therefore, that all science is merely a game can be discarded as a piece of wisdom too easily come by. But it is legitimate to enquire whether a science is not liable to indulge in play within the closed precincts of its own method. Thus, for instance, the scientist's continued penchant for systems tends in the direction of play. Ancient science, lacking adequate foundation in empiricism, lost itself in a sterile systematization of all conceivable concepts and properties. Though observation and calculation act as a brake in this respect they do not altogether exclude a certain capriciousness in scientific activities. Even the most delicate experimental analysis can be, not indeed manipulated while actually in progress, but played in the interests of subsequent theory. True, the margin of play is always detected in the end, but this detection proves that it exists. Jurists have of old been reproached with similar manoeuvres. Philologists too are not altogether blameless in this respect, seeing that ever since the Old Testament and the Vedas they have delighted in perilous etymologies, a favourite game to this day for those whose curiosity outstrips their knowledge. And is it so certain that the new schools of psychology are not being led astray by the frivolous and facile use of Freudian terminology at the hands of competents and incompetents alike?

Apart from the possibility of the scientific worker or amateur juggling with his own method he may also be seduced into the paths of play by the competitive impulse proper. Though competition in science is less directly conditioned by economic factors than in art, the logical development of civilization which we call science is more inextricably bound up with dialectics than is the aesthetic. In an earlier chapter we discussed the origins of science and philosophy and found that they lay in the agonistic sphere. Science, as some one has not unjustly said, is polemical. But it is a bad sign when the urge to forestall the other fellow in discovery or to annihilate him with a demonstration, looms too large in the work done. The genuine seeker after truth sets little store by triumphing over a rival.

By way of tentative conclusion we might say that modern science, so long as it adheres to the strict demands of accuracy and veracity, is far less liable to fall into play as we have defined it, than was the case in earlier times and right up to the Renaissance, when scientific thought and method showed unmistakable play-characteristics.

These few observations on the play-factor in modern art and science must suffice here, though much has been left unsaid. We are hastening to an end, and it only remains to consider the play-element in contemporary social life at large and especially in politics. But let us be on our guard against two misunderstandings from the start. Firstly, certain play-forms may be used consciously or unconsciously to cover up some social or political design. In this case we are not dealing with the eternal play-element that has been the theme of this book, but with false play. Secondly, and quite independently of this, it is always possible to come upon phenomena which, to a superficial eye, have all the appearance of play and might be taken for permanent play-tendencies, but are, in point of fact, nothing of the sort. Modern social life is being dominated to an ever-increasing extent by a quality that has something in common with play and yields the illusion of a strongly developed play-factor. This quality I have ventured to call by the name of Puerilism, as being the most appropriate appellation for that blend of adolescence and barbarity which has been rampant all over the world for the last two or three decades.

It would seem as if the mentality and conduct of the adolescent now reigned supreme over large areas of civilized life which had formerly been the province of responsible adults. The habits I have in mind are, in themselves, as old as the world; the difference lies in the place they now occupy in our civilization and the brutality with which they manifest themselves. Of these habits that of gregariousness is perhaps the strongest and most alarming. It results in puerilism of the lowest order: yells or other signs of greeting, the wearing of badges and sundry items of political haberdashery, walking in marching order or at a special pace and the whole rigmarole of collective voodoo and mumbo-jumbo. Closely akin to this, if at a slightly deeper psychological level, is the insatiable thirst for trivial recreation and crude sensationalism, the delight in mass-meetings, mass-demonstrations, parades, etc. The club is a very ancient institution, but it is a disaster when whole nations turn into clubs, for these, besides promoting the precious qualities of friendship and loyalty, are also hotbeds of sectarianism, intolerance, suspicion, superciliousness and quick to defend any illusion that flatters self-love or group-consciousness. We have seen great nations losing every shred of honour, all sense of humour, the very idea of decency and fair play. This is not the place to investigate the causes, growth and extent of this world-wide bastardization of culture; the entry of half-educated masses into the international traffic of the mind, the relaxation of morals and the hypertrophy of technics undoubtedly play a large part.

One example of official puerilism must suffice here. It is, as we know from history, a sign of revolutionary enthusiasm when governments play at nine-pins with names, the venerable names of cities, persons, institutions, the calendar, etc. *Pravda*[4] reported that as a result of their arrears in grain deliveries, three *kolkhozy* in the district of Kursk, already christened Budenny, Krupskaya and the equivalent of Red Cornfield, has been re-christened Sluggard, Saboteur and Do-Nothing by the local soviet. Though this *trop de zèle* received an official rebuff from the Central Committee and the offensive soubriquets were withdrawn, the puerilistic attitude could not have been more clearly expressed.

Very different is the great innovation of the late Lord Baden-Powell. His aim was to organize the social force of boyhood as such and turn it to good account. This is not puerilism, for it rests on a deep understanding of the mind and aptitudes of the immature; also the Scout Movement expressly styles itself a game. Here, if anywhere, we have an example of a game that comes as close to the culture-creating play of archaic times as our age allows. But when Boy-Scoutism in degraded form seeps through into politics we may well ask whether the puerilism that flourishes in present-day society is a play-function or not. At first sight the answer appears to be a definite yes, and such has been my interpretation of the phenomenon in other studies.[5] I have now come to a different conclusion. According to our definition of play, puerilism is to be distinguished from playfulness. A child playing is not puerile in the pejorative sense we mean here. And if our modern puerilism were genuine play we ought to see civilization returning to the great archaic forms of recreation where ritual, style and dignity are in perfect unison. The spectacle of a society rapidly goose-stepping into helotry is, for some, the dawn of the millennium. We believe them to be in error.

More and more the sad conclusion forces itself upon us that the play-element in culture has been on the wane ever since the 18th century, when it was in full flower. Civilization to-day is no longer played, and even where it still seems to play it is false play—I had almost said, it plays false, so that it becomes increasingly difficult to tell where play ends and non-play begins. This is particularly true of politics. Not very long ago political life in parliamentary democratic form was full of unmistakable play-features. One of my pupils has recently worked up my observations on this subject into a thesis on parliamentary eloquence in France and England, showing how, ever since the end of the 18th century, debates in the House of Commons have been conducted very largely according to the rules of a game and in the true play-spirit. Personal rivalries are always at work, keeping up a continual match between the players whose object is to checkmate one another, but without prejudice to the interests of the country which they serve with all seriousness. The mood and manners of parliamentary democracy were, until recently, those of fair play both in England and in the countries that had adopted the English model with some felicity. The spirit of fellowship would allow the bitterest opponents a friendly chat even after the most virulent debate. It was in this style that the "Gentleman's Agreement" arose. Unhappily certain parties to it were not always aware of the duties implicit in the word gentleman. There can be no doubt that it is just this play-element that keeps parliamentary life healthy, at least in Great Britain, despite the abuse that has lately been heaped upon it. The elasticity of human relationships underlying the political machinery permits it to "play", thus easing tensions which would otherwise be unendurable or dangerous—for it is the decay of humour that kills. We need hardly add that this play-factor is present in the whole apparatus of elections.

In American politics it is even more evident. Long before the two-party system had reduced itself to two gigantic teams whose political differences were hardly discernible to an outsider, electioneering in America had developed into a kind of national sport. The presidential election of 1840 set the pace for all subsequent elections. The party then calling itself Whig had an excellent candidate, General Harrison of 1812 fame, but no platform. Fortune gave them something infinitely better, a symbol on which they rode to triumph: the log cabin which was the old warrior's modest abode during his retirement. Nomination by majority vote, i.e. by the loudest clamour, was inaugurated in the election of 1860 which brought Lincoln to power. The emotionality of American politics lies deep in the origins of the American nation itself: Americans have ever remained true to the rough and tumble of pioneer life. There is a great deal that is endearing in American politics, something naïve and spontaneous for which we look in vain in the dragoonings and drillings, or worse, of the contemporary European scene.

Though there may be abundant traces of play in domestic politics there would seem, at first sight, to be little opportunity for it in the field of international relationships. The fact, however, that these have touched the nadir of violence and precariousness does not in itself exclude the possibility of play. As we have seen from numerous examples, play can be cruel and bloody and, in addition, can often be false play. Any law-abiding community or community of States will have characteristics linking it in one way or another to a play-community. International law between States is maintained by the mutual recognition of certain principles which, in effect, operate like play-rules despite the fact that they may be founded in metaphysics. Were it otherwise there would be no need to lay down the *pacta sunt servanda* principle, which explicitly recognizes that the integrity of the system rests on a general willingness to keep to the rules. The moment that one or the other party withdraws from this tacit agreement the whole system of international law must, if only temporarily, collapse unless the remaining parties are strong enough to outlaw the "spoilsport".

The maintenance of international law has, at all stages, depended very largely on principles lying outside the strict domain of law, such as honour, decency, and good form. It is not altogether in vain that the European rules of warfare developed out of the code of honour proper to chivalry. International law tacitly assumed that a beaten Power would behave like a gentleman and a good loser, which unhappily it seldom did. It was a point of international decorum to declare your war officially before entering upon it, though the aggressor often neglected to comply with this awkward convention and began by seizing some outlying colony or the like. But it is true to say that until quite recently war was conceived as a noble game—the sport of kings—and that the absolutely binding character of its rules rested on, and still retained, some of the formal play-elements we found in full flower in archaic warfare.

A cant phrase in current German political literature speaks of the change from peace to war as "das Eintreten des Ernstfalles"—roughly, "the serious development of an emergency". In strictly military parlance, of course, the term is correct. Compared with the sham fighting of manoeuvres and drilling and training, real war is undoubtedly what seriousness is to play. But German political theorists mean something more. The term "Ernstfall" avows quite openly that foreign policy has not attained its full degree of seriousness, has not achieved its object or proved its efficiency, until the stage of actual hostilities is reached. The true relation between States is one of war. All diplomatic intercourse, insofar as it moves in the paths of negotiation and agreement, is only a prelude to war or an interlude between two wars. This horrible creed is accepted and indeed professed by many. It is only logical that its adherents, who regard war and the preparations for it as the sole form of serious politics, should deny that war has any connection with the contest and hence with play. The agonistic factor, they tell us, may have been operative in the primitive stages of civilization, it was all very well then, but war nowadays is far above the competitiveness of mere savages. It is based on the "friend-foe principle". All "real" relationships between nations and States, so they say, are dominated by this ineluctable principle.[6] Any "other" group is always either your friend or your enemy. Enemy, of course, is not to be understood as *inimicus* or *ekhthros,* i.e. a person you hate, let alone a wicked person, but purely and simply as *hostis* or *polemios,* i.e., the stranger or foreigner who is in your group's way. The theory refuses to regard the enemy even as a rival or adversary. He is merely in your way and is thus to be made away with. If ever anything in history has corresponded to this gross over-simplification of the idea of enmity, which reduces it to an almost mechanical relationship, it is precisely that primitive antagonism between phratries, clans or tribes where, as we saw, the play-element was hypertrophied and distorted. Civilization is supposed to have carried us beyond this stage. I know of no sadder or deeper fall from human reason than Schmitt's barbarous and pathetic delusion about the friend-foe principle. His inhuman cerebrations do not even hold water as a piece of formal logic. For it is not war that is serious, but peace. War and everything to do with it remains fast in the daemonic and magical bonds of play. Only by transcending that pitiable friend-foe relationship will mankind enter into the dignity of man's estate. Schmitt's brand of "seriousness" merely takes us back to the savage level.

Here the bewildering antithesis of play and seriousness presents itself once more. We have gradually become convinced that civilization is rooted in noble play and that, if it is to unfold in full dignity and style, it cannot afford to neglect the play-element. The observance of play-rules is nowhere more imperative than in the relations between countries and States. Once they are broken, society falls into barbarism and chaos. On the other hand we cannot deny that modern warfare has lapsed into the old agonistic attitude of playing at war for the sake of prestige and glory.

Now this is our difficulty: modern warfare has, on the face of it, lost all contact with play. States of the highest cultural pretensions withdraw from the comity of nations and shamelessly announce that "pacta non sunt servanda". By so doing they break the play-rules inherent in any system of international law. To that extent their playing at war, as we have called it, for the sake of prestige is not true play; it, so to speak, plays the play-concept of war false. In contemporary politics, based as they are on the utmost preparedness if not actual preparation for war, there would seem to be hardly any trace of the old play-attitude. The code of honour is flouted, the rules of the game are set aside, international law is broken, and all the ancient associations of war with ritual and religion are gone. Nevertheless the methods by which war-policies are conducted and war-preparations carried out still show abundant traces of the agonistic attitude as found in primitive society. Politics are and have always been something of a game of chance; we have only to think of the challenges, the provocations, the threats and denunciations to realize that war and the policies leading up to it are always, in the nature of things, a gamble, as Neville Chamberlain said in the first days of September 1939. Despite appearances to the contrary, therefore, war has not freed itself from the magic circle of play.

Does this mean that war is still a game, even for the aggressed, the persecuted, those who fight for their rights and their liberty? Here our gnawing doubt whether war is really play or earnest finds unequivocal answer. It is the *moral* content of an action that makes it serious. When the combat has an ethical value it ceases to be play. The way out of this vexing dilemma is only closed to those who deny the objective value and validity of ethical standards. Carl Schmitt's acceptance of the formula that war is the "serious development of an emergency" is therefore correct—but in a very different sense from that which he intended. His point of view is that of the aggressor who is not bound by ethical considerations. The fact remains that politics and war are deeply rooted in the primitive soil of culture played in and as contest. Only through an ethos that transcends the friend-foe relationship and recognizes a higher goal than the gratification of the self, the group or the nation will a political society pass beyond the "play" of war to true seriousness.

So that by a devious route we have reached the following conclusion: real civilization cannot exist in the absence of a certain play-element, for civilization presupposes limitation and mastery of the self, the ability not to confuse its own tendencies with the ultimate and highest goal, but to understand that it is enclosed within certain bounds freely accepted. Civilization will, in a sense, always be played according to certain rules, and true civilization will always demand fair play. Fair play is nothing less than good faith expressed in play terms. Hence the cheat or the spoil-sport shatters civilization itself. To be a sound culture-creating force this play-element must be pure. It must not consist in the darkening or debasing of standards set up by reason, faith or humanity. It must not be a false seeming, a masking of political purposes behind the illusion of genuine play-forms. True play knows no propaganda; its aim is in itself, and its familiar spirit is happy inspiration.

In treating of our theme so far we have tried to keep to a play-concept which starts from the positive and generally recognized characteristics of play. We took play in its immediate everyday sense and tried to avoid the philosophical short-circuit that would assert all human action to be play. Now, at the end of our argument, this point of view awaits us and demands to be taken into account.

"Child's play was what he called all human opinions," says late Greek tradition of Heraclitus.[7] As a pendant to this lapidary saying let us quote at greater length the profound words of Plato which we introduced into our first chapter: "Though human affairs are not worthy of great seriousness it is yet necessary to be serious; happiness is another thing. . . . I say that a man must be serious with the serious, and not the other way about. God alone is worthy of supreme seriousness, but man is made God's plaything, and that is the best part of him. Therefore every man and woman should live life accordingly, and play the noblest games, and be of another mind from what they are at present. For they deem war a serious thing, though in war there is neither play nor culture worthy the name, which are the things *we* deem most serious. Hence all must live in peace as well as they possibly can. What, then, is the right way of living? Life must be lived as play, playing certain games, making sacrifices, singing and dancing, and then a man will be able to propitiate the gods, and defend himself against his enemies, and win in the contest". Thus "men will live according to Nature since in most respects they are puppets, yet having a small part in truth". To which Plato's companion rejoins: "You make humanity wholly bad for us, friend, if you say that". And Plato answers: "Forgive me. It was with my eyes on God and moved by Him that I spoke so. If you like, then, humanity is not wholly bad, but worthy of some consideration."[8]

The human mind can only disengage itself from the magic circle of play by turning towards the ultimate. Logical thinking does not go far enough. Surveying all the treasures of the mind and all the splendours of its achievements we shall still find, at the bottom of every serious judgement, something problematical left. In our heart of hearts we know that none of our pronouncements is absolutely conclusive. At that point, where our judgement begins to waver, the feeling that the world is serious after all wavers with it. Instead of the old saw: "All is vanity", the more positive conclusion forces itself upon us that "all is play". A cheap metaphor, no doubt, mere impotence of the mind; yet it is the wisdom Plato arrived at when he called man the plaything of the gods. In singular imagery the thought comes back again in the *Book of Proverbs,* where Wisdom says: "The Lord possessed me in the beginning of his ways, before he made any thing from the beginning. I was set up from eternity, and of old before the earth was made . . . I was with him forming all things: and was delighted every day, playing before him at all times; playing in the world. And my delights were to be with the children of men."[9]

Whenever we are seized with vertigo at the ceaseless shuttlings and spinnings in our mind of the thought: What is play? What is serious? we shall find the fixed, unmoving point that logic denies us, once more in the sphere of ethics. Play, we began by saying, lies outside morals. In itself it is neither good nor bad. But if we have to decide whether an action to which our will impels us is a serious duty or is licit as play, our moral conscience will at once provide the touchstone. As soon as truth and justice, compassion and forgiveness have part in our resolve to act, our anxious question loses all meaning. One drop of pity is enough to lift our doing beyond intellectual distinctions. Spring as it does from a belief in justice and divine grace, conscience, which is moral awareness, will always whelm the question that eludes and deludes us to the end, in a lasting silence.

Notes

1. A happy variation of the natatorial contest is found in *Beowulf,* where the aim is to hold your opponent under water until he is drowned.
2. It is probably significant that we no longer speak of "games" but of "sport". Our author may not have been sufficiently familiar with the development of "sport" in the last ten or twenty years, here and in America, to stress the all-important point that sport has become a business, or, to put it bluntly, a commercial racket. Trans.
3. Note G. K. Chesterton's dictum: If a thing is worth doing at all it is worth doing badly! Trans.
4. January 9th, 1935.
5. *Over de grenzen van spel en ernst in de cultuur,* p. 25, and *In the Shadow of To-morrow,* ch. 16.
6. Carl Schmitt, *Der Begriff des Politischen,* Hamburg, 1933.
7. *Fragments,* 70.
8. *Laws,* 803-4; cf. also 685. Plato's words echo sombrely in Luther's mouth when he says: "All creatures are God's masks and mummeries" (Erlanger Ausgabe, xi, p. 115).
9. viii, 22-3, 30-1. This is the Douay translation, based on the Vulgate. The text of the English A. V. and R. V. does not bring out the idea of "play".

The Emergence of Fun Morality

By MARTHA WOLFENSTEIN

A RECENT development in American culture is the emergence of what we may call "fun morality." Here fun, from having been suspect if not taboo, has tended to become obligatory. Instead of feeling guilty for having too much fun, one is inclined to feel ashamed if one does not have enough. Boundaries formerly maintained between play and work break down. Amusements infiltrate into the sphere of work, while in play self-estimates of achievement become prominent. This development appears to be at marked

Reprinted from the *Journal of Social Issues,* 7, 4 (1951), by permission of the author and the publisher.

variance with an older, puritan ethic, although as we shall see the two are related.

As a basis for the discussion of fun morality I shall present an analysis of ideas of child training of the past thirty-five years. In these one can observe a changing conception of human impulses and a related altered evaluation of play and fun which afford clues to the transformation of moral outlook. The changing ideas in child training will be taken as phenomena of American culture, as part of a larger set of adult attitudes. This paper will consist, then, of two parts: first, an analysis of a selected sample of child training literature, and second some hypotheses about a moral trend which it seems to illustrate.

Changing Themes in Infant Care. The ideas on child training which I shall present are taken from the publications of the United States Department of Labor Children's Bureau. These publications probably express at any given time a major body of specialized opinion in the field, though how far they are representative would have to be determined by further study of other publications. In taking these publications as indicative of certain changing attitudes, I leave undetermined to what extent these attitudes are diffused among parents and also to what extent parents' actual behavior with their children conforms to these ideas. Both of these topics would require further research.

The innovations in child training ideas of the past few decades may readily be related to developments in psychological research and theory (notably behaviorism, Gesell's norms of motor development, and psychoanalysis). However, the occurrence and particularly the diffusion of certain psychological ideas at certain periods is probably related to the larger cultural context. A careful study of the ways in which psychological theories have been adapted for parent guidance and other pedagogical purposes would show that a decided selection is made from among the range of available theories, some points being overstressed, others omitted, and so on.

The *Infant Care* Bulletin of the Children's Bureau, the changing contents of which I shall analyze, was first issued in 1914. The various editions fall into three main groupings: 1914 and 1921, 1929 and 1938, 1942 and 1945 (i.e., the most drastic revisions occurred in 1929 and 1942).[1] For the present purpose I shall mainly contrast the two ends of the series, comparing the 1914 edition with those of 1942 and 1945 (the two latter are practically identical), and skipping over the middle period. Thus I shall attempt to highlight the extent of the change rather than to detail the intermediate stages (which in any case show some complicated discontinuities).

As the infant embodies unmodified impulses, the conception of his nature is a useful index of the way in which the impulsive side of human nature generally is regarded. The conception of the child's basic impulses has undergone an extreme transformation from 1914 to the 1940's. At the earlier date, the infant appeared to be endowed with strong and dangerous impulses. These were notably autoerotic, masturbatory and thumb-sucking. The child is described as "rebelling fiercely" if these impulses are interfered with.[2] The impulses "easily grow beyond control"[3] and are harmful in the extreme: "children are sometimes wrecked for life."[4] The baby may achieve the dangerous pleasures to which his nature disposes him by his own movements or may be seduced into them by being given pacifiers to suck or having his genitals stroked by the nurse.[5] The mother must be ceaselessly vigilant; she must wage a relentless battle against the child's sinful nature. She is told that masturbation "must be eradicated . . . treatment consists in mechanical restraints." The child should have his feet tied to opposite sides of the crib so that he cannot rub his thighs together; his nightgown sleeves should be pinned to the bed so that he cannot touch himself.[6] Similarly for thumb-sucking, "the sleeve may be pinned or sewed down over the fingers of the offending hand for several days and nights," or a patent cuff may be used which holds the elbow stiff.[7] The mother's zeal against thumb-sucking is assumed to be so great that she is reminded to allow the child to have his hands free some of the time so that he may develop legitimate manual skills; "but with the approach of sleeping time the hand must be covered."[8] The image of the child at this period is that he is centripetal, tending to get pleasure from his own body. Thus he must be bound down with arms and legs spread out to prevent self-stimulation.

In contrast to this we find in 1942-1945 that the baby has been transformed into almost complete harmlessness. The intense and concentrated impulses of the past have disappeared. Drives towards erotic pleasure (and also towards domination, which was stressed in 1929-1938) have become weak and incidental. Instead we find impulses of a much more diffuse and moderate character. The baby is interested in exploring his world. If he happens to put his thumb in his mouth, or to touch his genitals, these are merely incidents, and unimportant ones at that, in his over-all exploratory progress. The erogenous zones do not have the focal attraction which they did in 1914, and the baby easily passes beyond them to other areas of presumably equal interest. "The baby will not spend much time handling his genitals if he has other interesting things to do."[9] This infant explorer is centrifugal as the earlier erotic infant was centripetal. Everything amuses him, nothing is excessively exciting.

The mother in this recent period is told how to regard autoerotic incidents: "Babies want to handle and investigate everything that they can see and reach. When a baby discovers his genital organs he will play with them. . . . A wise mother will not be concerned about this."[10] As against the older method of tying the child hand and foot, the mother is now told: "See that he has a toy to play with and he will not need to use his body as a plaything."[11] The genitals are merely a resource which the child is thrown back on if he does not have a toy. Similarly with thumb-sucking: "A baby explores everything within his reach. He looks at a new object, feels it, squeezes it, and almost always puts it in his mouth."[12] Thus again what was formerly a "fierce" pleasure has become an unimportant incident in the exploration of the world. Where formerly the mother was to exercise a ceaseless vigilance, removing the thumb from the child's mouth as often as he put it in, now she is told not to make a fuss. "As he grows older other interests will take the place of sucking."[13] (Incidentally this unconcerned attitude towards thumb-sucking is a relatively late development. The 1938 edition still had an illustration of a stiff cuff which could be put on the infant at night to prevent his bending his elbow to get his fingers to his mouth. The attitude towards masturbation relaxed earlier, diversion having been substituted for mechanical restraints already in 1929.)

This changing conception of the nature of impulses bears on the question: is what the baby likes good for him? The opposition between the pleasant and the good is deeply grounded in older American morals (as in many other ascetic moral codes). There are strong doubts as to whether what is enjoyable is not wicked or deleterious. In recent years, however, there has been a marked effort to overcome this dichotomy, to say that what is pleasant is also good for you. The writers on child training reflect the changing ideas on this issue.

In the early period there is a clear-cut distinction between what the baby "needs," his legitimate requirements, whatever is essential to his health and well-being, on the one hand, and what the baby "wants," his illegitimate pleasure strivings, on the other. This is illustrated, for instance, in the question of whether to pick the baby up when he cries. In 1914, it was essential to determine whether he really needs something or whether he only wants something. Crying is listed as a bad habit. This is qualified with the remark that the baby has no other way of expressing his "needs"; if he is expressing a need, the mother should respond. "But when the baby cries simply because he has learned from experience that this brings him what he wants, it is one of the worst habits he can learn." If the baby cries, "the mother may suspect illness, pain, hunger or thirst." These represent needs. If checking on all these shows they are not present, "the baby probably wants to be taken up, walked with, played with," etc. "After the baby's needs have been fully satisfied he should be put down and allowed to cry."[14] (This position remains substantially unchanged up to 1942.)

In 1942-45, wants and needs are explicitly equated. "A baby sometimes cries because he wants a little more attention. He probably needs a little extra attention under some circumstances just as he sometimes needs a little extra food and water. Babies want attention; they probably need plenty of it."[15] What the baby wants for pleasure has thus become as legitimate a demand as what he needs for his physical well-being and is to be treated in the same way. (*Cf.* a recent television advertisement in which Angelo Patri is quoted as saying: "Youngsters today need television for their morale as much as they need fresh air and sunshine for their health." *New York Times,* November 14, 1950.)

The question of whether the baby wants things which are not good for him also occurs in connection with feeding. The baby's appetite was very little relied on to regulate the quantity of food he took in the early period. Over-feeding was regarded as a constant danger; the baby would never know when he had enough. This is in keeping with the general image of the baby at this time as a creature of insatiable impulses. In contrast to this we find in the recent period that "the baby's appetite usually regulates successfully the amount of food he takes."[16] Thus again impulses appear as benevolent rather than dangerous.

Formerly, giving in to impulse was the way to encourage its growing beyond control. The baby who was picked up when he cried, held and rocked when he wanted it, soon grew into a tyrant.[17] This has now been strikingly reversed. Adequate early indulgence is seen as the way to make the baby less demanding as he grows older.[18] Thus we get the opposite of the old maxim, "Give the devil the little finger and he'll take the whole hand." It is now: "Give him the whole hand and he'll take only the little finger."

The attitude towards play is related to the conception of impulses and the belief about the good and the pleasant. Where impulses are dangerous and the good and pleasant are opposed, play is suspect. Thus in 1914, playing with the baby was regarded as dangerous; it produced unwholesome pleasure and ruined the baby's nerves. Any playful handling of the baby was titillating, excessively exciting, deleterious. Play carried the overtones of feared erotic excitement. As we noted, this was the period of an intensive masturbation taboo, and there were explicit apprehensions that the baby might be seduced into masturbation by an immoral nurse who might play with his genitals.

The mother of 1914 was told: "The rule that parents should not play with the baby may seem hard, but it is without doubt a safe one. A young delicate and nervous baby needs rest and quiet, and however robust the child much of the play that is indulged in is more or less harmful. It is a great pleasure to hear the baby laugh and crow in apparent delight, but often the means used to produce the laughter, such as tickling, punching, or tossing, makes him irritable and restless. It is a regrettable fact that the few minutes' play that the father has when he gets home at night . . . may result in nervous disturbance of the baby and upset his regular habits."[19] It is relevant to note that at this time "playthings . . . such as rocking horses, swings, teeter boards, and the like" are cited in connection with masturbation, as means by which "this habit is learned."[20] The dangerousness of play is related to that of the ever-present sensual impulses which must be constantly guarded against. (In 1929-38, play became less taboo, but must be strictly confined to certain times of the day. In this period the impulse to dominate replaces erotic impulses as the main hazard in the child's nature and the corresponding danger is that he may get the mother to play with him whenever he likes.)

In the recent period play becomes associated with harmless and healthful motor and exploratory activities. It assumes the aspect of diffuse innocuousness which the child's impulse life now presents. Play is derived from the baby's developing motor activities which are now increasingly stressed. "A baby needs to be able to move all parts of his body. He needs to exercise . . . At a very early age the baby moves his arms and legs aimlessly . . . As he gets older and stronger and his movements become more vigorous and he is better able to control them he begins to play."[21] Thus play has been successfully dissociated from unhealthy excitement and nervous debilitation and has become associated with muscular development, necessary exercise, strength, and control. This is in keeping with the changed conception of the baby in which motor activities rather than libidinal urges are stressed. For the baby who is concerned with exploring his world rather than with sucking and masturbating, play becomes safe and good.

Play is now to be fused with all the activities of life. "Play and singing make both mother and baby enjoy the routine of life."[22] This mingling of play with necessary routines is consonant with the view that the good and pleasant coincide. Also, as the mother is urged to make play an aspect of every activity, play assumes a new obligatory quality. Mothers are told that "a mother usually enjoys entering into her baby's play. Both of them enjoy the little games that mothers and babies have always played from time immemorial." (This harking back to time immemorial is a way of skipping over the more recent past.) "Daily tasks can be done with a little play and singing thrown in."[23] Thus it is now not adequate for the mother to perform efficiently the necessary routines for her baby; she must also see that these are fun for both of them. It seems difficult here for anything to become permissible without becoming compulsory. Play, having ceased to be wicked, having become harmless and good, now becomes a new duty.

In keeping with the changed evaluation of impulses and play, the conception of parenthood has altered. In the earlier period, the mother's character was one of strong moral devotion. There were frequent references to her "self-control," "wisdom," "strength," "persistence," and "unlimited patience." The mothers who read these bulletins might either take pride in having such virtues or feel called upon to aspire to them. The writers supposed that some mothers might even go to excess in their devoted self-denial. Thus the mothers were told that for their own health and thus for the baby's good they should not stay bound to the crib-side without respite, but should have some pleasant, although not too exhausting recreation.[24] The mother at this time is pictured as denying her own impulses just as severely as she does those of her child. Just as she had to be told to let the baby's hands free occasionally (not to overdo the fight against thumb-sucking), so she must be counselled to allow herself an intermission from duty. (In the 1929-39 period parenthood became predominantly a matter of know-how. The parents had to use the right technique to impose routines and to keep the child from dominating them.)

In the most recent period, parenthood becomes a major source of enjoyment for both parents (the father having come much more into the picture than he was earlier). The parents are promised that having children will keep them together, keep them young, and give them fun and happiness. As we have seen, enjoyment, fun, and play now permeate all activities with the child. "Babies—and usually their mothers—enjoy breast feeding"; nursing brings "joy and happiness" to the mother. At bath time the baby "delights" his parents, and so on.[25]

The characterization of parenthood in terms of fun and enjoyment may be intended as an inducement to parents in whose scheme of values these are presumed to be priorities. But also it may express a new imperative: you ought to enjoy your child. When a mother is told that most mothers enjoy nursing, she may wonder what is wrong with her in case she does not. Her self-evaluation can no longer be based entirely on whether she is doing the right and necessary things, but becomes involved with nuances of feeling which are not under voluntary control. Fun has become not only permissible but required, and this requirement has a special quality different from the obligations of the older morality.

Work and Play in American Culture: Some Hypotheses. I should now like to speculate on the connection between the attitudes revealed in this child training literature and a wider range of attitudes in American culture today. The extent of diffusion with respect to class, region, etc. of the attitudes I shall discuss would be a topic for further research.

The changing attitudes towards impulse and restraint, the changing treatment of play, the changing evaluation of fun which we have found in the child training literature would seem to have many counterparts in other areas of adult life. Play, amusement, fun have become increasingly divested of puritanical associations of wickedness. Where formerly there was felt to be the danger that in seeking fun, one might be carried away into the depths of wickedness, today there is a recognizable fear that one may not be able to let go sufficiently, that one may not have enough fun. In the recent past there has been an increased tendency to attempt by drinking to reduce constraint sufficiently so that we can have fun. Harold Lasswell has defined the super-ego as that part of the personality which is soluble in alcohol. From having dreaded impulses and being worried about whether conscience was adequate to cope with them, we have come round to finding conscience a nuisance and worrying about the adequacy of our impulses.

Not having fun is not merely an occasion for regret but involves a loss of self-esteem. I ask myself: What is wrong with me that I am not having fun? To admit that one did not have fun when one was expected to, arouses feelings of shame. Where formerly it might have been thought that a young woman who went out a great deal might be doing wrong, currently we would wonder what is wrong with a girl who is not going out. Fun and play have assumed a new obligatory aspect. While gratification of forbidden impulses traditionally aroused guilt, failure to have fun currently occasions lowered self-esteem. One is apt to feel inadequate, impotent, and also unwanted. One fears the pity of one's contemporaries rather than, as formerly, possible condemnation by moral authorities. In our book, *Movies, A Psychological*

Study,[26] Nathan Leites and I referred to this new obligatoriness of pleasure as "fun morality" as distinguished from the older "goodness morality" which stressed interference with impulses. We noted a particular type of current American film heroine, the masculine-feminine girl, whose major merit consists in making the achievement of fun not too effortful. She initiates the flirtation, keeps it casual, makes it clear that she does not require excessive intensity from the man. At the same time she supports his self-esteem by implying that she never doubts his resources for having fun, however cool or abstracted he may seem. She affords a relief from the pressures of fun morality.

David Riesman, in *The Lonely Crowd: A Study of the Changing American Character*,[27] has observed how extensively in business and professional life work and play have become fused. Activities formerly sharply isolated from work, such as entertainment, have become part of business relations. Aspects of the personality such as pleasingness or likeability, formerly regarded as irrelevant to work efficiency, have been increasingly called into play in working life. Relations with work associates have become less and less sharply distinguishable from relations outside of working hours. Thus there has been a mutual penetration of work and play. Work tends to be permeated with behavior formerly confined to after work hours. Play conversely tends to be measured by standards of achievement previously applicable only to work. One asks oneself not only in personal relations but now also at work: Did they like me? Did I make a good impression? And at play, no less than at work, one asks: Am I doing as well as I should?

In the past when work and play were more sharply isolated, virtue was associated with the one and the danger of sin with the other. Impulse gratification presented possibilities of intense excitement as well as of wickedness. Today we have attained a high degree of tolerance of impulses, which at the same time no longer seem capable of producing such intense excitement as formerly. Is it because we have come to realize that the devil does not exist that we are able to fuse play and fun with business, child care, and so on? Or have we developed (without conscious calculation) a new kind of defense against impulses? This defense would consist in diffusion, ceasing to keep gratification deep, intense, and isolated, but allowing it to permeate thinly through all activities, to achieve by a mixture a further mitigation. Thus we would have preserved unacknowledged and unrecognized the tradition of puritanism. We do not pride ourselves on being good and we secretly worry about not having enough fun. But the submerged super-ego works better than we know, interspersing play in small doses with work and applying a norm of achievement to play. Instead of the image of the baby who has fierce pleasures of autoeroticism and the dangerous titillation of rare moments of play, we get the infant who explores his world, every part of whose extent is interesting but none intensely exciting, and who may have a bit of harmless play thrown in with every phase of the day's routine. We get the adult whose work is permeated with personal relations and entertainment requirements, the impact of which is far from intensely pleasurable, and whose play-time is haunted by self-doubts about his capacity for having as much fun as he should.

I should like to add a further instance which epitomizes this tendency to fuse work and fun, manifestly to make work more agreeable, but in effect probably reducing the impact of fun. Recently a ten-year-old boy showed me one of his school books. It had the title "Range Riders" and showed on the cover a cowboy on a galloping horse. The subtitle was "Adventures in Numbers"; it was an arithmetic book. The problems involved cowboys, horses, and so on. The traditional image of the American schoolboy has been that he sits with a large text book propped up in front of him, a book representing the hard and tedious lessons which he wants to evade. And inside the text book he conceals a book of wild west stories, detective stories, or the like, which he is avidly reading. These two books have now been fused into one. I do not know whether this succeeds in making the arithmetic more interesting. But I have a suspicion that it makes the cowboys less exciting.

Postscript. Since the foregoing was written a new edition of the *Infant Care* bulletin was issued, in the fall of 1951. This perpetuates many of the tendencies of the 1942-45 editions, but also shows some changes. Fun morality remains prominent. The new parents are told that they are making a good start if they can enjoy their baby (p. 3). The child should learn that mother and father are "two people who enjoy each other" (p. 1). Introducing the baby to solid foods will be "fun" and "amusing" for the mother, and the baby will "enjoy the new experience more if you are having a good time" (p. 32). The mother should arrange the baby's bath so that it will be "the pleasant time it should be . . . If you feel hurried, bath time won't be the fun for either of you that it should be." (p. 64).

The difficulty of achieving fun, which, as we have observed, tends currently to worry adults, is now ascribed to the infant as well (following the general tendency to see the infant as the model of impulse life). The infant now may suffer from boredom. And this has become the main reason for autoerotic activities. The baby may suck his thumb out of "loneliness or boredom" (p. 57). He may rock or bang his head because of "boredom" (p. 56). In toilet training the baby the mother must take care that it does not become a "hateful bore" for him (p. 87). Masturbation is mentioned only in the section of toilet training: "sometimes a baby handles his genitals when he is on the toilet, or at other times when he is undressed" (p. 87). While it is not said explicitly that he does this out of boredom, we might infer it on an analogy with thumb sucking, rocking, and head-banging since we are told that the baby may also get bored on the toilet. Thus the autoerotic activities which were first derived from fierce impulses, later from less intense exploratory tendencies, now arise as an escape from boredom. The dwindling of impulsive intensity has proceeded further than before.

The exploratory impulse of the baby continues to be stressed. We have interpreted this as an attempt to conceive the child's impulsive endowment in harmless terms. But the puritanical condemnation of impulses seems to be catching up with this displacement. Bounds must now be set to the baby's exploration. "We know that if we leave him free to creep everywhere he'd get into trouble." Thus we must "set a limit" for the baby "while he explores" (p. 76).

There are still more striking signs that the belief in the dangerousness of impulses is breaking through the defenses that have been erected against it. In 1942-45 the view was advanced that the early gratification of the baby's demands led to the subsequent moderation of demands. There is now a conflict on this point. In some areas the precept is maintained, notably in relation to sucking and food preferences (pp. 57, 47). But in respect to the impulse to dominate it has been reversed. The apprehension of the twenties that the baby may get the upper hand if his parents give in to him reappears. The baby may get the parents "at his mercy by unreasonable demands for attention (p. 55). Although the baby's need for companionship and for being held when he cries is stressed (p. 53), the mother is also warned: "If you get in the habit of picking your baby up every time he whimpers, you may do more harm than good." The gratified demand is apt to grow rather than subsiding. The mother "may find her baby getting more and more demanding" (p. 54).

Thus the conflict about facing and accepting human impulses is far from solved. The attempt to dilute and diffuse impulses seems to lead, on the one hand, to doubts about adequate impulsive intensity, boredom and the difficulty of achieving fun. On the other hand, the anxiety that impulses in one form or another will tend to grow beyond control has not been successfully warded off.

Notes

1. My analysis is based on the six editions indicated. I was unable to obtain those of 1926 and 1940.
2. *Infant Care,* U. S. Department of Labor, Children's Bureau, Washington, D. C., 1914, p. 58.
3. *Ibid.,* p. 62.
4. *loc. cit.*
5. *loc. cit.*
6. *loc. cit.*
7. *Infant Care,* 1914, p. 61.
8. *loc. cit.*
9. *Infant Care,* 1942, p. 60.
10. *loc. cit.*
11. *loc. cit.*
12. *Infant Care,* 1942, pp. 59-60
13. *loc. cit.*
14. *Infant Care,* 1914, pp. 60-61.
15. *Infant Care,* 1945, p. 52.
16. *Ibid.,* p. 95.
17. *Infant Care,* 1914, pp. 60-61.
18. *Infant Care,* p. 30.

19. *Infant Care,* 1914, pp. 59-60.
20. *Ibid.,* p. 62.
21. *Infant Care,* 1942, p. 41.
22. *loc. cit.*
23. *loc. cit.*
24. *Infant Care,* 1914, p. 34.
25. *Infant Care,* 1945, pp. 1, 29, 38, 62.
26. Glencoe, Illinois: The Free Press, 1950.
27. New Haven: Yale University Press, 1950.

In Praise of Idleness

By BERTRAND RUSSELL

LIKE MOST of my generation, I was brought up on the saying 'Satan finds some mischief still for idle hands to do.' Being a highly virtuous child, I believed all that I was told, and acquired a conscience which has kept me working hard down to the present moment. But although my conscience has controlled my *actions,* my *opinions* have undergone a revolution. I think that there is far too much work done in the world, that immense harm is caused by the belief that work is virtuous, and that what needs to be preached in modern industrial countries is quite different from what always has been preached. Every one knows the story of the traveler in Naples who saw twelve beggars lying in the sun (it was before the days of Mussolini), and offered a lira to the laziest of them. Eleven of them jumped up to claim it, so he gave it to the twelfth. This traveler was on the right lines. But in countries which do not enjoy Mediterranean sunshine idleness is more difficult, and a great public propaganda will be required to inaugurate it. I hope that, after reading the following pages, the leaders of the Y.M.C.A. will start a campaign to induce good young men to do nothing. If so, I shall not have lived in vain.

Before advancing my own arguments for laziness, I must dispose of one which I cannot accept. Whenever a person who already has enough to live on, proposes to engage in some everyday kind of job, such as school-teaching or typing, he or she is told that such conduct takes the bread out of other people's mouths, and is therefore wicked. If this argument were valid, it would only be necessary for us all to be idle in order that we should all have our mouths full of bread. What people who say such things forget is that what a man earns he usually spends, and in spending he gives employment. As long as a man spends his income, he puts just as much bread into people's mouths in spending as he takes out of other people's mouths in earning. The real villain, from this point of view, is the man who saves. If he merely puts his savings in a stocking, like the proverbial French peasant, it is obvious that they do not give employment. If he invests his savings, the matter is less obvious, and different cases arise.

One of the commonest things to do with savings is to lend them to some government. In view of the fact that the bulk of the public expenditure of most civilized governments consists in payment for past wars or preparation for future wars, the man who lends his money to a government is in the same position as the bad men in Shakespeare who hire murderers. The net result of the man's economical habits is to increase the armed forces of the State to which he lends his savings. Obviously it would be better if he spent the money, even if he spent it in drink or gambling.

But, I shall be told, the case is quite different when savings are invested in industrial enterprises. When such enterprises succeed, and produce something useful, this may be conceded. In these days, however, no one will deny that most enterprises fail. That means that a large amount of human labor, which might have been devoted to producing something that could be enjoyed, was expended on producing machines which, when produced, lay idle and did no good to any one. The man who invests his savings in a concern that goes bankrupt is therefore injuring others as well as himself. If he spent his money, say, in giving parties for his friends, they (we may hope) would get pleasure, and so would all those upon whom he spent money, such as the butcher, the baker, and the bootlegger. But if he spends it (let us say) upon laying down rails for surface cars in some place where surface cars turn out to be not wanted, he has diverted a mass of labor into channels where it gives pleasure to no one. Nevertheless, when he becomes poor through the failure of his investment, he will be regarded as a victim of undeserved misfortune, whereas the gay spendthrift, who has spent his money philanthropically, will be despised as a fool and a frivolous person.

All this is only preliminary. I want to say, in all seriousness, that a great deal of harm is being done in the modern world by belief in the virtuousness of work, and that the road to happiness and prosperity lies in an organized diminution of work.

First of all: what is work? Work is of two kinds: first, altering the position of matter at or near the earth's surface relatively to other such matter; second, telling other people to do so. The first kind is unpleasant and ill paid; the second is pleasant and highly paid. The second kind is capable of indefinite extension: there are not only those who give orders, but those who give advice as to what orders should be given. Usually two opposite kinds of advice are given simultaneously by two organized bodies of men; this is called politics. The skill required for this kind of work is not knowledge of the subjects as to which advice is given, but knowledge of the art of persuasive speaking and writing, i.e., of advertising.

Throughout Europe, though not in America, there is a third class of men, more respected than either of the classes of workers. There are men who, through ownership of land, are able to make others pay for the privilege of being allowed to exist and to work. These landowners are idle, and I might therefore be expected to praise them. Unfortunately, their idleness is only rendered possible by the industry of others; indeed their desire for comfortable idleness is historically the source of the whole gospel of work. The last thing they have ever wished is that others should follow their example.

From the beginning of civilization until the Industrial Revolution, a man could, as a rule, produce by hard work little more than was required for the subsistence of himself and his family, although his wife worked at least as hard as he did, and his children added their labor as soon as they were old enough to do so. The small surplus above bare necessaries was not left to those who produced it, but was appropriated by warriors and priests. In times of famine there was no surplus; the warriors and priests, however, still secured as much as at other times, with the result that many of the workers died of hunger. This system persisted in Russia until 1917, and still persists in the East; in England, in spite of the Industrial Revolution, it remained in full force throughout the Napoleonic Wars, and until a hundred years ago, when the new class of manufacturers acquired power. In America, the system came to an end with the Revolution, except in the South, where it persisted until the Civil War. A system which lasted so long and ended so recently has naturally left a profound impress upon men's thoughts and opinions. Much that we take for granted about the desirability of work is derived from this system, and, being pre-industrial, is not adapted to the modern world. Modern technique has made it possible for leisure, within limits, to be not the prerogative of small privileged classes, but a right evenly distributed throughout the community. The morality of work is the morality of slaves, and the modern world has no need of slavery.

It is obvious that, in primitive communities, peasants, left to themselves, would not have parted with the slender surplus upon which the warriors and priests subsisted, but would have either produced less or consumed more. At first, sheer force compelled them to produce and part with the surplus. Gradually, however, it was found possible to induce many of them to accept an ethic, according to which it was their duty to work hard, although part of their work went to support others in idleness. By this means the amount of compulsion required was lessened, and the expenses of government were diminished. To this day, 99 per cent of British wage-earners would be genuinely shocked if it were proposed that the King should not have a larger income than a working man. The conception of duty, speaking historically, has been a means used by the holders of power to induce others to live for the interests of their masters rather than for their own. Of course the holders of power conceal this fact from themselves by managing to believe that their interests are identical with the larger interests of humanity. Sometimes this is true; Athenian slave-owners, for instance, employed part of their leisure in making a permanent contribution to civilization which would have been impossible under a just economic system. Leisure is essential to civilization, and in former times leisure for the few was only rendered possible by the labors of the many. But their labors were valuable, not because work is good, but because leisure is good. And with modern technique it would be possible to distribute leisure justly without injury to civilization.

Modern technique has made it possible to diminish enormously the amount of labor required to secure the necessaries of life for every one. This was made obvious during the War. At that time, all the men in the armed forces, all the men and women engaged in the production of munitions, all the men and women engaged in spying, war propaganda, or government offices connected with the War, were withdrawn from productive occupations. In spite of this, the general level of physical well-being among unskilled wage-earners on the side of the Allies was higher than before or since. The significance of this fact was concealed by finance: borrowing made it appear as if the future was nourishing the present. But that, of course, would have been impossible; a man cannot eat a loaf of bread that does not yet exist. The War showed conclusively that, by the scientific organization of production, it is possible to keep modern populations in fair comfort on a small part of the working capacity of the modern world. If, at the end of the War, the scientific organization, which had been created in order to liberate men for fighting and munition work, had been preserved, and the hours of work had been cut down to four, all would have been well. Instead of that the old chaos was restored, those whose work was demanded were made to work long hours, and the rest were left to starve as unemployed. Why? because work is a duty, and a man should not receive wages in proportion to what he has produced, but in proportion to his virtue as exemplified by his industry.

This is the morality of the Slave State, applied in circumstances totally unlike those in which it arose. No wonder the result has been disastrous. Let us take an illustration. Suppose that, at a given moment, a certain number of people are engaged in the manufacture of pins. They make as many pins as the world needs, working (say) eight hours a day. Some one makes an invention by which the same number of men can make twice as many pins as before. But the world does not need twice as many pins: pins are already so cheap that hardly any more will be bought at a lower price. In a sensible world, everybody concerned in the manufacture of pins would take to working four hours instead of eight, and everything else would go on as before. But in the actual world this would be thought demoralizing. The men still work eight hours, there are too many pins, some employers go bankrupt, and half the men previously concerned in making pins are thrown out of work. There is, in the end, just as much leisure as on the other plan, but half the men are totally idle while half are still over-worked. In this way, it is insured that the unavoidable leisure shall cause misery all round instead of being a universal source of happiness. Can anything more insane be imagined?

The idea that the poor should have leisure has always been shocking to the rich. In England, in the early nineteenth century, fifteen hours was the ordinary day's work for a man; children sometimes did as much, and very commonly did twelve hours a day. When meddlesome busybodies suggested that perhaps these hours were rather long, they were told that work kept adults from drink and children from mischief. When I was a child, shortly after urban working men had acquired the vote, certain public holidays were established by law, to the great indignation of the upper classes. I remember hearing an old Duchess say: "What do the poor want with holidays? They ought to *work*." People nowadays are less frank, but the sentiment persists, and is the source of much of our economic confusion.

Let us, for a moment, consider the ethics of work frankly, without superstition. Every human being, of necessity, consumes, in the course of his life, a certain amount of the produce of human labor. Assuming, as we may, that labor is on the whole disagreeable, it is unjust that a man should consume more than he produces. Of course he may provide services rather than commodities, like a medical man, for example; but he should provide something in return for his board and lodging. To this extent, the duty of work must be admitted, but to this extent only.

I shall not dwell upon the fact that, in all modern societies outside the U.S.S.R., many people escape even this minimum of work, namely, all those who inherit money and all those who marry money. I do not think the fact that these people are allowed to be idle is nearly so harmful as the fact that wage-earners are expected to overwork or starve.

If the ordinary wage-earner worked four hours a day, there would be enough for everybody, and no unemployment—assuming a certain very moderate amount of sensible organization. This idea shocks the well-to-do, because they are convinced that the poor would not know how to use so much leisure. In America, men often work long hours even when they are already well off; such men, naturally, are indignant at the idea of leisure for wage-earners, except as the grim punishment of unemployment; in fact, they dislike leisure even for their sons. Oddly enough, while they wish their sons to work so hard as to have no time to be civilized, they do not mind their wives and daughters having no work at all. The snobbish admiration of uselessness, which, in an aristocratic society, extends to both sexes, is, under a plutocracy, confined to women; this, however, does not make it any more in agreement with common sense.

The wise use of leisure, it must be conceded, is a product of civilization and education. A man who has worked long hours all his life will be bored if he becomes suddenly idle. But without a considerable amount of leisure a man is cut off from many of the best things. There is no longer any reason why the bulk of the population should suffer this deprivation; only a foolish ascetism, usually vicarious, makes us continue to insist on work in excessive quantities now that the need no longer exists.

In the new creed which controls the government of Russia, while there is much that is very different from the traditional teaching of the West, there are some things that are quite unchanged. The attitude of the governing classes, and especially of those who conduct educational propaganda, on the subject of the dignity of labor, is almost exactly that which the governing classes of the world have always preached to what were called the "honest poor." Industry, sobriety, willingness to work long hours for distant advantages, even submissiveness to authority, all these reappear; moreover, authority still represents the will of the Ruler of the Universe, Who, however, is now called by a new name, Dialectical Materialism.

The victory of the proletariat in Russia has some points in common with the victory of the feminists in some other countries. For ages, men had conceded the superior saintliness of women, and had consoled women for their inferiority by maintaining that saintliness is more desirable than power. At last the feminists decided that they would have both, since the pioneers among them believed all that the men had told them about the desirability of virtue, but not what they had told them about the worthlessness of political power. A similar thing has happened in Russia as regards manual work. For ages, the rich and their sycophants have written in praise of "honest toil," have praised the simple life, have professed a religion which teaches that the poor are much more likely to go to heaven than the rich, and in general have tried to make manual workers believe that there is some special nobility about altering the position of matter in space, just as men tried to make women believe that they derived some special nobility from their sexual enslavement. In Russia, all this teaching about the excellence of manual work has been taken seriously, with the result that the manual worker is more honored than anyone else. What are, in essence, revivalist appeals are made, but not for the old purposes: they are made to secure shock workers for special tasks. Manual work is the ideal which is held before the young, and is the basis of all ethical teaching.

For the present, possibly, this is all to the good. A large country, full of natural resources, awaits development, and has to be developed with very little use of credit. In these circumstances, hard work is necessary, and is likely to bring a great reward. But what will happen when the point has been reached where everybody could be comfortable without working long hours?

In the West, we have various ways of dealing with this problem. We have no attempt at economic justice, so that a large proportion of the total produce goes to a small minority of the population, many of whom do no work at all. Owing to the absence of any central control over production, we produce hosts of things that are not wanted. We keep a large percentage of the working population idle, because we can dispense with their labor by making the others overwork. When all these methods prove inadequate, we have a war: we cause a number of people to manufacture high explosives, and a number of others to explode them, as if we were children who had just discovered fireworks. By a combination of all these devices we manage, though with difficulty, to keep alive the notion that a great deal of severe manual work must be the lot of the average man.

In Russia, owing to more economic justice and central control over production, the problem will have to be differently solved. The rational solution would be, as soon as the necessaries and elementary comforts can be provided for all, to reduce the hours of labor gradually, allowing a popular vote to decide at each stage, whether more leisure or more goods were to be preferred. But, having taught the supreme virtue of hard work, it is difficult to see how the authorities can aim at a paradise in which there will be much leisure and little work. It seems more likely that they will find continually fresh schemes, by which present leisure is to be sacrificed to future productivity. I read recently of an ingenious plan put forward by Russian engineers, for making the White Sea and the northern coasts of Siberia warm, by putting a dam across the Kara Sea. An admirable project, but liable to postpone proletarian comfort for a generation, while the nobility of toil is being displayed amid the icefields and snowstorms of the Arctic. This sort of thing, if it happens, will be the result of regarding the virtue of hard work as an end in itself, rather than as a means to a state of affairs in which it is no longer needed.

The fact is that moving matter about, while a certain amount of it is necessary to our existence, is emphatically not one of the ends of human life. If it were, we should have to consider every navvy superior to Shakespeare. We have been misled in this matter by two causes. One is the necessity of keeping the poor contented, which has led the rich, for thousands of years, to preach the dignity of labor, while taking care themselves to remain undignified in this respect. The other is the new pleasure in mechanism, which makes us delight in the astonishingly clever changes that we can produce on the earth's surface. Neither of these motives makes any great appeal to the actual worker. If you ask him what he thinks the best part of his life, he is not likely to say: "I enjoy manual work because it makes me feel that I am fulfilling man's noblest task, and because I like to think how much man can transform his planet. It is true that my body demands periods of rest, which I have to fill in as best I may, but I am never so happy as when the morning comes and I can return to the toil from which my contentment springs." I have never heard working men say this sort of thing. They consider work, as it should be considered, a necessary means to a livelihood, and it is from their leisure hours that they derive whatever happiness they may enjoy.

It will be said that, while a little leisure is pleasant, men would not know how to fill their days if they had only four hours of work out of the twenty-four. In so far as this is true in the modern world, it is a condemnation of our civilization; it would not have been true at any earlier period. There was formerly a capacity for light-heartedness and play which has been to some extent inhibited by the cult of efficiency. The modern man thinks that everything ought to be done for the sake of something else, and never for its own sake. Serious-minded persons, for example, are continually condemning the habit of going to the cinema, and telling us that it leads the young into crime. But all the work that goes to producing a cinema is respectable, because it is work, and because it brings a money profit. The notion that the desirable activities are those that bring a profit has made everything topsy-turvy. The butcher who provides you with meat and the baker who provides you with bread are praiseworthy, because they are making money; but when you enjoy the food they have provided, you are merely frivolous, unless you eat only to get strength for your work. Broadly speaking, it is held that getting money is good and spending money is bad. Seeing that they are two sides of one transaction, this is absurd; one might as well maintain that keys are good, but keyholes are bad. Whatever merit there may be in the production of goods must be entirely derivative from the advantage to be obtained by consuming them. The individual, in our society, works for profit; but the social purpose of his work lies in the consumption of what he produces. It is this divorce between the individual and the social purpose of production that makes it so difficult for men to think clearly in a world in which profit-making is the incentive to industry. We think too much of production, and too little of consumption. One result is that we attach too little importance to enjoyment and simple happiness, and that we do not judge production by the pleasure that it gives to the consumer.

When I suggest that working hours should be reduced to four, I am not meaning to imply that all the remaining time should necessarily be spent in pure frivolity. I mean that four hours' work a day should entitle a man to the necessities and elementary comforts of life, and that the rest of his time should be his to use as he might see fit. It is an essential part of any such social system that education should be carried further than it usually is at present, and should aim, in part, at providing tastes which would enable a man to use leisure intelligently. I am not thinking mainly of the sort of things that would be considered "highbrow." Peasant dances have died out except in remote rural areas, but the impulses which caused them to be cultivated must still exist in human nature. The pleasures of urban populations have become mainly passive: seeing cinemas, watching football matches, listening to the radio, and so on. This results from the fact that their active energies are fully taken up with work; if they had more leisure, they would again enjoy pleasures in which they took an active part.

In the past, there was a small leisure class and a larger working class. The leisure class enjoyed advantages for which there was no basis in social justice; this necessarily made it oppressive, limited its sympathies, and caused it to invent theories by which to justify its privileges. These facts greatly diminished its excellence, but in spite of this drawback it contributed nearly the whole of what we call civilization. It cultivated the arts and discovered the sciences; it wrote the books, invented the philosophies, and refined social relations. Even the liberation of the oppressed has usually been inaugurated from above. Without the leisure class, mankind would never have emerged from barbarism.

The method of a hereditary leisure class without duties was, however, extraordinarily wasteful. None of the members of the class had been taught to be industrious, and the class as a whole was not exceptionally intelligent. The class might produce one Darwin, but against him had to be set tens of thousands of country gentlemen who never thought of anything more intelligent than fox-hunting and punishing poachers. At present, the universities are supposed to provide, in a more systematic way, what the leisure class provided accidentally and as a by-product. This is a great improvement, but it has certain drawbacks. University life is so different from life in the world at large that men who live in an academic *milieu* tend to be unaware of the preoccupations and problems of ordinary men and women; moreover their ways of expressing themselves are usually such as to rob their opinions of the influence that they ought to have upon the general public. Another disadvantage is that in universities studies are organized, and the man who thinks of some original line of research is likely to be discouraged. Academic institutions, therefore, useful as they are, are not adequate guardians of the interests of civilization in a world where every one outside their walls is too busy for unutilitarian pursuits.

In a world where no one is compelled to work more than four hours a day, every person possessed of scientific curiosity will be able to indulge it, and every painter will be able to paint without starving, however excellent his pictures may be. Young writers will not be obliged to draw attention to themselves by sensational pot-boilers, with a view to acquiring the economic independence needed for monumental works, for which, when the time at last comes, they will have lost the taste and the capacity. Men who, in their professional work, have become interested in some phase of economics or government, will be able to develop their ideas without the academic detachment that makes the work of university economists often seem lacking in reality. Medical men will have time to learn about the progress of medicine, teachers will not be exasperatedly struggling to teach by routine methods things which they learnt in their youth, which may, in the interval, have been proved to be untrue.

Above all, there will be happiness and joy of life, instead of frayed nerves, weariness, and dyspepsia. The work exacted will be enough to make leisure delightful, but not enough to produce exhaustion. Since men will not be tired in their spare time, they will not demand only such amusements as are passive and vapid. At least 1 per cent will probably devote the time not spent in professional work to pursuits of some public importance, and, since they will not depend upon these pursuits for their livelihood, their originality will be unhampered, and there will be no need to conform to the standards set by elderly pundits. But it is not only in these exceptional cases that the advantages of leisure will appear. Ordinary men and women, having the opportunity of a happy life, will become more kindly and less persecuting and less inclined to view others with suspicion. The taste for war will die out, partly for this reason, and partly because it will involve long and severe work for all. Good nature is, of all moral qualities, the one that the world needs most, and good nature is the result of ease and security, not of a life of arduous struggle. Modern methods of production have given us the possibility of ease and security for all; we have chosen, instead, to have overwork for some and starvation for the others. Hitherto we have continued to be as energetic as we were before there were machines; in this we have been foolish, but there is no reason to go on being foolish forever.

The Right to Be Lazy

By PAUL LAFARGUE

A DISASTROUS DOGMA.

A STRANGE delusion possesses the working classes of the nations where capitalist civilization holds its sway. This delusion drags in its train the individual and social woes which for two centuries have tortured sad humanity. This delusion is the love of work, the furious passion for work, pushed even to the exhaustion of the vital force of the individual and his progeny. Instead of opposing this mental aberration, the priests, the economists and the moralists have cast a sacred halo over work. Blind and finite men, they have wished to be wiser than their God; weak and contemptible men, they have presumed to rehabilitate what their God had cursed. I, who do not profess to be a Christian, an economist or a moralist, I appeal from their judgement to that of their God; from the preachings of their religious, economics or free-thought ethics, to the frightful consequences of work in capitalist society. . . .

Jesus, in his sermon on the Mount, preached idleness: "Consider the lilies of the field, how they grow: they toil not, neither do they spin: and yet I say unto you that even Solomon in all his glory was not arrayed like one of these." Jehovah the bearded and angry god, gave his worshipers the supreme example of ideal laziness; after six days of work, he rests for all eternity. . . .

In our society, which are the classes that love work for work's sake? The peasant proprietors, the little shopkeepers; the former bent double over their fields, the latter crouched in their shops, burrow like the mole in his subterranean passage and never stand up to look at nature leisurely.

And meanwhile the proletariat, the great class embracing all the pro-

---

An abridged version of *The Right to Be Lazy, Being a Refutation of the "Right to Work" of 1848,* by Paul Lafargue, translated by Charles H. Kerr (Chicago: Charles H. Kerr and Company).

ducers of civilized nations, the class which in freeing itself will free humanity from servile toil and will make of the human animal a free being,–the proletariat, betraying its instincts, despising its historic mission, has let itself be perverted by the dogma of work. Rude and terrible has been its punishment. All its individual and social woes are born of its passion for work. . . .

And if the miseries of compulsory work and the tortures of hunger have descended upon the proletariat more in number than the locusts of the Bible, it is because the proletariat itself invited them. . . .

Shame on the proletarians! Where are those neighborly housewives told of in our fables and in our old tales, bold and frank of speech, lovers of Bacchus? Where are those buxom girls, always on the move, always cooking, always singing, always spreading life, engendering life's joy, giving painless birth to healthy and vigorous children? . . . Today we have factory girls and women, pale drooping flowers, with impoverished blood, with disordered stomachs, with languid limbs . . . They have never known the pleasure of a healthful passion, nor would they be capable of telling of it merrily! And the children? Twelve hours of work for children! O, misery. But not all the Jules Simon of the Academy of Moral and Political Science, not all the Germinys of jesuitism, could have invented a vice more degrading to the intelligence of the children, more corrupting of their instincts, more destructive of their organism than work in the vitiated atmosphere of the capitalist factory.

Our epoch has been called the century of work. It is in fact the century of pain, misery and corruption.

And all the while the philosophers, the bourgeois economists–from the painfully confused August Comte to the ludicrously clear Leroy-Beaulieu; the people of bourgeois literature–from the quackishly romantic Victor Hugo to the artlessly grotesque Paul de Kock,–all have intoned nauseating songs in honor of the god Progress, the eldest son of Work. Listen to them and you would think that happiness was soon to reign over the earth, that its coming was already perceived. They rummaged in the dust of past centuries to bring back feudal miseries to serve as a sombre contrast to the delights of the present times. . . . The economists go on repeating to the laborers, "Work, to increase social wealth", and nevertheless an economist, Destutt de Tracy, answers: "It is in poor nations that people are comfortable, in rich nations they are ordinarily poor"; and his disciple Cherbuliez continues: "The laborers themselves in co-operating toward the accumulation of productive capital contribute to the event which sooner or later must deprive them of a part of their wages". But deafened and stupified by their own howlings, the economists answer: "Work, always work, to create your prosperity", and in the name of Christian meekness a priest of the Anglican Church, the Rev. Mr. Townshend, intones: Work, work, night and day. By working you make your poverty increase and your poverty releases us from imposing work upon you by force of law. The legal imposition of work "gives too much trouble, requires too much violence and makes too much noise. Hunger, on the contrary, is not only a pressure which is peaceful, silent and incessant, but as it is the most natural motive for work and industry, it also provokes to the most powerful efforts." Work, work, proletarians, to increase social wealth and your individual poverty; work, work, in order that becoming poorer, you may have more reason to work and become miserable. Such is the inexorable law of capitalist production.

Because, lending ear to the fallacious words of the economists, the proletarians have given themselves up body and soul to the vice of work, they precipitate the whole of society into these industrial crises of over-production which convulse the social organism. Then because there is a plethora of merchandise and a dearth of purchasers, the shops are closed and hunger scourges the working people with its whip of a thousand lashes. The proletarians, brutalized by the dogma of work, not understanding that the overwork which they have inflicted upon themselves during the time of pretended prosperity is the cause of their present misery, do not run to the granaries of wheat and cry: "We are hungry, we wish to eat. True we have not a red cent, but beggars as we are, it is we, nevertheless, who harvested the wheat and gathered the grapes." . . . Now they are at leisure and wish to enjoy a little of the fruits of their labor. . . .

Instead of taking advantage of periods of crisis, for a general distribution of their products and a universal holiday, the laborers, perishing with hunger, go and beat their heads against the doors of the workshops. With pale faces, emaciated bodies, pitiful speeches they assail the manufacturers: "Good M. Chagot, sweet M. Schneider, give us work, it is not hunger, but the passion for work which torments us". And these wretches, who have scarcely the strength to stand upright, sell twelve and fourteen hours of work twice as cheap as when they had bread on the table. And the philanthropists of industry profit by their lockouts to manufacture at lower cost.

If industrial crises follow periods of over-work as inevitably as night follows day, bringing after them lockouts and poverty without end, they also lead to inevitable bankruptcy. So long as the manufacturer has credit he gives free rein to the rage for work. He borrows, and borrows again, to furnish raw material to his laborers, and goes on producing without considering that the market is becoming satiated and that if his goods don't happen to be sold, his notes will still come due. At his wits' end, he implores the banker, he throws himself at his feet, offering his blood, his honor. "A little gold will do my business better", answers the Rothschild. "You have 20,000 pairs of hose in your warehouse; they are worth 20c. I will take them at 4c." The banker gets possession of the goods and sells them at 6c or 8c, and pockets certain frisky dollars which owe nothing to anybody: but the manufacturer has stepped back for a better leap. At last the crash comes and the warehouses disgorge. Then so much merchandise is thrown out of the window that you cannot imagine how it came in by the door. Hundreds of millions are required to figure the value of the goods that are destroyed. In the last century they were burned or thrown into the water.[1]

But before reaching this decision, the manufacturers travel the world over in search of markets for the goods which are heaping up. They force their government to annex Congo, to seize on Tonquin, to batter down the Chinese Wall with cannon shots to make an outlet for their cotton goods. In previous centuries it was a duel to the death between France and England as to which should have the exclusive privilege of selling to America and the Indies. Thousands of young and vigorous men reddened the seas with their blood during the colonial wars of the sixteenth, seventeenth and eighteenth centuries.

There is a surplus of capital as well as of goods. The financiers no longer know where to place it. Then they go among the happy nations who are loafing in the sun smoking cigarettes and they lay down railroads, erect factories and import the curse of work. And this exportation of French capital ends one fine morning in diplomatic complications. In Egypt, for example, France, England and Germany were on the point of hairpulling to decide which usurers shall be paid first. Or it ends with wars like that in Mexico where French soldiers are sent to play the part of constables to collect bad debts.[2]

These individual and social miseries, however great and innumerable they may be, however eternal they appear, will vanish like hyenas and jackals at the approach of the lion, when the proletariat shall say "I will". But to arrive at the realization of its strength the proletariat must trample under foot the prejudices of Christian ethics, economic ethics and free-thought ethics. It must return to its natural instincts, it must proclaim the Rights of Laziness, a thousand times more noble and more sacred than the anaemic Rights of Man concocted by the metaphysical lawyers of the bourgeois revolution. It must accustom itself to working but three hours a day, reserving the rest of the day and night for leisure and feasting.

Thus far my task has been easy; I have had but to describe real evils well known, alas, by all of us; but to convince the proletariat that the ethics inoculated into it is wicked, that the unbridled work to which it has given itself up for the last hundred years is the most terrible scourge that has ever struck humanity, that work will become a mere condiment to the pleasures of idleness, a beneficial exercise to the human organism, a passion useful to the social organism only when wisely regulated and limited to a maximum of three hours a day; this is an arduous task beyond my strength. Only communist physiologists, hygienists and economists could undertake it. In the following pages I shall merely try to show that given the modern means of production and their unlimited reproductive power it is necessary to curb the extravagant passion of the laborers for work and to oblige them to consume the goods which they produce.

THE CONSEQUENCES OF OVER-PRODUCTION

A Greek poet of Cicero's time, Antiparos, thus sang of the invention of the water-mill (for grinding grain), which was to free the slave women and bring back the Golden Age: "Spare the arm which turns the mill, O, millers, and sleep peacefully. Let the cock warn you in vain that day is breaking. Demeter has imposed upon the nymphs the labor of the slaves, and behold them leaping merrily over the wheel, and behold the axle tree, shaken, turning with its spokes and making the heavy rolling stone revolve. Let us live the life of our fathers, and let us rejoice in idleness over the gifts that the goddess grants us." Alas!, the leisure which the pagan poet announced has not come. The blind, perverse and murderous passion for work transforms the liberating machine into an instrument for the enslavement of free men. Its productiveness impoverishes them.

A good workingwoman makes with her needles only five meshes a minute, while certain circular knitting machines make 30,000 in the same time. Every minute of the machine is thus equivalent to a hundred hours of the workingwomen's labor, or again, every minute of the machine's labor, gives the workingwomen ten days of rest. What is true for the knitting industry is more or less true for all industries reconstructed by modern machinery. But what do we see? In proportion as the machine is improved and performs man's work with an ever increasing rapidity and exactness, the laborer, instead of prolonging his former rest times, redoubles his ardor, as if he wished to rival the machine. O, absurd and murderous competition!

That the competition of man and the machine might have free course, the proletarians have abolished wise laws which limited the labor of the artisans of the ancient guilds; they have suppressed the holidays.[3] Because the producers of that time worked but five days out of seven, are we to believe the stories told by lying economists, that they lived on nothing but air and fresh water? Not so, they had leisure to taste the joys of earth, to make love and to frolic, to banquet joyously in honor of the jovial god of idleness. Gloomy England, immersed in protestantism, was then called "Merrie Engand." Rabelais, Quevedo, Cervantes, and the unknown authors of the romances make our mouths water with their pictures of those monumental feasts[4] with which the men of that time regaled themselves between two battles and two devastations, in which everything "went by the barrel". Jordaens and the Flemish School have told the story of these feasts in their delightful pictures. Where, O, where, are the sublime gargantuan stomachs of those days; where are the sublime brains encircling all human thought? We have indeed grown puny and degenerate. Embalmed beef, potatoes, doctored wine and Prussian schnaps, judiciously combined with compulsory labor have weakened our bodies and narrowed our minds. And the times when man cramps his stomach and the machine enlarges its out-put are the very times when the economists preach to us the Malthusian theory, the religion of abstinence and the dogma of work. Really it would be better to pluck out such tongues and throw them to the dogs.

Because the working class, with its simple good faith, has allowed itself to be thus indoctrinated, because with its native impetuosity it has blindly hurled itself into work and abstinence, the capitalist class has found itself condemned to laziness and forced enjoyment, to unproductiveness and over-consumption. But if the over-work of the laborer bruises his flesh and tortures his nerves, it is also fertile in griefs for the capitalist.

The abstinence to which the productive class condemns itself obliges the capitalists to devote themselves to the over-consumption of the products turned out so riotously by the laborers. At the beginning of capitalist production a century or two ago, the capitalist was a steady man of reasonable and peaceable habits. He contented himself with one wife or thereabouts. He drank only when he was thirsty and ate only when he was hungry. He left to the lords and ladies of the court the noble virtues of debauchery. Today every son of the newly rich makes it incumbent upon himself to cultivate the disease for which quicksilver is a specific in order to justify the labors imposed upon the workmen in quicksilver mines; every capitalist crams himself with capons stuffed with truffles and with the choicest brands of wine in order to encourage the breeders of blooded poultry and the growers of Bordelais. In this occupation the organism rapidly becomes shattered, the hair falls out, the gums shrink away from the teeth, the body becomes deformed, the stomach obtrudes abnormally, respiration becomes difficult, the motions become labored, the joints become stiff, the fingers knotted. Others, too feeble in body to endure the fatigues of debauchery, but endowed with the bump of philanthropic discrimination, dry up their brains over political economy, or juridical philosophy in elaborating thick soporific books to employ the leisure hours of compositors and pressmen. The women of fashion live a life of martyrdom, in trying on and showing off the fairy-like toilets which the seamstresses die in making. They shift like shuttles from morning until night from one gown into another. For hours together they give up their hollow heads to the artists in hair, who at any cost insist on assuaging their passion for the construction of false chignons. Bound in their corsets, pinched in their boots, decollettė to make a coal-miner blush, they whirl around the whole night through at their charity balls in order to pick up a few cents for poor people—sanctified souls!

To fulfill his double social function of non-producer and over-consumer, the capitalist was not only obliged to violate his modest taste, to lose his laborious habits of two centuries ago and to give himself up to unbounded luxury, spicy indigestibles and syphilitic debauches, but also to withdraw from productive labor an enormous mass of men in order to enlist them as his assistants. . . .

Once settled down into absolute laziness and demoralized by enforced enjoyment, the capitalist class in spite of the injury involved in its new kind of life, adapted itself to it. Soon it began to look upon any change with horror. The sight of the miserable conditions of life resignedly accepted by the working class and the sight of the organic degradation engendered by the depraved passion for work increased its aversion for all compulsory labor and all restrictions of its pleasures. It is precisely at that time that, without taking into account the demoralization which the capitalist class had imposed upon itself as a social duty, the proletarians took it into their heads to inflict work on the capitalists. Artless as they were, they took seriously the theories of work proclaimed by the economists and moralists, and girded up their loins to inflict the practice of these theories upon the capitalists. The proletariat hoisted the banner, "He who will not work Neither shall he Eat". Lyons in 1831 rose up for bullets or work. The federated laborers of March 1871 called their uprising "The Revolution of Work". To these outbreaks of barbarous fury destructive of all capitalist joy and laziness, the capitalists had no other answer than ferocious repression, but they know that if they have been able to repress these revolutionary explosions, they have not drowned in the blood of these gigantic massacres the absurd idea of the proletariat wishing to inflict work upon the idle and reputable classes, and it is to avert this misfortune that they surround themselves with guards, policemen, magistrates and jailors, supported in laborious unproductiveness. . . .

For alleviation of its painful labor the capitalist class has withdrawn from the working class a mass of men far superior to those still devoted to useful production and has condemned them in their turn to unproductiveness and over-consumption. But this troop of useless mouths in spite of its insatiable voracity, does not suffice to consume all the goods which the laborers, brutalized by the dogma of work, produce like madmen, without wishing to consume them and without even thinking whether people will be found to consume them.

Confronted with this double madness of the laborers killing themselves with over-production and vegetating in abstinence, the great problem of capitalist production is no longer to find producers and to multiply their powers but to discover consumers, to excite their appetites and create in them fictitious needs. Since the European laborers, shivering with cold and hunger, refuse to wear the stuffs they weave, to drink the wines from the vineyards they tend, the poor manufacturers in their goodness of heart must run to the ends of the earth to find people to wear the clothes and drink the wines: Europe exports every year goods amounting to billions of dollars to the four corners of the earth, to nations that have no need of them.[5] . . .

But all to no purpose: the over-fed capitalist, the servant class greater in numbers than the productive class, the foreign and barbarous nations, gorged with European goods; nothing, nothing can melt away the mountains of products heaped up higher and more enormous than the pyramids of Egypt. The productiveness of European laborers defies all consumption, all waste.

The manufacturers have lost their bearings and know not which way to turn. They can no longer find the raw material to satisfy the lawless depraved passion of their laborers for work. In our woolen districts dirty and half rotten rags are raveled out to use in making certain cloths sold under the name of renaissance, which have about the same durability as the promises made to voters. At Lyons, instead of leaving the silk fiber in its natural simplicity and suppleness, it is loaded down with mineral salts, which while increasing its weight, make it friable and far from durable. All our products are adulterated to aid in their sale and shorten their life. Our epoch will be called the "Age of adulteration" just as the first epochs of humanity received the names of "The Age of Stone", "The Age of Bronze", from the character of their production. Certain ignorant people accuse our pious manufacturers of fraud, while in reality the thought which animates them is to furnish work to their laborers, who cannot resign themselves to living with their arms folded. These adulterations, whose sole motive is a humanitarian sentiment, but which bring splendid profits to the manufacturers who practice them, if they are disastrous for the quality of the goods, if they are an inexhaustible source of waste in human labor, nevertheless prove the ingenuous philanthropy of the capitalists, and the horrible perversion of the laborers, who to gratify their vice for work oblige the manufacturers to stifle the cries of their conscience and to violate even the laws of commercial honesty.

And nevertheless, in spite of the overproduction of goods, in spite of the adulterations in manufacturing, the laborers encumber the market in countless numbers imploring: Work! Work! Their superabundance ought to compel them to bridle their passion; on the contrary it carries it to the point of paroxysm. Let a chance for work present itself, thither they rush; then they demand twelve, fourteen hours to glut their appetite for work, and the next day they are again thrown out on the pavement with no more food for their vice. Every year in all industries lockouts occur with the regularity of the seasons. Over-work, destructive of the organism, is succeeded by absolute rest during two or four months, and when work ceases the pittance ceases. Since the vice of work is diabolically attached to the heart of the laborers, since its requirements stifle all the other instincts of nature, since the quantity of work required by society is necessarily limited by consumption and by the supply of raw materials, why devour in six months the work of a whole year; why not distribute it uniformly over the twelve months and force every workingman to content himself with six or five hours a day throughout the year instead of getting indigestion from twelve hours during six months? Once assured of their daily portion of work, the laborers will no longer be jealous of each other, no longer fight to snatch away work from each other's hands and bread from each other's mouths, and then, not exhausted in body and mind, they will begin to practice the virtues of laziness.

Brutalized by their vice, the laborers have been unable to rise to the conception of this fact, that to have work for all it is necessary to apportion it like water on a ship in distress. . . .

To force the capitalists to improve their machines of wood and iron it is necessary to raise wages and diminish the working hours of the machines of flesh and blood. Do you ask for proofs? They can be furnished by the hundreds. In spinning, the self-acting mule was invented and applied at Manchester because the spinners refused to work such long hours as before. In America the machine is invading all branches of farm production, from the making of butter to the weeding of wheat. Why, because the American, free and lazy, would prefer a thousand deaths to the bovine life of the French peasant. Plowing, so painful and so crippling to the laborer in our glorious France, is in the American West an agreeable open-air pastime, which he practices in a sitting posture, smoking his pipe nonchalantly.

NEW SONGS TO NEW MUSIC

We have seen that by diminishing the hours of labor new mechanical forces will be conquered for social production. Furthermore, by obliging the laborers to consume their products the army of workers will be immensely increased. The capitalist class once relieved from its function of universal consumer will hasten to dismiss its train of soldiers, magistrates, journalists, procurers, which it has withdrawn from useful labor to help it in consuming and wasting. Then the labor market will overflow. Then will be required an iron law to put a limit on work. It will be impossible to find employment for that swarm of former unproductives, more numerous than insect parasites, and after them must be considered all those who provide for their needs and their vain and expensive tastes. When there are no more lackeys and generals to decorate, no more free and married prostitutes to be covered with laces, no more cannons to bore, no more palaces to build, there will be need of severe laws to compel the working women and workingmen who have been employed on embroidered laces, iron workings, buildings, to take the hygienic and calisthenic exercises requisite to re-establish their health and improve their race. When once we begin to consume European products at home instead of sending them to the devil, it will be necessary that the sailors, dock handlers and the draymen sit down and learn to twirl their thumbs. The happy Polynesians may then love as they like without fearing the civilized Venus and the sermons of European moralists.

And that is not all: In order to find work for all the non-producers of our present society, in order to leave room for the industrial equipment to go on developing indefinitely, the working class will be compelled, like the capitalist class, to do violence to its taste for abstinence and to develop indefinitely its consuming capacities. Instead of eating an ounce or two of gristly meat once a day, when it eats any, it will eat juicy beefsteaks of a pound or two; instead of drinking moderately of bad wine, it will become more orthodox than the pope and will drink broad and deep bumpers of Bordeaux and Burgundy without commercial baptism and will leave water to the beasts.

The proletarians have taken into their heads to inflict upon the capitalists ten hours of forge and factory; that is their great mistake, because of social antagonisms and civil wars. Work ought to be forbidden and not imposed. The Rothschilds and other capitalists should be allowed to bring testimony to the fact that throughout their whole lives they have been perfect vagabonds, and if they swear they wish to continue to live as perfect vagabonds in spite of the general mania for work, they should be pensioned and should receive every morning at the city hall a five-dollar gold piece for their pocket money. Social discords will vanish. Bond holders and capitalists will be first to rally to the popular party, once convinced that far from wishing them harm, its purpose is rather to relieve them of the labor of over-consumption and waste, with which they have been overwhelmed since their birth. As for the capitalists who are incapable of proving their title to the name of vagabond, they will be allowed to follow their instincts. . . . It would, however, be necessary to put the public funds out of the reach of the capitalists out of due regard for their acquired habits.

But vengeance, harsh and prolonged, will be heaped upon the moralists who have perverted nature, the bigots, the canters, the hypocrites, "and other such sects of men who disguise themselves like maskers to deceive the world. For whilst they give the common people to understand that they are busied about nothing but contemplation and devotion in fastings and maceration of their sensuality,–and that only to sustain and aliment the small fraility of their humanity,–it is so far otherwise that on the contrary, God knows, what cheer they make; et *Curios simulant, sed Bacchanalia vivunt.*[6] You may read it in great letters, in the coloring of their red snouts, and gulching bellies as big as a tun, unless it be when they perfume themselves with sulphur."[7] On the days of great popular rejoicing, when instead of swallowing dust as on the 15th of August and 14th of July under capitalism, the communists and collectivists will eat, drink and dance to their hearts' content, the members of the Academy, of moral and political sciences, the priests with long robes and short, of the economic, catholic, protestant, jewish, positivist and free-thought church; the propagandists of Malthusianism, and of Christian, altruistic, independent or dependent ethics, clothed in yellow, shall be compelled to hold a candle until it burns their fingers, shall starve in sight of tables loaded with meats, fruits and flowers and shall agonize with thirst in sight of flowing hogsheads. Four times a year with the changing seasons they shall be shut up like the knife grinders' dogs in great wheels and condemned to grind wind for ten hours.

The lawyers and legislators shall suffer the same punishment. Under the regime of idleness, to kill the time, which kills us second by second, there will be shows and theatrical performances always and always. And here we have the very work for our bourgeois legislators. We shall organize them into traveling companies to go to the fairs and villages, giving legislative exhibitions. The generals in riding boots, their breasts brilliantly decorated with medals and crosses, shall go through the streets and courts levying recruits among the good people. . . .

If, uprooting from its heart the vice which dominates it and degrades its nature, the working class were to arise in its terrible strength, not to demand the Rights of Man, which are but the rights of capitalist exploitation, not to demand the Right to Work which is but the right to misery, but to forge a brazen law forbidding any man to work more than three hours a day, the earth, the old earth, trembling with joy would feel a new universe leaping within her. But how should we ask a proletariat corrupted by capitalist ethics, to take a manly resolution. . . .

Like Christ, the doleful personification of ancient slavery, the men, the women and the children of the proletariat have been climbing painfully for a century up the hard Calvary of pain; for a century compulsory toil has broken their bones, bruised their flesh, tortured their nerves; for a century hunger has torn their entrails and their brains. O Laziness, have pity on our long misery! O Laziness, mother of the arts and noble virtues, be thou the balm of human anguish!

APPENDIX

Our moralists are very modest people. If they invented the dogma of work, they still have doubts of its efficacy in tranquilizing the soul, rejoicing the spirit, and maintaining the proper functioning of the entrails and other organs. They wish to try its workings on the populace, *in anima vili,* before turning it against the capitalists, to excuse and authorize whose vices is their peculiar mission.

But, you, three-for-a-cent philosophers, why thus cudgel your brains to work out an ethics the practice of which you dare not counsel to your masters? Your dogma of work, of which you are so proud, do you wish to see it scoffed at, dishonored? Let us open the history of ancient peoples and the writings of their philosophers and law givers. "I could not affirm," says the father of history, Herodotus, "whether the Greeks derived from the Egyptians the contempt which they have for work, because I find the same contempt established among the Thracians, the Cythians, the Persians, the Lydians; in a word, because among most barbarians, those who learn mechanical arts and even their children are regarded as the meanest of their citizens. All the Greeks have been nurtured in this principle, particularly the Lacedaemonians."[8]

"At Athens the citizens were veritable nobles who had to concern themselves but with the defense and the administration of the community, like the savage warriors from whom they descended. Since they must thus have all their time free to watch over the interests of the republic, with their mental and bodily strength, they laid all labor upon the slaves. Likewise at Lacedaemon, even the women were not allowed to spin or weave that they might not detract from their nobility."[9]

The Romans recognized but two noble and free professions, agriculture and arms. All the citizens by right lived at the expense of a treasury without being constrained to provide for their living by any of the sordid arts (thus, they designated the trades), which rightfully belonged to slaves. The elder Brutus to arouse the people, accused Tarquin, the tyrant, of the special outrage of having converted free citizens into artisans and masons.[10]

The ancient philosophers had their disputes upon the origin of ideas but they agreed when it came to the abhorrence of work. "Nature," said Plato in his social utopia, his model republic, "Nature has made no shoemaker nor smith. Such occupations degrade the people who exercise them. Vile mercenaries, nameless wretches, who are by their very condition excluded from political rights. As for the merchants accustomed to lying and deceiving, they will be allowed in the city only as a necessary evil. The citizen who shall have degraded himself by the commerce of the shop shall be prosecuted for this offense. If he is convicted, he shall be condemned to a year in prison; the punishment shall be doubled for each repeated offense."[11]

In his "Economics," Xenophon writes, "The people who give themselves up to manual labor are never promoted to public offices, and with good reason. The greater part of them, condemned to be seated the whole day long, some even to endure the heat of the fire continually, cannot fail to be changed in body, and it is almost inevitable that the mind be affected." "What honorable thing can come out of a shop?" asks Cicero. "What can commerce produce in the way of honor? Everything called shop is unworthy an honorable man. Merchants can gain no profit without lying, and what is more shameful than falsehood? Again, we must regard as something base and vile the trade of those who sell their toil and industry, for whoever gives his labor for money sells himself and puts himself in the rank of slaves."[12]

Proletarians, brutalized by the dogma of work, listen to the voice of these philosophers, which has been concealed from you with jealous care: A citizen who gives his labor for money degrades himself to the rank of slaves, he commits a crime which deserves years of imprisonment.

Christian hypocrisy and capitalist utilitarianism had not perverted these philosophers of the ancient republics. Speaking for free men, they expressed their thought naively. Plato, Aristotle, those intellectual giants, beside whom our latter day philosophers are but pygmies, wish the citizens of their ideal republics to live in the most complete leisure, for as Xenophon observed, "Work takes all the time and with it one has no leisure for the republic and his friends." According to Plutarch, the great claim of Lycurgus, wisest of men, to the admiration of posterity, was that he had granted leisure to the citizens of Sparta by forbidding to them any trade whatever. But our moralists of Christianity and capitalism will answer. "These thinkers and philosophers praised the institution of slavery." Perfectly true, but could it have been otherwise, granted the economic and political conditions of their epoch? War was the normal state of ancient societies. The free man was obliged to devote his time to discussing the affairs of state and watching over its defense. The trades were then too primitive and clumsy for those practicing them to exercise their birth-right of soldier and citizen; thus the philosophers and law-givers, if they wished to have warriors and citizens in their heroic republics, were obliged to tolerate slaves. But do not the moralists and economists of capitalism praise wage labor, the modern slavery; and to what men does the capitalist slavery give leisure? To people like Rothschild, Schneider, and Madame Boucicaut, useless and harmful slaves of their vices and of their domestic servants. "The prejudice of slavery dominated the minds of Pythagoras and Aristotle,"—this has been written disdainfully; and yet Aristotle foresaw: that if every tool could by itself execute its proper function, as the masterpieces of Daedalus moved themselves or as the tripods of Vulcan set themselves, spontaneously at their sacred work; if for example the shuttles of the weavers did their own weaving, the foreman of the workshop would have no more need of helpers, nor the master of slaves.

Aristotle's dream is our reality. Our machines, with breath of fire, with limbs of unwearying steel, with fruitfulness, wonderful inexhaustible, accomplish by themselves with docility their sacred labor. And nevertheless the genius of the great philosophers of capitalism remains dominated by the prejudice of the wage system, worst of slaveries. They do not yet understand that the machine is the saviour of humanity, the god who shall redeem man from the sordidae artes and from working for hire, the god who shall give him leisure and liberty.

Notes

1. At the Industrial Congress held in Berlin in Jan. 21, 1879, the losses in the iron industry of Germany during the last crisis were estimated at $109,056,000.

2. M. Clemenceau's "Justice" said on April 6, 1880, in its financial department: "We have heard this opinion maintained, that even without pressure the billions of the war of 1870 would have been equally lost for France, that is under the form of loans periodically put out to balance the budgets of foreign countries; this is also our opinion." The loss of English capital on loans of South American Republics is estimated at a billion dollars. The French laborers not only produced the billion dollars paid Bismarck, but they continued to pay interest on the war indemnity to Ollivier, Girardin, Bazaine and other income drawers, who brought on the war and the rout. Nevertheless they still have one shred of consolation: these billions will not bring on a war of reprisal.

3. Under the old regime, the laws of the church guaranteed the laborer ninety rest days, fifty-two Sundays and thirty-eight holidays, during which he was strictly forbidden to work. This was the great crime of catholicism, the principal cause of the irreligion of the industrial and commercial bourgeoisie: under the revolution, when once it was in the saddle, it abolished the holidays and replaced the week of seven days by that of ten, in order that the people might no longer have more than one rest day out of the ten. It emancipated the laborers from the yoke of the church in order the better to subjugate them under the yoke of work.

The hatred against the holidays does not appear until the modern industrial and commercial bourgeoisie takes definite form, between the fifteenth and sixteenth centuries. Henry IV asked of the pope that they be reduced. He refused because "one of the current heresies of the day is regarding feasts" (Letters of Cardinal d'Ossat). But in 1666 Prefixus, archbishop of Paris, suppressed seventeen of them in his diocese. Protestantism, which was the Christian religion adapted to the new industrial and commercial needs of the bourgeoisie, was less solicitous for the people's rest. It dethroned the saints in heaven in order to abolish their feast days on earth.

Religious reform and philosophical free thought were but pretexts which permitted the jesuitical and rapacious bourgeoisie to pilfer the feast days of the people.

4. These gigantic feasts lasted for weeks. Don Rodrigo de Lara wins his bride by expelling the Moors from old Calatrava, and the Romancero relates the story:

Les bodas fueron en Burgos
Las tornabodas en Salas:
En bodas y tornabodas
Pasaron siete semanas
Tantas vienen de las gentes
Que no caben por las plazas

(The wedding was at Bourges, the infaring at Salas. In the wedding and the infaring seven weeks were spent. So many people came that the town could not hold them................).

The men of these seven-weeks weddings were the heroic soldiers of the wars of independence.

5. Two examples: The English government to satisfy the peasants of India, who in spite of the periodical famines desolating their country insist on cultivating poppies instead of rice or wheat, has been obliged to undertake bloody wars in order to impose upon the Chinese Government the free entry of Indian opium. The savages of Polynesia, in spite of the mortality resulting

from it are obliged to clothe themselves in the English fashion in order to consume the products of the Scotch distilleries and the Manchester cotton mills.

6. They simulate Curius but live like Bacchanals. (Juvenal.)
7. Rabelais "Pantagruel," Book II, Chapter XXXIV. Translation of Urquhart and Motteux.
8. Herodotus, Book II.
9. Biot. De L'abolition de L'esclavage ancien en Occident, 1840.
10. Livy, Book I.
11. Plato's "Republic," Book V.
12. Cicero's "De Officiis," I, 42.

The Great Emptiness

By ROBERT M. MACIVER

"IN THE sweat of thy face shalt thou eat bread." From this primal decree millions of human beings are now liberated. More and more men have more and more leisure. The working day grows shorter, the weekend longer. More and more women are released at an earlier age from the heavier tasks of the rearing of children, in the small family of today, where kindergarten and school and clinic and restaurant come to their aid. More and more people are freed for other things, released from the exhaustion of their energies in the mere satisfaction of elementary wants. No longer is the pattern so simple as that of Longfellow's blacksmith, who "something attempted, something done, has earned a night's repose."

Released from what? When necessity no longer drives, when people own long hours in which to do what they want, what do they want to do? Where necessity is heavy upon men, they yearn for the joys of leisure. Now many have enough leisure. What are the joys they find?

The shorter working day is also a different working day. Nearly all men work for others, not for themselves—not the way a man works who has his own little plot of earth and must give himself up to its cultivation. For many, work has become a routine—not too onerous, not too rewarding, and by no means engrossing—a daily routine until the bell rings and sets them free again. For what?

It is a marvelous liberation for those who learn to use it; and there are many ways. It is the great emptiness for those who don't.

People of a placid disposition do not know the great emptiness. When the day's work is done, they betake themselves to their quiet interests, their hobbies, their gardens or their amateur workbenches or their stamp collecting or their games or their social affairs or their church activities or whatever it be. When they need more sting in life, they have a mild "fling," taking a little "moral holiday." Some find indulgence enough in the vicarious

---

pleasure of snidely malicious gossip. Their habits are early formed and they keep a modicum of contentment.

But the number of the placid is growing less. The conditions of our civilization do not encourage that mood. For one thing, the old-time acceptance of authority, as God-given or nature-based, is much less common. Religion is for very many an ancient tale, "a tale of little meaning, though the words are strong," reduced to ritual or the moral precepts of the Sunday pulpit. There is little allegiance to the doctrine that every man has his allotted place. How could there be when competition has become a law of life? There is incessant movement and disturbance and upheaval. And with the new leisure there come new excitations, new stimuli to unrest.

So the new leisure has brought its seeming opposite, restlessness. And because these cannot be reconciled the great emptiness comes.

Faced with the great emptiness, unprepared to meet it, most people resort to one or another way of escape, according to their kind. Those who are less conscious of their need succeed in concealing it from themselves. They find their satisfaction in the great new world of means without ends. Those who are more conscious of it cannot conceal it; they only distract themselves from the thought of it. Their common recourse is excitation, and they seek it in diverse ways.

The first kind are go-getters. When they are efficient or unscrupulous or both, they rise in the world. They amass things. They make some money. They win some place and power. Not for anything, not to do anything with it. Their values are relative, which means they are no values at all. They make money to make more money. They win some power that enables them to seek more power. They are practical men. They keep right on being practical, until their unlived lives are at an end. If they stopped being practical, the great emptiness would engulf them. They are like planes that must keep on flying because they have no landing gear. The engines go fast and faster, but they are going nowhere. They make good progress to nothingness.

They take pride in their progress. They are outdistancing other men. They are always calculating the distance they have gained. It shows what can be done when you have the know-how. They feel superior and that sustains them. They stay assured in the world of means. What matters is the winning.

"But what good come of it at last?"
Quoth little Peterkin.
"Why that I cannot tell," said he,
"But 'twas a famous victory."

Victory for the sake of the winning, means for the sake of the acquiring, that is success. So the circle spins forever, means without end, world without end. Amen.

The second kind have it worse. They are the more sensitive kind, often the more gifted. They want their lives to have some meaning, some fulfilment. They want the feel of living for some worthwhile end. But often there is something wrong with the seeking. They too suffer from the intrusive ego. Their seeking lacks adequate sincerity. The need of success is greater for them than the need of the thing that is sought. If, for example, they pursue some art, the art itself counts less than the renown of the artist. They would be great artists, great writers, opera singers, pathfinders. They aim high, but the mark is higher than their reach. When they miss it they grow disillusioned. They are thrust back on their unsatisfied egos, and the great emptiness lies before them.

They try to escape, but they run from themselves. They try to forget, but their only recourse is an excitation of the senses. This stimulant needs to be incessantly repeated. The little spell of liberation, the false glow, the hour of oblivion, leaves them the more desolate and adds new tensions to the returning emptiness. Then there is leisure no more, no relaxedness, no return to the things they once loved, no lingering ease of quiet discourse with friends, no natural savor of living, no perception of the unfolding wonder of things. But instead they pass from excitation to a hollow release, from release to tension, from tension to new excitation. Nothing is itself any more. And no more at the end of the day do they sink peacefully into the marvelous process of slowly gathering sleep.

Once they were so eager to make life feel real; now they shun its reality and are driven to pursue phantoms, the will-o'-the-wisp of sense-spurred distraction, the unseeing ghosts of once clear-eyed joys, the phantom Aphrodite.

But it is not only the more cultivated, the more sophisticated, and the well-to-do with their more ample opportunities, who feel the great emptiness. In other ways it besets large numbers who, finding little satisfaction in the daily work, seek compensation in the leisure they now possess. There are many besides, people who win early pensions or otherwise can get along without toil through legacies or rents or other sources of unearned income, women who have no family cares—the new, unopulent leisure class.

They have no training for leisure. They have, most of them, no strong interests or devotions. The habits of their work time convey no meaning to the time of liberation. Most of them live in cities, in drab and narrow confines within which they revolve in casual little circles. They see nothing ahead but the coming of old age. They want to regain the feel of life. Time is theirs, but they cannot redeem it.

Soon they too betake themselves, in their various ways, to some form of excitation. Having no recourse in themselves, they must get out of themselves. They take the easy ways out because they see no alternative. They have never learned to climb the paths leading to the pleasures that wait in the realm of ideas, in the growing revelation of the nature of things, in the treasuries of the arts, and in the rich lore of the libraries. They must seek instead the quick transport, the dream, the adventure, in the tavern or where the gamblers meet.

They would cover the emptiness they cannot fill. They make a goal of what is a diversion. The healthy being craves an occasional wildness, a jolt from normality, a sharpening of the edge of appetite, his own little festival of the Saturnalia, a brief excursion from his way of life. But for these others the diversion becomes the way of life and diverts no more. For them the filled glass is not the cheerful accompaniment of pleasant reunions but a deceitful medicine for the ennui of living. For them the gambling venture is no mere holiday flutter but a never-satisfied urge that forever defeats itself.

In 1946, in straitened England, the then equivalent of half a billion dollars was placed in bets on the horses and the dogs. Besides which, vast sums changed hands on the results of football games. For hundreds of thousands of people the major news in the daily papers, day after day and month after month, was the lists of the winners and the betting odds. England was not, is not, alone in this respect. It is only that the figures happen to be more accessible.

A former addict explained in the London *Spectator* why men do it. The gambler, he said, "gambles because it provides an emotional tension which his mind demands. He is suffering from a deficiency disease, and the only antidote he knows is gambling." He is trying to escape the great emptiness. An English worker of the semi-skilled category once said to me: "A fellow has to do something, and what is there? Maybe I have a shilling or two in my pocket. Maybe I could buy an extra shirt. It's no go. So I put them on the dogs."

By these resorts people do not escape the great emptiness. What they get is a sequence of brief delusions of escape. In time the only thing they can escape to is what they themselves know for a delusion. The resort is only a drug to make them forget the disease. As with all such drugs, the dose must be continually renewed, and it becomes harder and harder to return to the pre-addict stage. They come to look on the great emptiness as something inherent in the very nature of things. That is all life is. Now they know the drug is a delusion, but they do not know that it has bred a deeper delusion.

There are other avenues of escape that, while they may still be delusive, have the merit of not being recognized as such. Which means that the escape is actually made. In every large city, and notably in those areas where people go to spend their retirement, where the climate is mild and sunny, all kinds of special cults flourish and new ones are frequently born. To these places repair the hucksters of the supernatural and find a ready market for their wares. There are to be found the prophets of mystical union, robed and turbaned preachers of the Light of Asia, interpreters of the Rosy Cross, exponents of the heavenly trance, new healers of the soul, tuners-in of the Infinite, operators in spiritual magics. Considerable numbers flock to them, some to seek a new sensation and then pass on, but some to stay and become disciples or devotees.

These last are the credulous ones, the unsophisticate, the suggestible. They search no more. The emptiness is filled. They have undergone a kind of hypnosis. They live in the nebula of their mystical dream. They meet reality no more. But at least, in a manner, they have found their peace.

Back in the days when unremitting toil was the lot of all but the very few and leisure still a hopeless yearning, hard and painful as life was, it still felt real. People were in rapport with the small bit of reality allotted to them, the sense of the earth, the tang of the changing seasons, the consciousness of the eternal on-going of birth and death. Now, when so many have leisure, they become detached from themselves, not merely from the earth. From all the widened horizons of our greater world a thousand voices call us to come near, to understand, and to enjoy, but our ears are not trained to hear them. The leisure is ours but not the skill to use it. So leisure becomes a void, and from the ensuing restlessness men take refuge in delusive excitations or fictitious visions, returning to their own earth no more.

Time and Silence

By MAX PICARD

TIME is interspersed with silence.

Silently one day moves onward to the next. Each day appears unnoticed as if God had just put it down out of His own quietness.

Silently the days move through the year. They move in the rhythm of silence: the content of the day is noisy, but the advent of the day is silent.

It is not so much the equal measure of the silence with which each day is newly born.

The seasons move in silence through the changing year. Spring does not come from winter; it comes from the silence from which winter came and summer and autumn.

One morning in spring the cherry tree stands full of blossom. The white blossoms seem not to have grown on the tree but to have fallen through the sieve of silence. No sound was heard; they glided gently along the silence and it was that that made them white.

The birds sang in the tree. It was as if the silence had shaken out the last sounds from itself. Birdsong is like the picked-up notes of silence.

Suddenly the green appears on the trees. As one tree stands green beside another, it is as if the green had passed silently from from one tree to another, as words pass from one to another in a conversation.

Pages 113-19 from *The World of Silence,* by Max Picard, translated by Stanley Godman, published by Henry Regnery Company, Chicago; published originally as *Die Welt des Schweigens* by Eugen Rentsch Verlag, Zürich. Reprinted by permission of the publishers.

Spring comes suddenly: man looks into the distance as if he could still see the harbinger who brought the spring in silence. In spring a man's eyes gaze into the distance.

The reality of spring is so gentle that it does not need to break through the solid walls of time with noise. It simply seeps through the chinks of time and suddenly appears.

Children playing on the square are the first to come through the chinks. Even before the blossoms they come along with their balls in the air and their marbles on the ground.

They suddenly appear not as from their parents' houses but as if were out of the chinks, along with spring. They throw their balls high up in the air; they shout aloud, these first harbingers of spring showing the way to the things of spring that follow on behind.

Behind all the sounds of spring is the silence of time. It is a wall throwing back the children's words like balls from the walls of the houses.

The blossoms on the trees make themselves so light, as if they wanted to settle on the silence, unnoticed by the silence itself; to be carried into the next spring in the ever-moving circle of the seasons, just as birds settle down on ships to be carried farther on.

Then, quite suddenly, the summer arrives.

The air is hot with the violence of its invasion. As if they had burst out from a covering, the things of summer suddenly appear in their fullness. But no one heard the summer come. It too was brought in silence. The covering enclosing the fullness of summer burst open in the silence. No one heard a sound when time put the summer down with a violent thud. Everything happened silently.

But now summer has appeared, everything begins to sound: the animal voices are stronger, people throw their words like balls; out of the gardens and taverns voices tumble as if the room inside were too narrow for them. It is the triumph of the sounds of summer over silence.

Silence is now hidden in the forest. The forest is like a green tunnel leading from the noise of summer into the silence. And as one sometimes sees lights in a tunnel, so the deer of the forest flash like light illuminating the silence.

Silence is now in a hiding place, but any moment it can come out and cover everything again. In the noon of a hot summer's day every sound of summer is absorbed by the all-possessing silence. It is sometimes as if the summer stands quite still. It stands so fast, as if it would never move again. Its image seems to be impressed on and to remain in the air.

Then after silence has taken a new breath the autumn comes.

Like birds clustering thick on the wires before their departure, the apples sit on the branches. Here and there when an apple falls to the ground there comes a moment of stillness. It is as if the silence had held out its hand to try and catch the apple.

The colours of the leaves and fruits become more vivid. It is almost as though, if one were to tear them, a sound would come out of them. The dark blue berries of the grapes are like the heads of crotchets. The song of the harvester lies concentrated in the dark crotchet-heads of the berries.

Everything moves closer to speech in the autumn: the silence itself seems to sound in between the songs of the harvesters.

In winter silence is visible: the snow is silence become visible.

The space between heaven and earth is occupied by silence; heaven and earth are merely the edge of the snowy silence.

Snowflakes meet in the air and fall together on to the earth, which is already white in the silence. Silence meeting silence.

People stand silent on the side of the street. Human language is covered by the snow of silence. What remains of man is his body standing in the snow like a milestone of silence. People stand still and silence moves between them.

Time is accompanied by silence, determined by silence. Its quietness comes from the silence that is enclosed within it. But the sound of measurable time, the rhythmic beat of time, is drowned by the silence.

Time is expanded by silence.

If silence is so preponderant in time that time is completely absorbed by it, then time stands still. There is then nothing but silence: the silence of eternity.

When there is no more silence left in time, then the noise of its as it were mechanically flowing movement becomes audible. Then there is no more time, only the impetus of its onward flow. Men and things are then as it were pushed on by the movement of time, taken up into its mechanical onward flow, no longer independent, but merely a constituent part of time itself. Men, things, and time compete against each other as in a race; as if they existed only as competitors in the race—"the race against time" and the race of time against men and things.

Without the silence that is in time, there would be no forgetting and no forgiving. Just as time itself enters into silence, so what happens in time enters also; and therefore man is led by the silence which is in time to forgetting and forgiving.

When time has been completely absorbed by silence, in Eternity, there can be nothing but the great forgetting and forgiving, for Eternity is permeated by the great silence into which everything that has ever happened falls and disappears.

It is true, the spirit stands above time and above the silence that is in time; it is the spirit that determines forgetting and forgiving. But it is easier for the spirit to forgive and to forget when it meets the silence in time: through the silence the spirit is reminded of Eternity, which is the great silence and forgiving.

The Ideology of Privacy and Reserve

By PAUL HALMOS

IN THE ERA of competitive liberalism, the Christian ideal of the uniqueness of the person has been over-stressed and the service of this ideal has popularised the display of mannerisms, styles and conventions suggestive of independent, self-sufficient personalities. From the more or less correct judgment that too much sociability is a mark of superficiality, it is quite unconsciously deduced that sociability itself is undignified and superficial. Let us not forget that Christian virtues have never been so prominently displayed, if at all, in connection with communal activities, gregarious desires and so on.[1] Neighborly love is pre-eminently an attitude of service and sacrifice without regard to mutuality in the relationship. Also, Christianity has been, to say the least, neutral to religiously non-committal group experience. When such experience displayed sufficient vitality to be suspected of paganism it was anxiously watched and at the first opportunity righteously criticised by the protagonists of the Christian churches. The unworldly ideals and disregard for other people's—the world's—opinion made the believers look upon their gregarious cravings, their search for companionship, as if they had been the signs of just another failure in virtue and a shallow desire for worldly pleasures. It is to be particularly remembered that the Christian archetype of virtuous living has been the life of the recluse mystic, not of the fraternal, congenial inspirer of groups and communities.[2] Berdyaev's excuse is a typical instance of some contemporary Christian attitudes: 'Kierkegaard's affirmation, that the Absolute divides rather than unites, is only true in so far as it applies to the division and union operative in everyday social life'.[3] But it is in everyday social life that integration on a more fundamental level is sought for; it is in everyday social life that the ravages of desocialisation have become unbearable. This fantasied virtuousness of isolation is a frequent theme of Christian moralists and Pascal's comments on it may be quoted as a fairly representative sample: 'I have discovered that all the unhappiness of men arises from one single fact, that they cannot stay quietly in their own chamber . . . men only seek conversation and entering games, because they cannot remain with pleasure at home. . . . But on further consideration, when, after finding the cause of all our ills, I have sought to discover the reasons of it, I have found that there is one very real reason, namely, the natural poverty of our feeble and mortal condition, so miserable that nothing can comfort us when we think of it closely'.[4]

Talcott Parsons distinguishes between the individualistic separativeness

---

of Catholic Christianity and of Protestant, in particular Calvinistic, Christianity. Of the former he writes: 'The whole medieval cast of mind favored ideas of corporate unity and conceived of the church as the central form of human life.'[5] The individualism of the Catholic Christianity was 'mitigated' by the 'sacramental dispensations of the church'.[6] And later on he states that although '. . . a certain "individualistic" character has been fundamental to Christianity from the beginning . . . this was greatly strengthened by the Reformation. Calvinism represents the extreme of the development of this individualistic element in one particular direction . . . its extreme anti-ritualism cut off the individual far more drastically than Luther ever did from the protecting, guiding hand of church and priest, which was felt especially in the confessional . . . other human beings were not merely useless to him, they might be positively dangerous, since however virtuous his outward conduct, any other human being, even the closest relative or friend, might be one of the damned. The net result was, as Weber puts it, an unheard-of "inner isolation of the individual",[7] which placed him squarely on his own responsibility in all things, and involved a radical devaluation, not to say mistrust, of even the closest human ties. God always came first.'[8]

The individualist ideology of the era of competitive liberalism secularised this Christian ideal, that is, the ideal of the moral autarchy of the individual.[9] Just as Christianity has not attached any moral significance to the bilateral or multilateral relationship as such, modern individualism also posits the ideal of perfection in a strong, self-sufficient person who is not incomplete in solitude and who is not craving for anything, let alone fellowship. The spectacle of corporate happiness is just as nauseating to the individualist as its impious, ephemeral jollity is suspect to the Christian. Furthermore, the vigorous, competitive *bellum omnium contra omnes* atmosphere of the age adds hostility to separativeness. Perhaps at no other juncture of human history has there been made so much of the uniqueness and sovereignty of the individual.[10] It is this ideological distortion upon which Harry Stack Sullivan commented, '. . . the delusion of unique individuality cuts off all communion that is not absolutely required by maturing necessities. . . . We see quite a number of people in whom effectual development of personality was arrested at this stage; the later matured needs for intimacy (inhering in the human biological equipment) having then been tortured into strange channels of maladaptive expression, and the autistic-magical interpersonal behavior evolved in delusions of reference, of persecution, and of grandeur, or along an uncertain course in which other people are treated as troublesome units transiently more or less useful to a flaming ambition to outdo everyone else in some particular field of accomplishment . . .'.[11]

It is in this atmosphere that man meets his fellowman. He may expect some benefit from his fellowman's approval or some harm from his displeasure, and even when their relationship is not coloured by business or professional interests the participants of the meeting keep a cautious eye on their prestige. It is not the prestige of wisdom, serenity and good-neighbourliness they are protecting but that of conspicuous consumption and status. Furthermore, there is the spiritual heritage of nineteenth-century *laisser faire et laisser perdre* individualism which prescribed an ideal of self-sufficiency and personal autarchy, an ideal which has since been incorporated into our conception of social worth: 'I may not show my need for you, for your love and approval, because I am supposed to be strong and independent of such things'.[12]

Since the feudal era the class-stratification of Western communities has become less and less rigid; the mobility of the individual, both upwards and downwards, is perhaps greater to-day than in previous civilisations. The jealous protection of one's status and the energetic upward pressure from the lower strata have produced greater sensitiveness and selectiveness in social participation. The economic and aristocratic symbols of class-superiority may not be brandished to-day with the same blind pride as in former centuries, yet position, rank and conspicuous consumption still act as perpetuators of an ideology of privacy and reserve. This is familiar enough in contemporary inter-class relationships, thought it must be noted that to-day discrimination on these grounds is more subtle and rarely explicit. Also, the extension of the media of social advancement into fields which were previously not recognised as such, e.g., the arts, sciences, sport, business and so on, has reduced the impenetrable exclusiveness of the aristocratic few. What is more significant, however, is that even within the limits of a more or less homogeneous neighbourhood the traditional selectiveness of inter-class relationships reappears to influence the social behaviour of individuals and families *in their own class:* accent, professional nuances, conspicuous consumption ('not being able to keep up with the Joneses') and so on, survived the age of hereditary privileges. Here it is of some interest to re-read Thornstein Veblen's diagnosis of our social life, which is, on the whole, still accurate: 'Through this discrimination in favour of visible consumption it has come about that the domestic life of most classes is relatively shabby, as compared with the éclat of that overt position of their life that is carried on before the eyes of observers. As a secondary consequence of the same discrimination people habitually screen their private life from observation. So far as concerns that portion of their consumption that may without blame be carried on in secret, they withdraw from all contact from their neighbours. Hence the exclusiveness of people, as regards their domestic life, in most industrially developed communities; and hence, by remoter derivation, the habit of privacy and reserve that is so large a feature in the code of proprieties of the better classes in all communities.'[13] We might add that in modern mass-society the bourgeois code of propriety is observed by the consolidated working classes through the latter's often pathetic conformity constitutes a grotesquely rigid and naïvely pretentious effort. The authors of 'The Peckham Experiment'[14] leave no doubt that the 'habit of privacy and reserve' is by no means the exclusive convention of the 'better classes'. The peasantry of feudal society did not practise formality or cherish reserve to the extent their present-day descendants do; the village folk of the fifteenth century, in Western Europe, did not yet attempt to imitate the 'good manners' of their rulers. To-day the formalism of social intercourse is very largely uniform in all classes of Western society, but while the leisure and amenities of the ruling classes leave ample time and energy for the observance of the refinements of social contact, the new bourgeoisie, the lower-middle and lower classes, have little or no margin of time and resources for living up to a code which, after all, requires all these things. To-day we often see 'county' manners and hospitality attempted on a bare living wage. This imitated congeniality is naturally tiresome to all participants and becomes, sooner or later, forbidding. In *Men Without Work*[15] we find the following telling passage: 'The Rhondda family does not consider that "keeping itself to itself" is a canon of respectability. Everyone knows its affairs, and if anything goes wrong, there is sympathy and help readily forthcoming from the home next door.' Indeed a gratifying spectacle of a well-integrated community life! By implication, however, we receive the writers' testimony that elsewhere 'keeping oneself to oneself' *is* a 'canon of respectability'.

Sociometric investigations have shown that the majority of positive choices in a community go to those with a higher socio-economic status.[16] This 'societal nucleation' around the more favourably placed and around leaders drains the positive choices from all quarters and deprives the majority of being wanted, of the experience of being sought after. There is also a 'nucleation' of rejection which is out of all proportion to the degree of inferiority in the status of the rejected. H. H. Jennings, working on a 'laboratory society', an approved school for girls, found this 'nucleation' of choices and rejections particularly distinct: 'The great disparity between the positive emotional expansiveness of the population towards the well-chosen and towards the isolated or near-isolated is found to be accentuated by the vastly greater extent to which they reject the latter as compared with the extent to which they focus rejection upon the well-chosen. The 46 well-chosen are given 724 positive choices by indivduals to 116 rejections; or 86 per cent positive to 14 per cent negative expressions. The 11 isolated or near-isolated are given 6 positive choices to 115 rejections by the membership, or 5 per cent positive to 95 per cent negative reactions.'[17] In this investigation socio-economic status of the members could hardly have influenced their motivations, yet the cumulative effect of 'nucleation' was very striking. On the other hand, socio-economic factors bring about the same pronounced 'nucleation' in communities where the underlying selectiveness is inspired by a competitive ambition and by a stubborn effort at self-validation through prestige-giving social contact. E.g. the relative number of votes received by children of the various social classes showed in one investigation[18] that children of all social classes tend to want children of the higher classes for friends, and not to want children of the lower classes as friends. Also, '. . . the children of the higher social classes were said to be good-looking, while those of lower social level were said to be not good-looking. Yet the fifth- and sixth-grade classrooms contained a number of blonde, blue-eyed Polish girls and stalwart, freckle-faced Scotch-Irish boys of lower-class families who would undoubtedly be picked as good-looking by adults who knew nothing of social backgrounds.'[19]

Georg Simmel said that our 'modern life is overburdened with objective content and material demands'. In his view riches, social position, learning, fame, exceptional capacities and merits 'stylise' our sociability and induce reserve. The 'pure humanity' and its 'capacities, attractions and interests' ought to be the only features which should be allowed to enter the social relationships of man.[20] Though the utopianism of this view is apparent it is in fundamental agreement with the conclusions of many recent writers. For instance, Erich Fromm's *The Fear of Freedom* contains the following passage: 'Modern man's feeling of isolation and powerlessness is increased still further by the character which all his human relationships have assumed. The concrete relationship of one individual to another has lost its direct and human character and has assumed a spirit of manipulation and instrumentality. In all social and personal relations the laws of the market are the rule. It is obvious that the relationship between competitors has to be based on mutual human indifference.'[21] Trigant Burrow's writings abound in observations to the same effect; e.g.: 'We may only *deal with* one another; we may not be *united as* one another. If there is conviviality and accord, it is not because of a phylic union between the organisms involved, but because momentarily the self-interest of each of us happens to correspond in its outward form.'[22] In a pamphlet *The Churches' Part in the Provision of New Centres of Community Life* (published by the National Council of Social Service, London, 1947), we read: 'Life in these days is so largely split up into separate sections and departments that we are apt to meet only those who share with us a common cause or a common pursuit. We meet for bridge, or in a ratepayers' association or Labour group, or for the study of economics, or the praise of Robert Burns; and in these meetings we know our associates in only that limited relationship—as bridge players or ratepayers or Labour politicians, as students or admirers of this or that: we do not meet other people just because they are people and in spite of our lack of a specific bond; nor do we meet under circumstances when any subject may be mentioned or any question raised.' The increasing complexity of our material culture depersonalises human relationships in many ways. Firstly, the heightened tempo of competition compels the individual to greater and greater specialisation of function and alienates him from the functions and interests of others; secondly, the specialist function comprises so much of the personality that many people are nowadays lawyers, shop-stewards or linguists first and persons second; thirdly, the narrow margin of leisure may well be spent in 'talking shop' or in social participation through the only remaining *lingua franca,* the playing of games; fourthly, competitiveness may not terminate at the end of the shift or of the official hours and may continue into leisure-time social life, though admittedly this is far more frequent in the middle and upper strata of society than in the lower classes. Could it be statistically assessed, the amount of social participation motivated by the desire for occupational, professional and social advancement would stagger us all. This is, of course, the most typical example of using other people as tools and ignoring them as persons.

Selectiveness on grounds of prestige when inspired by ideas of class, income, specialisation of function and so on has been considered in the foregoing section. There is, however, one specialisation of function which issues in a selectiveness of a peculiar and very significant kind: it remains to examine the somewhat different spectacle presented by selectiveness on intellectual grounds. It would be said that when the intellectual medium genuinely needed and sought by the *one* is alien to the *other* there can be no justification for condemning the former's selectiveness and withdrawal. Admittedly, it is not possible to define what should be taken as a 'genuine need'; nevertheless, selectiveness of this sort cannot be accepted as an *all-time* principle, which it undoubtedly is among many intellectuals of our age. Here the ideology of privacy and reserve is engendered by prestige-seeking intellectualism and rationalised by fervently repeated references to the ultimate values which the arts and sciences so obligingly represent. In Aldous Huxley's opinion, 'neighbours whom one never sees at close quarters are the ideal and perfect neighbours', and according to Cyril Connolly, '. . . from now on an artist will be judged only by the resonance of his solitude or the quality of his despair'. These are only two examples of the intellectual isolationism to which we refer here; no doubt similar pronouncements from a great variety of contexts could be cited.[23]

Apart from intellectual selectiveness there is also a widespread rationalisation of withdrawal under the pretext that privacy is superior to participation (cf. Pascal's remarks above). Isolation is 'splendid' and solitude is voluntarily suffered in a tower which is built of the noble material of ivory; and even when these attributes are coloured by sarcasm, the latter is aimed at a presumption of superiority. Superiority is thus associated with retirement. This type of 'ennobled' solitude often appears as a consolation for the loss of social approval and as a life-pattern it is frequently adopted in adolescence. 'The feeling of solitude arouses exaltation, for example, in the form, "From the watch tower of divine solitude I look down on the common herd". During adolescence such an orientation can be considered normal.'[24] And this is how Karen Horney formulates the latent views held by so many in contemporary society: 'Probably nobody can stand isolation without either *being* particularly strong and resourceful or *feeling* uniquely significant.'[25]

Evidently the man of a serene and solid *Weltanschauung* is held to be self-sufficient in his aloneness, finding comfort with ease in the contemplation of revealed truth, beauty and goodness. Here, as elsewere, it is made clear that the man who stays content in his own chamber has risen above the feeble and mortal condition of the many. Even if we were to accept such a portraiture of the exceptional few as faithfully accurate we would still have to recognise that the common man is more adept at imitating the externals of virtuous self-sufficiency than at grasping its essence, that is, assimilating the virtues which make sustained privacy and reserve not only possible but also legitimate.

In his search for the justification of his separativeness the intellectual has often attempted to postulate *a priori* principles of self-sufficiency. Graham Wallas, for instance, went as far as seriously affirming his belief in an 'instinctive need of privacy'. He argued that social participation requires a 'repeated emotional adjustment' which is an intolerable demand on our adaptability. But he 'gave himself away' when he said that 'Light chatter, even among strangers, in which neither party *gives himself away,* is very much less fatiguing than an intimacy which makes some call upon the emotions.'[26] (Italics mine.) Not being able to show where this instinctive need of privacy ends and where the instinctive need of fellowship begins, he tries to escape by recommending some magic recipe of a mixture of privacy and participation the composition of which he does not divulge. His attitude closely resembles that of Schopenhauer's shivering porcupines who suffered each other's pricks when too close together, from cold when too far from each other, and finally settled at a medium distance which, they thought, would secure a moderate measure of freedom from both these unpleasantnesses.[27]

There is, of course, a great deal of commonsense in all those views which advocate a compromise solution; after all, the *Principium Individuationis* requires a certain amount of elbow room and a certain degree of solitary incubation of ideas and affects. On the other hand, 'Let us answer ambition, that herselfe gives us the taste of solitarinesse. For what doth she shun so much as company? What seeketh she more than elbow-roome?' wrote Montaigne,[28] whose interpretation of intellectual separativeness is still accurate to-day: "They have gone backe that they might leap the better, and with a stronger motion make a nimbler offer amidst the multitude.'[29] This interpretation should be borne in mind when the merits of solitariness are compared with the virtues of sociability, and when a compromise solution is sought. But it is one thing to advise compromise to a hypersocial community submerged in interminable convivialities and another to preach it to a desocialised, and consequently sick, society. It may be, of course, that the convivialities with which Pascal was familiar were coarse, idle and therefore 'sinful'; it may be that the social surface of man's personality appeared 'pricky' to Schopenhauer; it may be that intimacy—'giving himself away'—was too great an emotional strain to Graham Wallas; we venture to suggest that, in these cases, the ideological affirmation of withdrawal from society was demanded by intra-psychic needs, i.e. the ideology of privacy and reserve underlying their pronouncements was a rationalisation of intra-psychic blockages erected in them by the mediated and direct influence of their social environment. These intra-psychic needs are the functions of the social-cultural value-systems which they concretise and perpetuate.

Recently, there has been a 'counter-reformation' of the individualist creed. The regimentation of life under totalitarian dictatorships enveloped many intellectuals who submitted their skills to the service of these régimes. Julien Benda wrote of these men: 'The modern "clerk" has entirely ceased to let the layman alone descend to the market place. The modern clerk is determined to have the soul of a citizen and to make vigorous use of it; he is proud of that soul; his literature is filled with his contempt for the man who shuts himself up with art or science and takes no interest in the passions of the state.'[30] Benda's charge against the intellectuals[31] is that they have become scribes to the tyrants and officiating priests to the mobs. He quotes Renan as saying, 'Man belongs neither to his language nor to his race, he belongs to himself.' Both attitudes, the classical individualism of the ninenteeth century and the individualism of the 'counter-reformation', on the one hand, and the impersonal political passions of the modern 'clerks', on the other, are ideological distortions. Between the evasions of a precious exclusiveness[32] and *La Trahison* there is a third way which is being sought in the pages of this enquiry.

The dialectic fluctuations since nineteenth-century liberalism, through twentieth-century collectivism and totalitarianism, to the individualism of the 'counter-reformation' continue facing us with forbidding, antithetical extremes and deny the right of way to explorers who seek a synthesis on a higher level. There is a blindness in these extremes—alas, a congenital attribute of extremes—which cannot anticipate new alloys of individualism. Whereas most individualists would agree that the so-called 'rugged' variety of their creed is dead, they uphold an individualism of a more up-to-date kind without expressly admitting the relativism of their *credo*. From the crucible of the present age a new individualism will have to emerge if the survival of the species as well as its continued regeneration through individual contributions is to be secured.

In our Western society, the basic pattern of living is rigidly home-centred; the daily and nightly retirement into solitude or the family circle shows up the only things which have remained really concrete and tangible to modern man: his freedom in privacy and his belonging to the family circle. One lives one's life in the family and one has social contacts, makes social excursions, instead of the other way round, that is, instead of living in society and withdrawing from it occasionally according to one's need. This discrimination may appear to many as a matter of perspective and of limited significance, but it is clearly more than that. The man of mass society regards his home as a base of operations; the base is, at least conventionally, thought to be constant, defined and reliable, whilst social contacts and social excursions are fortuitous, unpredictable. In other words, the basic social reality is the unpopulous modern family or the bachelor individual. The insularity of modern families is aided by the vast suburban developments of our great cities, in which, incidentally, it is difficult to see distinctive individuality being fostered by a staggering uniformity of the homes (three rooms upstairs, two downstairs, mass-produced, shoddy furniture, and so on) and of domestic routines. A variety in styles of life is hardly fostered by family separativeness and individuality under these conditions. The ideological defence of family insularity cannot be readily supported by aesthetic considerations. A criticism of its moral justification may be deduced from the following analysis.

The clan-morality of primitive communities shrank throughout the early civilisations and the narrower family loyalty of the patrician and the feudal lord took over. It was the feudal allegiance to the family crest which bourgeois society aped and adopted when tradesmen and artisans demanded from their sons and daughters that they uphold and enhance the honour of the family name. Of course, not all the bourgeois families realised the esoteric exclusiveness of the Forsytes, but the pattern was there to be reproduced even by those who were much less prominently placed. Urbanisation was a most fertile soil for this development. 'With the growth of urban forms of social organisation, links of kinship and of feudal dependence become less vivid and the house as headquarters of the family becomes more focal. Each family became an organisation in its own right, with its own private space. Because this space was more limited, at urban densities, than in the sparsely populated feudal countryside, it also became more exclusive, both physically and emotionally. The value of what is private was much increased. Private property and private enterprise were highly esteemed.'[33] In this era competition is not so much between individuals as between families, and hence Charles Madge is right in saying that 'There is an important distinction between family privacy and single person privacy.'[34] There is no single person privacy in the slum or even in a better placed populous family. The proletarianisation of the middle classes further extends the area within which single person privacy is a luxury. Thus it has come about that family privacy is a more conspicuous phenomenon than single person privacy.

Notes

1. 'Freedom is complete purity and detachment which seeketh the Eternal; an isolated, a withdrawn being, identical with God or entirely attached to God.' This is John Tauler's formula of Christian virtue (quoted by Aldous Huxley in *Ends and Means*, London, 1937, p. 5); undoubtedly there are many statements like this in Christian theological literature. Much has been made of the Aristotelian influence on Christianity, and one wonders how much of Aristotle's ideas on friendship has found its way into Christian Ethics. The following passage from *The Nicomachean Ethics* lays stress on mutuality in friendship in a manner which is alien to Christian moral philosophy.

'... but the term (Friendship) is not applied to the case of fondness for things inanimate because there is *no requital of the affection* nor desire for the good of those objects; it certainly savours of the ridiculous to say that a man fond of wine wishes well to it: the only sense in which it is true being that he wishes it to be kept safe and sound for his own use and benefit. But to the friend they say one should wish all good for his sake. And when men do thus wish good to another (he not reciprocating the feeling), people call them kindly; because Friendship they describe as being *"Kindliness between persons who reciprocate it"*. But must they not add that the feeling must be mutually known? for many men are kindly disposed towards those whom they have never seen but whom they conceive to be amiable or useful: and this notion amounts to the same thing as a real feeling between them. Well, these are plainly kindly-disposed towards one another: but how can one call them friends while their mutual feelings are unknown to one another? *to complete the idea of Friendship then, it is requisite that they have kindly feelings towards one another, and wish one another good ... and that these kindly feelings should be mutually known.*' (1155*b*-1156*a*.) (Translation by D. P. Chase, Everyman's Library, London,

1942, pp. 184-5. Italics mine.) In Aristotle's opinion friendship 'is a thing most necessary for life' and our need for it 'seems to be implanted in us by Nature'. That friendship, as defined by Aristotle, is not a central virtue in Christianity follows from the latter's failure to attach significance to mutuality in such a relationship.

2. A typical example of religious isolationism is quoted by William James in his *Varieties of Religious Experience* (London, 1935, p. 336): 'I had not fellowship with any people, priests, nor professors, nor any sort of separated people. *I was afraid of all carnal talk and talkers, for I could see nothing but corruptions*'. (From George Fox, *Journal*, Philadelphia, 1800, pp. 59-60—italics mine.)

3. *Solitude and Society,* Nicolas Berdyaev, London, 1938, p. 94.

4. *Pensées,* translated by W. F. Trotter, Everyman's Library, London, 1931, p. 39, para. 139.

5. *The Structure of Social Action,* The Free Press, Glencoe, Illinois, 1949, p. 53.

6. *Ibid.*

7. *The Protestant Ethic and the Spirit of Capitalism,* London, 1930, p. 108.

8. *Op. cit.*, p. 525.

9. By the use of terms like 'moral autarchy' or 'self-sufficiency' no more self-centredness is imputed to Christian attitudes than the pursuit of personal salvation and solitary communion may suggest.

10. Georg Simmel believed that this unprecedented emphasis on uniqueness is a defensive reaction of the individual against the overgrowth of material culture in metropolitan society and against the hypertrophy of 'objective contents'; '... life is composed more and more of these impersonal contents and offerings which tend to displace the genuine personal colorations and incomparabilities. This results in the individual's summoning the utmost uniqueness and particularization, in order to preserve his most personal core. He has to exaggerate this personal element in order to remain audible even to himself. The atrophy of individual culture through the hypertrophy of objective culture is one reason for the bitter hatred which the preachers of the most extreme individualism, above all Nietzsche, harbor against the metropolis ... The carrier of man's values is no longer the "general human being" in every individual, but rather man's qualitative uniqueness and irreplaceability'. (*The Sociology of Georg Simmel,* Glencoe, Illinois, 1950, pp. 422-3.)

11. 'A Note on the Implications of Psychiatry, the Study of Interpersonal Relations, for Investigations in the Social Sciences', *American Journal of Sociology,* May, 1937, Vol. XLII, No. 6. Some writers consider the individual's drive for power or 'quest for significance' as the basic motive of all social interests. The individuals '... are sociable in the degree to which their value is raised by joining together'. (*Man's Quest for Significance,* by Lewis Way, London, 1948, p. 73.) This view is not an explanation but a symptom of contemporary sociability. The true sequence between a 'quest for significance' and sociability is this: 'I wanted to be above all in order to be equal, to have in order to give, to be covered in order to be revealed. Beyond every goal lay another friendship'. (Stephen Spender in *World Within World,* London, 1951, p. 88.)

12. Much of our interpersonal manners requires revision, but this revision will probably follow the revaluation of our individualistic values. Lawrence K. Frank, whose comments on the problems of mental hygiene are usually very apt, states the case in the following: 'Instead of clinging to the traditional conceptions of individual autonomy and moral responsibility that were dependent upon a coherent culture for their effective operation, we must begin to think in terms of individuals caught in social confusion wherein individual conduct and ethics are no longer socially tolerable. The individual, instead of seeking his own personal salvation and security, must recognize his almost complete dependence upon the group life and see his only hope in and through cultural re-organization. The tradition of individual striving that was ushered in by the Renaissance has been the very process of this cultural disintegration, for the individual, in striving to be an individual, has broken down the inherited culture of common, shared beliefs and activities'. (*Society as the Patient,* New Brunswick, Rutgers University Press, 1949, p. 7.)

Mary Parker Follett's views are in fundamental agreement with the above: 'Many writers tell us that we are living in a barren age and deplore this as a sign of our degeneration. These writers look to the periods of creative energy in the past and find there their Leonardos and their Dantes; they then look around to-day and, seeing no Leonardos nor Dantes, deplore the unproductiveness of our modern civilisation. Such people make the mistake of connecting creativeness always and inevitably with individuals. They do not see that we are now at the beginning of a period of creative energy, but that instead of being the individual creativeness of the past which gave us our artists and our poets, we may now enter on a period of collective creativeness if we have the imagination to see its potentialities, its reach, its ultimate significance, above all if we are willing patiently to work out the method'. (*Dynamic Administration,* Bath, 1941, p. 94.)

13. *The Theory of the Leisure Class,* London, 1924, p. 112.

14. Pearse and Crocker, Chapter XIV, on *Social Poverty*. Dr. A. T. M. Wilson, reporting on a recent research into family behaviour, stated that 'Christian names are practically taboo, even among friends of long standing. Curtains in front rooms (which are seldom used) are usually left half drawn with the pattern facing outwards. Every effort is made to put high fences in the back gardens owing to the fear of being overlooked. The whole emphasis is on keeping the neighbors out rather than letting them in'. (*The Star, April* 25th, 1950.)

If further evidence of this 'social poverty' is needed, other daily papers provide ample material. E.g. 'It seems incredible, but in spite of the fact that all our cities are practically bursting their walls with social activities for young, middle-aged and old, a major problem still remains "people without friends". Doctors are worried because their loneliness makes their patients neurotic. Social scientists are scratching their brains out to find ways of supplying "social nurture" (which in essence means human friendship) for whole families cut off from contact with their kind'. (Louise Morgan in the *News Chronicle,* Feb. 2nd, 1950.) 'Blocks of council flats, new housing estates and divided houses have not yet developed the easy neighbourliness of long-established communities. The "keeping oneself to oneself" is still a too-marked characteristic of the lives of many urban and suburban married women. The effect of all this is very often to encourage young married women to park the baby and take up whole-time work in office or factory. I am convinced that the need for companionship is often as strong a motive here as the financial one'. (Peggy Jay in the *News Chronicle,* Feb. 24th, 1950.) And a sombre report: 'Grave Problem of Lonely Wives in London Suburbs.—The loneliness of wives in suburban London was referred to at a Barnet inquest yesterday...' (*News Chronicle,* June 9th, 1938.) The American scene does not appear to be very different if one is to judge from reports like these: 'Profit in Loneliness.—New York... Ten million people in the U.S. pay £12,500,000 yearly to the 100-odd agencies who make a business of bringing lonely people together.—B.U.P.' (*News Chronicle,* March 7th, 1949.) Or: 'New York will soon have a "lonely hearts" bureau run on scientific and non-profit-making lines, reports B.U.P. It will be known as the "Institute for Inter-personal Research" and will be headed by five prominent New York citizens....' (*The Star,* June 4th, 1947.) In many of these instances the social isolation of the wife, the mother is brought out. This is, of course, not an entirely recent development. Flaubert writes of Madame Bovary: 'Like sailors in distress, she gazed around with despairing eyes upon the loneliness of her life, seeking a white sail on the immensities of the misty horizon'. Yet nineteenth-century domesticity, its limitations and arduous tasks, were to be endured in more populous families at a time when the audience type of entertainment was not yet ubiquitous and the home was the focus of social participation.

15. A Report made to the Pilgrim Trust, Cambridge University Press, 1938, p. 276.

16. 'The Sociography of Some Community Relations', by George A. Lundberg and Margaret Lawsing, *American Sociological Review,* June, 1937, Vol. II, No. 3.

17. *Leadership and Isolation,* New York, 1943, p. 85.

18. *The Relation Between Family Social Participation and the Social Development of the Child,* by Bernice L. Neugarten, Doctoral Dissertation, University of Chicago Library, 1943, quoted in *Who Shall be Educated?,* by W. L. Warner, R. J. Havighurst and M. B. Loeb, London, 1946, pp. 85, 171.

19. *Ibid.*

20. 'The Sociology of Sociability'.

21. P. 102.

22. *The Neurosis of Man,* p. 111.

23. Cf. the following passage from Cyril Connolly's *The Unquiet Grave* (Hamish Hamilton, London, 1945): 'The more I see of life the more I perceive that only through solitary communion with nature can one gain an idea of its richness and meaning. I know that in such contemplation lies my true personality, and yet I live in an age when on all sides I am told exactly the opposite and asked to believe that the social and co-operative activity of humanity is the only way through which life can be developed. Am I an exception, a herd outcast? There are also solitary bees, and it is not claimed that they are biologically inferior.' And, after these apologetics of the nature-mystic, he gives a brilliantly concise picture of the nature-mystics' paradise: 'A planet of contemplators, each sunning himself before his doorstep like the mason-wasp; no one would help another, and no one would need help!' (p. 19). Yet he believes that 'Fraternity is the State's bribe to the individual; it is the one virtue which can bring courage to members of a materialist society. All State propaganda exalts comradeship, for it is this gregarious herd-sense and herd-smell which keeps people from thinking and so reconciles them to the destruction of their private lives' (p. 28). At the same time Connolly reveals a remarkable insight in the following passages: '... we are unkind about our friends and resentful of their intimacy because of something which is rotting in ourselves'. And, 'When we see someone living alone, like a beech-tree in a clearing, with no other signs of life around him... we can be sure that such a person is an ogre and that human bones lie buried under his roots' (pp. 29-30).

In fact, isolation is one of the afflictions of power. From which the false logic of the ambitious concludes, 'I want to be solitary that I may think myself powerful!'

'J'ai marché devant tous, triste et seul dans ma gloire,
Et j'ai dit dans mon coeur: "Que vouloir à présent?"
Pour dormir sur un sein mon front est trop pesant,
Ma main laisse l'effroi sur la main qu'elle touche,
L'orage est dans ma voix, l'éclair est sur ma bouche;
Aussi, loin de m'aimer, violà qu'ils tremblent tous,
Et quand j'ouvre les bras on tombe à mes genoux.

O Seigneur! j'ai vécu puissant et solitaire,
Laissez-moi m'endormir du sommeil de la terre!
Alfred de Vigny *(Moïse)*

One detects a streak of pride and of self-importance even in Proust's 'nous sommes irrémédiablement seuls'.

24. *Psychology of Women,* by Helene Deutsch, London, 1947, Vol. I, p. 75.
25. *Our Inner Conflicts,* p. 79.
26. *Human Nature in Politics,* London, 1948, p. 50.
27. *Parerga and Paralipomena,* Part II, para. XXXI.
28. *The Essayes of Michael Lord of Montaigne,* translated by John Florio, Book I, Chapter XXXVIII, 'Of Solitarinesse'.
29. Montaigne quotes, '. . . . usque adeone scire tuum nihil est, nisi te scire hoc sciat alter? which Florio translates as:

"Is it then nothing worth that thou doost know,
Unlesse what thou doost know, thou others show?"

Intellectual separativeness and withdrawal stands revealed: the intellectual employs his solitariness "to purchase unto himself" fame, power and "an imortall life".' Emerson felt this too, though he phrased it less sceptically: 'The soul environs itself with friends, that it may enter into a grander self-acquaintance or solitude; and it goes alone for a season, that it may exalt its conversation or society'. From the essay on Friendship (*The Works of Ralph Waldo Emerson,* London, 1899, pp. 80-92).

30. *The Great Betrayal (La Trahison des Clercs),* translation by Richard Aldington, London, 1928, p. 32.
31. This is, of course, an inaccurate rendering of the mediaeval 'clerk'; for brevity's sake, however, the two may justifiably be used to express the same idea.
32. The arch-precept of this autarchism is the injunction: *'Il ne faut pas s'engager';* it is interesting to follow up the spiritual ancestry of this attitude, e.g. 'Kierkegaard had spoken of the impossibility of genuine "existential" communication of the tragical solitariness of man; Sartre not only denies the possibility of communion, but regards love as a slavery so that "hell is the others" ' (from *The Crisis of the Human Person,* by J. B. Coates, London, 1949, p. 23).
33. 'Private and Public Spaces', by Charles Madge, *Human Relations,* Vol. III, No. 2, 1950.
34. *Ibid.*

The Pathology of Boredom

By WOODBURN HERON

IF YOU SHAKE the surface on which a snail is resting, it withdraws into its shell. If you shake it repeatedly, the snail after a while fails to react. In the same way a sea anemone which is disturbed by a drop of water falling on the water surface above it ceases to be disturbed if drops continue to fall; a bird stops flying away from a rustling motion if the motion is steadily repeated. Most organisms stop responding to a stimulus repeated over and over again (unless the response is reinforced by reward or avoidance of punishment). Indeed, the higher organisms actively avoid a completely monotonous environment. A rat in a maze will use different routes to food, if they are available, rather than the same one all the time. It will tend to avoid areas in which it has spent considerable time and to explore the less familiar areas.

Monotony is an important and enduring human problem. Persons who

Reprinted from *Scientific American,* Volume 196, Number 1 (January 1957), pp. 52-56, by permission of the author and the publisher.

have to work for long periods at repetitive tasks often complain of being bored and dissatisfied with their jobs, and frequently their performance declines. During the last war N. H. Mackworth of England made a series of researches for the Royal Air Force to find out why radar operators on anti-submarine patrol sometimes failed to detect U-boats. The operators usually worked in isolation, watching a radar screen hour after hour. Mackworth set up a comparable laboratory situation, requiring subjects to watch a pointer moving around a graduated dial and to press a button whenever the pointer made a double jump. The subjects' efficiency declined in the surprisingly short time of half an hour. As a result of this and other research the radar operators' tour of duty was shortened.

In this age of semi-automation, when not only military personnel but also many industrial workers have little to do but keep a constant watch on instruments, the problem of human behavior in monotonous situations is becoming acute. In 1951 the McGill University psychologist D. O. Hebb obtained a grant from the Defence Research Board of Canada to make a systematic study of the effects of exposure for prolonged periods to a rigidly monotonous environment. Hebb's collaborators in the project were B. K. Doane, T. H. Scott, W. H. Bexton and the writer of this article.

The aim of the project was to obtain basic information on how human beings would react in situations where nothing at all was happening. The purpose was not to cut individuals off from any sensory stimulation whatever, but to remove all patterned or perceptual stimulation, so far as we could arrange it.

The subjects were male college students, paid $20 a day to participate. They lay on a comfortable bed in a lighted cubicle 24 hours a day for as long as they cared to stay, with time out only for meals (which they usually ate sitting on the edge of the bed) and going to the toilet. They wore translucent plastic visors which transmitted diffuse light but prevented pattern vision. Cotton gloves and cardboard cuffs extending beyond the fingertips restricted perception by touch. Their auditory perception was limited by a U-shaped foam rubber pillow on which their heads lay and by a continuous hum of air-conditioning equipment which masked small sounds.

When we started the research we were not at all sure what aspects of behavior it would be most profitable to investigate. Accordingly we began with a preliminary run in which we merely observed the subjects' behavior and interviewed them afterward. Most of these subjects had planned to think about their work: some intended to review their studies, some to plan term papers, and one thought that he would organize a lecture he had to deliver. Nearly all of them reported that the most striking thing about the experience was that they were unable to think clearly about anything for any length of time and that their thought processes seemed to be affected in other ways. We therefore decided that the first thing to do was to test effects on mental performance.

We used three main methods of investigating this. One was a battery of oral tests involving simple arithmetic, anagrams, word association and so on.

This battery was given before the experiment, at 12, 24 and 48 hours during the isolation and finally three days afterward. Another battery of tests, given two days before and immediately after the isolation period, included copying a design with blocks, speed of copying a prose paragraph, substituting symbols for numbers, picking out what was odd in each of a series of pictures (for instance, one picture showed a man in a canoe using a broom instead of a paddle) and recognizing patterns embedded in a complex background. The third test used a recording of a talk arguing for the reality of ghosts, poltergeists and other supernatural phenomena. It was played to each subject during his isolation. We examined the individual's attitude toward supernatural phenomena before he entered isolation and after he had emerged.

On almost every test the subjects' performance was impaired by their isolation in the monotonous environment (and was poorer than that of a control group of students). The isolation experience also tended to make the subjects susceptible to the argument for the existence of supernatural phenomena. Some of them reported that for several days after the experiment they were afraid that they were going to see ghosts.

As the subjects lay in isolation, cut off from stimulation, the content of their thought gradually changed. At first they tended to think about their studies, about the experiment, about their personal problems. After a while they began to reminisce about past incidents, their families, their friends and so on. To pass the time some tried to remember in detail a motion picture they had seen; others thought about traveling from one familiar place to another and would try to imagine all the events of the journey; some counted numbers steadily into the thousands. (Incidentally, such experiences are commonly reported by persons who have been in solitary confinement for long periods.) Eventually some subjects reached a state in which it took too much effort to concentrate, and they became "content to let the mind drift," as one subject put it. Others said: "My mind just became full of sounds and colors, and I could not control it"; "I just ran out of things to think of"; "I couldn't think of anything to think about." Several subjects experienced "blank periods" when they did not seem to be thinking at all.

Not surprisingly, the subjects became markedly irritable as time went on and often expressed their irritation. Yet they also had spells when they were easily amused. In the interview afterward many of the subjects expressed surprise that their feelings could have oscillated so much, and that they could have behaved in such a childish way. They also said that they seemed to lose their "sense of perspective" while in the cubicle, and some subjects mentioned that at times they felt that the experimenters were against them, and were trying to make things exceptionally tough for them.

The subjects reported something else to which we at first paid no particular attention, but which was to emerge as the most striking result of the experiments. Many of them, after long isolation, began to see "images." One man repeatedly saw a vision of a rock shaded by a tree; another kept on seeing pictures of babies and could not get rid of them. Several subjects seemed to be "having dreams" while they were awake. Not until one of the experimenters himself went through the isolation experience for a long period did we realize the power and strangeness of the phenomenon. His report, and a review of the literature on other experiments in monotony, made clear that the experimental situation induced hallucinations.

The visual phenomena were similar to those experienced after taking the intoxicating drug of the mescal plant (mescal buttons), which is a ceremonial practice of some Indian tribes in the Southwest. They have also been reported in experiments in which subjects were exposed for long periods to blank visual fields or flickering light.

Our subjects' hallucinations usually began with simple forms. They might start to "see" dots of light, lines or simple geometrical patterns. Then the visions became more complex, with abstract patterns repeated like a design on wallpaper, or recognizable figures, such as rows of little yellow men with black caps on and their mouths open. Finally there were integrated scenes: *e.g.*, a procession of squirrels with sacks over their shoulders marching "purposefully" across the visual field, prehistoric animals walking about in a jungle, processions of eyeglasses marching down a street. These scenes were frequently distorted, and were described as being like animated movie cartoons. Usually the subjects were at first surprised and amused by these phenomena, looked forward eagerly to see what was going to happen next and found that the "pictures" alleviated their boredom. But after a while the pictures became disturbing, and so vivid that they interfered with sleep. Some of the subjects complained that their eyes became tired from "focusing" on the pictures. They found sometimes that they could even scan the "scene," taking in new parts as they moved their eyes, as if they were looking at real pictures.

The subjects had little control over the content of the hallucinations. Some kept seeing the same type of picture no matter how hard they tried to change it. One man could see nothing but dogs, another nothing but eyeglasses of various types, and so on. Some subjects were able to realize visions of objects suggested by the experimenter, but not always in the way they were instructed. One man, trying to "get" a pen, saw first an inkblot on a white tablecloth, then a pencil, then a green horse, finally a pen.

The hallucinations were not confined to vision. Occasionally a subject heard people in the "scene" talking, and one man repeatedly heard a music box playing. Another saw the sun rising over a church and heard a choir singing "in full stereophonic sound." Several subjects reported sensations of movement or touch. One had a feeling of being hit in the arm by pellets fired from a miniature rocket ship he saw; another, reaching out to touch a doorknob in his vision, felt an electric shock. Some subjects reported that they felt as if another body were lying beside them in the cubicle; in one case the two bodies overlapped, partly occupying the same space. Some reported feelings of "otherness" or "bodily strangeness"; trying to describe their sensations, they said, "my mind seemed to be a ball of cotton wool floating above my body," or "something seemed to be sucking my mind out through my eyes."

After emerging from isolation, our subjects frequently reported that "things looked curved," "near things looked large and far things looked small," "things seemed to move," and so on. We therefore made some systematic tests of their visual perception. The most striking finding was that when subjects emerged after several days of isolation, the whole room appeared to be in motion. In addition there was a tendency for surfaces to appear curved, and for objects to appear to be changing their size and shape. Asked to match a disk that was handed to them to one in a row of disks of various sizes 12 feet away, the subjects consistently chose a larger disk than did control subjects.

We recorded changes in the electrical activity of the brain in these subjects by means of electroencephalograms made before, during and after the isolation period. There was a tendency for some slow waves, which are normally present in sleep but not when an adult is awake, to appear after a period of isolation. In addition, the frequencies in the region of the principal brain rhythm slowed down.

The overt behavior of the subjects during the experiment was, of course, carefully recorded. Most of the subjects went to sleep fairly soon after they had been placed in the cubicle. After waking they showed increasing signs of restlessness. This restlessness was not continuous but came in more and more intense spells, which were described as being very unpleasant. The subjects appeared eager for stimulation, and would talk to themselves, whistle, sing or recite poetry. When they came out for meals, they tended to be garrulous and attempted to draw the experimenters into conversation. In moving about, as when they were led to the toilet, they appeared dazed and confused, and had increasing difficulty in finding their way about the washroom.

As an outgrowth of the general experiment, we have begun some tests to find out the effects of restriction of just one sense. We tested six subjects who wore the frosted visors constantly but who otherwise were allowed to pursue comparatively "normal" activities. Unfortunately the results of this experiment are not "pure," because the restriction of vision greatly restricted their movements and opportunity for other stimulation. These subjects developed visual hallucinations and also experienced some disorders of visual perception when the visors were removed.

Prolonged exposure to a monotonous environment, then, has definitely deleterious effects. The individual's thinking is impaired; he shows childish emotional responses; his visual perception becomes disturbed; he suffers from hallucinations; his brain-wave pattern changes. These findings are in line with recent studies of the brain, especially of the reticular formation in the midbrain [see "Pleasure Centers in the Brain," by James Olds; SCIENTIFIC AMERICAN, October, 1956]. In some way the reticular formation regulates the brain's activity. The recent studies indicate that normal functioning of the brain depends on a continuing arousal reaction generated in the reticular formation, which in turn depends on constant sensory bombardment. It appears that, aside from their specific functions, sensory stimuli have the general function of maintaining this arousal, and they rapidly lose their power to do so if they are restricted to the monotonously repeated stimulation of an unchanging environment. Under these circumstances the activity of the cortex may be impaired so that the brain behaves abnormally.

The results of our experiments seemed to throw light on a number of practical problems. For instance, studies in France and at Harvard University have indicated that hallucinations are fairly common among long-distance truck drivers. After many hours on the road they may begin to see apparitions such as giant red spiders on the windshield and non-existent animals running across the road, which frequently cause accidents. Similar phenomena have been reported by aviators on long flights: Charles Lindbergh described some in his autobiography. It is not improbable that some unexplained airplane and railroad accidents have been occasioned by effects of prolonged monotonous stimulation.

A changing sensory environment seems essential for human beings. Without it, the brain ceases to function in an adequate way, and abnormalities of behavior develop. In fact, as Christopher Burney observed in his remarkable account of his stay in solitary confinement: "Variety is not the spice of life; it is the very stuff of it."

3
"Too Much or Too Little?"

How much leisure is there today? And how different in kind is the leisure we now enjoy from that of a generation ago?

We have brought together some reports on crucial aspects of leisure—the amount of time people have, and the number of resources that can be employed in leisure-time activities. The time available for a man's leisure can be measured in at least two ways: the number of hours he works each week (and by subtraction the number of hours that he does not); and the length of his life. Wolfbein and Zeisel reveal the increase in leisure through the reduced workweek, increased work life, and the growth in the number of the retired—those who experience leisure as a full-time occupation. The article from Fortune *presents basic data on how money is spent for what products in the leisure market.*

One heroic effort to measure the uses of leisure-time is contained in a study by George Lundberg, Mirra Komarovsky, and M. A. McInerny; it was conducted in the 1930s, the period in which the era of the "Leisure Classes" was coming to an end. Until then the rich set leisure styles and the others tried to make enough money to adopt them. But by now, due to uneven increases in leisure time (with the workers benefiting the most, professional and executive groups the least), due to increases in workers' discretionary spending power, and due to the spread of recreational facilities, there is little inherent exclusiveness left; in this sense class leisure has become mass leisure.

This does not mean that there are no class differences but only that these differences are more sociological than economic. Clyde White and Alfred Clarke report on two surveys, and Robert Dubin examines the meaning of work for blue-collar workers.

At the other pole is "Society." Here too work may lack meaning. We present accounts of the leisure habits of two groups regarded as "High Society" by whites and Negroes, respectively. Cleveland Amory describes the professional idlers at a time when sumptuousness in America reached its peak. Frazier's account taken together with Amory's makes clear that High Society, whether Negro or white, has stringent rules, even in its profligacy. We catch a glimpse of the world where leisure is the distinguishing characteristic.

The Workweek in American Industry 1850–1956

By JOSEPH S. ZEISEL

ONE of the most persistent and significant trends in the American economy in the past century has been the continuing long-term decline in the work-week in industry. From an average of about 66 hours worked in 1850—the equivalent of 11 hours a day, 6 days a week—the workweek in nonagricultural industries declined to nearly 40 hours in 1956—generally 8 hours a day, 5 days a week. A similar sharp reduction in the workweek on farms has also been reported. This dramatic reduction in hours worked has been accomplished by taking part of the fruits of increasing productivity in the form of greater leisure.

The length of the workweek is a basic factor in measuring the Nation's economic well-being. The amount of goods and services that we produce, when related to the number of persons at work and the length of the work-week, provides an estimate of our productiveness. The amount of leisure that we can afford should be considered as an element of our standard of living. Goods and services, produced and purchased by time worked, make up part of our high standard of living; leisure, also purchased, in effect, by work, is another part. Both income and leisure must be considered when assessing the level of living of the American population.

Source of Workweek Data. Not much comprehensive, reliable information on hours of work is available for the period before World War II. Data for individual industries have been compiled for a number of decades and rough estimates made of overall hours worked in broad sectors of the economy for the past century. One such series of estimates on average weekly hours worked,[1] covering the period 1850-1940, is presented in chart 1. These data are rough at best. Also, as with all long-term series, the comparability of the data is compromised by changing employment classifications and industry definitions. Nevertheless, the series provides a reasonably satisfactory indication of levels and long-term trend.[2]

For more recent years, the U. S. Department of Labor's Bureau of Labor Statistics has published annual data on average weekly hours for manufacturing industries, starting in 1919, and for mining, contract construction, and for a few sectors of transportation and public utilities, trade, and service, starting at various later dates.[3]

In 1941, the Census Bureau began collecting data on hours of work for all employed persons (agricultural and non-agricultural workers, including groups excluded from Bureau of Labor Statistics figures—workers in agriculture, the self-employed, unpaid family workers, and household workers).

Reprinted from the *Monthly Labor Review,* Volume 81, Number 1 (January 1958), pp. 23-29. Courtesy U. S. Department of Labor.

The Census data are collected through a household sample survey, and attempt to measure all of the hours worked by individuals in the survey week.

The Bureau of Labor Statistics data come from payroll records of establishments and measure the number of hours worked in a given industry. Both of these types of data are valuable; BLS data have the advantage of being fairly precise estimates of average hours worked by industry, obtained from a relatively large sample of establishments. Census data, on the other hand, have broader coverage and provide estimates of all hours worked by individuals; however, they are not based on records and the respondents sometimes cannot remember or do not know the hours worked by other members of the household.

Long-Term Trends. The workweek for the overall economy had declined from about 70 hours in 1850 to 44 hours in 1940. (See chart 1.) Current

Chart I—Estimated Average Weekly Hours of All Persons Employed in Agricultural and Nonagricultural Industries, 1850-1940 (10-Year Intervals) and 1941-56 (Annual Averages)[1]

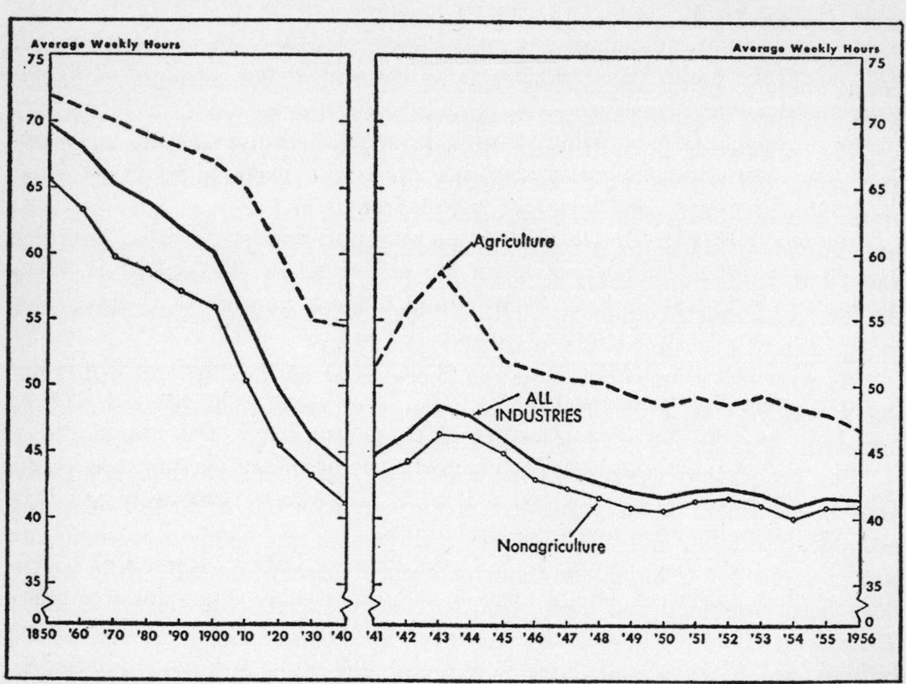

[1] All employed persons, including the self-employed and unpaid family workers.

Source: 1850-1940, Dewhurst and Associates, America's Needs and Resources, 1955; 1941-56, U. S. Bureau of the Census.

hours data published by the U. S. Bureau of the Census (which are not entirely comparable with the data before 1941) indicate that the workweek for the economy in 1956 averaged 41.5 hours.

The reduction in hours of work has not been a straight-line trend. The decline after 1900 was at a much greater rate than in the previous half century. In nonagricultural industries, hours of work declined by about 10 hours between 1850 and 1900–from 66 hours to 56 hours. The rate of decline appears to have been much greater in the period 1850 to 1870 than from 1870 to the turn of the century. In the next four decades, reductions in the workweek were much sharper than in the previous half century. Between 1900 and 1940, the workweek in nonagricultural industries declined from 56 hours to about 41 hours, an average of almost 4 hours per decade. The sharpest declines occurred between 1900 and 1920, when average workweek in nonagricultural industries dropped about 5 hours every 10 years. After rising sharply during World War II to a peak in 1943, the workweek declined again, starting in 1944, and continued downward in the postwar period; in 1956, it was 40.9 hours.

Of course, even where the overall trend appears relatively smooth, this is not typical of the movement of hours of work for individual industries. The average obscures the declines occurring–at an irregular pace–in a number of industries. Rather than showing a regular rate of decline in hours, individual industries tend to move from plateau to plateau, and ordinarily each new level prevails for a period of years.[4]

Hours of work also tend to fluctuate quite sharply with changes in economic activity. In the depression years of the 1930's, for example, hours of work declined sharply, but had recovered somewhat by 1940.

The workweek in agriculture has also been reduced sharply over the 100 years, but the rate of decline in the earlier years was much more moderate than in nonagricultural industries. By 1910, the workweek in agriculture was about 65 hours a week compared with 72 in 1850. Between 1910 and 1930, agricultural hours declined by about 5 hours per decade, reaching the level of about 55 hours in 1930. No significant decline in the workweek in agriculture occurred between 1930 and 1940.

As with other industries, hours of work in agriculture rose sharply during World War II. Following the war, the workweek on farms resumed its long-term decline, reaching about 47 hours in 1956.

For production workers in manufacturing, BLS annual data are available on the length of the workweek going back to 1919, and also, there are estimates for 1909 and 1914. In order to provide a roughly consistent historical series for other major industry groups, several available BLS series have been combined and these data, for selected years, are shown in chart 2. Data on hours for mining and transportation, communications, and public utilities, which are combinations of industry series, are estimates and subject to revision. However, they provide some indication of both trend and level of hours worked. Moreover, in conjunction with the other series, they indicate which were the "leading" and "lagging" industries in reduction of hours, and the degree to which individual industry sectors have contributed to the total decline in the workweek in the past several decades.

Length of Workweek Since 1929. Hours of work dropped in all of the major nonagricultural industries during the depression, but they appear to have declined much more sharply in some industries than in others. The workweek in manufacturing and mining dropped by nearly 10 hours between 1929 and 1934, to levels of about 35 hours and 30 hours, respectively. A sharp decline in hours during the period also appears to have occurred in

Chart II—Trend of Average Weekly Hours in Five Nonagricultural Industries, Annual Averages, Selected Years

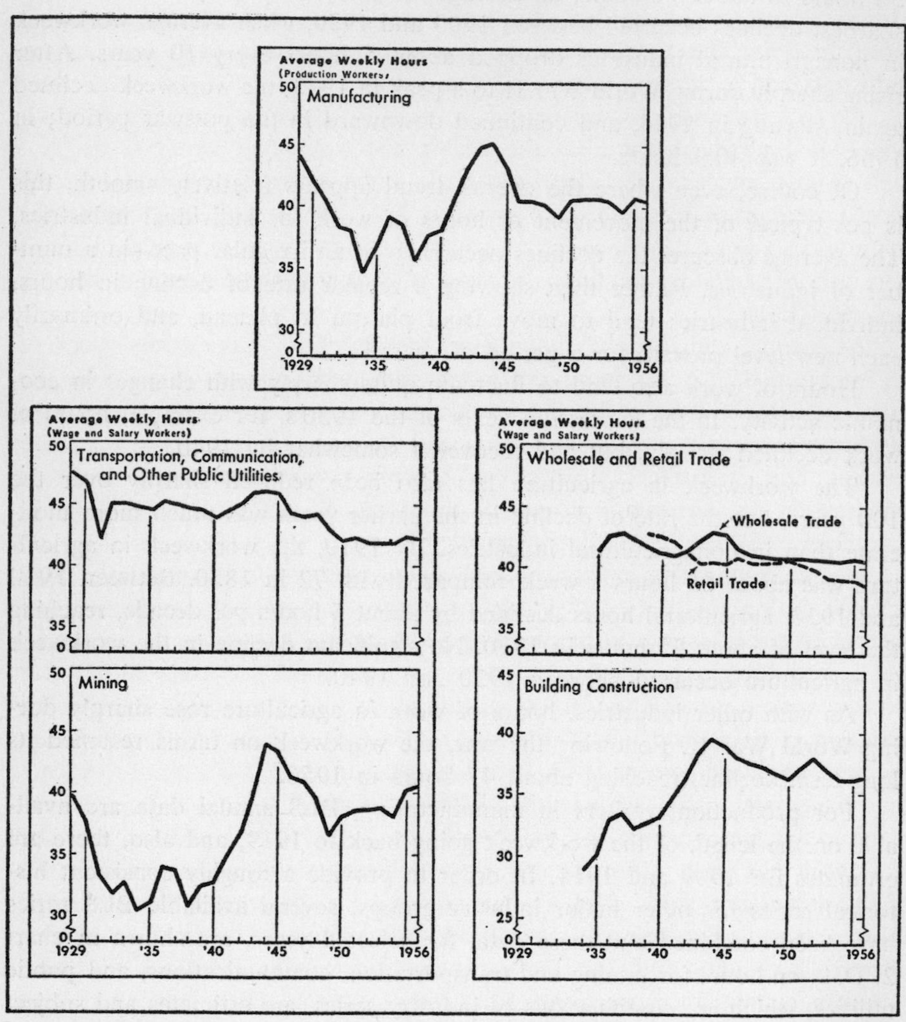

construction. The average workweek in building construction was about 29 hours in 1934. Weekly hours for union workmen in construction are reported to have declined by about 3 to 4 hours from 1929 to 1934. Hours of work in most industries picked up for a few years in the mid-thirties, but declined again in the severe recession of 1937-38. The few series available for hours of work in service industries during this period indicate a more moderate rate of decline.

Weekly hours of work generally rose again after the low point of 1938 and continued to a peak in World War II. The average workweek for all nonagricultural industries appears to have resumed its long-term decline in the postwar period. Census estimates of hours of work of all persons in nonagricultural industries declined 1.4 hours between 1947 and 1956. However, the workweek has shown no declining trend in manufacturing since the war. The downward trend has been resumed in trade and service industries and in transportation and communications.[5]

Factors Affecting Trends in the Workweek. Back in the 19th century, widespread public concern for the health and welfare of workers, particularly women and children, plus early trade union activity, were probably the most important factors in reducing weekly hours of work. This concern was expressed in State laws restricting hours of work for women and children and in laws regulating conditions of work in certain industries such as mining and railroading.

As income and levels of living rose, the desire for more leisure became an important factor. As more and more workers in industry rose above the mere subsistence level of income, it became possible for larger proportions of the labor force, through labor union activity, to indicate a desire for more leisure. This was especially true as sharply rising productivity made it unnecessary for increased leisure–in the form of a shorter workweek–to completely displace real income gains.

It is unlikely that significant reductions in the workweek could have been effected during the past century were it not for the amazing productivity of the American economy. Without rising productivity, reductions in the workweek would have resulted in reduced output. Rapidly rising output per worker made it possible to support a rapidly expanding population on a rising standard of living with fewer hours of work. One estimate is that ". . . in the past, about 60 percent of the increase in productivity has gone into higher real wages and about 40 percent into more leisure."[6]

Another factor which has on several occasions led to a reduction in the workweek has been a share-the-work philosophy. This was especially true of the depression of the 1930's when pressure for sharing the work through shorter workweeks gained considerable momentum. During this period, effective maximum limits on the workweek for certain groups were established in National Recovery Administration codes, in State legislation, and in the Fair Labor Standards Act of 1938. The Federal legislation resulted in the widespread adoption of premium pay for many persons in interstate commerce, for work beyond the standard workweek. The 40-hour workweek became standard for much of industry during this period.

As might be expected in a period of virtually full employment, little significant pressure for sharing the work has developed in the postwar period.[7] And, since most industries schedule workweeks of less than 48 hours, long hours threatening workers' health and safety no longer constitute a problem for any significant proportion of the labor force.

In manufacturing, where workweeks of 40 hours or less have become the general rule, no significant trend in hours has been apparent, on the whole, since 1947. The reduction in hours has been effected mainly in those nonmanufacturing industries where workweeks were above 40 (as in railroads), rather than in industries where the workweek has declined below 40 hours. In fact, the sharp reductions in hours during the past 3 decades have been mainly in those industries which, at the beginning of the period, were well above 40 hours.

There are at present relatively few industries scheduling less than 40-hour weeks.[8] But there has been indication of a growing demand by unions for shortening of the scheduled workweek below 40 hours–especially in manufacturing.[9]

Reduction in the Farm Workweek. Significant reductions have occurred since World War II in the workweek of both self-employed farmers and wage and salary workers on farms. As a result, hours of work in agriculture since the war have declined more rapidly than in nonagricultural industries, a reversal of the pre-World War II trends. Throughout the past century, the average workweek in agriculture has been much longer than in nonagricultural industries; moreover, the differential was widening throughout the period 1850 to 1940. In 1850, the difference was 6 hours, but by 1940, the difference was about twice as great. Between 1947 and 1956, the workweek declined by 4 hours in agriculture compared with 1.4 hours in nonagricultural industries.

This decline in farm hours, combined with a sharp and persistent reduction in the size of the farm work force and its ratio to total employment, has played an important part in the decline in average hours for the whole economy. Between 1850 and 1950, the percentage of the Nation's work force on farms declined from almost 70 percent to under 12 percent.[10] The decline in farm employment has had a greater effect on reducing overall hours of work than is indicated by the magnitude of the drop in total farm employment, because the employment decline was especially sharp among self-employed farmers, who have always worked much longer hours than the "hired hands." Census estimates for 1956, for example, indicate that farmers and farm managers in 4 sample months during the year averaged between 10 and 15 hours more per week than did farm laborers and foremen.[11]

Part-Time Workers. Another factor which has been important in reducing the average workweek in recent years has been the increasing number and proportion of part-time workers in American industry. The proportion of the work force in nonagricultural industries employed 1 to 14 hours increased from 3.2 percent in 1940 to 4.5 percent in 1956. At the same time, the proportion working 35 hours or more declined from about 83 percent in 1940 to about 79 percent in 1956. Recent Census data indicate that this general pattern is representative of all major nonagricultural industries.[12] This trend is even more evident in agriculture. Between 1940 and 1956, the proportion of those working from 1 to 14 hours increased from 2.1 percent of total agricultural employment to 6.3 percent.

The rise in the number of part-time workers in nonagricultural industries is to a large extent the result of the rapid increase in the number of married women workers over 35.[13] Many of these women prefer part-time work, and employers, faced with a tight labor market, have provided part-time jobs.

Dual Jobholding. A labor force trend which has operated recently to offset the long-term decline in average hours worked is the increase in dual jobholding. Information on this point is available only for a few periods. An estimated 3.6 million persons, or 5.3 percent of the total employed, held more than one job in July 1957, as compared with 1.8 million dual jobholders, or 3 percent of the employed total, reported in a survey in July 1950.[14] Some part of the increase reported may have been the result of improved measurement techniques, but the magnitude of the increase indicates a significant uptrend.[15] This increase can be related directly to the continued expansion in the trade and service industries, which have provided opportunities for spare-time work in the evening and on Saturdays. Such extra jobs held in trade and service industries tripled between 1950 and 1956—from 350,000 to over a million. Another significant factor that has increased the supply of spare-time workers is the continuing downtrend in the normal full-time workweek in some sectors of the economy. Rising consumer prices during this period were probably an added factor in influencing workers to take a second job.

Labor Force Participation of Women 35 Years Old and Over and Percent Having Part-Time Jobs, Annual Averages, 1940, 1947, and 1956

Year	Number in labor force (thousands)	Percent of female population in labor force	Percent of labor force	Percent of employed women working less than 35 hours
1956	12,878	35.3	18.3	26.4
1947	8,373	27.7	13.6	23.4
1940	5,755	21.9	10.3	*

*Not available.
Source: U. S. Department of Commerce, Bureau of the Census.

Paid Vacations, Holidays, and Sick Leave. Most of the factors which have been summarized above directly affect the data on average weekly hours. But one of the most important developments of recent decades affecting hours actually worked, but not hours "paid for," has been the introduction and rapid spread of vacations with pay, paid holidays, and sick leave—time paid for but not worked. Relatively few companies provided paid vacations for wage earners (as opposed to salaried personnel) in the 1920's and it is not likely that they inaugurated many of these benefit programs during the early 1930's, when many companies had to cut labor costs. However, organized labor pressed for these benefits, and with improved business conditions in the latter half of the decade of the thirties, these programs began to spread. Their spread received its main impetus during World War II, as a result of several decisions of the National War Labor Board, and through the continued efforts of organized labor.

Although few comprehensive data are available on the amount of time paid for but not worked, some surveys provide a clue to trends in this regard.[16] Rough estimates of the average number of hours per week involved can be computed. On the basis of these estimates, the number of hours per week in nonagricultural industries paid for under programs of paid vacations, holidays, and sick leave, would appear to total about 3 hours in 1956, an increase of 1 hour in the past decade and about 2½ hours since 1929. Or, in other words, the number of days of paid vacation, holidays, and sick leave in nonagricultural industries averaged about 20 days in 1956,[17] a gain of about 6 days in annual paid vacations, holidays, and sick leave since 1947.

Implications of Current Trends. The desire for more leisure is often cited as the major reason for past reductions in the workweek in the United States, and will certainly be a major factor in the future. With continually rising real income, people can increasingly "afford" leisure. However, it is not at all clear that, for all individuals, rising income and the ability to afford more leisure will necessarily be translated into demand for more leisure. The recent rapid increase in dual jobholding has occurred during a period of near full employment and a rapid rise in real wages. Moreover, dual jobholding is by no means concentrated among lower income persons alone. For example, a recent Census survey shows that the percentage of professional and technical workers who held two jobs at the same time in mid-1957 was about the same as for non-farm laborers.[18] The percentage of dual jobholding among craftsmen was higher than among operatives and service workers. Because a rising proportion of workers are employed in professional and technical occupations, further increases in dual jobholding may be in prospect.

Other factors also will affect future trends in the length of the workweek. Hours worked in agriculture as well as in nonagricultural industries other than manufacturing, mining, and construction have been declining in the past decade, and the long-term decline in agricultural employment has also continued. This should result in further declines in average hours of work in the economy. Furthermore, technological advances may support the trend toward a shortened workweek. In addition, labor force predictions indicate a large increase in the numbers of teen-age youth and married women seeking part-time work.[19] Moreover, the increase in the practice of granting holidays and vacations with pay, as well as paid sick leave, seems likely to continue to reduce the average number of hours actually worked during the year. Thus, whether or not the standard workweek is reduced further as a direct result of collective bargaining, a number of factors are operating which will tend to lower the average number of hours worked per week and per year.

Notes

1. J. Frederic Dewhurst and Associates, America's Needs and Resources–A New Survey (New York, The Twentieth Century Fund, 1955), p. 1073.

2. Other estimates of hours of work for the period 1840 through 1890 are available from a special Congressional report (S. Rept. 1394, 52d Cong., 2d sess., 1893, Part 1, pp. 178-179) and, for 1890-1926, from Real Wages in the United States, 1890-1926, by Paul H. Douglas (Boston, Houghton Mifflin Co., 1930). Both of these sources agree in general with the trend of hours indicated in chart 1.

3. For a detailed list of industries for which hours data are available plus information on date of origin, see Guide to Employment Statistics of BLS–Employment, Hours and Earnings, Labor Turnover (Bureau of Labor Statistics, 1954).

4. Harry A. Millis and Royal E. Montgomery, Labor's Progress and Some Basic Labor Problems (New York, McGraw-Hill Book Co., 1938), p. 465.

5. Unpublished Census data indicate a decline of about 1½ hours between 1947 and 1956 in service industries, and 1 hour in finance, insurance, and real estate.

6. William Haber, The Shorter Work Week Issue (in Addresses on Industrial Relations–1957 Series, Bull. 25, Ann Arbor, Mich., University of Michigan, Bureau of Industrial Relations, 1957).

7. In this connection, see Layoff, Recall, and Work-Sharing Procedures, Pt. IV (in Monthly Labor Review, March 1957, pp. 334-335).

8. See Wages and Related Benefits, 17 Labor Markets, 1955-56 (BLS Bull. 1188, 1956), table B-3, p. 54. A 1956 survey of 17 labor market areas indicates that only 7 percent of the sample of plant workers were on less than a 40-hour schedule.

9. Five papers presented at the AFL-CIO Conference on Shorter Hours of Work were excerpted in the Monthly Labor Review, November 1956 (pp. 1263-1275).

10. Statistical Abstract of the United States, 1957 (U. S. Bureau of the Census), p. 195.

11. Annual Report on the Labor Force, Current Population Reports, Series P-50, No. 72, U. S. Bureau of the Census, p. 8.

12. Hours of Work in the United States: 1955, Current Population Reports, Series P-50, No. 63, U. S. Bureau of the Census, table B.

13. See Labor Force Projections to 1975 (in Monthly Labor Review, December 1957, pp. 1443-1450).

14. Multiple Jobholding: July 1957, Current Population Reports, Labor Force, Series P-50, No. 79, U. S. Bureau of the Census, p. 1.

15. It is important to note that an increase in dual jobholding will have different effects on the Census and BLS series. Under BLS procedures, when a man who works 40 hours a week at his regular full-time job takes on a part-time job of 10 hours in another industry, this would not affect average hours of work in his primary industry, but the average workweek in the industry of the secondary job would be reduced, since the individual is counted there as an employee working only 10 hours a week. Under the Census survey technique of collecting employment and hours data, the individual would be counted as working 50 hours a week and all 50 hours would be assigned to the industry of primary employment. Total man-hours would be increased by the same amount under either method of counting, however.

16. For example, Fringe Benefits, 1955 (Washington, D. C., Chamber of Commerce of the United States, Economic Research Department, 1956).

17. This figure may be somewhat high, since firms which reported in the Chamber's sample tended to be mainly large concerns, and in industries where fringe benefit policies have been more liberal traditionally.

A BLS survey of the feasibility of measuring the cost of fringe benefits in manufacturing, applying to the year 1953, and various National Industrial Conference Board surveys, suggest an average of paid holidays, vacations, and sick leave totaling somewhat less–possibly 15 to 16 days per year in 1956, or about 2.5 hours per week.

18. See text footnote 14.

19. Labor Force Projections to 1975, op. cit.

The Changing Length of Working Life

By SEYMOUR L. WOLFBEIN

"THE EXPECTATION OF LIFE" has been of keen interest to the public as a whole and to workers in many professional fields for a long time. It is a ranking index of a Nation's well-being; it is the key to measuring man's progress in controlling his biological environment. In much the same way "the average length of working life"—the ages at which men begin and end their work careers and the span of their lives they spend as gainfully occupied members of the labor force—represents a key indicator of a Nation's social and economic welfare. The educator or the person interested in the maintenance of child labor standards may focus on the "age of accession"—the age at which young people make their entry into the work force. The actuary, the expert on pension plans, the practitioner in the field of industrial relations may concentrate on the "age of separation"—the age at which men exit from the labor force. All of these persons, plus the economist who has to measure the manpower potential of a population, the businessman interested in the size and composition of consumer expenditures and many others will watch the changes in man's total span of working life—and the years of his life he spends in retirement. Similarly, the facts of working life represent a key to measuring man's progress in controlling his economic environment, for one of the hallmarks of a country's standard of living is the extent to which it can increase the amount of goods and services per capita while permitting later ages of accession (more education and training for young people) and earlier ages of voluntary exit from the labor force (more years of retirement).

Five years ago, the U. S. Department of Labor's Bureau of Labor Statistics constructed a series of Tables of Working Life which depicted the changing length and pattern of working life among men in the United States.[1] This paper presents for the first time the new BLS Table of Working Life for 1950 and compares it with similar materials for prior periods.

These Tables of Working Life are very similar to the familiar standard life tables. The life table is a statistical device for summarizing the mortality experience of a population of some particular period of time. For this purpose, the life table starts with a group of persons—usually 100,000—born alive and follows it through successive ages as it experiences the attrition caused by death. A number of significant measures can be obtained from such a table, the most familiar of which is "life expectancy"—the average number of years of life remaining after each specified age. The Table of Working Life also follows through successive ages the experience of an

Reprinted from *Proceedings* of the Seventh Annual Meeting of the Industrial Relations Research Association, Detroit, Michigan, December, 1954, pp. 248-257, by permission of the author and the publisher.

initial cohort of 100,000 at birth. In addition to showing attrition caused by mortality, however, it also shows the number who may be expected to work or seek work over their life span. From these materials it is possible to find the rates at which persons enter and exit from the labor force and to calculate a "work-life expectancy"—the average years of labor force activity remaining after each specified age.

This paper will 1) discuss briefly the basic structure of working life among men as it prevailed in 1950, 2) summarize some of the important developments which have occurred since the turn of the century, and 3) describe what happened during the past decade under conditions of mobilization and high levels of economic activity. These materials will then serve as the general context for discussion by the experts of some of the consequences of the changing length of working life—their manpower implications, industrial relations effects and results in terms of changing patterns of income and expenditures.[2]

STRUCTURE OF WORKING LIFE

1. Back in 1900 there were about 3 million people 65 years of age and over; in 1950 they numbered a little over 12 million—four times as high. In 1900 people 65 years and older accounted for one in every twenty-five of the population; in 1950 they accounted for one in every twelve. The great reduction in mortality experience which took place during the past half century and which served to bring about this significant increase in the number of older persons also resulted in the general population curve which can be observed from the Tables of Working Life (column 2). Attrition due to mortality is very low at the earlier ages, gradually increases during youth and middle age and becomes progressively more rapid after men reach their fifties. Mortality experience has improved so much, however, that a third of the initial cohort born is still alive at age 60-64 years; more than a fifth is still alive at age 70-74.

2. At the turn of the century more than one out of every five young boys 10-15 years of age were workers; by 1950 the Census Bureau had for a long time stopped enumerating labor force activity for anyone under 14 years because of the very small number of persons working below that age. This has resulted, among other things, in a marked aging of our labor force. In 1900 the median age of the male work force was 33.3 years; in 1950 it was 38.5 years. This trend also reflects, of course, the very marked increase in the age at which young men make their entry into the labor force. The labor force curve (see columns 3, 4 and 5 of Table I) rises rapidly during the late teens and early twenties when most men normally begin their work careers. However, at 1950 levels and rates, the average American male does not enter the labor force until he is between his 18th and 19th year of life. Between about age 25 and 55 practically all men are in the labor force, the exceptions consisting almost entirely of those unable to work. After the mid-fifties, the labor force declines rapidly. In 1950, four-fifths of the men

60-64 years of age were still in the labor force; the proportion drops to two-thirds for the age group 65-69 and to two-fifths in the age group 70-74.

3. Fifty years ago there was very little difference between a man's working life span and his total life span. Life expectancy was comparatively short

Table I—Abridged Table of Working Life, Males, 1940, 1947, and 1950*

(1)	(2)	(3)	(4)	(5)	(6)	(7)	(8)	(9)	(10)
Age interval	*Number living of 100,000 born alive*: In population	*In labor force*: Number	*In labor force*: Percent of population	Accessions to the labor force (per 1,000 in population)	*Separations from the labor force (per 1,000 in labor force)*: Due to all causes	Due to death	Due to retirement	*Average number of remaining years of*: Life	Labor force participation
x to x+n	${}_nL_x$	${}_nLw_x$	${}_nw_x$	$1000\,{}_nA_x$	$1000\,{}_nQ^s_x$	$1000\,{}_nQ^d_x$	$1000\,{}_nQ^r_x$	$\mathring{e}_x$	$\mathring{e}w_x$
	(Within age interval			(Between successive age intervals)				(At beginning of age interval)	
					1940				
10-14	461,865	6,196	†	431.0	8.2	8.2	—	—	—
15-19	458,100	205,229	44.8	441.6	12.0	12.0	—	51.3	45.8
20-24	452,589	405,067	89.5	68.0	14.9	14.9	—	46.8	41.3
25-29	445,845	429,795	96.4	7.9	17.6	17.6	—	42.4	36.8
30-34	438,014	425,750	97.2	—	28.0	21.9	6.1	38.0	32.3
35-39	428,373	413,808	96.6	—	37.8	29.7	8.1	33.7	28.0
40-44	415,611	398,155	95.8	—	53.3	42.1	11.2	29.6	23.8
45-49	398,028	376,933	94.7	—	80.2	60.8	19.4	25.5	19.8
50-54	373,582	346,684	92.8	—	117.8	85.9	31.9	21.8	16.0
55-59	340,970	305,850	89.7	—	211.6	115.7	95.9	18.3	12.4
60-64	299,545	241,134	80.5	—	376.7	148.9	227.8	15.1	9.2
65-69	248,456	150,316	60.5	—	495.5	191.8	303.7	12.2	6.8
70-74	189,583	75,833	40.0	—	576.4	262.4	314.0	9.6	5.6
75 and over	232,278	44,830	19.3	—	—	—	—	—	—
					1947				
10-14	475,284	18,320	†	524.1	5.8	5.8	—	—	—
15-19	472,525	259,889	55.0	346.7	9.5	9.5	—	52.6	47.4
20-24	468,041	421,237	90.0	67.2	11.3	11.3	—	48.0	42.8
25-29	462,739	447,931	96.8	6.9	12.6	12.6	—	43.5	38.2
30-34	456,917	445,494	97.5	—	20.7	16.6	4.1	39.0	33.6
35-39	449,323	436,293	97.1	—	32.5	24.4	8.1	34.5	29.1
40-44	438,330	422,112	96.3	—	47.9	36.7	11.2	30.2	24.8
45-49	422,149	401,886	95.2	—	75.6	56.3	19.3	26.0	20.7
50-54	398,186	371,508	93.3	—	106.7	82.1	24.6	22.1	16.9
55-59	365,102	331,878	90.9	—	160.5	115.1	45.4	18.6	13.2
60-64	322,102	278,618	86.5	—	354.7	148.6	206.1	15.3	9.7
65-69	267,931	179,782	67.1	—	501.8	189.2	312.6	12.4	7.0
70-74	204,978	89,575	43.7	—	544.3	258.8	285.5	9.9	5.9
75 and over	263,826	60.944	23.1	—	—	—	—	—	—
					1950				
10-14	477,806	21,000	†	483.5	5.3	5.3	—	—	—
15-19	475,282	251,899	53.0	354.0	8.5	8.5	—	53.6	47.9
20-24	471,255	418,003	88.7	73.3	9.8	9.8	—	48.9	43.2
25-29	466,652	448,453	96.1	6.0	10.7	10.7	—	44.4	38.6
30-34	461,671	446,436	96.7	—	15.1	14.1	1.0	39.8	34.0
35-39	455,169	439,693	96.6	—	23.3	21.3	2.0	35.2	29.3
40-44	445,488	429,450	96.4	—	42.6	33.4	9.2	30.8	24.9
45-49	430,539	411,165	95.5	—	70.9	51.5	19.4	26.6	20.6
50-54	408,140	382,019	93.6	—	116.3	77.4	38.9	22.6	16.6
55-59	375,956	337,608	89.8	—	195.5	109.7	85.8	19.0	13.0
60-64	332,858	271,612	81.6	—	337.2	142.3	194.9	15.7	9.7
65-69	279,537	180,022	64.4	—	485.9	180.1	305.8	12.7	7.2
70-74	217,261	92,553	42.6	—	558.6	247.5	311.1	10.1	5.9
75 and over	287,742	61,289	21.3	—	—	—	—	—	—

*Labor force data for 1940 have been adjusted to allow for a revision in Census Bureau enumeration procedures introduced in July 1945.

†In accordance with current Census definitions, only persons 14 years of age or over are enumerated in the labor force. No meaningful percentage of the population in the labor force could therefore be computed for the age interval 10-14 years.

Prepared by: U. S. Department of Labor, Bureau of Labor Statistics, Division of Manpower and Employment Statistics, November 19, 1954.

and only a small proportion of the population survived to the age which we now consider conventional for retirement. Moreover, in an agrarian economy where self-employment predominated, those who reached an older age were often in a position to continue in some active productive role. In fact, for most workers there was no sharp break in employment as we know it now.

Exits from the labor force have a much different and more distinctive pattern today. Labor force withdrawals are classified as a) due to death and b) due to "retirement"[3] (see columns 6, 7 and 8 of Table I). Separations are comparatively low in the early ages and these are due mainly to deaths. In fact, death is a more important reason for separation from the labor force than retirement in all ages up to 55. Thereafter, the retirement rate moves up sharply. *Among men, the retirement rate more than doubles between ages 55-59 and 60-64 and reaches its peak in the age group 65-69 years.*

The concentration of labor force retirements among men in their sixties is due only partly to the progressive increase in disability among older persons. Available evidence, in fact, suggests that disability for work-force activity rises with age in a much smoother pattern, not unlike mortality. In actual fact, of course, the ages at which men withdraw from the labor force are tied much more to prevailing employer attitudes toward employment of older workers and the conventional retirement age of 65 which is found in State old age assistance laws, Federal programs (Railroad Retirement and Social Security) and private pension plans.

LENGTH OF WORKING LIFE

4. Changes in the length of life combined with developments affecting the structure of working life—particularly the later entries into and the earlier exits from the labor force—have brought about some very striking effects on the length of working life of the American male (cf. Table II).

Table II—Average Life and Work-Life Expectancy for Men, 1900-2000

	AT BIRTH			AT AGE 20		
YEAR	Average life expectancy	Average work-life expectancy	Average years outside labor force	Average life expectancy	Average work-life expectancy	Average years in retirement
1900*	48.2	32.1	16.1	42.2	39.4	2.8
1940	61.2	38.3	22.9	46.8	41.3	5.5
1947	64.2	41.6	22.6	48.0	42.8	5.2
1950	65.5	41.9	23.6	48.9	43.2	5.7
2000†	73.2	45.1	28.1	53.8	45.1	8.7

*For white males in 11 original death registration States.

†Estimated by assuming continuation of labor force participation rates by males as they prevail today except for drop of 10 percentage points among men 65 and over; assumes continuation of mortality trends which have prevailed from 1920 to 1950 (cf. Social Security Administration Actuarial Study No. 33).

5. The difference between the "average number of remaining years of life" and the "average number of remaining years of labor force participation" (columns 9 and 10 of Table I) represents the average time spent in retirement. Thus under 1950 mortality and work-force patterns:

A man of 20 would average	48.9	years of life
and	43.2	years of working life
leaving	5.7	years of retirement
A man of 60 would average	15.7	years of life
and	9.7	years of working life
leaving	6.0	years of retirement

In fact, for all the age groups below 65 years, the average difference between life and work life is around 6 years (5.7 years). In other words, under 1950 mortality and labor force conditions, men could look forward to spending about 6 years of their lives in retirement. After age 65, the gap between total life and work life narrows considerably, because people who continue to work past that age apparently tend to continue as workers until they die. Needless to say these figures are averages: they include the young man who dies while still a member of the labor force and thus spends zero years in retirement and the man who lives long enough to put in a protracted period of retirement.

6. The contrast with 1950 experience is very marked. Under 1900 mortality and work-force patterns:

A man of 20 would have averaged	42.2	years of life
and	39.4	years of working life
leaving	2.8	years of retirement
A man of 60 would have averaged	14.3	years of life
and	11.5	years of working life
leaving	2.8	years of retirement

Under 1900 mortality and worker participation patterns, therefore, a man averaged around three years of his life in retirement (2.8 years). *Thus, during the first fifty years of this century, the average amount of years spent by men in retirement has doubled.* And as can be seen from Table II, if all of these trends persist into the future, the average number of years in retirement will go up to about 9 years (8.7 years). *Past and current trends, therefore, point to a tripling of the average number of years men spend in retirement between 1900 and 2000.*

7. It is instructive to examine a little more closely how the doubling of the number of years spent in retirement was achieved between 1900 and 1950. As can be seen from Table II and the few figures presented above, average life expectancy of a 20-year old man went up from 42.2 years in 1900 to 48.9 years in 1950—a very substantial increase in expectation of life of nearly seven years. At the same time the average number of years of working life also went up—from 39.4 to 43.2 or 3.8 years. But the duration of working life did not go up as much as the duration of life, permitting a corresponding increase in the duration of time spent in retirement as well.

Thus, despite the marked delay in entry into the labor force on the part of young people and earlier exits from the labor force on the part of older people, men today put in more years of work than did their counterparts 50 years ago. And further, despite more years of labor force activity, men today spend more of their lives in retirement than did their 1900 counterparts—the answer to this seeming paradox being the added years of total life we have today.

8. These points are sharpened by looking at the figures in Table II which presents data on life and work life expectancy at birth. This information enables us to note the expectancies for both life and working life from birth (instead of for some later working age) and to examine the difference between those two expectancies which represents the *total* number of years spent outside the labor force (instead of just the number of years spent in retirement).

Between 1900 and 1950 life expectancy at birth went up from 48.2 years to 65.5 years—more than 17 years added to the average man's expected lifetime.[4] At the same time, the average number of years of work-life went up from 32.1 to 41.9 years—an increase in work-life expectancy of just short of a full ten years. Thus, again, despite the sizable reductions in labor force participation rates at both ends of the age scale, men today put in a decade more of work than their 1900 counterparts. The manpower potential of a group of 100,000 men living and working under 1950 conditions is hundreds of thousands of man-years more than a similar group operating under 1900 conditions. This is a factor which is frequently overlooked when simple comparisons are made of how age-specific worker rates have changed during the past 50 years.

9. The point is often made that with protracted periods of education and training during youth and high rates of retirement in older age, more of our years are spent in "nonproductive" status and a smaller and smaller group must provide for these non-worker activities. This point should be viewed against the many additional years of labor force input which men currently provide. It should also be tempered by another fact shown by Table II. Under 1900 conditions men could expect to average about 16 out of their 48 years of life outside of the labor force—about one-third of their total life time spent as nonworkers. In 1950 they averaged about 23½ out of the 65½ years of their life outside the labor force—also about one-third. To summarize, then, men today spend no greater proportion of their lives outside the labor force than they did in 1900; the longer life afforded them permits both more time as workers and more time for education and training at one end of the age scale and more retirement at the other.

THE IMPACT OF CHANGING LEVELS OF ECONOMIC ACTIVITY

10. The data and brief analytical summaries presented so far have emphasized the fundamental long-term changes in working life among men which have evolved over the past fifty years. "Evolved" is perhaps the best way to put it, because such factors as the basic structure of the labor force or mortality rates change very slowly over time. As is true in so many other fields, however, shorter range changes do take place around the secular

trend and often give added perception of some of the factors which affect the length and pattern of working life. If the experience of the 1940's (as portrayed in Table I) is any guide, the ebb and flow of working life in the shorter run appears to correspond very closely to alternations in economic activity, especially as they are reflected in changing employment opportunities.

11. The contrasting work-life patterns for 1940 and 1947 illustrate this point very well. The 1940 pattern looks almost like an exaggerated picture of the secular trends described above. After a decade of severe dislocation of economic activity and reduced employment opportunity, 1940 worker rates at both ends of the age scale were very low. Thus a worker rate of about 45 percent for the age group 15-19 years in 1940 contrasts with one fully 10 percentage points more in 1947 when economic activity and employment were at high levels. In 1940 young men were at a competitive disadvantage in job competition; very few (about 6 percent) who went to school had part-time employment. In 1947, many young people held full-time jobs; over a fifth who were enrolled in school were also employed.

In addition, the retirement pattern shifted markedly between 1940 and 1950. The continuation of high employment in the postwar period led many men in their fifties and sixties to remain at work. (The Social Security Administration reported a total of 842,000 men 65 years of age and over entitled to OASI benefits continued in covered employment in 1947.) Higher postwar wages and prices may also have contributed to later retirement ages. At any rate the retirement rate for men 55-59 years of age, for example, fell from 96 per thousand to 45 per thousand between 1940 and 1947—more than a 50 percent drop.

Thus, the sharp change in economic climate between 1940 and 1947 actually resulted in a reversal of the long-term trend: Age of entry into the labor force went down; age of exit from the labor force went up. As a result, the span of working life under 1947 conditions increased over that of 1940 by 1½ years (Table II). Life expectancy also moved up—by 1.2 years. This time, however, the working life span went up more than total life expectancy, so that the average number of years spent in retirement actually went down slightly between 1940 and 1947 (from 5.5 to 5.2 years)—also a reversal of the long term trend. Between 1940 and 1947, the manpower potential of a group of 100,000 men went up more than a third of a million man-years of labor force activity, an increase of almost ten percent.

12. By 1950 the employment situation had again changed. The country was not, of course, in the midst of any depression, but April 1950 (the month for which the Tables of Working Life apply) was only a couple of months away from the peak period of postwar unemployment (4.7 million in February 1950). Worker rates among the young men were below those of 1947, but nowhere near as low as those of 1940. Worker rates for older men were also down, and in some cases closer to the 1940 than to 1947 levels. All this added up to a return to the observed secular trends: later entry, earlier exit from the labor force; longer duration of working life, but

even longer duration of total life—and a consequent increase in average duration of years spent outside of the labor force, including retirement. As can be seen from Table III presented below, for all ages the trend 1940-47-50

Table III—Average Number of Years of Life in Retirement, Male Workers 1940, 1947, and 1950—By Age

AGE	1940	1947	1950	AGE	1940	1947	1950
15-19	5.5	5.2	5.7	45-49	5.7	5.3	6.0
20-24	5.5	5.2	5.7	50-54	5.8	5.2	6.0
25-29	5.6	5.3	5.8	55-59	5.9	5.4	6.0
30-34	5.7	5.4	5.8	60-64	5.9	5.6	6.0
35-39	5.7	5.4	5.9	65-69	5.4	5.4	5.5
40-44	5.8	5.4	5.9	70-74	4.0	4.0	4.2

were along these lines: Between 1940 and 1947 earlier entry into and later exit from the labor force combined to effect a substantial reduction in average years spent in retirement; by 1950 the situation was reversed so that the gap between work life and total life was above not only 1947 levels, but had already surpassed the 1940 levels as well. And throughout the decade of the 1940's while labor market participation rates experienced marked short run changes in response to economic change, reductions in mortality continued and added years not only to man's total life span but to the man-years of labor force input as well.

Notes

1. First published in Wolfbein, Seymour L., "The Length of Working Life" in *Population Studies,* December 1949 (Printed in Great Britain). A detailed exposition of the substance and techniques of this work was presented in *Tables of Working Life,* Bulletin No. 1001 of the Bureau of Labor Statistics (Aug. 1950) from which some of the descriptive materials here are taken.
2. The labor force life tables presented here were constructed by Stuart H. Garfinkle, Labor Economist at Bureau of Labor Statistics. Mr. Garfinkle is now doing pioneer work in developing companion tables of working life for women.
3. Separations due to "retirement" as shown in the Tables include all exits from the labor force other than death, e.g. because of old age, disability, eligibility for pension, long duration unemployment, etc.
4. The reason why the increase in life expectancy at birth between 1900 and 1950 is so much longer than for, say, age group 20, is that the major reductions in mortality during this period took place among infants and young children.

$30 Billion for Fun

By THE EDITORS OF *FORTUNE*

FULL OF VIGOR and promise, the leisure and recreational market today is one of the largest and most complex in the entire U.S. economy. It already

Chapter X from *The Changing American Market,* by the Editors of Fortune.

measures about $30.6 billion, which is half again as much as the American consumer spends on clothing or shelter, and twice what he lays out for new cars or home goods. Its components are a hodgepodge of smaller markets, some wholly interdependent, others closely related but antagonistic, still others totally unrelated. The market would also be a sure bet to become the fastest growing in the U.S. economy but for its endless contradictions.

For the leisure market, whether looked at piecemeal or as a whole, is above all a perverse thing. For example, in the economist's book, leisure spending should exactly reverse the pattern of food spending—that is, as total income rises the share spent on food should go down, the share on leisure up. That did not happen with food, as already observed. Neither has it happened so far with leisure, whose share of disposable consumer income has actually declined from 14 per cent in 1947 to about 12 per cent in 1953, despite the phenomenal rise in income. As to specific markets, who would have supposed that U.S. drinkers would so neglect their opportunities that the national liquor bill would actually fall in a period of rising population and income? Outlay for all alcohol sagged badly after 1947, and did not recover past the 1947 level until 1952. And who would have predicted at the end of the war that the movie industry would not share in the greatest of American booms? Yet movie admissions have dropped by a thumping $340 million since 1947.

If these two segments of the leisure market had merely followed the rise in dollar income since 1947 the total market would be past the $35-billion mark; and the fact that they did not demands explanation. As for alcohol, its relative decline reflects two other phenomena, i.e., the long tendency of Americans to switch from hard liquor to beer, and the shrinking capacity of individual drinkers. The absolute decline of the movies is chargeable first of all to another leisure component, television. But the larger explanation, more applicable to the leisure market than to any other, is that the consumer's preferences are strongly influenced by habits, by social trends, and by other factors that have little connection with how much time he has or how much money is in his pocket.

Fortunately, for the future of leisure spending, these perversities are not all on the down side. They may influence a particular leisure item suddenly to take off, as home-workshop equipment has done since the war; and they have caused the share of leisure spending to rise at times when the economists might confidently have expected a fall. Far from denying the promise of the leisure market, these apparent contradictions merely suggest that that market requires detailed study; for it follows the movements of the whole economy as though connected by a loose and flexible tether.

All Fun in Two Parts. The term leisure activity or expenditure, as used here, means one that is undertaken by choice, not of necessity, and is pursued for its own sake, not merely to avoid some other and larger expenditure. The definition admittedly has leaks: for example, is tobacco a voluntary pleasure or a compulsion? (*Fortune* considered it more the latter than the former, and excluded it.) Definitely excluded, however, are a multitude of necessary activities often accompanied by a minor pleasure component. Cooking, for example, to some few people is both an art and a joy, but its primary purpose for most Americans is keeping alive. Likewise excluded are most home-betterment and do-it-yourself activities by the homeowner, who usually engages in them not for fun but because he cannot afford or cannot wait for a professional. The only two around-the-house activities that meet the test are gardening and home workshops, both of which tend to be carried on as an end in themselves.

The leisure market becomes more intelligible if it is viewed in two parts:

First, the heart of that market is $18 billion of unmistakable leisure-recreational expenditures on spectator amusements, spectator and participant athletics, hunting and fishing, gardening, domestic recreational travel (including vacations and weekends), foreign pleasure travel, boating, games and toys, certain books, magazines, and newspapers, etc. This is the heart of the market in several respects: it is the largest part, the most dynamic, and it has the greatest potential for growth.

A secondary group, totaling a little over $12.6 billion, is made up of consumer expeditures for alcohol ($8.9 billion), expenditures for television (including repair), radios, records, and musical instruments ($2.7 billion), and casual eating out for pleasure (estimated at $1 billion).

This separation is primarily a matter of convenience, indulged in for two purposes. First, it gets the massive component for liquor (substantially a tax component) off to one side, lest it obscure the more interesting changes that are taking place in other, smaller items. And it also follows the consumer's own budgeting practice, separating those items that he clearly labels as recreation from those that often show up in other parts of his budget. For example, television is generally considered a household expenditure, and outlays for alcohol—especially beer—tend to get mixed up with food purchases.

Table I—The Leisure Market in Motion

SELECTED LEISURE EXPENDITURES
(in millions of dollars)

Category	1947	1953
Movies	1,594	1,252
Nondurable toys and sports supplies	910	1,209
Books and Periodicals	927	1,230
Foreign travel	597	1,144
Dining out	854	1,030
Durable toys and sports equipment	906	1,108
Boats	500	800
Flowers, seeds, plants	475	684
TV repair	140	533
Sports events, etc.	410	408
Golf, bowling, etc.	415	539
Hotels and motels	230	422
Race tracks	255	377
Power tools	31	209

Sources: Department of Commerce except for *Fortune* estimates, developed from trade sources, of dining out, boats and power tools.

The sharpest fact about the postwar leisure market is the growing preference for active fun rather than mere onlooking. Movies were down by some $375 million between 1947 and 1953, while all the items related to active pursuits showed gains ranging from respectable to spectacular.

Once the separation has been made, however, some more vivid distinctions between the two groups begin to appear. All the active, premeditated pursuits are in the first group; those in the second are enjoyed casually, without forethought, mainly in the home, and always in postures ranging from sitting to prone. Moreover, the first group also contains the items that are active in the economic sense, while those in the second are comparatively static.

To look for a moment at the items of the second group, liquor spending has risen scarcely at all since 1947; and the trends in social drinking already noted offer little promise that alcohol will attract more than its present share of consumer income over the next few years. As for casual dining out for pleasure, the percentage of food consumed away from home has sagged since shortly after the war. The phenomenal rate of homebuilding and the growth of suburbia had a lot to do with that. While the percentage of diners-out who do so by choice (seeking a break in the cooking-and-cleaning-up routine) appears to be on the rise, the net effect of both tendencies will probably be to maintain eating-out expenditures at about the same share of income—so long as total income at least holds steady. If income should drop significantly, this is one of the first expenses the consumer would trim.

The only really vigorous item in the second group is the TV-radio-record component, whose prospective bounce comes almost entirely from color television just around the corner. Color could yield a TV gain of perhaps $500 million within the next four or five years. However, this potential increase merely points up the lack of buoyancy in the second group, for a $500-million boost would raise the group as a whole by only 4 per cent. And a mere 6 per cent drop in liquor spending—which went down more than that between 1947 and 1949—would wipe out the entire hoped-for gain from color TV.

Doers of the Word. The great trend in the leisure market over the past two decades was foreshadowed by a 1934 report on what people would like to do with their leisure time, as opposed to what they did. In that year the National Recreation Association, a professional group concerned primarily with standards for municipal parks and playgrounds, published a study entitled "The Leisure Hours of 5,000 People," showing the following orders of preference:

Did	*Would Like to Do*
1. Reading newspapers and magazines	1. Tennis
2. Listening to radio	2. Swimming
3. Going to movies	3. Boating
4. Visiting or entertaining	4. Golf

Did	*Would Like to Do*
5. Reading books (fiction)	5. Camping
6. Auto riding	6. Gardening
7. Swimming	7. Playing music
8. Writing letters	8. Auto riding
9. Reading books (non-fiction)	9. Theatregoing
10. Conversation	10. Ice skating

While the findings should not be taken too literally (tennis, for example, has never gained the popularity that its ranking above would imply), the preference for getting up and doing, instead of merely sitting around, is unmistakable. Eight of the ten most common leisure activities were sedentary; while of those most aspired to, all but one were active pursuits.

This itch to do things rather than sit and watch has actually cut down spending at the box office during the nation's greatest prosperity. Total admissions to all spectator sports and amusements (except horse racing) slumped from over $2 billion to about $1.6 billion between 1947 and 1953, while the civilian population fourteen years of age and over increased by 7 per cent, prices by 16 per cent, and consumer income by nearly half. The decline in the movies has already been noted, but other amusements that lost ground included baseball and hockey (both down 25 per cent), and theatres and concerts (down 2 per cent). Almost alone among the spectator sports was horse racing, where total receipts of pari-mutuel (including admissions, track and government percentages, etc.) rose from $255 million in 1947 to $380 million in 1953. But since the gambling feature attracts customers who know not a foal from a fetlock, horse racing from the customer's viewpoint almost becomes an active sport.

Now, Americans have not forgotten how to have fun sitting down. Through high-fidelity recording they probably hear more good music, and through television see more sports events, plays, skits, movies, etc., than in the 1920's, that golden age of the box office. They are merely seeing them, at comparatively small out-of-pocket cost, at home. And nothing so sharply whets the hunger to do, rather than watch, as a heavy schedule of TV-viewing.

This lust for exertion shows up in items ranging from small to very large. Between 1947 and 1953, home workshop tools went up from less than $50 million to over $200 million, and commercial recreation (whose major components are bowling and golf green fees and instruction) increased from $350 million to nearly $470 million. Over the same period the whole class of non-durable receation items (including games and toys, sporting ammunition, still and movie film, golf balls, etc.) increased from $900 million to $1.2 billion. A similar class of durable items, composed primarily of wheeled goods (such as bicycles), cameras, sporting arms, fishing rods and reels, golf clubs, and similar athletic paraphernalia, rose from $900 million to $1.1 billion; and boating expenditures went up by more than half, from a roughly estimated $500 million in 1947 to perhaps $800 million last year.

These figures alone do not reflect adequately the extent to which some of the active sports have grown. The $800-million boating figure includes the cost of boats and motors, fuel, upkeep, insurance, etc.—in short, most of the expense that a man shoulders in becoming a boatowner. But total expenditure on fishing, for example, cannot be measured by the sale of fishing tackle. The largest expenditures in fishing are the cost of travel, the fisherman's lodging, and the food and liquor he consumes.

The most massive item in the primary leisure group is that for domestic recreational travel, which by *Fortune's* estimates rose from $5.4 billion in 1947 to $8 billion in 1953. The major subtotals of the $8-billion figure are auto expense, a little under $2 billion; train, plane, and bus fares, about $1 billion; food and lodging, nearly $4 billion; and vacation homes, perhaps another $600 million. The rest consists of incidental purchases, mainly clothing and luggage (but not including sports equipment), made in preparation for vacation and other pleasure travel.

All of this huge travel item falls on the active side of the ledger, for much of it is incurred for outdoor sports, and the rest is spent on sightseeing —which is not a sedentary pastime. The same is true of foreign pleasure travel, up from about $600 million in 1947 to $1.1 billion in 1953, but with this major difference: the bulk of foreign pleasure travel is for sightseeing and related purposes, with a smaller portion—mainly fishing, hunting, and skiing trips to Canada—going for active outdoor sports.

Time on My Hands, With Pay. Granting that most Americans have long had this hankering for movement and active recreation, they could satisfy the desire only after three conditions were met: they had to have the time (meaning time off from work), the money, and the facilities.

The time has slowly been coming their way. For twenty-five years the average work week has declined gradually, from nearly fifty hours in 1929 to a trifle under forty-two hours in 1953. Moreover, these averages are distorted by those traditional sunup-to-sundowners, the agricultural workers, and by the inclusion of overtime, which is piled on top of the five-day, forty-hour week now enjoyed by well over half of all U.S. workers. Indeed, overtime has the unusual effect of increasing consumer income without necessarily increasing leisure expenditures, for the overtime worker has more money to spend but less leisure time in which to spend it. If agricultural workers and overtime are discounted, the average basic U.S. work week is very close to forty hours.

A sharp rise in paid holidays has accompanied this drop in the work week. A recent study of labor contracts covering six million workers in both manufacturing and non-manufacturing industries—out of perhaps 20 million covered by contracts—showed that nearly 80 per cent received six or more paid holidays a year. As holidays are granted to a broader group of workers, and as those who now receive them get more, the current $1.5-billion figure for holiday and weekend trips (out of $8 billion for all domestic pleasure travel) should show lively growth.

The biggest boon to the leisure market, however, has been the phenomenal growth of vacations with pay. Production workers have been the major new beneficiaries, since as far back as 1937 over three-fourths of all office and retail employees (to take an especially favored group) were already enjoying them. In that same year only about 40 per cent of production workers were covered by paid-vacation plans, granting an average of about

Table II—Hours Down, Vacations Up

THE WORK-WEEK AND VACATIONS, WORKING TIME*
(in average hours per week)

1929	1941	1947	1953
49.7	45.4	43.5	41.9

VACATIONS
(in millions of weeks)

1929	1941	1947	1953
17.5	30.0	48.5	60.5

*Including agricultural workers.

Sources: Working time—1947 and 1953 from Bureau of the Census; 1929 and 1941 from Twentieth Century Fund, adjusted to Census levels by *Fortune.*

Vacation time—Estimated by *Fortune* from intermittent surveys of vacation policies by B.L.S. and employment data of the Department of Commerce. The level was linked to the number of vacation weeks reported by the Bureau of the Census in postwar years in its surveys of the labor force. The total number of vacation weeks is very probably understated because the Census vacation data are merely by-products of employment surveys which, e.g., may fail to interview persons away on vacation.

The two trends, down in hours and up in paid vacations (practically all the vacations above are with pay), help different segments of the leisure market, shorter hours promoting casual leisure pursuits while vacations encourage heavy travel expenditures. Since 1929 the average gain has been about one leisure day per week from shorter hours, and nearly one week per year from vacations.

one week. During the war the percentage jumped to about 80; and today perhaps 90 per cent of all production workers are covered by such plans, the average vacation approaching two weeks. The whole U.S. working force received in 1953 over 60 million weeks[1] of vacation time—substantially all with pay—against less than 18 million in 1929.

Beyond doubt, the leisure market benefited from this increase in leisure time: the question is why did it not benefit more. The answers again display the trickiness of that market. Most of the gain in leisure time has come from the reduction of working hours, the five-day week, and more holidays. Only a few leisure pursuits will fit this "bits-and-pieces" time—for which there are other strong claimants. On the average, the time spent en route between home and work is probably greater today than before the war, especially if the home is in suburbia. And seven million owners of new homes are discovering how many things there are around the house to fix, replace, improve, and otherwise spend time on.

While these factors do not apply with the same force to vacation leisure time, other factors do. The wage earner accustomed to receiving one week of vacation, and budgeting for it, has a whole set of habit patterns to change when he suddenly gets two weeks. At first his budget may lead him to spend the extra time at home. Later he may extend his vacation travel, but with a determined effort to keep down the added cost. And since his travel expense to any given point is the same whether he goes for one week or two, almost never will his vacation spending increase as fast as his vacation time.

The Thin, Even Spread. Overshadowing both these points, however, is the fact that the people who have made the most gains in leisure time do not have the most leisure dollars. The time gains of recent years have gone first of all to factory workers, service employees, and others who lay out 11 or 12 per cent of their income on leisure instead of 15 or 16.

The ability of Americans to spend far more for fun than for clothing or shelter of course stems from the spectacular increase in consumer income, up from the $160-billion to $170-billion neighborhood just after the war to nearly $250 billion last year (though about half the increase was due to price rises). But the share of this income devoted to leisure and recreation behaves as no other major consumer market does.[2] In food, clothing, housing, home goods, or cars, there is always some point along the income scale beyond which the consumer spends a smaller share of income for that particular class of goods. But the share for leisure and recreation, as demonstrated earlier in chart form, starts climbing at an average income somewhere between $3,000 and $4,000—and keeps going up.

Thus the rulers of the leisure market are those families with incomes of over $4,000; and their number has increased mightily. In 1929 only 20 per cent of the family units enjoyed incomes of over $4,000 (expressed in 1953 dollars) and received some 54 per cent of all income. In 1953 over 45 per cent of the family units were above $4,000 and garnered over 72 per cent of the income. In other words, nearly half the nation's 51 million family units and nearly three-quarters of the income were on the up slope of the leisure-market curve.

The Laggard. Again the tantalizing question appears: why didn't leisure spending grow to, say, $35 billion or $40 billion? For, as noted earlier, a rise in real income should increase the leisure market's share.

A partial answer lies in the details of income redistribution. The general income reshuffling brought about by taxation and other factors has slowed the expansion of the upper-bracket groups who spend most for leisure, while raising many of the erstwhile low-income families past the $4,000 mark for the first time. Thus today's leisure dollars are spent by more people, but the leisure market's share of total spending has been held down by income redistribution. It is the *character* of the leisure market that has changed: the yacht splurge of the late 1920's is replaced by the outboard boom of today.

This may explain why leisure's share of total income did not rise; but why did it go down? The fact that two individual leisure items, liquor and movies, have been hamstrung by special difficulties provides part of the answer; but force of habit plays a still larger part. As remarked in the discission of vacations, all consumers spend this year's income with last year's habits. This tendency of leisure expenditures to lag behind income changes can be seen frequently over the past twenty-five years. Leisure spending did not fall so fast as income just after the 1929 crash or start to climb so quickly in 1934. During the 1938 recession, and the momentary faltering of 1949, the percentage of income spent on leisure went up.

So long as real income keeps rising, the share that goes to the leisure market will probably never achieve its full potential.[3] Thus the economists' dictum that leisure spending should increase faster than income probably needs that standard hedge, "in the long run." And the long run, in this instance, will probably arrive only if income ceases to rise for two or three years.

Man-Made Opportunity. The change in U.S. leisure activities in the last decade or so is reflected in the growth of facilities, especially those for active sports. The National Recreation Association estimates that the number of

Table III—Leisure Spending Outpaces Family Income

	PER CENT OF INCOME SPENT ON LEISURE IN 1953	
Income* Group	Per Cent of Income* Spent on All Leisure Items	Per Cent of Income* Spent on Leisure, Excluding Alcohol, TV, Dining Out
$0-$1,000	14.8	9.0
$1,000-$2,000	13.1	7.7
$2,000-$3,000	11.7	6.6
$3,000-$4,000	11.6	6.5
$4,000-$5,000	12.2	7.1
$5,000-$7,500	13.7	8.0
$7,500-$10,000	15.0	8.9
$10,000 and over	16.1	9.6

*Consumers' cash Income after taxes.

Source: Fortune.

The level of leisure spending, charted as a percentage of 1953 cash income, reaches its low point just under 12 per cent for families making about $3,000, then rises steadily. As in other markets, the high percentage of leisure spending by the lowest income groups (including many youngsters and oldsters without dependents) merely shows that many spend more than they make.

playgrounds, swimming pools, beaches, and similar public recreation areas increased from 21,500 to about 37,500 between 1940 and 1950. Where facilities did not rise, neither did the sales of corresponding sporting goods. Municipal tennis courts, for example, did not increase substantially in the decade of the 1940's—nor did outlays for tennis equipment. On the other hand, an increase of 20 per cent in softball diamonds and nearly 40 per cent in baseball diamonds yielded a growth of about two and one half times in sales of baseball and softball equipment.[4]

Playground and similar facilities, however, affect leisure activities more than they do leisure expenditures, since the only consumer spending involved is for sports equipment. Much more important to consumer leisure expenditure are the larger state and national parks, including national monuments, shrines, forests, etc., that require heavy travel expenditure by visitors.

A number of new areas have come under the jurisdiction of the National Park Service since 1929, some by the creation of new parks (Great Smoky, Everglades, Olympic, etc.), some by transfer from other government agencies. The number of visitors has soared—from 21 million in 1941, to 25 million in 1947, to 46 million in 1953. But since Park Service appropriations have not nearly kept pace with the increase in both areas and visitors, the national parks today are faced with a grave crisis.

A national park such as Yellowstone, Bryce Canyon, or Great Smoky, for all its awesome scenic attractions, cannot be fully used without access roads, camp grounds, lodges, overnight cabins, restaurants, water supply, comfort stations, etc.—not to mention trained personnel. The existing national parks, monuments, etc., especially the ones now underdeveloped, could accommodate a vastly larger number of vistors than they now do —*if* there were a sharp increase in personnel and facilities. Lacking such an increase, overcrowding will limit the number of visitors and result in serious physical deterioration of the parks themselves.

Land of Waters. If Americans of a few generations hence begin to develop webbed hands and feet, they can blame it on their forefathers' love for the water. Three of today's largest and fastest-growing outdoor sports—fishing, boating, and swimming—are water sports; most summer homes and cottages are built near water, which is also necessary to most camping and to a great deal of U.S. hunting (of ducks and geese, for example); and the number of pleasure trips that are journeys toward water would almost suggest that the U.S. is a desert. While traditional coastal and lake areas have shared in this growth of water recreation, the big push has come from the creation of new inland waters.

The TVA system, lying mainly within Tennessee, Kentucky, and Alabama, has created in a lake-poor region more than a score of artificial lakes and a total water area of 600,000 acres and 10,000 miles of shorelines. In addition, the Army Engineers have completed ninety-three reservoirs, ranging from a few hundred acres to over 300,000 acres in size, located for the most part in the Southeast, the Middle West, and the Southwest. The grand total is further swelled by a number of lakes created by other public and private power dams.

These lakes have made fishing, not hunting, the favorite U.S. outdoor sport. Two decades ago hunting licenses exceeded fishing licenses by over a million, 5,900,000 to 4,850,000. In 1953 the totals were 17,650,000[5] for fishing, 14,800,000 for hunting. (The issuance of licenses alone yielded the states over $75 million in revenue that year.)

The Future of Leisure. Although the leisure market probably will *not* keep exactly in step with the economy in the next few years, any forecast of leisure spending still demands careful statement of the assumptions as to the amount and distribution of consumer income. Here are three possibilities:

If consumer income were to level off (income distribution remaining unchanged), leisure spending should continue to rise slowly for two or three years to about $33 billion, as leisure habits catch up with economic facts.

If real consumer income keeps going up at the 1947-53 rate through 1959 and is distributed about as in 1953, then leisure spending could rise from the present $30.6 billion to a little over $39 billion. This assumes that the increase in income will lift more consumers into heavy-leisure-spending brackets, and thus implies that leisure spending's share of total expenditure will also increase. Finally, if the persistent tendency of leisure spending to lag behind changes in income were to keep the leisure share the same as today, the figure would be about $37.5 billion. This figure, or something close to it, is the most likely from a general economic standpoint–i.e., at most, leisure spending will rise moderately, but at best it will not realize all its potentials if income grows rapidly.

A Little More Liquor. The question, then, is whether this additional $7 billion is likely to be spent, in fact, on individual leisure items. In the secondary leisure group, amounting to $12.6 billion, a gain of about $500 million should come from color TV, perhaps $100 million from records and record players, $100 million from dining out, and possibly $300 million from liquor. As for the small gain in liquor (small, that is, compared to the $9-billion liquor component), it is true that the social trends that set back liquor sales after 1947 are still in evidence. But since all of the dollar decline in liquor sales took place by 1949 and has since been followed by a slow rise, it is not unreasonable to expect a $300-million increase by 1959. On the other hand, if per capita consumption holds up, population growth alone would mean an increase of $1 billion in liquor spending.

Several items within the $18-billion primary leisure group–notably spectator sports and amusements (including movies), and books, magazines, and newspapers–show limited promise, though they should all rise moderately, but others should rise substantially. Gardening, up from about $500 million in 1947 to almost $700 million in 1953, should reach perhaps $900 million by 1959, since the largest gardening expenditures come when a new home is first being landscaped and planted, and the housing boom as yet shows no signs of tapering off. Home power tools should grow from the present $200 million to say, $300 million, with the 1947-53 growth rate flattening a bit as this market shifts toward a replacement basis.

Outdoor recreation seems sure to enjoy healthy growth. Total boat expenditures may surpass $1 billion by 1959, against 1953's figure of $800 million; and the durable and nondurable recreational goods market, which rose from $1.8 billion in 1947 to nearly $2.3 billion in 1953, should show about the same growth, and perhaps even reach $3 billion, by 1960.

The Migrants. All in all, there might be a $2-million advance in the $9 billion spending on primary leisure other than travel, but the biggest promise of new leisure expenditure lies in foreign and domestic vacations. Foreign pleasure travel, up by about $100 million a year over the last six years to the present $1.1-billion figure, should rise to $1.5 billion by 1959 or 1960, assuming present travel costs. And domestic vacation spending will probably rise from the present $8 billion to about $10 billion. These projections follow the 1947-53 pattern, when vacation spending grew faster than leisure expenditures as a whole and accounted for about half the total increase.

But foreign and domestic pleasure travel could increase still more. If North Atlantic air-tourist fares could be brought down to perhaps $350 for a summer-season round trip, foreign travel might soar another $500 million, to $2 billion. Cheaper steamship passage would not have the same effect, for most Americans have only two or three weeks of paid vacation. One possibility for a further increase in domestic travel lies in the expansion and refurbishing of such facilities as the national parks and inland waters, and the creation of new facilities. If both things are done, the estimate for domestic pleasure travel could be boosted another $1 billion, to $11 billion, within the next five to six years. And both these travel conditions will help to determine whether the 1959-60 leisure market reaches only $35 billion or rises above $37 billion.

This discussion of where the leisure market will be five years hence serves to outline one of that market's peculiarities, the fact that it promises to outperform the economy in nearly every conceivable circumstance—whether the economy is rising rapidly, rising slowly, holding steady, or even declining.

The other peculiarity of the leisure market is its dependence on time. Theoretically, if the American people had not lengthened their vacations at all since 1929, the increase in production—and income—that would have resulted from this extra labor time would have been roughly $5 billion. However, the *demand* created by the longer vacations has expanded the vacation market by more than $5 billion. Extra leisure time tends to result in extra leisure spending. Thus the leisure market may eventually become the dynamic component of the whole American economy. For while consumer appetites for necessities may become sated, where is the limit to the market for pleasure?

Notes

1. This minimum estimate is derived from Census Bureau postwar surveys of the labor force, not especially designed to yield vacation data. The actual number of vacation weeks per year may be as high as 80 million. *Fortune's* prewar estimates are also tied to the Census surveys.

2. The exception is the luxury market, which behaves like the leisure market and of course often overlaps it.

3. This may also apply to a rise in dollar income offset by higher prices; for the consumer tends to measure his leisure spending, much more than his necessity spending, in dollars unrelated to the price level.

4. Golf is a special case. The rise in all golf expenditures from about $82 million in 1939 to $230 million in 1953 reflects increased use of golf courses, especially private courses, which were "underused" during the depressed Thirties.

5. There are more fishermen than this, of course. No state (except California) requires a license for salt-water fishing, and many states exempt farmers, children under a certain age, and other special groups from the license requirement.

The Amount and Uses of Leisure

By GEORGE A. LUNDBERG, MIRRA KOMAROVSKY and MARY ALICE McINERNY

THE GENERAL pattern of life for any given group is determined primarily by three factors, namely, the activities engaged in, the amount of time devoted to each, and the more customary relationship of these activities. The broad outlines of the rhythm and pattern of life for the population as a whole are readily apparent to casual observation. The peak loads of transportation, the rush hours of eating establishments, and the opening and closing of shops are objective indexes of the general scheme of life in any urban or suburban community. There is reason to believe, however, that this pattern varies considerably both as to content and time sequence among different demographic and occupational groups. Especially is this true with regard to leisure activities. The routine and sequence of the major paid occupations have been studied with some fullness by economists and efficiency experts. Such studies range from general inquiries into hours of work to specific job analyses. But the uses of leisure time, being presumably subject to the relatively "free" choice of individuals, and therefore supposedly largely unstandardized, have never been subjected to detailed study from the standpoint of the individual or the special group.

The ideal method of securing a detailed record of activity would presumably be to assign an investigator (preferably unseen) with a stop watch and a motion picture camera to follow an individual during every minute of the twenty-four hours, or at least during his waking hours.[1] Since this technique is not generally practicable in the present stage of social research, we are forced to rely on the next most adequate method, namely, the individual's own account of his activities. Certain difficulties with this method at once present themselves. First of all, it is necessary to secure the voluntary coöperation of a number of people of different classes in what is likely to seem to them an unjustifiable invasion of their privacy, and likewise a study of little interest to them individually. In this connection the usual problems of representative sampling are also encountered. Secondly, such a record must rely more or less on the memory of the person keeping it even though he makes notations every few hours. Thirdly, the accurate description of an activity in brief words and the subsequent interpretation of these records is fraught with obvious difficulties. The problem of defining such terms as work and leisure in objective terms was discussed in the first chapter. Furthermore, several activities may be carried on at the same time and may overlap

From Chapter IV, *Leisure: A Suburban Study,* by George A. Lundberg, Mirra Komarovsky and Mary Alice McInerny.

in various ways. All of these difficulties and many others have been encountered in the present study and are fully recognized.

At the same time it should be noted that these difficulties are no greater in a statistical study such as we have here attempted than they are in the voluminous nonstatistical discussions of the same subject. The difficulties only seem less in the latter because rigid definitions of activities and units of time can be largely avoided. Our technique of meeting these difficulties and attempting to reduce them to a minimum is described elsewhere. To supplement the data regarding the more or less public uses of leisure, . . . we induced several thousand people [in Westchester County, New York] to keep detailed diaries for us regarding their actual activities for periods ranging from one day to seven days. The information secured from these diaries, representing a total of some 4,460 days as voluntarily recorded by 2,460 different individuals, constitutes the bulk of the subject matter of the present chapter.[2]

The activities of a people are subject to a great variety of classifications according to the purpose at hand. We have been governed in our classifications by considerations of what was found objectively possible on one hand and certain practical considerations on the other. In the latter connection we had in mind the possible value of the data to educators, social workers, and other community leaders in indicating the feasibility and desirability of proposed community programs. Adult education is, for example, at present receiving much attention. What groups today have time available for such education and when do they have such time? What activities which today occupy leisure time might be displaced by an expansion of adult education programs? To what extent can further recreational, educational, or artistic facilities be profitably expanded in view of present habits of leisure? What changes in these habits would appear to be possible and desirable? A consideration of present uses of time is the first step toward answers to these questions.

THE PLACE OF LEISURE IN THE GENERAL PATTERN OF LIFE

Before proceeding with a detailed analysis of daily life we should glance at the general organization of activity for a longer period. In the first place, there is some variation in activities with the seasons, chiefly during the months of June, July, and August. The traditional functioning of the schools during the other nine months tends in a large measure to impose considerable routine and uniformity upon a large portion of the entire community. This is perhaps especially true in the suburbs, where children are not only more prevalent, but also more dominating, in community life. The chief variation in activity during the summer season is the prevalence of vacations varying in length from a week to a month. The other principal variation in the week-day routine is the occurrence of special holidays. We shall consider vacations and special holidays in later chapters, and confine ourselves here to a consideration of work days and ordinary week-ends.

Excluding vacations, we may say that the year for most people in Westchester consists of 280 working days, 52 Saturday afternoon holidays, 52 Sundays, and 7 special holidays.[3] Thus 85 days (including the half holidays) per year constitute the standardized time allowance for leisure in an industrial civilization. This appears to be somewhat more than were allowed in ancient Egypt or in ancient Athens but a good deal less than in ancient Rome and Tarentum.[4] Our present holiday pattern is a combination of the Hebrew Sabbath with the Greek-Roman festivals, plus a half-day per week concession of our own resulting from the efficiency of the machine. The Saturday half-holiday was apparently first introduced under pressure from labor organizations.[5] More recently it has probably been adopted as a feeble reaction against the doctrine of work as a virtue, and in any case it is undoubtedly destined to be considerably augmented in the near future. As this manuscript goes to press a series of industrial codes propose a general shortening of working hours in the interest of industry itself as well as of society as a whole. The lag in this development is to be accounted for chiefly on the grounds of habit and an individualistic profit economy. We have traditionally labored so hard to avoid the danger of physical want that we find it difficult to rest when the danger is past.

THE USES OF TIME

We have seen that the dominant pattern of activity with respect to time is 280 working days grouped into five-and-a-half-day parcels interspersed with a day and a half of holiday. From our study in Chapter II of the general population groupings and from our general knowledge of the significance of these groupings from the standpoint of variations in the uses of leisure time, we secured the diaries from members of the groups represented in Table I. This table together with Tables II and III indicate the chief classifications and conclusions to be drawn from the data.

The Nonleisure Activities. For our purposes in the present study we have separated all activities into the two main categories of leisure and nonleisure. We have included in the latter category those activities which are usually considered in a high degree obligatory or necessary to the maintenance of life and which are on the whole instrumental to other ends rather than ends in themselves. Also, they are the activities which general current attitudes do not regard with that peculiar emotional tone with which they regard leisure. Each specific activity has, however, been separately tabulated so that anyone who disagrees with our classification of them by these two main categories may recombine them according to any plan which he considers more relevant to his own purposes.[6]

Proceeding on this basis we find that work and sleep are for the great majority of people still the two major, as well as the most stable, individual items of time expenditure. We may at the outset, therefore, consider what part of the twenty-four hours are devoted to each of these activities.

If one drives through almost any residential area of Westchester between

*Table I—The Mean Number of Hours Per Day Devoted to Leisure and Nonleisure Activities**

OCCUPATIONAL GROUP	TOTAL			
	No. of Cases	No. of Days	Non-leisure Hours	Leisure Hours
	1	2	3	4
Labor†	70	258	18.3	5.7
White-collar‡	494	1,482	17.0	7.0
Professional and executive	97	307	17.2	6.7
Unemployed	95	285	14.6	9.0
Housewives	107	425	14.7	9.2
High school students	1,544	1,544	16.6	7.4
College students	53	159	17.2	6.8
Entire Group	2,460	4,460	16.6	7.4

OCCUPATIONAL GROUP	MALE					
	No. of Cases	No. of Days	Non-leisure Hours	Leisure Hours	S. D. of Leisure Mean§	S. E. of Leisure Mean
	5	6	7	8	9	10
Labor†	10	30	17.2	6.8	1.3	±.40
White-collar‡	268	804	16.7	7.3	3.2	±.32
Professional and executive	97	307	17.2	6.7	2.1	±.21
Unemployed	71	213	14.2	9.2	3.8	±.45
Housewives	....	....	......	....	....	....
High school students	773	773	16.6	7.4	3.3	±.27
College students	53	159	17.2	6.8	1.9	±.26
Entire Group	1,272	2,286	16.6	7.4	....	....

OCCUPATIONAL GROUP	FEMALE					
	No. of Cases	No. of Days	Non-leisure Hours	Leisure Hours	S. D. of Leisure Mean	S. E. of Leisure Mean
	11	12	13	14	15	16
Labor†	60	228	18.4	5.6	1.4	±.20
White-collar‡	226	678	17.4	6.6	2.7	±.27
Professional and executive	....	....	......	....	....	....
Unemployed	24	72	15.7	8.3	2.2	±.45
Housewives	107	425	14.7	9.2	2.2	±.25
High school students	771	771	16.6	7.4	3.1	±.25
College students	....	....	......	....	....	....
Entire Group	1,188	2,174	16.8	7.2	....	....

*"Nonleisure" has here been used to include sleep, paid work, care of household and children, care of self, transportation, and other items which the record indicates are primarily instrumental or incidental to the other activities rather than ends in themselves. Leisure includes all other activities. The daily averages are based on the total leisure and the total nonleisure for five workdays plus one Saturday and one Sunday, divided by seven, except in the case of high school students, where the figure for an additional Sunday per week is used instead of Saturday.

The significance of the differences in the average number of hours of leisure for the different groups has been tested by the formula $\sigma(m_1 - m_2) = \sqrt{(\sigma m_1)^2 + (\sigma m_2)^2}$. All the differences of 0.6 hours or more are statistically significant and in cases where the standard errors of the means are small, differences of as little as 0.3 hours are also significant.

†"Labor" includes males who used this term in designating their occupation. The females in this category consist mostly of factory women and about a dozen housemaids.

‡This white-collar group consists chiefly of office employees of a public utility company, excluding executive positions.

§The Standard Deviations and Standard Errors given in this table are based on the number of cases stated in columns 5 and 11 with the following exceptions: White-collar, male and female, 100 cases each; female labor, 47 cases; housewives, 78 cases; and high school students, male and female, 154 cases each. All samples were selected at random.

the hours of midnight and 6:00 A.M., it will be apparent that for large numbers of people those hours are set aside for sleep. This conclusion is corroborated by a detailed study of the time diaries.[7] The time spent in sleep and the activities incidental thereto are for the population as a whole the most stable single activity not only with regard to amount of time consumed but also with regard to the uniformity in the time of day devoted to it. We may say that in any general study of human activity in Westchester we may eliminate at the outset the hours 10:00 P.M. to 7:00 A.M. With slight variations at either extreme, these are the hours set aside by the overwhelming majority of the population for sleep. Individual parties, small groups, or transients at an occasional road house or lunch wagon, a policeman here and there, represent the chief exceptions. On Saturday night and Sunday morning there is a tendency to advance by an hour or two the schedule given above. But for most purposes one-third of the twenty-four hours are accounted for at the outset as indicated above.

The amount of time devoted to work and its distribution is not so uniform. For the gainfully employed (about 36 percent of the whole population at the time of this study[8]) a high degree of uniformity obtains. Thus the peak load of traffiic to the city occurs between the hours of seven and eight. Before this hour several trains have already taken a certain number to their work. In addition to this index, time diaries covering over two thousand working days for the gainfully employed revealed that in general the work day begins around 9:00 A.M. and that the preceding half-hour is mainly occupied by transportation to work. Even more pronounced in uniformity is the hour of closing at 5:00 P.M. By far the greatest peak load of the day on commuting trains is between 5:00 and 6:00. Thus the hours 9:00 to 5:00, interrupted by an hour for lunch usually between 12:00 and 1:00, from Monday to Saturday noon, represents the standard work time for the gainfully employed.

Another large group of the population for which the work day is standardized with high uniformity is the school children (about 20 percent of the population). From approximately 8:45 to 4:00 Monday to Friday, inclusive, during the months of September to June, inclusive, this group is in school. The gainfully employed and the school children constitute together about two-thirds of the population. For the overwhelming majority of these two major elements of the population we may say that the hours from midnight to 5:00 in the afternoon on week days are occupied by sleeping, eating, and work (classifying school attendance as work), together with the activities incidental to each, such as dressing, washing, and transportation. Leisure pursuits tend to fall during the hours from 7:00 to 12:00 P.M. for the gainfully employed and from 4:00 to 11:00 P.M. for the school children on work days.

The remaining third of the population consists for the most part of housewives. Their hours of work and leisure are very much more irregular than that of the classes we have just considered. Their work, consisting principally of preparation of meals and care of the house and children, tends to fall into two periods, namely, from 7:00 to 10:00 in the morning and from 5:00 to 8:00 in the evening. Their diaries designate an average of thirty hours per week devoted to household and children (the principal item of work for this class) as against about forty hours work per week indicated by gainfully employed women. A great deal of irregularity is present in this pattern for housewives, however. The combination and overlapping of activities among this group also makes difficult any accurate classification of the various activities and the time devoted to each.

We may then summarize the quantitative aspect of nonleisure activities of the 2,460 individuals from whom we received records as follows (See Tables I and II):

1. Of the approximately seventeen hours a day consumed by the nonleisure activities, all classes spend on the average from eight to nine hours in bed. The laboring man and the unemployed of both sexes indicate the largest average time devoted to sleep. But the differences are not great. (See Table II.)

Table II—The Mean Number of Hours Per Day Devoted to the Principal Nonleisure Activities

	SLEEP	PAID WORK* 7 day Basis	PAID WORK* 5½ day Basis	CARE OF SELF	TRANS-PORTATION	HOUSEHOLD AND CHILDREN	TOTAL NON-LEISURE
	1	2	3	4	5	6	7
Labor:							
Male	9.0	5.9	7.5	0.8	0.9	0.6	17.2
Female	8.3	6.7	8.5	1.0	1.0	1.4	18.4
White-collar:							
Male	8.3	6.4	8.1	0.7	0.8	0.5	16.7
Female	8.2	5.9	7.5	1.0	1.1	1.2	17.4
Professional and executive:							
Male	8.2	6.2	7.9	0.7	1.2	0.9	17.2
Unemployed:†							
Male	9.1	2.2	2.8	0.7	0.5	1.7	14.2
Female	8.9	1.0	1.2	1.0	0.7	4.1	15.7
Housewives‡	8.6	0.1	0.0	1.0	0.8	4.2	14.7
High school students:§							
Male	8.7	6.0	7.5	0.7	0.7	0.5	16.6
Female	8.7	5.6	7.2	0.9	0.6	0.8	16.6
Male college students	9.5	5.6	7.1	0.6	1.1	0.4	17.2

* The figures in column 2 are based on the total number of hours paid work for five working days, one Saturday and one Sunday divided by 7. Column 3 is based on the same data but divided by 5½.

†Unemployed was defined as without regular employment.

‡The corresponding figures in the study of Oregon farm women (*op. cit.*) were: sleep, 8.5; care of self, .7; transportation, .3; household and children, 10.6; total nonleisure, 20.1.

§The figures in columns 2 and 3 for high school and college students refer to school work. Only in the case of males was there an item for paid work amounting to half an hour a day.

2. The gainfully employed according to their own testimony devote from seven and a half to eight and a half hours a day to their work for five and a half days per week. This amount of time does not vary greatly between different classes, though it tends to be highest for white-collar men and unskilled women.
3. Housewives devote a little more than four hours a day to household and

children but this work is distributed over the seven days. If we consider this for comparative purposes on a five and a half day basis the "work" item rises to about five and a half hours a day as against seven and a half for white-collar women and eight and a half for factory and shop girls, housemaids, and other unskilled women.

4. The other nonleisure activities consist for the most part of a daily item of from one half to one hour for transportation and a similar amount of time devoted to "care of self"—washing, shaving, bathing, dressing, etc.
5. Altogether these nonleisure activities occupy an average of between fifteen and eighteen hours a day. Actually they occupy from seventeen to twenty hours during five and a half days with Saturday afternoon and Sunday off, for most of the gainfully employed. It amounts on the upper extreme to an average of 18.2 hours for housemaids and factory girls as compared to 14.8 hours for housewives[9] and unemployed men.
6. Conversely, we find that the amount of leisure varies from five and a half hours per day for housemaids and factory girls to somewhat over nine hours for housewives. Here again we must remember that in the case of factory girls this leisure time comes mainly on Saturday afternoons and Sundays and amounts to only about an hour a day during week days. The amount of leisure of the housewife is not only larger by three and a half hours a day than that of the unskilled working woman but the leisure time is more evenly distributed.

Suburban housewives are conspicuously of the leisure class. They are also the most ready to assure the investigator that they have "no leisure at all." It is clear that, just as the paid work of the gainfully employed is frequently mixed with leisure and recreational elements, so the leisure of such groups as housewives is frequently occupied with more or less obligatory activities which no longer yield the peculiar satisfactions which we associate with leisure pursuits.

For the population as a whole, in so far as our sample is representative, the amount of leisure averages a little more than seven hours a day on a weekly basis. We turn now to a consideration of how this leisure is spent.

The Leisure Activities. We have seen that the people of Westchester spend an average of about seventeen hours a day on sleep, work, and various necessary minor activities connected with these main consumers of time. There remains an average of seven hours a day devoted to various leisure pursuits. What are the principal activities which occupy these hours?

Ninety percent or more of the leisure of all classes (except students) is divided between seven activities, namely, eating, visiting, reading, public entertainment, sports, radio, and motoring. (See Table III.) With a few exceptions they consume time in the order named.

Eating[10] is the principal and most stable single item. It occupies on the average an hour and three-quarters a day.

Next in importance for all classes is visiting. It varies from an average of forty-five minutes a day, for male students, to two and a half hours a day for housewives. The average for the whole group is an hour and a half a day.[11]

Third in importance with regard to the amount of leisure time devoted to it is reading. There is an exception to this ranking in the case of students, which is accounted for by the fact that most of their reading is connected with their school work and therefore was listed under "work." Unskilled women show the lowest average time, 38 minutes a day spent in reading as a leisure pursuit, which is closely approximated by high school girls with an

Table III—The Mean Number of Minutes Per Day Spent on Certain Leisure Pursuits

Leisure Pursuits	*White-Collar* Male 1		*White-Collar* Female 2		*Professional and Executive* Male 3		*Housewives* Female 4		*Labor* Male 5		*Labor* Female 6	
No. of Cases	268		276		97		107		10		60	
No. of Days	804		678		307		425		30		228	
	Min.	*Per cent of Total Leisure*	*Min.*	*Per cent of Total Leisure*	*Min.*	*Per cent of Total Leisure*	*Min.**	*Per cent of Total Leisure*	*Min.*	*Per cent of Total Leisure*	*Min.*	*Per cent of Total Leisure*
Eating	114	26	116	29	106	26	106	19	101	25	109	32
Visiting	81	18	94	24	79	19	151	27	94	23	74	22
Reading	61	14	43	11	74	18	84	15	95	23	38	11
Entertainment	45	10	48	12	15	4	44	8	35	9	29	9
Sports	34	8	19	5	40	10	16	3	35	9	20	6
Radio	34	8	18	5	22	5	29	5	32	8	45	13
Motoring	20	5	25	6	15	4	10	2	12	3	13	4
Clubs	8	2	3	1	10	2	61	11	0	0	0	0
Miscellaneous	35	8	33	8	40	10	50	9	5	1	8	2
Total	438	99	399	101	401	98	551	99	409	101	336	99

*The comparable figures for Oregon farm housewives (Agricultural Experiment Station, Corvallis Oregon, *Bulletin* 256, November, 1929) are as follows: eating, 76; visiting, 69; reading, 58; entertainment, 5; sports, 6; radio, 9; clubs, 30; miscellaneous, 51; total, 304.

	Unemployed Male 7		*Unemployed* Female 8		*H. S. Students* Male 9		*H. S. Students* Female 10		*College Students* Male 11		*Total* 12	*Mean* 13
No. of Cases	71		24		773		771		53			
No. of Days	213		72		773		771		159		4,460	
	Min.	*Per cent of Total Leisure*	*Min.*	*Per cent of Total Leisure*	*Min.*	*Per cent of Total Leisure*	*Min.*	*Per cent of Total Leisure*	*Min.*	*Per cent of Total Leisure*	*Min.*	*Min.*
Eating	109	20	119	24	101	23	104	23	98	24	481,311	108
Visiting	111	20	138	28	53	12	90	20	45	11	399,209	90
Reading	128	23	78	16	44	10	40	9	44	11	252,858	57
Entertainment	28	5	43	9	44	10	53	12	20	5	186,806	42
Sports	67	12	24	5	86	19	38	9	95	23	173,838	39
Radio	52	9	31	6	45	10	35	8	37	9	150,375	34
Motoring	15	2	19	4	14	3	10	2	2	1	68,622	15
Clubs	5	1	7	1	9	2	9	2	15	4	55,311	12
Miscellaneous	37	7	42	8	48	11	65	14	51	13	169,571	38
Total	552	99	501	101	444	100	444	99	407	101	1,937,901	435

average of 40 minutes, white-collar women with 43 minutes, and high school boys with 44 minutes. All the other classes devote from one to two hours a day to this activity. The average for the whole group is 57 minutes.

Public entertainment varies considerably from group to group in its importance as a leisure pursuit but in most cases falls into fourth place.[12] Women indicate more time spent in this way than do men, with the exception of the unskilled labor group. Professional and executive men devote the least time (fifteen minutes) to this pursuit. Unemployed men and unskilled laborers spend about twice as much, and students, the white-collar class, and housewives spend about three times as much time. In the case of housewives, also, club activities take precedence over public entertainment as a leisure pursuit. An average of an hour a day for club activities is indicated by housewives, whereas this is an activity of negligible importance to all other classes. The average for public entertainment for the whole group is 42 minutes.

The amount of time devoted to active participation in sports also varies considerably. Male college students devote the most time (about an hour and a half a day) to this activity with high school boys a close second. Men spend more time than women on sport. Housewives devote the least time (an average of 16 minutes per day) to this activity. Professional and executive men average forty minutes a day, the unemployed indicate over an hour and others spend an average of about half an hour daily on sports. The average for the whole group is 39 minutes but only about 60 percent of the different groups indicated participating at all, except students and unemployed men.[13]

The average number of minutes a day spent by the whole group on listening to the radio is 34. Unemployed men spend more time in this way than any other class, an average of 52 minutes for the whole group. Forty-five percent spent no time on radio, however, which means that the actual average for those who spent time in this way was about an hour and a half a day. White-collar women spend the least time (18 minutes) in this way, and more than half of them indicated no time spent on the radio. Professional and executive men also neglect the radio: the average time is 22 minutes, and less than half of this group use the radio; the rest spend an average of about half an hour day on this activity. Housewives, high school students, and the unskilled are the principal radio fans both in percentages participating and in time spent.

Listening to the radio is frequently combined with other activities such as reading newspapers or doing housework. The figures used above represent the time devoted to the radio as the only, or at least the major, activity. For example, "reading and radio" is classified under "reading"; "talked and listened to radio" under "visiting"; and so on. The peculiar practice of leaving the radio playing during the entire evening while a complete set of other activities takes place—eating, conversation, reading, cards, dancing, and housework—clearly indicates the incidental nature of much radio listening. This practice also explains the enormous amount of time spent on the radio as indicated by special studies of radio listening in which the entire time spent within hearing distance of a playing radio has been estimated.[14] For our present purpose it was deemed more significant to consider only time spent consciously and deliberately listening to the radio and so designated by the informant himself.

Finally there is motoring which receives an average allotment of fifteen minutes of the day's leisure. The range is from ten to twenty-five minutes.[15]

In addition to the above activities in which all, or a large proportion of the people engage to a greater or lesser degree, there is a tremendous variety of pursuits in which comparatively few engage, but on which these few may spend considerable time. These activities have for the most part been thrown together in Table III under the caption of "miscellaneous." A detailed list of all of these activities would fill several pages.[16] Such general groupings as "visiting" and "public entertainment" are also blanket terms covering a wide variety of activities, each of which was separately designated in the diaries and tabulated under more detailed headings. Unless, however, a considerable proportion of the whole group engaged in the activity, it would be misleading to compute an average time expenditure for this pursuit for the group as a whole. Thus, a computation of the amount of time spent in active participation in some art by the unskilled of both sexes during a total of 258 days revealed a daily average of less than three minutes or about twenty minutes a week. For purposes of comparing different groups with respect to their relative degree of participation in the arts, such a figure may have value. But for our present purpose we are more interested in the question as to what proportion of the whole group indicate any participation whatever in the activity. For example, we are more interested in the fact that only 42 percent of professional and executive men devoted any time to church than in the fact that the daily average per person per day of time spent by this class on this activity was eleven minutes, or seventy-seven minutes a week. We turn, therefore, to a consideration of the more detailed and less general activities which we have grouped above under the heads of "visiting," "public entertainment," and "miscellaneous."

The principal items separately tabulated under the head of "visiting" were cards and dancing. The average daily amount of time spent on cards varies from five minutes for students to 58 minutes for housewives. But with the exception of housewives, over 60 percent of each of the other groups spent no time on cards. Among housewives only 34 percent indicated no time spent in this way. This means that for the 66 percent of all the housewives studied, namely, those who played cards at all, the average time per day devoted to it would be about 75 minutes or over eight and a half hours a week. Likewise, the unemployed of both sexes indicate an average of about 45 minutes a day spent on cards. But 60 percent of this class do not play cards so that the actual amount of time spent by those who do play is nearer two hours a day. Over 60 percent of the white-collar class do not devote any time to cards. The daily average for those who do play is consequently raised from approximately 25 minutes for the whole group to about 45 minutes a day for the group participating.

In summary, it may be said that somewhat over 60 percent of the whole group studied spend no time on cards. The remaining 40 percent average from three-quarters of an hour to an hour and a quarter a day on this activity. It is an activity most popular among housewives, a higher proportion of whom engage in this activity and who also spend more time per day on it than any other class.

Women of every class with the exception of housewives spend twice as much time as men in dancing. From 75 to 90 percent, however, indicated no time spent on this activity. The average for the whole group is about two and a quarter hours per week for women, excluding housewives, and less than half that time for housewives and men. The fact is that dancing is an activity engaged in with frequency by only about 15 percent of the population who spend about eight hours a week on it.

The other items besides cards and dancing which we have grouped under the general head of "visiting" are the parties, dinners, teas, calls on neighbors and friends, conversation, and other social intercourse of a non-business character.[17] This sociability item is a fairly large one ranging from a maximum of an hour and 38 minutes a day for housewives to 40 minutes a day for unskilled women and high school students. It is for all classes a large and more constant item than either cards or dancing. Possibly both of the latter activities have sometimes been included by the keeper of the diary under more general heads such as "sociability," "party," etc. Consequently we have grouped them together in our main tabulation under the head of "visiting."

The main items in our "miscellaneous" category are church attendance,[18] active participation in the arts, correspondence and telephoning on non-business subjects, idling, and a scatter of other activities not easily classified. The church receives the greatest attention from housewives, who devote an average of about two hours per week to this institution and its work; other classes average a little more than half this amount. The activity is not included at all, however, in from one-fifth to two-thirds of the diaries of different classes. Of the unskilled women 80 percent indicate participation in church work as against about 50 percent for housewives, 53 percent for white-collar men and unemployed women, 70 percent for white-collar women, and 42 percent for professional and executive men. Among high school students, girls devote twice as much time as boys to this activity, the average for the former being about 80 minutes per week.

Apparently only a small proportion of the population participates actively in any of the fine arts or crafts. In this category was classified all active artistic performance whether done in class or at home, such as playing some instrument, writing poetry, embroidering, woodcarving, painting, and so on. Only about 10 percent of any class indicated spending some time on such activities. Of those who did designate such participation nearly all indicated that they spent less than an hour a day on it.

The number of cases upon which most of the above comparisons of occupational groups are based is entirely too small to make the results valid as more than tentative hypotheses for further study. If carried out for larger numbers and for more homogeneous groups, over longer periods of time, the results might yield generalizations of basic importance regarding leisure behavior. For example, a question of great scientific, as well as practical, interest is this: As the amount of leisure increases, how is the proportion of time spent on different activities affected? This is a question which has been widely studied with respect to pecuniary income and expenditure under the caption of "Engel's Laws." Engel undertook on the basis of extensive studies of the budgets of workingmen's families to determine how variation in income affected the proportion spent for food and other common items. Hundreds of similar studies all over the world have since been made. The importance of the same kind of generalizations regarding the expenditure of leisure time is obvious. If we compared adequate samples of the uses of leisure of those who have much of it with those who have little, it should be possible to draw certain tentative conclusions regarding some of the principles governing leisure behavior.

Some such correspondences may be noted in Table III. For example, the figures show that as the amount of leisure increases the proportion of the total spent on eating decreases for all classes. If we consider only extremes and compare, for example, housewives with unskilled women (the highest and the lowest respectively in amounts of leisure), we find that the following generalization hold true: As the amount of leisure increases, the proportions spent on eating, sports, radio, motoring and public entertainment decrease, while the proportions spent on visiting, reading, and clubs increase. The same generalizations hold true if we compare unemployed women (having next to the largest amount of leisure) with unskilled women (lowest in amount of leisure), except with respect to the proportion of time devoted to sports. Again, the rule as first stated is found to apply to a comparison of housewives and white-collar women, two groups with a difference of 2.6 hours of leisure per day.[19]

If we compare unemployed men with professional and executive men (the highest and the lowest, respectively, in amounts of leisure), we have to revise the above generalization as follows: As the amount of leisure increases the proportions spent on eating, motoring, and club activities decrease, but the proportions spent on all other items increase. If we attempt comparisons between groups with less difference in the absolute amount of leisure we encounter increasing irregularities and exceptions, as was to be expected.

Thus, housewives have the most leisure (9.2 hours) and also spend a larger proportion (27 percent) of it on visiting than does any other group. This suggests that as the amount of leisure increases, the proportion spent on visiting also increases. But white-collar women with less leisure (6.6 hours) than unemployed women (8.3 hours) and high school girls (7.4 hours) spend a higher proportion (24 percent) of it on visiting than do the latter classes. Similar exceptions occur to a great many of the more refined comparisons, especially where the differences in the amounts of leisure between the groups is not large and where we encounter important group differences in age, sex, cultural background, and economic status.

The most general conclusion which we might tentatively suggest on the basis of the whole body of data is that increased leisure for women means an increased proportion of time spent on visiting, reading, and club work, while men tend to spend greater proportions not only on visiting and reading, but also on public entertainment, sports, and radio. The statistical insignificance of some of the differences on which this conclusion is based must again be emphasized. At the same time, the logical consistency and compatibility of all the results of the analysis of these diaries with common sense observation and other reliable knowledge should be noted.[20] To verify the tentative generalizations here suggested, there is needed, first, a study of larger samples of individual groups which are economically, as well as culturally, homogeneous. Secondly, we need studies of the variations in the expenditure of leisure according to cultural status, with economic status held constant. That is, groups of similar pecuniary income, but of different occupational and educational status, should be compared with respect to their quantitative and qualitative leisure schedules. Thirdly, the same type of comparisons should be made by age and sex rather than by income to determine the relative significance of such variables as sex, age, occupation, education, and income in determining the proportion of leisure expended on different pursuits. Such a study on a really comprehensive basis would yield generalizations of basic importance regarding leisure behavior.

The above study of over 4,400 days of human activities as they occurred in the lives of several thousand individuals exhibit an amazing uniformity of objective content and pattern in the midst of what is from another point of view almost infinite diversity. The qualitative variety within the quantitative uniformity exhibited by our behavior records is, of course, just as important a subject for study. Indeed, we may say that perhaps the broadest single conclusion regarding the uses of time by different groups is this: The type of activity, the time spent on it, its sequence in the pattern, and even, perhaps, the subjective response it arouses in the individual, are quite similar, but their qualitative differences as objective events may be very great. For example, sleeping is an activity in which all classes engage to about the same extent, at about the same time, and presumably with approximately the same subjective satisfaction; but for some classes it means lying upon pillows of down in clean, well-ventilated, and artistic surroundings, while for others it means reposing upon a rude couch or park bench amid dirt and squalor. Yet both satisfy the same basic need. Likewise, our diaries reveal a high degree of uniformity for all in such activities as eating and work.

They do not reveal the difference between the elaborately served meal in the millionaire's mansion and the dinner in the laborer's flat. The subjective satisfaction may be the same in both cases. The work of the bank president and that of the bricklayer frequently occupy the same hours, and both cause fatigue and the need for rest and recreation. The broad categories of activity are highly uniform among all classes.

The same holds true to a high degree of the recreation of these classes. Thus we find from our diaries that nearly all classes participate to some extent in nearly all activities. The attempts of lower classes to imitate the upper and their ability to do so as a result of our technical ingenuity is common knowledge. Thus, all classes spend considerable time in reading; but there is great variety in what they read, as we shall see in a later chapter. Most classes report a fairly uniform amount of time spent on sports, public entertainment, and the radio. But in some cases, for example, this time record represents golf played on a private golf course in the middle of the afternoon with a caddy, at a gross cost of from $10 to $50 a round; in others the same game is played on the adjoining public course after a day of arduous labor, at a total cost of $1; or it may represent pitching horse shoes in the back yard. "Went to the theater" may mean a highly sophisticated play in New York City, or a Wild West movie. The same holds true for nearly the whole gamut of recreational and leisure pursuits, as subsequent chapters will show.

We have reviewed in preceding chapters the characteristics of the people themselves, the conditions under which they live and the multiplicity of their recreational facilities and activities. The present chapter has indicated the more general patterns of life with special emphasis on the time devoted by different classes to different activities. It remains to consider some of the qualitative and subjective aspects of these experiences. What are some of the more common combinations of these activities and under what conditions are they regarded as especially satisfying? In short, what do these people consider a good time?

"GOOD TIME" PATTERNS

As an approach to this question a schedule was circulated chiefly among high school students asking for a brief account of the most enjoyable occasion within the past year which they could recall. In addition to certain objective questions regarding time, place, companions, and activities, each student was also asked to state his own idea as to why he enjoyed this occasion. The results of the first part of the inquiry appear in Table IV.

We find that in the overwhelming majority of these 796 cases, some other place than home was the scene of the pleasant occasion reported. Only 5 percent of the boys and 17 percent of the girls had their "best time" at home. Almost equally pronounced is the preference for sports and outdoor activities, though here also the boys are more nearly unanimous than are the girls. The chief difference between the preferences of boys and girls is in

Table IV—Place, Companionship, and Activities on Occasions Considered a "Good Time" by High School Students

	MALE	FEMALE
Number of cases	318	478
Place	Percent	Percent
Home	5	17
Elsewhere	95	83
Companionship		
Alone	1	1
Couple	5	3
Small group (3 to 10)	59	55
Large group (more than 10)	31	34
Activities		
Sports	73	55
Outings	26	26
Party	3	18
Excursion	9	9
Theater	9	8
Reading	2	3
Dancing	7	19
Amusements (Recreation parks)	8	12
Music	2	5
Driving	2	8

the more frequent mention of parties and dancing by the latter. With respect to companionship we find that the small group of from three to ten persons is by far the most popular. Next in importance is the large group. Very few high school people have memorably good times alone or with a single companion.

The study of a smaller group of adults (about fifty) with the same schedule shows the same preference for the outdoors away from home. At least two-thirds of this group describe outings of some kind as the occasion of their "best time." As will appear later we find in this group more occasions where a single couple of opposite sex constituted the group and where good conversation was mentioned as the main activity. A more adequate account of the real form and content of the good-time pattern both for children and adults can, however, be secured from a consideration of actual cases including the participant's own estimate of his reasons for finding the occasion enjoyable. We turn, therefore, to a consideration of such instances.

The thrill of a new experience is, among high school students at least, frequently the element which makes a "good time."[21] One high school boy, the son of an Italian plasterer, designated a trip to the Bronx zoo as the scene of a memorable afternoon because on this occasion he had his first ride on a horse and fed a seal. Another describes his best time as taking place on a farm and remarks: "I had never ridden a horse before and liked it very much." The pleasure of a new experience is also reflected in the frequency with which the learning of something new is mentioned as being the reason for an occasion being pleasurable. "I learned to swim and to dive," says a girl of fourteen, the daughter of a laborer. Another says, "I enjoyed it because that day I learned to swim and because that was the first time I ever knew how." "I liked swimming at that particular time," says a third, "because I was taking lessons and was improving greatly." "I always enjoy anything I do for the first time," says a fourth, "whether it is successful or not."

The suggestion of physical danger is also a big factor in making an activity pleasant. Thus the various roller coasters at Playland and Coney Island receive mention as affording much pleasure. One boy of sixteen after designating riding the Jack Rabbit at Coney Island as the occasion of a pleasant afternoon explains: "The Jack Rabbit is a little railway on which you first go up a steep hill and then down. This gives plenty of excitement especially for the girls and young boys." Likewise, a girl enjoyed a boat ride because "the waves were very high and the boat rocked from side to side. At first I was afraid but when I got used to it I didn't want to go home." Likewise, a boy describes an accident while coasting as the best time he can recall. After hitting a rock and a tree and upsetting the entire party with minor casualties he remarks with emphasis: "This is the best time I ever had in spite of my split lip."

Somewhat similar in psychological background is perhaps the following account of a good time by a boy of thirteen: "The play was going off good when someone made an uncalled-for remark and put me into a fit of laughter, and then I forgot my part and was alive instead of dead. But still I think I had the best time then."

Sometimes the pleasurable element in an occasion was the release from customary norms of conduct. For example, one girl reports: "We played many games that would seem ridiculous to us now such as tag, hide-and-seek, and other baby games. The reason why I enjoyed it was because everyone acted with enthusiasm and none acted too old or too young to join in the games."

Competitions for prizes are frequently mentioned as the reason for enjoying an occasion. The more analytical frankly admit that the reason for their enjoyment was that they appeared to good advantage. Says one boy of sixteen, after designating a certain baseball game as the one especially pleasurable occasion: "I played extremely well and made a good impression upon my fellow playmates." "I hit a home run," is the simple and sufficient reason another boy enjoyed a ball game.

Sometimes such occasions arouse dreams of future careers. "I like baseball," says one boy, "because I wish to play on some big team some day." Another enjoyed a jazz orchestra practice for a similar reason. At other times the past is brought back. "I enjoyed this hunt," says an Italian boy of sixteen, "because it brought back memories of the old pioneer days when men had to hunt in order to eat."

The good times of high school boys are associated to an overwhelming degree with outdoor sports. Among the girls, parties frequently receive mention. For example:

> All had gathered at the home of the hostess. We were giving her a surprise sweet-sixteen party. After she had arrived and found everything so unexpected we presented her with birthday gifts which she opened. A little later the radio was turned on and everyone began to dance. After we tired, some of the guests played the piano and guitar, also the ukulele. When the clock struck 10:30 p.m., the hour our hostess was born, a buffet dinner was served. I enjoyed this party the most because of its simplicity and sincereness.

"I enjoyed it [a birthday party]," says another, "because they were all about the same age as myself and the crowd was not a rough bunch. The girl who gave the party was also nice because she treated everyone alike and made you feel at home."

Occasionally an intellectual event is designated as the best time. A girl of fifteen, the daughter of a bricklayer, describes one such occasion: "Our ancient history class went down to the Metropolitan Museum of Art in Central Park. We devoted most of our time to the Egyptian part and the rooms on the Stone Age. We then went to the Automat for lunch and later returned to the Museum. We visited the Obelisk and came home." A few (chiefly girls) designated concerts as memorable occasions, some as listeners and some as participants. A few students likewise refer to the satisfaction of solitude. "I enjoy walking through the woods alone," said one boy in describing why he had a good time on this occasion. "I like the air, beauty and solitude of the country," said another. Enjoyment of nature is frequently mentioned. But on the whole it must be admitted that esthetic experiences are not frequently emphasized as among the major forms of a good time of high school people.

In a number of cases the release from unhappy family situations receives mention as the reason for enjoying an occasion. A carpenter's daughter, sixteen years of age, describes a trip to a farm and says: "I enjoyed this very much because it made me forget all my troubles at home with my big sisters and brothers." Another describes a trip to the seashore with swimming, and dancing and says: "I enjoyed that day a whole lot. It made me forget some of the home troubles that my mother and dad have most of the time."

The pressure of economic circumstances is also reflected occasionally. One girl after describing a good time at the Wilson Woods swimming pool remarks, "The only objection is that it is too expensive to go to this pool and often I have to go during the free period when it is too crowded." One boy of eighteen, the son of a telephone linesman, after describing a very commonplace outing says: "It was about the first real outing I ever went on and it certainly was an enjoyable experience."

Release from school and its discipline is still appreciated. The following laconic account is of the classical tradition: "The beginning of vacation. No home work. Had all day to play and did not have to wash your ears and get dressed up."

Congenial companions, coöperative activity, a departure from every-day routine, and the stimulus of a game—these may be said to be the almost universal requirements of a good time for people of the high school age. The following description of an afternoon trip to Rye Beach is perhaps typical of thousands of "good times" in Westchester.

In the morning the boys and I cleaned the car which was very dirty. There was fun in it with everyone giving a helping hand. On our way to the beach we sang and ate ice cream. As we reached the beach we rushed to the water and played games for a couple of hours. We then visited the amusements. On returning we ate our lunch and called it a day.

Among adults we find as previously noted a more frequent reference to the so-called serious pleasures, or at least adults show a tendency to give a more sophisticated rationalization of their enjoyments. Also, the sex pattern which receives almost no mention among high school students is frequently mentioned among adults. For example, take the following description by a college student of a good day in the woods with the girl friend:

Hiked four hours in the morning—gay repartee. Lunch for two hours, with some romping and display of affections. Some more hiking, much more leisurely—and talk. Home, followed by visit to some mutual friends. My lady companion was a young intelligent girl of whom I am quite fond, and whose company I always enjoy. Both of us like vernal surroundings and naturally find great enjoyment in hiking. During the hike, we discussed topics of interest to us both such as the significance of the increased insanity rate in the U. S., Rousseau's natural man, the meaning of civilization, the validity of psycho-analysis, sex problems of today, etc. Thus this day was most pleasant for me for three reasons: (1) I was with a girl whose company I enjoy; (2) a vernal background, with a sunny atmosphere encouraging gayety of spirit; (3) discussion of topics that allowed for the expansion of my ego through showing my "erudition" on vital topics. Also, the evening gathering with friends provided a pleasant social ending to a "perfect day."

A variation of this pattern is reported by a male teacher of twenty-four as follows:

Traveled with two classmates—men of my age—from New York to Massachusetts. Called on three women slightly younger than ourselves—all college students, charming, clever and—ah!—pretty. We were fêted comfortably, played bridge and danced a bit. Then we visited a neighborhood "movie" house and enjoyed a clever comedy entitled "Annabelle's Affairs." Immediately thereafter we took the femmes home. Kissed goodby, and wended our way homeward. We had had, we all thought, one of the finest—if not the finest—times of our short lives. We all like outdoor traveling and enjoyed driving the car in shifts of an hour each. We each had a special liking for the company of the particular woman we went to visit. Bridge was a special hobby to us—and we all played a fair game. Dancing filled the gaps. The theatre filled another—and gave us each a chance to get better acquainted. The trip home was somewhat tiresome but we succeeded in making it enjoyable by a little good riding, and exceptionally clear roads—and a little nap here and there. After a good night's rest we all vowed we'd do it again any day in the year. Wouldn't almost anybody?

As the years roll by the above pattern loses some of its vigor and variety. A man of forty-nine, a social worker, gives the following account, and incidentally drops a hint for recreation officials:

> The day was memorable because of the radiance of an early summer morning and the natural beauty of scenery. It was just an uneventful, ordinary day such as one spends in the mountains while on vacation but it gives me the most vivid pleasure in recollection of all my varied recreations during the year. In the company of a friend who is mentally and spiritually congenial to me we hiked for three hours, then sat down to rest and to enjoy nature. We discussed at times the latest books we had read or discussed subjects in which we were mutually interested. At noon we cooked our lunch and rested, observing the birds, rabbits and squirrels around us. In the afternoon we made a leisurely descent from the summit of the mountain enjoying the sunset and its gorgeous reflections on the gathering rain clouds. I liked this day chiefly because:
>
> 1. I was on vacation and was carefree.
> 2. I had a congenial companion whose silences I enjoyed as well as her conversation.
> 3. There was the great natural beauty of clouds, trees, sunshine, dazzling air, etc.
> 4. And *most important of all:* because our recreation had *not* been planned or directed by *anybody*. We went where and when we felt like it and had no predetermined destination.

Some of the same elements of enjoyment are found in the case of the tired advertising man of twenty-six who reports as follows on a week-end at the seashore:

> Looked forward to the two day week-end as a good rest. Therefore planned no specific activities. Found pleasure in sopping up sunshine varied by short periods of invigorating cold water swims resulting in complete contentment. The fact that the second couple fitted our mood and did not insist on excessive activity, conversation, etc. probably helped make the occasion a success.

It should not be assumed, however, that the adult male always finds his enjoyment in such philosophic, not to say vegetarian, calm. He also enjoys his golf, and his orgies. Thus, one memorable night extending from 7 P.M. to 4 A.M. is described by one young man. With three men friends the following schedule was followed:

> (1) To .... for a real Hungarian meal. (2) To the .... for a rotten movie. (3) to .... Restaurant (Irish Speakeasy). (4) To .... (Italian Speakeasy). (5) To .... (Mixed Speakeasy and Furnished Rooms). (6) To the .... (Walter Winchell's favorite speakeasy). (7) Don't remember name of this place. (8) Child's Savoy Restaurant for Coffee, etc. Then into Central Park Subway home.
>
> The meal was good. The movie rotten, but we were in "good time" mood and we left the theater mimicking the Doug Fairbanks, Jr. Hinglish Haccent. The liquor was very good stuff—I didn't feel sick the next day. We just ran wild over town and gave vent to some pent up energies, emotions, desires, drives, and what nots. Our Hinglish Haccent Haccompanied Hour Hiccups.

The women concur in the above estimates of the outdoors, motoring, hikes, and picnics. In fact, all of the above descriptions of outings could be multiplied in large numbers with women as authors. They also like their golf and swimming. But they occasionally find their best time in the theater, and report being "carried off into a world of beauty." Otherwise their reports differ from the men's chiefly in the more frequent reference to parties, dances, and social affairs (weddings, family reunions, etc.). Thus one housewife (and registered nurse) of forty-five reports:

Drove all day Friday to a wedding. Helped to get everything going in the proper way. A quiet very informal wedding. Served the wedding cake to guests and met *very* charming people, as *real* artists, etchers, and musicians. Saw bride off. Went into town and window shopped. Returned to home of very old resident and heard about the real old people. Looked over many very well taken photos. At sun down we drove out and watched the moon come up over the water. Drove all day Sunday to return home.

The homecoming and reunion at Christmas time is still a joyful occasion to this single woman of thirty-eight:

It began with the decoration of the tree on Christmas Eve, the children helping. On Christmas day, friends came in the afternoon. The elements of joy in this occasion for me were: (1) My homecoming and reunion with my family and friends (I had been away some months). (2) The happiness of the children in their gifts to which I had contributed. (3) The general excitement of a festive occasion in our family.

The routine of dining and dancing is under certain conditions still a "best time" even to the graduate student of twenty-one. She describes an evening at Central Park Casino:

I knew nearly all of the women and several of the men present. The dance was a nice size and the Casino has a gay and festive appearance. My escort was most congenial and attractive. (We all like to be proud of our friends.) We both love to dance.

Most of the enthusiasm for dancing and all of the references to cards, however, come from the humbler occupational groups, and especially from the Negroes. Bridge, whist, and dancing are repeatedly mentioned by the latter as the occasion of their best times. A messenger of twenty-four writes:

The game was whist. I enjoy the game because I usually hold good cards. Also we were evenly matched. The food was well prepared and I was extremely hungry at the time. The evening was cool and ideal for dancing. Also it is a good way to relax, exercise, and become acquainted with girls.

Another says:

I enjoyed playing bridge. I led the game thruout. I turned two grand slams. I got so much fun out of teasing my opponents. I enjoyed the wine because I drank just about enough to make me forget my worries.

Finally, and as evidence that traditional celebrations still have their followers, we may cite the following report from a colored gentleman of thirty-two regarding a memorable Independence Day.

Bought fire works and had a friendly battle. I enjoyed above activities first because I am used to having said fun from childhood and this being the first time I had the occasion of entering into same since those youthful days made it that much more enjoyable in every respect. I am sure it is the best time I can remember spending with such joyful results. It ended when one friend of ours had his pants leg blown off.

The above cases are, of course, little more than random selections, from about a thousand documents. Recreational patterns are almost infinitely varied and what is a very enjoyable activity at one time may be a bore under different circumstances. An electrical engineer calls attention to this fact in a very excellent statement which we may very properly use as a summary. After reporting as his "best time" a three-day trip with his wife to visit their best friends he remarks:

This is a tough questionnaire to fill out because there are different kinds of "best times" such as (1) Times of abandon and hilarity, as at a party of some kind, (2) Reunions and the like with friends and relatives, (3) Vacations and the like, (4) Periods of satisfaction over the progress or outcome of some activity or specific endeavor.

Every person could undoubtedly give a half dozen widely different occasions which he could truly designate as enjoyable. It is interesting to note that in spite of this fact a study of even a comparatively small number of cases reveals such striking preponderance of certain patterns as is reflected in the above tabulation and illustrations. There is evidence also that, greatly as the details of each may vary between different ages and classes, they have a certain elemental similarity. The main patterns are present among practically all groups. People engage in them in response to certain common needs. It is probably safe to assume that relative to the capacities of each the difference in daily amounts of leisure between any of the other classes is group, these activities yield essentially the same type of satisfactions.

SUMMARY AND CONCLUSION

We have attempted above to arrive at a schedule of time expenditure for different classes in a community. Such schedules of money expenditures have been extensively collected. It has long been customary to calculate per capita incomes for occupational groups, communities, and nations. Likewise, calculations have been made of the relative portions of that income which is spent by different groups for various goods and services. These schedules of average income and expenditure are felt to be of significance in describing planes and patterns of living. They are also used as the basis of estimates of the relative material well-being of different groups.

We have proceeded above on the theory that the distribution of time expenditure is an even more important index to the pattern of life, and possibly to the social well-being of the group, than is the distribution of money expenditure. It is true that in the present case the total income is constant. All ages, races, and classes have a daily time income of twenty-four hours at their disposal. But the amount of leisure time and its expenditure varies within fairly wide limits among different groups. It might, under other social conditions and under another system of ideals, be very widely different from what it is. For example, the full allotment of time might be spent on work for pecuniary status and on the eating and sleeping necessarily instrumental to such work. Under these condtions work and pecuniary prowess become an end in themselves rather than a means to other ends. On the other hand, the amount of time devoted to work for pay might be very much less than it now is. Indeed, such a time seems to be immediately impending. In any case, it is the size of this leisure time income and its expenditure which has concerned us in this chapter.

The justification for such study is found in one of the most general and deep-seated beliefs of the race, namely, the conviction that the main satisfactions of life are to be found in the time and the activities which remain when work (of the type considered above), sleep, and the activities necessarily incidental thereto are done. On the basis of this axiom, implicit in the behavior of people themselves, questions of the social well-being of groups must ultimately be measured largely in terms of the amount of leisure which they have and the uses they make of it. That these factors are in turn largely conditioned by economic considerations of work and pecuniary income is obvious. But this does not alter the importance of studying the way in which people spend their time.

A comparative study of the leisure income of these different groups reveals an extreme difference of over three and a half hours a day. Housewives have that much more leisure than gainfully employed unskilled women. If we leave out of consideration these extremes and also the unemployed, somewhat less than an hour. The distribution of leisure is, therefore, from any point of view very much more equitable than the distribution of material wealth.

When we look at the expenditure of this leisure we find that quantitatively, at least, there is also considerable uniformity in this respect. We find that over 90 percent of the leisure of all classes (except students) is consumed by eight types of activity, namely, eating, visiting, reading, public entertainment, sports, radio, motoring, and club activities.

Speaking very generally and tentatively, our study of the relative proportion of the total leisure spent by different groups on each of these classes of activity shows that as the total amount of leisure increases, the proportion spent on eating, sports, radio, and motoring tends to decrease, while the proportion spent on visiting, reading, clubs, and miscellaneous activities tends to increase. The proportion spent on public entertainment tends to remain constant or to fluctuate irregularly. Quite apart from questions of social well-being (which is here taken to mean only a high degree of achievement of whatever goals are sought), such a study of budgets of time expenditure constitutes a basic record of human behavior, and thus forms the raw material for scientific generalization.

The different occupational groups for which we have accumulated data on time expenditure also represent to some extent economic classes. Thus our group of unemployed consists of recipients of public or other relief or, at least, an economically submerged class. Only slightly better off is a group of unskilled laborers. The white-collar class and the professional and executive groups represent for the most part classes of increasing degrees of economic sufficiency. In addition, we have included samples of two important population groups dependent for the most part upon the other four classes, but different from them with respect to their schedules of time expenditure. These are the housewives and the school children.

Perhaps our most important practical conclusion from the data presented in this chapter is that the difference of greatest significance in the leisure of the various groups lies not in the total amounts nor in the distribution of that leisure between different activities. The most meaningful difference lies in the qualitative variations between the activities which we have been compelled to classify under the same captions. For example, we have determined the amount of time devoted by different groups to listening to the radio. From one point of view this activity is the same whether the hour is spent listening to the Philharmonic-Symphony in an all-Beethoven program or to the jazziest of the jazz orchestras. Yet we must recognize, from another point of view, a vitally and socially significant difference in the two cases, unless we are to set aside the time-tested value scale of the race in this field of experience. That scale of values is, of course, ultimately only a set of differential behavior patterns, built, like all other behavior patterns, on the basis of what has been found to be more or less permanently agreeable to the organism. They are, therefore, subject to the same kind of objective study as other behavior.[22] In the meantime, and for practical purposes, we need be concerned only with the fact that the experience of the race has yielded us such a scale of values. The main object of man's efforts and institutions, including science, is the achievement of the higher of these aims.

The relevance of this reasoning, and indeed its fundamental importance to the concrete situation we have studied must be apparent. Unless we can posit the social significance of quantitative and especially qualitative differences in leisure pursuits, the principal *raison d'être* for such institutions as the Recreation Commission, the Park Commission and all other educational and promotional services having to do with the raising of recreational standards disappears. The existence of these services is based on the assumption that it does make a socially significant difference whether, for example, children sing "Polly Wolly Doodle," or a Bach chorale. We know that people read what they have opportunity to read, that they listen to, and perform, the music which is available to them. The question is, shall the guidance and the opportunity be provided by such agencies as the school, the public library, and the recreation commission or by cheap magazine stands and cabarets. We have shown that the qualitative variety in pursuits of leisure is perhaps greater and more significant than the quantitative; the latter is largely beyond local control and hence outside the province of recreation and park commissions. The true opportunity of such organizations lies in the possibility of improving quality.

Notes

1. Behavior during sleep has been so studied by means of automatic cameras and clocks. See H. M. Johnson, "Is Sleep a Vicious Habit?" *Harper's Magazine,* CLVII (Nov., 1928), 731-41.

2. A number of similar studies of farm women have been made in recent years under the general direction of Miss Hildegarde Kneeland and of the Bureau of Home Economics, U. S. Department of Agriculture. *See especially* "Use of Time by Oregon Farm Homemakers," in Agricultural Experiment Station, Corvallis, Oregon, Bulletin 256, November, 1929. Similar studies, all of them of farm women, are reported in the following bulletins of Agricultural Experiment Stations: Bulletin 221, Rhode Island State College, Kingston, R. I., September, 1929; Bulletin 234, State College of Washington, Pullman, Washington, July, 1929; Bulletin 247, South Dakota State College, Brookings, S. D., March, 1930; Bulletin 146, University of Idaho, Moscow, Idaho, January, 1927. We have used essentially the same technique as used in Miss Kneeland's studies and, for the group to which her study was devoted, namely housewives, our broad categories of classification are sufficiently similar to permit comparison. Another study "How Workingmen Spend Their Time," by G. E. Bevans (Ph. D. Thesis, Columbia, 1913), employs a technique which does not permit comparison of his results with ours. These are the only published data on the subject that have come to our attention. Seventeen dissertations on the general subject are, however, announced in the *American Journal of Sociology* in its most recent list of student dissertations. Other comparable studies under way are those by Janet Fowler Nelson of the International Y. W. C. A. and one under the auspices of der Sozialpsychologischen Erkebungstelle des Psychologischen Instituts der Universität Wien.

3. New Year's Day, Washington's Birthday, Memorial Day, Independence Day, Labor Day, Thanksgiving Day, and Christmas Day. Other days, such as Lincoln's Birthday, Columbus Day, and Armistice Day are widely observed by special exercises but are not generally occasions for abstinence from work. In addition there are numerous church holidays observed by special groups.

4. C. D. Burns, *Leisure in the Modern World* (New York: Century, 1932), p. 260. This author gives the following estimates: Egypt, 53 days; Athens, 50 to 60 days; Tarentum more holidays than work days; Rome, "about one-third of the days of the year were *nefasti,* unlucky for work." These comparisons are of somewhat dubious value because of the much greater diffusion of leisure among all classes in modern times.

5. For an account of this development see Marion C. Cahill, *Shorter Hours: a Study of the Movement since the Civil War* (New York: Columbia Univ. Press, 1933).

6. Our original tabulations of leisure activities contain 17 categories as follows: active arts, church, club, correspondence and telephoning, cards, dancing, idle, meals, miscellaneous, motoring, public entertainment, radio, reading, sociability (visiting), sports, study, unaccounted for. On account of the negligible relative amount of time devoted to some of these activities they have for the most part been thrown into the "miscellaneous" category in our tables. Cards, dancing, and sociability have, however, been classified under "visiting."

7. According to our diaries, over 90 percent of the adults of all classes and both sexes arise on week days between 7:00 and 8:30 A.M. and retire between the hours of 10:00 P.M. and 1:00 A.M. The modal hour of arising is between 7:30 and 8:00 A.M. (Housemaids indicate half an hour earlier.) The hour of retiring is more varied, but 65 percent retire between 11:00 P.M. and 12:30 A.M., most of them in the last half hour of this period. On Saturday the peak for retiring is still between 12:00 and 12:30, but 20 percent retire after 1:00 A.M. as against 1.5 percent retiring after this hour on work days. Furthermore, about a third of those who retire after 1:00 A.M. do not get to bed until after 3:00 A.M. This tendency is especially evident among the white-collar class which in our records include disproportionately large numbers of young people. There is a corresponding skew upward in the rising hour on Sunday when the peak comes between 9:00 and 9:30 A.M. The hour of rising on Sunday is also more varied than on week days. Retiring hours on Sunday night are practically the same as on work days.

8. According to the Federal Census of 1930 about 43 percent were engaged in gainful occupations. However, at the time of this study about 8 percent were unemployed.

9. It should be noted, however, that our sample of housewives, being secured largely from the members of women's clubs is undoubtedly biased in the direction of the middle and upper

classes and therefore in the direction of more leisure than the housewives of the lower economic classes. The same should probably be said for all our classes inasmuch as only the literate could keep the required record. Also, the studies of the Department of Agriculture *(op. cit.)* show the farm housewife's leisure to occupy a little over three hours per day.

10. The classification of the activity of eating occasioned considerable difficulty. From one point of view it might have been excluded, in large part, at least, from the category of leisure, as a necessary and instrumental activity. On the other hand it is almost always the occasion for visiting and conversation and is chiefly a relaxation from work. Since it is a large and stable item of time expenditure, however, we have chosen to classify the routine eating of meals alone or with members of the household in a separate category under leisure. Such entries as "dinner party," "entertained friends at dinner," "served refreshments to friends," "refreshments with friends after theater," etc., are, however, included in the category "visiting."

11. This category includes cards, dancing, visiting with neighbors, friends, or members of the family, conversations, social affairs not classifiable as public entertainment or under other specific categories, and teas, luncheons, and dinners when the sociability factor is conspicuously emphasized as compared to the daily routine of meals. Some of the types of visiting are further discussed on a later page.

12. This category refers to passive entertainment at public places, e.g., attendance *as a spectator* at sports, movies, theaters, concerts, fashion shows, lectures, museums, amusement parks, etc. Active participation in entertainments at public places is classified under the head of the activity itself; e.g., "went swimming at the Y" is classified under "active sports"; "read in the library" under "reading"; "did pottery at the County Center" under "active arts"; "danced at a hotel" under "visiting", etc.

13. The fact that only 60 percent mentioned participating in sport during the days they were keeping our diaries (3 successive days in most cases) does not, of course, prove that they never participate in sports. To the extent that some people do not participate at all in the activities here listed, the group averages here given are below the actual average for the groups participating. Assuming that our diaries are equally representative for each group, however, the general average here used is satisfactory as a basis of comparing different groups with respect to the relative amount of time devoted to a given activity.

14. Thus Kirkpatrick *(Attitudes and Habits of Radio Listeners)* reports an average of about three hours a day on this basis. Furthermore, from 30 to 50 percent of those keeping our diaries reported no time spent listening to the radio, which means that the actual time spent by those who listened at all would be nearer one hour per day. But the difference in definition used by Kirkpatrick and other students of the subject as compared with our method of definition and classification as noted above undoubtedly accounts chiefly for the difference.

15. This category aims to include only motoring for pleasure as contrasted to "transportation" as a nonleisure activity. That is, such entries as "went driving"; "drove out into the country," etc., were classified under motoring. Considerable difficulty was experienced in making this separation especially in case of motoring to and from places of amusement. Such transportation is frequently in urban areas a necessary evil incidental to recreational pursuits, and consequently we have classified such necessary transportation in most cases under *transportation* rather than under *motoring.*

16. For example, the Hobby Show, held under the auspices of the Recreation Commission and the Kiwanis Club of Mt. Vernon in 1933, listed 72 separate classes of exhibits grouped into 12 sections. Besides drawing, painting, and the commoner crafts, there were listed collections of leaves, insects, stones, shells, stamps, post cards, coins, autographs, advertising buttons, and cigar bands.

17. *See* footnote 10 regarding the category of "eating."

18. This includes services, prayer meetings, Sunday school and other events directly connected with the church and religion. Purely social affairs under church auspices, such as bridge parties for church funds, are excluded.

19. It may be argued that the relation here noted between the amounts of leisure and its use is not the concomitant of variations in the amount of leisure but of other factors such as occupation, wealth, education, etc. But this objection is equally applicable to Engel's laws or any other similar statement of concomitant variations. That is, the observed variations in expenditure with variations in income are not invalidated or vitiated by the unquestionable fact that variations in income are themselves associated with variations in occupation, education, leisure, and other factors. The relative priority of some factors or antecedents in a given end-result is another question which involves fundamental problems in the philisophy of causation. In the meantime we are at liberty to select any factor in which we happen to be interested as an independent variable and regard the others as dependent. The fact that the above objection is not usually raised with respect to such formulations as Engel's laws but is likely to occur in similar statements regarding leisure is merely the result of our preoccupation with economic factors.

20. A favorite criticism in this connection of nearly all of this kind of research, in some quarters, is that it merely proves what "everybody knows." The answer is that a large proportion of the most laborious and painstaking labor of all science consists of (1) verifying or disproving what the scientist himself and probably most other people *think* they already know and (2) determining the degree to which it is or is not so. A further justification for the verification of what "everybody knows" is that techniques developed and tested in cases where the results are already known are then applicable to similar studies of situations which nobody knows.

21. A classification of 320 statements of high school students as to why a given occasion was enjoyable showed the following elements emphasized: new experience 21 percent; thrill and excitement 15 percent; friends and fellowship 15 percent; personal achievement 14 percent; good food 12 percent; beauty of nature 8 percent; freedom from home and school routine 8 percent; music, singing, etc., 8 percent.

22. We are not here concerned with philosophical questions of the "intrinsic" merit of different culture forms. We merely accept the value-scale broadly recognized, for whatever reason, throughout Western civilization over a considerable period of time.

Social Class Differences in the Uses of Leisure

By R. CLYDE WHITE

STUDIES have been made of the kinds of activities in which people engage at leisure, and some effort has been made to relate the use of leisure to broad occupational groups.[1] Recent developments in social class theory, however, have not been related to the subject. Does the class position of an individual affect his choice of leisure activities? Is his class position reflected in what he does in his leisure?

In a given district most children go to the same or similar schools. The same machines for communication are available to all people. These things make for uniformity. But there are a range of choice in schools and a very wide range of choice in communication. Ways of using leisure are matters partly of free choice and partly of obligations recognized, and the conditions for making the choices or recognizing the obligations exist in the individual's subculture.

The thesis of this paper is that the use of leisure is a function of class position and that the differentiation increases with age up to maturity.

Leisure is defined as all the time in a day when the individual is not sleeping, eating, or working. Attending school is equivalent to work for children or young people. Nine principal categories were used: leisure spent in parks and playgrounds; in group-work agencies financed by the community chest; in church; in museums; in libraries; at home; in ethnic groups; and in commercial amusements. These were broken down into thirty-one specific choices; remaining items (amounting to 6.6 per cent of the total) were put into the category "Other."

Reprinted from *The American Journal of Sociology*, Volume 61, Number 2 (September 1955), pp. 145-50, by permission of the author and the publisher.

In addition to information on what people did at their leisure during the week preceding the interview, information on the occupation of the head of the family, the sources of family income, and the kind of residential neighborhood was obtained for computing an Index of Status Characteristics (ISC).[2]

The Sample. The sample was a number of census tracts in Cuyahoga County, representative as to income, education, racial composition, distribution of occupations, condition of housing, and the age distribution of the population. Census tracts in which the median income was $5,000 or more were not used. Within each census tract the families to be interviewed were selected by a random method. Fourteen census tracts were chosen, and 673 usable schedules were obtained. The households contained 1,741 persons over six years of age.

Some use has been made of data obtained in another study of how junior high school students use their leisure. This study was based upon matched pairs of upper-middle- and upper-lower-class students and contained five pairs of boys and fourteen pairs of girls. It provided information on the amount of time students gave to various leisure pursuits in a given four days.

Table I gives the social class distribution of the families in the primary sample. This sample probably has too many lower-class families: to represent the population more accurately, there should be about 2 per cent in the upper class and about 10 per cent in the upper middle class.

Table I—Social Class Distribution of Families

SOCIAL CLASS	FAMILIES	PER CENT
Upper Middle	46	6.8
Lower Middle	184	27.3
Upper Lower	360	53.5
Lower Lower	83	12.3
Total	673	99.9

In the following analysis the data will be dealt with in four classes: upper middle, lower middle, upper lower, and lower lower.

General Patterns in the Use of Leisure. The number of activities per person during the week ranged as follows: for males, 5.1 for the upper middle class to 4.7 for the upper lower; for females, 5.5 for the upper middle to 4.3 for the lower lower. The difference in number of activities for males is small and may have no significance, but that for females is large and might be found in larger samples. This may reflect the amount of leisure when both sexes and all ages are considered together. If so, the upper middle class is likely to have more leisure. This possibility, however, is not supported by data from junior high school students. The amount of leisure per day in this study was found to be 8.5 hours for upper-lower-class boys and 8.1 for upper-middle-class boys; and for the girls the corresponding figures were 8.4 for the upper lower class and 7.1 for the upper middle. The difference for the girls is statistically significant.

The percentage of persons who engage in a particular kind of leisure activity varies widely among the social classes. Table II gives the use rates per 100 persons in each class.

Table II—Rates of Use of Leisure per 100 Persons of All Ages, by Social Class

MEANS OF USING LEISURE	Male UM	Male LM	Male UL	Male LL	Female UM	Female LM	Female UL	Female LL
Parks and playgrounds	1.6	7.0	12.2	23.0	1.9	6.7	6.8	16.4
Community-chest services	9.8	12.7	11.4	18.6	7.7	11.2	8.8	12.3
Church	49.2	68.4	66.2	76.1	53.8	73.8	81.1	82.8
Museums	1.6	3.1	1.2	7.1	0	4.1	1.6	4.9
Libraries	21.3	20.6	13.7	11.5	17.3	25.1	19.1	12.3
Home	339.3	274.6	272.8	254.0	374.5	298.9	288.1	258.2
Ethnic-racial organizations	4.9	6.1	8.5	0.9	3.8	3.7	9.4	0.8
Lecture-study	9.8	4.8	3.3	5.3	19.2	7.5	2.5	4.1
Commercial amusements	68.9	82.9	82.0	82.0	76.9	56.9	58.0	56.0

(USE OF LEISURE PER 100 BY SEX AND SOCIAL CLASS)

The rate of use of parks and playgrounds by class rises sharply from the upper-middle-class rate through other classes for both males and females. The same regular progression is shown in attendance at church services and, with slight variations, for a single class in rates for community-chest services, museums, and ethnic-racial organizations. For libraries, home activities, and lecture-study courses the trend is reversed and decreases from the upper middle downward. The rates for commercial amusements differ: low for upper-middle-class males and on a higher level for the other three classes; for females exactly the reverse, indicating a high rate for upper-middle-class females and a lower and almost even rate for the others.

The analysis was carried further by the discovery of certain patterns of leisure in the analysis by sex in the age groups six to seventeen and eighteen and over. These are shown in the use of parks and playgrounds, community-chest-agency activities, church, libraries, home games, radio, television, phonograph, reading, lecture-study, movies, and all other commercial amusements added together.

Chi-square tests of correspondence between observation and expectancy were made for male and female series separately, first by comparing the upper-middle pattern with the pattern of each of the other classes, then the lower middle with upper lower, and lower lower, and, finally, upper lower with lower lower. In only one pair of patterns for the younger age group, the LM-LL, was there a significant difference. Consequently, these are not presented. The inference is that children and adolescents are less aware of or habituated to social class behavior than those eighteen years of age and older. The general patterns of the younger groups are similar for all classes except the male LM-LL pattern.

In the older groups the behavior of the several classes is markedly divergent. Table III shows the chi squares with the corresponding values of *P* for 10 degrees of freedom in each pattern. (Any *P* larger than 0.05 is considered in this study to be too large to indicate statistical significance.)

Table III—Class Pairs and the Chi Squares for Discrepancies of Patterns, By Sex (Age Eighteen and Over)

CLASS PAIRS	MALE Chi Square	MALE P	FEMALE Chi Square	FEMALE P
UM-LM	19.86	.05—	14.55	.05+
UM-UL	38.05	.01—	39.04	.01—
UM-LL	43.26	.01—	30.86	.01—
LM-UL	21.19	.05—	20.35	.05—
LM-LL	60.83	.01—	17.98	.05+
UL-LL	20.67	.05—	22.13	.05—

For the six patterns chi square increases regularly with the spread between the two classes being compared. There is less regularity in female patterns. UM-LM and LM-LL differences are not significant at the 5 per cent level, but in all other comparisons the differences are significant beyond the 5 or 1 per cent level, though the patterns show unevenness in direction of size of differences. The data demonstrate a clear tendency toward divergence in the use of leisure among the classes for males and considerable evidence of such among the females.

Specific Patterns in the Use of Leisure. The behavior of two classes of the same age and sex group with respect to a single leisure-time activity was compared in two-by-two contingency tables.

Comparisons were made first for the younger part of the sample, that is, ages six to seventeen, by sex, as shown in Table IV. Of 23 pairs for the males,

Table IV—Comparison of Class Differences in a Single Activity Ages 6-17, By Sex (df-1)

CLASS	MEANS OF USING LEISURE	MALE Chi Square	MALE P	FEMALE Chi Square	FEMALE P
+UM-LM*	Home games	........†	....	5.39	.05—‡
+UM-LM	Phonograph	10.67	.01—	15.39	.01—
+UM-UL	Phonograph	4.98	.05—	13.79	.01—
+UM-LL	Phonograph	7.88	.01—	19.04	.01—
+UM-LM	Radio	7.78	.01—	6.17	.05—
+UM-LL	Radio	4.13	.05—	7.91	.01—
+UM-LM	Television	6.40	.05—	3.30	.05+
+UM-UL	Television	5.02	.05—	2.89	.05+
+UM-LL	Television	4.56	.05—	3.46	.05+
+UM-LM	Reading	....	....	4.06	.05—
+UM-LL	Reading	4.05	.05—	5.67	.05—
+UM-LM	Movies	6.73	.01—	7.92	.01—
—LM-UL	Parks—playground	5.66	.05—	6.31	.05—
—LM-UL	Church	6.61	.01	....	....
—LM-LL	Home games	8.62	.01—	....	....
—LM-UL	Home games	12.33	.01—	....	....
+LM-LL	Television	7.25	.01—	....	....
—LM-UL	School library	5.83	.05—	7.10	.01—
—LM-UL	Reading	5.12	.05—	....	....
—LM-LL	Movies	6.28	.05—	4.74	.05—
—UL-LL	Movies	5.57	.05—	3.98	.05—
—LM-LL	Parks—playground	4.24	.05—	....	....

*A plus or minus sign to the left of the symbols in the "Class" column indicates that the first symbol had more participation than expectancy or less.

†Dash indicates "obviously not significant."

‡Minus sign indicates beyond the level stipulated—a plus after .05 indicates that P is greater than .05 and that difference is not significant.

22 show significant differences, and in 14 pairs out of 23 for females the differences in frequency of a specified use of leisure are significantly different from chance variations.

Table V—Comparison of Class Differences in a Single Activity Age Eighteen and Over, By Sex

		MALE		FEMALE	
CLASS	MEANS OF USING LEISURE	Chi Square	P	Chi Square	P
+UM-UL*	Public library	4.12†	.05—‡	........§	....
+UM-LM	Home games	6.34	.05—	6.97	.01—
+UM-UL	Home games	9.51	.01—	7.30	.01—
+UM-LL	Home games	24.62	.01—	22.88	.01—
+UM-LM	Phonograph	10.94	.01—	6.52	.05—
+UM-UL	Phonograph	18.93	.01—	17.76	.01—
+UM-LL	Phonograph	9.47	.01—	16.78	.01—
+UM-LM	Radio	14.01	.01—	....	....
+UM-UL	Radio	22.21	.01—	20.97	.01—
+UM-LL	Radio	21.81	.01—	27.06	.01—
+UM-LL	Television	8.80	.01—	....	....
+UM-LM	Reading	6.12	.05—	....	....
+UM-UL	Reading	8.15	.01—	11.88	.01—
+UM-LL	Reading	11.67	.01—	3.22	.05+
+UM-LM	Lectures	14.99	.01—	3.51	.05+
+UM-UL	Lectures	25.87	.01—	17.58†	.01—
+UM-LL	Lectures	11.78	.01—	3.15	.05+
+UM-UL	Movies	8.13	.01—	4.87	.05—
+UM-LL	Movies	6.75	.01—	7.05	.01—
+UM-UL	Theater	4.56†	.05—	14.50†	.01—
+UM-LL	Theater	7.27†	.01—	4.19†	.05—
—UM-UL	Tavern	4.33	.05—	....	....
—UM-LL	Tavern	10.97	.01—	....	....
+LM-UL	Public library	7.84	.01—	4.18	.05—
+LM-LL	Public library	2.73	.05+	4.35	.05—
+LM-LL	Home games	11.05	.01—	9.89	.01—
+LM-UL	Phonograph	....	....	4.12	.05—
+LM-LL	Phonograph	....	....	5.50	.05—
+LM-UL	Radio	3.50	.05+	29.89	.01—
+LM-LL	Radio	3.31	.05+	32.48	.01—
+LM-LL	Television	18.19	.01—	30.57	.01—
+LM-UL	Reading	....	....	23.48	.01—
+LM-UL	Movies	6.23	.05—	2.79	.05+
+LM-LL	Movies	4.00	.05—	4.54	.05—
+LM-UL	Theater	3.73	.05+	8.13	.01—
+LM-LL	Theater	75.09†	.01—	15.75†	.01—
—LM-UL	Tavern	10.03	.01—	....	....
—LM-LL	Tavern	25.26	.01—	....	....
+UL-LL	Home games	10.01	.01—	9.95	.01—
+UL-LL	Television	4.37	.05—	56.42	.01—
—UL-LL	Tavern	8.15	.01—	3.14	.05+

*A plus or minus sign to the left of the symbols in the "Class" column indicates that the first symbol had more participation than expectancy or less.

†Number of persons in the two classes participating in this activity is 10 or less. Chi square was computed only to show direction of the present data which are believed to hold for larger samples.

‡Minus sign indicates beyond the level stipulated—a plus after .05 indicates that *P* is greater than .05 and that the difference is not significant.

§Dash indicates "obviously not significant."

The patterns for these young people are clear but somewhat irregular, like the blurred general patterns for young people mentioned above. Yet upper-middle-class boys use the phonograph, radio, television, reading, and movies proportionately more than do the boys of any of the other social classes. The same tendency exists for females except in the case of television. This form of entertainment or education is used with about the same frequency among females in all social classes. For males the value of *P* for television is .05—, which means it is barely significant. The lower-middle-class boys tend to use leisure in the same way, except that they use the school library more than boys of the upper lower and lower lower classes; but differences are much less marked among females of all classes.

The tests of difference in a single activity for persons eighteen years of age or older, like the general patterns in Table III, show much more regularity than they do for the young people, as seen in Table V. The evidence in this table that leisure activities are a function of social class is much stronger than in Table IV. Comparisons for males show significant differences in 34 out of 41 pairs, and among females the differences are significant in 28 out of 41 pairs. As shown by the size of chi square, the differences in descending order from upper middle class toward lower lower class for men are regular in the case of the use of home games, reading, theater, and tavern. Again the patterns are less clear for females. Taverns as a place to spend leisure are used by rising proportions of males when one moves from the upper middle class to each of the others.

Time Given to Various Uses of Leisure. The amount of time which individuals devote to specific activity in their leisure is probably as important as the choice of activity, providing as it does information on intensity of informal education.

While it proved impracticable to get estimates of time for specific activities from persons interviewed for the primary sample, the information was obtained in the more restricted junior high school study. One school was predominantly upper middle class and the other predominantly upper lower class. These two classes gave the tone and atmosphere to the schools. Random samples of twenty boys and twenty girls were taken at each school, and then in so far as possible matched pairs were used. Matching was done on sex, age, I.Q., and grade. Many cases were lost in the matching process, and in the end there were only five pairs of boys and fourteen pairs of girls. Two interviews were held with each child, and the home was visited. Table VI gives some of the time averages. The total number of hours for each sex is almost the same for upper-lower-class children as it is for those of the upper middle class, but the children of the upper lower class had about three hours more leisure during the four-day period than did those of the upper middle class; they devoted almost twice as many hours to radio, television, movies, and sports as did the upper middle class and correspondingly less to each of the other activities. The fact that the upper middle class spent more time on remunerative work and home duties than did the upper lower is a little surprising. However, the large difference in use of time was in recreation.

Table VI—Mean Amount of Time Spent in Certain Leisure Activities

MEANS OF USING LEISURE	MEAN NUMBER OF HOURS Male UM	UL	Female UM	UL
Church, reading, and school homework	5.3	1.0	4.7	4.1
Radio, TV, movies, and sports	12.0	21.7	7.7	14.1
Remunerative work and home duty	5.0	3.0	9.7	8.1
Total	22.3	25.7	22.1	26.3

Recreation of various sorts was divided into four categories, and chi squares for two-by-four tables were computed for each matched pair to determine whether the patterns for the use of time by the two classes were significantly different. In only one of the matched pairs of the boys were the differences not significant, and in three of them the differences were significant beyond the 1 per cent level. The time patterns for pairs of girls were not significantly different for six pairs, but for the other eight the differences were significant beyond the 1 per cent level in five and beyond the 5 per cent level in three.

Age and Sex Discrepancies. Why do the leisure activities of young people show such irregular patterns between social classes? And is there any way of accounting for the less well-defined patterns of leisure activities among adult females?

It is clear that the tendency to choose leisure activities on the grounds of membership in a particular social class begins in adolescence and becomes more pronounced in maturity. To test this hypothesis, the two middle classes were put together and the two lower classes were also put together to produce relatively large numbers of cases. Then chi-square tests for nine types (8 degrees of freedom) of activities were made for persons six to eleven years of age, twelve to seventeen years of age, and eighteen years of age and over. The chi squares were, respectively, as follows: 12.65, 17.01, and 51.83. As people get older and settle into the ways of the class to which they belong, they choose leisure activities which are congenial to their class.[3] The growing divergence between the uses of leisure by the middle class and lower classes is clear. Class differences are reflected by young people but are not fixed until maturity.

A reasonable explanation of the irregular variations in leisure activities of adult females is that most of them were housewives. The class of the family was determined on the basis of the head of the family, generally a man. While there is a strong tendency for men to marry within their own social class, some marry outside it, and the women bring their own family background into the new family. Hence, greater heterogeneity among the females of the sample is to be expected. Yet the class of the husbands is attributed to them, which results in an apparent confusion in the selection of leisure pursuits but which actually are probably inconsistent with their original family background.

In concluding, it may be observed that these findings have practical import for the planning of leisure services by both public and private agencies. They might also be taken into account by the manufacturers of communication equipment in planning marketing procedures.

Notes

1. George A. Lundberg, Mirra Komarovsky, and Mary Alice McInerny, *Leisure: A Suburban Study* (New York: Columbia University Press, 1934), esp. chap. iv.
2. W. Lloyd Warner, Marchia Meeker, and Kenneth Eells, *Social Class in America* (New York: Science Research Associates, 1949), esp. chap. x. Graduate students in the School of Applied Social Sciences of Western Reserve University did the field work on this study and assisted with the tabulation in the spring, 1953.
3. It would have been desirable to run a similar test for persons eighteen to twenty-four years of age had the sample lent itself to that test.

Leisure and Occupational Prestige

By ALFRED C. CLARKE

LUNDBERG'S observation, made twenty years ago, that social scientists have paid little attention to the problems of leisure,[1] holds true today with few exceptions, even though living habits have been altered by the further reduction of the work week.[2] Much of the previous research has been approached from a recreational, community, or welfare point of view. Many of these studies appeared in the middle thirties when the enforced leisure of the depression years stimulated communities to become increasingly concerned with the way in which people spent their hours away from work. Moreover, few studies have attempted to consider leisure in terms of the larger cultural context. For example, are the dominant values of the culture reflected in the differential use of leisure time? Is there a systematic relationship between social status and leisure styles? Does the occupational structure influence the ways in which work-free time is spent? Research evidence bearing on these and similar questions is extremely limited. In addition, the question

---

Reprinted from *American Sociological Review*, Volume 21, Number 3 (June 1956) pp. 301-7, by permission of the author and the publisher. (Copyright 1956 by the American Sociological Society.) This is a revision of a paper read at the annual meetings of the Ohio Valley Sociological Society, April, 1955. Originally titled, "The Use of Leisure and Its Relation to Levels of Occupational Prestige."

can be raised whether present leisure-time patterns are accurately portrayed by past research. It would appear probable that in recent years increasing amounts of spare time, accompanied by rising income levels, might tend to equalize the frequency of participation in many spare-time activities among different segments of the population. Perhaps certain alleged differences in leisure behavior are more apparent than real. It may well be, as Denney and Riesman suggest, that mass leisure has emerged so suddenly that we tend to interpret it by drawing on the stereotypes of an earlier era.[3]

The present research views leisure activity as an aspect of social stratification. It focuses on the role of leisure as a part of the life-styles of individuals occupying different prestige levels.

THE STUDY DESIGN

Although levels of prestige have been delineated in varied ways, it was felt that an occupational referent would provide a meaningful standard upon which leisure behavior could be based.[4] The North-Hatt Occupational Prestige Scale was selected as the instrument best suited to the requirements of the present study.[5] Through the use of this scale it was possible to translate the prestige level of individuals into a numerical score. A second instrument was constructed to measure certain configurations of leisure behavior. It included a section on frequency of participation in different types of leisure activities, a set of questions concerning preferences and attitudes, several items pertaining to membership in voluntary organizations, and a section of relevant background items. This instrument, in questionnaire form, was pretested on 100 male respondents randomly selected from the Columbus City Directory.

Since this study sought to delineate the nature of the relationship existing between different prestige levels and leisure styles, rather than focusing on the stratification system of a particular community, a sampling technique providing similar numbers of cases at different occupational levels was chosen. A design of this type would appear to have broader applicability for the study of social stratification in general, and could enable research findings to transcend local configurations with greater ease.

The selection of respondents was confined to urban, adult males, in order to increase the homogeneity of the sample so that significant differences in leisure among the strata studied could be more readily identified. Cutting points were established along the continuum of occupational scores dividing them into five prestige levels, and within these categories five separate random samples were selected. These samples encompassed the total range of occupational prestige. It should be noted that the term "prestige level," as used in this study, was defined as a category of persons with occupations of somewhat similar prestige status. They do not, therefore, represent "social classes" in the sense of clearly distinguishable categories "set off from one another." The limits of the categories were determined by the investigator and were chosen to facilitate analysis of the data.[6]

THE SAMPLES

The basic plan of the sampling technique was to obtain a random sample of at least 100 respondents at each of the five occupational levels. It was necessary at this point to estimate how many cases would have to be selected in order to yield these 100 respondents at each level. The distribution of occupational scores of respondents in the pre-test offered a basis for this estimate. The smallest number of returns occurred at the lowest prestige level. Only four persons from this group in the pre-test sample of 100 returned the questionnaire. Thus, in order to obtain 100 returns in the lowest prestige category, at least 2500 cases would be needed in the total sample. In order to allow for partially completed returns, approximately 3000 potential respondents were systematically selected from the Columbus City Directory and the name, address, and occupation of each was placed on a separate card.[7] The cards were then sorted by occupations into five prestige levels, yielding the distribution shown in the first row of Table I.

Pattern of Questionnaire Returns. In order to satisfy the requirements of

Table I—Questionnaire Returns by Occupational Prestige Level

	PRESTIGE LEVELS					
SAMPLE PROCEDURE	I	II	III	IV	V	TOTAL
Number in sampling population	192	348	1113	789	568	3010
Number of questionnaires sent	192	250	250	375	550	1617
Number delivered to addressees	180	234	226	331	475	1446
Number returned	134	128	112	117	108	599
Per cent returned*	74.4	54.7	49.5	35.3	22.7	41.4
Number of usable cases	130	122	110	109	103	574

*Percentages are based on the number of questionnaires returned which presumably were received by potential respondents. The percentages do not include questionnaires which were returned because of faulty addresses.

the sampling design, two mailings were necessary. In the first mailing, questionnaires were sent to persons at each level. As the returns of this mailing were received, it was noted that the frequency of completed returns varied directly with occupational prestige level. In other words, the higher the prestige level, the higher the frequency of returned questionnaires. Due to the operation of this factor, the first mailing did not produce the needed 100 cases at Levels IV and V. Additional names were then randomly drawn from the replacements in these levels. The returns from the second mailing were sufficient to produce the number of cases needed at these lower levels and increased the total sample to 574 usable cases, as summarized in Table I.

When the specific occupational information contained in the returned questionnaires was evaluated, it was found, in some instances, that the initial prestige rating, based on a brief occupational description in the City Directory, no longer applied. This necessitated a reassignment of some cases to either a higher or lower prestige category.[8] Although the research design called for limiting arbitrarily the number of cases in each level to 100, it was later thought best to utilize every completed questionnaire returned. Thus, the number of respondents varies from one level to another, and the total frequencies exceed 100 cases in each of the five prestige levels.[9] It should also be noted that throughout the classification of the data, five initial prestige categories were kept separated. The several samples were never combined and never treated as representative of a single universe.

THE FINDINGS

In the analysis of the data the first area of concern involved two related questions:

1. Is the frequency of participation in specific leisure-time activities significantly associated with occupational prestige levels?
2. If such association exists, in which prestige level is participation in a given activity most frequent?

For this analysis the chi-square test of significance was applied to relative frequencies of participation of the five samples. The results are summarized in Table II.

Table II—Leisure Activities by Prestige Level Participating Most Frequently

	PRESTIGE LEVEL PARTICIPATING MOST FREQUENTLY					
ACTIVITY	I	II	III	IV	V	LEVEL OF SIGNIFICANCE
Attending theatrical plays	X					.001
Attending concerts	X					.001
Attending special lectures	X					.001
Visiting a museum or art gallery	X					.001
Attending fraternal organizations	X					.001
Playing bridge	X					.001
Attending conventions	X					.001
Community service work	X					.001
Reading for pleasure	X					.001
Studying	X					.001
Entertaining at home	X					.01
Attending motion pictures	X					.05
Out-of-town weekend visiting (overnight)		X				.001
Attending football games		X				.001
Attending parties		X				.001
Playing golf			X			.001
Working on automobile				X		.01
Watching television					X	.001
Playing with children					X	.001
Fishing					X	.001
Playing card games other than bridge and poker					X	.001
Playing poker					X	.01
Driving or riding in car for pleasure					X	.01
Attending auto theater					X	.01
Spending time in tavern					X	.01
Spending time at zoo					X	.05
Attending baseball games					X	.05

As an inspection of this table indicates, significant differences were found to exist between occupational prestige and leisure use.[10] Most of the relationships were linear or near-linear in nature, that is, individuals with higher scores were more likely to participate frequently in some types of leisure pursuits and infrequently in others.[11]

Several relationships, however, were curvilinear. For example, the number of times a year the respondents played golf increased along with their prestige ratings—until the middle status group was reached. At this point the frequency of participation began to decline with higher occupational scores. Within this middle group the highest degree of participation occurred among those who classified themselves as "salesman." This would appear to be consistent with the wide spread conception that golf offers an excellent opportunity for pursuing business relations under informal and pleasant surroundings. It should also be noted that among the participant sports, golf represents perhaps the most pertinent example of how an activity is being transformed from the exclusive pastime of a few wealthy individuals to a popular pastime for many, representing diversified backgrounds in income and social status. The possible instrumental nature of this activity suggests, however, that membership in the "right" golf club could still be accepted as an important index of social status.

While examination of individual spare-time activities is useful in understanding leisure behavior, the design of this study also permitted an analysis of certain broader dimensions of leisure use. At this point the focus will shift to a consideration of these configurations.

Spectator-Type Activities. Although value-judgments differ considerably regarding the desirability of certain forms of amusement, the passive-spectator nature of some leisure pursuits has probably received more widespread criticism than any other facet of contemporary leisure behavior. While few people dispute the merits of participation in physical activities, there are those who seem to consider "spectatoritis" as a new national affliction. The idea is current that most Americans spend most of their spare time in a spectator role.

Information collected in this study, however, does not substantiate this observation. The respondents were asked to indicate the spare-time activities taking up most of their leisure time. An analysis of the responses when classified as "spectator" and "non-spectator" types,[12] revealed that the majority of respondents at each level devoted most of their leisure time to non-spectator activities. The data in Table III show the non-linear nature of this relationship. The largest proportion of respondents who spent most of

Table III—Percentage of Respondents Devoting Most of Their Leisure Time to Spectator Type Activities, by Prestige Level*

TYPE OF LEISURE ACTIVITY		PRESTIGE LEVEL I	II	III	IV	V
	N	120	96	126	98	96
Spectator		25.7	22.9	41.3	36.1	23.9
Non-spectator		74.3	77.1	58.7	63.9	76.1
Total		100.0	100.0	100.0	100.0	100.0

*Percentages are based on the number of respondents giving the necessary information. No data cases were excluded.

their leisure hours as spectators (41.3 per cent) occurred at the middle occupational level. This percentage decreased markedly as the upper and lower segment of the prestige continuum were approached. Only about 25 per cent of the respondents at Levels I and V devoted most of their spare time to activities that could be classified as constituting "spectatoritis." These findings appear to cast serious doubts on the validity of current conceptions concerning the allegedly ominous portions of time consumed by such activities.

Commercialized Leisure. Another criticism frequently leveled at the American leisure pattern is an alleged dominance of commercialized amusements. Hollywood movies, night clubs, and dance halls are sometimes defined as threatening the "basic values of the society." However, the empirical basis for this observation seems to be indeed limited. The surprisingly small proportion of respondents for whom commercial types of recreation occupied most of their leisure hours is shown in Table IV. It will be noted that the

Table IV—Percentage of Respondents Devoting Most of Their Leisure Time to Commercial Type Activities, by Prestige Level

TYPE OF ACTIVITY		PRESTIGE LEVEL I	II	III	IV	V
	N	124	98	130	104	99
Commercial		3.8	4.2	7.7	7.9	10.1
Non-commercial		96.2	95.8	92.3	92.1	89.9
Total		100.0	100.0	100.0	100.0	100.0

percentages representing these respondents varied inversely with prestige level.[13] As little as about 4 per cent of the persons in Level I specified activities which could be included in the commercial category. The proportion of respondents in this category increased to about 10 per cent at Level V. Even though commercialized recreation has become one of the nation's largest business enterprises, it still does not occupy a large share of the leisure time of the adult population.

Craftsmanship. In his provocative book, *The Lonely Crowd,* David Riesman advances the hypothesis that competence in craftsmanship during leisure hours may have developed new meanings in contemporary American society.

The man whose daily work is glad-handing can often rediscover both his childhood and his inner-directed residues by serious craftsmanship. An advertising man, involved all day in personalizing, may spend his week ends in the craftsmanlike silences of a boatyard or in sailboat racing. . . . But the craft-skill is valued more than ever before for its own sake, as in the case of the Sunday painter. . . . Certainly many people now have the leisure and encouragement to pursue crafts who never did before. . . .

There is a widespread trend today to warn Americans against relaxing in the featherbed of plenty, in the pulpy recreations of popular culture, in the delights of bar and coke bar, and so on. In these warnings any leisure that looks easy is suspect, and craftsmanship does not look easy.[14]

Some of the data collected in this study bear upon these observations, and perhaps in some measure support them. Craftsmanlike activities, which appeared throughout the list of leisure pursuits consuming most of the respondents' spare-time, were separately tabulated.[15] The results of this

Table V—Percentage of Respondents Devoting Most of Their Leisure Time to Craftsmanlike Activities, by Prestige Level

		PRESTIGE LEVEL				
		I	II	III	IV	V
TYPE OF ACTIVITY	N	124	98	130	104	99
Craftsmanlike activities		19.9	21.4	21.9	23.2	30.3
Other types of activities		81.1	78.6	78.1	76.8	69.7
Total		100.0	100.0	100.0	100.0	100.0

analysis are shown in Table V. These data suggest that craft interest tends to vary inversely with prestige level. An interesting relationship appears when these frequencies are compared with the percentages of respondents devoting most of their time to commercial types of recreation. (See Table 4.) The proportion of respondents who frequently participate in craftsmanlike activities is greater than the per cent who participate chiefly in commercial forms of amusement. This relationship holds for each occupational level studied.

It is difficult, of course, to know how much significance should be attached to this emphasis on craftsmanship, because comparable data indicating the percentage of those who engaged in this activity in previous years are not available. Therefore little can be said concerning a possible trend in this direction. Even though increased sales of home-workshop equipment and the phenomenal increase in "Do-It-Yourself" literature may be partially explained by such correlative factors as the increase in home ownership and certain characteristics of suburban living, it may well be that competence in craft skills has developed new meanings for many persons.

Use of Added Leisure Time. It was thought that additional insight into the use of leisure would be attained by analyzing responses to the question: What would you do with an extra two hours in your day? An analysis of these responses may reflect both an individual's attitude toward the appropriate use of leisure time as well as certain subcultural differences regarding the proper use of leisure. These choices were readily classified into eight categories. The findings are summarized in Table VI.

An inspection of the data shows that the respondents in the higher and lower groups would use this extra time in quite different ways. For example,

Table VI—Response to the Question, "What Would You Do With an Extra Two Hours in Your Day?" by Prestige Level, in Percentages

	PRESTIGE LEVEL				
	I	II	III	IV	V
ACTIVITY N	128	102	133	109	102
Relax, rest, loaf, sleep	24.7	31.1	26.7	32.9	39.7
Read, study	27.9	18.7	14.8	11.2	12.8
Work at job	19.8	13.8	14.0	8.3	9.1
Work around house	8.5	7.9	12.3	18.4	15.7
Spend time with family, play with children	4.3	11.8	7.3	7.5	4.9
Watch television	0.0	1.9	2.5	5.6	6.9
Other leisure activities	7.1	4.1	10.8	6.1	3.2
Don't know	2.3	5.8	8.3	6.4	3.9
No answer	5.4	4.9	3.3	4.6	3.8
Total	100.0	100.0	100.0	100.0	100.0

the modal response category for the highest status group indicates that these persons would use the time to read and study, while the highest proportion of those at the other extreme of the prestige continuum replied they would use the extra two hours to rest, loaf and relax. The proportion of persons at Level I who would use this time to work at their jobs is almost as great as the percentage who would relax and rest. It would seem that for a somewhat greater proportion of the higher than the lower prestige groups, an extra amount of leisure would serve largely as an extension of the main activities of life.

Further analysis of these responses reveals that the amount of time which would be spent "working around the house" also tended to vary inversely with prestige level. The percentage of persons who stated they would watch television increased as occupational level decreased. Interestingly, no one in the higher group would use this time to watch television.

Many of the above responses would seem to support the conclusion that a substantially greater proportion of the higher prestige groups would use this hypothetical increase in leisure time largely to implement their business and professional interests. While many interpretations of this pattern are perhaps tenable, it would appear that differential levels of aspiration might account for some of these differences. Perhaps other differences reflect the fact that unlike occupations place widely different demands and expectations upon the role incumbent. It may well be that through the process of attaining higher occupational status, it becomes increasingly difficult to dissociate business interests from leisure pursuits. At the extreme, this process would seem to be most clearly demonstrated in those cases where the practice of a man's profession becomes so important to him, aside from pecuniary considerations, that it becomes his avocation as well as his vocation.

This study sought to delineate some of the relationships between prestige levels and leisure behavior. Systematic differences were found between the frequency of participation in certain types of leisure activities and levels of occupational prestige. Most of the relationships were linear or near-linear.

Some of the preceding data strengthen the findings of earlier research regarding relationships between social status and leisure use. However, other data suggest the emergence of new patterns. Perhaps competence in certain leisure pursuits, notably craftsmanship, has developed new meanings for many persons. Perhaps the alleged domination of spare-time activities by commercial forms of recreation needs to be re-evaluated. Furthermore, the conception of the man at leisure as chiefly a spectator—a non-participant—may be a major distortion of fact.

In spite of much current research directed toward the delineation of different life-styles, most investigations have largely overlooked the institutionalization of leisure. Since it is highly probable that the amount of leisure will continue to increase in the future, this aspect of present-day life in American society assumes increasing proportions and significance. This would seem to indicate that social scientists must eventually recognize that it is as important to understand the leisure-time aspect of American society as it is to understand the economic, familial, religious, or political aspects.

Notes

1. G. A. Lundberg, M. Komarovsky and M. A. McInerny, *Leisure: A Suburban Study,* New York: Columbia University Press, 1934, p. 8.

2. American leisure is obviously a broad subject with many facets and many definitions. In this study the term is used essentially in the same manner as conceptualized in the following statement by Lundberg: Leisure is "the time we are free from the more obvious and formal duties which a paid job or other obligatory occupation imposes upon us. In accepting this definition we are not overlooking the interdependence of work and leisure. Such terms are merely pragmatic ways of designating aspects, rather than separate parts, of life. It remains a fact, however, that nearly all people can and do classify nearly all their activities according to these two categories in a way that is deeply meaningful to themselves. . . . As such the categories are . . . useful for our purpose." (Lundberg, *et al., op. cit.,* pp. 2-3.)

There are, however, other researchers who feel that leisure should also be considered as an attitude of mind rather than merely spare time. For a discussion of this point of view, see Reuel Denney and David Riesman, "Leisure in Urbanized America," in Paul K. Hatt and Albert J. Reiss, Jr. (editors), *Reader in Urban Sociology,* Glencoe: The Free Press, 1951, p. 470.

3. Denney and Riesman, *op. cit.,* p. 315.

4. Occupational prestige is generally regarded as the most satisfactory and probably the most valid index of social status. For example, Warner and his associates found a high correlation between occupation and other measures of "social class." A multiple correlation of occupation, source of income, house type and dwelling area, with subjective judgments of community informants (Evaluated Participation) was .972. A zero-order correlation of .91 was obtained between occupation alone and Evaluated Participation.

5. This scale was based on ratings of occupations by a cross-section of the American population interviewed by the National Opinion Research Center. There were, of course, some occupations encountered in this study which did not appear in the North-Hatt scale. Final ratings of all occupations not mentioned on the scale were the average of individual ratings made by five sociologists asked to compare and equate these occupational titles with those in the scale and to assign corresponding present ratings to them.

6. The range of scores in each of the five prestige levels include: Level I, 82-96; Level II, 75-81; Level III, 67-74; Level IV, 55-66; Level V, 44-54. The chief factor underlying the choice of the intervals was an effort to reflect major occupational groupings. Thus, the scores represented by Level I include, for the most part, professional persons. Level II encompasses largely managers, officials, and proprietors, while Level III includes sales and clerical workers as well as white-collar employees generally. Skilled craftsmen and kindred workers comprise the major portion of Level IV, while service workers, semi-skilled and unskilled laborers make up most of the lower prestige level.

7. It should be noted that several factors restricted the City Directory from yielding a random sample in the strict sense of the term. For example, the directory was over a year old. Obviously, the population had changed to some extent during the interim. Also, some names may have been initially omitted. The representativeness of the sample is therefore decreased to the extent that these and similar factors were operative.

8. The final totals after this reassignment were: Level I, 128; Level II, 102; Level III, 133; Level IV, 109; Level V, 102.

9. Additional details concerning the sample and its logic are presented in the writer's unpublished doctoral dissertation, *The Use of Leisure and Its Relation to Social Stratification*, The Ohio State University, 1955.

10. Eight activities included in the questionnaire were not significantly related to occupational prestige. They were: hunting, bowling, working in garden, out-of-town visiting (not over-night), listening to radio, loafing, doing odd-jobs around home, attending picnics, fairs, exhibitions.

11. The direction of these relationships was examined by assigning arbitrary weights to the frequency categories as follows:

Almost daily 4; about once a week, 3; about 1 to 3 times a month, 2; less than once a month, 1; rarely or never, 0.

Obviously, participation in certain activities such as baseball, fishing, etc., depends largely upon the season of the year. In such cases the respondents were asked to "place an X in one of the columns to indicate how often you usually do these things *during the regular season*."

Mean scores on all activities were computed for each prestige level. Using this procedure it was possible to estimate if differential participation varied directly or inversely with prestige level.

12. Among the activities included in the "spectator" category were: watching television, attending motion pictures, lectures, plays and musical events, attending various sports events e.g. football, baseball, basketball, boxing, wrestling, and auto races.

13. Some of the activities included in the "commercial" category were: bowling, attending theatrical plays, motion pictures, playing pool or billiards, spending time in a cafe or tavern, attending a night club, dancing, attending sports events. If the event or activity generally involved the payment of a fee, it was classified as "commercial."

14. David Riesman, *The Lonely Crowd*, New York: Doubleday and Company, Inc., 1953, pp. 333-336.

15. Among the activities classified as "craftsmanlike" were: model building, sculpturing, painting, and various forms of woodworking.

Industrial Workers' Worlds

By ROBERT DUBIN

In an urban industrial society it seems more than pertinent to inquire into the world of industrial workers. We are here concerned with defining this world in terms of the significant areas of social experience. For each area of experience our basic object is to determine whether it represents a life interest of importance to the worker. In particular, we will focus attention on work and the workplace to determine its standing as a central life interest to workers in industry.

The impact of industrialization and urbanization on human behavior is empirically noted and theoretically accounted for in the general sociological literature. Microscopic studies of industrial organizations and of "human relations" within them are producing their own observations and generalizations. The bodies of knowledge in general sociology and in industrial sociology are at variance on critical points. This study presents one part of a larger research linking general and industrial sociology. The linkage is made through an intensive study of the "central life interests" of industrial workers.

Introduction. It is a commonplace to note that work has long been considered a central life interest for adults in most societies, and certainly in the Western world. Indeed, the capitalist system itself is asserted to rest upon the moral and religious justification that the Reformation gave to work, as Weber and Tawney have pointed out. (8, 9) Our research shows that for almost three out of every four industrial workers studied, work and the workplace *are not* central life interests.

This result is surely not startling to the general sociologist. He has already noted that the social world of urban man is continuously subdivided into areas of activity and interest, with each social segment lived out more or less independently of the rest. It seems highly plausible that the urban world, with its emphasis upon secondary and instrumental social relations, might indeed be one in which work has become secondary as a life interest.

The one large subject matter illuminated by industrial sociologists in the past decade has been the human relationships that surround job and task performance in the formal organizations of modern life. (5, 6, 11) We are generally led to believe that informal human relationships at work are impor-

---

Reprinted from *Social Problems*, Volume 3, Number 3 (January 1956), pp. 131-42, by permission of the author and the publisher. (Copyright 1956 by the Society for the Study of Social Problems.) This paper won a Helen L. DeRoy Award. This is the first of a series of reports on research conducted under a grant from the National Mental Health Institute of the United States Public Health Service. The larger study has the general title, "Mental Health and Social Structure of the Work Situation." Grateful acknowledgment is made for the grant of funds.

tant to the individual industrial man—he finds that the informal work society presents opportunities for intimate and primary human interaction. Our research indicates that only about 10% of the industrial workers perceived their important primary social relationships as taking place at work. The other 90% preferred primary interactions with fellow men elsewhere than on the job!

This finding should jolt the industrial sociologist, if duplicated in subsequent studies. The result will be an important corrective to the naive assumption that complex and rational organizations of modern society, through which most of the society's business gets done, are effective or not as the human relations of their members are "good" or "bad."

In an era when loyalty is in the vocabulary of even the common man, the ways in which members become attached to, and thereby loyal toward, an organization are of central interest. Our research findings indicate that more than three out of five industrial workers have strong job-oriented preferences for those sectors of their experience that involve either a formal organization or technological aspects of their personal environment. This result (again perhaps surprising to the human relations expert) suggests that strong bonds of organization may be forged out of the impersonal aspects of work experience that attach the individual more or less firmly to his company or workplace.

These three problems taken together, then, are the subject of this report: (a) work as a central life interest; (b) the role and importance of primary social relations on the job; and (c) some sources of organizational attachment.

Theory. The theory underlying this study involves five basic points: (a) the axiom that social experience is inevitably segmented; (b) the assumption that an individual's social participation may be necessary in one or more sectors of his social experience but may not be important to him; (c) the logical conclusion that adequate social behavior will occur in sectors of social experience which are mandatory for social participation by the individual but not important to him; (d) the second conclusion that in situations of necessary but unimportant social participation the most direct and obvious features of the situation become bases for the individual's attachment to that situation; and (e) the third conclusion that primary social relations take place only in situations where the social experience is valued by the individual.

The axiom with which we start scarcely needs elaboration. The segmented character of experience is revealed in the round of daily activities where one kind of activity succeeds another; in the succession of days, and particularly the weekend days when leisure-time activity replaces remunerative work; in the physical separation of such significant locales as place of residence and place of work; and in the numerous autonomous organizations that serve special, and sometimes very esoteric, interests in our lives. This by no means exhausts the illustrations of ways in which social experience is divided into discrete parts, but it should serve adequately to demonstrate the reasonableness of our initial axiom.

It is equally obvious that participation in some segments or sectors of social experience may be necessary but not important to an individual. The significance of this assumption rests on the definition of important social experience. We are here concerned with a subjective state of mind. Some social experience is important because it is valued by its participants; some is important because it is necessary as a means towards an end, though slightly valued in itself. The ceremonial banquet for awarding football letters to the college team may be valued as public recognition of achievement. The meal eaten at the banquet is important, too, but only as the justification for naming the ceremony, not for its nutritive value or esthetic appeal. The kind of importance we are concerned with is illustrated by the ceremony, not the meal.

This assumption tells us that social experience is differentially valued. The form in which it is stated emphasizes the fact that participation takes place in some experiences because it is necessary and not because the activity is itself valued. We could equally well state the axiom as follows: only a portion of all social experience is important or valued by its participants. We have chosen the first formulation because it gives greater emphasis to the subject matter of this research—the fact that remunerative work may be required by the society but that this does not guarantee that it will be viewed as important or valued by workers.

Three propositions or generalized predictions follow from our two axioms. The first is that individuals will exhibit adequate social behavior in sectors of social experience in which participation is mandatory but not valued. This proposition, when converted to hypothesis form, becomes empirically testable. In its proposition form it makes a general prediction for any and all individuals. In the form of a hypothesis the prediction is limited to the particular data of the study and the actual empirical indicators used. For example, this proposition in our study becomes the following hypothesis: a significant proportion of industrial workers will rate non-job interests high in their value orientation on the Central Life Interests questionnaire. Our hypothesis as a prediction is completely consonant with the general proposition, but it is also directly related to the data of our study. The hypothesis is the bridge between the general proposition and the empirical data marshaled in testing the proposition. Any proposition can be converted to an indefinite number of hypotheses. Consequently, no confirmation of a single hypothesis can establish any proposition. The confirmed hypothesis does, however, lend support to the proposition. Our research findings lend support to the three propositions set forth. We are not, of course, asserting that the propositions are thereby proven.

The second proposition or general prediction is that an individual's attachment to a situation in which his social experience is not valued by him will be to the most physically and directly obvious characteristics of that situation. The pertinent hypotheses that flow from this proposition will be set forth below.

The third general prediction in proposition form is that primary human relations take place only in situations where the social experience is valued by the individual. By "primary human relations" we mean, of course, the relationships that occur in groups where the interaction is face-to-face, continuous, intimate, and shared over a wide range of subjects. The directly related hypotheses will be stated below.

Research Procedure. This study was conducted in 1952-53 in three middle-western plants employing a total of approximately 1,200 workers. The companies are located in different communities ranging in size from 35,000 to 125,000, all clearly urban units. The largest company makes industrial equipment, employing about 600 workers on two shifts in a wide and typical range of metal manufacturing and equipment assembly operations. The smallest company manufactures industrial, dress, and novelty gloves of cloth and leather with a work force of approximately 200 employees, who were represented by an A.F. of L. union. The third company produces printed and novelty advertising items and employs about 400 people.

Active cooperation was secured in each plant to carry on the total study, which included observation of work performance and work behavior, the anonymous completion of a series of separate questionnaires administered over a period of time and completed by 491 workers, and intensive recorded interviews with a sample of 120 selected employees.

We will report here the results of the Central Life Interests questionnaire only. This questionnaire was designed to determine whether the job and workplace were central life interests of workers or whether other areas of their social experience were important to them. We defined "central life interest" as the expressed preference for a given locale or situation in carrying out an activity. After a pretest, forty questions were selected for the Central Life Interests (CLI) schedule.

Each question represented an activity that had an approximately equal likelihood of occurring in connection with some aspect of the job or workplace, or at some definite point in the community outside of work. A third choice was added that represented an indifferent or neutral response to the question. An example of a typical question is the following:

I would most hate

–missing a day's work

–missing a meeting of an organization I belong to

–missing almost anything I usually do

The forty questions used dealt with the formal aspects of membership and behavior in organizations, the technological aspects of the environment, the informal group life experiences, and general everyday experiences.
Each question was individually scored as a job-oriented response, as a non-job-oriented response, or as an indifferent response. The questions that applied to each of the four areas were then scored as separate groups by

summing the responses to the individual questions in each group. Those workers who chose a work-related response on at least half the questions in each group and answered the remaining ones with a non-job or indifferent response, or who had at least 70% of their answers made up of a combination of job-oriented and indifferent responses, were designated job-oriented workers. The remaining workers were designated non-job in their outlook because they responded with more emphasis upon non-job and indifferent choices. The indifferent response is not utilized as a separate category in this report.

By the same scoring procedure and using the same criteria a total classification was secured for each worker. This indicated whether he was job-oriented or non-job-oriented in his total pattern of responses on all forty questions.

Work As a Central Life Interest. Previous researchers have generally assumed that work must be a central life interest because so many are engaged in it. We make quite a different assumption about work. We assume that holding a job is simply evidence of adequate performance above some minimal level that justifies continued employment by the company. In short, we assume that social behavior is adequate in this sector of social experience. For us the research question becomes one of determining to what extent the job and its locale are central life interests to workers.

It will be recalled that our first proposition is that individuals will exhibit adequate social behavior in sectors of social experience in which participation is mandatory but not valued. Remunerative work is mandatory both in the general sense that most male adults (or female heads of households) are expected to work for a living and in the specific sense that each job is surrounded by many imperatives and requirements for its performance. We have thus assumed that continued employment is evidence of adequacy of social behavior and that holding a paying job is evidence of mandatory participation in the two senses mentioned.

Our hypothesis can now be stated as follows: a significant proportion of industrial workers will be classified as non-job-oriented when central life interest is measured with the CLI questionnaire.

Considering the pattern of responses to all the questions, we found that only 24% of all the workers studied could be labelled job-oriented in their life interests. (N = 491, for this and all other percentages reported here.) Thus, three out of four of this group of industrial workers did not see their jobs and work places as central life interests for themselves. They found their preferred human associations and preferred areas of behavior outside of employment.

If this finding holds generally, the role and significance of work in American society has departed from its presumed historical position. Factory work may now very well be viewed by industrial workers as a means to an end—a way of acquiring income for life in the community. The factory as a locale for living out a lifetime seems clearly secondary to other areas of central life interest. The factory and factory work as sources of personal satisfaction, pride, satisfying human associations, perhaps even of pleasure in expressing what Veblen called the "instinct of workmanship," seem clearly subordinated in the American scene. The general and specific implications of this finding will be examined in the last section of this paper.

Work and Informal Social Relations. Our third general prediction of human behavior in proposition form was that primary human relations take place only in situations where social experience is valued by the individual. From the test of our first hypothesis we have strong evidence that the workplace does not provide social experience that is valued more highly than other experiences. It would follow, then, that we may expect a significant proportion of industrial workers to be non-job-oriented with respect specifically to informal group experiences when measured on the relevant portion of the CLI questionnaire. This is the hypothesis derived from the above proposition.

Informal group experiences are those relations between people that are not directly a product of an official relationship in an organization or related positions in a division of labor. Illustrative of informal social relations are those involving small talk, leisure-time behavior, friendship interactions, and affectional attachments. Questions such as the following were asked:

I would rather take my vacation with
–my family
–some friends from work
–by myself

The people I would be most likely to borrow money from are
–the people I know around town
–anyone who would lend it to me
–the people I know here in the plant

It hurts me if I am disliked
–by the people at work
–by the people around town
–by anyone I know

In all a total of fourteen questions were used to sample informal group experiences. A job-oriented or non-job-oriented score was secured for each worker for the informal group experience sector in accordance with the procedure set forth above.

Only 9% of the industrial workers in the sample prefer the informal group life that is centered in the job. Nine out of ten of those studied clearly indicated that their preferred informal human associations and contacts were found in the community, among friends, and in the family.

The industrial sociologist has been impressive in demonstrating the informal group life of people associated together at work. But the relative significance of this kind of human experience in relation to the full round of life has never before been considered. If our findings are at all typical—and general sociology theory would predict the findings to be of this sort—

then the workplace is not very congenial to the development of preferred informal human relationships.

Much action research and some company policy has implicitly or explicitly been grounded in the simple-minded assumption that improving, enriching, or facilitating the development of informal group life is both desirable as a goal (to develop "happy" workers) and necessary as a means (to improve production, decrease turnover, etc.). Now it can perhaps be suggested that, on balance, such well-intended efforts may be misdirected. The workplace is not the breeding ground of preferred informal human relationships; deliberate efforts to make it so may be relatively ineffectual. The possible exception, perhaps, is the one worker in ten who sees the job environment as his most likely source of desired informal group life.

The immediately preceding hypothesis tested its underlying proposition by asking questions directly about primary or informal social relations. We can make another test of the proposition by focusing upon the part of it that deals with valued social experience. One of the direct ways of getting at valued social experience is to ask questions that deal with activities giving pleasure, satisfaction, or general rewards, which may be pursued in varying places and at varying times. For questions dealing with this area we have used the designation of "general experience." In terms of this approach to our third proposition, the hypothesis becomes: a significant proportion of industrial workers will not respond to work as a valued social experience when this is tested by the general experience section of the CLI questionnaire. Questions dealing with general experience include those concerning "the most important things I do," "the most pleasant things I do," "my ideas about getting ahead," "my worries," and "my interests." General experience was sampled in a total of nine questions on the basis of which each worker was classified as job-oriented or non-job-oriented in this area.

Only 15% of the workers give job-oriented preferences. The rest—about eleven in thirteen—saw experiences of theirs that were sampled in the study as taking place somewhere away from the workplace.

It is immediately suggested that the emotional impact of work and the work environment seems to be remarkably low in terms of general life experiences. Not only is the workplace relatively unimportant as a place of preferred primary human relationships, but it cannot even evoke significant sentiments and emotions in its occupants. These two conclusions may, of course, be related. A large proportion of emotionally significant experience takes place in primary group relationships. If the informal work group is a matter of relative indifference to workers, then it is reasonable that general social experiences of emotional importance will not take place with high frequency in the workplace.

It seems fair to conclude that our hypotheses have been supported. When measured in terms of valued social experience, the workplace is preferred by only 15% of the workers studied. When measured in terms of primary human relations, only 9% of the workers report that the workplace provides their preferred associations. Thus, in terms of the workplace as a testing ground, we can conclude that the underlying proposition may well be valid: primary human relations take place only in situations where social experience is valued by the individual. Obviously, many more tests of this proposition must be made, but the present tests encourage its future exploration.

Some Bases of Organizational Attachment. Max Weber has pointed out that, in formal organizations based upon rational authority with staff units organized in bureaucracies, the staff members are loyal to the legally established impersonal order of the organization. (10) By implicit extension of this idea we can see immediately the possibilities of other sources of organizational attachment for members. In particular, we can examine the possibility that organizational attachment can be a product of the formal organization and its operations, and of the technology which surrounds work.

Our second general proposition was set forth in the following manner: an individual's attachment to a situation in which his social experience is not valued by him will be to the most physically and directly obvious characteristics of that situation. From our data we propose to test this in terms of experience in formal organizations and experience with technology.

The choice of these two kinds of experiences is based on clear grounds. Both kinds of experiences are direct and obvious. We have many daily evidences of our participation in an organization. We arrive at its building from home, enter into a specified location, do required jobs under the direction of organization supervisors, work with machines and equipment under operating conditions that are special to the work, and have our time spent and output measured and recorded as a basis for remuneration.

We know from the first portion of this study that a significantly large percentage of the industrial workers studied do not value the work situation in terms of its opportunities for informal group experiences and for general affective experiences. This suggests that the workplace provides an excellent opportunity to test our second proposition, because it generally meets the condition that it does not provide valued social experience for a large proportion of its participants. We can derive the following hypothesis from that proposition: a significant proportion of industrial workers will score job-oriented for their organizational experience when measured on the organizational section of the CLI schedule.

A sampling was made of typical relationships between members and organizations. Experience in the formal sector includes a number of different relationships between an organization, its officials, and its members. Hiring, joining, firing, disciplining, rewarding, directing, and ordering are illustrative of relationships of this sort. Some of these relationships were covered in the study and on the basis of his responses to seven questions, each worker was rated as job-oriented or non-job-oriented in the formal sector.

More than three out of five of the workers were scored as job-oriented with respect to their experiences in organizations: 61% chose their companies as the most meaningful context to them when their life experiences in organizations were brought into their focus. Put another way, the most significant formal organization when judged in terms of standard and typical organizational ties and bonds is the employing one, the industrial company.

This conclusion should not be confused with the notion that these workers are saying they necessarily like their employer or the company for which they work. No such questions were included. The questions asked placed emphasis only upon choosing that situation or organizational context in which a particular behavior was best carried out, or in which the worker would most like to have it happen. Thus, he was asked to choose between getting a job promotion or "becoming a more important member in my club, church, or lodge"; between workplace or "an organization I belong to" as the locale where praise received produces greater happiness; between regretting most "missing a day's work" or "missing a meeting of an organization I belong to." These choices serve to illustrate the questions asked in order to seek information on attachment to the formal organizations in workers' lives. Like all the questions asked, those in the formal sector were designed to determine the central life interests of workers.

We may conclude, then, that the workers studied were not confusing a liking for their company or its officials with a preference for their workplace as the most important formal organization in their lives. It seems reasonably clear that a significant majority of these workers believed that the companies in which they worked provided the important or preferred opportunities for organizational experience. Further important implications of this finding will be examined below.

The second test of the general proposition underlying this section can be made through the following hypothesis: a significant proportion of industrial workers will be job-oriented for their experiences with technological aspects of their environments when measured on the technological section of the CLI questionnaire.

A sampling was made of experiences involving the relations between people and the technical aspects of their environment. The questions probing this aspect of experience gave the workers the opportunity to select the place or situation most preferred or desired for behavior directly involving relations with machines or technical operating conditions. The technical sector of experience was defined as that involving the relationships between an individual and his actual work operations. Tool, equipment, and machine maintenance; concern with job and operating techniques; overcoming operating problems; minimizing waste; accuracy of operations; quality of materials; and cleanliness and care of operations are illustrative of the kinds of relationships between an individual and technical aspects of his environment. These relations were sampled and another score on job vs. non-job orientation was secured for each worker for the technological sector of experience, based on a total of ten questions.

In the technological sector, 63% of the respondents were scored as job-oriented. This is the highest proportion of job-oriented responses for any of the sectors of experience examined. It certainly seems notable that almost two out of every three of the workers studied identified their workplace as the locale of their preferred relationships with the purely technical aspects of their environment.

The meaning of this finding can, perhaps, be made clearer when we examine some of the kinds of questions asked. For the statement, "I don't mind getting dirty," the alternative responses were: "while working at home," "at anytime if I can wash up afterwards," "while working at the plant." The introductory phrase, "I most enjoy keeping," was followed by these choices of response: "my things around the house in good shape," "my hand tools and workspace on the job in good shape," "my mind off such things." Additional questions in this area included:

Noise bothers me most
- –when working at home
- –when working at the plant
- –hardly ever

When I am doing some work
- –I am usually most accurate working at home
- –I seldom think about being accurate
- –I am usually most accurate working at the plant

It will be noted that an attempt was made to select those kinds of technical considerations that would have an equal likelihood of being relevant to the non-job and job environments. We feel certain that the high percentage of job-oriented responses is not the product of a bias in the questions asked that tended to favor the job environment.

The fact that the technological sector of experience is the most clearly job-oriented one suggests the desirability of a fresh appraisal of this dimension of social experience. In the past there has been considerable concern with the general meaninglessness of industrial work derived directly from a technology that makes work itself monotonous, repetitious, mechanical, and fragmentary. The human consequence of this has been generally assumed to be indifference, alienation, rebellion, or even personal disorganization and possibly mental disorder.

We can, however, return to one of Durkheim's important theoretical points and see another possible analytical approach to the problem of technology. (3) It will be recalled that Durkheim stressed the organic solidarity that made whole the individual units, tasks, and jobs in a given division of labor. He was emphasizing, of course, the necessary unity and integration that must bind together the divided and separate tasks and functions constituting the given division of labor. Without such unity the parts cannot mesh properly with each other, with the result that the planned-for outcome (product or service) will not be forthcoming.

To Durkheim, this organic solidarity was a non-consensual one. People who were part of a given division of labor did not necessarily share with other members of it either a sense of common enterprise or a body of common values. To be sure, Durkheim clearly saw that consensus was essential to social unity, as his concept of mechanical solidarity illustrates. The connections between the two forms of social bond were a central research interest of his, but remain even to this day a set of mooted issues.

It may now be possible to suggest that industrial employment is one of the important focal points in our society for experiences with technical environments. This kind of experience has meaning in a sociological sense because it signifies the interdependence of man with man even where there is no necessary common ground of values shared between them. The urban environment is heterogeneous–in values, in the backgrounds of its residents, and in their daily experiences. Diversity is one of the hallmarks of urban life. But underpinning this heterogeneity and diversity is a fundamental human interdependence that flows from the far-flung division of labor. The real experiencing of this interdependence and sensing of it comes from the daily job. On the job the urbanite learns more directly and acutely than anywhere else how dependent he is upon those about him. There may follow from this the unity of interdependent action that is such an impressive feature of industrial work. This can often be achieved even in spite of lack of consensus, as Goode and Fowler neatly demonstrated in their study of an industrial plant. (4)

The characteristics of industrial work that are alleged to be disturbing to the individual (monotony, repetitiveness, mechanistic character, and overspecialization) are the very features that make obvious to its participants the nature of symbiotic or technological interdependence. In short, industrial work may be functional for the society because it sharply etches for the individual some awareness of the division of labor and its resultant interdependence.

Both of the hypotheses derived from our second proposition have been supported. This suggests that the proposition has merit. It certainly must be subjected to further test, but we now have some prospect that the tests will continue to sustain the general prediction about human behavior that it represents.

Conclusions. The industrial workers' world is one in which work and the workplace are not central life interests for a vast majority. In particular, work is not a central life interest for industrial workers when we study the informal group experiences and the general social experiences that have some affective value for them. Industrial man seems to perceive his life history as having its center outside of work for his intimate human relationships and for his feelings of enjoyment, happiness, and worth. On the other hand, for his experiences with the technological aspects of his life space and for his participation in formal organizations, he clearly recognizes the primacy of the workplace. In short, he has a well-developed sense of attachment to his work and workplace without a corresponding sense of total commitment to it.

In a more general sense this study has been designed to provide empirical tests for three propositions. We have evidence to believe that these propositions are worthy of further testing. It now seems reasonable to believe that individuals will exhibit adequate social behavior in sectors of social experience in which participation is mandatory but not valued. Where the social experience is not valued, the individual may still become attached to the situation of the experience in terms of the most physically and directly obvious features of that situation (as we examined it, the formal organization and its technology). Finally, we would predict that primary human relationships develop only in situations where the social experience is valued by the individual.

Implications and Speculations. Several years ago the Corning Glass Company celebrated its centennial with a conference whose proceedings have been published under the title of *Creating an Industrial Civilization.* (2) This suggests a theme for drawing implications from this study in a speculative vein. The emphasis is upon the future and the creative task that lies ahead.

Viewed from the standpoint of industrial management there are two broad and contradictory influences at work in the society. Work is no longer a central life interest for workers. These life interests have moved out into the community. Yet work was presumably once a central life interest. Much management activity in personnel and industrial relations is implicitly directed at restoring work to the status of a central life interest. Management's efforts and the main drift of social developments work at directly contrary purposes.

The second contradictory influence centers on the location of primary human relationships in the total social fabric. Some groups in management have accepted a philosophy and developed social engineering practices summed up in the phrase "human relations in industry." The major purpose of this movement is to center primary human relationships in work and make it functional for productivity. At the same time it seems evident that primary human relations are much more likely to be located at some place out in the community. The management efforts again seem to be at odds with social reality.

The first dilemma is perhaps best highlighted in the pronounced frustration that management practitioners experience with the relative failure of their efforts to engender a sense of participation in their work forces. Many have become convinced that it's all a matter of communication and semantics. If simple language is chosen, comic-book presentation is used, and volume of impact is raised, then employees will feel they are part of the "company team," a phrase commonly used. Other efforts have been directed at "participant management" and its latter-day descendant, "group dynamics." Here the chief goal seems to be to make a central life interest out of work by permitting some sharing by employees of decisions affecting their work routines.

None of these efforts have been crowned by remarkable success. Indeed, the group dynamics technique, which has much research background and a number of practical applications, seems singularly sterile. When the research findings indicate that the technique has not produced a material change in the output of an experimental group over an "old-fashioned" control group, the group dynamics approach is justified on the ground that it is easier on the emotional hide of those who are subjected to it.

Perhaps the issue is really not one of human manipulation after all. All the communication effort and group dynamics in the world will not alter the basic drift in our society away from a central life interest in work. Some of the older personnel techniques of supporting after-work activities, bowling leagues and bird-watching clubs, may really be more sensible. Company involvement in a constructive way in community affairs, in the non-work activities of its own employees as well as in a general sense, might be a more significant way to enhance attachment of employees to their company. Perhaps the basic problem is not one of central life interest in work after all, but one of enhancing the sense of attachment of participants to social organizations in which participation is necessary but not important to them. These are all questions that are suggestively derived from this study. They may be examined with profit.

The second dilemma has an interesting intellectual history in which theorizers and researchers, having established the concept of primary group and primary social relations (1, 7), proceeded to apply it indiscriminately to all kinds of social organizations. Whyte in his finest study (12) gave us a magnificent picture of primary relations in boys' gangs (community, not work, organizations). He has since attempted to discover the same primary group life in industry (11), with much less certainty of the results obtained. At least in this writer's opinion we have a good deal of evidence that there are non-official as well as official, or informal along with formal, relations in a business organization. But to call these "primary social relationships" may do grave injustice to a perfectly good concept.

It may very well be that those efforts of any managerial group in any kind of organization to center primary group life for a majority of employees in the workplace are misplaced. If our evidence is substantiated in other studies, the community is the locale of preferred primary social relations. To attempt to shift the locale to the workplace may be trying to reverse a social development that is not alterable in that direction.

This may not be an entirely undesirable prospect. Weber emphasized the impersonality and efficiency of modern bureaucratic organization. The efficiency can remain along with the impersonality, providing there are other points in the society where the primary social relations can be experienced.

The general conclusion of the Corning Glass Conference was that the problem of creating an industrial civilization is essentially a problem of social invention and creativity in the non-work aspects of life. Our great social inventions will probably not come in connection with work life; they will center in community life. This research certainly suggests the importance of this insight.

References

1. C. H. Cooley, *Social Organization,* New York: Scribner, 1924.
2. *Creating an Industrial Civilization,* Eugene A. Staley, ed., New York: Harper Bros., 1952.
3. Emile Durkheim, *Division of Labor in Society,* Glencoe, Ill.: Free Press, 1947.
4. W. J. Goode and I. Fowler, "Incentive Factors in a Low Morale Plant," *American Sociological Review,* 14 (October, 1949), 619-624.
5. George C. Homans, *The Human Group,* New York: Harcourt, Brace and Co., 1950.
6. F. J. Roethlisberger and W. J. Dickson, *Management and the Worker,* Cambridge: Harvard University Press, 1934.
7. Georg Simmel, *The Sociology of Georg Simmel,* K. H. Wolff, ed., Glencoe, Ill.: Free Press 1950.
8. R. H. Tawney, *Religion and the Rise of Capitalism,* New York: Harcourt, 1926.
9. Max Weber, *The Protestant Ethic and the Spirit of Capitalism,* London: Geo. Allen and Unwin, Ltd., 1930.
10. Max Weber, *Theory of Social and Economic Organization,* New York: Oxford University Press, 1947.
11. W. F. Whyte, *Human Relations in the Restaurant Industry,* New York: McGraw-Hill Book Co., 1948.
12. W. F. Whyte, *Street Corner Society,* Chicago: University of Chicago Press, 1943.

"Society": Status Without Substance

By E. FRANKLIN FRAZIER

THERE is a phase of the world of make-believe of the black bourgeoisie which requires special treatment, namely, the activities of those persons who constitute its "society." Although Negro "society" was not created by the Negro press, it is the Negro press which feeds and perpetuates the illusions of this element in the black bourgeoisie. The activities of "society" are not simply a form of social life engaged in for pleasure and friendly social intercourse. They are engaged in primarily in order to maintain status or as a part of the competition for status. The activities of "society" serve to differentiate the black bourgeoisie from the masses of poorer Negroes and at the same time compensate for the exclusion of the black bourgeoisie from the larger white community. However, the behavior and standards of consumption which are maintained by "society" generally lack the economic base which such activities presuppose. "Society" thus provides one of the main escapes from the world of reality into a world of make-believe.

1. Evolution of "Society". "Society" among Negroes had its roots among the house servants who enjoyed a certain prestige among the other slaves on the plantation during their social gatherings. An ex-slave, who wrote his autobiography after escaping to freedom, has provided a vivid account of the status of this group on a plantation.

It was about ten o'clock when the aristocratic slaves began to assemble,

Chapter 9 from *Black Bourgeoisie,* by E. Franklin Frazier.

dressed in the cast-off finery of their master and mistress, swelling out and putting on airs in imitation of those they were forced to obey from day to day.

House servants were, of course, "the stars" of the party; all eyes were turned to them to see how they conducted, for they, among slaves, are what a military man would call "fugle-men." The field hands, and such of them as have generally been excluded from the dwelling of their owners, look to the house servants as a pattern of politeness and gentility. And indeed, it is often the only method of obtaining any knowledge of the manners of what is called "genteel society"; hence, they are ever regarded as a privileged class; and are sometimes greatly envied, while others are bitterly hated.[1]

After Emancipation, some of the social distinctions which had grown up among the slaves continued to function. Negroes who were free before the Emancipation Proclamation or who could boast of a distinguished family background set themselves apart from the masses of freedmen and constituted a distinct upper social class. Many of them boasted of their "blood," which generally referred to their white ancestry. A mulatto witness of the history of Negroes during the years following the Civil War has left a rather satirical account of the emergence of "society" among them in the nation's capital.

There is another element in this strange heterogeneous conglomeration, which for want of a better name has been styled society and it is this species of African humanity which is forever and ever informing the uninitiated what a narrow escape they had from being born white. They have small hands, aristocratic insteps and wear blue veins, they have auburn hair and finely chiselled features. They are uneducated as a rule (i.e.) the largest number of them, though it would hardly be discovered unless they opened their *mouths* in the presence of their superiors in intellect, which they are very careful not to do. In personal appearance, they fill the bill precisely so far as *importance* and pomposity goes–but no farther. They are opposed to manual labor, their physical organization couldn't stand it, they prefer light work such as "shuffling cards or dice" or "removing the spirits of Frumenta from the gaze of rude men" if somebody else becomes responsible for the damage. Around the festive board, they are unequalled for their verbosity and especially for their aptness in tracing their ancestry. One will carry you away back to the times of William the Silent and bring you up to 18 so and so, to show how illustrious is his lineage and pedigree. His great, great grandfather's mother-in-law was the Marchioness So and So and his father was ex-Chief Justice Chastity of S. C. or some other southern state with a polygamous record.[2]

Washington became, in fact, the center of Negro "society" and retained this distinction until after the first World War. This was owing partly to the fact that until the mass migrations of Negroes to northern cities, Washington with around 90,000 Negroes had a larger Negro community than any city in the United States until 1920. The pre-eminence of Washington as the center of Negro "society" was due more especially to other factors. Because of its relatively large Negro professional class, including teachers in the segregated public school system, doctors, dentists, and lawyers, and large numbers of Negroes employed in the federal government, Negroes in the nation's capital had incomes far above those in other parts of the country.

This enabled Washington's "colored society" to engage in forms of consumption and entertainment that established its pre-eminence among American Negroes. Moreover, the Negro "society" which developed in Washington was composed of the upper-class mulattoes who, in fleeing from persecution and discriminations in the South, brought to Washington the social distinctions and color snobbery that had been the basis of their ascendancy in the South.

The first World War, which initiated a period of increased social as well as physical mobility in the Negro population, set in motion social and economic forces that inaugurated a new stage in the evolution of Negro "society." First, family background and color snobbishness based upon white ancestry became less important for membership among the social elite. Although in Charleston, South Carolina, in Atlanta, Georgia, in New Orleans, and in other southern cities, Negro "society" might continue to boast of the white or mulatto ancestors, in New York, Chicago, and Detroit, those who were becoming "socially" prominent were beginning to ask, "What is his profession?" or "What is his income?" Even in Washington, where a light complexion had been so important in "society," these questions were being asked. "Blue veins" and "auburn hair and finely chiseled features" were beginning to be ridiculed as a basis of social prominence. A newspaper edited by a pure black Negro carried articles each week showing up the foibles of the mulattoes who constituted Negro "society."[3]

During a decade or so following the first World War, in both northern and southern cities education and occupation increasingly supplanted family background and a light complexion as a basis for admission to the social elite among Negroes. For example, in New York, Chicago, and Philadelphia, Negroes who had constituted Negro "society" because they were mulattoes and acted like "gentlemen" were pushed aside because they were engaged in personal services. The Negro doctors, dentists, lawyers, and businessmen, who could not boast of white ancestors or did not know their white ancestors, were becoming the leaders of Negro "society." Even if they did not act like "gentlemen," they were able to imitate white "society" in their standards of consumption and entertainment. In fact, they tended to ridicule the so-called "culture" and exclusiveness of the older Negro "society."

During this transition period in the development of Negro "society," the "socially" prominent among Negroes were developing the new social values and new orientation towards the American environment that have become characteristic of Negro "society" at the present time. Although among isolated enclaves in the Negro communities of both southern and northern cities there is an attempt to constitute a "social" elite after the manner of the older Negro "society," such Negroes are generally looked upon as curiosities. Family background has little significance in Negro "society" of the present day, although there is an unavowed color snobbishness which has ceased to have much importance. Education from the standpoint of fundamental culture has completely lost its significance. There is still a certain snobbishness in regard to one's occupation, but the most important thing about one's occupation is the amount of income which it brings. Therefore, at the present time, Negro "society" is constituted largely of professional and business men and women with large incomes that enable them to engage in conspicuous consumption. From time to time the incomes of these Negro professional men who are "socially" prominent are revealed to have been derived from traffic in narcotics and performing abortions, while it is difficult at times to determine whether "socially" prominent businessmen are engaged in legitimate or illegitimate business.[4]

2. The Gaudy Carnival. One may get some idea of the nature of "society" in the make-believe world of the black bourgeoisie from an article entitled "Society Rulers of 20 Cities," which was published in the May, 1949 issue of *Ebony*. The rulers of "society" included five wives of physicians, three wives of dentists, three women school teachers, two wives of morticians, a social worker, the owner of a newspaper, the wife of a lawyer, a banker's daughter, a concert pianist, and the wife of a college president. Of course, there are Negro women in these cities who would challenge the "social" ascendency of these so-called leaders, since there is much competition to be known as a ruler of "society." In northern cities, especially, there are wives of politicians and businessmen who, because of their ability to engage in conspicuous consumption, would not accept these so-called leaders. Nevertheless, the rulers of "society" reported in *Ebony* are representative, on the whole, of the leaders in "society" among the black bourgeoisie both with respect to the source of income and the style of life of this element among the black bourgeoisie.

One of the rulers of colored society, a physician's wife who works every day, is celebrated for her three big parties each year. The ruler of society in a southern city has gained fame because she entertains Negroes who have a national reputation. Another has gained notoriety because she is a friend of Lena Horne and gave a cocktail party for the famous movie actress. A former social worker is reported to have won her position in "society" because certain white writers and white "playboys" have paid attention to her. Another gave lavish debutante parties for her daughters. A southern ruler of society seemingly won eminence because her husband gave her a Cadillac automobile and a mink coat. The eminence of one school teacher in society seems to stem from the fact that she gives expensive parties and drives a Mercury automobile. A physician and his wife who had been to Europe proved their "social" eminence by giving a "continental" dinner consisting of nine courses for fifty-six guests which required four hours and thirty-five minutes to consume. In one case the reader learns that a particular ruler of "society" is noted for receptions in her home, the walls and ceilings of which, including the bathroom, are covered with mirrors. Details are supplied concerning the other rulers of "society" who own Cadillacs, have elaborate recreation rooms, and supply unlimited food and liquor to their guests.

For that section of the black bourgeoisie which devotes itself to "society," life has become a succession of carnivals. In cities all over the country, Negro "society" has inaugurated Debutante Balls or Cotillions which provide an opportunity every year for the so-called rich Negroes to indulge in lavish expenditures and create a world of fantasy to satisfy their longing for recognition. Very often these "rich" Negroes mortgage their homes in order to maintain the fiction that they are able to indulge in these vast spectacles of make-believe. In Philadelphia the Debutante Ball known as the "Pink Cotillion" is reputed to excel all others in the country. At this Debutante Ball, noted for the money spent on decorations and the expensive gowns and jewels worn by the women, an award is made each year to some distinguished Negro. This award consists of a diamond cross of Malta. During the years 1949, 1950, and 1951, the diamond cross of Malta was presented successively to Marian Anderson, Dr. Ralph Bunche, and Mrs. Mary McCleod Bethune.[5] The Debutante Balls are written up in the Negro press, with pictures, in order to show the splendor and wealth of those who participate in this world of make-believe.[6]

The Debutante Balls are only one manifestation of the carnival spirit of Negro "society" which never slackens, especially since the black bourgeoisie has been enjoying unusual prosperity during recent years. The weekly accounts in the Negro press of the activities of Negro "society" are invariably stories of unbridled extravagance. These stories include a catalogue of the jewelry, the gowns, and mink coats worn by the women, often accompanied by an estimate of the value of the clothes and jewelry, and the cost of the parties which they attend. One constantly reads of "chauffeured" Cadillac cars in which they ride to parties and of the cost of the homes in which they live. The carnival spirit of Negro "society" with its emphasis upon conspicuous consumption has permeated the Negro colleges, where the fraternities and sororities compete with each other to excel in the amount of money spent for flowers, decorations and entertainment. It was reported in the Negro press that during the Christmas holidays in 1952, nine Greek letter societies meeting in four cities spent $2,225,000.[7] Most of the persons attending the college fraternities and sororities were not, of course, college students, but as the article stated, top "social" and intellectual leaders. For these top "social" and intellectual leaders, the fraternities and sororities represented their most serious interest in life.

3. Playing Seriously. For a large section of the black bourgeoisie, their activities as members of "society" are their most serious or often their only serious preoccupation. Their preoccupation with "society" has its roots in the traditions of the Negro community in the United States. As we have seen above, in their position of house servants during slavery, Negroes acquired from their white masters notions of what constituted "social" life or "society." After emancipation they continued in the role of personal servants, and therefore saw the white man only in his home or when he was engaged in recreation. They never saw the white man at work in the shop or factory and when he engaged in the serious matter of business. As a consequence they devoted much time and much of their meager resources to attempting to carry on a form of "social" life similar to the whites'. For many Negroes, it appears that "social" life became identified with the condition of freedom. "Social" life among the masses of Negroes was a free and spontaneous expression of their desire to escape from the restraints of work and routine. But for those who set themselves apart as Negro "society," "social" life became a more formalized activity. Among the Negro elite as well as among the masses, "social" life acquired a significance that it did not have among white Americans.

The great significance which "social" life has for Negroes has been due to their exclusion from participation in American life.[8] The numerous "social" clubs and other forms of voluntary associations which have existed among them provided a form of participation that compensated for their rejection by the white community. At the same time these various "social" clubs have been a part of the struggle of Negroes for status within their segregated communities. The elite, who have set themselves apart as Negro "society" and have attempted to maintain an exclusive "social" life, have been extremely conscious of their inferior status in American life. For them "social" life has not only provided a form of participation; it has represented an effort to achieve identification with upper-class whites by imitating as far as possible the behavior of white "society."

The exclusion of middle-class Negroes from participation in the general life of the American community has affected their entire outlook on life. It has meant that whites did not take Negroes seriously; that whites did not regard the activities of Negroes as of any real consequence in American life. It has tended to encourage a spirit of irresponsibility or an attitude of "play" or make-believe among them. Consequently, Negroes have "played" at conducting their schools, at running their businesses, and at practicing their professions.[9] The spirit of play or make-believe has tended to distort or vitiate the ends of their most serious activities. For example, in a number of cities where Negro doctors have been excluded from joining the white professional associations, they have set up "reading societies," supposedly to offset such exclusion. But, on the whole, these "reading societies" have turned out to be "social" clubs for drinking and playing poker. Playing, then, has become the one activity which the Negro may take seriously.

In fact, great importance is attached to "Negro society" in the Negro press because it is a serious preoccupation among the black bourgeoisie. One can get some notion of its importance from an editorial in the September, 1953, number of *Ebony* entitled "Is Negro Society Phony?" The editorial asserts that those who say that Negro "society" is a pretense are envious of those who have been accepted by "society." It goes on to show that members of American white "society" have achieved entrance in the same manner as the members of Negro "society." Then the editorial points out that people like Dr. Bunche, Louis Armstrong, Marian Anderson, Mary

McCleod Bethune, and Joe Louis have won their places in Negro "society" by achievement. The article concludes with the statement that brains rather than blood should be the basis for admission to Negro "society" and that if this is made the basis of acceptance, then Negro youth will seek recognition by Negro "society." It seemingly never occurred to the writer of the editorial that Negroes with brains would prefer not to seek escape in the world of make-believe of the black bourgeoisie.

The exaggerated importance which the black bourgeoisie attaches to "society" is revealed in the emphasis placed by the Negro press upon the "social" aspects of events concerning Negroes. When it was announced recently that a Negro businessman had been named a member of the American delegation to the United Nations, it was stated in a leading Negro publication that he was invading the "glittering international UN scene—the most exclusive and powerful *social* set in the world."[10] The news item added that the nominee had "already made plans to acquire new formal wear" and that he was preparing his wardrobe for his entrance into the United Nations. In fact, generally when white middle-class people have sought the co-operation of the black bourgeoisie in some serious community project, they have found it difficult unless it could be interpreted as a "social" event. For example, such liberal middle-class white groups as the League of Women Voters and League of Women Shoppers have constantly complained that they could not interest middle-class Negro women. On the other hand, let us take the following account of an interracial group of women who raised money for the fight against infantile paralysis. There appeared in the February 25, 1954, issue of *Jet,* under the section labeled "People Are Talking About," the statement that $1,500 was raised by a group of fifteen white and colored "society" women who wore over $500,000 worth of furs and gowns.

Anyone who achieves any distinction in any field may become a "socialite" in the Negro press. It is not simply that, as a Negro journalist stated, "anybody not in the criminal class can get a 'personal' or 'social' note in the Negro paper."[11] This suggests only a small-town attitude which may be found among any people. In making a "socialite" of a Negro, the Negro press is attributing to him or to her the highest conceivable status and recognition. For example, when a Negro anthropologist, who never attended "social" functions, gave a lecture in Chicago, the account in the Negro press referred to him as a "socialite." Consequently, one learns in the Negro press that wives of gamblers, policemen, waiters, college professors, doctors, lawyers, petty civil servants, and public school teachers are all "socialites"—often when their husbands are not so designated. It should be pointed out, however, that being called a "socialite" in the Negro press is generally regarded as a high compliment by the members of the black bourgeoisie, whatever may be their occupations.

As a consequence of the prestige of "society," many Negro professional men and women take more seriously their recreation than their professions. Once the writer heard a Negro doctor who was prominent "socially" say that he would rather lose a patient than have his favorite baseball team lose a game. This was an extreme expression of the relative value of professional work and recreation among the black bourgeoisie. At the same time, it is indicative of the value which many Negro professional men and women, including college professors, place upon sports. Except when they are talking within the narrow field of their professions, their conversations are generally limited to sports—baseball and football. They follow religiously the scores of the various teams and the achievements of all the players. For hours they listen to the radio accounts of sports and watch baseball and football games on television. They become learned in the comments of sportswriters. Often they make long journeys in order to see their favorite teams—white or Negro—play baseball and football games. Although they may pretend to appreciate "cultural" things, this class as a whole has no real appreciation of art, literature, or music. One reads, for example, under what "People Are Talking About," in the September 2, 1954, issue of *Jet,* that a "wealthy" Negro doctor in Detroit is planning to install a "Hammond organ" on his "luxurious yacht." The decor of their homes reveals the most atrocious and childish tastes. Expensive editions of books are bought for decoration and left unread. The black bourgeoisie, especially the section which forms Negro "society," scarcely ever read books for recreation. Consequently, their conversation is trivial and exhibits a childish view of the world.

The prominent role of sports in the "serious playing" of Negro "society" stems partly from certain traditions in the Negro community. It reflects to some extent the traditions of the "gentleman" who engaged in no serious work. But in addition, preoccupation of Negro "society" with sports is related to its preoccupation with gambling, especially poker. This latter preoccupation is especially significant because it is related to the religious outlook of the black bourgeoisie, especially Negro "society."

4. From Church to Chance. The black bourgeoisie can not escape completely from the religious traditions of the Negro masses, since many of those who are achieving middle-class status have come from the masses. They are often haunted by the fears and beliefs which were instilled in them during their childhood. However, they are glad to escape from the prohibitions which the Baptists and Methodists placed upon dancing, card playing, and gambling. They want to escape from the concern of the Baptists and Methodists with sin and death and salvation. The middle-class Negro is like the "suburban agnostic" with whom Mary Kingsley compared the missionary-made African, who keeps the idea of the immortality of the soul and a future heaven but discards the unpleasant idea of hell.[12] The middle-class Negro will tell you that he believes in a Supreme Being, some vague entity who runs the universe, and the immortality of the soul, but he does not believe in hell because he thinks that man has his hell on earth. As a rule, the black bourgeoisie do not give themselves to reflection on these matters. They are regarded as impractical and unpleasant questions which should be left to a few "queer" Negroes, who should spend their time more profitably in making money. An outstanding educated Negro minister, who is a sort of a mystic, was generally regarded with amusement by the black bourgeoisie, and he sought a more congenial audience in an interracial church and as a visiting preacher in white colleges.

When the middle-class Negro abandons the traditional religion of his ancestors, he seldom adopts a new philosophical orientation in regard to existence and the world about him. Since he is as isolated intellectually as he is socially in the American environment, he knows nothing of humanistic philosophy and he rejects materialism because of his prejudices based upon ignorance. Negro intellectuals have nothing to offer him, since they have never developed a social philosophy, except perhaps a crude and unsophisticated opportunism. Therefore, as a rule, the middle-class Negro is the prey of all forms of spiritualism. He avoids the fantastic extravagances of Father Divine's cult, partly because lower-class Negroes are associated with it. He concedes, however, that Father Divine "does some good" because his followers are "honest and faithful domestic servants." Nevertheless, the black bourgeoisie are interested in "psychic" phenomena because, according to them, "scientists do not know everything." Therefore, the little reading in which they indulge is often concerned with "faith healing" and popular accounts of "psychic" phenomena. In some cities it has become a fad for members of Negro "society" to make a novena though they are not Catholics, and they have reported that this religious exercise has resulted in their securing a dress or mink coat which they have always desired.

Without the traditional religion of the Negro and a philosophy to give them an orientation towards life, the black bourgeoisie, especially the element among them known as Negro "society," have often become the worshippers of the God of Chance. This new faith or dependence upon chance finds its extreme expression in their preoccupation with gambling, including the "numbers" (the illegal lotteries in American cities), betting on horses, and more especially poker. At one time the black bourgeoisie regarded the "numbers" as a lower-class form of gambling and restricted themselves to betting on horses. Likewise, playing poker was formerly regarded by them as a pastime for the sporting element among Negroes. But with the emergence of the new Negro "society," playing the "numbers" has become respectable. This is not strange, since some members of "society" derive their incomes from the "numbers." Therefore, it is not unusual for Negro professional men and their wives to play the "numbers" daily. Even the wives of Negro college professors are sometimes "writers" or collectors of "numbers" for the "numbers racket."

But poker has become the most important form of recreation for members of "society" among the black bourgeoisie. In fact, poker is more than a form of recreation; it is the one absorbing interest of Negro "society." It is the chief subject of conversation. Negro "society" women talk over the telephone for hours on the last poker game. According to an article in *Ebony,* March, 1953, the bane of many "society" editors is that "social" affairs turn into poker games, though the latter "can be exciting" when the stakes involve "homes, lots, and automobiles." Even a chance encounter of members of Negro "society" will lead to a poker game. Moreover, poker has tended to level all social barriers among Negroes. At the richly furnished homes of Negro doctors, chauffeurs, waiters, and gasoline station attendants gather with college professors to play poker. So important has poker become among the black bourgeoisie that the measure of a man has become the amount of stakes which he can place at a poker game.

In many cities of the United States, the black bourgeoisie usually spend their weekends in what might be called "poker marathons" or "poker orgies" which last sometimes from Friday night until Monday morning. Some poker players who still have old-fashioned religious ideas may leave the poker table long enough to go to church, because, as they say, they believe in God. But usually most of them, being refreshed with food, remain throughout the "marathon." Some college professors boast of leaving the poker table and going directly to lecture to their classes on Monday. Likewise, Negro surgeons have been heard to boast of leaving the poker table and going directly to perform an operation. Because of their devotion to poker, some middle-class Negroes form groups and journey periodically from city to city in order to engage in these gambling orgies. News of these orgies, with details emphasizing the high stakes played are the main topic of conversation among Negro "society." The importance of poker may be measured by the fact that some middle-class Negroes assert that poker is the one thing in life that prevents them from going crazy.

Notes

1. Austin Steward, *Twenty-Two Years a Slave, and Forty Years a Freeman* (Rochester: Allings and Cory, 1857), pp. 30-32.
2. Manuscript document by John E. Bruce in the Schomburg Collection, New York.
3. It is difficult to find a file of *The Washington Bee*, which published these attacks on the mulattoes.
4. See St. Clair Drake and H. R. Clayton, *Black Metropolis.* (New York: Harcourt, Brace, 1945), pp. 470 ff.
5. See *Jet*, December 27, 1951.
6. See, for example, pictures of Dr. Bunche being presented with the diamond cross of Malta in *The Philadelphia Tribune*, January 2, 1951.
7. See *The Pittsburgh Courier. Washington Edition*, January 10, 1953.
8. Compare Gunner Myrdal, *An American Dilemma.* (New York: Harper & Bros., 1944), pp. 918-19, 952-55.
9. Once I was asked to write a criticism of an article which a Negro had written in a scientific journal. The dean of a Negro college, who read the article and my criticism, objected to what I wrote on the grounds that I had treated the article in the scientific journal seriously!
10. See *Jet*, August 12, 1954, p. 6. Italics mine.
11. Cited in Mydral, op. cit., p. 919.
12. Mary H. Kingsley, *Travels in West Africa, Congo Francais,* Corisco and Cameroons. (London: Macmillan, 1897), pp. 660-661.

Tuxedo Park—Black Tie

By CLEVELAND AMORY

IN VIEW of the importance of clubs in the resort way of life, it is not surprising that more than once resorts have been founded which have been all-club; the greatest of these in America, all club and some five thousand yards wide, was Tuxedo Park, or, as it became more familiarly called, Tuxedo. Located forty miles northwest of New York City in the rugged but picturesque Ramapo Hills overlooking Tuxedo Lake, Tuxedo was incorporated in 1886, originally as a hunting and fishing resort—in the words of its founder, a "short-season place between New York and Newport." Gradually Tuxedo, which was between New York and Newport seasonally but not geographically, became not a resort at all; old-time resorters deserted it because they found it too hot in the summer and too cold in the winter and, in between, neither one thing nor the other. Nowadays, though still clubbable, it is nothing more or less than a year-round community outside of New York which, like the ancient resort of Nahant outside of Boston, still clings to its age-old reputation but is really a social ghost town.

No other community in this country, however, ever started off on a grander social scale and therefore no other may be said to have fallen so hard. Today, with its turreted cottages either in the hands of tax-free institutions or going to wrack and ruin in private hands, with its so-called "Young-Marrieds" living in Stable Row (converted stables of the great estates), and with more than forty families refusing to belong to its heavily mortgaged Club (to which in its great days all belonged), Tuxedo has been called, with some justice, the Graveyard of the Aristocracy. Nonetheless, no other community of its size—roughly two hundred families—still attracts so much curiosity, and no one who has ever lived in Tuxedo for any length of time has ever been allowed to forget it. Governor Thomas E. Dewey, a resident of Tuxedo many years ago, recalls that the most definite bit of advice he ever received concerning his proposed active entry into politics was to get out of Tuxedo. "No one," he was told, "could be elected to anything from such a social place."

The late Price Collier, who made his home in Tuxedo from 1898 until his death in 1915, once said, "The best society of Europe is success enjoying an idle hour or so; the best society here is idleness enjoying its success. . . . Society, to be permanently interesting, must be made up of idle professionals, not of professional idlers." Today Mrs. Price Collier, who ranks as Tuxedo's First Lady, believes that in its great days Tuxedo Park came at least close

---

Reprinted from *Harper's Magazine,* Volume 205, Number 1228 (September, 1952) pp. 80-90, by permission of the author and the publisher. (Copyright 1952 by Cleveland Amory). An expanded version of this article appears in the author's book, *The Last Resorts* (New York: Harper & Brothers, 1952), pp. 79-121.

to her husband's ideal but that it is now far from it indeed. Now ninety-two years old, she has in her lifetime traveled all over the world ever since she first went to China with her father, Warren Delano, at the age of two. "Tuxedo," she says, "has changed more than any place I know of. My father used to say, 'This place is perfection,' and I remember the wife of the Old Squire telling me, 'If you live in Tuxedo one year, you will meet everybody you've ever heard of.' I don't mean to sound crotchety, but, oh dear me, what a change!"

Mrs. Collier, who now spends her winters in two rooms of the Tuxedo Club's bachelor quarters, has of course seen this change at first hand. So, too, has Miss Dorothy Kane, one of the last who still cottages at Tuxedo in the old sense. "I guess you might say," she says, "that I'm a lady—to use an absolutely extinct word." Tuxedo's younger contingent is also vocal. Mrs. Eric Archdeacon, a relative newcomer to the Park, is firm. "Mentally," she says, "Tuxedo has always been constipated. I always think of this place as a beautiful cemetery." Jay Rutherford, scion of a distinguished Tuxedo family and a young man who in 1927, at the age of nine, was editor and publisher of the only newspaper the Park has ever had, is more philosophical. But today he sees vast changes from the Golden Days of his paper which, though it lasted only six months, maintained, right to the end, a circulation of an even four hundred.

"It's the most beautiful place in the world," he says, "but it's full of midgets. The midgets are trying to hold down the tent—and the kings are all gone."

The story of Tuxedo Park goes back to the first Pierre Lorillard, original prince of the snuff and tobacco empire, who, in 1814, foreclosed a mortgage upon part of the Tuxedo territory. This Pierre I was a true empire-builder of the old school. On his death in 1843 one newspaper coined the word "millionaire"—which had never before been used—and another newspaper was moved to remark, "He led people by the nose for the better part of a century and made his enormous fortune by giving them to chew that which they could not swallow." His descendant Pierre Lorillard IV came into the possession of 600,000 acres around the present Tuxedo partly by inheritance, partly by buying out others, and partly by defeating his own relatives at poker.

Starting in September 1885, Pierre Lorillard IV proceeded rapidly. It was in the days before strict immigration and labor laws, and Lorillard imported 1,800 workmen direct from Italy. On the almost deserted property, which was then known as the Erie Railroad's "Wood Pile," the first thing these workers had to do was build a small city of shanties for themselves—like an army in barracks. Lorillard, though a severe man socially, was a remarkable general of his army. "He talked rapidly," his architect Bruce Price once said, "and thought twice as fast as he talked and wished his order carried out at a speed that equaled the sum of both." Once, as Lorillard was leaving Price's office he called back, "By the way, make it four cottages instead of two. Show me the plans for them tomorrow and break ground for them next Monday." Incredibly enough, since the workmen had only the simplest equipment and the winter was a severe one, eight months to the day from the September thirtieth start, Lorillard had a 7,000-acre park fenced with eight-foot barbed wire, thirty miles of graded dirt and macadam road, a complete sewage and water system, a park gatehouse described by the architect as looking "like a frontispiece to an English novel," a broad-verandaed clubhouse staffed with English servants, twenty-two casement-dormered English-turreted cottages, each surrounded by a square of new green lawn; and also two blocks of stores, a score of stables, four lawn tennis courts, a bowling alley, a swimming tank, a boathouse, an icehouse, a dam, a trout pond, and a hatchery. The total cost was $1,500,000. On Memorial Day, 1886, three special trains from New York brought seven hundred guests and Tuxedo Park was opened for inspection.

Nothing had been left to chance. Even the streets of the workers' shanties had been named circumspectly; one was "Fifth Avenue," another "Broadway"; the mess hall was "Delmonico's." During the construction of the Park the grounds were carefully guarded and, warned the New York *World,* "Woe to the unlucky stranger who strays across the posted boundaries." As far back as October Lorillard had completed the membership list of his Club. Described at the time as "a guide to Who was especially Who in the Four Hundred," it consisted of William Waldorf Astor, T. Burnett Baldwin, George S. Bowdoin, Lloyd S. Bryce, William P. Douglas, Robert Goelet, John G. Heckscher, Henry H. Hollister, C. Oliver Iselin, Granville Kane, William Kent, Lawrence Kip, Herman R. LeRoy, Pierre Lorillard, Pierre Lorillard, Jr., Ogden Mills, Herbert C. Pell, Allen T. Rice, F. Augustus Schermerhorn, and William R. Travers. These members sported the Club badge which, designed to be worn as a pin, was an oakleaf of solid gold. At first Lorillard had intended to own all the cottages himself and rent them out to his friends, but gradually he was persuaded to parcel them out for purchase on a sort of social first-come, first-served basis. No one who was not a member of the Club was allowed to buy property; the first outsider to be admitted was Sir Roderick Cameron, the British Consul in New York.

From miles around the country folk gathered to witness the coming of the New York trains on the opening day. On their arrival at the Tuxedo station, the seven hundred guests were directed to newly painted coaches and Brewster wagonettes which, sporting the Tuxedo colors with their leaf-green bodies and bright yellow-gold wheels, waited to take the visitors on tour. Architecturally the original idea of Tuxedo had been to blend everything into the surrounding woods; the shingled cottages were stained russets and grays, and the gatehouse, as well as the post office, drugstore, and market, all were patched with lichen and moss and were supposed to look a thousand years old. Beds of flowers lined the roads. As the coaches and wagonettes drove around the Park, private Tuxedo policemen, chosen for their height and good looks, pointed the way; Tirolean hatted game-keepers, also in Club uniform, darted in and out of the forest on a regular in-and-out schedule; and out on the lake, crews in blue and white sailor suits manned eight-oared sight-seeing barges. From one hilltop a red flag flew; Lorillard's idea of this flag, said *Harper's Weekly,* was that it would serve as "a warning to hesitating lovers that the beauty of the place will turn their thoughts to love."

The high point of the visit, which included a luncheon reception, an afternoon of sports, and an evening dance before the special trains returned, was the trip to the new Club, or the Old Club as it is called today. Until the time of Tuxedo the few country clubs which existed were relatively simple, small-roomed farmhouse affairs. Tuxedo's Club was something else. Although it would seem primitive by today's standards—there were a hundred bedrooms and only one private bath—it was the marvel of its time. A square wooden building, surrounded by porches, it boasted a large paneled living room, long leather sofas, and wide open fireplaces burning five-foot logs; everywhere the appointments were the last word in smartness. Hallmen, footmen, and waiters were in full Tuxedo Club livery, green with gold-striped waistcoats; the service was excellent and the food generally reported to be the best this side of Paris.

Of all the features of what to Tuxedoites will always remain their beloved Old Club the most remarkable was its large circular ballroom, eighty feet in diameter, which was actually a separate building from the main Club and was connected to it by a long corridor. This ballroom had not only a parquet floor which was reputed the best dance floor of its time, but also a handsome domed ceiling supported on a set of Corinthian columns. Behind these columns were built-in divans, or high-chair seats, which were reserved for the Tuxedo dowagers who, complete with lorgnettes, spent the dance evenings happily strafing their offsprings. Finally, opposite the entrance of the ballroom, was a stage fully equipped with footlights, drop-curtains, and all the trimmings. There was some irony in connection with this stage since when James Brown Potter proposed the actor Kyrle Bellew for membership in the club, there was such consternation that a special *ad hoc* committee was called of the Tuxedo Governors. Immediately they passed a rule that no actor should ever be permitted to become a member of the club—a rule which has never been erased from the books.

The only feature of Tuxedo society which has continued intact to the present day, the annual Autumn Ball, is still the opening gun of each New York debutante season; a debutante who receives an invitation to it feels confident that she is a member of New York's inner circle. This ball has a justly famous place in the history of American Society, for it was at the first Autumn Ball in October 1886, that young Griswold Lorillard, son of Pierre IV, wore the tailless dress coat to which the resort gave its name. Today all Tuxedoites agree that, once having seen the coat, "everyone wanted one like Grizzy's," but how the coat came to be worn in the first place, or even whether it was first worn at Tuxedo, can still start an argument in any resort society. Some resorters trace the origin of the coat to James Brown Potter's visit to the Prince of Wales, who wore a somewhat similar smoking jacket; some to the late E. Berry Wall, King of the Dudes, who was put off the dance floor of the Grand Union Hotel in Saratoga for wearing such a coat; and some to an anonymous leader of Irish Society who sported the coat at a dance at one of the Bowery's Chowder and Marching Clubs; perhaps the simplest explanation is that given by Newport's young Louis Lorillard, great great grandson of Pierre IV. "I've always heard," he says, "that they just got tired of sitting around on their tails, so they cut them off."

Two things, however, are certain. One is that the coat which Griswold Lorillard wore was designed by his father and was a scarlet satin-lapeled affair which was tailored, if not tailed, along the lines of the pink coats worn by hunters riding to hounds. The other is that the coat was not an instant success. The society journal *Town Topics* claimed that Griswold Lorillard looked "for all the world like a royal footman" and that he and his friends who wore the coats "ought to have been put in straitjackets long ago." Even today it is an ironical fact that in society the word "tuxedo" is itself taboo, the use of "dinner jacket" in its stead being mandatory.

The immediate success of Tuxedo Park, entirely apart from its coat, was a phenomenon of the great resort era. In social prestige Tuxedo quickly outranked other New York resorts such as Richfield Springs and Sharon Springs, Lake Placid and Lake George, and even challenged mighty Saratoga; soon Tuxedo was a rival of Newport itself. Any Tuxedoite, merely by showing his gold oakleaf pin, could have any Erie train, even those which did not stop except at the largest stations, stop at Tuxedo, and Mrs. William Pierson Hamilton, daughter of the elder J. P. Morgan, even had her own railroad station; the last before Tuxedo, it was called "Sterlington" and dutifully the Erie trains stopped there as they did at "Arden," the station beyond Tuxedo belonging to the railroad king, E. H. Harriman.

Gradually, however, there began to be intimations that all was not well with Society's Utopia. The first chink to appear in the Tuxedo armor occurred in 1892 when Julia Ward Howe, author of "The Battle Hymn of the Republic," journeyed up from Newport and made a visit to the Park. On her return she was asked by her daughter, Newport's beloved Maud Howe Elliot, what she thought of the place. Replied Mrs. Howe briefly: "White of an egg." This opinion, coming from one of the social oracles of the age, was widely repeated at the time. Although Tuxedoites knew they could expect no quarter from confirmed Newporters—Pierre Lorillard IV had deserted Newport to found Tuxedo—they also suffered at this time a severe blow from within. This occurred with the report handed in to the executive committee of the Tuxedo Park Association from another committee which was headed by William Waldorf Astor and was entitled "The Committee Appointed to Examine into the Original Historical Names of the Tuxedo Region." This sort of search for the historic is, of course, a familiar defense in which all the great resorts have indulged in order to take the edge off the purely social; in Tuxedo's case the report, which still reposes in the Tuxedo Club safe and which was supposed to prove that the name Tuxedo meant "beautiful view"—an opinion widely held by Tuxedoites—unfortunately disclosed that the original Indian name must have been P'tauk-Seet-tough, meaning "The Home of the Bear."

Also it was becoming apparent that "The Home of the Bear" was by no means a perfect habitat for sport. Article I of Tuxedo's Constitution had clearly stated that the resort was established "for the protection, increase, and capture of all kinds of game and fish," and a gallant effort subsidized by Lorillard's money was made to carry this out. Fishing, expected to be Tuxedo's main sport, was the first to suffer. Originally Tuxedo Lake had a reasonable supply of black bass; unfortunately German carp were soon added under the mistaken idea that they would breed and that the carp fry would furnish good bass food. Instead the grown-up carp, hungry in the meantime, ate first the bass fry and then the bass themselves. In the matter of game Tuxedo had an even more difficult time. Though no expense was spared and ring-necked pheasant from New Jersey, quail from North Carolina, and wild turkey from Texas were imported with abandon, all either found Tuxedo's eight-foot fence no bar to their desire for less social areas or else became so tame that sportsmen lacked the heart to molest them.

Tuxedo's white-tailed deer, also an imported item from New Jersey, were particularly pacific. In the early days a favorite story of the Park was of the occasion when a group of eager sportsmen, out from New York to Tuxedo for the first time, were suddenly thrilled by the sight of a doe springing through the woods. Up went their guns, only to come down again when, sighting closer, the sportsmen observed that the animal wore, handsomely bowed around her neck, a large red ribbon.

Still Tuxedo refused to give up. Failing in its fish and game the Park turned to other endeavors. In short order the Park built not only a mile-long, electrically-lit toboggan slide—which was the subject of a famous Tuxedo short story entitled "A Kiss in the Toboggan"— but also a racetrack complete with a grandstand for horse shows and dog shows. On the lake the Park went in heavily for canoeing and sailboating in the summer, and in the winter for both curling and ice skating; old-timers recall with relish the "black ice" days when the lake froze over. Tuxedoites skated as romantically as they tobogganed, often in the evenings by lantern light, later coming in, two by two, to the Club's hot-spice punch and sugared doughnuts.

In 1889, Tuxedo had its first golf course, one which has always been regarded by Tuxedoites as the second oldest in the country, junior only to St. Andrews at Yonkers. Southampton, Saratoga, Bar Harbor, Hot Springs, and White Sulphur are among the resorts which dispute the claim. In 1894, by which time the Park had a new course, Tuxedo sent out invitations to an inter-club match. Four teams competed, St. Andrews, Boston's Brookline Country Club, Southampton's Shinnecock Club, and Tuxedo—with St.

Andrews winning. Following this match, which was the major social sporting event of its day, the country's golf craze began in earnest; the days of the so-called "gentleman champions," as were the days of Tuxedo itself, were numbered.

One sport has to this day been kept almost entirely safe from democracy, and Tuxedo played, characteristically, a stalwart role in its promotion. Known as court tennis—not to be confused with lawn tennis or squash tennis, squash or squash racquets, or even just plain racquets—the sport has exceptionally complicated rules and is so aristocratic that it has been played at only a handful of racquet clubs and private courts. From the time when the Park installed its court, in 1899, the Tuxedo fathers of the game appeared to realize that they had in their hands the last sport of the last resorts—in other words, a gentleman's sport, as lawn tennis and golf once were, and one which so few people could understand, let alone have any facilities for practice, that it was almost possible to announce yourself as champion without playing at all. (Even if you did have to play, the chances were good that your opponent would not know the rules, and if he did know the rules, the chances were even better that he would not know how to keep score; no game can be played without a "marker" or umpire, and even then the scoring is so complicated that many people have played for years without understanding it.)

At first serene in their Club Championship, in which good Tuxedoites happily took turns in sharing the honors, Tuxedo gingerly started in 1903 its famous Gold Racquet Championship. For the first year and for two years following, this was won, satisfactorily enough, by the neighboring Hudson Valley player Charles B. Sands, a young man who kept the game even more in the family by playing both under his own name and the alias "E. Edwards." When the outlander Jay Gould, however, came over from Lakewood in 1906 and won, not only that year but also for the next two years, the tournament was abandoned, and although it was revived in 1926 following the retirement of Gould—some idea of the sport may be gained from the fact that Gould was amateur champion for twenty straight years—Tuxedo took no chances. The tournament was revived only on condition that no one who had won the national championship could also play for the Gold Racquet.

In the booming nineteen-twenties Tuxedo, believing that the old order would continue *ad infinitum,* dug in. A new clubhouse with long stone lines, contrasting sharply with the old square wooden building, was designed by John Russell Pope; a new swimming pool replaced the old swimming tank; and the resort ushered in a new generation of millionaires—the "bad" millionaires in the view of the old "good" millionaires. By this time also Tuxedo led all other resorts in the recognition of a new difficulty, the servant problem. Because of the Park gatehouse rigmarole—by which no visitor to Tuxedo can get by the gate policemen until his purpose has been checked by telephone with his destination—servants found it extremely difficult to entertain their boy friends; their boy friends in turn usually persuaded them to leave for more accessible areas. Still remembered at Tuxedo today is Newell Tilton's bon mot on a subject which became far from funny with the passing years. "We have ten servants," said Tilton, "five coming and five going."

The era of the twenties was ushered in by at least one specific tempest in the Tuxedo teapot. The year was 1921 and the resort was in a turmoil. Word was passed around that one of the Park's most charming ladies was writing a book; furthermore, as the dark story went, she was putting all her friends in it. Fortunately the fears were unfounded. The book, published in 1922, was *Etiquette;* the author, Mrs. Price Post, better known as Emily. For many years the literary advisor of Funk and Wagnalls had tried unsuccessfully to persuade Mrs. Post, who was the daughter of the architect of Tuxedo and the author of several novels contrasting European with American standards, to undertake such a book; Mrs. Post had steadfastly refused. One day the Funk and Wagnalls man surreptitiously left another book on the subject, published by Doubleday, in Mrs. Post's Tuxedo cottage. Picking it up one night, Mrs. Post was horrified with its gaucheries. "Doubleday!" she says today, recalling the event. "Doubleday! And I knew they were ladies and gentlemen, too!"

Mrs. Post was never one to brook gaucheries. Among other distinctions, she had been named, at the age of eighteen, by Ward McAllister, as one of the ten ladies in New York who could gracefully cross a ballroom floor alone; furthermore, she had learned the art, wearing a sandbag on her head, at Miss Graham's Finishing School for Young Ladies—a school which also taught, in the same manner, the art of curtseying. The next day Mrs. Post sat down and began her book, and today *Etiquette,* born in Tuxedo Park, is currently in its seventy-seventh edition. Mrs. Post herself, who no longer lives in the Park, still ranks as Tuxedo's most distinguished ex-hostess.

"Tuxedo was the most formal place in the world," she declares. "Nobody ever waved or hello-ed or hi-ed at Tuxedo. You bowed when you shook hands and the manners at the balls were something wonderful. You never slopped. You sat up perfectly straight. And first names were considered very bad form. You might be Johnny in private, but you were Mr. Jones in public. There were only five men in Tuxedo who called me Emily—and never in formal Society."

From the beginning, Tuxedo was for its size the most attractive of all resorts to royalty; even today a spare Hapsburg or a miscellaneous Hohenzollern may be flushed, along with the tame quail, from almost any given spot in the Tuxedo woods. In the memory of Tuxedo old-timers, however, one regal visit of the winter of 1927 still stands out. The visit began quietly enough when Mrs. Charles E. Mitchell, wife of the National City banker, innocently playing a double concerto on the piano in her New York home, was summoned to the telephone to receive a long-distance call from Louisville, Kentucky; the call was from a former acquaintance, a man she knew so slightly that she hardly recalled his name. The man informed Mrs. Mitchell that he was on tour with Queen Marie of Romania and that Her Majesty was coming to New York and would like very much to visit Mrs. Mitchell in Tuxedo rather than stay in a New York hotel. When Mrs. Mitchell asked how many people there were in the Queen's party, the man informed her that there were sixteen—including nine servants.

At first Mrs. Mitchell, relatively new to the ways of visiting royalty at resorts, was sure the whole thing was a hoax. Her Tuxedo cottage was closed for the winter and neither she nor her husband had ever met the Queen of Romania. She merely said politely she should be delighted, hung up the telephone, and returned to her double concerto. But at dinner she received a telegram from the same man who had telephoned her. The telegram was to the point: HER MAJESTY WISHES ME TO EXPRESS HER DEEP APPRECIATION FOR THE HOSPITALITY WHICH YOU AND MR. MITCHELL HAVE SO VERY KINDLY OFFERED WHICH SHE ACCEPTS WITH PLEASURE.

To this day Mrs. Mitchell does not know how she did it. The telegram arrived Thursday night; the Queen and her army were to arrive in Tuxedo Saturday afternoon. Mrs. Mitchell's Tuxedo cottage had no linen or silver in it, the water and electric lights were turned off, and winter shutters boarded all the windows. She does recall, however, her very first step—which was to wire the go-between and ask if Her Majesty preferred seclusion or if she wished to be entertained. Promptly she received an answer in the form of her second wire of the evening—one which contained a list of friends Her Majesty would be happy to see. "It was," says Mrs. Mitchell, recalling the incident, "an abbreviated little yellow edition of the *Social Register*."

By Saturday afternoon the Mitchells were ready on their doorstep—royalty at resorts must always be greeted from outside, rather than inside, one's cottage—when the Queen and party, accompanied by the sirens of police escorts, screamed up the Tuxedo hills. During the entire visit only two mishaps occurred. At the first dinner a novice butler spilled a melon of ice cream down the back of Princess Ileana—who, since the Queen's luggage did not arrive until the next day, was wearing Mrs. Mitchell's black velvet Chanel dress—and midway in the visit Master Craig Mitchell's American cocker spaniel, bit Her Majesty's dog in the behind. There was also one error in protocol. This occurred at the first dinner when the Queen found herself seated at Mr. Mitchell's right; actually, of course, she should have been on his left—or, in other words, Mr. Mitchell should have been at *her* right.

Evidently such discrepancies did not trouble the Queen at all. Shortly before leaving she confided, with what a friend described as her "infectious wink," that she had completely forgotten the matter of the dinner protocol. "Mr. Mitchell has been so royal," she said, "that I felt common."

In many ways the recent story of Tuxedo Park can be summed up in the story of the last of its great estates. Known as "Duckhollow House," a beautiful white Georgian building, directly across the Lake from the Club, it consists, among other things, of twenty-five air-conditioned rooms, an all-mirrored master bathroom, a movie theatre, a swimming pool, a life-size granite Buddha, a boathouse, an electric motorboat, and 300,000 dollars' worth of shrubbery; the total cost was $2,250,000 in 1937. Designed by Architect T. Markoe Robertson, this charming cottage was presented to Mr. and Mrs. Angier Biddle Duke as a wedding present by their parents, the Duke and St. George families. Following the divorce of this couple, "Duckhollow House" was sold to Mr. and Mrs. John Astor Drayton, also of Tuxedo. When Mr. and Mrs. Drayton also reached the end of their marriage, "Duckhollow House" was again resold, but on this occasion for the first time the cottage came into ownership which, by Tuxedo standards, involved an outsider. The new owner, Nathan Berkman, a wealthy New York tax consultant, was charmed with "Duckhollow House." When, however, he went down to his boathouse and put out to sea at a fast ten knots in his forty-battery electric motorboat—since the lake is the source of the Park's drinking water all boats have to be electric—he was promptly informed by letter from the Tuxedo Park Association that since he did not belong to the Tuxedo Club, and the Tuxedo Club claimed exclusive use of the lake for its members, he could not use the lake.

Berkman was promptly disenchanted. Having no desire to buck the Club for membership he was, as a tax consultant, a man who knew his way around in law books; when the Club threatened with an injunction, he decided to fight back. He not only traced deeds to the lake far beyond those the Tuxedo Park Association had ever heard of—one being a manuscript map made for George Washington—but he also declared that if the Club sued him he was prepared to maintain that if the lake was indeed a private reservoir then it must have an eight-foot fence around it—the same height of fence, ironically enough, which surrounds Tuxedo Park and, even more ironically perhaps, surrounds "Duckhollow House." Finally both the Park Association and Berkman dropped both suits and threats of suits and Berkman was once more permitted to put out to sea. "I found," he says today, above the puttering of his forty batteries, "that I had no less and no more privileges to the lake than the Club itself."

Today at Tuxedo, if the situation in the lake is fraught with peril, the situation in the Club itself is even more so. In the early days so great was the prestige of being a member of the Club's fifteen-man Board of Governors that these Governors cheerfully paid the deficit, which often ran as high as $80,000 a year, out of their own pockets; no statement was ever even rendered to ordinary members. The depression, however—along with the fact the new Club was vastly more expensive than the old—brought an end to this situation. Today's Clubhouse is now supported by all manner of desperate measures, including renting out the premises to the employees of Time, Inc., for a so-called "Time Out." While such heterogeneous outsiders enjoy using the tradition-hallowed facilities, insiders have not taken kindly to the change, and even the trusted old employees of the Club, men like "Chris," "Scott," and "Carter," all of whom have served more than forty years, view the present with distaste and the future with alarm.

Furthermore, coupled with dangerous money-raising programs has come another modernism which to elderly Tuxedoites is equally dangerous—a sort of social inflation in the electing of members. Recently Tuxedoite Charles Coulter of "Wee-Wah" cottage, following the election of a new member of whom he did not approve, announced that he would never cross the threshold of the Club again, and while the Club pondered this blow Coulter's motion was promptly seconded by action on the part of Mrs. E. John Heidsieck of "To the Point." Following the election of a member of whom she did not approve, Mrs. Heidsieck, daughter of the late railroad man James J. Hill, ordered the portrait of Pierre Lorillard V removed from the Club's ballroom; in her opinion Tuxedo's beloved Squire, who was her second husband and of whom she was the second wife, should not have to view, even from the wall, the sort of modern goings-on in the Club he loved so well.

For a while the space was blank. Then quietly one day in the place of Squire Lorillard a new portrait was hung, and all good Tuxedoites breathed a sigh of relief when it turned out to be the familiar, chop-whiskered visage of the greatest of all the Gods of the Club, the Titan of Tuxedo himself, the late George F. Baker. In the opinion of old Tuxedoites no man in his life ever personified better than the great banker the virtues of the era which had passed; in their opinion, also, no man after death was so eminently fitted to warn the moderns, by the stern, disapproving look from the wall, of the wages of their sins.

Tuxedo could not have made a better choice. Certainly the career of Banker Baker, who lived from 1840 to 1931, was the antithesis of the modern, high-pressure, publicity-charged success story of today. Whether or not he was, as Tuxedoites claim, "third or fourth richest man in the history of the country," he was certainly the only man of his eminence who ever led a life so secretive that in the course of his ninety-one years he granted just one newspaper interview and made just two speeches which might even be considered public (six words to the Bond Club, "Thank you and God bless you"; six words to the Tuxedo Club following his gift of a golf house, "God bless you and thank you").

In 1910 at the age of seventy, Baker took up for the first time smoking, drinking cocktails, and golf. Stories of his latter-day links efforts are still part of Tuxedo conversation. Among other things if Baker wished a round before dinner, the train stopped right at the first tee of the golf course. Once playing in the pouring rain with Edward E. Loomis, a man thirty years younger than he, Baker insisted on continuing a tied match. "Mr. Baker," gasped Mr. Loomis, "you are a wonder for a man of your age." Baker teed up his ball. "The difference between you and me," he said, "is that I never began to dissipate until I was seventy."

But even at golf the banker could not forget himself entirely. On losing a ball he would become so distressed that he would hunt for it with his caddy as long as there was even a remote hope of finding it. Nor were tees items to be taken lightly. One of the banker's golfing companions, a Tuxedo "little brother of the rich," made a practice of surreptitiously placing broken tees where Baker would find them; the disappointment on Baker's face on picking up one of these tees was, according to this "little brother," something to see. To players following Baker around the course, the Titan's game, a severe point of which was to let no one else through, was little pleasure indeed.

One Saturday afternoon when the course was crowded and Baker, at eighty-five, was being slowly pushed up a hill by the strong arm of his caddy, a fellow-Tuxedoite cupped his hand in desperation. "Mr. Baker," he called out, "I've got to catch a train." Then, dropping his hand, he added, "Monday morning."

During the boom nineteen-twenties Tuxedo joined with the entire country in trying to figure each day the result of the bull market on Baker's personal fortune. When, for example, the First National Bank stock, of which it was common knowledge in the Park that Baker owned some 25,000 shares, touched $8,500 a share, they quickly multiplied it out and found Baker worth $212,500,000 in that stock alone; they knew that besides he was also the largest single stockholder in such companies as American Telephone and U. S. Steel. Few of Baker's friends at Tuxedo actually banked with him. The story was that it took $100,000 to open an account and even today, since the bank is primarily a banker's bank—one for other banks and corporations—the average individual bank balance is something over $300,000.

Although in 1929, 97 per cent of Baker's total fortune was in common stocks, he had but one complaint to make when the market broke. Sick in bed, he begged to be allowed to go downtown. "This is my ninth panic," he protested. "I have made money in every one of them." The following year, true to his word, Baker made, by the estimate of *Fortune* magazine, $50,000,000 at a time when he was ninety years old.

In the last two years of his life, though suffering from diabetes, Baker attended no less than 150 directors' meetings, his favorites being those of companies on the so-called "tontine" system. At these meetings the directors present divide the fees of directors absent; Baker, characteristically, especially enjoyed such meetings in inclement weather. Unfortunately they proved the death of him. In the last week of his life he attended four directors' meetings. At the final one, of the Consolidated Gas Company, which was held on a bad day, he caught the cold which led to the pneumonia from which, two days later, on May 2, 1931, he died.

4

The Runaway Weekend—Mass Leisure

For most of us, leisure means doing something—hobbies, sports, games, entertainment, amusements, recreational activities. The chapters in this section describe a few of these activities and give a composite picture of mass leisure—a picture which is then examined critically.

Highly representative of mass leisure is sports, a vast business for spectators and participants alike, which Gregory Stone and Roger Kahn see as a reflection of the tensions in American society.

Hobbies constitute another of the major leisure-time activities. In the past, leisure provided, for those who could afford eccentricities, ample room to express them, and harmless obsessiveness could well be absorbed (particularly among English eccentrics). Ornamental hermits abounded. Today's pursuit of hobbies seems less compulsive and less involuted; if we follow a hobby at all we tend to be more practical about it: we join a hobby club, subscribe to its magazine, conform to expert advice, and most important, express our interests which may even save us money, such as do-it-yourself. "What's Happening to Hobbies" describes this professionalization; included also is a report on do-it-yourself issued by the Department of Commerce.

A vacation is that time of the year which is most clearly one's leisure time and there are a great many ways to spend one. Leslie Stephen described, almost a hundred years ago, the folly of most people's choice of activities. Stone and Taves describe one form: camping out when one does not have to.

On the surface of much leisure are trivial preoccupations—listening to popular music, arguing about the appeal of a movie star. Topics change but the conversation and preoccupation remains the same. This top layer of life is examined in "Notes on a Natural History of Fads."

Hardly a fad, yet fad-like, is America's preoccupation with organizations. Ever since Tocqueville made the observation, it has seemed that Americans are a nation of joiners. The extent to which this is true is shown by Charles Wright and Herbert Hyman.

Any and all activities may provide leisure and gratification; hence from knowing what a person is doing one cannot say that he is at leisure. The perfect enjoyment of leisure lies somewhere between addiction and indifference. Drinking is perhaps one of the most ambiguous activities—it may be leisure, or work, or an addiction; Riley, Marden, and Lifshitz help unravel the mixed motivations.

The fact that there are rules in leisure as elsewhere seems paradoxical. Such rules are most important and least discussed in the area of sex, as Nelson Foote points out in his discussion of the rules of this game.

Pieper, Lynes, Swados, and Riesman provide a kind of finale to this book. One conclusion reached is that this age of mass leisure would be helped if a way were found to endow work with some of the qualities of leisure and leisure with some of the qualities found in work.

The real problem may be the one that William Faulkner once mentioned (cf. Paris Review, *12. p. 45):*

> *One of the saddest things is that the only thing a man can do for eight hours a day is work. You can't eat eight hours a day nor drink eight hours a day nor make love eight hours a day—all you can do for eight hours is work. Which is why man makes himself and everybody else so miserable and unhappy.*

American Sports: Play and Dis-Play[1]

By GREGORY P. STONE

SOCIETY has often been likened by its students to a game, but, like other more frequently encountered social science metaphors such as the machine or the organism, the game itself is usually unquestioned. Its significance is only to be found in that which it represents. Thus the well known "game theory" of von Neumann and Morgenstern, for example, contributes to our knowledge of economic behavior or, more recently, political behavior and conflict. Little, if anything, has been said about what our economic or political life can tell us of games or play. Or, concurrent with its representational value, the game is interpreted as a "childish thing." George Herbert Mead has shown how play and the game may be viewed symbolically as phases in the emergence of selfhood, and Jean Piaget has studied with admirable care the relation between the child's orientation to the rules of the game and his larger moral development. These efforts are mentioned not to detract in any way from their value but rather to indicate something of the circumlocution that has seemingly attended our studies of play and games. The substantive investigation of play has been largely eschewed by social scientists. Consequently, there is little to *report* here about American sport, but much to *suggest*.

Jan Huizinga in his remarkable little study of man, the player,[2] notes that play is certainly prior to culture, for all young animals may be observed to gambol and frisk about. But puppies and kittens may at times be envied. Animal play is not interpreted. Ernst Cassirer would have said their play is responsive, not responsible. Man, on the other hand, imbues his play with meanings and affect, arranges it, stylizes it. And in America, at least among the "middle mass" of the large cities and suburbs, the old styles of play seem somehow to apply no longer, while the new emergent styles are not yet widely apprehended and nowhere clearly understood. Play is often conceived in archaic restraint and carried on in frenzies of unrestraint. Americans are uneasy with play, sometimes inept. Even in their discussions of leisure, as David Riesman has observed,[3] many of our people seem uncomfortable. Nor are sociologists immune to such discomfort. Nelson Foote, in a recent plea for a "social science of play," apparently felt constrained to protest his "deadly seriousness."[4] The uneasiness that accompanies our view of play may well afford the simplest and most efficient explanation for the lack of social science inquiries into the nature of play. At the same time, and in the light of the ambivalence and anomalies it suggests, it may afford a fruitful point of departure for our own discussion of American sport.

Reprinted from *Chicago Review*, Volume 9, Number 3 (Fall 1955), pp. 83-100, by permission of the author and the publisher.

Huizinga rested his case for the thesis that civilization develops *in* and *as* play largely upon his detection of an agonistic component—a competition or contest—in various phases of life among diverse civilizations. Yet what is relevant here is not only that play is a contest or that it manifests tension and uncertainty, but that it is also *contested.* Play both embraces the contest and is caught up in the larger contests, tensions, ambivalences, and anomalies of society. A brief glance at the history of sport and play in Western civilization demonstrates this. As our social organization has shifted from a system of estates, through a system of production and classes, to a pattern of consumption and masses; play and sport have always been affected by the cleavages and processes built into such organizational patterns. The significance of archery for the early maintenance of aristocratic power lay behind most of the medieval bans against such sports as football, golf, and bowling. In a sense the pre-eminent place assigned to production in the nineteenth century had the effect of insulating sport and play or restricting most sports to the playgrounds of the leisure classes and placing sports in the hands of amateurs who would perform conspicuously and graciously to gain the esteem and deference of exclusive class-linked audiences. Nor has the massification of sport, implying its commercialization and professionalization, emerged uncontested on the contemporary scene. Professional sport experienced many early setbacks in its struggle to break out of the dignified amateurism and exclusiveness of the nineteenth century.

The point is this: because of their intrinsic agonistic character and the fact of their involvement in the "agony" of the larger society, sport and play are fraught with anomalies. A consideration of some of these anomalies should reveal something of the significance that sport and play have for Americans.

The Production and Consumption of Sport. The anomalous quality of sport may be seen at once when its industrial or economic character is placed over and against its appeal as a product to be consumed. In 1950 less than one-half of 1 per cent of all workers were professional athletes (0.02 per cent). This category did, however, increase sharply from 1940 to 1950, when it increased 61 per cent, a greater increase than the other professional occupations taken together (37.4 per cent) and greater than the increase of the labor force taken as a whole (25.2 per cent). From 1910 to 1940 the proportions of persons employed in amusement, recreation, and related services has almost doubled; but it is still less than 1 per cent of the total labor force. Within this small segment of the labor force the most notable change in specific occupations has occurred in the professional and semiprofessional groupings which comprised well over half of all workers in the industry in 1910, but comprised only about one-quarter of all the workers in the industry in 1950. Although it is difficult to interpret these census data accurately because of the heterogeneity of some of the categories concerned, they may well attest to the proliferation of related occupations that seems to have characterized the growth of sport in America.

As a matter of fact, sport would seem to present a unique occupational morphology among American industries. Those engaged first hand in the production of the commodity—the game or the match—constitute a minority within the industrial complex, while those engaged in the administration, promotion, and servicing of the production constitute a sizable majority. The occupational structure of the industry has the character of an inverted pyramid.

We may note in passing an additional peculiarity of the occupational character of sport. It would seem to be readily apparent that the occupation is one in which the work cycle differs from that of most occupations. Specifically, the worker has a relatively short productive work life, and generally his occupational experience does not qualify him for any other skill.[5] Currently the aversion to "subject matter men" in some educational circles may merely reflect larger trends in social mobility. As Riesman suggests, it would seem that there is "a new pattern in American business life: if one is successful in one's craft, one is forced to leave it"[6]—the "subject matter" may, in fact, be losing its significance for mobility in professional and business occupations. The athlete, however, is involved in different mobility patterns. As opposed to the "skills of gregariousness and amiability," it is proposed that "skill democracy . . . based on respect for ability to do something tends to survive only in athletics."[7] Not only are the athlete's opportunities for mobility considerably constricted by the intrinsic brevity of his career, but, once that brief career has ended, he leaves it whether he is successful or not. Perhaps the career of the boxer may dramatize, if not precisely speak for, the case of the professional athlete in America:

> Boxers find further that, despite their success in the sport, their careers terminate at a relatively early age . . . Since boxing has been the vocational medium of status attainment and since they have no other skills to retain that status, many boxers experience a sharp decline in status in their postboxing careers. As an illustration, of ninety-five leading former boxers (i.e., champions and leading contenders), each of whom earned more than $100,000 during his ring career, eighteen were found to have remained in the sport as trainers or trainer-managers; two became wrestlers; twenty-six work in, "fronted for," or owned taverns, two were liquor salesmen; eighteen had unskilled jobs, most commonly in the steel-mills; six worked in the movies; five were entertainers; two owned or worked in gas stations; three were cab-drivers; three had newsstands; two were janitors; three were bookies; three were associated with the race tracks (two in collecting bets and one as a starter); and two were in business, one of them as a custom tailor.[8]

When these findings are regarded in light of the fact that the chances of success in boxing are, indeed, relatively slim, the negligible opportunity for larger social success to be found in boxing circles is sharply underscored. Specifically, of a sample of 127 fighters whose careers were traced from 1938 on, 84.2 per cent remained in the local preliminary or semiwindup category; 8.7 per cent became local headliners; and 7.1 per cent achieved national recognition. It does not seem unreasonable to surmise that similar barriers confront other professional athletes in their quest for ultimate success.

Moreover, the more "purely" economic status of sport is certainly not impressive. Specifically, the share of the national product contributed by amusement, recreation, and related services in 1953 was only about one-half of 1 per cent. Perhaps of some importance is the fact that the motion picture industry accounted for more of this proportion of the national product from 1937 to 1952, but that a reversal occurred in 1953. This was not a sudden shift. Rather, it is discernible throughout the period. In 1937 motion pictures contributed 5.3 per cent of the national product for all service industries, while other amusement, recreation, and related services contributed 3.6 per cent. In 1950 the figures were 3.7 and 3.3 per cent respectively; and in 1953, 2.9 and 3.3 per cent. However, the precise contribution to this reversal made by sport cannot be determined from the data at hand.

In 1948, the last date for which figures are available, of all businesses classed as amusements only 13 per cent comprised establishments devoted to sport; 9.4 per cent of the total payrolls of such businesses went to employees of the sporting industry; and business receipts for sport comprised only 7.3 per cent of the receipts for all amusement establishments.

As over and against the relatively insignificant place that sport occupies in the American industrial complex, the place it assumes in American consumption is awesome. Here consumption must be writ large. It extends, of course, beyond the sheer purchase of a seat at the game or contest. We read, hear, and view sport in America. The pervasiveness of our interest may be readily documented. Glancing at my morning paper, the *Detroit Free Press,* I note that five pages are given over to sporting news (roughly four hundred column inches excluding advertising) and two and one-half pages to news of business and industry (roughly two hundred and forty column inches). Available back issues acknowledge that this morning's paper was not at all unrepresentative. Recently I had the occasion to make a crude estimate of gross sales (newsstand and subscriptions) of a national sports weekly. These approximate three-tenths of 1 per cent of all business receipts for sports establishments in 1948. When advertising income for this single magazine is added, we may begin to realize the tremendous disparity between the production costs and consumption expenditures for sport in America.

Unfortunately no studies have been made of the function of sport for the American consumer. We can only speculate. We suspect, for example, that the sports pages in the daily newspaper are important for many consumers primarily because they provide some confirmation that there is a continuity in the events and affairs of the larger society. A certain reassurance may be gained from following sporting news that is not possible from following current events, the continuity of which is not readily discernible for many readers. In addition to imposing order upon the vicissitudes of the larger uncertain social scene, the consumption of sports may have the latent function of bringing continuity into the personal lives of many Americans. Team loyalties formed in adolescence and maintained through adulthood may serve to remind one, in a nostalgic way, that there are areas of comfortable stability in life—that some things have permanence amid the harassing interruptions and discontinuous transitions of daily experience. Certainly the personal identities of those who have followed the St. Louis Browns and, especially, the Philadelphia Athletics—members of the original National Association of Baseball Players—have not been unaffected by the change of identity incurred by these teams.[9] But these are speculations. Research is needed to explore the various ramifications. Finally, in this regard, may not the boxing fan "suffer" somewhat more than the baseball fan? The Cleveland Indians can always come back next year, or this year, but Joe Louis never can.

Work and Play. Disparities revealed by our objective overview of the industrial character of American sport may be both reflections of and contributions to the tension between work and play in American life. Work has been for a century or more the means par excellence of acquiring the treasured symbols of our society. There has been no ethical alternative. Furthermore, Max Weber has demonstrated that the ethic of work in America was fortified early by the sanctions of Protestantism. The consequences are clear. We know that athletics were at their lowest ebb in England during the Puritan rule and that of Charles II. Such tendencies have survived in the contrasting views American Protestant and Catholic churches have maintained toward lotteries, gambling, or gaming. Only in the 1920's did the American Protestant churches relax their rules toward such games, and then it was with the stipulation that they be played for amusement only. Risk and gain were cemented in the context of work, never in the context of play. The workplace and the playground were sharply set apart. During the nineteenth century and on into this century, perhaps (as Riesman has somewhere suggested) up to the death of Henry Ford, work and play stood at a distance. The distances between the child and the man, the sexes, the home and the factory or the office, the gentleman and the worker, the Protestant and the Catholic, night and day, Saturday and Sunday—all recorded the gap between work and play.

Now the distances diminish. Long pants no longer signify the adult male, and, as the symbols of adulthood are captured by children, youth creeps into middle age—men of forty-five are "boys." Women are now engaged in all occupations, and boys and girls enter the schools hand in hand through the same doors. The factory becomes a ranch house; the home, a tool shop. The leisure class that inspired the irony of Veblen has become a leisure mass. Religion embraces science and psychoanalysis, and diverse churches unite in national committees. Increments of pay lure the working man out of the day into the night. Saturday no longer mobilizes the household. All these mitigations of distance are ramified in the world of sports and play. For with the loss of the social frame that once insured their separation, work and play have spilled over their former bounds and mingle together in American life. However, the amalgam is new, untested, strange. Traces of the old distance remain and are expressed in vital anomalies.

Consider how Americans speak of sport. Baseball, basketball, football, golf, hockey, and tennis—these sports are "played." The participants are "players." Huizinga speaks of the superfluous character of play, its disinterestedness, its extraordinary and unreal character. "It is never a task."[10] Certainly the sports mentioned here are unreal—a sort of "voluntary hallucination," as Nelson Foote has put it.[11] Yet precisely those sports that are "played" have become work in America. Here is the matrix of professional athletics.

However, the "players of sport" are not, literally, "sportsmen"! Sportsmen are hunters and fishermen, archers, skiers, yachtsmen, or campers. Note that these sports are never "played," nor may they assume the character of work. They are peopled almost entirely by amateurs. When they do become work, they become occupations that bear no reference to leisure. Fishing is a primary *industry*. Another alternative permits such sports to become tutorial in character. "Working sportsmen" can be guides, tutors, or counselors.

There are, of course, exceptions. Boxing, bowling, and wrestling, for example, are not "played"; but note the extraordinarily difficult path each has had to follow to gain public acceptance as a professional sport. Every state in the union has at one time outlawed "prize fights," and it was not until 1917, when boxing became an integral part of the U.S. Army's physical training program, that legal bans were significantly relaxed. The American Bowling Congress is in no small measure the outcome of a social movement designed to secure public respect for the sport. Wrestling can scarcely be considered a professional sport. Occasionally amateurs and professionals participate together in the contest as in the case of golf. But the mingling of "players" and "workers" does not proceed boldly and undisguised. It is cloaked in the guise of a teacher-student relationship. The "pro" is usually attached to some country club, though he may seldom "work" at that club. The unattached "pro" is still relatively rare.

For the most part in America sports that were once work are never played, but these engage the "players"—the amateurs. *Sports that were never work are always played, and these engage the "workers"*—the professionals.[12]

The intertwining of work and play is carried over into daily life. More and more we work at our play and play at our work. Reuel Denney, Everett Hughes, and David Riesman have observed again and again that our play is disguised by work and vice versa. Consequently, we begin to evaluate our leisure time in terms of the potential it has for work—for us to "do it ourselves," and we evaluate our work in terms of the potential it has for play. I have noted in another discussion my son's remark that he wants to be a sociologist so he can hunt, fish, and play golf. This betrays a process of stylization—a process that becomes exacerbated in periods of transition from one pattern of social organization to another. Huizinga asks, "Is not the birth of a style itself a playing of the mind in its search for new forms?"

He notes in the same passage that "a style lives from the same thing as does play, from rhythm, harmony, regular change and repetition, stress and cadence."[13] Perhaps in our groping for new forms of work to replace the old in an age where production is being replaced by consumption as a central organizing phase, the play style, being the most fundamental style, is most readily available and the one with which we have been most intimate for the greater part of our lives. Thus, we endow our work with qualities of play. Yet the old limitations upon play are not easily forgotten, and often we may stylize our work, for example, with the idiom and phraseology of sport, omitting to carry over and apply the ethic. Crucial moral problems are posed, then, for a significant number of Americans. We can play at our work for the enjoyment of it, thereby enriching it; or we can play at work to conceal it from ourselves, thereby shrugging off responsibility for it.[14] Similarly, our stylization of play with the work form may ennoble or debase it. Certainly the ultimate ethical outcome is not at all clear.

The Battle Between the Sexes. Sport would appear to be caught up in the contest of the sexes in American life as well as in the contest between work and play. In viewing American sport the observer may be suddenly impressed with the "masculine bias" of his observations. When I asked one of my colleagues what he thought about the general function of sport in American life, he thought first of hunting and fishing, and described the function of sport as providing a vehicle of "escape" from civilization—a way for the *boys* to go out, drink, and avoid shaving. His wife maintained that he was "like a little boy" when he went fishing. Apparently my colleague embarks upon a flight from adulthood and, inferentially, responsible sexuality, when he goes on his fishing trips. I would prefer to discern a more positive quality in his "irresponsible fishing." Women, above all, are taboo on hunting and fishing trips.[15] The masculine symbolism of hunting and fishing is clear (even though women are now capturing some of the symbols—they have their hunting fashions and styles), and the hunter or fisherman may not be trying to "escape" anything. Perhaps men go on such trips to accentuate their masculinity and independence (responsibility)—to be more male than they are—rather than to "escape" responsible sexuality. But, paradoxically, man owes his maleness to women, i.e., a man is only a man because he differs from women. The sexes are intrinsically dependent upon one another for their identity. It is in a striving for autonomy and independence that Thurber's "battle between the sexes" is conceived, and it is a battle that can never, by definition, be won, although at different times and in different places one of the contestants may win a temporary advantage. The hunting or fishing trip may be viewed merely as a tactic in the battle, and I suggest that the hunter or fisherman is striving to achieve an autonomous masculinity with his hunting or fishing companions. This is often reinforced by the decorum of the trip which prohibits going in to the town tavern "on the make," although getting drunk is quite within bounds. Even erotic revery may be censored at the camp fire. Preferably the revery is autonomously masculine and often consists solely of heroic hunting legends and myths where men only play the role of heroes.

In discussing the function of American sport my colleague distinctly confined his remarks to the purpose it served himself and other men. We have little knowledge of the feminine player or sporting enthusiast (in 1950, 540 of the 10,230 professional athletes were women), except that many "feminine players" are "masculine females." We have even less knowledge of the female spectator, and least knowledge of the spectator of female players.

Let us consider the female fan. Her plight is effectively dramatized by an uncertain, confused, and querulous letter addressed by a female fan to a sports columnist who writes in my daily newspaper:

> I'm a woman who has loved baseball all of her life. When I was nine or 10 I remember keeping box scores of all the games. My father's friends were always amused and gladly would explain the game to me.
>
> But now that I'm older, what happens? Did you ever notice men when women talk baseball to them? They put on a frozen smile and try to change the subject or get away from you.
>
> I still like baseball. But what fun is it for women to take an interest in it when they can't discuss it with men who know more about it?
>
> If baseball is slipping, it's the men who are making it slip . . . by not including women fans in their baseball conversations.[16]

Age and sex are the fundamental anchorages of personal identity. That both are problematical vis-à-vis their validation in sport and play is underscored in the letter quoted above. Perhaps the female fan, even more than the male hunter or the fisherman, is engaged in a quest for sexuality.[17] At least elements of this possibility may be found in the contest between players and spectators that is waged in the wrestling arena.

In the case of wrestling it is my impression that I see more females in the background of my TV set when I view wrestling matches than when I view other games and contests. Fortunately I have been able to get some confirmation for this impression from David Riesman, who has found evidence for this in interviews carried on in a recent Kansas City study (unfortunately for us the interviews were not directly concerned with sport).

One wonders about the attraction wrestling has for the female spectator. Some who are psychoanalytically oriented might suggest the sadistic qualities of wrestling and consider the vicarious gratification derived from viewing the match. This seems not at all convincing to me. It merely attaches a different name to what is going on, for one thing; but, for another, boxing is certainly a bloodier sport, although the boxer's code imposes a suppression of overt manifestation of pain upon the contestants while the wrestler's code demands that pain, fear, viciousness, and unsportsmanlike conduct be overtly expressed. Yet these expressions are intentionally farcical, and I can not permit myself to believe that our women spectators are enchanted by the farce. This, as we shall see, does not mean that the farce is inconsequential.

Other observers have noted the sexual representations inherent in various wrestling holds. Guessing that women spectators are middle-aged and, therefore, were introduced to sex in a period before, as Nelson Foote has put it, sex became play,[18] these observers have speculated that the woman spectator of wrestling experiences vicarious gratification from the pain inflicted by one (male) wrestler upon the other (male) in the sexually suggestive position. This kind of analysis makes somewhat more sense to me than the first, but it presupposes too much about the kind of woman (age, etc.) who attends the matches.

Let me return to the conception of wrestling as a deliberate and contrived farce. Wrestling is a mockery of the spectator; and, when many spectators are women, it is women who are mocked. This may partially explain what I would call the "femininization" of wrestling. Although wrestlers appear in many parts on the arena stage—Indians, Arabian sheiks, atavistic monstrosities, and futuristic supermen—the role of the femininized wrestler is most relevant here. His mere presence in the sports arena is another manifestation of sexual tension along Thurberian lines. Moreover, in his mockery of the demonstrative, vociferous female spectator, the wrestler, has, in fact, become a woman. The female wrestler completes the cycle of the farcical femininization of the sport. Naively we might ask whether the mockery of the female will reintroduce the male to the wrestling audience.

Such remarks suggest a final matter that must be considered before we close our discussion of sport and play, namely, the problem posed by the spectacular elements of American sport.

Games and Spectacles. To this point we have largely treated various ways in which larger social tensions modify the character of American sport. Now we must turn to possible modifications of sport that are intrinsically generated. We would contend that all sport is affected by the antinomial principles of play and dis-play. These principles, in turn, summarize the contrasting character of games and spectacles, and historically have come to represent basic differences between whole societies. In a sense the glory of ancient Greece is expressed by play and the game, the vainglory of Rome by the spectacles and dis-play of the Caesars. Thucydides observed that the brilliant Spartan commander, Brasidas, was received by the multitudes at Scione with honor befitting an athlete. Moreover, competition for the Olympic crown never threatened the status of the most highborn competitor. In contrast, any Roman patrician appearing in public as a charioteer was stigmatized, and Roman names were conspicuous by their absence from the gladiatorial lists. The difference was, of course, never so dramatically clear-cut. Tendencies toward dis-play are to be found in the late history of ancient Greece, and tendencies toward play in the early history of Rome. The illustrations, however, do lay bare the noble character of the game as opposed to the ignoble character of the spectacle.

Play and dis-play are precariously balanced in sport, and, once that balance is upset, the whole character of sport in society may be affected. Furthermore, the spectacular element of sport may, as in the case of American professional wrestling, destroy the game. The rules cease to apply, and the "cheat" and the "spoil-sport" replace the players. Yet even here counterforces are set in motion. If we may, discontinuously, resume our analysis of wrestling, we would note that there is always the "hero" who attempts to defeat the "villain" within the moral framework of the rules of the game. It is a case of law *versus* outlaw, cops and robbers, the "good guys" *versus* the "bad guys." Symbolically the destruction of the game by the spectacle has called into existence forces of revival which seek to re-establish the rules, but these forces are *precisely* symbolic–representative. They are seldom able to destroy the spectacular components of the dis-play. They are part of the spectacle itself.

The point may be made in another way. The spectacle is predictable and certain; the game, unpredictable and uncertain. Thus spectacular dis-play may be reckoned from the outset of the performance. It is announced by the appearance of the performers–their physiques, costumes, and gestures. On the other hand, the spectacular play is solely a function of the uncertainty of the game. The spectacular player makes the "impossible catch"–"outdoes himself." He is *out of character*. The "villains" and "heroes" of the wrestling stage are *in character*. Consequently their roles have been predetermined. The denouement of the contest has been decided at its inception, and the "hero" is unlikely to affect the course of events.

These things would seem to lie at the base of the American humanist's aversion to many aspects of contemporary sport and play. The game, inherently moral and ennobling of its players, seems to be giving way to the spectacle, inherently immoral and debasing. With the massification of sport spectators begin to outnumber participants in overwhelming proportions, and the spectator, as the name implies, encourages the spectacular–the display. In this regard the spectator may be viewed as an agent of destruction as far as the dignity of sport is concerned.[19] There is a tension between the morality of the game and the amorality of the spectator (immoral in its consequences). There are many examples of this, but perhaps the most striking is the case of Maurice, "The Rocket," Richard, spectacular offensive player for the Montreal Canadiens. Fines were of dubious value for bringing "The Rocket" into line following his frequent infractions of the rules ("immorality"), for his fans would inevitably raise funds sufficient to overcompensate for his losses. This action alone tends to break down the morality of the game. However, the ultimate disparity between the immoral demands of the spectator and moral demands of the game was achieved, when, as we know, Montreal experienced its worst riot in recent years in public response to the suspension of "The Rocket" for the remainder of the hockey season.

But we cannot reverse the tide of history. Massification and the consumption of American sport will be with us yet a while. Perhaps one of the most pressing problems facing the social science analyst of sports in America is the problem of how the spectator becomes caught up in the dignity of the game he witnesses to the extent that his consumership of sport is ennobling rather than debasing. Only when that problem is solved and the solution is applied will play become a legitimate ethical alternative to work in America.

In Conclusion. I have attempted here to demonstrate how certain tensions in American society–between production and consumption, work and play, and between the sexes–and how the tension between play and dis-play contained within sport, itself, cast sport in a uniquely American mold. Now, at the end of the discussion, I wonder to what extent the consequences of these tensions for the character of sport are, in fact, uniquely American. I suspect that few of them are, and that they may be found in most of the nations we bring together in the application of that cumbersome concept, "Western civilization." All these remarks attest to the lack of ease and the discomfort with which many of us view sport and leisure. Our arrangements and stylizations of sport and play do not permit us to look upon the game with the same understanding and sympathy that, let us say, Plato experienced in his view of play and the game:

> Though human affairs are not worthy of great seriousness it is yet necessary to be serious; happiness is another thing. . . . I say that a man must be serious with the serious, and not the other way about. God alone is worthy of supreme seriousness, but man is made God's plaything, and that is the best part of him. Therefore every man and woman should live life accordingly, and play the noblest games, and be of another mind from what they are at present. For they deem war a serious thing, though in war there is neither play nor culture worthy the name, which are the things *we* deem most serious. Hence all must live in peace as well as they possibly can. What, then, is the right way of living? Life must be lived as play, playing certain games, making sacrifices, singing and dancing, and then a man will be able to propitiate the gods, and defend himself against his enemies and win in the contest.[20]

I would doubt that Americans would be the only people today made uneasy by those words. But this in no way restricts the implications of our discussion. A social science of play *is* needed in America. Without its contributions the ways in which we spend our growing leisure time may never be ennobled.

Notes

1. The author is extremely indebted to Dr. James D. Cowhig of the Michigan State Department of Mental Health for a critical reading of this paper, and, especially, for his preparation of relevant census materials.

2. Jan Huizinga, *Homo Ludens: A Study of the Play Element of Culture* (London: Routledge and Kegan Paul, Ltd., 1949).

3. David Riesman, "Some Observations on Changes in Leisure Attitudes," *Individualism Reconsidered* (Glencoe, Illinois: The Free Press, 1954), p. 202.

4. Nelson Foote, "Comments on 'The Consumer in the New Suburbia,' by William H. Whyte, Jr.," in Lincoln Clark (ed.), *Consumer Behavior* (New York: New York University Press, 1954), p. 114. He says, "I am deadly serious about this. I would propose that there be a social science of play. On the level of empirical findings, Americans don't know what to do with themselves. When they have free time, they become frantic to kill it."

5. There may be some exceptions to this statement. Thus, the career pattern: player to coach to athletic director, that prevails in American football seems to be acquiring its counterpart in

baseball. However, the career of Hank Greenberg in baseball remains the exception. Compare, for example, the work cycle of the professional athlete with that of the other professions. Even in the other "notorious professions," e.g., motion picture acting, the productive work life is considerably longer, as a listing of the ages of many Hollywood "glamor girls and boys" will testify. Moreover, the obsolete movie star can always be revived, while the obsolete athlete never can. The myth that sport is a channel of social mobility for disprivileged ethnics may well be reexamined in this light. Notoriety and fame are short lived and differ radically from privilege and dignity.

6. David Riesman, Nathan Glazer, and Reuel Denney, *The Lonely Crowd* (New York: Doubleday Anchor Books, 1954), p. 154.

7. *Ibid.*, p. 84.

8. S. Kirson Weinberg and Henry Arond, "The Occupational Culture of the Boxer," *American Journal of Sociology*, LVII (March, 1952), p. 469.

9. Since the original appearance of this article the community identifications of the Boston Braves, the Brooklyn Dodgers, and the New York Giants have also been transformed.

10. Huizinga, *op. cit.*, p. 8.

11. Foote, *op. cit.*, p. 114.

12. The above analysis was suggested in a conversation with a former colleague, Joanne B. Eicher, now of Boston University.

13. Huizinga, *op. cit.*, p. 186. See also Kenneth Burke's wonderful discussion of style in his *Permanence and Change* (Los Altos: Hermes Publications, 1954), pp. 50-58.

14. David Riesman, "Some Observations on Changes in Leisure Attitudes," *op. cit.*, p. 218.

15. Here I am exaggerating somewhat for effect. Certainly there are female hunters and fisherwomen, but these seem still to be the exception. The "invasion" of females into such predominantly male play forms as hunting and fishing signals a new phase of the "battle between the sexes" which I am unable to analyze here.

16. *Detroit Free Press*, June 30, 1955, p. 33.

17. In a personal note to the author David Riesman has written, "It seems to me that both among men and women there is a growing fear of homosexuality and the avoidance of certain sports for women is a way of avoiding this fear." This provides an alternative explanation of some of our observations, but we would like to reiterate that the problem may also be aggravated by the *loss* of sexual identity precipitated by what Riesman might call the "homogenization of the sexes." Thus, rather than avoiding homosexuality, many Americans may be attempting to discover "who" they are in sexual terms. Again only research can resolve such different interpretations. [Since the original appearance of this article, some evidence has been gathered to bear out some of the above contentions; cf. Gregory Stone and Marvin Taves, "Research into the Human Element in Wilderness Use." Reproduced elsewhere in this volume.]

18. Nelson Foote, "Sex as Play." Reproduced elsewhere in this volume.

19. Research in Minneapolis has subsequently convinced the author that the consequences of spectatorship are not exclusively *de-moralizing*. In many respects spectatorship and participation have similar consequences in the mass society. Cf. Gregory Stone, "Some Meanings of American Sport," *Sixteenth Annual Proceedings* of the College Physical Education Association (Columbus, Ohio, 1957), pp. 6-29.

20. Plato, *Laws*, vii, 796.

Money, Muscles—and Myths

By ROGER KAHN

THE BONDS that connect half-a-hundred recreations in America are a credo, which is competition, and a name, which is sports. No other single thread runs through them. Nothing else joins the skier crouching against a winter sky with the catcher squatting in the heat of August. No other tie binds the golden honeymooner pitching horseshoes in the spring at St. Petersburg

---

Reprinted from the *Nation*, Volume 185, Number 1 (July 6, 1957), pp. 9-11 by permission of the publisher.

with the halfback plunging through cold autumn mud at Notre Dame. There is no further link between the Puerto Rican who spars daily in a cramped Manhattan gymnasium and the Ford vice-president who sails weekly on Lake St. Clair off Grosse Pointe.

Without the risk of oversimplification, the enveloping rise of sports in the United States during the past thirty years can, I think, be explained rather briefly. A society wholly involved in competition had an increasing quantity of spare time thrust upon it. Was there a more logical mass outlet for the new afternoons and days of American leisure? Occasionally an orchestra trounces Beethoven and a novelist routs the English language, but compared to Joe Louis trouncing Max Schmeling and the Brooklyn Dodgers routing the New York Giants, these are small, subtle skirmishes. Real competition, the kind that makes a salesman spring for a fourth round of martinis, is duplicated best upon the playing fields. You either make the sale or you lose it. You either hit safely or you make out.

The commercial area of sports, with which I am most concerned, goes considerably deeper than that in reflecting society. Big-time sports have underscored the relentless trend toward the big devouring the small. Major league baseball expands while minor league baseball shrinks. More than fifteen million people watch Oklahoma win a televised football game while City College of New York drops football as hopeless and altogether too costly.

I don't intend to offer a history of the growth of sports in America, but it is essential to a knowledge of present conditions to realize that as recently as twenty-five years ago, there was a place for the individual promoter. If he was, say, a boxing man, he had only to provide for the local sports editor each Christmas, issue free tickets to selected political hacks and control his sense of outrage when a fight was fixed before his eyes. Then, if he had a hall, he was in business and eventually he could send his son to Harvard. Today there is no place for the small promoter in boxing or in any other major sport.

With the exception of New York and Chicago, there is room for only one team in each major league city. As a result, a franchise is a natural monopoly. All sixteen franchises are controlled by the American League and by the National League, which work in consort. Only one racetrack can operate profitably in an area at any time. Various state commissions, which cooperate with one another, write the rules that govern racing. As for prizefights, the federal government is now trying to prove that the International Boxing Club controls all championships and stands in restraint of trade. Every important track meet comes more or less directly under the supervision of the Amateur Athletic Union. The National Collegiate Athletic Association oversees all college athletic policy and dictates a TV football code to networks. In an era of bigness and centralization, sports are both big and centrally run.

The listing of these commercial sports, plus basketball, hockey, tournament golf and tennis, as a string of monopolies is not in itself an indictment.

Through legalisms which I have been unable to grasp, the Supreme Court ruled that boxing is subject to restraint-of-trade laws, which baseball is not. Legalistics aside, what is repugnant about the monopoly pattern is the unvarying adoption of paternalism. In big-time sports, the player has no significant rights.

Baseball is organized as rigidly as a totalitarian state, even to having a commissioner at its head who rules, presumably, by divine right and from whom there is no appeal. Leagues are grouped in one of seven classifications and each division, except the majors, must accept specified salary limits. Directing and preserving this complex structure has become so involved that it requires a body of by-laws ten times longer and considerably more pompous than the U. S. Constitution.

From a solely practical standpoint, it is a waste of emotion to pity a professional baseball player. Major league salaries run from the $6,000 paid most rookies to the flat $100,000 Ted Williams earns. The average on a successful team such as the Dodgers runs to slightly better than $18,000 a man for six months' work. Minor league salaries drop off toward the $125 monthly bottom, but in these prosperous times even the poorest minor league club-owner finds that he must bid in one way or another against aircraft factories and every other industry that advertises "Strong boy wanted for job with good future."

As league and team sports, professional basketball, football and hockey repeat the general outline of baseball and in no case are the athletes kept in serfdom. Even in the National Hockey League, where the family of a multi-millionaire named James Norris has a dominant interest in three of the six teams, the average player earns $7,500.

Most athletes seem satisfied with the owners' largesse, but it is noteworthy that generosity increased all around after major league baseball players banded together and hired a lawyer. The attorney has won some fringe benefits, but the owners retain the trump card. An athlete must accept the team's final salary offer or not play. A skillful bargainer may win a battle but never a war.

Several years ago Carl Furillo, Brooklyn's monolithic right fielder, so harried Branch Rickey, a suave man who was then directing the club, that Rickey agreed to give him $16,500 of the team's cash and a prize Angus bull of his own. It is an anti-climactic point and one which still drives Furillo to rage that the bull was never delivered.

Bigness and paternalism in sports are with us permanently, I suppose, and should be accepted in the same spirit with which we accept A.T. & T. Yet there is a profound difference between industry at large and the sports industry in particular. Sports feed directly upon legend. To preserve legend, they must operate behind a curious moral facade.

"Well, the company grossed a couple million last year," is enough of a justification to keep many successful business men from troubling themselves with questions about their presence on earth. With the big sports promoter there must be more. Victory, sportsmanship and tradition all cloud the profit and loss ledger. Baseball is "The Game" and football is "the natural outgrowth of competitiveness at a time when young men are at their physical prime" and boxing is "the basic, primal conflict." These catch-phrases guard the legend but in themselves are not enough.

The most fascinating and least reported aspect of American sports is the silent and enduring search for a rationale. Stacked against the atomic bomb or even against a patrol action in Algeria, the most exciting rally in history may not seem very important, and for the serious and semi-serious people who make their living through sports, triviality is a nagging, damnable thing. Their drive for self-justification has contributed much to the development of sports.

There is an appalling shortage of genuine myth in this country's background. There are semi-myth figures such as Washington, minor-myth figures such as Paul Bunyan, nonsense-myth figures such as Superman, but there is no Roland, no Arthur, no Siegfried. Obligingly and profitably, sports promoters have thrown their hirelings into the breach. Hollywood offers Ava Gardner as Aphrodite; sports gives us Babe Ruth for Zeus.

The number of adolescent boys who would like to be Mickey Mantle is beyond calculation. Compare it with the number who would like to be Robert Frost. (I also imagine that the number of teen-age girls who would rather be Ava than Marianne Moore is considerable.) Fortunately for the promoters, sports have been even more successful than Hollywood in providing enduring myth images. Bust lines sag, chins grow flabby and last spring's Aphrodite becomes this winter's Helen Hokinson girl. Sports heroes are less susceptible to time.

Steve Ketchel was a fine boxer thirty years ago, but as a myth image he has taken on more depth and beauty in death than he ever possessed in life. It was Ketchel's posthumous luck to become the motivator of a Hemingway short story in which one character says: "I never saw a man as clean and as white and as beautiful as Steve Ketchel. There never was a man like that. He moved just like a tiger and he was the finest free-est spender that ever lived, Steve Ketchel, and his own father shot him down like a dog."

Other athletes have become myths through briefer images. An Illinois halfback named Red Grange is safe for history as The Galloping Ghost. Grantland Rice, who created a profusion of images, gave birth to four at once when he took a Notre Dame backfield named Layden, Miller, Crowley and Stuhldreher and began a story, "Outlined against a blue-gray sky, the Four Horsemen rode again."

With this sort of thing constantly bobbing up, and with a public eager for godheads, suitable for self-identification, sports people long ago learned to believe that, cash aside, their field was a thing apart.

"I can remember a brutally hot afternoon last summer," Ford Frick, the commissioner of baseball, starts one story, "when I was walking near a post office in Manhattan. I noticed three letter carriers struggling under heavy loads, but all the while smiling and chatting. As I neared them, I realized that they were discussing Willie Mays and the New York Giants. Baseball had done that. With all their troubles and on this brutally hot day, they were happy because they were talking about The Game." Smaller baseball officials frequently tell smaller, but parallel, stories.

Somehow, over the years, it has worked. Somehow there does seem to be something different about baseball, or football, or horse racing; something cleaner, something closer to youth, something vaguely better than what we are doing at the moment. The sweep of legend and the impact of competitiveness have been such that virtually every American over the age of two, thinks, talks, watches, plays or competitively resists sports.

But the feeling of essential shallowness can never be erased, a fact dramatically illustrated several years ago in Cincinnati. Heywood Hale Broun, son of the late newspaper columnist, was then a sportswriter assigned to cover the Brooklyn Dodgers. It was a June day, fresh with spring and burdened with a long double-header. "What am I doing in Cincinnati," Broun said aloud in the press box, "watching a ball game on a day like this when I ought to be home walking with my wife and kids." Broun silently closed his typewriter, caught the next train for New York and has since become an actor.

Big-time sports, on television or off, are unimportant as Woody Broun knew but, in mid-century America, they are an inevitable natural product and a symptom of the times.

What's Happening to Hobbies?

By ERIC LARRABEE

HOBBIES, in a few words, are not what they used to be. Originally the name itself derived from hobby-horse, with all its foolish connotations, as though to have a hobby were to pursue a private passion with the frivolous concentration of a child riding a toy animal. Out of a more recent past the term comes to us clothed in associations from a rigorous, Calvinist ethic which held that even relaxation must be energetic. An active hobby, in the imagery of the old school, stood for a secure, though vigorous, tranquility of spirit: *viz.* Franklin Roosevelt poring over his stamps, or Winston Churchill building brick walls and painting pictures. Yet such security as theirs in time

Reprinted from *The New York Times Magazine*, December 27, 1953, by permission of the publisher.

and confidence comes mainly to the very young or very old, so that at a lesser level the most durable symbol for hobbies has surely been an ancient mariner in whiskers, showing a small boy how to put ships in bottles.

In the orderly, competitive context of the Protestant nineteenth century, where a compulsion neurosis could be a virtue, a hobby was the logical device to make time-killing both pointless and productive. It had to be pointless or it would be indistinguishable from work; it had to be productive or it would be bad for one's character. Hence the truly outrageous hobbies which represented revolt against that world in terms the world could understand—like building a model of Chartres cathedral out of toothpicks; or assembling the world's most complete collection of streetcar transfers; or writing the history, geography, economics, and literature of a wholly imaginary continent. Hence also—for individuals who were not, like a Roosevelt or Churchill, born to leisure with an abundance of energy—the assumption that hobbies could be defined as unnecessary or irrelevant, or by their quality of arts-and-craftsy make-work. Tying your own trout flies was a hobby, but fishing was not.

Similarly, for a youngster an electric train was an educational toy; for a grown-up to own one was either a hobby or a sign of senility. Hobbies were to be expected of the retired or the immature, and—since most ideas of play derive from childhood, as normally the only period when play is a full-time activity—their childish character had become forbiddingly stylized. A hobby was instructive, or it developed manual skill, or it followed the pattern of collecting and classifying that had been a respectable basis for scientific discovery in the previous hundred years. The prototype of the hobbyist was the grimy schoolboy who brought snakes and beetles to class in his pockets, or filled his home with the smell of evil brews from a chemistry set, or daubed banana oil on spindly model airplanes. These were respectable pursuits for a child, but when he grew up he would be expected to be a great naturalist, or discover chlorophyll, or design jet engines—and reconstruct his habits of play accordingly. Even the motto, "Happy the man whose work is his hobby," assumed that the fully-engaged adult could tell one from the other.

But since those simple days a lot has happened. Recently I asked Nathan Polk, of Polk's Hobbies in New York—the largest dealer in hobby materials of its kind in the world—what were the current trends in his business, and his immediate reply was that he didn't know exactly what his business was. "Is golf a hobby," he said, "is reading a hobby? The whole thing's intangible." Mr. Polk went on to explain the rule-of-thumb methods by which he decides whether or not a given hobby falls within his jurisdiction, but in so doing he found it necessary to mention the background of spare-time manners and customs which condition his choice. It is a remarkably different one from the social situation in which hobbies originated, and it compels Mr. Polk to be highly selective. Wherever there used to be hard-and-fast lines between hobbies and mundane, utilitarian affairs there are now whole new categories of activity that are partly hobbies and partly not—for instance, eating.

Formerly the consumption of food would have been called a necessity, or the opposite of a hobby, but it is no longer treated as though it were. Enormous energies used to be expended on their kitchens by women who had few other outlets for their sense of competence and creativeness, but now that such efforts are unnecessary there are housewives who replace them with a playful, corner-cutting enterprise. The straightforward, no-nonsense, meat-and-potatoes American diet has been snowed under in an avalanche of cookbooks filled with exotic recipes—German, Chinese, Jewish, French, Italian, Barbecue, Casserole, Wine Lover's, or Ulcer Diet—and sophistication is so far out of hand that a margarine company has thought it wise to take an ad in a supermarket magazine to describe the making of garlic bread. (You might say that for many *not* eating has become a hobby, with the consequent deluge of calorie-reduced flour, calorie-reduced soft drinks, calorie-reduced chocolate cookies, and even calorie-reduced beer.) This isn't just woman's work, either. The man who wants to make life comparably difficult for himself has only to go to a sporting-goods store (*sic!*) and buy what Mr. Polk called a "barbecue kit"—a packaged unit of mortar, ironwork, and instructions—wherewith to fill his weekends with the ritual of preparing elaborate hamburgers and basking in the formalized ridicule of his guests.

Many hobbies, on the other hand, have lost their time-killing status and turned deadly earnest. The home workshop is now far less likely to be a source of inlaid cigarette boxes and rustic cuckoo clocks than of substantial items of family furniture. Young-married couples who may have learned to do cabinet work as a hobby would far rather do it for themselves than pay for it, at present prices, especially now that equipment and supplies have been made easier to get and to use. After they have acquired the appropriate power tools, an extraordinary number go on to build all or part of their own houses—which is making your home your hobby with a vengeance. This large-scale return to the tinkering tradition has created a new industry to service it—with the ungainly name of "Do-It-Yourself"—and has caused the merchandisers of building materials to take a new look at their market. In Brooklyn, this fall, five free lectures on home-furnishing materials and techniques are being offered by the Paint and Wallpaper Dealers Association. In California, which always goes the rest of the Union one better, the Pan Pacific Do-It-Yourself Show exhibited separate pieces of fur that can be assembled into a do-it-yourself mink coat.

Once the hobbyist was presumed to be an amateur, in the best and worst senses of the word. Now you seldom know when a hobby stops being for fun and becomes professional. Even the schoolchildren who make hobbies of science have succeeded remarkably well in keeping up with it, and this during a decade in which science has progressively lifted itself above the common reach into lavishly equipped laboratories. The teen-agers can now build Wilson Cloud Chambers, to see cosmic rays for themselves as only graduate students at universities could before. One New Jersey boy had his family television set prepared for color almost as soon as the broadcasting companies announced it, and a Long Island girl repeated in her family washtub the experiments of the General Electric scientist which led to artificial rain-making. Probably the prize in this department goes again to California, where a group of five high-school physics students in El Cerrito made a cyclotron. Worked, too.

Strangely enough, as new-style hobbies have arisen, the old seem not to have declined. Some of them, quite to the contrary, have become big-time. Those little balsa-wood and rice-paper contraptions, which used to fly on the power of a wound-up rubber band, today have developed into gasoline-driven craft of silk-covered aluminum; the newest have jet engines, fly under radio control at 160 miles per hour, and cost as much as $20,000 apiece. When the 21st annual National Model Airplane Meet was held last year (in, of course, California) there were a mere thousand enthusiasts present, but they were drawn from a total for the whole country—not counting the millions who still stick to the old-fashioned wind-by-hand models—of 500,000 identifiable fanatics. The business of supplying them with model planes and parts has multiplied by five or six times since the end of World War II, and estimates of its national volume were reported by the *Wall Street Journal* to fall between $10 and $30 million a year.

As with model airplanes, so elsewhere. "Never before at any time," said Mr. Polk, "have so many people bought, either to construct or shape, so many hobby materials." New hobbies, in some cases, seem to revivify old ones (just as photography, for instance, has been revived by color film, stereo-cameras, and inexpensive flash equipment). Mr. Polk defines his areas of interest as "spare-time activities serving the whole family," but starting with children in (a) educational and manipulative toys, through (b) the model building stage to the point of (c) entering and bordering fully on the arts and crafts (Polk's Hobbies has three major fields, though they are subordinate to the second category, in model railroads, ship models, and toy soldiers or scale military models). Yet, in spite of phenomenal growth in the under-ten-years market, Mr. Polk claimed that "in the past few years the greatest development has been in the arts and crafts—by the numbers."

By this cryptic phrase, said Mr. Polk, he meant the ready-to-paint sets of artists' materials in which the canvas not only has a picture sketched on it but a number in each area corresponding to the color to be put there. The raw simplicity of this gimmick seems to have appealed to thousands upon thousands who had wanted to be Sunday painters, as President Eisenhower is, but had never dared to try. From easel painting the technique spread to "American traditional" black metal trays, to wastebaskets, and eventually to needlepoint. "For a small investment," said Mr. Polk, "you get a useful object in the house." He had asked his salesmen to estimate how many customers graduated from the numbered system, even after ten or twenty tries, to painting on their own with colors and subjects of their individual choice; the answer was about 10 per cent—"the greatest boon," said Mr. Polk, "to the art field in general."

What seems to be going on here is a major readjustment in national leisure habits, a change so pervasive that nothing can stand in its way—including television. "We felt it, all right," said Mr. Polk, "but very quickly the Metropolis has learned to be selective about television. We figure that we're now losing only an hour a day of the time of TV owners, instead of the five or six we were losing when it first came into the area." The present state of hobbies, if nothing else, should refute the prophets of spectatoritis, the disease which was going to reduce the mass-media audience to an imbecility of non-participation. "People are turning more to personal activity sports," said the sales manager of a sporting-goods company early this year, "away from the big spectator games." "Five years of television," says an official of one of the country's largest merchandisers of musical equipment, "have done more for our business than thirty-five years of radio ever did."

In a boom as big as the present one, everything booms. My impression is that numbers of the older generation's hobbies have declined, in the sense that most people I know have given up model-building, collecting butterflies, or carving soap, in favor of assembling high-fidelity radio-phonographs, building bookcases, painting their own apartments, reading up on the history of the Civil War, or writing articles like this one. Yet, at the same time, I'm reasonably certain there are so many new family units in the United States (half as many bachelors as fifty years ago), so many more hours of spare time available (six times as many people getting three-week vacations as in 1946), and so much more money to spend on non-essentials, that any specific loss is more than accounted for in the general gain. It works the other way, too. The lush prosperity of the model aircraft business may not mean that enthusiasm for model aircraft is proportionately greater than it used to be, but only that model aircraft enthusiasts, like everyone else, are prospering.

The awe-inspiring spectacle that the figures reflect is the birth of a new leisure class, not a minority that gives all its time to play but a majority that gives play part of its time. In the Western world this phenomenon is unprecedented (less so, perhaps, in the less work-minded and conscience-ridden areas of Africa and the Orient), and its delivery has been attended by confusion. So sharply divergent are the views of renascence and decay in American culture that, even if we knew to the last detail what *had* happened to hobbies in the past few years, we would not know what to make of it. With the astonishing increase in free time—that is, time that has been "paid for" by work, rather than merely unemployed time—has come a mushrooming demand for leisure services of every kind: highbrow along with vulgar, hobbies plus amusements undreamed-of as such, the traditional recreations plus a host of new ones. Everywhere the statistics are equally overwhelming and impossible to interpret. Here is a selection, again from the *Wall Street Journal,* whose reporting of popular culture is the most informative to be found, and itself an index of the importance that leisure has come to occupy in the national economy.

Item: There are five times as many Americans taking lessons in ballroom dancing as there are students in colleges and universities.

Item: The amount spent in Florida on deep-sea fishing is greater than the combined grosses of the state's citrus and cattle industries.

Item: Though the number of golf courses has declined from 5,500 to 4,970 (as real estate was needed for new houses), the number of golfers has increased 25 per cent in the past ten years.

Item: The sum of American money spent yearly on dogs is greater than the total personal incomes of the population of Vermont.

Item: In St. Louis, Missouri, there are more pleasure boats registered with the U. S. Coast Guard than there are in Boston.

Item: At the end of a winter weekend two years ago, business men in North Conway, New Hampshire, estimated that skiers in the area served by the town had spent one million dollars.

Item: Michigan last year licensed 61,000 people to hunt with the bow and arrow.

And so it goes.

What is one to conclude from these exuberant manifestations? First of all, I think, that the hobbyist as such is an archaic figure. He was the product of a world which tried to separate existence into semantically air-tight categories, where work was serious and play was not, but both tended to be workful. Now we are more prone to hope that work and play may intermingle, and both be playful. As a nation, we are saturating ourselves in leisure so indiscriminately that we need no longer pretend we know one form of it to be better for our psyches than another. Any distraction may be more of a hobby than it looks, and all hobbies may not be the bagatelles they seem. It may still be true that "every man needs a hobby," to the extent that everyone needs more than one skill, needs to get away at intervals from the skill by which he earns a living, and needs skill even in effecting that escape. But it is not true to the extent that true leisure and true work, as far as they aid the individual to realize himself, can never be fully separated. "Happy the society," perhaps, "whose members can no longer tell their hobbies apart."

Apparently hobbies are still favorably situated in the American hierarchy of values. The ability to do-for-oneself is still admired, the devotion of the individualist to his pet enthusiasm is still respected, and the inventive potentialities of the amateur are still recognized as valid. But the use of leisure time is a growing national preoccupation, and the vocabularies of behavior which the hobbyist once had to himself are now widely understood. Hobbies, in losing their exclusiveness, can achieve their justification. If all the devices of spare-time self-amusement require competence and practice, just as hobbies do, then the word can be abandoned at the same time that the incentives in which it originated are accepted. If, in a sense, stock-car racing is a hobby, playing croquet is a hobby, belonging to organizations is a hobby, listening to phonograph records is a hobby, betting on the horses is a hobby, or staring out the window on a sunny day is a hobby, then the arts of civilized living are the greatest hobbies of them all.

With one caveat: only those may disown the hobby approach who have learned from it the omnivorous interest, the constant curiosity, the ever-replenished wonder before the new-born day that made one American the greatest hobbyist of history. "There is not a spring of grass that shoots," wrote Thomas Jefferson to his daughter, "uninteresting to me."

The Do-It-Yourself Market

Prepared by U. S. DEPARTMENT OF COMMERCE

INCREASED earnings and more leisure hours have provided millions of Americans with both the income and the time for many new interests and activities. One of the most important of these new interests is the Do-It-Yourself trend which includes home carpentry, painting and decorating, gardening, and other activities in and around the home. Because of its diversity, no overall measurement of the size and scope of the Do-It-Yourself market has been made, either by Government or by private industry.

However, many separate estimates of current and potential sales of particular categories of merchandise have been made by research organizations, industries, trade associations, and trade and consumer publications. The information on estimated sales volume and other statistical data is necessarily based on such estimates. It is not offered as official Government data but as the best available information from several private industry sources indicating characteristics of the Do-It-Yourself market.

Reasons for the Growth of the Do-It-Yourself Market. Do-It-Yourself activities have received impetus—in addition to the stimulus of higher incomes and more leisure time—from several factors, such as:

1. Today more than 55 percent of all homes are owner-occupied. This figure was 44 percent in 1940. Owner's pride of possession makes him spend more time and money on his home.

2. The "flight to the suburbs"—the substantial shifts in population in recent years to the outlying sections of our metropolitan areas—has resulted in a trend to outdoor living and a demand for the tools and products used outdoors.

3. Home owners in this new "Suburbia" are typically younger couples,

From "Summary of Information on The Do-It-Yourself Market," *Business Service Bulletin,* Number 84 (November 1954). Courtesy U. S. Department of Commerce, Small Business Administration. Prepared by Robert J. Bond.

with larger than normal families and with earnings in the middle income brackets.

4. Home ownership by these younger couples, who are enthusiastic advocates of Do-It-Yourself, has been encouraged and made more feasible by the prevailing more liberal extension of credit through mortgage insurance by the Federal Housing Administration and the Veterans' Administration.

5. The Do-It-Yourself market for these new homeowners is greatly stimulated because a great many of their homes were built on an expandable basis—an attic to be finished, a garage, carport or breezeway to be added, or a basement to be finished as a recreation room. When older homes are bought, these new younger homeowners undertake many similar renovation projects on the Do-It-Yourself basis.

6. The Do-It-Yourself trend has been greatly stimulated by the fact that skilled labor is hard to get and costs more than ever before.

7. During the war years, millions of men in the Armed Forces and women in war plants became familiar with the use of tools. The younger generation has learned much about woodworking and metalworking in school.

The Do-It-Yourself way of improving and beautifying the home, both inside and out, the search for new recreation outlets in the hobby fields, the increased activities in home dressmaking—all are a part of the new way of life. It has affected the sale of many products ranging from paint to power lawn mowers.

The information in this Bulletin has been compiled to provide retailers with a better appreciation of the importance of this Do-It-Yourself market, currently estimated at $6 billion a year, and to indicate successful methods of realizing potential sales.

Do-It-Yourself activities can be broadly grouped as follows:

1. Structural home improvements
2. Home decoration (painting, wallpapering)
3. Home furnishing (furniture making and finishing, slip covering)
4. Gardening and grounds maintenance
5. Home dressmaking and sewing
6. Hobbies (model building, cabinetmaking)

The Home Workshop. The market for home-type power tools has mushroomed since the end of World War II. It has been estimated that 11 million homes in America now have workshops.

Manufacturers have redesigned their products for easier use by the home workman and provide plans, drawings, and guides for a wide variety of products. Plans and materials in kit form can be bought for boats, houses, airplanes, automobiles, and tractors.

The rental of tools has become big business. One Cincinnati dealer reported billings in 1953 of $28,000 in tool rentals. Many stores are also building a profitable business in the rental of waxers, polishers, and sanders.

(Much of the following information on power tools is based on the results of a survey of the industry made by Arthur D. Little, Inc., an industrial and engineering firm of Cambridge, Massachusetts.)

1. The multipurpose bench tool has had a most dramatic increase from a sales volume of approximately $2,250,000 in 1948, the first significant year, to about $24,000,000 in 1953. This tool drives four or five machines from a single power plant. It not only economizes on space (important in many basement work shops) but also saves the costs of additional motors and starter switches. Often the motor and starter switch price practically equals the machine price. One motor driving four machines, a drill, saw, lathe, and sander, would eliminate the purchase of three motors, a saving of possibly $100.

The multipurpose tool should be sold on the basis of the buyer's individual need. The machine which will be used most should be the basis of this tool with all other units as components.

2. Single-purpose bench tools—arbor saws, drill presses, band saws, jig saws, jointers, sanders, grinders, shapers, and lathes—increased from about $15,000,000 sales volume in 1946 to about $40,000,000 in 1953.

3. Portable electric tools—drills, saws, sanders, polishers, routers, and grinders—have zoomed from around $6,000,000 sales volume in 1946 to about $95,000,000 in 1953.

BENCH HOME-TYPE TOOLS. The following table indicates the current relative importance of the various types of bench tools:

TYPE	PERCENT OF TOTAL DOLLAR SALES	PERCENT OF TOTAL UNIT SALES	TYPE	PERCENT OF TOTAL DOLLAR SALES	PERCENT OF TOTAL UNIT SALES
Arbor saws	40	36	Jointers	5	9
Drill presses	16	18	Sanders and grinders	4	5
Band saws	13	14	Shapers and lathes	2	2
Jig saws	10	16			

Sales of accessories—dado heads, arbor extensions, blades, bits, drills, etc. —make up about 10 percent of total dollar sales. About 60 percent of the bench home-type tool production moves through wholesalers and 40 percent directly to chains and large retailers.

Of the amount handled by wholesalers about 85 percent is sold to hardware retailers and 15 percent to miscellaneous outlets.

PORTABLE HOME-TYPE TOOLS. The following table indicates the current relative importance of the various types of portable electric tools:

TYPE	PERCENT OF TOTAL DOLLAR SALES	PERCENT OF TOTAL UNIT SALES
Drills	51.5	80
Saws	24.5	16
Sanders & polishers	12	3
Grinders	2	1

Sales of accessories – blades, bits, drills, sanding attachments, etc. – are approximately 10 percent of the total dollar volume.

About 50 percent of the portable home-type power tools produced are sold through wholesalers and about 40 percent are sold directly to chains. The remaining 10 percent moves to retailers (other than chains) either directly or through manufacturers' agents.

Of the amount handled by wholesalers about 70 percent is sold to hardware retailers and 30 percent to miscellaneous outlets.

SEASONAL PATTERNS. In terms of 100 percent representing the monthly average, the following table indicates the sales pattern by months of all home-type power tools.

January	125%	April	96%	July	80%	October	89%
February	107	May	90	August	87	November	102
March	120	June	81	September	83	December	140

Hand tools are, of course, essential equipment for a home workshop. A well-equipped workshop might represent an investment of several hundred dollars in hand tools of all kinds—screw drivers, saws, hammers, chisels, wrenches, drills, pliers, and files.

A wide variety of materials are worked on in the home workshop.

Industry estimates that 350 million square feet of fir plywood, representing 10 percent of the industry's production, were used in Do-It-Yourself activities in 1953, an increase of 160 percent since 1946. Average annual sales per us U. S. household of lumber and building materials for Do-It-Yourself activities are estimated at over $60.

The plywood industry, through trade associations, has been particularly active in the Do-It-Yourself field. A wide selection of dealer selling aids is made available, including a 3-D viewer to help customers visualize things they can make with plywood and a handy panel rack which displays for self-selection the small sized panels for workshop use. Plans for making hundreds of products from plywood are available at nominal cost from manufacturers and trade associations.

Aluminum has been specially engineered for use with standard woodworking hand or power tools. Available in sheets, rods, tubes, bars, and strips, it can be worked just like wood—sawed, drilled, planed, and jointed —for a great variety of products ranging from wheelbarrows to wastebaskets. A self-selection display stand is available from one manufacturer. Although introduced only last year, annual sales of this Do-It-Yourself aluminum already amount to several million dollars.

Amateur furniture makers are enthusiastic about foam rubber, now available by the yard and in shapes for chair seats, pillows, and back rests.

New products and adaptations of old products are constantly being introduced for the home workman trade; to mention only a few—plastic upholstery material that can be cut and sewed like fabric, plastic laminates for counter tops, plastic screening and fiberglass panels for partitions.

Painting and Decorating. Industry estimates that the home workman will buy 150 million gallons of paint this year, 75 percent of the industry's production for nonindustrial use. Consumer analysis surveys by newspapers in six cities showed an average by cities of 80 percent of inside and 60 percent of outside household paint jobs were done by "Do-It-Yourselfers." Manufacturers have stimulated this market by introducing new products such as the fast-drying latex-base paint and new easy-to-use tools such as paint rollers, compressed-air spray guns for home use, and paint in pressure cans for small jobs.

Estimates in the trade are that yearly sales of the paint roller will reach 8 million units this year—some $24 million worth at retail.

The wallpaper industry has also introduced new easy-to-apply products such as pre-trimmed and packaged paper, washable plastic-coated paper, and paper with adhesive already applied to the back. Sales in 1954 to the Do-It-Yourself trade are estimated at 150 million rolls, about 60 percent of the industry's production as compared with 28 percent 10 years ago, according to an estimate by *American Home* magazine.

Customer preferences by type of paper are estimated by *Wallpaper Magazine* as follows:

	Far West	*Eastern Seaboard*	*Midwest*	*South*
Fully-trimmed	73%	68%	62%	42%
Pre-pasted	13	16	12	20
Semi-trimmed	4	11	18	33
Plastic-coated	10	5	8	5

New floor and wall tiles of asphalt, cork, rubber, and a variety of plastics have been introduced, and sales to the amateur ran about $116 million last year. Sales of asphalt tiles for the Do-It-Yourself market are estimated this year at 500 million square feet, roughly one-half of the industry's production, according to industry estimates.

Gardening and Grounds Maintenance. The "flight to the suburbs" with its companion trend to outdoor living has caused a boom in gardening supplies and equipment of all kinds with 1953 sales totalling almost $700 million, up $200 million since 1947. An estimated 18 million home owners now do their own landscaping.

According to *Business Week,* power lawn mower sales are currently at a yearly rate of over $100 million which is 20 times the 1940 rate. Hedge trimmers, power cultivators, chain saws, and garden tractors have enjoyed excellent sales. Garden implements have been introduced in special sizes and with special handles for female gardeners.

Home Dressmaking and Sewing. The piece goods business in 1953 amounted to an estimated $400 million plus approximately $100 million in sewing notions—thread, fasteners, and trimmings. The 1953 sales volume in paper patterns was $40 million—about 85 million patterns, twice the rate in prewar years.

Some 1.8 million sewing machines were sold for domestic use in 1953, swelling the total in use in the United States to about 32 million.

A survey by the New York University School of Retailing of the customers of a New York department store indicated that over 40 percent had made their own draperies.

Sources of Information. A number of consumer magazines devote substantial sections of each issue (in some instances, practically the whole issue) to articles of the "how-to-do-it" or "how-to-make-it" type. Many of these articles are of interest to the retail merchant as they are good sources of promotional ideas and indicate the materials and products for which demand may be stimulated. Among these magazines are: *American Home, American Magazine, Better Homes and Gardens, Homecraft and the Home Owner, House Beautiful, House and Garden, Ladies' Home Journal, McCall's, Mechanix Illustrated, Popular Mechanics, Popular Science, Sunset,* and *Woman's Home Companion.*

The following selected list of articles which appeared in the indicated publications are representative of other types of articles of interest to retailers, as they discuss the extent of the market and include merchandising and promotional information.

Building Supply News. 5 Wabash Avenue, Chicago 3, Ill.

This magazine carries a "Do-It-Yourself Profit Parade" section with many helpful merchandising ideas, e.g., "The Three Markets for Do-It-Yourself Sales," "Basic Policies for Do-It-Yourself Trade," and "How To Promote and Display Idea Literature and Plan Books" in the October 1954 issue. Also available are:

Sweat Equity or Owner Built Market.
Display for Profit.
How To Sell the Do-It-Yourself Market.
How To Make Money on Tool and Equipment Rentals.

Business Week. 330 West 42nd Street, New York 36, N.Y.

For Rent: Just About Everything (with table), p. 43, March 13, 1954.
The New Look in Home Power Tools: Do-It-Yourself is Tamed for the Timid (with illus.), p. 150, March 20, 1954.
The Sap Is Running in Do-It-Yourself, p. 122, March 27, 1954.
Build It Yourself, p. 52, October 18, 1952.
Wallboard for Amateurs (with illus.), p. 78, November 29, 1952.
Armstrong's Housefull of Ideas With One Aim: Sell the Fixup Market (with 10 illus.), p. 66, February 14, 1953.
Do-It-Yourself Ideas—on Parade: Big Turnout at New York Show (with 5 illus.), p. 32, March 21, 1953.
Making Up to Do-It-Yourself (with 7 illus.), p. 42, July 4, 1953.
Week-end Contracting, p. 102, July 11, 1953.
Reynolds Metals Offers Do-It-Yourself Aluminum, p. 54, October 31, 1953.

Curtain and Drapery Department Magazine. Hall Publishing Company, 230 Fifth Avenue, New York 1, N.Y.

How To Be Handy With Plastics, p. 130, January 1953.

Burdine's "Do-It-Yourself" Center, p. 90, October 1953.

For Handymen Only, p. 52, November 1953.

Display as I See It, p. 30, April 1954.

Tapping the Do-It-Yourself Market, p. 36, April 1954

Building Do-It-Yourself Sales, p. 36, April 1954.

Fortune. 9 Rockefeller Plaza, New York 20, N. Y.

Fun, a $30 Billion Market, June 1954.

Furniture Age. 4733 Broadway, Chicago 40, Ill.

Hudson Draws 60,000, April 1954.

Homecraft and the Homeowner. 154 East Erie Street, Chicago 11, Ill.

Digest of Do-It-Yourself Research, available on request.

Digest of Summertime Activities, available on request.

Modern Packaging. Emmett Street, Bristol, Conn.

Self Selling Packaging Is Working a Revolution in the Hardware Store, September 1954.

Printers' Ink. 205 E. 42nd Street, New York 17, N. Y.

4 Do-It-Yourself Trends, October 2, 1953.

Do-It-Yourself Urge Takes Hold, May 21, 1954.

Retailing Daily. Fairchild Publications, 7 East 12th Street, New York 3, N. Y.

Detroit Retailers Jumping on Do It Yourself Bandwagon, February 5, 1954.

Do It Yourself Market March 24 and 25, 1954.

Stores. National Retail Dry Goods Association, 100 W. 31st Street, New York 1, N. Y.

Do It Yourself Market, October 1953.

Tide. 2160 Patterson Street, Cincinnati 22, Ohio. Biweekly.

Circuses, 3D Spur Do It Yourself, August 1954.

Do It Yourself: From a Fad to a Stable and Lucrative Market, July 17, 1954.

Time. 540 N. Michigan Avenue, Chicago 11, Illinois.

Do It Yourself—the New Billion Dollar Hobby, August 2, 1954.

The Wallpaper Magazine. 114 East 23rd Street, New York 16, N. Y.

3 Part Survey of Wallpaper Selling. March, April and May 1954.

In addition to the above, articles on the Do-It-Yourself market of particular interest to retailers frequently appear in trade publications of many other industries, for example: *Hardware Age, Hardware Retailer, Hobby Merchandiser,* and *Craft, Model and Hobby Industry.*

For a complete listing of trade papers, periodicals and magazines in the related fields, the following guides, which are available for reference in many libraries, may be consulted: *N. W. Ayer and Son's, Directory of Newspapers and Periodicals,* published by N. W. Ayer and Son, West Washington Square, Philadelphia, Pa.; *Standard Rate and Data Service,* published by Standard Rate and Data Service, Inc., 1740 Ridge Avenue, Evanston, Ill.

Industrial Arts Index, published by the H. W. Wilson Company, 950 University Avenue, New York 52, N. Y. and *Readers Guide to Periodical Literature,* published by the H. W. Wilson Company, 950 University Avenue, New York 52, N. Y., are good sources of information on additional pertinent articles which have appeared in periodicals.

Vacations

By "A CYNIC" [LESLIE STEPHEN]

Mr. Creech, it is said, wrote on the margin of the *Lucretius* which he was translating, "Mem.–When I have finished my book, I must kill myself," and he carried out his resolution. This story, true or false, is reported by Voltaire as characteristic of English manners, and represents a current French theory as to our national tastes. Life in England, if we may venture to draw the moral of the anecdote, is a dreary vista of monotonous toil, at the end of which there is nothing but death, natural, if it so happen, but if not, voluntary, without even a preliminary interval of idleness. To live without work is not supposed to enter into our conceptions. We are nothing but machines employed to execute a particular duty; and when that duty is done, we think it better to break up the machine than to allow it to rust into gradual decay. In this opinion we may, if we please, see nothing but French prejudice, or rather nothing but a particular case of that utter want of appreciation with which rival nations regard each other. Each people can understand the more serious occupations of its neighbour, but finds it hard to enter into its amusements. Everybody wants to eat and drink and sleep, but everyone has his own peculiar notion of pleasure. Seeing the spare time of foreigners employed on purposes for which we care little, we fancy that they must be intolerably bored. A sporting man imagines that life must be unendurable in a country where there are no horse-races, no prize-fights, and no *Bell's Life* to chronicle the glories of the turf or the cricket-ground. Yet, unreasonable as all such prejudices are said to be, we can sympathise to some extent with the feelings of the Frenchman in England. We can guess at the horror which overwhelms him if he has arrived on a Saturday night, and turns out for a Sunday walk along the streets of London. Imagining, as he would naturally

Reprinted from the *Cornhill Magazine,* Volume 20, Number 116 (August 1869), pp. 205-214.

imagine, that he is witnessing our mode of employing a day set apart for relaxation, he would shudder on picturing to himself the more serious moments of a nation whose pleasure so strongly resembles the settled gloom of other races. On holidays, we are just capable, it would seem, of creeping along our streets in funereal processions, and relieving our woes by draughts of gin and "porter-beer." How is his imagination to paint the horrors of our working days? and is it strange if suicide seems to him to be the most fitting termination of such melancholy lives?

Let us suppose, however, that our friend recovers from this shock to his nerves, and penetrates the rough outside of English life. Will that domestic hearth, whose pleasures we are accustomed to celebrate, strike him as compensating by its glowing warmth for the chill fog without? If, for example, he is fortunate enough to receive an invitation to one of those cheerful entertainments called evening parties, is he likely to be raised to an almost unbearable pitch of exhilaration? The theory on which they are constructed seems to imply the existence of an amazing faculty for amusement. We apparently consider it sufficient to cram into a room twice as many people as it will comfortably hold, to make them all happy. We love each other so much that we can't pack too tight. By squeezing a number of apples into a press we can produce cider; and it is apparently believed that in a sufficiently crowded mass of humanity, raised to the proper temperature, there takes place a kind of social fermentation, possessing a certain spiritually intoxicating influence. There is so much brotherly love, I suppose, permeating our constitutions, that it only requires pressure to bring it out. And therefore it may be from some peculiar moral perversion that in my case, and some others which I know, the fermentation somehow takes place the wrong way; it all turns sour; and besides detesting the gentleman who stands on my toes, and the other one whose bony framework is imprinted in my back, I suffer from a general misanthropy on such occasions, and receive awful revelations of the depths of human folly. That some persons are happy is perhaps probable; flirtations, for example, may take place at evening parties, as they certainly do in shipwrecks, in hospitals, in the interior of omnibuses, and other scenes of almost universal misery: but when I look round, with the conventional compromise between a scowl and a simper, I fancy that I catch many answering symptoms of disgust on the faces of fellow-sufferers. The true final cause of evening parties, it may be urged, is not pleasure, but business; they are frequented, as the Stock Exchange is frequented, with a view to ulterior profit, rather than with any expectation of immediate returns in the shape of amusement. They are the markets at which we extend our social connections; and, perhaps, if Mr. Mill be right, do a little in the way of slave-dealing. That people should hypocritically continue to express pleasure in attending them, if melancholy, is only in accordance with our usual practice in social grievances. We could not get on without a little lying; and, so long as music is not added to the other torments provided, I am ready to bear my part of the suffering with such stolid indifference as I can command.

We may suppose, however, that our foreigner is ready to extend his researches a little further. If he believes as implicitly as a man ought to believe in the thorough trustworthiness of the British press, he will learn that the Derby is the true national holiday. Its pleasures are so great that even our legislators relax in its favour their habitual regard to the duties of their station. It illustrates all our best qualities; our manly spirit of play, our power of self-government, our wonderful facility for keeping order without the presence of the military, our genuine politeness and felicitous combination of boisterous good-humour with freedom from anything like horseplay, and so on. And yet, I think, a sensible man will mentally ask himself, on his return, what on earth so many thousands of people went out to see? That some answer must be found follows from the well-attested though melancholy fact that many persons have been to see the Derby twice; but what that answer is, I have never been able to discover. I do not speak of gamblers or professional persons; their motive is plain enough; though it may be observed, by the way, that nothing is so strong a proof of utter mental vacuity as a love of gambling; it is the pursuit of excitement pure and simple by a man who is capable of no nobler interest, and accordingly it is found to exist most strongly in savages, who, having nothing to do, will play for their scalps, and in those classes which most nearly approach the savage type in modern society and are forced to find a field for energies running to waste in field-sports, betting, and other such barbarous amusements. We can, however, dimly understand why a man should frequent a place where he is winning or losing thousands of pounds. But we may fairly assume that ninety out of a hundred attendants on Epsom Downs have no serious pecuniary interest, that they only know a horse as a four-legged animal generally forming part of a cab, and consequently that the mere sight of twenty such animals galloping for two or three minutes is not very exhilarating. Yet for this, at any rate, ostensible reason, they undergo a day of pushing and squeezing in railways and carriages, they are assailed by all manner of predatory humans, they stand for hours in rain, wind, and dust, and a large minority find their only intelligible pleasure in getting drunk. That, however, they might do at home; and it is not the motive of ladies or of many other persons who expose themselves to the inflictions of the day. I can understand the pleasure of a prize-fight or a bull-fight; I can believe that a gladiatorial show, when you had suppressed all humane feeling, must have been one of the most absorbing, if one of the most horrible, of amusements. I can even appreciate, though I have never shared, the pleasure of going to see a man hanged, or still more of seeing martyrs burnt. In all these there is a real spectacle of human suffering, and when they are properly managed, of human heroism, which may properly affect our sympathies. Athletic sports of all kinds are worth seeing, when we understand anything about them, as they possess something of the same interest without the counterbalancing horrors; but to see horses pass you like a flash of lightning gives to the mass of the crowd no pleasure that would not come equally from witnessing the throwing of dice or the drawing of a lottery. It is merely a question of whether a red or a blue jacket is first at a certain post. And, to be short, in accordance with the celebrated precedent of Artemus Ward, I treat the inquiry into the causes of this strange pleasure as a conundrum and give it up.

One conclusion, however, may be drawn, which is tolerably evident from other considerations. When a student is learning to paint, one of the great difficulties is to teach him what it is that he really sees. When he sits down before a landscape, it is twenty to one that he will try to represent, not the image of which he is supposed to be immediately conscious, but something which other people have persuaded him that he ought to see and must see. He does not copy the direct impression on his senses, but some imaginary object, which, without knowing it, he has constructed partly from observation and partly from a long series of traditions and inferences and arbitrary associations. In the same way, one of the most difficult of things is to know what we really enjoy. We do something which we have been always taught to consider as a convivial proceeding, and fancy that we are in a high state of enjoyment. Nothing is easier in practice, though in theory nothing should be more difficult, than to deceive people about their own emotions, and to cheat them into a belief of their own happiness. This is the difficulty which lies at the bottom of all our conventional modes of enjoyment, and till somebody has the courage to unravel the complex web of associations which conceals us from ourselves, we go on stupidly suffering, in the sincere conviction that sixty minutes of weariness and vexation of spirits make up an hour of happiness. Many thousands of persons at the present moment are enjoying, or pretending to themselves that they are enjoying, a holiday. They will come back almost tired to death of their pleasures, and delighting to return to their business, and yet they will persuade themselves and others that they have passed an inconceivably agreeable vacation. To convince oneself of their mistake, it is enough to watch the British tourist at his so-called amusement. Of all the dreary places in this world, none, perhaps, is more depressing to a philanthropic mind than the ordinary English watering-place. That the lodging-house is a torment has become notorious. A workhouse or a gaol is bad enough; but their inmates are scarcely in more melancholy quarters than those gloomy rooms, at once bare and frowzy, with a large shell and a china shepherdess on the mantelpiece, a picture of the lord-lieutenant of the county on the walls, a slatternly landlady downstairs, and a select party of parasitical insects in the bedrooms, in which the English paterfamilias consumes uneatable food, and tries to recall London to his imagination by reading the *Daily Telegraph,* from its glowing leaders to its interesting advertisements. Mariana found the moated grange bad enough; but she was not tormented, so far as we know, with barrel-organs. Sailors confined through the winter to their ships in the Arctic seas are generally pitied; but they have a greater variety of amusements than the visitor of some miniature of London *super mare*. An ocean steamer appears to its passengers for the time as about the culminating point of human weariness; yet even there, if there is more sea-sickness, there is also more society and more excitement in the incidents of the voyage. A grown-up man cannot make mud-pies, or build castles in the sand with wooden spades, and he is not, as a rule, passionately devoted to donkey-riding. Yet, so far as I have been able to discover, either from personal observation or from a careful perusal of the pages of contemporary novels and newspapers, these seem to be the main amusements provided for an intellectual public. It is true that some persons are brutal enough to amuse themselves by shooting gulls, in the spirit, I suppose, of the lady who, in one of Mr. Browning's poems, smashes a beetle, because, being wretched herself, she dislikes witnessing the enjoyment of other living beings. I rejoice that their cruelty is to be checked; but one cannot but ask oneself, what then are they to do?

Following the Briton abroad, we find him scarcely the better off for powers of enjoyment. Let any intelligent persons strike into the tracks of a party of Mr. Cook's tourists and study their modes of passing the time. Watch them in picture-galleries, at churches, or in celebrated scenery, and try to determine whether their enjoyment be genuine, or a mere conventional parade. Two or three painfully notorious facts are enough to settle the question. The ordinary tourist has no independent judgment; he admires what the infallible Murray orders him to admire; or, in other words, he does not admire at all. The tourist never diverges one hair's breadth from the beaten track of his predecessors, and within a few miles of the best known routes in Europe leaves nooks and corners as unsophisticated as they were fifty years ago; which proves that he has not sufficient interest in his route to exert his own freedom of will. The tourist, again, is intensely gregarious; he shrinks from foreigners even in their own land, and likes to have a conversation with his fellows about cotton-prints or the rate of discount in the shadow of Mont Blanc: that is, when he imagines himself to be taking his pleasures abroad, his real delight consists in returning in imagination to his native shop. The tourist, in short, is notoriously a person who follows blindly a certain hackneyed round; who never stops long enough before a picture or a view to admire it or to fix it in his memory; and who seizes every opportunity of transplanting little bits of London to the districts which he visits. Though all this has been said a thousand times, the same thing is done more systematically every year, until one is inclined to reverse the old aphorism, and declare that every man is a hypocrite in his pleasures. We are supposed to travel mainly in search of the beautiful and the picturesque; and yet the faculty which takes pleasure in such things is frequently in a state of almost complete atrophy. Writers of poetry and florid prose have now for many years been singing the praises of lovely scenery, and it is considered disgraceful to be unmoved by mountains, lakes, and forests: but I suspect that four people out of five share Dr. Johnson's preference of the view at Charing Cross to the most charming of rural landscapes. Why, indeed, should it be otherwise? At Charing Cross there is something which we can all understand; there is that peculiar manufactory in which Mr. Matthew Arnold delights; there are omnibuses, and cabs, and beggars, and policemen, and shop-windows, and newspaper placards; and every one of those objects has a certain interest for the intelligent cockney. There is a long succession of little dramas, which appeal in one way or another to his sympathies, and a gratuitous exhibition of all the articles which are supposed to be suitable for his wants. Why should he go to look at a variety of green objects whose names and uses are a mystery to him, or to stare at a big cliff with a mass of ice on top of it, whose very size he is unable to appreciate? I believe that the appreciation of scenery, like that of art, requires careful study, and that a man must familiarize himself with natural objects and their various properties before he can understand the charms which they have for those who have grown up amongst them. To take a raw Londoner and, with no previous training of mind or eye, to place him in the midst of the finest scenery, is to subject him to an unfair trial. He has not acquired the inward sense to which it appeals; he has passed a life in a wilderness of dingy bricks and mortar, and regards the sun chiefly as a substitute for gaslights; it is no wonder if he feels as bewildered and awkward as the countryman transplanted from the fields to Cheapside; and turns from the real beauties to congenial talk with his fellows, or at best, to admire some freak of nature which he can partly understand—a cliff that seems to be tumbling over, or a rock shaped like a human head. It is said that a man who has grown up amongst the "great unwashed" feels that the first ablution to be a species of ingenious torture; and we cannot expect that the accumulated grime and soot of London streets will fall off at once on our immersion in the country. Indeed, to be honest, I think that there is something strained in our assumed love of scenery. For a change, it is well enough; Switzerland is an admirable relief to the Strand, for those who have a touch of true mountain fire; but even they would, I think, if they were honest, generally agree that in the long run the Strand is a pleasanter view than the Rhone Valley, and human nature a better ingredient in a picture than hills and woods. Both Lamb and Wordsworth, in the opinion of most people, went to extremes; but Lamb showed, to my mind, a healthier and more genuine taste in his love of London than Wordsworth in his love of the Lakes.

This, however, is beside the point. I care not what people's tastes may be, so long as they express them candidly and gratify them sincerely. But how are we ever to persuade people to enjoy themselves rationally, when they are in a secret conspiracy to hide their real likings from themselves and the world? And how are people to be made sincere? How am I to persuade a man that he sees what is before his eyes—that he likes the tastes which really please his palate—that he is comfortable, when his senses are all gratified, and not when somebody else tells him that they ought to be gratified? We suffer from such an inveterate habit of self-deception on all these points, that the task is almost hopeless. A lad may often be seen smoking a cigar, whilst turning green in the face and qualmish in the stomach, and not only declaring that he likes it, which is intelligible, but even proving it to his own entire satisfaction. If it were not for this strange faculty of self-imposition,

I doubt whether anybody would ever learn to smoke; it accompanies us through life; grown-up men may often be observed who affect a dislike—supposed, for some strange reason, to be creditable—to anything sweet, and who as soon as the ladies have disappeared fall upon preserved fruits and bonbons with a marvellous appetite. How many similar practices are common in more serious matters need hardly be pointed out. How would managers of concerts get on, or preachers of sermons draw congregations, or artists sell their pictures, if we did not spontaneously conspire to impose upon ourselves in regard to our own likings? But it is useless to point out how many of the arrangements by which society is knit together depend upon this tacit consent to the manufacture of factitious pleasures.

Let us, however, ask this one question. Assuming that a man is so eccentric as to really wish to enjoy himself, and not to persuade other persons that he is enjoying himself, how may he best set about it? And it may be admitted, in spite of the general rule, that there are in fact many persons who really like evening parties, and horse-races, and watering-places, and foreign tours, and that, without a certain substantial foundation of genuine enjoyment, the mere figment, the empty simulacrum of pleasure, would not be so permanent as it is. One great element of the satisfaction derived is, of course, the merely negative pleasure of indolence. We like to obtain a good background of utter inertia with which to contrast the ordinary activity of our lives. It may, however, be doubted whether any European nations are capable of doing nothing to perfection; and the English, next to the Americans, are probably the most incapable race in the world. The Eastern can placidly reduce himself to a state of temporary absorption into the infinite, or allow visions to float before his imagination as formless and transitory as the smoke from his narghili. At rare moments we may enter that elysium far enough to guess at its pleasures. Our blood may be charmed into "pleasing heaviness,"

Making such difference 'twixt wake and sleep,
As is the difference betwixt day and night,
The hour before the heavenly harnessed team
Begins his golden progress in the east.

But the waking comes quickly; and the dreams are not altogether easy. They are crossed by figures savouring unpleasantly of reality, and bringing with them disagreeable whiffs from the outer life. The nearest approximation that I have ever observed in holiday-makers to this blissful state of dreaminess is in those harmless enthusiasts who sit in punts on the Thames under some transparent pretence of fishing. The rush of the cool waters, the swaying of the weeds in the deep stream, the soft beauty of the quiet gardens and woods that slope to the bank, produce a mesmeric influence; the monotonous bobbing of the float is designed, as I imagine, to discharge a similar function to that of the metal disk which "electro-biologists" used to place in the hands of their victims; the act of gazing at it dazzles the eye and helps to distract the attention from outward things. The dim legends which still float about that at some former periods a punt-fisher has been known to have a bite, or even to catch a gudgeon, serve partly as an excuse, but chiefly to make the repose more delectable by the faint suggestion of a barely possible activity. It soothes without exciting the patient, as the distant plunge of the surf helped the lotus-eater to enjoy his indolence by a half-formed reminiscence of his long-past labour "in the deep mid-ocean."

It is given to few persons to enjoy such repose for long. We cannot lower our vital powers like the animals which lie torpid through the winter. There is a certain amount of energy always being generated within, and we are forced to discover some kind of channel into which it may be directed. That channel should be as different as possible from our ordinary walks in life; for rest means to us, not a simple repose, but the use of a different set of activities. The fault of our tourists is, that they have about as much ingenuity in discovering an outlet for their energies, as a man who, after ploughing in the fields all day, should at night take a turn on the treadmill by way of relaxation. And it must be confessed that, if a man has no love of art, does not care about nature, is thoroughly indifferent to books, and is fitted for no society except that in which he was born, it is rather difficult to supply him with a satisfactory object of amusement. A very large number of Englishmen (and I dare say of other persons) are fit only to be human mill-horses, plodding along one weary round. When you turn them out for a run in the fields, they instinctively fall into the same mechanical circling, and prove that they are cramped in nature as well as by physical constraint. They resemble that fabulous animal the "brock," whose two right legs were half the length of his left legs; and who could, consequently, only live on the side of a conical hill, which he was obliged to be perpetually perambulating in the same direction. Yet few men are so stupefied that they cannot, by a little care, select some, more or less satisfactory, hobby—a selection in which the whole secret of judicious holiday-making may be said to consist. And here is one counterbalancing benefit in the lamentable natural deficiency of which I have been speaking. Our pleasures, I have said, are as artificial as a lady's hair is sometimes asserted to be; we live by rule instead of by instinct, and fashion our amusements after some arbitrary model. Yet it is also true that almost any amusement may in time become amusing. We smoke, as boys, purely out of imitation; but the acquired habit becomes as strong as a primary instinct. A man who will take up any special pursuit, from whatever motives, will end by loving it, if he only acts his part with sufficient vigour. The real misfortune is, that not only do people deceive themselves as to their pleasures, but that they only half-deceive themselves. They have a suppressed consciousness of their own hypocrisy, and therefore their occupation never generates a genuine passion. My first rule would be, take up some amusement for which you have a natural taste; and my second, act in any case as energetically as if you had one, and in time a very satisfactory artificial taste will be generated. It should, of course, give as much scope as possible for varied and long-continued pursuit; but devotion to any hobby whatever is preferable to a cold-blooded dawdling in obedience to general fashion after nothing in particular. Thus, for example, I remember reading the adventures of a gentleman who had made it the object of his spare hours to see big trees. Why he had hit upon that particular fancy did not appear; he was not a botanist, nor a timber merchant, nor in any other pursuit which had any particular reference to trees. So far as I remember he was, at his normal state, a hard-working clergyman. But he had trees on the brain. He dreamt, at his spare moments, of trees hundreds of feet in height, and covering acres with their shade; when he had a day or two to spare, he visited the finest trees in England; when he had a longer holiday, he travelled through the Continent in search of big trees. On one happy occasion he crossed the Atlantic, sailed up the Amazon, and penetrated the tropical forests of South America in the hope of finding some worthy object of his idolatry. Before this he had doubtless reached California by the Pacific Railway, and paid his respects to the gigantic pines in the Yosemite Valley. It is easy to imagine, not to play upon words, how this topic would branch out into all kinds of minor inquiries; how he would collect books on trees, pictures of trees, and statistical facts about trees; how, at moments when the composition of sermons was heavy upon his hands, the vision of some monster of the forest would float before his eyes, and enable him to return with fresh vigour to his work; how he would gradually acquire the pleasure of being the greatest living authority on one particular subject; and how he would look down from the heights of a genuine passion upon the miserable creatures who wander aimlessly and hobbilessly through the world, in obedience to the arbitrary dictates of the British traveller's bible.

The happy man who has selected his hobby always excites my admiration; whether it is sporting, or art, or athletic pursuits, or antiquarianism, or what not, he is at least able to boast of a genuine enjoyment. To be perfect, it should be happily contrasted with the regular pursuits of his life, so as to give a proper relaxation to his faculties. We are all more or less in the position of those artizans whose physical frames are distorted by one special kind of labour, and like them, are in want of something to call a different set of muscles, physical or spiritual, into play. But some energetic pursuit is at all events a blessing, and nothing seems less wise than to ridicule those who have hit upon some pleasure, however unintelligible to the rest of mankind, which may fill their leisure hours.

Unluckily most people are stupid. Every genuine hobby is speedily surrounded by a crowd of mock articles. The man who hunts and likes it, as Mr. Trollope has told us, is counterfeited by numbers who hunt and don't like it. One enthusiast goes to a picture gallery because he loves art, and fifty because they have succeeded in persuading themselves that they love it. Half the accepted creeds in the world are not what people believe, but what they believe that they believe. Other feasts than the theatrical are made off pasteboard dishes, with guests quaffing deep draughts of emptiness from tinsel cups. Vacations are less a time of enjoyment than a time of general consent to be bored under a hollow show of enjoyment. The best hope for many of us is that by pretending very hard, the pretence may come to have a sort of secondary reality; and as a large part of the pleasure derived from any pursuit consists in the recollection of our performances, and in the stories which they enable us to repeat to our friends, that satisfaction is open to those who never really enjoy the original pleasure, but believe in their own assertions after they have made them half-a-dozen times. There comes a time when the past sham is almost as good as the past reality, and a man persuades himself that his report of his own ecstasies is more or less founded on facts. Meanwhile a little more sincerity would be a good thing, for it would at least deliver many devotees of the genuine pleasures of foreign travel from those worst of bores—their own countrymen.

Camping in the Wilderness

By GREGORY P. STONE and MARVIN J. TAVES

BEHIND EVERY VIEW of whatever event lies a perspective. Often comprised of unstated assumptions, such a perspective sharply curtails the range and quality of statements that can be formulated about that event. We suspect that the forester sees and explains the forest differently than does the recreating tourist. We know that the sociologist's view and words are different from both.

Our very slight acquaintance with the perspective of forest conservation leads us to guess that one component—one implicit assumption—holds that the worlds of man and nature are separate and that the "laws" which govern events in each domain are irreconcilable and independent. There are profound consequences for forestry. For example, in 1952, 94 per cent of the nation's forest fires were man caused. Of these 61 per cent were due to human negligence. No one today would investigate forest fires only as natural catastrophes, their explanations to be sought in the study of "nature's laws." Some, however, may see forest fires only as a dramatic, fortuitous intersection between the "laws of man" and the "laws of nature."

It is not enough to conceive such instances as a mere overlapping of the domains of nature and man. To put it bluntly, man is not unnatural, the bear natural; buildings unnatural and beaver lodges natural.[1] Man is natural in at

---

Originally titled, "Research into the Human Element in Wilderness Use." Reprinted from *Proceedings, Society of American Foresters,* 1956, pp. 26-32, by permission of the authors and the publisher. (Copyright 1956 by the Society of American Foresters.)

The authors acknowledge the assistance of Holgar Stub, J. Eugene Haas, and Keith Lovald, graduate students in the Department of Sociology, University of Minnesota, in the interviewing on which many of the findings in this study have been based. They are also indebted to William L. Hathaway, graduate student in the Department of Political Science, University of Minnesota, for his valuable assistance in the coding of the interview materials and his useful suggestions for the formulation of many of the ideas presented here. Donald P. Duncan and Frank D. Irving of the University of Minnesota's School of Forestry offered helpful suggestions in their critical readings of a preliminary draft. Finally, the authors are indebted to the Quetico-Superior Wilderness Research Center and the Lakeland Foundation who sponsored this research. Without their help, this paper could not have been written.

least two senses. First, he has a natural history. His activities at any one time have evolved out of the activities of some former time. Second, he qualifies as an object of scientific study. To study the intrusions of a tree blight, the ecology of a fern, or the natural history of the beaver, and, at the same time, to neglect or merely opine about the human effect upon the wilderness as well as the reciprocal effect upon human life unnecessarily warps the forester's view of the events around him and hampers him seriously in his professional conduct.

Thus, the major purpose of this paper is to present a view of man in the wilderness and an agenda of research problems that concern sociology. Hopefully, in such a way, the perspectives of those active in forestry and the disciplined scrutiny of wilderness areas can be broadened and reinforced.

Several interviews have supplemented our personal experiences to inform the questions we will raise. The interview materials are of three kinds. First, short schedules report the socio-economic characteristics, character of trip, composition of party, and wilderness experience and imagery of 36 persons in 20 different wilderness parties, mostly canoeists, in the Quetico-Superior area during June and July, 1956. These schedules were directly administered at a frequently used truck portage into Basswood Lake. Second, nine mailed questionnaires were helpfully completed and returned by members of the American Forestry Association's "Trail Riders of the Wilderness" in the area during July. Thus, 45 persons representing 21 groups were contacted formally. Third, informal interviews were conducted with lodge guests, guides, and service personnel in the area. One of the authors and his family also participated in a canoe trip into Quetico Provincial Park early in September to gain additional insights and information.

Cautions about the interpretation of these data must be entered here. The materials are probably not representative of persons entering wilderness areas. Informants were not selected as a sample, but largely on the basis of their accessibility to the interviewers.[2] Moreover, the cases are so few that statistical tests of significance have often been precluded from the analysis, and frequency distributions may be misleading. Finally, conditions for interviewing were not conducive to optimum reporting. Informants were literally caught on the run between portage bus and launch. What follow, therefore, are research leads informed rather than confirmed by interviews and participant observation.

WILDERNESS CAMPING GROUPS

Any empirical investigation requires prior classification of its subject matter. We turn, then, at once to the characteristics of the wilderness campers studied.

Demographic characteristics.—Almost half of our interview respondents came from small cities between ten and one hundred thousand in population, about a quarter from larger cities, and another quarter from towns and villages. Yet, many of these small towns and cities were metropolitan suburbs. Thus, almost 60 per cent of those interviewed lived within a 40 mile radius of metropolises greater than half a million in population. The remainder–mostly from Iowa, Nebraska, and the Dakotas–were not of metropolitan origin. Informants came from the territory of Alaska and thirteen states. Although 30 of the 45 came from four nearby states–Illinois, Indiana, Iowa, and Minnesota–New Yorkers and Californians represented both coasts, and canoeists came from as far south as Kentucky and Missouri. What we may term the "wilderness clientele of Quetico-Superior" is primarily metropolitan and potentially national in character.

Eleven all-male groups and 10 mixed male and female groups were contacted. One female camping party, apparently made up of college co-eds, was observed on our canoe trip, and we expect the incidence of female outings in wilderness areas to increase in the future.[3] Even so, four-fifths of our informants were men.

The struggle to maintain bans on air travel into the Superior Forest continues. Those opposed to the bans argue that the area will ultimately be accessible only to canoeists, necessarily very young, and that older people will be deprived of the wilderness experience. A lodge hostess claimed, "Younger people go on canoe trips or camp out. But, when they get to be about thirty-five, they have money and stay at resorts." An operator of another resort and two lodge roustabouts confirmed this view, stating that lodge patrons were usually in their forties and fifties, while canoeists were in their teens and twenties.

Our data suggest that these impressions may be incorrect. Ages of canoeists ranged from fifteen to the early sixties. Although the modal age, representing one-fifth of the cases, was 22.5 years, the median age was 34.4, and the mean age was 35.4. We observed fourteen groups of canoeists during our trek in the wilderness and estimated that six included members in their thirties or older. Among those administered interviews or questionnaires, five were not canoeists. Three were on their way to a wilderness resort, and their ages (25, 38, and 46) did not differ markedly from the ages of canoeists. The other two were visiting a private cabin in the area. Both were in their early thirties.

We do not contend that the potential wilderness clientele will be unaffected by present air travel bans. Rather, our data show that current impressions about which specific segments will be affected may be in gross error.

Marital and parental status were also analyzed. Five married couples were interviewed, and four had no minor children at home. One couple left six minor children at home during the wilderness trip. Twenty-one informants were married. Of these, eight were without minor children at home, eight more had minor children at home, but did not take them into the wilderness area, and five were accompanied by minor children. One formerly married canoeist was accompanied by a nephew, and one widower reported one minor child at home. Twelve informants were single.

Wilderness travel is an exclusive recreation. Sociological research has established that one's occupation is the best single index of his place in community prestige arrangements (8), and Table 1 shows the occupational distribution of the informants, indicating their high social standing. Education data confirm the high status of canoeists. More than half had either completed college or received graduate degrees. The modal educational category included persons with graduate degrees and represented somewhat more than a fourth of those interviewed. Only one respondent had not completed high school.

Table I—Occupations of Forty-Five Wilderness Campers

OCCUPATION	NUMBER	PERCENT
Professionals	9	20
Engineers and other trained industrial technicians	10	22
Business executives	5	11
Managers and proprietors	4	9
Clerical and sales	3	7
Craftsmen	2	4
Air Force pilot	1	2
High school students	3	7
College students	4	9
Housewives	4	9
Totals	45	100

Camping and canoeing experience.—The 36 persons interviewed personally were asked about their previous canoeing and camping experience. Fourteen had no previous experience which might facilitate their immediate wilderness travel, and more than half were in the Quetico-Superior area for the first time. However, only one of the 20 groups represented by these interviews was without an experienced outdoorsman in the main party, and that group had employed a professional guide. Seven groups were completely composed of persons without prior Quetico-Superior experience. We shall see later that experienced campers and canoeists typify particular kinds of camping groups, while novices are more often found in other kinds of groups.

Kinds of groups.—Sociological group analysis examines many different variables, but we will touch only upon three variables in this place.

First, there is the size of the wilderness expedition. No informant was a "loner." The modal size, representing eight of the 21 groups formally contacted, was two. The median and mean size, however, were 4.3 and 4.4 persons respectively. Although there was no relationship between size and previous camping experience in general, specific experience in the Quetico-Superior area, as may be seen from Table 2, was inversely associated with group size. By noting the size of the group, a forester may be able to estimate the proportion of locally experienced campers.

Table II—Association Between Size of Wilderness Party and Previous Camping Experience in the Quetico-Superior Area

PREVIOUS CAMPING EXPERIENCE IN THE QUETICO-SUPERIOR AREA	SIZE OF WILDERNESS PARTY*	
	Two	Three or more
Experienced	9	6
Inexperienced	5	15
Totals*	14	21

$x^2 = 4.375$ $p < .05$

*One informant did not report the size of his party.

A second distinguishing feature of the camping group is the duration of its outing. Of the 21 groups investigated, the mean, median, and modal duration corresponded almost exactly at six and one-half days. Again, there was no significant association between this variable and general camping experience, but there was a highly significant association with Quetico-Superior experience. Table 3 shows that all informants making trips of five

Table III—Association Between Duration of Wilderness Trip and Previous Camping Experience in the Quetico-Superior Area

PREVIOUS CAMPING EXPERIENCE IN THE QUETICO-SUPERIOR AREA	DURATION OF WILDERNESS TRIP		
	5 days or less	*6 days*	*7 days or more*
Experienced	0	7	9
Inexperienced	14	3	3
Totals	14	10	12
	$x^2 = 14.431$*	$p < .001$	

*Because of the low expected frequency (4.4) in one cell, the Chi-Square has been corrected by subtracting 0.5 from every difference between expected and observed frequencies in the computation.

days or less were not experienced in that particular wilderness area. Trips of six days occupied about twice as many former Quetico-Superior campers as newcomers, and, in the case of trips of one week or more, this ratio increased to three to one.

These relationships have implications for the scheduling of patrolling activities in the forest. Such activities might be adapted to the type of camping groups known to be in the area. Several highly practical and concrete research problems are suggested. Among these, we include whether the frequency of forest accidents is a function of the kinds of groups utilizing the forest, and hypothesize that the frequency of forest accidents relative to the number of campers in the area decreases as the distance from points of entry into wilderness areas increases, because of the greater proportions of experienced campers in groups taking longer trips. Also we ask whether there is any temporal distribution of such groups during the camping season to which patrolling activities might be geared.

Perhaps the preeminence of married informants means that wilderness trips are largely family affairs. When the groups were analyzed by type of member relationships, we found this to be the case. Six types were discerned. First, the "Trail Riders of the Wilderness" constituted a special kind of group by itself. Second, there were three groups of adult-supervised younger boys. Third were five groups composed of male friends and acquaintances. The fourth category included four parties consisting of man and wife only. A fifth type was comprised by three groups including married couples and their married friends and, in one case, children of the campers. The final type was made up of five groups whose members were related by marriage and/or extended kinship bonds, e.g., siblings, cousins, nephews, etc., and, in two instances, friends of the larger extended family. Thus, 12 of the 21 groups consisted of members related by marriage or by birth.

The bearing of such differences in social relations on the size of the groups studied is evident from the typology itself. Generally, the shortest trips were made by the male friendship groups, and the longer trips by the supervised parties. Family and kinship camping parties were about evenly divided between those making the longer and shorter wilderness treks.

Sociologically, the most significant finding here is that 17 of the 21 groups were either families and their extensions or intimate friendship groups. Many of us are interested in what might be called the therapeutic value of the wilderness (7). By this, some persons have in mind only the psychological consequences *for the individual* of his wilderness experience. We would like to supplement this point of view. Among many psychiatrists and social psychologists, mental health is apprehended as a function of one's interpersonal relations (11, 14). The family and the friendship are crucial interpersonal relations in this respect. Consequently, to strengthen such groupings—which sociologists find to have been weakened by the impact of industrialization and city living—may be as important for therapy and even the prevention of mental disturbance as ministering to the disturbed individual *qua* individual. Certainly, the wilderness experience extends the opportunity for strengthening intimate social bonds as we shall see.

The point may be illustrated. There was a story going the rounds of wilderness personnel about a businessman who had selected a secluded part of the forest to sit alone and reflect upon a recent severe financial setback. A wilderness worker unwittingly stumbled upon the man who was in tears at the time. Unembarrassed, the man explained that he had "come up here to recharge my batteries." Much has been made locally of this story is epitomizing the wilderness experience. In our view, the experience of one of our informants who had come to the wilderness with his son after the boy's return from the military, "to get to know my son again," is just as germane. Moreover, we emphasize that wilderness travel is not an individual enterprise. None of our informants made his trek alone.

PLANNING THE WILDERNESS TRIP

That the wilderness is a context for the joint enterprise of intimates is also reflected in responses made by our informants to a question asking how they first learned about the area. Thirty-two of 44 responding to the question heard about the area from relatives, friends, or work associates. Four of these supplemented such information with promotional literature. Four others engaged in activities, such as camp counseling or business, which took them into the area, and only eight—all of them "Trail Riders"—relied primarily on promotional materials.

Because of the length of time involved, planning the trip may itself provide an occasion for reenforcing bonds of intimacy. Only five of 40 informants indicating the length of their planning activity spent less than a month in the process. Fourteen spent one or two months; 14, more than two months but less than a year; and seven spent a year or more. Twenty-three persons volunteered additional comments upon the planning process itself, most indicating that it was a joint affair accomplished in the design of vacation plans. However, three informants saw themselves as promoters of their wilderness venture and three as playing a passive role in the process, leaving the planning largely up to others. Only two informants said that they had availed themselves of outfitters' assistance in the planning stage.

These sketchy notes on planning suggest at least two problems for future study. First, planning may have consequences for the integration of intimate groups, because extensive and careful consideration of wilderness trip details necessarily reveals the personal characteristics of the participants much more than the planning of a "commercialized vacation" where the personal needs of the vacationer—eating, sleeping, etc.—are provided for by service personnel. Planning and the wilderness experience provide the sociologist with a kind of laboratory situation in which primary group processes and functions may be fruitfully investigated.[4] Second, the "lay promoters" of wilderness travel could well be studied to determine whether they have characteristics enabling their ready identification by those interested in disseminating wilderness values among the population at large.

IMAGERY OF THE WILDERNESS

These remarks lead us directly into a consideration of the motivation of wilderness travelers. We view motives as vocabularies appropriate for the explanation of behavior in specified social situations (2, 4, 11, 12). To discern these vocabularies, we asked 36 informants in personal interviews to tell us in their own words why they were in the wilderness. Analysis disclosed five broad categories of reasons which, taken together, depict the imagery of the wilderness held by those who visit it.

The wilderness as a locale for sport and play.—Mentioned by about seven-tenths of the informants, this theme envisions the wilderness as a place for two fundamentally different kinds of activities: sport and play. These terms are employed in a special sense. Play we regard, along with Jan Huizinga, as superfluous in character, a disinterested, extraordinary and "unreal" activity. Most important, "it is never a task." (10). Play, in its pure form, stands apart from work. When our informants spoke of the wilderness as a place to have fun, relax, or take it easy, their responses were classified as play. Sport, for one thing, may link play with some work form, and, in this respect, there are two major sport modes. First, there are those sports that mark transformations of the play form into work—professional and otherwise subsidized athletics. In these sports spectators usually outnumber participants. Second, there are sports that are transformations of the work form into play.[5]

Earlier one of us put it this way:

Consider how Americans speak of sport. Baseball, basketball, football, golf, hockey, and tennis–these sports are "played." The participants are "players.". . . Yet precisely those sports that are "played" have become work in America. . . . However, the "players of sport" are not, literally, "sportsmen"! Sportsmen are hunters and fishermen, archers, skiers, yachtsmen, or campers. Note that these sports are never "played," nor may they assume the character of work [and retain their identity as sport]. They are peopled almost entirely by amateurs. When they do become work, they become occupations. Fishing is a primary *industry.* (*13*).

Participation is extensive in those sports that constitute transformations of a work form into play, such as fishing and camping, and spectators are practically nonexistent. Moreover, most such sports are conducted in the outdoors, many adaptable to wilderness areas. Now that leisure time is on the increase and people are frequently anxious about how to employ it as a source of personal dignity, the appropriateness of the wilderness for participant sport is striking. For participation in the game is inherently moral in character, while spectacular sport, implying spectatorship, is often destructive of morality (13). We regard morality, in this sense, merely as a body of rules governing conduct. The participant sportsman incorporates such rules in his conception of himself; the spectator often revels in the infraction of the rule and actively cultivates it. The case of present-day wrestling is pertinent.

Our informants were evenly divided in their conceptions of the wilderness as a place for sport and for play, some regarding it as both. Fishing–a play upon work and the most frequently mentioned sport–is fun for some and a grim affair for others.

The wilderness as a fascination. About sixty percent of the informants regarded their entry into the wilderness as a response to a kind of "call of the wild." Usually, the "call" was thought to be specific to the Quetico-Superior area, often based on some former experience in the wilderness. Frequently, too, it was a summons to adventure. Many informants were impelled to embark on the wilderness trip as a form of exploration, to satisfy their curiosities, or to gain a new experience. Others attached a general positive value to the outdoors. A few were attracted by special qualities of the wilderness usually aesthetic in nature, and one person viewed the "call" as a summons to combat–a challenge to struggle with the elements.

The wilderness as a sanctuary.–Somewhat more than a third of the informants used this image as a rationale for their trips.

Perhaps informants employing the images mentioned before are "looking forward" to their experience, while those thinking of the wilderness as a sanctuary are "looking backward" during their trip. Yet, we hesitate to call this theme an escape *motif*. The notion of "escape" often connotes a personal avoidance pattern, suggesting a characterological flaw. We wish to "escape" this implication. "Escape" is also construed to be a psychological defense mechanism, as "escape into fantasy," but what is at point here is the social character of the wilderness experience. Our informants may be "escaping" one set of relationships, but they are entering another. Leaving the impersonal city, the telephone ring, the monotony of work, and the mass media of communication behind, they enter the highly personalized, face-to-face, often unpredictable enterprise of the camping party. They find in the wilderness the opportunity to be "alone with others." Several informants made this explicit. One canoeing bridegroom explained, "We wanted to get away by ourselves for a honeymoon." A member of another group elaborated, "I like to get away from people, the newspaper, and the radio, so I can be alone with my wife." Still another said, "I wanted to find a nice secluded place where I could be with my friends and get away from it all." In conceiving the wilderness as a sanctuary, the person leaves the established routines of daily life for the more intimate spontaneities of the camping group, he surrenders one set of intimacies for another, or he merely changes the setting of existing intimate relations.

Fishing, hunting, and camping trips have frequently been regarded as male mechanisms of escape. We can hardly conceive that men depart on such ventures looking over their shoulders. The data offer support for our scepticism. Table 4 shows that the proportion of members of male friendship

Table IV—Difference in Proportions of Members of Male Friendship Groups and Members of Other Camping Parties Employing an Image of the Wilderness as a Sanctuary

WILDERNESS IMAGERY	GROUP CATEGORY			
	Male friendship groups		*Other camping parties*	
	Number	Percent	Number	Percent
Wilderness as sanctuary	1	11	12	44
Other imagery	8	89	15	56
Totals	9	100	27	100

$p_1 - p_2 = 1.7$ z. The probability is .0446 that the difference in proportions can be attributed to sampling.

groups conceiving the wilderness as a sanctuary is significantly less than the proportion of members of other groups holding that image of the wilderness.[6] Rather, it is family and kinship groups and those who act as supervisors of young people who view the wilderness as a sanctuary. Whole families take refuge in the wilderness, and, since each of the three adult supervisors interviewed held this image of the wilderness, perhaps *individuals* take refuge in wilderness occupations.

The wilderness as a heritage. Somewhat more than a fourth of the respondents conceived the wilderness as a heritage, dedicating themselves in a mission to pass it on to others. One informant put it this way:

> I came here to take my children into the wilderness and to commune with nature. We've been out camping, and we want our children to experience it, and their children, and their children after them.

For some, the wilderness trip was part of the socialization of the child; for others part of the socialization of wives or friends. Of course, some of these were "stuck with an unwanted heirloom." One housewife muttered, "I was roped in." Then, she quickly, more loudly added, "But I wanted to go."

The wilderness as personal gratification.—About a fifth of the informants viewed the wilderness as a means of gratifying diverse individual wants. Some felt that the wilderness experience answered a vague unformulated human need. One saw the wilderness as a vehicle for "realizing himself"—what we might term autonomous recreation. Another undertook the experience to toughen himself physically, and still another was vicariously gratified by his association with youngsters:

> Men like myself, businessmen and others who work under pressure, need to be able to get away from it all once in a while. Besides, being with all these boys every summer keeps me feeling younger. I see myself in them all the time.

Adequate social-psychological analysis of such responses requires considerably more intensive interviewing than was feasible in this pilot study.

A frequency distribution of these wilderness images is provided in Table 5. Single images were rarely maintained by respondents, although four saw

Table V—Distribution of Wilderness Images Held by Thirty-Six Campers

WILDERNESS IMAGES	Number	Percent
Locale for sport and play	25	69
Fascination	21	58
Sanctuary	13	36
Heritage	10	28
Personal gratification	7	19

the wilderness only as a locale for sport and play, four only as a fascination, and one each as exclusively a sanctuary or heritage. Usually the view of the wilderness in terms of sport and play was combined with its fascination, its value as a refuge, or a heritage. It was also common to find the images of the wilderness as a fascination and a sanctuary combined.

Such imagery is not always validated in actual experience, and some informants volunteered information about how prior images had been corrected by the trip. For some, the sport of camping involved "playing at" more work than had at first been envisioned. One canoeist remarked, "There were good chances to fish, but I only did it two hours. There was too much to do." Another informant said all he did was eat, and a companion chimed in, "Yes, between eating, and paddling, and putting up camp, one did little else." Still, the experience eventuated not only in revised imagery, but in some instances in a new respect for winderness etiquette and the acquisition of wilderness skills.

We think that new campers should be directly indoctrinated by foresters in wilderness etiquette and skills. Brochures are too often consulted in the reminiscing period that follows the camping activity, and many of the misfortunes of wilderness camping that we observed—using cardboard cartons as packs in rainy country, losing all one's supplies to marauding bears on the first day out, or trying to portage a 180 pound boat (supplied, incidentally, by experienced outfitters), and a seven and one-half horsepower motor over a two mile portage—seemed most unnecessary. Yet, among those volunteering relevant comments, six stated definitely that they would return. Certainly, others will also return, hopefully more considerate, more skillful, and wiser campers.

THE SOCIOLOGY OF CAMPING

Several additional problems are raised by these observations. Although they refer specifically to camping and its related activities, they touch on broader areas of sociological theory and research. In the space available, they cannot be extensively discussed, but the more salient may be listed and briefly examined.

Small group research.—The wilderness camping group is of necessity a small group, and currently there has been considerable interest in the general study of small groups (9). There are at least three rationales for such study. First, the small group is seen as a social microcosm so that presumably much can be learned about the larger society from its analysis. Second, large social structures are thought to be tied together in part by the functioning of small groups. Third, one's conception of self is formed, maintained, and altered in the matrix of close intimate relations.

An abiding question in small group research asks how an organization arises—how the activities of members become geared into one another so that a so-called "system" is established. Establishing a set of complementary activities—a division of labor—among the members of a camping group is undoubtedly an operation on which the success of the venture stands or falls. Mutual recriminations among the campers we observed seemed invariably to stem from some unsatisfactory apportionment or carrying out of camping tasks.

There are three group variables which condition the harmonious achievement of a division of labor.

First, there is size. The harmony of camping venture is imperiled beyond some numerical upper limit. Large numbers will undoubtedly hinder a joint working out of any division of labor. They can also militate against an apportionment of tasks commensurate with available talents and skills. When this happens, gaps and lulls in camp activities will arise permitting the attention of campers to be diverted from the task at hand to one another's performances so that some members may find themselves with time on their hands and feel left out of the collective enterprise. Others may censure such unavoidable idleness, attributing it to shirking.

Second, there is the articulation of previously established social relations with the interpersonal relations that arise in the wilderness outing. Camping relationships among peers, such as friends and acquaintances, may be more seriously affected by the size of the party than more clearly defined relationships such as man and wife, adult supervisor and youngsters, or father and son. We hypothesize that the more clearly established the dominance-submission in the relations of campers to one another *prior* to their camping trip, the more easily and smoothly will a workable division of labor be achieved during the camping activity. The nature of prior dominance-submission, e.g., whether it has been formally constituted as authority, as in the case of a scoutmaster or a camp counselor, or informally constituted as influence, as in a friendship, is important here also.

Third, there is the intimacy of the camping outing. Erving Goffman, in a remarkable study of what he calls "impression management," notes that front- and back-stage regions nicely divide the places in which we make our impressions upon others from the places in which such impressions are contrived (6). The bath-room, for example, is back-stage; the living-room, front-stage. Different comportment, language, gestures, and obligations obtain in these two regions, but one salient distinguishing feature is that the audience which we wish to impress is denied access to back-stage. In a sense, this is what makes propriety possible in our daily lives. What is unique about the camping trip is the difficulty of keeping these regions distinct. The toilet is completed almost always within the perceptual range of others—one's back-stage is always accessible to others. Camping unmasks its participants. This unmasking effect frequently generates tensions among the members of the camping party, and stands in need of sociological study. By such a study, the broad problem of how intimacies are formed, sustained, and fail would be greatly informed.

Social solidarity.—The central problem of sociology is the nature of the social bond—how people are held together in association, and the analysis of camping can shed light on at least two facets of social solidarity.

First, there is the solidarity of the camping party. Every in-group presupposes some out-group, and groups are consolidated by the presence of some outside, usually antagonistic form. The "combat metaphor," evoked by most campers at one time or another to describe their wilderness experience is pertinent. A trip in the wilderness is apprehended as a struggle, and this struggle sustains the solidarity of the camping party, but only so long as the struggle is with nature—so long as the enemy is without rather than within.

Second, camping contributes to the solidarity of the larger society which rests, in part, upon the maintenance of a community of experience among persons. To maintain the community of experience, people must share, as William James put it, both knowledge about and acquaintance with similar salient events. On this basis, they can enter into association without necessarily having been introduced.

Knowledge about similar events is provided by the mass media. One can ask almost any stranger about sports or popular TV programs, and, because the stranger possesses relevant information, the conversation will be sustained, sometimes transformed into a more enduring relationship. Knowledge about similar events makes us available to one another.

Acquaintance with similar events is provided by certain pervasive experiences—the work experience, the military, the courtship, the blizzard of '88. These are marked by a dominant mood which mobilizes sympathies and mutual appreciations among those having the experience. Such persons need not have participated together in the experience. Consequently, borrowing again from Goffman, they may be called *colleagues.* As he says, "colleagues share a community of fate." (4). Wilderness travelers are colleagues in this sense. Blair Fraser provides a clue to our meaning:

> When we set out from Basswood Lake for the second leg of the journey . . . our food weighed 180 pounds. We had to carry every ounce of it over the long portage into Lake Kahshahpiwi—half a mile up a rocky mountainside, another half mile down again, with a soggy bog cupped in the middle at the summit. Anyone who has gone over this portage is entitled to membership in the Kahshahpiwi Club, an exclusive organization which offers its members no privileges whatsoever. (5)

Again colleagues, even though strangers, easily enter into relationships with one another. They are mutually available.

The role of knowledge about and acquaintance with camping in sustaining the community of experience shared by members of the larger society needs extensive research.

Occupational sociology.—We have largely examined here possible research on campers or wilderness clientele. There is also a personnel. The study of occupations by sociologists has grown rapidly in recent years. Persistently, they seek what is common among occupations, and one commonalty is that all involve contingencies—points at which outside relations impinge upon the work career. A common contingency involves the relation between the work career and family life (1).

We cite here only the manner in which the contingency of family and work affects the career of the guide to exemplify the problems occupational sociologists may find in the wilderness. The career of the guide is entered early in life, usually during the teens. The guide may free-lance or work through an established resort. At any rate, his seasonal goal is "a hundred days" which nets him between $1,500 and $2,000 plus tips. Formerly he was able to supplement this income by trapping or work in other primary industries. These are now declining industries for the most part. Trapping, as one guide put it, "doesn't pay any more. It's a dying occupation. There are thousands of muskrats around here. You get thirty-five or fifty cents a pelt, and it's not worth it." Today's guide, then, is faced with a limited income. Yet, he may be tied to the wilderness, as we have said, because it is his sanctuary.

At some point he may be faced with the decision to marry. The bachelor guide avoids the contingency we are discussing here, as does the married guide—until the children begin to arrive. Usually in his early or middle thirties, with four or five children, he must question his career. He painfully acknowledges the uncertainties of a seasonal occupation, and the family contingency usually forces him out. Now, he finds himself on the labor market, unskilled and disadvantaged by age.

Social problems arising from this single occupational contingency underscore the need for research into wilderness occupations. Certainly, foresters can recognize many contingencies of their own careers.

Social resources.—Often we view our forests as natural resources, implying only their economic value. Yet, the recreational use of many forested areas has already superseded their industrial use. The forest, consequently, may be viewed as a social resource.

Just as our social life provides stressful situations, like career contingencies, so does it provide resources which may be used to offset such stresses. The provision of these resources is vital to the national mental health. Throughout this paper we have touched upon the ways in which the wilderness experience affects the self-conception of the wilderness camper. The effect is pervasive because of the intimate nature of the camping enterprise.

Most of the propositions of social psychology are built on two general axioms: one, that the person sees himself as others see him; the other, that one has as many selves as he has group affiliations. A rough measure of intimacy is the relative number of group affiliations that are brought into play in a social relationship. A supermarket cashier need only known the amount of money in our hand and the value of the groceries in our bag, and we know no more about her than that she has rung up our purchase correctly, and will give us the proper change and allotment of gift stamps. In her eyes, we see ourselves as a customer; in our eyes, she sees herself as a cashier. Among intimates, however, our affiliations at home, work, church, and in politics enter in. What is reflected in the eyes of intimates is the whole self—the network of a significant segment of all one's group affiliations. Consequently, the intimate relationship provides us with the opportunity to form that more extensive and integrated conception of self that is so vital to mental health, but presumably so difficult to achieve in a specialized world. Clearly, the wilderness experience is relevant.

SUMMARY AND CONCLUSION

In conclusion, we wish to bring together all the foregoing observations as a prospectus of social research on the human element in wilderness use. On the one hand, we have suggested a set of four major problems which would seem to be of direct relevance to forestry as well as sociology:

1. A study of the demography of the wilderness—the residence, sex, age, family status, occupation, and education of those venturing into wilderness areas. We need to know what segments of our population avail themselves of the wilderness experience.

2. A study of the different forms of wilderness camping groups in terms of size, the duration of their trips, and the kinds of social relations they bring with them into the wilderness. Since the varieties of camping groups are comprised of different proportions of members experienced in wilderness camping, and, since they are probably temporally distributed over the camping season, the identification of such groups would seem important for the disposition of wilderness patrolling and other activities of the forester. Moreover, since such groupings are composed of intimates in large measure, the social psychological consequences of participation in them are probably pro-

found and contribute greatly to any therapeutic effects the wilderness experience might have.

3. A study of the planning and design of the wilderness trip. There are several implications of such a study. These include the identification of those campers who are promoting the wilderness in the population at large, the knowledge of how best to prepare the novice for his experience, and the detection of how the planning experience, usually a long and intimate one, functions to form and cement or disrupt close personal association.

4. A study of the imagery of the wilderness. To know why people venture into the wilderness is to be better able to evaluate the full range of consequences of their experience.

On the other hand, we have shown how the study of wilderness activities can inform four important areas of contemporary sociological research: (1) the study of small group interaction; (2) the study of social solidarity; (3) occupational sociology; and (4) the study of social resources for mental health.

Posing these problems and pointing out the sociological areas within which they may be studied has scarcely begun to tap the research possibilities afforded by the wilderness experience. However, this can mark the beginning of a closer collaboration between sociologists and foresters. Hopefully, in the near future, they will embark upon a joint research venture that can only result in the vast enrichment of both disciplines.

References

1. Becker, Howard S. 1953. Some contingencies of the professional dance musician's career. Human Organization 12: 22-26.

2. Burke, Kenneth. 1954. Permanence and change. Hermes Publications, Los Altos, Calif.

3. Callois, Roger. 1955. The structure and classification of games. Diogenes No. 12: 62-75.

4. Foote, Nelson. 1951. Identification as a basis for a theory of motivation. Amer. Soc. Review 16: 14-21.

5. Fraser, Blair. 1955. We went La Verendrye's way. MacLean's Magazine.

6. Goffman, Erving. 1956. The presentation of self in everyday life. University of Edinburgh Soc. Sci. Research Centre Monograph No. 2. Edinburgh, Scotland.

7. Gordon, J. Berkeley. 1952. Psychiatric values of the wilderness. The Welfare Reporter 6.

8. Hatt, Paul K. 1950. Occupation and social stratification. Amer. Jour. Soc. 55: 533-543.

9. Homans, George C. 1950. The human group. Harcourt, Brace and Co., New York.

10. Huizinga, Jan. 1949. Homo Ludens: A study of the play elements of culture. Routledge and Kegan Paul, Ltd., London.

11. Lindesmith, Alfred R. and Anselm L. Strauss. 1956. Social psychology. The Dryden Press, New York.

12. Mills, C. Wright. 1940. Situated actions and vocabularies of motive. Amer. Soc. Review 5: 904-913.

13. Stone, Gregory P. 1955. American sports: play and dis-play. Chicago Review. 9: 83-100.

14. Sullivan, Harry Stack. 1940. Conceptions of modern psychiatry. The William Alanson White Psychiatric Foundation, Washington, D. C.

Notes

1. Note carefully that these are not preference statements. Aesthetically, some of us may prefer the beaver lodge to the cracker box house in the metropolitan suburb.

2. Our own canoe trip demonstrated that future samples should be drawn from universes of groups rather than individuals.

3. Women are capturing the symbols of the outdoors previously monopolized by men. They have their outdoor fashions *(13)*. A count of advertisements showing female models in outdoor magazines during the whole history of their publication would afford a useful index of this "feminization of the outdoors."

4. There is nothing inherently good or psychologically beneficial about intimacy. Familiarity may breed contempt so that the members of a wilderness camping party may get to know one another "all to well." These problems require careful examination.

5. One of the authors owes a long overdue debt of gratitude to his former associate, Joanne B. Eicher, now of Boston University, for first suggesting this fruitful line of analysis. Those interested in the general problem of sport and play might also review the valuable article by Roger Callois *(3)*. For example, outdoor sports, skiing, and mountain climbing are referred to as a type of game he calls *ilinx* or vertigo, i.e., they constitute "an answer to one's need to feel the body's stability and equilibrium momentarily destroyed, to escape the tyranny of perception, and to overcome awareness." *(3)*. Perhaps this is one source of the fascination on the part of many campers, usually novices, with the instability of the canoe and the mysterious threatening uncertainties of the bear.

6. Since we are not interested in the association between these variables, but only in the difference in proportions, a one-tailed test of significant difference was employed instead of the Chi-square. The computation of the standard error of the difference in proportions was corrected for small sample size.

Notes on a Natural History of Fads[1]

By ROLF MEYERSOHN AND ELIHU KATZ

THE STUDY of fads and fashions[2] may serve the student of social change much as the study of fruit flies has served geneticists: neither the sociologist nor the geneticist has to wait long for a new generation to arrive.

Fads provide an extraordinary opportunity to study processes of influence or contagion, of innovative and cyclical behavior, and of leadership; this has been long recognized by social thinkers, most of whom tended, however, to regard fads and fashions as one form of permanent social change.[3]

To regard change in fads exclusively as a prototype of social change is to overlook several fundamental distinctions. In the first place, the process by which fads operate is typically confined to particular subgroups in society, and, although fads may change violently and swiftly, the subgroup remains the same; the network of fad communication usually remains stable. On the other hand, patterns of communication that create new social movements—for example, a new religious sect—also create a new social structure; here both the content and the network of communication are new. This distinction is well made by Blumer, who points out that social movements, unlike fads, usually leave stable organizations in their wake:

> Not only is the fashion movement unique in terms of its character, but it differs from other movements in that it does not develop into a society. It does not build up a social organization; it does not develop a division of labor among

Reprinted from *The American Journal of Sociology*, Volume 62, Number 6, "The Uses of Leisure" (May 1957), pp. 594-601, by permission of the publisher. (Copyright 1957 by the University of Chicago.) This is a publication of the University of Chicago Center for the Study of Leisure.

its participants with each being assigned a given status: it does not construct a new set of symbols, myths, values, philosophy, or set of practices, and in this sense does not form a culture; and finally, it does not develop a set of loyalties or form a we-consciousness.[4]

Popular music illustrates this distinction.[5] Every few months a new "content" in the form of new hits flows through the same "network" of distributors (disk jockeys, etc.) and consumers (primarily teen-agers and other radio audiences). While an occasional song may attract some distributors or consumers who are not regularly a part of the system—for example, the recently popular song "Moritāt" from Brecht and Weill's *Threepenny Opera* found high-brow listeners outside the regular music audience—these stray elements usually get out as quickly as they came in. The popular-music world as a whole remains unchanged and goes on as before to produce its continuous cycle of discontinuous hits.

Each new fad is a *functional alternative* for its predecessor: this hit for that hit, this parlor game for that one. On the other hand, the processes involved in broader social changes, such as religious conversions, an increase in the birth rate, or a movement toward suburban living, are too complex to permit simple substitution. Following Merton, who, in arguing against the functional indispensability of a social structure, points out that the range of possible variation is more relevant,[6] one may say that in fashion the range of functional alternatives is far greater than in other domains of social change.

Perhaps this is so because fashions are found in relatively superficial areas of human conduct—in the trivial or ornamental. Many more changes have occurred in the styling of automobiles (e.g., in the length of tail lights) than in their engines.[7] In a brilliant essay on fashion Simmel discusses the selective process whereby some cultural items are subject to fashion and others not, and he points out that the former must be "independent of the vital motives of human action."

> Fashion occasionally will accept objectively determined subjects such as religious faith, scientific interests, even socialism and individualism; but it does not become operative as fashion until these subjects can be considered independent of the deeper human motives from which they have risen. For this reason the rule of fashion becomes in such fields unendurable. We therefore see that there is good reason why externals—clothing, social conduct, amusements—constitute the specific field of fashion, for here no dependence is placed on really vital motives of human action.[8]

Triviality, of course, does not refer to the amount of emotion, affect, and functional significance surrounding an object but rather to its life-expectancy, its susceptibility to being *outmoded*. Every object has a finite and estimable life-span; a pair of nylon stockings may last a few weeks, a dress a few years, an automobile a decade or two, a house much longer. It is one of the characteristics of fashion that replacement is made before the life-span ends. Such objects are acquired without regard for their durability. This is one definition of "conspicuous consumption."

Hence we arrive at one possible indication whether an item is a carrier of fashion. Simmel has illustrated this point very well:

> When we furnish a house these days, intending the articles to last a quarter of a century, we invariably invest in furniture designed according to the very latest patterns and do not even consider articles in vogue two years before. Yet it is obvious that the attraction of fashion will desert the present article just as it left the earlier one, and satisfaction or dissatisfaction with both forms is determined by other material criteria. A peculiar psychological process seems to be at work here in addition to the mere bias of the moment. Some fashion always exists and fashion per se is indeed immortal, which fact seems to affect in some manner or other each of its manifestations, although the very nature of each individual fashion stamps it as being transitory. The fact that change itself does not change, in this instance endows each of the objects which it affects with a psychological appearance of duration.[9]

Since most fads are of a minority or subculture, they may of course exhibit contradictory or countervailing trends all at once. While the fashion system as a whole may rely on an incompleted life-span for a part of its *élan,* certain subsystems of fashions operate in the opposite way. Thus, the trend today may be to trade in perfectly usable automobiles; yet there are those who drive nothing but antique automobiles. Such people attempt to *exceed* the structural limits of this particular item, and their possessions are as much a part of the fashion system as the latest, newest, the "most unique."[10]

Several approaches to the study of fads can be distinguished. One is concerned with the function of fashion generally for society, groups, and individuals. There has been considerable interest in the question why one group rather than another is the carrier of certain fashions; for example, in most societies women are the agents of fashion in clothes, though occasionally, and particularly in deviant societies, it is the men. Simmel relates this to the presence or absence of a class system and/or the need to call attention to one.[11]

Fashions have also been examined in terms of their specific content, and many attempts have been made to relate a particular trend, style, or motif to a *Zeitgeist,* a "climate of opinion," or an ideology. The unit under examination is a particular rather than a general fashion, as, for example, in the area of dress, in which a great many attempts have been made to relate style to *Zeitgeist.* Flügel has recorded a number of such connections, such as the shift after the French Revolution from clothes as display of ornament to clothes as display of body—which he attributed to the naturalism of the period.[12]

A third approach to fashion deals not with the content of fashions but with the network of people involved. A fashion "system" may be seen in the interaction among producers, distributors, and consumers, which works as a spiral-like closed circuit. Studies have been made, on the one hand, of the several "relay stations," the producers of fashions (such as the designers, the "tastemakers"), and the media that serve them. On the other hand, there has been research on the economics of fashion and on the channels of information and advice that impinge on consumer decisions,[13] attention usually focusing on individual choices or "effects" without emphasizing the flow from the mass media to groups and, within groups, from person to person. The latter can be done only by beginning with a specific fashion, A or B, tracing its diffusion, as in a fluoroscopic examination, from one consumer to the next.

A fourth approach to the study of fashions, one which differs from the three cited above, though it operates within their orbits, seeks to determine the origin of a given item, the conditions of acceptance by the first participants (the "innovators"), the characteristics of those whom the innovators influence, the shifts from minority to majority acceptance, its waning, and where it goes to die. This is its natural history. The natural history of any phenomenon which is ephemeral and which comprises a specific content (e.g., popular music) with its particular network (e.g., the flow from song writers, to publishing companies, to record companies, to disk jockeys, to teen-agers, to juke-box listeners, etc.) can obviously be studied. It is based on the premise that different *stages* of a fad can be isolated. In the past this premise has been used in studies of crowds, race riots, lynching mobs, and even political movements, all of which have been described in terms of discrete evolutionary steps, isolated according to their patterns of person-to-person interaction.[14] Each stage, furthermore, has been described as paving the way for the next stage.

Fads and fashions, too, have been subjected to such analysis. Almost every textbook in social psychology points out how aspirants to social mobility continually try to pre-empt the symbols of higher status, thereby forcing their former holders to search ever for replacements. This is how the story of fashions, and sometimes of all consumer purchasing, is usually told.[15] While it is certainly likely that one function of fashion is in the display of social ascent and that one network for its transmission is from the upper classes downward, the extent to which this traditional view of fashion remains valid cannot be told without refined empirical study—without tracing the diffusion of particular fads and fashions in time and through their relevant social structures.

In the continuing absence of such refined empirical data, this paper presents on the basis of crude observations some notes on the stages in the natural history of any fad; beginning at the point where some change has just begun to occur, it traces very roughly the fad's probable course.

Fads are not born but rediscovered.—Where do new fads come from? In many instances they have existed all along but not as fads. For example, in the past several years a large number of songs that went under the collective title of "Rhythm and Blues" rose to the top of the "hit parade." Now these songs and this type of music were not new. The music industry had known about them for many years, largely under the title "race records." They had been produced for consumption by a Negro audience, a number of small record companies and publishers devoting themselves almost exclusively to this market. Trade journals carried separate ratings for such music, ranking each new song according to its popularity within this special category.

Then, all of a sudden, "rhythm and blues" songs invaded the general market, and "feedback points" (including the disk jockeys, fan clubs, listings of sheet-music sales, record sales, juke-box sales, etc.) all began to indicate a new trend.[16] This particular new trend had existed for a good long time but in a different audience. It had been a little pocket in the music world as a whole which sustained it not as a fashion but as a "custom." What happened was that minority music was becoming majority music.

These minority social systems seem to feed many kinds of fashions to the majority. This is true not only of racial groups: the word "minority" is here used in the sense of engaging only a small segment of the population. Some "minorities" are more likely to be fashion-feeders, of course; the classic view of fashion assumes that a minority either in the upper classes or tangential to them engages in certain choices, and these are then "discovered" and made fashionable by lower strata.

This process exists in a variety of fields. The hog-breeding industry, for example, has cyclical trends, and in time a number of "dimensions" of hogs are altered in the prize-winning or champion hogs. Hogs may be well larded or have relatively long legs—results produced by variations in breeding. Some hog-breeders seem to ignore the going fashion, but most of them breed "what the public wants," making appropriate annual changes in breeding. But every once in a while the mantle of fashion descends on one of the ignorers of fashion; he becomes the fashion leader, and his hogs set the style.[17]

In areas of life where "new" products are in demand or vital to the continuation of the industry, such "discoveries" are clearly more frequent. Since fashions serve a symbolic function and must be recognized in order to be transmitted, their greatest motility is likely to be found in those areas which are most visible. Thus, changes in dress are likely to be more frequent than in underclothes. Furthermore, the search for something new—what Simmel has called "exceptional, bizarre, or conspicuous"[18]—will be greater there.

In the popular-music industry, where such a search is conducted on a monthly basis, the life-span of a "hit" being approximately that long, new discoveries are essential. Hence, every pocket of the musical world is sooner or later "discovered." "Rhythm and blues" is one of many such pockets, if more successful than some of the others; for a time African songs were hits; South American music has followed this pattern; hillbilly music shows the same trend; even classical music was "discovered" when suddenly the first movement of a Tchaikovsky piano concerto exploded all over America.

Minorities not only provide material to majorities but are also an integral part of the total system. Not only do they offer a pretest—"If it goes well in Tangiers, maybe it has a chance here!"—but they are also a shelf and shelter for dangerous or threatening ideas. Mark Benney suggests that bohemias serve this function. For urban societies their bohemias are a kind of social laboratory. Here something new can be tried out—because it is expected—

without threatening either the bohemian minority or the urban population as a whole. The city watches, Benney suggests, and confers respectability on what it likes. Wrought-iron furniture, Japanese scrolls, charcoal-gray flannel suits, not to mention new literary forms and ideological movements, have indeed been bred in these quarters.

The tastemakers.—While the community, the music industry, or the clothing world as a whole may watch and wait for new ideas in many places, the task of scouting seems to fall to one particular set of people. By the nature of their tasks, they must be intimately acquainted with two worlds, the majority and the minority. Fashions, for instance, are often transmitted by the homosexual element in the population or by others who have entree into different realms, Proustian characters who share the values of several groups.

A good example in the popular-music industry is the success of the current artist and repertoire director (the "A&R Man") at Columbia Records, Mitch Miller. A concert oboist himself, he was thoroughly trained as a serious musician. With an established reputation and a semibohemian personality which manifests itself in harmless ways, such as the wearing of a beard and keeping odd hours, he has been able to utilize good judgment in the popular-music world not only by being better educated but by having a far broader range of minorities to draw on for inspiration. Thus he is familiar with the attributes of French horns and harpsichords, with echo chambers and goat bells, and has been able to use all to full advantage. One reason for his using esoteric "effects" is that in the music industry any popular hit is immediately copied, but his arrangements have been made so complex by the use of such "gimmicks"—as the music industry calls them—that imitation is very difficult. In addition of course, the gimmicks have given Columbia Records a unique reputation.[19]

In any case, certain individuals in society are equipped to scout for new ideas and products to feed the various fashion systems. What is perhaps more important is to examine the fate of the original producer of the particular minority "custom" once it has been "exported" and translated into a fashion.

The exporter becomes self-conscious.—At some time in the past Parisian clothes were "discovered" and made fashionable throughout "society" in other countries. Before that, undoubtedly, a stable relationship existed between the Paris *couturières* and their customers, and designs were made with a very particular "audience" in mind. In the course of "discovering" these designs, one element which probably attracted the early innovators was precisely the product which emerged from this relationship. But, once discovered, what happened? As Simmel said, "Paris modes are frequently created with the sole intention of setting a fashion elsewhere."[20] The exporter becomes self-conscious, tries to appeal to his wider circle of customers, and *changes* the product. Another well-known example is found in oriental porcelain. In the nineteenth century, European art collectors "discovered" Chinese and Japanese pottery, and in a very short time the potters began manufacturing "export ware," creating an industry quite separate from the production of domestic "china." Another example is the shift from the 1954 to the 1955 MG car; the most popular British car in this country, the MG had been designed in a somewhat old-fashioned way, with a square hood; but recently the British Motor Company decided to build it more along the lines of the latest American styles.

There are, of course, some occasions when the exporter does not become self-conscious. This would be most true where there is no return for more: composers who work folk songs into concert music, like Mozart, Beethoven, and Béla Bartók, do not affect the folk "producers."

What happens to the original consumers is not clear. Those who find their own customs—pizza or Yiddish melodies or canasta—becoming widely popular undoubtedly enjoy some sense of pride as well as mixed feelings about the inevitable distortions and perhaps yield to the temptation to make some accommodation from then on in the hope of being "picked up" once again.

Statistical versus real fashions: a case of pluralistic ignorance.—Who can say that something is a fashion? Who knows about it? It may happen that a number of people in various parts of this country, for a variety of reasons, will all buy a certain item. They may all "go in" for "rhythm and blues" music or good musical sound reproduction or raccoon-skin caps, all unaware that others are doing the same thing.

Such situations, in which no one realizes that others are doing the same thing, probably occur all the time. They are similar to what social psychologists have called "pluralistic ignorance," a state in which nobody knows that others maintain an attitude or belief identical with their own.[21] If this coincidence persists long enough, however, the point will be reached at which one cannot help noticing the unself-conscious, "inner-directed" activity of large numbers of people in making identical choices.[22] At this point the phenomenon which had been statistical becomes a real fad; here another important stage is reached—the labeling of a fad.

The label and the coattail.—The birth of a fad is really accompanied by two labels; the phenomenon is given a name, and it is named as a fad. The fad is defined as real and in consequence becomes so.

Such a definition, however, must be made not only real but public. It must be translated from the specialized professional, business, or trade vocabulary into more popular terms—in short, into a label or a slogan.

While there are certainly plenty of labels which do not represent fads, there are no unlabeled fads or fashions. It is usually through the label that the fashion acquires fame—even beyond its consumer audience. Thus the "New Look," "hi-fi," "motivation research," "automation," and "charcoal gray."

The ground swell immediately after the labeling is caused partly by the activities of indirectly related enterprises. Machines that yesterday were ordinary phonographs and radios are suddenly called "hi-fi"; coonskin headgear becomes Davy Crockett caps; a lever makes of an industrial machine "automation"; an ordinary open-ended question converts a public opinion survey into "motivation research."

Thus the coattails which dress the fashion. Although the original minorities—whether devotees of recordings of high quality and accurate sound reproduction or Negroes who have been hearing certain kinds of "pop" music for years—may not recognize the $29.95 portable radio as "hi-fi" or the ordinary hit of the week as "rhythm and blues," the respective producers have found something that "works," and every commodity within labeling distance has a chance to be included.

The flow.—Where the various fashions find their victims depends on their specific nature. Beginning in the minority, the fad is "discovered," then is labeled, and ultimately reaches the mass audiences. In the case of clothing, there is sometimes a stage, mentioned by Simmel and later by contemporary social psychologists and sociologists, which precedes or accompanies the labeling process, when the fashion is adopted by a group of acknowledged respectability. The fashion is perhaps borrowed from a fringe group within the society, or even outside it, and touted as an "esoteric" discovery. But in a society such as ours very little can be kept private, and providing clues to "better living," tips on the stock market, and advice on clothing, furniture, and virtually every other artifact is the professional job of all the media of communication. Thus, a product associated with a respected group or class is likely to spread, through being publicized, to other groups as well. From here it moves to groups which aspire to be like the advocates. These are not necessarily lower in status, although often so described. It may be that the lower group innovates—as in the "do-it-yourself" fad, a phenomenon which all farmers and lower-income groups have been aware of all their lives—but it is more likely to be a somewhat esoteric group, as the bohemians who flocked to New York's Greenwich Village after World War I, followed by the middle-class New Yorkers after World War II.

Regardless of the direction of the flow, for a time the original possessors of a fashion-to-be will maintain the fashion for themselves and their kind. But after a time the innovation will cross the boundary line of the groups who adopted it and pass into other groups, in the process losing some of its distinguishing characteristics.

The old drives in the new.—The story of fads is, then, one of constant change. The process of change occurs necessarily at every point, leaving, as it were, a vacuum when the fashion departs for its next point. Eventually, the vacuum is filled, even to overflowing, by its successor. When a fad has reached full bloom, its distinguishing features become so blurred that some are totally lost. If everything is called "hi-fi," nothing is high-fidelity. Furthermore, if more than just certain classes are *aficionados,* the self-conscious among the class-conscious will want something new for themselves.

Thus, at some point before a dress design hits the Sears-Roebuck catalogue, a sports car the secondhand automobile dealer, and a modern chair the suburban rummage sale, once again it is time for a change.

The feedback.[23]—Producers notoriously see an undifferentiated audience before their eyes. They tend so often just to count that they miscalculate demand. William McPhee and James Coleman have suggested that, while one group may be oversaturated with a fad, another may be very receptive—and only accurate reporting (feedback) about each group can tell the whole story.[24] For example, since teen-agers are the major purchasers of records and sheet music and the major investors in juke boxes, and since these three commodities are the major tests of demand consulted by the producers, teen-agers can make or break a song. Disk jockeys also play a role in feedback, but it is primarily the "top" jockeys with the large teen-age followings who are the key informants. Yet there is another audience for popular music to whom the producers have almost no access—the daytime radio listeners: the housewives, traveling salesmen, commuters. Their tastes are thus inferred —of all places—from teen-agers!

In other words, the skewed feedback of the music industry is responsible in part for the volatility of its fads; exaggerating as it does the tastes of an already erratic group considered as its primary audience, its fads fluctuate beyond all expectation. With perfect information, a normal distribution of tastes can be expected at most times and for most things. In certain industries, and among certain subgroups, the distribution is less likely to be normal, in part due to the pressures for new commodities, to the superficiality of the appeals themselves, to the publicity accompanying every product, and, in the case of teen-agers, to their unstable moods. When information comes only or largely from teen-agers, who are at the fringes of the distribution curve, so to speak, then the music industry is rendered excessively phrenetic. Kurt and Gladys Lang, in studying the Chicago MacArthur Day parade of 1951, found that the television reporting of this rather slow-moving and dull event was systematically distorted to give the impression of a vast crowd, a glorious spectacle, and an unremitting enthusiasm.[25] Here, as in the case of the popular-music industry, the requirements to hold an audience from switching to another station or channel or losing interest in popular music or a given song force such emphasis on the manic.

Hence, while the feedback from consumer to producer makes, at first, for a frenzied increase in a fashionable product, it may also make for a more rapid saturation than is warranted or, if the gauge is placed somewhere else in society, for an oversupply.

Notes

1. Some of the ideas presented in this paper were formulated several years ago in discussions with colleagues then at the Bureau of Applied Social Research, Columbia University, notably James Coleman, Philip Ennis, William McPhee, Herbert Menzel, and David Sills. We are also grateful to David Riesman and Mark Benney, both at the University of Chicago, for critical comments.

2. We choose to ignore the distinction between the two concepts made by previous writers and perhaps most clearly stated by Sapir, who regarded fads as involving fewer people and as more personal and of shorter duration than fashions. He described a fad, furthermore, as "something unexpected, irresponsible of bizarre" and socially disapproved (cf. Edward Sapir, "Fash-

ion," *Encyclopaedia of the Social Sciences* [New York: Macmillan Co., 1937], III, 139-44). We apply both terms to transitory phenomena that involve a large number of people or a large proportion of members of a subculture.

3. The long-standing interest among social thinkers in fads and fashions is seen, for example, in Tarde, who contrasted fashion with custom and showed that the transformation of tradition and custom is made possible by the form of imitation known as fashion (see Gabriel Tarde, *The Laws of Imitation* [New York: Henry Holt & Co., 1903], chap. vii). Sumner regarded a large array of human activities, beliefs, and artifacts as fashions and considered them essential determinants of the *Zeitgeist* (see William Graham Sumner, *Folkways* [Boston: Ginn & Co., 1907], esp. pp. 194-220). Park and Burgess treated fashion as a form of social contagion and as one of the fundamental ways in which permanent social change is brought about (see Robert E. Park and Ernest W. Burgess, *Introduction to the Science of Sociology* [Chicago: University of Chicago Press, 1924] chap. xiii).

4. Herbert Blumer, "Social Movements," in *New Outline of the Principles of Sociology*, ed. A. M. Lee (New York: Barnes & Noble, 1946), pp. 217-18. While fashions do not create social organizations, there is some evidence that a new set of symbols, myths, etc., is apparently often built up in the course of a fashion movement. "Bop talk," for example, could be considered a language built up by the participants of the "bop" fad, and, although extrinsic to the music itself, it nevertheless contributed to "we-consciousness."

5. Examples in this paper which deal with popular music are based in part on the general conclusions of an unpublished study of disk jockeys carried out at the Bureau of Applied Social Research by William McPhee, Philip Ennis, and Rolf Meyersohn.

6. Robert K. Merton, *Social Theory and Social Structure* (Glencoe, Ill.: Free Press, 1949), p. 52.

7. Eric Larrabee and David Riesman, "Autos in America: Manifest and Latent Destiny," in *Consumer Behavior*, Vol. III, ed. Lincoln H. Clark (New York: Harper & Bros., 1958).

8. Georg Simmel, "Fashion," *International Quarterly*, X (October, 1904), 135, reprinted in the *American Journal of Sociology*, 62, 6 (May, 1957), p. 544. All subsequent references refer to this edition.

9. *Op. cit.*, p. 556.

10. It is to such countervailing minority movements that Sapir applies the word "fad." "A taste which asserts itself in spite of fashion and which may therefore be suspected of having something obsessive about it may be referred to as an individual fad" (*op. cit.*, p. 139).

11. *Op. cit.*, pp. 130-55. Cf. pp. 541-58 in this issue. See also Talcott Parsons, "An Analytical Approach to the Theory of Social Stratification," reprinted in *Essays in Sociological Theory Pure and Applied* (Glencoe, Ill.: Free Press, 1949), pp. 166-84; cf. Bernard Barber and Lyle S. Lobel, " 'Fashion' in Women's Clothes and the American Social System," in *Class, Status and Power*, ed. Reinhard Bendix and Seymour M. Lipset (Glencoe, Ill.: Free Press, 1953), pp. 323-32. For an interesting historical discussion relating manners to milieu see Harold Nicolson, *Good Behaviour* (London: Constable & Co., Ltd., 1955).

12. J. C. Flügel, *The Psychology of Clothes* (London: Hogarth Press, 1930), chap. vii.

13. See, e.g., Elihu Katz and Paul F. Lazarsfeld, *Personal Influence* (Glencoe, Ill.: Free Press, 1956).

14. E.g., Blumer enumerated the stages of crowd behavior as follows: from "milling" to "collective excitement" to "social contagion" (*op. cit.*, p. 202).

15. The following may be a typical account: "In recent years status objects of a technical kind have appeared in the home, such as washing, cleaning and polishing machines, and elaborate heating and cooking apparatus. In the United States appliances to provide an artificial climate in the home are the latest in a series of status-conferring devices" (Dennis Chapman, *The Home and Social Status* [London: Routledge & Kegan Paul, 1955], p. 23). A discussion of the importance of fads in television sets may be found in Rolf Meyersohn, "Social Research in Television," in *Mass Culture*, ed. Bernard Rosenberg and David Manning White (Glencoe, Ill.: Free Press, 1957).

16. New trends are reported at least once a week. The uncertainty of prediction in combination with the fact that financial investments are made on the basis of such prediction bring it about that any and all shifts and flutters are exaggerated, and large-scale predictions are made for each and every one of them. This is of course true of all businesses, but many of them (e.g., the stock market) are kept from excesses by various control agencies (e.g., the Securities and Exchange Commission).

17. This example draws on material presented in a term paper dealing with fashions in hog-raising, by Samuel R. Guard, formerly a graduate student, Committee on Communications, the University of Chicago.

18. *Op. cit.*, p. 545.

19. In a recent essay on jazz and popular music, Adorno argued that its various forms, whether they be called "swing" or "bebop," are identical in all essential respects and distinguishable by only a few trivial variations, formulas, and clichés. He considers jazz a timeless and

changeless fashion (Theodor Adorno, "Zeitlose Mode: Zum Jazz," *Prismen: Kulturkritik und Gesellschaft* [Frankfurt: Suhrkamp Verlag, 1955], pp. 144-61).

20. *Op. cit.*, p. 545.

21. Cf. Floyd H. Allport, *Social Psychology* (Boston: Houghton Mifflin Co., 1924).

22. An amusing portrayal of the consequences of large masses of people doing the same thing at the same time, such as crossing the George Washington Bridge on a Thursday afternoon, may be found in Robert Coates's short story, "The Law," a description of the law of averages and what might happen to it some day.

23. This world itself has become something of a fad!

24. "Mass Dynamics," *PROD*, I,4 (March, 1958).

25. "The Unique Perspective of Television," *American Sociological Review*, XVIII (February, 1953), 3-12.

Voluntary Association Memberships of American Adults

By CHARLES R. WRIGHT and HERBERT H. HYMAN

Introduction. Several recent studies have demonstrated the need for a thorough reappraisal of the commonly held belief that Americans are a nation of joiners. For example, Komarovsky[1] and Axelrod[2] have provided evidence for urban dwellers, to whom such behavior has been especially attributed, that membership in a large number of associations is not characteristic of many Americans and is far from universally distributed throughout the various segments of the population.

Unfortunately, most investigators of the problem have had to work within serious limitations imposed by the nature of their data. In some instances, the sampling procedures available to the investigator could not provide adequate data.[3] In other instances, while the researcher was fortunate enough to have access to representative samples, the findings relate to such circumscribed and limited universes as small local communities, a single metropolis, or one social class within a particular city.[4] What has been missing in the literature is evidence of the voluntary association memberships of Americans in general and of important sub-groups within the nation, derived from adequate sampling of the general population. The present paper provides data that partially meet this need.

More specifically, the paper presents evidence bearing on the following problems: (1) the pattern of membership in voluntary associations of adult Americans in general, and of specific sub-groups, such as racial and religious minorities; (2) some correlates of membership which might be considered determinants, for example, socio-economic status, urban or rural residence;

Reprinted from the *American Sociological Review*, Volume 23, Number 3 (June 1958), pp. 284-294, by permission of the authors and the publisher.

and (3) some of the correlates of membership which might be considered consequences of significance to theories about such functions of voluntary association membership for society as interest in politics, voting, and charitable activity.

Method and Data. Solutions of these problems are provided by secondary analysis of recent survey data, where the universes studied often approximate the national adult population and where the samples have been drawn through probability designs. Through good fortune, a number of nationwide and local surveys conducted by the National Opinion Research Center[5] have contained one or more questions on voluntary association memberships. These items provide substantial information on the actual magnitude and pattern of voluntary association membership of the American people and of sub-groups within the general population. Secondary analysis of these surveys can also provide evidence about numerous sociological determinants of membership, which have figured in past speculative discussions but have seldom been supported by much empirical data, for example, the effect of urbanization upon membership. In addition, the surveys often contain data on possible determinants of membership which have rarely been treated, either speculatively or empirically, in past writings. Thus data are available on various situational factors which might facilitate or impede membership and participation, such as parenthood, residential mobility, travel time to work, and the like. For many of these latter analyses, it is necessary to consult sample surveys which were conducted on local rather than national populations, but here too all the inquiries have the merit of being based on large samples drawn by a probability design. Therefore, though limited to the cities or counties involved, they still constitute reliable evidence concerning hypotheses based on representative sampling. Finally, by secondary analysis tabulation of voluntary association membership is possible, not only by hypothesized determinants, but also by the customary questions asked in such surveys about attitudes, opinions, interests, conduct, and so on. In this manner, some empirical perspective can be obtained on the fundamental question of the functions of organizational membership for citizens in a democratic society.

Admittedly there are serious limitations to such secondary analysis. Foremost among these is the reliance put upon questions not primarily designed for the study of voluntary association memberships. Since data on such memberships were only incidental to the primary purposes of the surveys, the questioning in this area is not as thorough as would be desired. Furthermore, the wording of questions about membership varies from study to study, hence complicating the analysis. Nevertheless, we believe that these inherent limitations of secondary analysis are more than offset by the gains which have been outlined above.

The bulk of the analysis to be presented is based on two national probability samples of the adult, non-institutionalized population of the United States, over 21 years of age. The first sample contains 2,809 men and women, and the second 2,379. The studies were conducted in the years 1953 and 1955. In addition to the national data, findings on voluntary association membership were available for representative samples from NORC studies of the following localities: a large metropolitan area (New York metropolitan area represented by a probability sample of 1,053 cases drawn in 1951); a medium sized Western metropolis (Denver represented by a probability sample of 920 cases obtained in the spring of 1949); a small city and surrounding county (Findley and Hancock County, Ohio, represented by 535 cases drawn in May, 1952). The local findings on magnitude of membership and its social distribution are not presented in detail, although, where confirmation or contradiction occurs, some brief reference will be made. They will be used to examine hypotheses about particular variables, however, which are not demonstrable on a national scale.

FINDINGS

Memberships of Americans. Data from the national surveys confirm the conclusions drawn by previous researchers based on local studies, which showed that a sizeable group of Americans are not members of any voluntary associations and that only a minority belong to more than one such organization. Table 1 presents data from two surveys, one of which inquired about the voluntary association membership of *any* member of the family, the other survey pertained to activities of the respondent himself. Calculated

Table I—Membership in Voluntary Associations for Two National Cross-Sections of American Adults, 1953 and 1955

Number of Voluntary Associations	Percentage of Families Whose Members Belong to Organizations as Indicated (1953)*	Percentage of Adults Who Were Themselves Members of the Organizations, as Indicated (1955)†
None	47	64
One	31	20
Two	12	9
Three	5	4
Four or more	4	3
Unknown	1	0
Total	100% (2,809)	100% (2,379)

*"Does anyone in the family belong to any sort of club, lodge, fraternal order, or union with ten or more members in it?" If *yes,* "What organization? Any other?" (Source: NORC Survey 335.)

†Union membership is *not* included in these data because the interviewing on organizational membership during this part of the survey concerned associations other than union. The question was, "Do you happen to belong to any groups or organizations in the community here? If *yes,* "Which ones? Any other?" (Source: NORC Survey 367.)

either way, voluntary association membership is not a major characateristic of Americans. Nearly half of the families (47 per cent) and almost two-thirds of the respondents (64 per cent) belong to no voluntary associations. About a third of the families (31 per cent) and a fifth of the respondents belong to only one such organization. Only about a fifth of the families (21 per cent) and a sixth of the respondents (16 per cent) belong to two or more organizations. These findings hardly warrant the impression that Americans are a nation of joiners.[6]

Data on the types of organizations to which Americans belong are also revealing. In the 1953 survey, which contained an account of organizations to which any family member belonged, only two (unions and fraternal or secret societies) have relatively large memberships, 23 per cent and 19 per cent respectively. Next in order are neighborhood-ethnic-special interest groups (8 per cent), veterans' organizations (7 per cent), civic organizations (5 per cent), church sponsored organizations (3 per cent), youth organizations (2 per cent), and professional and learned societies (2 per cent). These findings provide national perspective on the data recorded by former studies of local populations, such as the Detroit Area Study, in which unions and fraternal organizations also accounted for more of the citizens' voluntary memberships than any other type of association.[7]

Table II—Voluntary Association Memberships of Racial and Religious Subgroups Based on National Samples

(A) FAMILY DATA (1953)	*PER CENT OF FAMILIES WHOSE MEMBERS BELONG TO:*			
	No Organization	*One*	*Two or More*	*N (100%)*
Race*				
Negro	60	29	11	279
White	46	31	23	2,472
Religion†				
Jewish	31	37	32	99
Catholic	44	34	22	579
Protestant	49	30	21	1,992

(Source: NORC Survey 335.)

(B) RESPONDENT DATA (1955)	*PER CENT OF RESPONDENTS WHO BELONG TO:*			
	No Organization	*One*	*Two or More*	*N (100%)*
Race‡				
Negro	73	18	9	229
White	63	20	17	2,139
Religion§				
Jewish	45	25	30	71
Protestant	63	20	17	1,701
Catholic	69	17	14	519

*Figures exclude 58 cases of other races or of unknown race.
†Figures exclude 139 cases who report some other religion or none at all.
‡Figures exclude 11 cases of other races.
§Figures exclude 88 cases who report some other religion or none at all.
(Source: NORC Survey 367.)

Racial and Religious Subgroups. Table 2 presents figures on the membership patterns for two types of subgroups within American society: racial and religious. Comparison of Negro and white respondents shows that voluntary association membership is somewhat more characteristic of whites than Negroes. Less than half (46 per cent) of the white families and 63 per cent of the white respondents belong to no associations in contrast to 60 per cent of the Negro families and 73 per cent of the Negro adults. And nearly a quarter (23 per cent) of the white families belong to two or more organizations in contrast to only 11 per cent of the Negro families.

Differences in rates of membership also distinguish the major religious subgroups of the population. Whether measured on a family or individual basis, the highest rate of membership is found among the Jews. On a family basis, the next highest participants in voluntary associations are the Catholics (56 per cent), and the least active are the Protestants (51 per cent). Data on individual memberships, however, are different, with a higher percentage of Protestants than Catholics belonging to any organizations.

Interesting comparisons with national data on memberships of religious subgroups are available from the local studies of New York City and Denver. In both cities the ordering of memberships agrees with the national sample on individual memberships: the rate of membership is highest for Jews, next for Protestants and lowest for Catholics. In New York, 64 per cent of the Jewish respondents reported membership in at least one voluntary association, 54 per cent of the Protestants and 37 per cent of the Catholics. In Denver, the membership rates were 77 per cent for Jews, 65 per cent for Protestants and 55 per cent for Catholics. Thus the Catholic membership rates in these urban settings appear lower than those of the Jews and Protestants, as in the 1955 national survey.[8]

Social Stratification and Membership. On the local level, several studies have demonstrated a relationship between the social status of the respondent, as measured by a variety of indices, and membership in voluntary associations.[9] These studies generally agree that there is an increase in the percentage of memberships in formal associations the higher the status of the respondents. The magnitude of the difference in membership between classes varies considerably, however, from study to study. For example, Komarovsky found that 60 per cent of working class men in her sample of New Yorkers belonged to no voluntary association in contrast to only 53 per cent of white collar workers. Similarly Dotson's study of families in New Haven reported that 70 per cent of the working class adults in his sample belonged to no organizations. On the other hand, Bell and Force in a recent study of San Francisco report that even in low status neighborhoods about three-quarters of the men belong to at least one formal group.

Data from the national samples support the correlation between social status and membership. Table 3 presents data on the membership of the 1955 sample classified by five indices of social status: family income, education of respondent, interviewer's rating of family's level of living, occupation of head of household, and home ownership. Whichever index of status is used, an appreciably higher percentage of persons in higher status positions belong to voluntary associations than do persons of lower status. For example, fully 76 per cent of the respondents whose family income falls below 2,000 dollars do not belong to any organizations in contrast to only

48 per cent of those whose income is 7,500 dollars or more. Furthermore, there is an increase in the percentage of persons who belong to *several* organizations as social status increases. For example, only 7 per cent of the lowest income group belong to two or more associations in contrast to 30 per cent of the highest income group. Similar findings are obtained from inspection of the data on education, level of living, occupation, and home ownership, as examination of Table 3 reveals.[10]

Table III—Indices of Stratification and Voluntary Association Membership, 1955*

	PER CENT WHO BELONG TO:			
	No Organization	One Organization	Two or More	No. of Cases (100%)
A. Income level				
Under $2,000	76	17	7	385
2,000-2,999	71	17	12	304
3,000-3,999	71	18	11	379
4,000-4,999	65	21	14	450
5,000-7,499	57	22	21	524
7,500 and over	48	22	30	328
B. Education				
0-6 years	83	12	5	348
7-8 years	73	17	10	522
9-11 years	67	20	13	495
12 years	57	23	20	610
1-3 yrs. of college	46	24	30	232
4 yrs. college or more	39	25	36	170
C. Level of living (Interviewer's rating)				
Very low	92	7	1	125
Below average	81	14	5	580
Average	61	22	17	1,318
Above average	43	25	32	288
Very high	18	18	64	44
D. Occupation				
Professional	47	24	29	259
Prop., mgrs., officials	47	24	29	294
Farm owners	58	28	14	265
Clerical and sales	59	21	20	240
Skilled labor	68	19	13	447
Semi-skilled labor	77	14	9	492
Service	73	18	9	142
Non-farm labor	79	16	5	155
Farm labor	87	13	0	54
Retired, unemployed	77	11	12	35
E. Home ownership				
Owns home	57	22	21	1,407
Rents	75	16	9	968

*Data exclude union membership. (Source: NORC Survey 367.)

One set of findings warrant special mention. The pattern of voluntary association membership among different occupational levels indicates even less participation among blue collar workers than had been noted in previous local studies. For example, from 68 to 87 per cent of the blue collar workers belong to no organizations (not counting union membership), in contrast to 59 per cent of the white collar workers and 47 per cent of the businessmen and professionals. The higher rate of voluntary association membership among businessmen and professionals is clearly documented by the national data, which show that 29 per cent of the members of these two occupational categories belong to two or more organizations, in contrast with only 5 to 13 per cent of the blue collar workers. These data extend to the national level a relationship noted by Komarovsky in her New York study, namely that it is only in the business and professional classes that the majority is formally organized.

Urbanization and Voluntary Association Membership. Voluntary associations customarily have been identified as characteristic of the urban way of life, and membership in such associations has been assumed to be more common for city residents than rural people. Recent observers, however, have noted that the spread of urbanization in America is reducing such differences between city and country. Williams,[11] for example, has noted that "Formally organized special-interest associations are most highly developed in urban areas, but have increasingly pervaded the open country as well." Nevertheless, we have lacked specific information on the differential rates of voluntary association membership of residents of various sized communities. A breakdown of national survey data provides considerable information on this question.

From the 1953 national survey it is possible to determine the number of association affiliations of family members living in counties of varying degrees of urbanization, taking the size of the largest city in the county as a crude index of its degree of urbanism. Three types of counties can be examined: (1) highly urbanized counties, those with at least one city of 50,000 population or more; (2) moderately urbanized, with at least one city of 10,000 to 50,000 population; and (3) least urbanized, having no city of 10,000 or more. Examination of the memberships of residents of these three types of counties reveals that only 57 per cent of the families who live in highly urbanized counties have members in at least one voluntary association, 53 per cent of those in moderately urbanized counties, and 41 per cent of those living in the least urbanized or predominantly rural counties. Thus some correlation appears between the degree of urbanization and voluntary association membership, although the difference between the most urban and least urban counties is not great.

But the type of county is only a crude index of the social atmosphere within which the citizen lives. Within each county, for example, there are areas of more *and* less urban nature. Therefore a finer breakdown is desirable in order to determine more precisely the relationship between urbanism and membership in voluntary associations. Table 4 presents data on membership according to urban, rural non-farm, and rural farm residences within each type of county.

Table IV—Urbanism and Voluntary Association Membership, 1953

Per Cent of Families Whose Members Belong to:	PLACE OF RESIDENCE								
	Metropolitan Counties (with City of 50,000 or more)			Other Urbanized Counties (with City of 10-50,000)			Primary Rural Counties (Have No Town of 10,000)		
	Urban Residence	Rural Non-Farm	Rural Farm	Urban	RNF	RF	Urban	RNF	RF
No organization	42	40	67	46	46	53	54	52	70
One organization	33	37	21	36	34	28	27	24	21
Two or more organizations	25	23	12	18	20	19	19	24	9
Total	100%	100%	100%	100%	100%	100%	100%	100%	100%
Cases	1,394	193	48	294	115	134	110	264	252

(Source: NORC Survey 335.)

Several interesting findings emerge. First, it appears that, with one exception (rural farm residents in moderately urbanized counties) the relationship between urbanization of county and membership in voluntary associations persists. That is, more of the residents of highly urbanized counties belong to organizations than do persons living in similar types of neighborhoods but in less urbanized counties. For example, only 42 per cent of the urbanites in highly urbanized counties belong to no organization, in contrast with 46 per cent of the urbanites in moderately urbanized counties, and 54 per cent in the least urbanized.

Secondly, within each type of county, rural farm residence is more closely associated with non-membership than is either rural non-farm or urban residence. For example, within highly urbanized counties 67 per cent of the rural farm residents belong to no voluntary association, in contrast to only 40 per cent of the rural non-farm residents and 42 per cent of the urbanites.[12]

Third, there is *no* appreciable difference between the membership rates of urbanites and rural non-farm residents within any type of country. This finding, in connection with the second, suggests an interesting hypothesis about the spread of urbanism into American suburan and rural areas. If the countryside were becoming urbanized then one might expect that rural-urban differences would be minimal in counties which contained large cities and maximal in counties still rural. Such is not the case, at least with respect to voluntary association membership. True, the urban pattern of membership prevails in rural non-farm areas but it does not extend to rural farms. Furthermore, an anomaly (requiring further substantiation) appears in that rural farm persons living in *moderately* urbanized counties resemble their urban and rural non-farm neighbors more than do ruralites in either highly urbanized or heavily rural counties. Perhaps this finding means that rural-urban differences in general are polarized—being greatest in both highly urban and highly rural counties and least in partially urbanized areas.

Some Situational Determinants of Membership. In this section some data from the Denver survey are examined to clarify certain situational factors which might be presumed to affect urban participation in voluntary associations. Specifically, data are presented on the effect of length of residence in the community, length of residence at the same address, type of residence (for example, single family dwelling versus apartment), travel time to work, and family status (for example, single, married with children or without children). The presumed influence of such factors is illustrated by the hypothesis that long-time residents in the community or in the neighborhood are more likely to be involved in formal organizations. Or, persons living in apartments might be expected to participate less in voluntary associations than those living in single family dwellings. Persons who spend less time commuting to work, it may be argued, should have more time to devote to organizations and therefore should show a higher incidence of membership. Similarly, single men and women, who are unencumbered by children, might have more spare time and hence be more apt to belong to voluntary groups. Table 5 presents data which fail to support several of these arguments.

Table V—Some Situational Determinants of Voluntary Association Membership: Evidence From Denver Survey

	Percentage of Each Type Who Belong to Voluntary Associations	No. of Cases in Base
A. Residential history		
Born in Denver or lived there at least 20 yrs.	65	504
Lived in Denver less than 20 years.	62	404
Lived in Denver at present address over 20 years	63	200
Lived at present address for 5 to 20 years	67	346
Lived at present address less than 5 years	60	358
B. Residential mobility		
Moved to Denver from place of under 2,500 population	61	272
Moved from place of 2,500 to 25,000 population	60	205
Moved from place larger than 25,000	64	281
C. Type of residence		
Single family house, rented	57	81
Multiple family dwelling, rented	59	165
Apartment building, rented	60	117
Owned, all types of dwelling	67	512
D. Travel time to work		
45 minutes or more daily	60	81
35-44 minutes	70	185
30-34 minutes	64	256
25-29 minutes	66	192
Less than 25 minutes	57	205
E. Family status		
Men: Not married	66	79
Married, no children under 18 yrs. old	74	182
Married, with children under 18 yrs. old	82	162
Women: Not married	51	149
Married, no children under 18 yrs. old	53	174
Married, with children under 18 yrs. old	56	174

(Source: Denver Community Survey, NORC-12B.)

None of the residential factors shows a systematic relationship with the incidence of affiliation with voluntary associations. For example, persons born in Denver are hardly more likely to belong to voluntary associations than those who have arrived recently.[13] Apartment dwellers are slightly more likely to be voluntary association members than persons renting houses. Commuters who spend more than 45 minutes getting to work are about as likely to belong to organizations as are those people who have to travel only 25 minutes or less.

Only two of these situational factors—home ownership and family status —seem related to voluntary association membership. Home ownership as a determinant of membership, as brought out above, is related to social stratification. The data on family status show that married persons are more likely to be members of organizations than single persons; and that men and women with children are more likely to be members than childless couples. One might hypothesize that children—and perhaps the expectation of children —draw adults into participation in the voluntary associations in the urban community. This finding corroborates that of Janowitz in his study of Chicago residents in which he notes that neighborhood involvement often centers around activities connected with the rearing of children in a metropolis. As Janowitz remarks, on the neighborhood level, "children are not only the best neighbors in the community but they lead their parents to neighborhood community participation and orientation."[14]

Civic Involvement of Voluntary Association Membership. In this final section, data from the Denver Survey are presented which demonstrate psychological and behavioral differences between citizens who are members and those who are not members of formal organizations. Admittedly the data do not indicate that such differences can be attributed solely to the respondents' patterns of associational membership. Clearly several factors already established as correlates of membership (for example, high socio-economic status, occupation, place of residence) may also account for differences in political interest, voting and charitable acts of members and non-members. The authors feel, however, that comparison of members and non-members without controlling these associated factors is proper insofar as the purpose is solely to *describe* the differences between persons who are or are not members of voluntary associations, regardless of the ultimate causes of such differences.[15] Hence Table 6 presents simple comparisons between the formally organized and unorganized, concerning their interest in political topics, voting records, and contributions to charity.

Several measures of interest in public affairs (including presidential elections, unemployment, labor relations, minority problems, public schools, and city planning) indicate that persons belonging to voluntary associations are more concerned with such topics than are non-members. For example, fully 84 per cent of the Denverites who belonged to any voluntary association said they took a great deal of interest in presidential elections, in contrast with only 73 per cent of the non-members. And members were more likely than non-members to be interested in city planning, 50 per cent to 31 per cent respectively.

Table VI—Political Interests and Behavior Associated with Voluntary Association Membership: Evidence From Denver Survey, 1949

	PERSONS WHO WERE MEMBERS OF:	
	No Organizations	One or More Organizations
A. Per cent who said they take "a great deal" of interest in:		
Presidential elections	73	84
Unemployment in the U.S.	53	57
The Denver public schools	33	50
City planning in Denver	31	50
Labor relations	31	45
The situation of Denver Negroes	23	35
B. Per cent who voted in each of the following elections:		
1944 Presidential	36	40
1946 Congressional	27	36
1947 City charter	15	24
1948 Primary	24	34
C. Per cent who report making a contribution to the Community Chest in Denver	56%	72%
Total cases	335	585

(Source: Denver Community Survey, NORC-12B.)

Political interest is backed by participation in the political process, insofar as participation is measured by voting. Data on behavior in four elections—the 1944 Presidential, 1946 Congressional, 1947 City Charter, and 1948 Primary—indicate in every instance a greater percentage of voting among Denverites who were members of voluntary associations than among non-members.

Finally, in the non-political sphere of community life, charity, 72 per cent of the persons belonging to associations reported having made a contribution to the Community Chest in Denver, in contrast to 56 per cent of the non-members.

Thus three separate measures—interest in social issues, voting, and support of community charities—show that voluntary association participants are more involved civically than the non-members. Further research might fruitfully be addressed to such questions as the following: (1) to what extent does the citizen's interest in public affairs lead him to join voluntary associations; (2) to what extent do the voluntary associations contribute to their members' interest in public affairs; (3) to what extent is membership in one or more voluntary associations functional for the citizen who has a great deal of interest in public affairs. Questions of this order, however, fall beyond the scope of this secondary analysis.[16]

Notes

1. Mirra Komarovsky, "The Voluntary Associations of Urban Dwellers," *American Sociological Review*, 11 (December, 1946), pp. 686-698.

2. Morris Axelrod, "Urban Structure and Social Participation," *American Sociological Review*, 21 (February, 1956), pp. 13-18.

3. For example, Komarovsky's study was based on responses of persons contacted at places of employment or other organizational meetings, hence not purporting to be a representative sample of New York adults. *Op. cit.*

4. For example, see the following studies: Scott Greer, "Urbanism Reconsidered: A Comparative Study of Local Areas in a Metropolis," *American Sociological Review*, 21 (February, 1956), pp. 19-25; Wendell Bell and Maryanne T. Force, "Urban Neighborhood Types and Participation in Formal Associations," *American Sociological Review*, 21 (February, 1956), pp. 25-34; Herbert Goldhamer, "Some Factors Affecting Participation in Voluntary Associations," unpublished Ph.D. dissertation (microfilmed), University of Chicago, 1942; Morris Axelrod, *op. cit.;* Floyd Dotson, "Patterns of Voluntary Association Among Urban Working Class Families," *American Sociological Review*, 16 (October, 1951), pp. 687-693; Mirra Komarovsky, *op. cit.* Thus Greer's study used two census tracts within Los Angeles; Bell and Force employed four tracts within San Francisco; Goldhamer's study is confined to Chicago, Axelrod's to Detroit, Dotson's to New Haven, and Komarovsky's to New York City.

5. The authors wish to acknowledge their indebtedness to N.O.R.C. and to its director, Clyde Hart, who made the data available for secondary analysis, and to Jack Feldman, who provided many special tabulations.

6. To some extent, the open-ended form of the questions in the national studies might have reduced the proportion of memberships reported insofar as respondent recall might be faulty. There is some indication, however, that the impact of question format was not great in this instance. In the Denver study a card listing several types of organizations was handed to the respondent before he reported memberships. Under these conditions, 36 per cent of the Denverites reported that they belonged to no organizations, including unions. In the 1953 national survey, which used an open-ended question, 39 per cent of the urbanites living in large cities (1,000,000 or more) and 42 per cent of those living in any sizeable city (50,000 or more) reported no organizational memberships, including unions, for anyone in their family.

Obviously, primary research on voluntary association membership would require more and different questioning in this area, including check lists of organizations, investigation of the meaning of "belonging" to the respondent, etc. The data used in the current secondary analysis, however, were obtained from studies in which information on membership was only incidental to the primary purposes of the surveys, for which the open-ended questions sufficed. Confidence in the interpretation of the findings as indicative of low membership among Americans is increased through the use of data from *several* national and local surveys, which support one another, in general, despite variations in the wording of questions.

Of course, this is not to dispute the fact that, from a *comparative* point of view, Americans may be more prone to such membership than other national groups. Such a mode of analysis is illustrated, for example, by Arnold Rose, *Theory and Method in the Social Sciences*, Minneapolis: The University of Minnesota Press, 1954, pp. 72-115.

7. Axelrod, *op. cit.* Also see *A Social Profile of Detroit: 1952.* A report of the Detroit Area Study, Ann Arbor: The University of Michigan Press, 1952, pp. 13-19.

8. These findings are consistent with those reported by Bell and Force, *op. cit.*, from their study in San Francisco during 1953. They not only found that Protestants were more likely than Catholics to belong to formal associations but also that the relationship persisted even when economic level was controlled.

9. See, for example, Komarovsky, *op. cit.;* Dotson, *op. cit.*, and Bell and Force, *op. cit.*

10. Data from the 1953 sample on family participation in voluntary associations generally corroborated the findings presented above and hence are not reproduced here. In addition, several of the local studies contain data in support of the relationships described. For example, home ownership data were available in Denver and provided an opportunity to examine the influence of this factor within an urban setting. Here, as on the national level, home owners were more likely to be members than were renters, 67 per cent versus 59 per cent respectively. And in New York, families employing domestic help were more likely to be members than those without help, 73 per cent versus 45 per cent.

11. Robin Williams, *American Society: A Sociological Interpretation*, New York: Alfred Knopf, 1951, pp. 467-468.

12. The higher incidence of organizational membership among urban residents in contrast with their rural neighbors also was evident in the Hancock County, Ohio survey. In this survey a distinction was made between the residents of a small town (Findley, pop. approximately 24,000) and persons in the surrounding county. Fifty-six per cent of the Findley townspeople belonged to some voluntary association, in contrast to 49 per cent of the ruralites. For a recent summary of some surveys on rural memberships see Raymond Payne, "Some Comparisons of Participation in Rural Mississippi, Kentucky, Ohio, Illinois, and New York," *Rural Sociology*, 18 (June, 1953), pp. 171-172.

13. These data are consistent with those obtained in Hancock County, Ohio where 51 per cent of the persons who had resided in the county for 20 years or more were members of voluntary associations, 57 per cent of the 10-19 year residents were members, 58 per cent of the 5-8

year residents, and 57 per cent of the persons living there less than five years. The survey was conducted in May 1952. On the other hand, Zimmer, in a study of married men in a mid-western community of 20,000, found that membership in formal organizations increased directly with length of time in the community. Zimmer's relationship persisted within age, occupational and educational control categories. See Basil Zimmer, "Participation of Migrants in Urban Structures," *American Sociological Review,* 20 (April, 1955), pp. 218-224. And a recent study in Spokane, Washington indicates a relationship between mobility and voluntary association membership; see Howard Freeman, Edwin Novak and Leo Reeder, "Correlates of Membership in Voluntary Associations," *American Sociological Review,* 22 (October, 1957), pp. 528-533.

14. Morris Janowitz, *The Community Press in an Urban Setting,* Glencoe, Ill.: The Free Press, 1952, p. 124. Janowitz's remark is made in connection with family structure as a determinant of readership of the community press, but its import extends to other forms of involvement in community activities.

15. For a discussion of the differential demands of descriptive vs. explanatory analysis see Herbert Hyman, *Survey Design and Analysis: Principles, Cases and Procedures,* Glencoe: The Free Press, 1955, especially pp. 121-124.

16. For examples of earlier theoretical and empirical work on the functions of voluntary association membership, see Rose, *op. cit.*; and Bernard Barber, "Participation and Mass Apathy in Associations," in Alvin Gouldner (ed.), *Studies in Leadership: Leadership and Democratic Action,* New York: Harper and Brothers, 1950, pp. 477-504.

The Motivational Pattern of Drinking

By JOHN W. RILEY, JR., CHARLES F. MARDEN,
and MARCIA LIFSHITZ

THE question of motivation is clearly one of the most important theoretical and practical problems in the study of drinking behavior. Perhaps its most crucial aspect is to determine whether the motivation of those who become alcoholics differs from so-called "normal" drinkers. There seems to be little doubt that the drinking motivation of the true alcoholic, when he has reached that stage, is in the nature of an irresistible compulsion. In fact, it may be said that the compulsive desire to drink has become the main motivation in his life. It is generally agreed, however, that the stage of true alcoholism is preceded by many years of drinking. Are the motivations of the pre-alcoholic different in the first place? If so, what are the potentially dangerous motivations? If not, do the motivations change during the course of the drinking history from those which are not potentially dangerous to those which are? Or do individual differences in physiological reaction to alcohol, regardless of motivation, predispose some to follow a non-disorganizing path in their drinking history, while others become alcoholics?

As a result of a nation-wide survey of public attitudes and knowledge concerning the drinking of alcoholic beverages,[1] certain data were acquired which constitute material pertinent to this problem. The purpose of the present communication is to present this material and to indicate its implications

---

Reprinted from *Quarterly Journal of Studies on Alcohol,* Volume 9, Number 3 (December 1948), pp. 353-62, by permission of the author and the publisher.

with reference to the larger basic problem stated above. The data are the verbalized responses of consumers of alcoholic beverages to the question, "What would you say is your main reason for drinking?" It is recognized at the outset that such data have limitations. Verbal responses to questions of motivation may be rationalizations—due either to the desire of the respondent to provide a reply which is morally approved or to the well-known fact that often we honestly do not know why we do certain things. On the other hand, the data here presented have the virtue of being based upon a cross-section sample of the entire American public, sufficiently large to permit comparison breakdowns of the responses within significant categories of the population.

A survey of this sort, however, obviously does not permit comparison of alcoholics with nonalcoholics. The direct value of the data from the viewpoint of the central problem stated at the outset is, consequently, limited. Why Americans drink and the variations in motivation among different population groupings based on age, sex, and frequency of drinking can only hint at a relationship between motivation and tendencies toward alcoholism. Since, however, there is increasing emphasis on drinking histories as a continuum, any and all further material on the motivations of drinking are grist to the mill. Insofar as our results tend to confirm researches into the motivations of drinking by other approaches and techniques, they contribute to scientific agreement. Insofar as they differ, they challenge resolution of the differences by the application of more exacting methods.

Of the entire sample (2,677), 65 per cent (1,744) indicated that they sometimes drank alcoholic beverages.[2] The reasons they gave for drinking are presented in terms of main classifications in Table 1. The replies pointed

Table I—Reported Reasons for Drinking

	PER CENT OF DRINKERS	
Social reasons		43
Sociability	38	
To keep husband company	2	
On festive occasions	2	
Brought up with it	2	
As business courtesy	1	
	45*	
Individual reasons		41
Makes me feel good	16	
I like it	12	
Quenches thirst	6	
Stimulates appetite	4	
Other health reasons	4	
	42*	
Both social and individual reasons		6
Other reasons		2
No reason given		8
		100% equals (1,744)

*These apparent discrepancies are due to the fact that more than one answer was possible within the major categories.

to a major division into reasons which are called social, where the respondents attribute their drinking mainly to the stimulus of the social situations in which their drinking takes place; and to reasons called individual, where the respondents attribute the main reason to the pleasurable effects or consequences of their drinking. The total replies divide approximately equally into these main divisions. The very fact that they fell easily into this twofold division suggests the basic significance of these categories of motivation.

Much more frequently than any other single reason, people say they drink "to be sociable." While some few respondents reserve drinking for festive occasions such as weddings and christenings, and others consider drinking a necessary adjunct in business contacts, the bulk of social reasons for drinking were stated in general terms—"just to be sociable," or "because all our friends drink," or "to be a good sport."

Within this general grouping, however, were included persons who drink because otherwise the social situation threatens mild ostracism, and others who are apparently merely following the dictates of fashion. While these distinctions are not clear-cut enough to be handled statistically, they suggest possible clues for approaches to the larger question.

The following are some of the answers of those who seem most influenced by the fear of group pressures.

A young New Yorker, recently discharged from the army: "Liquor is always sold in the places I frequent. You can't have a soda in a night club. It's just not done."

A Pennsylvania housewife: "People think you're dead if you don't drink."

A well-to-do professional woman, wife of an architect, New York City: "I hate to make a fuss about refusing. I don't like to be a poor sport."

A poor, elderly, west-coast farmer: "Just to be a good fellow. You make people mad if you don't."

The following are typical replies of those for whom the normative pressures of the group, be it custom or fashion, describe the main reasons given.

The wife of a Kansas City service-station attendant: "Sometimes when we have company I drink it to be sociable."

A young rural Wisconsin schoolteacher: "I guess just to be sociable. I don't care for it at all. I just choke it down."

A linesman for the telephone company in a southern town: "All of our friends drink, so we drink too."

A young nurse: "I goes to the dance hall and everybody else is drinking, so I just drinks too."

Students of family life will be interested in the special class of answers which are headed "keep husband company." While the percentage of such replies is small, it seems significant that, of all of the various and special reasons which are given for drinking, as many as 2 per cent of the drinkers —which of course means a much larger percentage of wives—offered this as a main reason for their drinking. This may well reflect the tendency for a common sharing of recreational interests in the emerging companionship marriage and indicates an active effort of wives in this direction.

Half of the drinkers, however, report that they drink for other than social reasons, such as to feel better, to quench thirst, to stimulate appetite or digestion, or to keep in good health. Some simply say they like to drink. While most of the categories under this second major classification are sufficiently specific to be self-explanatory, the general heading "makes me feel good," ascribed to one drinker out of every six, covers a variety of responses. Typical answers range from drinking for relaxation or for euphoric effect to drinking as an escape from worries, responsibilities and frustration.

A domestic employee in an Oklahoma town: "A bottle of beer makes me feel rested after a hard day's work. Then I can get up and clean my house."

A building contractor in Charlotte, N.C.: "When I drink I feel important."

A young man, unemployed, in Peoria, Ill.: "I drink because of disappointments in life. I don't want to face reality."

A Georgia farmer: "Drinking takes me right on up. Then I'se just forgets this world."

A salesman of electrical appliances in New York City: "Why do I drink? To keep alive."

Of still greater significance to the basic problem of why people drink is the comparison of the relative weights of social and individual reasons when various population groupings are examined. In interpreting the following comparisons it should be recalled that the population as a whole—that is, adults 21 years of age or older—was divided approximately equally between these two main reasons.

Table II—Reported Reasons for Drinking, By Sex

	Male (%)	Female (%)
Social reasons	33	55
Individual reasons	49	31
Both	7	6
Other reasons	2	1
No reason given	9	7
100% equals	(953)	(791)

Women give social reasons far more frequently than men, as Table 2 shows. Similarly, comparisons based on age (Table 3) show the individual

Table III—Reported Reasons for Drinking, By Age

	21-25	26-35	36-45	46-55	56+
	(PER CENT IN EACH AGE CLASS)				
Social reasons	51	46	44	39	38
Individual reasons	36	37	40	43	47
Both	3	7	8	6	5
Other reasons	2	1	1	3	1
No reason given	8	9	7	9	9
100% equals*	(213)	(482)	(432)	(303)	(308)

*This table omits six respondents whose age was not ascertained.

reasons becoming consistently more frequent with each successive age group, while the younger the respondents the more common is the emphasis on social reasons. The newer addition to the drinking population—women and younger people—tend to be social drinkers.

Since the differences in motivation between the sexes were so striking, and particularly in view of the finding reported previously that in recent years there has been a much "greater proportional increase in the number of drinkers among women than among men,"[3] the data of Table 3 were further refined. When sex is held constant within each age group it becomes readily apparent that the consistent relationship between age and motivation for drinking is largely contributed by women, although even among men there is a slight tendency to assign "individual" reasons for drinking with increasing age. Table 4 thus shows the distribution of men and women of

Table IV—Individual Reasons for Drinking, By Age and Sex

Age Class	Male (%)	Female (%)
21-25	45	25
26-35	47	28
36-45	50	30
46-55	49	33
Over 55	50	41

various age groups who drink for "individual" reasons. Among men, almost as many in the youngest group drink for physical effect as in the oldest age group. On the other hand, only 25 per cent of the youngest women drinkers, but as many as 41 per cent of the oldest, give individual reasons for drinking. Obviously, then, if drinking customs are changing more rapidly among women than among men, this occurs mainly through the influence of social pressures, particularly among the younger women. Sixty-one per cent of the women drinkers in the 21-25 age group say they drink only for social reasons.

Another profile of the data, leading to a similar general interpretation, is noted when the reasons given for drinking are related to frequency of drinking. Table 5 shows clearly that the greater the frequency of drinking,

Table V—Reasons Reported for Drinking Compared with Frequency of Drinking

	Daily Drinker	3-5 times a week	1-2 times a week	2-3 times a month	Once a month	Less than once a month
	(PER CENT IN EACH CATEGORY OF FREQUENCY)					
Social reasons	20	26	36	50	52	67
Individual reasons	59	55	46	36	32	23
Both	8	8	9	4	6	3
Other reasons	3	....	1	1	3	2
No reason given	10	11	8	9	7	5
100% equals*	(225)	(231)	(398)	(297)	(222)	(358)

*This table omits 13 respondents whose frequency of drinking was not ascertained.

the greater is the proportion of individual as distinct from social reasons for drinking. The trends are not only consistent but the range of variability is wide: 67 per cent of those who claim to drink very occasionally give social reasons for their drinking, whereas only 20 per cent of the daily drinkers claim to be socially motivated.

The relationship between frequency of drinking and motivation was examined separately for men and for women in order to determine more accurately the source of the sharp differences noted in Table 5. Apparently,

Table VI—Reasons Reported for Drinking Compared with Frequency of Drinking, by Sex*

	Daily Drinker	3-5 times a week	1-2 times a week	2-3 times a month	Once a month	Less than once a month
MALES	(PER CENT IN EACH CATEGORY OF FREQUENCY)					
Social reasons	21	25	31	39	43	54
Individual reasons	56	56	51	46	41	35
Both	8	7	10	5	4	2
Other reasons	3	1	1	1	3	2
No reason given	12	11	7	9	9	7
100% equals	(174)	(164)	(237)	(138)	(107)	(122)
FEMALES						
Social reasons	18	27	45	60	61	73
Individual reasons	70	51	38	27	23	18
Both	6	10	7	4	9	3
Other reasons	....	....	....	....	3	2
No reason given	6	12	10	9	4	4
100% equals	(51)	(67)	(161)	(159)	(115)	(236)

*This table omits 13 respondents whose frequency of drinking was not ascertained. Note also the small bases for some of these percentages. They are presented for comparative purposes only. Individual figures should be interpreted cautiously.

as Table 6 shows, among both men and women, the more frequently one drinks the greater is the tendency to drink for individual reasons or physical effect rather than for sociability. Again, however, consistent with the observation that recent changes in drinking customs are more strongly influencing women, the relationship between frequency of drinking and motivation is more pronounced among female respondents than among males.

Finally, although sociability is fully as important a reason for drinking as is physical effect, in terms of proportional distribution of responses by the population, nevertheless the tendency for more seasoned drinkers to assign individual reasons for drinking suggests a difference in the strengths of the two motivational patterns. To test this hypothesis, the reasons people gave for drinking in legally dry areas were compared with those expressed in the rest of the country (the wet areas). The results (Table 7) clearly support

Table VII—Reported Reasons for Drinking in Wet and Dry Areas

	Wet (%)	Dry (%)
Social reasons	46	29
Individual reasons	39	48
Both	6	6
Other reasons	1	4
No reason given	8	13
100% equals	(1,531)	(213)

the hypothesis. Where alcoholic beverages are hard to get, a much larger proportion of people drink for individual than for social reasons. Conversely, where alcoholic beverages are easily available, sociability is the more frequently reported reason for drinking. Even in dry areas, however, 29 per cent of the drinkers are willing to go to the trouble to secure liquor although they drink just to be sociable.

Implications and Significance of the Findings. Despite the theoretical limitations of these data as indices of "true" motivation, the impression grows, after qualitative and internal consistency analysis, that the respondents, on the whole, stated quite frankly and without reservation their main reason for drinking, within the limits of conscious awareness. Furthermore, the statistical stability of the data, particularly in comparisons among various population segments, as noted above, is in itself impressive evidence of the meaningfulness of individual responses at the level of everyday articulation.

Within this framework of interpretation the data support three hypotheses related to motivation for drinking. In the first place, they suggest the feasibility of applying standard analytical procedures to this aspect of the problem of consumption of alcoholic beverages. While further research is obviously needed, particularly in the direction of deeper probing into the mechanisms of motivation, the conceptual value of this twofold classification as a starting point is clearly indicated.

Secondly, the data lend powerful support to the hypothesis that drinking is as directly motivated by the influence of social pressures as it is by acquired inner drives. (The modifying word "directly" has been used since there can be little argument that all drinking is affected indirectly by social factors.) Of all the people who state that they sometimes drink, more than two out of five assign main motivation to group pressure.

Thirdly, the relative weight of external social pressures versus inner acquired drives varies widely between different classes of drinkers. Direct social pressure is much more influential in motivating the drinking of women compared with men; the young compared with the old; and the occasional or infrequent compared with regular drinkers. On the other hand, seasoned and regular drinkers tend to state that their reasons for drinking lie more within themselves than in the direct pressures from the group situation.

While neither the data themselves nor the hypotheses they support relate directly to the problem of the compulsive drinker, they do, however, pertain to the question of prevention. If it be assumed that drinking in general cannot be eliminated from our society, the search becomes one for effective controls directed at the clearly demonstrable problem aspects of drinking—drunkenness and alcoholism. Since the above findings document in statistical terms the proposition that social pressures play a large part in motivating drinking, they also by indirection indicate that social pressures can be brought to bear to limit drinking. But what type of social pressure is here involved? It is probably not custom—except in the case of those who descend from particular ethnic backgrounds. It is something too short-lived for that.

It is certainly not institutional pressure, since with few exceptions the basic institutions of our times denounce drinking, however much the individual members may not practice what the mores admonish. It is rather the kind of transitory social pressure which characterizes so much of the personal behavior of people in a rapidly changing social order when the old mores are outmoded and new mores, or authoritatively sanctioned rules of behavior, have not replaced them. From this point of view the effective control of the problem aspects of drinking requires the establishment of new authoritative group sanctions, founded on science and supported by the basic institutions. In the meantime anything which can be done to alter the one-way influence on drinking patterns of these temporary normative pressures will point in the same direction.

The possibility of introducing such changes may be illustrated by the pamphlet admonition emphasized by the National Committee for Education on Alcoholism, a suggestion perhaps not so trivial as it may at first sound:

> *Never insist on anyone taking a drink.* Following this simple rule of etiquette may have greater consequences than you know. If all hosts and hostesses heeded it, the problem of alcoholism might be greatly reduced.

The effect of instituting such a small change in fashion, for example, as the serving of both alcoholic and nonalcoholic beverages at gatherings, and in such a manner that either choice seems appropriate, might be, in the long run, far-reaching. Certainly for the "dry" alcoholic (the alcoholic who has regained his sobriety) it would have immediate significance, for he knows, as his host and friends frequently do not, that he must not take one drink. In addition, there are those adults who do not like to drink, or have been ordered not to drink for physical reasons, but "choke it down just to be sociable." Finally, and probably of greatest significance, are the younger people who have not become regular consumers of alcoholic beverages or have not yet accepted the proposition that drinking always goes with sociability. Science has not discovered how to distinguish the potential alcoholic from those who may drink within controllable limits all their lives. Until it does, the trend toward the automatic association of drinking with sociability must take its place in the complex of factors contributing to the problem of alcoholism.

Notes

1. Conducted for Rutgers University by the National Opinion Research Center. The larger survey was sponsored by the New Jersey Commission on Alcoholism and the Research Council on Problems of Alcohol. The present report was made possible by funds granted by the Research Council of Rutgers University. The interpretations are the authors' and do not necessarily reflect the opinion of any of the sponsoring groups.

2. Toward the close of the interview, the respondents were handed a card on which were listed various kinds of alcoholic drinks and were asked, "Which of these do you sometimes drink?" Those who indicated one or more beverages were further asked how often they drank of each. It should be understood that the definition of "drinker" here is very wide, covering the individual who drinks once a year at Christmas as well as the alcoholic, a few of whom showed up unmistakably in the sample.

3. Riley, J. W., Jr., and Marden, C. F. The social pattern of alcoholic drinking. Quart. J. Stud. Alc 8:265-73, 1947.

Sex as Play

By NELSON N. FOOTE

THE new Kinsey volume provides evidence toward a few more conclusions than its authors care to draw about sex as a magnet of interest in America. It is the purpose of this paper to draw these conclusions.

Among the lower mammals, sexual intercourse appears to be rather thriftily apportioned through the mechanism of female periodicity in a manner which maximizes the probability of conception. The Malthusian principle that nature reproduces offspring in excess may apply also to the over-production of ova and spermatozoa, but except in *homo sapiens,* it conspicuously does not apply to the frequency of copulation. (p. 609)[1] Only humans are lavish in this respect, and only among humans as a consequence can sexual conjugation be elaborated so extensively as a cultural interest independently from the function of procreation.

One of the salient but underrated Kinsey findings about human sexual behavior is how much of it there is.

The conditions mainly responsible for this unique distinction are two: the human female will accept intercourse at almost any time, not merely at her period of ovulation, and the stimuli which evoke desire among both men and women are primarily symbolic rather than physiological. Thus it is given in nature that human beings should develop conscious longings (or aversions) for sexual experience on its own account, neither because they are driven by irrepressible instinct nor by rational calculation of distant consequences. The view that sex is fun can therefore hardly be called the invention of immoralists; it is everyman's discovery.

Contraception completes the divorce of sexuality from procreation, but as can be seen, only in part accounts for it. "No appreciable part of the coitus, either in or out of marriage, is consciously undertaken as a means of effecting reproduction." (p. 313) The ease with which pregnancy may be avoided is conveyed by these striking statistics:

> We have a sample of 2094 single, white females . . . who had had coitus and on whom we have data concerning pregnancy. They had had 476 pregnancies . . . The 2094 single females who had had coitus had had it approximately 460,000 times. This means, approximately, that one pregnancy had resulted from each 1000 copulations. But considering the effectiveness of modern contraceptives and the exceedingly few failures which we have recorded for the condom and diaphragm when properly used, there is, today, practically no necessity for such a pregnancy rate in pre-marital coitus (p. 327)

The great market for contraceptives, of course, is among the married,

---

Reprinted from *Social Problems,* Volume 1, Number 4 (April 1954), pp. 159-63, by permission of the author and the publisher. (Copyright 1954 by the Society for the Study of Social Problems.)

and no more evidence than census figures on family size is needed to prove their contemporary effectiveness. Contraception, however, appears to have been a well-nigh universal practice among human beings—who have, according to the ethnologists, devised an immense array of schemes for keeping down their numbers, including abortion and infanticide. Only recently have the means for purposeful segregation of sex and family—for rational decisions on family size—become reliable and widely accessible; but the wish to pursue the two interests separately has always and everywhere been evident.

Dr. Kinsey's work demonstrates how important objective research can be to the intelligent revision of social policy. Most of the force of the two reports has come from the near-puritan rigor with which he and his associates have held to their ideal of thorough, factual investigation. And it is significant that most of the reaction against them has been directed likewise at the validity of their interviewing and sampling methods, or the discipline with which they have held to a narrowly-specified research problem. Only improbably large rectifications of the published percentages could alter the bearing of this intensive documentation upon recognition that, in the United States, what is preached and what is practiced sexually are widely discrepant. Revelation of such gaps is the first step in closing them.

Kinsey himself enlarges upon the significance of only one of the discrepancies between profession and practice which his findings throw into relief. In terms of the letter of the law, most adult Americans are sexual offenders, and in multiple ways. He has piled up so much evidence in his first two volumes to exhibit the magnitude of this official hypocrisy that it is difficult to imagine of what he will compile his next volume on sexual offenders and offenses. Sociologists in particular are conscientiously bound to renew the question of when a law, like the Volstead Act, becomes illegitimate and its enforcement unjust.

Not directly but implicitly Kinsey highlights a second quite different ambiguity or ambivalence of American sexual culture. Our popular vocabulary for describing sexual behavior has been compounded of about equal parts of euphemism and obscenity, and popular attitude and sentiment have followed the same dualism. Among both his male and female subjects, the interviewers found many who knew only the lewd words for features of their own anatomy and physiology. Perhaps no sex educator up to now has been as successful in imparting to discussion of sex the straightforward, unemotional language of the scientist. Condensation of his findings in our most widely-circulated family magazine was in this sense a high-water mark in the advancement of public sanity about sex. The speakers of matter-of-fact on this subject now so squarely confront the partisans of obscenity-euphemism that resolution of the issue seems unavoidable much longer. Even if the schools continue to default, the mass media will complete the job of vanquishing sexual ignorance.

Another salient finding, of the second report especially, is the steady decline of the ancient double standard in sexual morality. It is evidenced in several quite different kinds of data which convey an impressive sense of internal consistency:

a) the steady decline of prostitution (p. 300)

b) extension of pre-marital coital activities among females to levels more nearly comparable to those in the male (p. 324)

c) increasing percentages of marital copulations leading to orgasm decade by decade (p. 380)

d) steady approach to equivalence of male and female in pre-marital petting and marital sex play techniques (p. 245, 362)

e) increasing percentages of marital and female extra-marital coitus (p. 436 ff.)

f) declining male insistence upon female virginity at marriage (p. 323)

g) some decline in frequency of marital coitus, implying more mutual consent and less unilateral male demand. (p. 359, 397)

Such evidence agrees with the observations to be made of the equalization of male and female roles in social and economic life—the declining authority of fathers, access of women to better jobs, removal of legal and political disadvantages of women, and the decline of segregation of the sexes. As equality of opportunity for women has tended to replace exploitation in society at large, fair play has been replacing chastity as the badge of honor in the interpersonal relations of the sexes.

Not all the consequences of reducing male power and female dependency have been clearly anticipated, and not all of them have been equally welcome. It might be argued that an effective majority have favored such trends as the three outlined above—pressure for relaxation of legal prohibitions, freer and franker public discussion, and increased economic and social opportunity—or they would have not occurred. But even the more liberal moralists tend to boggle when they contemplate the recognition of sex as a legitimate form of play. Kinsey documents its emergence and importance as such, but goes no further himself in reflecting upon the meaning of its prevalence than to note:

> There is no doubt that coitus, both before and after marriage, is had primarily because it may satisfy a physiologic need and may serve as a source of pleasure for one or both of the individuals who are involved. (p. 313)

One could speculate upon whether it is the puritan tendency to frown upon play or the puritan tradition that sex is intrinsically sinful, or both in combination, which still obscure and confuse the significance of the manifest situation. As our advertisers imply daily in a thousand ways, the attractions of sex make it the favorite form of play for millions of Americans. Why do not our thinkers go on from there to contemplate the kind of social life which might result from formal recognition of this fact, rather than implicitly or explicitly reverting to the prejudice that sex as play is bound to be sinful or at best amoral? Is it because to grant its status as play is felt to legitimize its pursuit without restraint? If so, the thinker does not understand the nature of play.

For play—any kind of play—generates its own morality and values. And the enforcement of the rules of play becomes the concern of every player, because without their observance, the play cannot continue; the spoilsport is sternly rejected. To be sure, the development of rules intrinsic to the game itself does not guarantee that they will be the same rules outsiders would like to impose, and when outsiders repress the play itself as illicit, the development of rules can hardly occur at all. But the social psychologists of play, from Spencer and Groos to the present, all seem to agree that no system of government whatever can approach play in making the enforcement of rules the felt interest of every participant.

With regard to sex, an example may clarify this point. A male student not long ago spent a year doing academic work in Sweden. He had learned that in that enlightened country the double standard is almost extinct, and women both permit and are permitted the same liberties as men in premarital relations. This knowledge excited in him the hope of enjoying such an unrestrained orgy of self-gratification as other college males only dream of. After a series of frustrating and bewildering encounters with some Swedish young women, however, he was left a sadder and wiser person, for he found himself disgraced and outcast as an oaf and a boor. He had not played the game correctly nor had he realized how strictly its rules are enforced in that highly moral and law-abiding country. It is not that he was mistaken about the greater sexual freedom of Scandinavia, but that coming from an American background, he did not rationally foresee the context through which order and responsibility are nonetheless maintained.

Exploration of the morals and values which might emerge from the forthright public acceptance of sex as play is obviously a task for extended research. Only a few speculations on the lines such research might follow are legitimate or possible here. Two intriguing avenues for investigation of ethical developments are visible, and two with regard to emergent values:

The dynamics of obligation and commitment: The freedom with which an interpersonal relationship is entered conditions the faith with which its implicit moral obligations are kept, both psychologically and legally, as in the marriage contract itself. The force which the rule of reciprocity gives to commitments engendered by the voluntary exchange of sexual intimacy has been often noted but little studied systematically. Increasing awareness of the power of this rule stands out among the objections given by the younger generation to pre-marital intercourse except with a person to whom engaged. Though half (53%) of the married females in Kinsey's sample had experienced pre-marital coitus, 46% of these had confined their coitus to the fiance. (p. 292) The play *The Moon is Blue* scrutinizes this subtle point as no research study to date has done.

The counterfeiting of intimacy: Sociologists and critics alike have belabored the theme of the lonely individual in mobile, urban society. Sex stands for many lonely people as the symbol of the intimacy they crave, but when they reach for the symbol, the substance may yet elude them. The writer has argued elsewhere[2] that the Freudian derivation of the social from the sexual should be read in reverse. Even within happy marriage, variations in sexual response are indicative of fluctuations in the level of trust attained between partners. Thus intimacy is not an inheritance but a social-psychological achievement; it is the acme of communication and exposure of self. Every act of human coitus has something of the quality of a drama; it commences with some form of pursuit and may be climaxed by total intimacy, but often is not. By itself, sex cannot substitute for intimacy; at best it then becomes mutual masturbation, a counterfeit currency of interpersonal relations. In *Virginibus Puerisque,* Robert Louis Stevenson put the issue well with his essay on "Truth of Intercourse." In the area of life where the self is most at stake, where anxiety and dissembling form a vicious circle, social-psychological research could offer much by identifying the conditions of trust, relaxation and confidence. So-called learning theory has not begun to touch this problem—though, to look at the bright side, many young people have learned intuitively how to achieve genuine intimacy with skill and grace. If it can be learned, it can be taught.

Sexual competence as a developmental process. Though their bearing is still only dimly understood, it is the improvement of specific social conditions to which we must look for explanation of trends in sexual functioning, in the life of the individual and in society at large. Kinsey reflects the influence of cultural development by his emphasis upon the orgasm. Orgasm among women is unnecessary for procreation, and it is doubtful if the females of any other species achieve orgasm at all. Though he dwells with loving care upon all its physical details, his data disclose how vital social-psychological conditions are to its incidence. Two per cent of his sample, to illustrate, were able to achieve orgasm by sheer fantasy. (p. 174) As mentioned, marital frigidity at large has declined each decade; moreover, frequency of orgasm mounts regularly with length of marriage. (p. 384) Those who accuse Kinsey of reducing sexual behavior to merely animal functioning (translation by friendly critics: not straying outside the field of his competence) miss the many indications of his interest in the conditions optimal for female orgasm, each of which is a lead for research on the development of sexual competence through social experience. Rise in orgasm capacity is not due to constitutional alterations. Recognition of the significance of these findings opens the door to further investigation and experimentation to identify the conditions optimal for the realization of full sexuality. The first condition, of course, is that it be taken as a value, as Kinsey himself appears to take it, along with a mounting majority of his fellow-citizens.

The elaboration of sex as a cultural interest: It is only realistic to recognize the orgasm as the basic index of individual sexual development. But culture does not simply condition individual behavior; culture itself evolves. And with the release of American sexual behavior from the tabu upon valuing it as play, the anthropologist may soon have at hand for study a considerable efflorescence of cultural innovation. Dr. Kinsey's chapter on psychological factors in sexual response is quite unimaginatively limited to the most literal and direct stimuli to sexual arousal; pornography, for example, gets twice the attention of serious literature and art. (p. 670 ff.) In an America which is coming to honor leisure and play, however, not only is our interest in sex capable of infinite elaboration through all the arts, but intercourse itself is likely to gain recognition as an art. Women may then still retain some lesser degree of psychic responsiveness than men, as Kinsey believes, but anxiety and awkwardness will be the exception.

1. Otherwise unidentified page notations refer to Alfred C. Kinsey *et al., Sexual Behavior in the Human Female,* Philadelphia: W. B. Saunders Co., 1953.
2. Nelson N. Foote, "Love." *Psychiatry.* 16 (August, 1953), 245-251.

Leisure as Contemplation

By JOSEPH PIEPER

THE 'WORKER' is characterized by three principal traits: an extreme tension of the powers of action, a readiness to suffer *in vacuo* unrelated to anything, and complete absorption in the social organism, itself rationally planned to utilitarian ends. Leisure, from this point of view, appears as something wholly fortuitous and strange, without rhyme or reason, and, morally speaking, unseemly: another word for laziness, idleness and sloth. At the zenith of the Middle Ages, on the contrary, it was held that sloth and restlessness, 'leisurelessness', the incapacity to enjoy leisure, were all closely connected; sloth was held to be the source of restlessness, and the ultimate cause of 'work for work's sake'. It may well seem paradoxical to maintain that the restlessness at the bottom of a fanatical and suicidal activity should come from the lack of will to action; a surprising thought, that we shall only be able to decipher with effort. But it is a worth-while effort, and we should do well to pause for a moment to enquire into the philosophy of life attached to the word *acedia*.

In the first place *acedia* does not signify the 'idleness' we envisage when we speak of idleness as 'the root of all vice'. Idleness, in the medieval view, means that a man prefers to forgo the rights, or if you prefer the claims, that belong to his nature. In a word, he does not want to be as God wants him to be, and that ultimately means that he does not wish to be what he really, fundamentally, *is. Acedia* is the 'despair from weakness' which Kierkegaard analysed as the 'despairing refusal to be oneself'. Metaphysically and theologically, the notion of *acedia* means that a man does not, in

Chapter 3 from *Leisure the Basis of Culture,* by Joseph Pieper, translated by Alexander Dru.

the last resort, give the consent of his will to his own being; that behind or beneath the dynamic activity of his existence, he is still not at one with himself, or, as the medieval writers would have said, face to face with the divine good within him; he is a prey to sadness (and that sadness is the *tristitia saeculi* of Holy Scripture).

And then we are told that the opposite of this metaphysical and theological notion is the notion 'hard-working', industrious, in the context of economic life! For *acedia* has, in fact, been interpreted as though it had something to do with the economic ethos of the Middle Ages. Sombart, for example, treats it as though it were the fault of the lazy stay-at-home as compared with the industrious worker—though Max Scheler criticized his view. And some of Sombart's successors even go so far as to translate *acedia* as 'stick-in-the-mud'—as well say 'lack of business enterprise' or even 'lack of salesmanship'. All this, however, is less painful than the eager attempt of the apologist to make Christian teaching square with a passing fashion, which in this case involves interpreting the Church's view of work in terms of modern activism—with the result that *vivere secundum actum est quando exercet quis opera vitae in actu* is actually translated as 'life *in actu* consists in this, that one is busy and occupied with practical affairs' . . . as if Aquinas did not hold that contemplation was an *opus vitae*!

No, the contrary of *acedia* is not the spirit of work in the sense of the work of every day, of earning one's living; it is man's happy and cheerful affirmation of his own being, his acquiescence in the world and in God—which is to say love. Love that certainly brings a particular freshness and readiness to work along with it, but that no one with the least experience could conceivably confuse with the tense activity of the fanatical 'worker'.

Who would guess, unless he were expressly told so, that Aquinas regarded *acedia* as a sin against the third commandment? He was in fact so far from considering idleness as the opposite of the ethos of work that he simply interprets it as an offence against the commandment in which we are called upon to have 'the peace of the mind in God'.

But what has all this, one might well ask, to do with the question? *Acedia* was reckoned among the *vitia capitalia,* as one of the seven capital or cardinal sins, for they were not called 'capital' because of the best-known rendering of *caput*; *caput* certainly means 'head', but it also means 'source' or 'spring'—and that is the meaning in this case. They are sins from which other faults follow 'naturally', one is tempted to say, as from a source. Idleness—and this is how we get back to the question—idleness, according to traditional teaching, is the source of many faults and among others of that deep-seated lack of calm which makes leisure impossible. Among other faults, certainly, and one of the children of *acedia,* is despair, which amounts to saying that despair and the incapacity for leisure are twins—a revealing thought that explains, among other things, the hidden meaning of that very questionable saying, 'work and don't despair'.

Idleness, in the old sense of the word, so far from being synonymous with leisure, is more nearly the inner prerequisite which renders leisure impossible: it might be described as the utter absence of leisure, or the very opposite of leisure. Leisure is only possible when a man is at one with himself, when he acquiesces in his own being, whereas the essence of *acedia* is the refusal to acquiesce in one's own being. Idleness and the incapacity for leisure correspond with one another. Leisure is the contrary of both.

Leisure, it must be clearly understood, is a mental and spiritual attitude —it is not simply the result of external factors, it is not the inevitable result of spare time, a holiday, a week-end or a vacation. It is, in the first place, an attitude of mind, a condition of the soul, and as such utterly contrary to the ideal of 'worker' in each and every one of the three aspects under which it was analysed: work as activity, as toil, as a social function.

Compared with the exclusive ideal of work as activity, leisure implies (in the first place) an attitude of non-activity, of inward calm, of silence; it means not being 'busy', but letting things happen.

Leisure is a form of silence, of that silence which is the prerequisite of the apprehension of reality: only the silent hear and those who do not remain silent do not hear. Silence, as it is used in this context, does not mean 'dumbness' or 'noiselessness'; it means more nearly that the soul's power to 'answer' to the reality of the world is left undisturbed. For leisure is a receptive attitude of mind, a contemplative attitude, and it is not only the occasion but also the capacity for steeping oneself in the whole of creation.

Furthermore there is also a certain happiness in leisure, something of the happiness that comes from the recognition of the mysteriousness of the universe and the recognition of our incapacity to understand it, that comes with a deep confidence, so that we are content to let things take their course; and there is something about it which Konrad Weiss, the poet, called 'confidence in the fragmentariness of life and history'. In the same entry in his Journal he refers to the characteristically precise style and thought of Ernst Jünger, with his fanaticism for the truth—Jünger, who really seems to tear the mystery out of a thing, coldly and boldly, and then lay it out, neatly dissected, all ready to view. His passion for tidy formulae 'is surely the very reverse of contemplative, and yet there is something idle in it, idleness concealed within the sublime exactitude of thought—as opposed to the true idleness which lets God and the world and things go, and gives them time . . .'!

Leisure is not the attitude of mind of those who actively intervene, but of those who are open to everything; not of those who grab and grab hold, but of those who leave the reins loose and who are free and easy themselves—almost like a man falling asleep, for one can only fall asleep by 'letting oneself go'. Sleeplessness and the incapacity for leisure are really related to one another in a special sense, and a man at leisure is not unlike a man asleep. Heraclitus the Obscure observed of men who were asleep that they too 'were busy and active in the happenings of the world'. When we really let our minds rest contemplatively on a rose in bud, on a child at play, on a divine mystery, we are rested and quickened as though by a dreamless sleep. Or as the Book of Job says 'God giveth songs in the night' (Job xxxv, 10). Moreover, it has always been a pious belief that God sends his good gifts and his blessings in sleep. And in the same way his great, imperishable intuitions visit a man in his moments of leisure. It is in these silent and receptive moments that the soul of man is sometimes visited by an awareness of what holds the world together:

> was die Welt
> Im innersten zusammenhält

only for a moment perhaps, and the lightning vision of his intuition has to be recaptured and rediscovered in hard work.

Compared with the exclusive ideal of work as toil, leisure appears (*secondly*) in its character as an attitude of contemplative 'celebration', a word that, properly understood, goes to the very heart of the meaning which I am concerned to put before you. Leisure is only possible, to recall what has already been said, to a man at one with himself, but who is also at one with the world. Those are the 'presuppositions' of leisure, for leisure is an affirmation. Idleness, on the contrary, is rooted in the omission of those two affirmations.

Leisure, it may be re-stated, is not just non-activity, it is not the same as quiet and peace, not even inward quiet and peace, though there is a silence in the dialogue of love to which it might be compared. Something of this is conveyed in Hölderlin's fragment *Leisure,* where he compares himself to a loving elm standing in a peaceful meadow, while the delight of life plays about him, embracing him like a vine:

> ich stehe im friedlichen Felde
> Wie ein liebender Ulmbaum da, und wie Reben und Trauben
> Schlingen sich rund um mich die süssen Spiele des Lebens.

God, we are told in the first chapter of Genesis, 'ended his work which he had made' and 'behold, it was very good'. In the same way man celebrates and gratefully accepts the reality of creation in leisure, and the inner vision that accompanies it. And just as Holy Scripture tells us that God rested on the seventh day and beheld that 'the work which he had made' was 'very good'—so too it is leisure which leads man to accept the reality of the creation and thus to celebrate it, resting on the inner vision that accompanies it.

The strongest affirmation of this agreement is the celebration of a feast, where 'to celebrate', as Karl Kerényi says, is 'the union of peace, contemplation and intensity of life'. In all religions, the meaning of a feast has always been the same, the affirmation of man's fundamental accord with the world; and its purpose is to express this accord and man's participation in the world in a special manner. Feast days and holy-days are the inner source of leisure. It is because leisure takes its origin from 'celebration' that it is not only effortless but the direct contrary of effort; not just the negative, in the sense of being no effort, but the positive counterpart.

And *thirdly,* leisure stands opposed to the exclusive ideal of work *qua* social function. A break in one's work, whether of an hour, a day or a week, is still part of the world of work. It is a link in the chain of utilitarian functions. The pause is made for the sake of work and in order to work, and a man is not only refreshed *from* work but *for* work. Leisure is an altogether different matter; it is no longer on the same plane; it runs at right angles to work—just as it could be said that intuition is not the prolongation or continuation, as it were, of the work of the *ratio,* but cuts right across it, vertically. *Ratio,* in point of fact, used to be compared to time, whereas *intellectus* was compared to eternity, to the eternal now. And therefore leisure does not exist for the sake of work—however much strength it may give a man to work; the point of leisure is not to be a restorative, a pick-me-up, whether mental or physical; and though it gives new strength, mentally and physically, and spiritually too, that is not the point.

Leisure, like contemplation, is of a higher order than the *vita activa* (although the active life is the proper human life in a more special sense). And order, in this sense, cannot be overturned or reversed. Thus, however true it may be that the man who says his nightly prayers sleeps the better for it, nevertheless no one could say his nightly prayers with that in mind. In the same way, no one who looks to leisure simply to restore his working powers will ever discover the fruit of leisure; he will never know the quickening that follows, almost as though from some deep sleep.

The point and the justification of leisure are not that the functionary should function faultlessly and without a breakdown, but that the functionary should continue to be a man—and that means that he should not be wholly absorbed in the clear-cut milieu of his strictly limited function; the point is also that he should continue to be capable of seeing life as a whole and the world as a whole; that he should fulfil himself, and come to full possession of his faculties, face to face with being as a whole.

That is the sense in which the powers necessary to enjoy leisure are among the fundamental powers of the human soul. Like the gift of contemplation in which the soul steeps itself in being, and the capacity to raise up the mind and heart and 'celebrate', in the full religious sense of the word, leisure is the power of stepping beyond the workaday world, and in so doing touching upon the superhuman life-giving powers which, incidentally, almost, renew and quicken us for our everyday tasks. It is only in and through leisure that the 'gate to freedom' is opened and man can escape from the closed circle of that 'latent dread and anxiety' which a clear-sighted observer has perceived to be the mark of the world of work, where 'work and unemployment are the two inescapable poles of existence'.[1]

In leisure—not of course exclusively in leisure, but always in leisure—the truly human values are saved and preserved *because* leisure is the means whereby the sphere of the 'specifically human' can, over and again, be left behind—not as a result of any violent effort to escape, but as in an ecstasy (the ecstasy is indeed more 'difficult' than the most violent exertion, more 'difficult' because not invariably at our beck and call; a state of extreme tension is more easily induced than a state of relaxation and ease *although* the latter is effortless); the full enjoyment of leisure is hedged in by paradoxes of this kind, and it is itself a state at once very human and superhuman. Aristotle says of leisure, 'A man will live thus, not to the extent that he is a man, but to the extent that a divine principle dwells within him.'[2]

Notes

1. Richard Wright in *Die Umschau,* vol. 1, no. 2, pp. 214-16.
2. Nichomachean Ethics, 10, 7 (1177b).

Time on Our Hands

By RUSSELL LYNES

RECENTLY I discovered among some papers that my mother had stowed away in a deserted file a clipping from a magazine of the 1920s. It was headed "Schedule for a One-Maid House." The house, it said, "has seven rooms: a living-room, dining-room, porch, kitchen, maid's room and bath, three bedrooms, and two baths." The schedule starts with:

6:45 A.M. *Wash and Dress*

and ends with:

8:00 P.M.*Plans for the evening will be adapted to the household convenience.*

Bridget, if that was her name, was busy in the intervening hours with cleaning, cooking, bed-making, baking, and polishing silver and brass. Her respite came sometime between 1:30 and 3:00 P.M. when, according to the schedule, she was to "clear table, wash dishes, go to own room to rest, bathe, and change dress." At 3:00 she was back in the kitchen, "ready to answer door, etc."

Leisure was not much of a problem for Bridget at work in a one-maid house. Her schedule covers six days (on Saturday it says: "Bake cake for Sunday") and like everyone else she had Sunday as her only day off. (She doesn't seem to have had "maid's night out" on the customary Thursday.)

The familiar picture of the maid on her day off was of a girl dressed "fit to kill" on her way to meet her friends at church. The equally familiar picture of the man of the house was father asleep in a hammock buried under the Sunday paper. Leisure in those days was merely a restorative for work.

Now leisure has become work in its own right . . . and a worry to lots of earnest Americans.

Last year at the commencement exercises at New York University a clergyman said to the graduating class: "America can be undone by her misuse of leisure. Life is getting easier physically, and this makes life harder morally."

There are, of course, a great many professional and business men who wonder what all this talk about leisure is; somehow it is no problem to them —or so they think. There are also a good many women, especially young married women, who would give their heirlooms for a few minutes to themselves. They have only to wait.

But leisure is making some thoughtful people uneasy. In January the American Council of Churches met in Columbus to discuss the spare time of our increasingly urbanized populace. The Twentieth Century Fund is deep in an investigation of leisure and the University of Chicago is (with the help of Ford Foundation funds) making a study of the nature of leisure and how people use it. Corporations not only worry about the leisure of their employees; they do something about it. Schoolteachers and social workers and local politicians worry about it, about footloose youngsters, about long summer vacations for teen-agers, and about juvenile delinquency. City planners, safety experts, highway engineers watch the growing number of hours when families are not at work and feel they have to go somewhere. Where? To what extent is the boredom of leisure responsible for young drug addicts, for the common cold, for muggings on city streets?

Every new scientific development, whether it is aimed at saving our skins or washing our dishes, leads in one way or another to reducing still further the sweat of the public brow. The four-day week which looms on the immediate horizon (and which causes such consternation in the corporate breast) is, of course, less the product of labor's demands than of manufacturing genius. Machines not men have created the three-day weekend, and men are worried about what to do with it. Not long ago the Oil, Chemical, and Atomic Workers Union made a survey of its membership. It asked them: ". . . if and when the Union enters a bargaining program for shorter hours" how would they like this additional leisure to be distributed? Would a housewife, for example, "want her husband at home three consecutive days?" Good question.

The attitude of many large corporations has been somewhat different. They have attacked the problem of employee leisure head on. They have provided all sorts of sports facilities, music clubs, theater groups, and bowling leagues. IBM has its own golf courses for its employees. Bell and Howell has baseball fields lighted for night games. Ford's River Rouge plant has an indoor shooting range, tennis courts, baseball diamonds (nine of them), and horseshoe pits. Corning Glass has its own museum, visiting repertory theater, and changing exhibitions, in addition to automatic bowling alleys, basketball courts, and dancing classes.

Business is not sentimental about the new leisure. "Many of these off-the-job or after-hours activities," the head of employee relations for General Motors has said, "have not only a therapeutic value, but can actually sharpen or increase employees' skills." And the President of Bell and Howell has said, "Everyone in the organization gains from a well-planned recreational program."

How to Keep the Idle Rich From Committing Suicide. But these efforts to sponge up the ocean of the so-called leisure time which has engulfed us can only put a few drops in the bucket. The truth is that while the new leisure has come on us fairly gradually, it has found us not at all prepared. If we are to cope agreeably with it, we are going to have to change our minds about some shibboleths and even some rather basic beliefs. To do this, we need to understand what has happened to the pattern of our leisure and where it is likely to lead.

Leisure is not a new problem born of automation, but it is a new problem for a great many kinds of people who were never much concerned with it when Bridget was working her seventy- or eighty-hour week in the one-maid house. America has had a leisure class since the industrialization of our country began, and in the 1850s the art critic James Jackson Jarves complained in shocked tones of the number of scions of wealthy families who threw themselves into rivers because they were so bored that life seemed not worth living. (Mr. Jarves wanted to interest such young men in the arts as a suitable outlet for their energies and money.) These young men, whom we would call the idle rich, had on a large scale the same problem that nearly everybody in America has today on a small scale. In its simplest terms, the primary problem of leisure is how to avoid boredom.

We used to be more accomplished at being bored than we are today, or at least we seem to have taken boredom with better grace in the days of party calls and decorous parlor games. We assumed a high moral tone toward leisure, and in some respects this tone persists. "The devil finds work for idle hands," our parents said and shook their heads; and when they said, "All work and no play makes Jack a dull boy," they meant, of course, that Jack should work most of the time but not quite all of it. Primarily leisure was thought of as a way to get a man back on his feet so that after Sunday he could put in sixty or so productive hours from Monday through Saturday. Leisure for women (few women in those days had jobs) was something quite else–it was the custody of culture and good works. Women in their spare time were expected to cultivate the arts, foster the education of their children, and play the role of Lady Bountiful in the community.

It was a neat division of family functions and a tidy way of life. Father's leisure was restorative; mother's was extremely productive. But more has changed than just the roles of men and women; the whole complex machinery of leisure has changed.

Briefly the changes are these:

In the last few decades what had started about a century ago as a trickle of people from the country and small towns to the cities became a torrent. Cities filled like cisterns and overflowed into suburbs, and as we shifted from a predominantly agricultural economy to a predominantly industrial one, we changed the nature of much of our leisure from what might be called a natural one to an artificial one, from pleasures provided by nature to pleasures concocted by man. Ways of using leisure began to come in packages—in cars, in movies, in radios, and most recently in television sets, and what was once the sauce only for the city goose became the sauce for the country gander as well. City culture is now within easy reach of everyone everywhere and everyone has the same access to talent that only a few decades ago used to be reserved for the rich and the urbane.

During the time when we were changing from a rural to an urban culture, the length of the work-week fell from sixty hours or more to forty or thirty-five. Gradually the five-day week became an almost universal reality, and the four-day week is on the immediate horizon. With more leisure time, men have, quite naturally, taken on some of the household chores that only a short while ago they wouldn't have been caught dead at, and have assumed some of the cultural responsibilities which were once the domain of their wives. They have also, with time on their hands and cars at their disposal, turned again to many kinds of rural recreation . . . to fishing and hunting, especially, but also to sailing and skiing. The most solitary of all sports, fishing, is also the most popular of all sports with American men.

The Cash Value of the Devil's Work. But the greatest assault on old patterns of leisure and on the shibboleths about devil's work for idle hands, has been industry's discovery that it needs the consuming time of workers as much as it needs their producing time. In an economy, geared as ours is to making life comfortable for everyone, it is essential to business that people have time to enjoy their comfort and to use up the things that make life comfortable.

A tremendous part of our production plant is committed to promoting leisure—to automobiles, to television sets, to time-saving gadgets, to sports equipment, and to hundreds of services which are unnecessary to life but which contribute to relaxed living. Our economy, in other words, is more and more involved with Time Off. Think of the industries, the purveyors of pleasure, that would collapse if we were to go back to the sixty-hour week. It looks as though we were far more likely (and not because of pressures from labor but the demands of technology and automation) to go to a twenty-eight hour week.

Urbanization, the shorter working day and week, and the changing roles of the sexes have, heaven knows, produced tremendous changes in the ways Americans live. But the premium put on the consuming time of the worker by our economic system presents us with a tidily packaged moral dilemma. When idleness is a public virtue, what becomes of the moral value of work? What are we going to substitute for the old adages on which we were brought up? What are we going to tell our children? What will happen to the economy if we go on saying that virtue is its own reward, that work is good for the soul, and that leisure is only a reward for toil? What happens to the Calvinist ethic?

This is a problem I would rather refer to a dilettante than to an economist or a clergyman or certainly to an engineer. The economist would consider it from the point of view of wealth, the clergyman of the after life, and the engineer of production. The dilettante can be counted on to look at it from the point of view of life, liberty, and especially the pursuit of happiness.

A Special Kind of Lover. I would like to contend in all seriousness, at this moment when there is such a cry for engineers and when our theological seminaries are bursting at the doors, that what we need is more dilettantes. Compared with good dilettantes, good engineers and good clergymen are a dime a dozen. Every newspaper account of the engineering shortage is contradicted by another story of how big corporations are hoarding engineers the way people hoarded butter during the war. Recently, Dr. Robert J. Havighurst of the University of Chicago made it quite clear that the number of engineers and technologists being trained in our technical schools is more than adequate to our needs; the shortage, he said, is in good teachers. In the long run our civilization will be measured more accurately by our know-why than by our know-how.

It is probably because in the triumvirate of our ideals—life, liberty, and the pursuit of happiness—the last of these has always seemed to our Calvinist society rather naughty, that we have come to look down our noses at the dilettante. We have dismissed him as a trifler; we have despised him as a parasite on other people's work, the fritterer, the gadfly. But there was a time when the word dilettante was by no means the term of opprobrium it has become.

Originally *dilettante* meant a lover of the fine arts (it comes from the Latin word for delight) and it was used to distinguish the consumer from the producer. Its application spread beyond the arts in England, and in the eighteenth century the Society of the Dilettanti was a club of influential men interested not only in the arts but in the sciences and in archaeology. It meant the man of intellectual curiosity who devoted part of his time to the intelligent cultivation of the arts and sciences, to the resources of leisure and the satisfactions of the mind.

If you transplant the idea of the eighteenth-century dilettante from England to America, you discover that he was Thomas Jefferson and Benjamin Franklin—one a farmer who dabbled in architecture and introduced a new style to America, the other a printer who dabbled in natural science and flew a kite into a thunderstorm. You discover several others who got together and started a talkfest that became the Philosophical Society of Philadelphia, and others who, dabbling in the arts, somehow founded a string of distinguished museums across the nation and filled them with masterpieces, and, of course, a good many bad guesses. These men were dilettantes. There is no other word that fits them.

In the nineteenth century the word came on hard times. "The connoisseur is 'one who knows,' as opposed to the dilettante who 'only thinks he knows'," said F. W. Fairholt in the 1850s. Fairholt, an antiquary who wrote among other things *A Dictionary of Terms in Art,* was, there is no question, a connoisseur, and like all experts he was impatient of non-scholars who pretended to the delights he reserved for himself and his kind. A connoisseur, he said, "is cognisant of the true principles of Art, and can fully appreciate them. He is of a higher grade than the amateur, and more nearly approaches the artist." In his definition of an amateur he puts the emphasis on his "skill" as a performer and his non-professionalism, just as we do today, and in his definition of the dilettante, while he acknowledges the seriousness of the original meaning of the word, he bemoans the dilettante's pretentiousness and his use of the arts for purposes of social climbing. He admits (as people who consider themselves connoisseurs today rarely admit, however far they may go in buttering up the dilettante for their own purposes) that the arts need the enthusiasm that the dilettante's support brings to them.

The trouble (and it is a trouble) is that, with the decline of the word *dilettante,* there is no word left to describe the enthusiast who is more serious than the fan, less knowledgeable than the connoisseur, and hasn't the skill that makes an amateur. (The amateur is, after all, basically a performer.) What we need in our society, I contend again, is more real dilettantes, and we need to extend the meaning of the word to many delights besides the arts and sciences.

The dilettante is just a consumer. He is a man who takes the pursuit of happiness seriously, not frivolously, and he works at it. He is part sensualist, part intellectual, and part enthusiast. He is also likely to be a proselytizer for those causes in which his interests are involved, and to be rather scornful of those people who do not take their pleasures seriously and who are passive instead of active in the cultivation of them. But whatever else he may be he is not lazy. He may or may not have a job that he finds interesting, but he does not use his leisure in a miscellaneous and undirected fashion. He knows what he wants out of life and will go to a lot of trouble to get it. Primarily, in Voltaire's sense, he wants to cultivate his own garden.

The Crank on Quality. You will find dilettantes everywhere and in every aspect of our culture. I found one a few weeks ago driving a taxi in New York. He was a man in his early sixties.

"I only drive this hack three days a week," he said. "The other four days I go fishing. I like to fish and I'm pretty good at it."

By the time he had delivered me home I knew what he fished for at what times of year, what bait he used and where and in what weather, and which were the best fishing boats and captains going out of New York harbor. I asked him what he did with all the fish he caught.

"I got a son-in-law runs a saloon," he said. "I give them to his customers."

Probably the most common and in some ways the most accomplished of American dilettantes is the baseball fan, though the national pastime is being crowded out of its position as top banana of entertainment these days by serious music. The baseball fan knows his subject with something very close to genuine scholarship. He is an expert in the minutiae of its history and understands the nuances and subtleties of its performance. He takes as much pleasure from the refinements of its details as from the outcome of any single game, and he enjoys the company of others with whom he can argue the relative virtues of performance and make comparisons with other similar situations. He demands skill on the field of a truly professional caliber, and he lets his displeasure with anything less be known in the most direct and uncompromising manner. He is, by and large, a less tolerant dilettante than the one whose interest is devoted to art, for his expert eye is less subject to changes in fashion. Unquestionably without him the standards of baseball would long since have gone to pot.

The simple fact is that the dilettante is the ideal consumer, not ideal, perhaps, from the point of view of those producers who would like their customers to accept their products with blind confidence, but ideal from the point of view of maintaining standards of quality . . . whether material or cultural. He takes his functions as a consumer seriously. He takes the trouble to know what he likes and to sort out the shoddy and the meretricious from the sound and reasonable. If he is a dilettante of music, for example, he demands the best performance from his record-player. He is unimpressed by an intimation mahogany cabinet in the Chippendale manner, but he knows that the components of his hi-fi equipment are the very best that he can afford. (He can, in fact, be credited with the very great improvement in mass-produced sound equipment; it was his interest in high-fidelity that spread the word to the general public and raised the level of public acceptance.)

We are likely to associate the dilettante only with the arts, which is one reason why he has such a bad name in America. In the rambunctious and expansive days of the nineteenth century when America was growing and fighting its way across the continent, toil was man's business; culture was left to women. So were most other refinements of life, and the arts were thought of as sissy and men who showed any interest in them as something less than virile. A man who didn't sleep through a concert or an opera was regarded with suspicion. It was only when a man retired from business that it was considered suitable for him to spend his money on art—not necessarily because he liked it or knew anything about it but because it gave him social prestige. Except in a few Eastern Seaboard cities, the arts were women's work, and there was no time and place for the dilettante.

The Ascent of Babbitt. The nature of our new-found leisure is rapidly changing the old stereotypes. The businessman who doesn't make some pretense at an interest in culture, who doesn't support the local symphony and museum, who isn't on the library board or out raising money for his college is looked upon as not doing his duty, much less serving his own interests. Babbitt isn't Babbitt any more. Babbitt is by way of becoming a dilettante. A lot worse things could happen to him. In no time at all being a dilettante will not be considered un-American.

The point at which the dilettante becomes an "expert" but not a "professional" is an indistinct one. Two successful businessmen who have, in their leisure time, become naturalists of considerable reputation are an officer of J. P. Morgan & Co., R. Gordon Wasson, who has recently produced an important book of original research on mushrooms, and Boughton Cobb, a textile manufacturer who is one of the world's leading authorities on ferns. A few years ago an ancient language known to scholars as "Minoan Linear B" that had had scholars completely at sea for years was "broken" by an English architect, Michael Ventris, for whom cryptanalysis was a leisure activity. These three men became experts, not professionals, dilettantes in the best sense, not amateurs.

Obviously not many men in any generation are going to be able to extend their leisure activities to such levels of distinctions. But leisure without direction, without the satisfaction of accomplishment of some sort is debilitating to anyone brought up in an atmosphere, like ours, in which the virtues of work have been so long extolled and are so deeply imbedded in our mythology. The greatest satisfaction of the dilettante is not in doing but in discovering, in discriminating, and in enjoying the fruits of his knowledge and his taste.

There will, of course, always be those who can only find satisfaction in making something, the eternal do-it-yourselfers, the cabinetmakers, and needlepointers, and gardeners, and model builders, and rug hookers. These are the amateur craftsmen who often achieve professional competence. There are also those who will find their only satisfactions apart from work in sensuous pleasures, in sports, and food and drink, and love. The dilettante finds his satisfactions primarily in the mind. He is the ideal traveler, the perfect audience, the coveted reader, and the perceptive collector.

Is He a Highbrow? But he is not by any means necessarily a highbrow. Indeed the ideal dilettante is not. He may be a professional intellectual or he may not, but he does not pose as what he isn't. His tastes and his knowledge may well run to abstruse and esoteric things, to the dances of Tibet or the jewelry of pre-Columbian Mexico, but they may just as well run to the square dance and baseball cards. The dilettante of jazz, the man who knows the names of the instrumentalists in all of the great bands of the last thirty years, is as important a dilettante as the man who knows his Mozart by Koechel numbers. It is genuine, not simulated, enthusiasm that counts. The function of the dilettante is to encourage a high degree of performance in whatever field of interest happens to be his, to be an informed, but by no means conventional, critic, and to be a watchdog. He must be both an enthusiast and an irritant who will praise what measures up to his standards and needle producers into doing as well as they know how, and better. He is an incorrigible asker of hard questions. He keeps controversy in our culture alive, and if he is sometimes proved to be dead wrong, he is at least never dead on his feet. He is the want-to-know-why man and the traditional anathema of the know-how man.

Several months ago I found myself in an argument, or the beginnings of one, in a radio interview with a well-known broadcaster. "Our colleges need to produce more and better trained men," he said, and I countered with the suggestion that they needed to produce better educated men. "We need experts," he said.

"We need dilettantes," I replied, and the word so surprised him that he gingerly changed the subject to safer ground.

I would like to change my position, but only slightly. What we need are trained men with the capacity for being dilettantes. There can be no argument with the fact that an industrialized society must have a great many highly trained men and women with specialized knowledge and skills. But in this country the consumers and the producers are the same people; all of us work both sides of the economic street. We are, the great majority of us, the part-time idle rich, and no nation, so far as I know, has ever found itself in such a position before. Ours is a society in which no man's nose need be permanently to the grindstone, and where every man is a potential dilettante.

We have thought of our know-how as our most exportable commodity, and when somebody else demonstrated, moon-fashion, a superior know-how, we took it as a blow to our "national prestige." In fact our most exportable commodity has been a cultural one, a way of life that balances work and leisure for almost everyone and distributes the fruits of labor with astonishing, if not complete, evenness. Our most effective know-how has been in the production of leisure, a commodity filled with promise and booby traps. It is the engineer with his slide rule who knows how to produce leisure, but it is the dilettante who knows how to use it and make it productive.

It will be as dilettantes and consumers that we will, in the long run, determine the quality of our culture. We will determine not only the gadgets of our civilization but the fate of its arts as well. We will determine whether the pursuit of happiness has, after all, been worth it.

Less Work—Less Leisure

By HARVEY SWADOS

I regard the five-day week as an unworthy ideal . . . More work and better work is a more inspiring and worthier motto than less work and more pay . . . It is better not to trifle or tamper with God's laws.

—John E. Edgerton, President of the National Association of Manufacturers (1926).

Reprinted from the *Nation*, Volume 186, Number 8 (February 22, 1958), pp. 153-58 by permission of the publisher. (Copyright 1958 by the Nation Company.)

TIMES HAVE changed since the gentleman quoted above invoked the Deity in opposition to Henry Ford's revolutionary five-day week. Not that hard-pressed executives ceased thereafter to cite divine guidance as the source of their labor relations. A decade after Mr. Edgerton pointed to the Lord, sit-down strikers at the largest rubber plant in the world, Akron's Goodyear plant, provided one of the first tests of the new C.I.O., and in a nineteen-below-zero St. Valentine's Day blizzard, the scraggly crowd of determined workers marched up Market Street into the teeth of the gale. Little more than a year later, in March, 1937, the 10,000 workers of the Akron Firestone plant struck after four years of futile effort to get the company to recognize their union. Harvey Firestone was at his estate in Miami Beach. The teletype from Akron to Harbel Villa kept Mr. Firestone informed, but, we are assured by the authorized Firestone biographer, it "did not alleviate his feeling of distress at this cleavage. 'When the strike broke out in Akron it jarred me for a day or two. Then I concluded there must be some reason for it and that we could not help it, but the thing we should do was not to fight it but to stand on what we thought was right and then let matters stand, as it was God's will we were to have a strike and there was a good reason for it, and it would be righted in the right time. . . .' "

In the Akron of today, it is hard indeed to realize that it was only twenty years ago that Harvey Firestone sent that philosophical message to his son, that it was only twenty years ago that the Firestone strikers threw up shacks of canvas, wood and tin as picket shelters at the freezing factory gates. Now this industrial city is clean, prosperous and not slum-ridden, and to the casual visitor the workers themselves are transformed, too; they are no longer the grimly huddled proletarians of those terrible and dramatic days. At a glance, they seem to epitomize the publicity ideal of the smiling middle-class American. And the union that helped to lead them out of the pit of the depression, the United Rubber Workers, is today not merely a well-housed and comfortably situated fraternal organization; it is a democratically-operated, decently-administered labor union, properly and profoundly concerned with the naggingly complex problems of its membership, and still so proud of its militant origins that it disputes with its big brother union, the Auto Workers, the claim to originating the weapon of the sit-down strike.

Just as it is hard to realize that the affable, self-assured workers cruising Akron's streets in late-model cars are often the same men who pounded up those streets as defiant strikers two decades ago, so it is hard to believe that much of the present leadership of their union, from President L. H. Buckmaster on down, consists of the very same men who founded the union and endured beatings and imprisonment in the course of their early struggles. Yet you will bump into them as you travel around town—George Bass in the International Office, Joe Childs at a restaurant, Jack Little at a meeting of his local; men whose names are already legendary, but who give the impression—along with the union's rank-and-file activists and "politicians"—of being more worried about the immediate future than proud of their accomplishments in what is already the remote past. Indeed, one might almost be tempted to characterize this mood, particularly among the rank and file, as one of uncertainty, of tentativeness of direction, of lack of confidence in whatever the ultimate goals may be. It is a mood strikingly different from the explosive élan of those who went out and built the C.I.O. because they were convinced beyond question that they were going to convert the rotten life of the American worker into the good life.

Ever since those dismal depression days, a portion of Akron's rubber workers have worked a six-hour day and a six-day week. The six-hour day was first instituted by the companies as a work-sharing (or poverty-sharing) device, but soon became so popular with the workers that they wrote it into their union constitution (one of their constitutionally-enshrined objectives is "To establish the six-hour day and the thirty-hour work-week with wage increases to compensate for the shorter time so that there will be no reduction in weekly earnings from such action"), and into their contracts with the Big Four of the rubber industry. Today it is an emotionally-charged article of belief, and even the most cursory inquirer in Akron soon becomes convinced that the delegate from Local 101 to the union's 1956 Los Angeles convention was hardly exaggerating when he cried from the floor: "We in the six-hour plant regard it as almost a religion."

It is this unique long-time experience with the shorter work-day that has lately made Akron a focus of interest as a possible forecast of what all America will be like in the era of the less-than-forty-hour week, an era that presently seems inevitable even if the Deity should once again be invoked by those who oppose its arrival. Already the town has been researched and written-up by *Fortune* and the *Wall Street Journal,* and it is increasingly referred to by those who write about and ponder the problems that will attend the shorter work-week: will people use the increased leisure wisely? will workers tend to hunt up second jobs? what will the social effects eventually be?

Unquestionably, the outlines of the social pattern of the future are here to be seen. But the first thing the visitor learns is the complexity of that pattern, and certainly before we are so brash as to generalize from this unique industrial instance we should at least note some of the special factors that must be taken into consideration in any speculation about the uses of leisure.

First, although about 30,000 rubber workers do work a six-hour day, six days a week, with the plants operating four shifts a day, they represent only about 15 per cent of the employees of the rubber industry. Most rubber workers, by special contractual agreements, are now on a straight eight-hour day with premium pay if they work the sixth day.

Second, even in some of the six-hour shops there are departments or divisions (mostly the crafts) which work eight-hour shifts.

Third, in only two cities outside Akron do Rubber Workers' locals have six-hour contracts.

(These first three points acquire a special significance when you realize that the hourly rate for the eight-hour man is contractually lower, even for the same work, than that of the man in the six-hour plant—but that he may take home somewhat more money if his plant regularly works a sixth or overtime day. To put it mildly, the union membership is not united on the question of which working day is better.)

Fourth, Akron cannot be regarded as a typical American industrial city, if only because its population is virtually homogeneous with a relatively small percentage of immigrants. They call Akron "the capital of West Virginia." It would seem obvious that people who have come up by the thousands out of the hill country to make steady money building tires are going to use their leisure somewhat differently from those who came over from Europe to make ladies' garments or pig iron, but also to escape oppression and to build a future for their children.

Fifth, the city is relatively characterless—partly because the Southerners are still so deeply rooted in their home country that they return at every opportunity, and partly because the rubber barons have not seen fit to dispense largesse in any considerable amount in the community which produces their wealth or to indulge locally in those leisure-class hobbies which have given other cities their symphonies and art galleries.

Sixth, it seems most unlikely that any general shortening of working hours across the country will follow the unique Akron pattern. More probably we are going to see unions pressing for work-weeks like the Garment Workers' seven-hour, five-day week, or the Auto Workers' momentarily-abandoned, but very much alive proposed eight-hour, four-day week. The difference in effect of each system is almost incalculable. For example, who is going to be more willing and able to work at a second job: the man who works a six-hour, six-day week, or the one who will work an eight-hour, four-day week?

Seventh, there has been no large-scale, careful study of the uses of leisure by Akron rubber workers. With the exception of a cursory union survey, there has not been an attempt to find out exactly how many of them hold down a second job. Therefore, given the complexity of the six-hour-eight-hour pattern, no one can say with confidence that the man who works shorter hours does in fact lead a measurably different life—in terms of what he does with his off-hours—than his fellow on the more traditional eight-hour day. In all honesty we must be limited at this point to impressionistic hunches and conjectures, which in the present instance are based on observation and on conversation with workers.

What can we learn from the experience of these Americans who have been living with the short work-day for a generation? Quite a lot. First of all, the research director of the Akron Chamber of Commerce estimates that there are about 52,000 women workers in an Akron labor force of 195,000 persons. Now it is true that one out of three in the national labor force of some 65,000,000 is a woman, and that the Akron ratio is apparently somewhat smaller. But when you remember that Akron is primarily a city of heavy industry, the figure is staggering—particularly when you learn that some 60 per cent of the Akron working women are married. In short, 30,000 housewives in this irea are not only housewives but wage-earners too, and not on an emergency wartime basis but as steady workers, accumulating seniority, looking for paid vacations and working toward retirement pensions alongside their men.

Not exactly alongside, however. The wife in Chicago or New York who works will probably leave home with her husband in the morning and meet him at home for supper. Not so in Akron, where the four six-hour rubber-plant shifts make it easier for the wife to work a shift which will still enable her to keep house, and for the husband to work one which will enable him to baby-sit while his wife works. If, in addition, he has a *second* job, which as we will see is often the case, he is going to be able to spend only a few hours a week alone with his wife. Their children, often looked after by grandma or by baby-sitters, are causing heads to shake anxiously over increasing juvenile delinquency. Togetherness is never going to penetrate very far into the household where the adults are holding down multiple jobs; for every three marriage licenses issued here last year, there was one suit filed for divorce. And we have to bear in mind that this looks more and more like a permanent phenomenon, as working wives strive not just for that extra paycheck (the federal government takes a healthy bite out of it every year), but for security, for hospitalization, medical care, vacations, pensions.

We might note parenthetically at this point that a Gallup poll taken last year indicated that, on a national basis, women were opposed to the idea of a four-day week by a three-to-one margin. No reasons were given, but it seems only logical that a housewife who normally puts in a twelve-hour day and must continue to do so (like the farmers, who were predictably opposed to the four-day week by a four-to-one margin) would resent such a lightening of the burden of others. Besides, there is the fear that the husband who is off for three days may become less responsible, drink more, run around more. Nevertheless, I should be very much surprised if a poll were to show anything like this feeling among the women of Akron, who have learned from experience that the shorter day gives them more of what they want—even if it is only the opportunity to go out and become wage-earners themselves.

What else have the Akron rubber workers been doing with those extra hours? The stroller down South Main Street on a Monday evening, when the stores are open late, will get one or two ideas, provided he isn't run over (per capita auto registration here last year was second only to Los Angeles). Husbands and wives are clustered in the brilliantly-lit do-it-yourself supermarkets, picking over wall-coverings for the bathroom and floor-coverings for the rumpus room. Home ownership is high—seven out of ten Akron families live in their own homes—and men who work only six hours a day can put in a good deal of time fixing and repairing, building a garage, paving a driveway, adding an extra room.

The bowling alleys are jammed, the poolrooms do well, the neighboring waters are stocked with power boats, and last year Summit County sold the fantastic number of 67,400 hunting and fishing licenses to local residents (there are a little over 300,000 people in Akron).

The churches can't complain, either. The people up from West Virginia, Kentucky and Tennessee take their religion seriously, many of them tithe as a matter of course and of conscience, and they go in heavily for revivalism and fundamentalism. The Temple of Healing Stripes has free bus service to its Divine Healing Services; evangelists hold Old Fashioned Brush-Arbor Revivals and show Signs! Wonders! Miracles! every night in the summertime; and Rex Humbard is supervising construction of the Cathedral of Tomorrow, Calvary Temple, The Largest Church Auditorium Built In This Generation.

Other cultural manifestations are somewhat more muted. Living theatre is practically non-existent, there is no professional symphony, and although the Public Library is good, one can search the city in vain for a bookshop devoted to selling new books. (There are, to be sure, several which specialize in ecclesiastical tracts of various denominations, and a shop in the very shadow of a rubber plant which, despite the protestations of its owner that he caters to a steady clientele of "bookworms," seems to attract primarily young workers looking for what the proprietor calls "strictly legal" sex and girlie books.)

At this level, then, Akron rubber workers do not seem to spend their extra off-hours very differently from their brothers across America. What the others are doing, *they* are doing—and then some. We can even say this of the one big question not touched on thus far, the second job. A Federal Census Bureau survey published in the summer of 1957 found some 3,700,000 persons to be multiple job-holders. This figure is about double what it had been six years before, and it works out to about 5.5 per cent of the country's total employed.

Now there cannot be a single person in Akron who would claim—although everyone is guessing—that the percentage of rubber workers holding down two jobs is that low. Best guesses seem to agree that anywhere from one in seven down to one in five rubber workers hold a second full-time job, with a small fraction even managing two jobs on different shifts at different rubber plants. In addition, something like 40 per cent engage in some sort of part-time outside work. With such a discrepancy between the Akron picture and the national picture, the inference would seem obvious, although there are many rubber workers who heatedly deny it: the shorter day, even with a higher pay scale, increases the number of men who obtain second jobs as garage attendants, taxi drivers, bellhops, grocers, butchers, clerks, insurance salesmen, realtors, brokers, barbers, repairmen, bakers—yes, and engineers too.

I am afraid that what I have said thus far has a cold and clammy ring to it; but the general picture must be clear before we can attempt to understand its meaning in the lives of the individual actors—the workers themselves. It is to be expected that *Time,* surveying the "moonlighting" (two-job) situation, should point out that there are those who "hail moonlighters as heirs to the spirt of the nation's founders and insist that hard work never hurt anybody." But when Arthur Schlesinger, Jr., asserted last fall that "The most dangerous threat hanging over American society is the threat of leisure . . . and those who have the least preparation for leisure will have the most of it," one wonders whether he realized that it was the *enforced* leisure of the layoff that was soon to threaten American workers, and that all too often it was the memory of previous enforced leisure that was driving them into moonlighting, into destroying their leisure by racing from one job to the other while the jobs were still there to be had?

It is unlikely that Mr. Schlesinger was thinking in these terms. One can agree with his warning only if one takes a long-term view; it can hardly be immediately comforting to those workers who have not accumulated sufficient seniority to avoid being laid off in the current slump, like the two ladies with fourteen years' seniority who sat biting their lips, jobless, in an Akron coffee shop. Or (to cite a perhaps less suspect source), like Kenneth Marxmiller of the Caterpillar plant in Peoria. "It affects my wife more than me," said Mr. Marxmiller to a *Life* reporter (January 27, 1958). "She just sits and cries. . . ."

Nor is it likely that Mr. Schlesinger could foresee how rapidly his analysis would be vulgarized into the grossest sort of caricature. The *Saturday Evening Post* of January 11, 1958, has a short story entitled Holiday for Howie and subtitled: *At first glance it seemed terrific, a four-day work week! But when he found there was a catch in it. . . .* The catch, it turns out, is that Howie rapidly gets bored with all that leisure. He takes to sleeping late on those long weekends, and when his wife declines to go gallivanting around the country with him (her responsibility to house and children continues on his days off), he looks up an old school friend, now a rich bachelor leading an idle, dissolute life. They drink together, which is what Howie had been looking forward to, but the friend reveals that he is not really happy or free; he is drinking himself to death from boredom and loneliness. Shocked, Howie goes to the beach to Think Things Out:

> He hadn't learned to handle time. All he could do was try to kill it. . . . And all the while, crazily, more time being made. Household gadgets to save time for the housewife, for what? So that she can spend the afternoon playing cards? And all the freeways built to save time, for what? So that people traveling at breakneck speed can get home ten minutes earlier to have an extra cocktail before dinner? And science adding years to a man's life, for what? So that at eighty he can learn to dance? . . . Speed, and time to be filled, is that all our civilization has contributed? He felt like crying and he didn't know why.

Lying there, Howie discovers the secret—Time opens out for him into Eternity. He hurries home to explain this to his wife—a large order—and to tell her that he has decided to take a second job, one which will fill two of his three free days, because:

"... Time is not for me. Some people can handle it. I can't...."

"Oh, Howie." There was love and admiration in her muffled voice. And vague regret.

"Cheer up, Doll. Think what we can do with the extra money—lots of things. Think what we can get—a new car, with all the gadgets! Color TV! Air conditioning! We'll really be living! Smile, Doll!"

It is characteristic of the corrupt sub-literature of the mass media, as it used to be of Fascist propaganda, that it is thoroughly capable of seizing on some of the most agonizing and centrally important human problems and distorting them into grotesque and semi-comic horror stories, which relate only weirdly to the way people really think and feel.

Then what do the workers believe? Every Akron worker with any consciousness of his position in society starts with one unalterable and clearly-understood premise: he is a member of a declining labor force. On November 1, 1951, the Goodrich plant in Akron had 11,475 employees on its rolls; on May 4, 1956, it had 8,500 employees. It is true that the company moved some of its operations to more modern and hence more competitive plants elsewhere, as well as to plants working eight-hour shifts (with lower hourly rates); but this only serves to sharpen the worker's realization that automation, rationalization and continually developing industrial technology are, before his very eyes, cutting down on the number of human beings needed to manufacture goods.

He sees himself in a situation not unlike that of the farmer. With productivity steadily increasing at the rate of about 3 per cent a year, he will be able to protect himself and his family only by moving from the manufacture of goods to the delivery of services, as the farmers have gradually moved to the cities (the two-job situation can be partially interpreted as the beginning of such a shift—very often the second job is a service job, whether it be cutting hair or selling real estate), or by spending less hours per week producing goods. I was not too surprised to hear several workers say that they believed eventually the government would have to subsidize labor as it has subsidized the farmer. "You can call this socialism if you want," one added aggressively. "The point is the problem is bigger than we are and it has to be solved in a big way."

Here again is something the Akron worker has come to see: the problem of the shorter work-week, of increased leisure versus a second job, is bigger than he is, it is bigger even than his 220,000-member union, and it has implications that may make it too big even for his senior partner, the million-membered Auto Workers Union, whose lead he has traditionally followed (although the development of the plastic industry and of such products as foam rubber and pliofilm are making Akron somewhat less directly dependent on Detroit's prosperity). And he is badly split.

He is split not only when an eight-hour local opposes a six-hour local (the international union, which has been seriously trying to achieve work-week uniformity so that it can bargain across the country for pay-rate uniformity, presented its program clumsily to the last convention and was voted down by the six-hour men and the abstainers). He is split in discussions within his own local. And most serious and pregnant of all, he is sorely split in his own mind.

Every rubber worker with whom I spoke was agreed that the rising unemployment in Akron would vanish at once if all men working second jobs were to leave them. Were they therefore agreed that all two-jobbers should be compelled to give up the second job? No.

Again, no one knows for sure, but there seems to be a consensus that the men who are out moonlighting are mostly in the thirty-five to fifty age bracket. Men older than that often have their homes paid off; their wants are more modest; they are looking forward to retirement and pension. They are over the hump. The youngsters in the six-hour shops have never worked any longer hours; this seems plenty long enough to spend in a filthy, noisy place where the acrid stench of hot rubber is never absent. And some of them can and do go to Akron University while they are working. It is the men who remember the depression who apparently comprise the bulk of the two-jobbers—they and the young men with wives and children who have concurrent payments to meet (sometimes of staggering amounts) on house, car, TV, furniture and appliances. And, as the very men who oppose the two-job frenzy demand: "Can you blame them?"

What is wrong, then, with a man going out and getting a second job? In reply the workers themselves will tell you horror stories far more shocking than any dreamed up by a slick fictioneer. They will tell you of a Negro worker found to have twelve years of seniority at one rubber plant and thirteen at another, and finally forced to choose between them, when the fact that he had been working seventy-two hours a week not for a few months, but for a dozen years, was brought to light. They will tell you of workers taking second jobs at small independent eight-hour rubber shops and being told frankly by their new boss that he had secured contracts on the basis of their working for him for less than the union scale in the Big Four. They will tell you of two men splitting an eight-hour shift at a gas station in their "leisure" time, and thus depriving one job-hunter of full-time work. They will tell you of their brother union members driving cabs for scab wages, cutting hair for scab wages, painting houses for scab wages. They will tell you of their terrible shame when a member of their union's policy committee was found working a second job as a salesman in a department store even while the store was being picketed by the Retail Clerks' union for not paying a decent minimum wage. They will insist that the rubber companies themselves look the other way when a worker takes a second job (unless his efficiency is drastically lowered), because they know that the man with two jobs will be less likely to attend union meetings, that he will more easily accede to downgrading, that in general he will be far less militant than the man who relies solely on the income from his job in the rubber plant.

And then, almost in the same breath, they will say that this is a free country; that you can't stop a man from trying to get ahead; that if a man wants to drive himself to death for the privilege of sleeping in a $30,000 house it is his privilege; and that it is only reasonable for a man still as basically insecure as an industrial worker to make it while he can, to catch up while times are still good, to acquire some of the luxuries while they are still within his grasp.

Is this a preview of America's (and indeed the industralized world's) future? As the work-week shrinks, will we be treated to the spectacle not of thousands, but of millions of workers scrambling to undercut one another, protected in the primary job by their union and bidding their labor for secondary employment at ruinously low rates? Will leisure become a term of mockery covering *longer* hours spent in working to obtain, and then to replace, household objects carefully engineered for rapid obsolescence? On this point, at any rate, some of the workers mix faith and optimism. They tend to agree, although they put it differently, with the magazine *Factory Management and Maintenance* (November, 1956), that the "Crux of the matter, on either a four- or five-day week, is whether general economic conditions and the worker's pay scale would put pressure on him to carry a second job for the added income, or allow him to enjoy the added leisure of a four-day week with a single job."

But the road toward that happy day is going to be, and is now, hard, rocky and painful. "Certainly it should not be expected that there should be eight hours of pay for six hours of work," Goodyear's Board Chairman P. W. Litchfield and President E. J. Thomas told their employees in 1953. Despite the fact that they did not invoke the Deity, they were not fooling. Employers generally are going to resist the better pay-less hours onslaught with everything they've got; unions will be forced by the logic of the situation to carry that onslaught forward with everything they've got.

When the dust has settled—and a good many human beings have suffered in the struggle to achieve it—we will probably find ourselves in the era of the shorter work-week. *Then* Mr. Schlesinger's warning of a populace trained to work but not to live will be seen in all its force—and in all likelihood it may be too late to do anything about it in a missile-maddened, consumption-crazy society premised on lunacy and buttressed by hypocrisy. It is not to be expected that the unions, deeply absorbed as they are in daily grievance wrangles and protracted contractual fights, are going to devote themselves to thoroughgoing studies and forecasts of the leisure hours of their membership. Besides, as one tough but weary old militant put it to me ruefully: "We've been so worried these past years about subversives that we haven't hired or inspired any of the young hotheads. The banks and the law firms aren't afraid of the independent-minded kids—they snap them up—but we've been scared of radicals here in the union and as a result we're not attracting the kind of minds who could help us plan for a different future, the way we used to attract them when we were first organizing."

The problem of what two hundred million of us will do with our increasing leisure time—and just as we have been watching Akron, so two billion will be watching the two hundred million—is so awesome in its magnitude as to be terrifying. Isn't that all the more reason for it to capture the imagination of our younger generation of social scientists, as the conquest of other worlds is supposed to be capturing the imagination of the physical scientists?

We must persist in the confidence that the best of the new intellectuals will break free of the internal isolationism, the exclusive concern with career and family, which has preoccupied them in common with most Americans for the past decade and more, and will undertake audaciously the task of outlining a social order in which both work and leisure will be rationally based. What is needed is a social order in which, most important of all, the masses of man will be protected against the swelling flood of "entertainment" opiates in order that they may be energized to search freely for new patterns of spontaneous living for themselves and their children.

Leisure and Work in Post-Industrial Society

By DAVID RIESMAN

To THE REST of the world, the American has characteristically appeared as someone who could not stand being idle or alone, someone who rushes about, whether in work or play, and is preternaturally restless. Tocqueville for instance observed, "No men are less addicted to reverie than the citizens of a democracy."[1] It is important to recall this pre-industrial image of America lest we assume that industrialization, the automobile, or television are responsible for what Clifton Fadiman deplores as "the decline of attention": the "American" way preceded the inventions which gave that way added scope. Like Tocqueville, Lewis Mumford, in his remarkable book, *The Transformations of Man,*[2] discusses these changes from Old World to New World life, suggesting that the Americans, released by social and geographic space from age-old limits and norms, have exhibited from the beginning an

---

This paper is developed from a lecture, given January 27th, 1958, in a series on "The American Future" sponsored at the University of Chicago by the Division of the Social Sciences and the College. It is a publication of the Center for the Study of Leisure, established at the University under a grant from the Ford Foundation. In footnotes I have sought to take account of some of the points raised in the question-and-answer period which followed the lecture. I have drawn on an earlier article, "Abundance for What?" in *Problems of United States Economic Development, vol. I.* (New York: Committee on Economic Development, 1958), pp. 223-234; reprinted in the *Bulletin of Atomic Scientists,* vol. 14 (1958), pp. 135-139.

exuberance and vitality, a romantic strenuousness, that in their respective ways both Emerson and Whitman represented and celebrated.

I MASS LEISURE: THE END OF SUMPTUARY TRADITIONS

At the present time, two processes are going on simultaneously. On the one hand, a decline of exuberance is just barely noticeable in America, making itself felt particularly among the more highly educated and the well-to-do in a loss of appetite for work and perhaps even for leisure. On the other hand, the spread of industrialization and of the mass media are bringing both the residual pockets of traditionalism within this country and the great areas of it outside into a more "American" pattern. Whatever a nation's political or religious ideology, mass culture continues to spread, even ahead of industrialization, bringing the disruption of old ways and the lure of a new hedonism (as most dramatically seen in the cargo cults of the Pacific islanders which combine a nativist revival with the belief that the white man's goods can be obtained, without the white man himself, by appropriate rituals[3]).

I recently saw a documentary film focused on a family living in the hills of Tennessee in the 1930s–a family with many children and many dogs, eking out a bare existence. Despite efforts to insure minimal schooling, knowledge of the outside world scarcely percolated. Today, despite remaining pockets of abysmal misery, many of the very Tennessee shacks where, before the coming of the TVA, life resembled that in other peasant and pre-industrial cultures, are equipped with television aerials that now bring in not only the local boys who made good with a guitar, like Elvis Presley, but all the insignia of making good which pass as currency in the nation at large: cars, clothes, washers (which are often put on the front porch), and general styles of life and leisure. Some of the farms even in this area have become nearly as over-mechanized, and hence engaged in "conspicuous production," as the richer agricultural areas of the North; horses and mules are disappearing, and the South is catching up with the rest of the country in per capita ownership of automobiles. (In that sense, the North is finally winning the Civil War, whatever resistances can be focused around racism—a theme that W. J. Cash already foresaw in his prophetic book, *The Mind of the South.*)

Indeed, Southerners coming North, white or Negro, Caribbean or native, have replaced the immigrants from Southern Europe as fodder, not for the machines of production so much as for those of consumption; for coming from a pre-industrial culture they lack sales resistance, let alone consumer sophistication: entering, if not the high-wage economy, at least the high-credit one, they are being "processed" as consumers, while escaping, because of their late arrival, some of the drill and exhausting hours that met earlier pre-industrial cadres entering the work force of industrial society.

They enter a society which has over the past eighty years taken in the form of leisure or free time approximately a third of the gains in productivity which industrialism and organization have achieved. (The average work-week now hovers around forty hours, as contrasted with seventy hours in 1850 and, in many industries and on the farms, nearly as much as that as late as 1920.) When the Bantu who works, let us say, in Johannesburg, has attained an increment over his old standard of living, he is likely to quit and return to the reservation; few of these Americans have a reservation to return to;[4] consequently, the Americans remain rather steadily at work while having time enough left on their hands for learning how to spend money in accordance with, and just beyond, their new wages.

This injection at the bottom is, I believe, responsible for much of the American economy of leisure, and more than makes up for the withdrawal of those people in the educated strata (whose attitudes we shall discuss more fully later) who no longer find in the purchase of possessions a sufficient agenda for living. (There still remain in America some more or less permanently underprivileged enclaves, principally among the old, the infirm, and among the less agile and mobile Negroes and poor whites in the South.)

But it is those who have recently been released from underprivilege by mass production and mass leisure who have gained, along with an often meaningless political vote, an often influential voice in the direction of consumption and hence of production. It is, for instance, the very millions whom Henry Ford helped release from drudgery who eventually defeated his ascetic and still rural canons of taste; it is they who like borax furniture or juke-box culture; their aesthetic is akin to that of all deracinated peasants whose folk culture crumbles at the first exposure to mass-produced commodities.[5]

Even in countries formerly run by an elite or presently run by a dictatorship, the same democratization and vulgarization of taste make themselves felt. The British mass press and the Butlin Holiday Camps are more than the equal of our Hearst papers and our own vacation "culture."[6] Likewise, although the newly urbanized in the Soviet Union may read a few more books and go to fewer movies, and will surely spend less time aimlessly driving about, their Parks of Culture and Rest are hardly more elevating than Coney Island; their privileged youth appears to be even more bored and delinquent; and the documentary realism of their art and its general lack of subtlety are being steadily outgrown in America. What distinguishes the Soviet Union is that it still has the goal of catching up with America and still possesses millions of unsatiated and eager buyers.

II TECHNOLOGICAL OVERPRIVILEGE

As many thoughtful people have recognized, our society offers little in the way of re-education for those who have been torn away from their traditional culture and suddenly exposed to all the blandishments of mass culture —even the churches which follow the hillbillies to the city often make use of the same "hard sell" that the advertisers and politicians do. In the past, the relatively voluntary nature of the immigration to this country, and the belief in progress of natives and immigrants alike, have tended to blind us to the casualties of transplantation. There are a few exceptions. For example, in the 1930s I admired the Rust brothers, inventors of the cotton picker, who hesitated to market their invention because they were worried about technological unemployment among Southern workers. (They were as unconvinced of the gospel of progress as were the members of the Advisory Committee which recommended under Oppenheimer's leadership against proceeding with the H-bomb.) It is ironical to reflect that this invention came along just in time to save some Southern fields from utter desertion—not only because Negroes and poor whites were leaving for the cities in the North but also because the cotton picking machine, as a form of conspicuous production, frees its operator from work which has long been considered dirty work and thus raises the status of the operator: it is the counterpart on the production side of today's Tennessee shack, electrified and gadget-filled. Even so, I think that the Rusts' scruples were well taken: people should not be ruthlessly torn away even from their incapacities and given the industrial bends: this country is rich enough and inventive enough to make social provision for a moratorium and retraining in those instances where uprooting is inescapable.

For many people today, the sudden onrush of leisure is a version of technological unemployment: their education has not prepared them for it and the creation of new wants at their expense moves faster than their ability to order and assimilate these wants.[7]

III THE CONSERVATIVE BELIEF IN PROGRESS

In the mercantilist era, and even today in the countries of grinding poverty, the creation of new wants has been a first step towards a better life and wider horizons of choice. But in the United States today, the belief that one cannot stop invention, cannot stop technological progress, has itself become a tradition, indeed a form of realistic insanity, or what C. Wright Mills calls "crackpot realism." Although adult Americans, contrary to European impression, are not dazzled by machines as such—but simply want to have those appurtenances that betoken an appropriate style of life—we are nevertheless half-willing slaves of the machine process itself. Even big business, thanks to the anti-trust laws and to the potential competition of small business, does not quite have sufficient control of the market to plan to its own liking the sequence of applied technology. A fortiori, it seems inconceivable to Americans that we could reduce the aggression our technology keeps up against our traditions and the texture of our lives—and we can always use the competition of the Russians to counter any tendency within ourselves to relax the rate of growth or to question the belief in growth as a value per se.

To be sure, the optimism of the booster was once much stronger in America than it is now. The ideal of manifest destiny, which took us across the continent and held the South bound to the Union in the Civil War, infects now only those perpetually adolescent males who are eager to conquer space or the planet Venus.[8] But the booster psychology has for so long been built into our culture and into our patterns of individual and group achievement that we tend to take for granted the notion that growth in population, in assets, in national income, is inevitable if not always desirable. Imagine the outcry, for instance, and not only from Catholics, against any suggestion that people be encouraged in this country to practice birth control, let us say, by removing the tax concession for child dependents or by instituting a sales tax on children's toys and clothes, or even by pointing out forcefully to people some of the less happy consequences of an exploding population.[9] For most Americans still believe that the future can take care of itself, or at any rate that we are not required to do anything to make it easier, less crowded, less full of friction, for our decendants. (In the same way, on a far smaller and simpler and less controversial issue, it seems almost impossible to cut down the growth of our autos in size and horsepower, let alone to forbid them from entering our downtown areas without good cause shown. Instead, everything else has to adjust to the auto: our central cities must tear down homes and tear up parks to provide those highways that, as Mumford has often pointed out, only brings more cars in an endless vicious spiral.)[10]

In other words, we have become a conservative country, despite our worldwide reputation for seeking novelty, in that we are unable to envisage alternative futures for ourselves. In an illuminating essay, John Kouwenhoven has suggested that a certain style of extrapolative thinking and designing is characteristically American.[11] He referred there to the way we have laid out our cities in gridiron blocks, to our assembly lines and consecutive sections, to our skyscrapers in serried stories. He pointed to our continuous flow of comic strips, movies, the stanzas of our popular music; he might have added our football cheers, and our seriatim credits and terms as one passes through the educational plant. Though no one of these is unique to America, it can be argued that our way of thinking tends to be extrapolative: we add one story to another, one thing to another, one frame to another: we think in terms of additives.

IV THE ABYSS OF LEISURE

So, too, it has been until recent years in the field of leisure time—so much so that my collaborators and I in *The Lonely Crowd* took it for granted that it was impossible to reverse the trend towards automation; we assumed that the current efforts to make work more meaningful—which by and large succeeded only in making it more time-consuming and gregarious but not more challenging—might as well be given up, with the meaning of life to be sought henceforth in the creative use of leisure. We failed to see, in the famous Marxist phrase, that "quantity changes into quality" and that there would come a point where additional increments of leisure would prove more stultifying than satisfying and that the mass of men would be incapable of absorbing any more.

The situation confronting Americans—and, as already indicated, in due course the rest of the industrially advanced countries also—is historically unprecedented. In pre-industrial cultures leisure is scarcely a burden or a "problem" because it is built into the ritual and groundplan of life for which people are conditioned in childhood; often they possess a relatively timeless attitude towards events. Likewise, the tiny leisure classes of the past would sometimes be able to absorb what seems like an overdose of leisure because they lived in an era when work itself was thought demeaning and when free citizens engaged in physical and intellectual self-cultivation and in the arts of war and government—they, so to speak, exercised their leisure on behalf of the whole society. During this era, which lasted throughout most of history, it was inconceivable that the mass of men could support a large and growing leisure class, let alone join such a class themselves. Yet today we live in such a world. The rich and leisured are no longer drastically set apart, but seek for the sake of their souls as well as their public relations to work with relative sobriety and consume with relative modesty and inconspicuousness; thus, they no longer set an example for either good or ill.[12]

At the present time, the closest thing we have to the traditional ideology of the leisure class is a group of artists and intellectuals who regard their work as play and their play as work. For such people, and for the larger group of professional people whom we shall discuss later, work frequently provides the central focus of life without necessarily being compartmentalized from the rest of life either by its drudgery and severity or by its precariousness. At best, the painter may always be seeing and the poet and writer always envisaging, although with greater or lesser intensity and concentration.

V WORK AS A PSYCHOLOGICAL STABILIZER

Such considerations and reconsiderations led the Center for the Study of Leisure to decide in 1957 to examine the prospects of the four-day week in manufacturing industry and to initiate conversations with union officials concerning the bearing of such a pattern of work on the leisure activities of the workers. At that time Walter Reuther and the UAW were contemplating such a week and other union leaders were also interested in it as a possibility. We were curious about the effects on employees of receiving an unexpected and unplanned-for dividend of leisure. Accordingly, when a small aircraft parts manufacturer in Southern California unilaterally decided to give its employees a four-day week at the beginning of each month, with Monday off (to be made up by working one Saturday at the end of the week), Rolf Meyersohn, Research Director of the Center, went to the spot and began to question workers concerning their reactions to the new plan. The periodic interviewing of these employees is presently under way; and *in medias re* it is, of course, not possible to say just what the research will turn up. But, so far, it would seem that the employees have accepted the idea of a four-day week readily enough and without Puritan inhibitions or misgivings; the only major problems appear to arise from the fact that the rest of the family is not as yet on a similar schedule. One could argue indeed that Southern California can absorb increments of leisure more readily than can other parts of the country: many of the employees have camps in the hills or boats in the water.

In fact, in a Roper Poll taken in the summer of 1957 concerning attitudes towards a possible four-day week, it turned out that there were some distinct regional differences as well as differences among people of different age and economic levels (although differences in education were the most pronounced). Strikingly enough, in the Far West a third of the respondents would use an additional day to take another job—in part apparently to get still more money to spend in the remaining time off or in a later stage of the life cycle. Contrastingly, the Southerners were least able to come up with ideas about what they would do with the extra day: do-it-yourself was less in evidence, as were hobbies, sports, and trips. College graduates incidentally were the most trip-prone: 47% would take trips as against 19% who had had only a grade school education; likewise, the college graduate also had a far greater interest in participant sports. Older people (who are also people of lesser education) were somewhat more worried about the possibility that people would get soft and lazy while younger people were somewhat more likely (27% to 19%) to believe that with the extra time people would relax more, enjoy themselves more, and be happier.

On the whole, this survey did not turn up great eagerness for an extra day (nor did a somewhat comparable Gallup survey). In our own more limited inquiries we have discovered many wives who are aghast at the thought of having their husbands around the house for a still-longer "lost weekend" —and not a few husbands who are not notably eager for what they term "honey-do" days; that is, days at home when their wives ask them, "Honey, do this!" and "Honey, do that!"

An informal poll of a union local (conducted by James Carper) found that the leaders did want a shorter work week whereas the rank and file did not. This was interpreted as suggesting that the leaders, better educated and more enterprising, feel cramped for time to do everything they want to—to read more books, to see more of their families, to take more adult education courses. Such men already had many hobbies, including being union leaders. But the less active members (no doubt including many who might tell the union leaders that they "lack time to go to meetings") had no similar feeling of wanting the days to be longer. Such men, asked what they would do with an extra day, sometimes say, "sleep"; others could use it in hunting season—and already did so to the dismay of the foreman.

Union leaders have pointed out to me that a lack of any experience with extensive leisure may be responsible for the frequent breakdown and anomic reactions among men forced to retire, regardless of the medical and recreational facilities that may be provided for the retired. Moreover, these officials have envisaged the impact of automation on their industry as well-nigh complete, and they have described to me what was already occurring: namely, the creation of many jobs which consist of little more than half-attentive dial watching of nearly self-corrective automatic machinery—machinery which, if it does break down, requires the services of specialists.[13] Envisaging a continuing decline in working hours, either through a four-day week or the six-hour day of the rubber workers, these thoughtful men have felt that leisure has to take up the slack in work, providing both the challenges and the variations of monotony that can no longer be found in work.

Certainly, there is plenty of evidence that even as things stand, unskilled industrial workers do not like their work, although some enjoy the companionship it provides.[14] In a study by Nancy Morse and Robert Weiss,[15] some 80% of such workers stated they they, in effect, kept on working for lack of alternatives, not for positive satisfactions. These workers were asked whether they would go on working even if there were no financial need to do so, and they said they would, although also indicating that the job itself (and in many cases any job they could imagine) was boring and without meaning in its own terms. This clinging to the job is not simply a legacy of the Puritan ethic: it is rather a legacy of industrialism itself, of the old structures it has destroyed and the new structures it has created. Nor, in Mr. Weiss's opinion, is it merely the feeling of shame in not having a job which is involved (although this is certainly an element). Work may not be an active presence in the life of these workers, but its absence would be an active absence. Or, more accurately, it is not so much "work" that would be missed as having a job: it doesn't have to be, and should preferably not be, hard work, nor need it even be gregarious work, but rather the self-definition (these data refer only to male workers) that comes from holding a job and the punctuations of life provided by regular employment. Putting together the still incomplete data from the four-day week studies and from the study by Nancy Morse and Robert Weiss, it would seem that there is a difference in kind between a four-day or three-day week and a no-day week—a difference which leisure in its present versions and for people of this level of education cannot possibly fill.[16] These workers, in other words, are too intelligent and too well educated to accept the routine of most factory work, while being still a long way away from the education of the artist or intellectual who can in some measure create his own work with a minimum of outside structuring.[17]

Such considerations concerning the limits of leisure suggest that it might be easier to make leisure more meaningful if one at the same time could make work more demanding. When work itself is infiltrated with leisure (as it is today in many jobs where the time-study man has been stymied), leisure may lose its savor, often becoming not much more than a continuation outside the plant of the sociability and inanity that go on within the plant. It might be slightly less difficult to reorganize work routines so that they became less routine, more challenging, and hence more instructive, than to cope all at once with the burdens placed on leisure by the evaporation of the meaning of work. This evaporation has occurred as a result of the same commercial and industrial developments that have turned leisure from a communal affair, celebrated by festivals or other shared activities, into an individualized pursuit, hence a "problem." Thus, we have lost not only, as already indicated, the folk traditions that have in many cultures integrated work and leisure, but also those that have integrated leisure with the community's framework (in Fromm's terms) or orientation and devotion. In this situation, I believe that we cannot take advantage of what remains of our pre-industrial heritage to make leisure more creative, individually and socially, if work is not creative, too. And not only have we lost the folk and peasant traditions: we are rapidly losing those which have developed under industrialism itself—whether of the John Henry variety or of the free-swearing, free-swinging construction engineer who gets roads and dams built: such legends hold little allure in an opulent society, even when building continues at a rapid pace. It is from the Soviet Union that the story comes of a mill foreman who, though complaining of his pay, says he "must be content with the 'thrill of producing something anyway.' "[18] Though he may have been speaking in part for the record, there is no doubt that production remains exciting for many where industrialism is the unfinished business of a rising power. Americans, however, cannot artificially recreate that atmosphere; we cannot make factory or other industrial and commercial work over on the model of army basic training or campcraft just to make it hard (though in fact many workers do enjoy making a game of output, for instance, working up the line on an assembly-line, in order to establish control and dramatize their activity). One alternative is to redesign our factories with an eye to the educational or challenging quality of each job, following the example set by some industrial units which have eliminated assembly lines and are giving workers larger units to assemble, or what is sometimes termed "job enlargement." The march of specialization which had originally been based on steam production but has in our day become an end in itself with its own dynamic and momentum could thereby be reversed.[19] Undoubtedly, work flows could be redesigned to maximize the demands on the worker's intelligence, while retaining present advances in making work quiet, free of dirt, and relatively unstrenuous.[20]

VI LEISURE — SOCIETY'S BLOTTING PAPER

It has become clear that post-industrial society no longer requires arduous and routinized work on the one hand, or, on the other hand, that kind of seemingly varied work, such as that of the salesman, in which the worker is compelled to exploit his own personality. Nevertheless, I have been arguing that Americans remain too unequivocally the children of industry, even when automation threatens to disinherit us, for us to be able to resort to leisure as a counterbalance for the deficiencies of work. Even so, leisure is coming to occupy for adults something of the position the school already occupies for youngsters, of being the institution which seems "available" to bear the brunt of all society's derelictions in other spheres. Thus, just as schools are asked to become quasi-parental, quasi-custodial, quasi-psychiatric, and quasi-everything else, filling in for tasks other institutions leave undone or badly done, with the result that the schools often cannot do their job of education adequately; so leisure is now being required to take up the energies left untapped everywhere else in our social order, with the result that it often fails in its original task of recreation for most of us most of the time and of creativity for some of us some of the time. The hopes I had put on leisure (in *The Lonely Crowd*) reflect, I suppose, my despair about the possibility of making work in modern society more meaningful and more demanding for the mass of men—a need which has come upon us so rapidly that the taste of abundance we have had in the past now threatens to turn into a glut.

My despair on this score, I must add, was not greatly alleviated by the feeling in the group of union leaders mentioned above that it was impossible either to get unions or management in the least interested in making work more humanly satisfying. I hoped the union leaders might cooperate with management in, so to speak, turning the engineers around, and forcing them to design men back into their machines rather than out of them. In this connection, I recall talking with aircraft engineers who were irritated with the "human factor," and eager to put a machine wherever a man might go wrong, rather than to design equipment that maximized the still enormous resourcefulness of the human mind. I recall the highway engineers who designed thruways that would look good to other engineers or to engineering-minded Americans—until the death toll made them realize that boredom could be a greater danger to man than speed and obstacles. And I thought of the subdividers who bulldozed down all trees to make it easier to build a road or a suburb, with no authorities around to forbid such wanton simplification of their own task along with such destruction of history and life. As the discussion with the union officials continued, it became clearer to me that the workers themselves were too much of this same school of engineering thought really to believe in the reorganization of industry.[21] The kind of utopia of meaningful work pictured in Percival and Paul Goodman's book, *Communitas,*[22] made no sense to them.

In this perspective, the rebellion of workers against modern industry is usually mere rebellion, mere goofing off. Many are quite prepared to go on wildcat strikes (Daniel Bell notes that in 1954-55 there were forty such in just one Westinghouse plant in East Pittsburgh); they are quite prepared to deceive the time-study man and to catch forty winks on the night shift, and otherwise to sabotage full production while still "making out" in terms of the group's norms—being in this like students who might cheat on exams or cut classes but could not conceive of reorganization of the curriculum or of asking for heavier assignments. The great victory of modern industry is that even its victims, the bored workers, cannot imagine any other way of organizing work, now that the tradition of the early nineteenth century Luddites, who smashed machines, has disappeared with the general acceptance of progress. We must thus think of restriction of output and other sabotage of production as mere symptoms.[23]

Furthermore, the resentment which manifests itself in these symptoms helps engender a vicious circle, since it confirms the opinion of management that workers must be disciplined by bringing them together in great factories and subjecting them to the relentless pressure of assembly lines—as against the possibility, for instance, that work could be decentralized so that workers would not have to commute long distances and could proceed more at their own pace and place.[24] In the high-wage industries given over to "conspicuous production," management has the resources to be concerned with the amenities of work—the group harmony, the decor, the cafeteria and other ancillary services—and to make provision for the worker's leisure, such as bowling teams, golf courses, and adult education courses too; in fact, a whole range of extracurricular pleasures and benefits. Sometimes these benefits include profit-sharing, but they are much less likely to include decision-sharing, for of course managers object less to giving away money, especially money that would otherwise go to stockholders or to the government in taxes, than to giving away power and prestige and freedom of action to workers whose unionized demands reflect merely their discontent and scarcely at all their desires for reconstruction.[25]

It is obvious in addition that managers are not free to reorganize their plants in order to provide their workers with a more satisfying work environment, if this might risk higher costs, unless their competitors are prepared to go along. Yet competition is not the whole story, for the situation is hardly better and is often worse in nationalized industries in Great Britain and Western Europe generally, while the situation of industrial workers in the Soviet Union today reminds one of the worst excesses of the Victorian era and the earlier days of the Industrial Revolution in the West. Managers of whatever ideological stripe seek to measure themselves against a single, unidimensional standard by which they can judge performance and thus are drawn to simplified work routines and an unremitting drive for maximum output. To open the possible consideration of factories as making not only things but also men, and as providing not only comfort and pay but also challenge and education, this would itself be a challenge to the way we have assimilated technology for the last three hundred years; and it would compel us to search for more Gestaltist and amorphous standards, in which we were no longer so clear as to what is process and what is product. There have, to be sure, been paternalistic employers (such as the Lowell mills in the 1840s or the Pullman plant a half-century ago) concerned with the education and uplift of their operatives—often to the eventual resentment and unionization of the latter (who felt it was enough to have to work for the bosses without imitating their preferred inhibitions). But these were efforts to compensate outside the plant for the dehumanization regarded as inevitable within. What I am asking for now is hardly less than reorganizing work itself so that man can live humanely on as well as off the job.

VII STRENUOUS WORK

The work of the managers themselves, of course, striving to get out production in the face of technical and human obstacles, is seldom boring, although if the product itself is socially valueless, a point may be reached where work upon it, despite technical challenges, is felt as stultifying. Indeed, one could argue that the great disparities of privilege today are in the realm of the nature of work rather than in the nature of compensation: it has proved easier partially to equalize the latter through high-wage and tax policies than to begin at all on the former, which would require still greater readjustments. In that brilliant precursor of much contemporary science-fiction, Aldous Huxley's *Brave New World,* the lower cadres are given over to fairly undiluted hedonism while serious work and thought are reserved for the ruling "Alphas." Likewise, a recent science-fiction story once more illuminates the issue (it is my impression that science-fiction is almost the only genuinely subversive new literature in wide circulation today[26]) : this is a story by Frederick Pohl called "The Midas Plague" which pictures a society in which the upper classes are privileged by being allowed to spend less time and zeal in enforced consumption; they are permitted to live in smaller houses and to keep busy fewer robots in performing services for them.[27] Their ration points–rations to extend rather than to limit consumption–are fewer; their cars are smaller; the things and gadgets that surround them are less oppressive. Best of all, they are allowed to work at work rather than having to spend four or five days a week simply as voracious consumers. That is, as one rises in the status system by excelling at consumership, one is allowed a larger and larger scope for what Veblen called the instinct of workmanship.

As already indicated, the world presented in "The Midas Plague," as in so much science-fiction, is all too little a fiction. For, if we except a number of farmers and skilled workers, such as tool and die makers, it is the professional and executive groups who at present have the most demanding and interesting work and for whom, at least until retirement, leisure is least a time to kill. The study by Nancy Morse and Robert Weiss referred to earlier indicates that on the whole these groups find most satisfaction in their work. A survey by *Fortune* last year showed that top executives, despite giving the appearance of being relaxed and taking it easy as our mores demand, work an average of sixty hours a week or more. In many other fields, the leisure revolution has increased the demands on those who service the leisure of others or who have charge of keeping the economy and the society, or considerable segments of it, from falling apart. High civil servants and diplomats probably work as hard or harder than ever–indeed it is not easy today to imagine writers like Hawthorne or Trollope holding civil service sinecures as a way of supporting themselves as novelists. Many priests and ministers, with expanding parishes and congregations, and with more and more expected of them in the way of ancillary services, find themselves as busy as any top executive. The same is true of a good many teachers and professors who are presumably training others to spend their leisure wisely! Physicians are notorious for their coronaries and their lack of care for their own health and comfort: as the public has more and more time to spend with doctors (often a kind of window shopping on themselves) and as there are fewer doctors in proportion to wealth and population, the medical men are forced to work seventy hours a week to pay for their monopoly position, their glamor, their high incomes, and their prestige. (The doctors at least have aides and antibiotics to help them out, but teachers and other ill-paid service workers have no similar labor-saving devices.) All in all, as I have suggested, those who are privileged in being able to choose their own work are becoming increasingly underprivileged with respect to leisure and perhaps also with respect to the pace at which, in the face of the waiting customers, they must respond to the demands upon them. A polarization is occurring between the toiling classes and the leisure masses.

In our egalitarian society, however, it would be surprising if the attitude of the masses did not influence the classes (there are of course also influences running the other way). As I remarked at the outset, I have the impression that a general decline is occurring in the zest for work, a decline which is affecting even those professional and intellectual groups whose complaint to their wives that they are over-worked has often in the past been a way of concealing the fact that their work interested them rather more than did their wives. To return to the case of the doctors, for example, there is some slight evidence that application lists to medical school are no longer so full, a decline which is attributed to the belief among young people that medical education is too arduous and takes too long before one is stabilized on a plateau of suburban life and domesticity.[28] Similar tendencies would appear to be affecting those already in medical school. Howard S. Becker and Blanche Geer report (from the study of medical education at the University of Kansas being carried out under the direction of Professor Everett C. Hughes) that the teaching faculty complains that the students are no longer as interested in the more theoretical or scientific aspects of medicine: three-quarters of them are married and, instead of sitting around waiting for night duty or talking about their work, they are eager to go home, help the wife get dinner, and relax with television.

Likewise, there is evidence that young men in the big law firms, although they still work harder than most of their clients, do not glory in putting in night work and weekend hours as they once did. And several architects have told me that similar changes are showing up even in this field, which is famous for the enthusiasm of its devotees and the zest for work built up during *charettes* at architectural school. (Possibly, this may reflect in part the loss of the enthusiasm of the crusade on behalf of "modern" and the routinization of what had once been an esoteric creed.)

If such tendencies are showing up in the professions to which, in the past, men have been most devoted, it is not surprising that they should also be appearing in large-scale business enterprise. Though top executives may work as hard as ever—in part perhaps because, being trained in an earlier day, they can hardly help doing so—their subordinates are somewhat less work-minded. The recruiters who visit college campuses in order to sign up promising seniors or graduate students for large corporations have frequently noted that the students appear at least as interested in the fringe benefits as in the nature of the work itself; I would myself interpret this to signify that they have given up the notion that the work itself can be exciting and have an outlook which is not so very different from that of the typical labor union member: they want and expect more but not so very much more than the latter. Certainly, if fiction is any clue (of course, it is at best an unreliable clue) to prevailing attitudes, the current crop of business novels is revealing, for it indicates a marked change from an earlier era of energetic if ruthless tycoons. In *The Man in the Grey Flannel Suit,* for instance, the hero, Tom Rath, chooses the quiet suburban life and domesticity over the chance for large stakes and large decisions, but possible ulcers, in a big broadcasting company. He does so after discovering that his boss, powerful and dynamic, is estranged from everything in life that matters: from his wife, his daughter, and himself—his work is only an escape. Likewise, in *Executive Suite,* there is an analogous picture of the old tycoon who is wedded to his work and isolated by it, contrasted with the young hero whose work is at once not so strenuous and more playful and "creative."

The movement to the suburbs is of course a factor in these developments, especially now that young men move to the suburbs not only for the sake of their wives and young children and the latter's schooling but also for their own sake. It is hard, for example, for a scientific laboratory to maintain a night-time climate of intense intellectual enthusiasm when its professional cadres are scattered over many suburbs and when the five-day week has become increasingly standard throughout American life (outside of a few universities which cling to the older five and a half day pattern). The sport-shirted relaxed suburban culture presents a standing "reproach" to the professional man who works at night and Saturdays instead of mowing the lawn, helping the Little League baseball team, and joining in neighborly low-pressure sociability. The suburbs continue the pattern of the fraternity house in making it hard for an individual to be a ratebuster or an isolate.

It is difficult to form a just estimate of the extent and scope of these changes. It is not new for the older generation to bewail the indolence of the young, and there is a tendency for the latter to maintain much of the older ethic screened by a new semantics and an altered ideology. Moreover, Americans in earlier periods were not uniformly work-minded. In Horace Greeley's account of his famous trip West in 1859 (which ended in his interviewing Brigham Young), he commented with disgust on the many squatters on Kansas homesteads who, in contrast to the industrious Mormons, sat around improvidently, building decent shelter neither for themselves nor for their stock (they sound a bit like Erskine Caldwell types).[29] Similarly, the correspondence of railroad managers in the last century (and railroad managers were perhaps the most professional managerial groups as they were in charge of the largest enterprises) is full of complaints about the lack of labor discipline; this is one reason that the Chinese were brought in to work on the transcontinental roads. There were, it is evident, many backsliders in the earlier era from the all-pervading gospel of work, and the frontier, like many city slums, harbored a number of drifters.[30] Today, in contrast, the gospel of work is far less tenacious and overbearing, but at the same time the labor force as a whole is post-industrial in the sense of having lost much of its pre-industrial resistance to the clock and to factory discipline generally.[31]

VIII STRENUOUS LEISURE

So far, I have largely been discussing the uneven distribution of leisure in terms of differential attitudes towards work in different occupational groups. In comparison with the achievements of our occupational sociology, however, we have little comparable information concerning the sociology of leisure. For instance, we have very few inventories of how leisure is actually spent (apart from fairly complete information concerning exposure to the mass media). Pitirim Sorokin before World War II[32] and more recently Albert J. Reiss, Jr.[33] have tried to get people to keep diaries which would include accounts of their day-by-day use of leisure time; but these suffer from faulty memory and stereotyping (people often say, "one day is just like another," and report accordingly) as well as from omissions of fights and other improper activities. A more systematic study than most, by Alfred Clarke, found that radio and TV listening were the top two activities for both upper and lower prestige groups, followed by studying in the upper group and do-it-yourself activities in the lower.[34] The latter spend much more time just driving around, as well as polishing the car; they also spend much more time in taverns. Only in the upper group do people go out to parties, as against simply dropping in on a neighbor to look at TV or chat in the kitchen; and going to meetings is also largely confined to the upper group. In both groups, commercial recreation outside the home, such as going to the movies, plays little part. This and other, more impressionistic studies point to the conclusion that the busier people, the professional and executives and better-educated groups generally, also lead a more active life in their time away from work; as the saying goes, they work hard and play hard. In Reiss's study, for example, there turned up a surgeon at a leading hospital who went to mass every morning, then to the hospital, then to attend to his private practice; he belonged to about every community organization, and he and his wife entertained three or four nights a week. Contrastingly, at the other end of the social scale, the unemployed as we know from several studies have in a psychological sense no leisure time at all; they, and the underprivileged generally, do not belong to voluntary associations (churches and unions are an occasional exception); they live what is often a shorter life on a slower timetable.

At the same time, as I have indicated above, it is among the less privileged groups relatively new to leisure and consumption that the zest for possessions retains something of its pristine energy. Consumership which is complex if not jaded among the better-educated strata seems to be relatively unequivocal among those recently released from poverty and constriction of choice (although since the recession began, some of the latter may feel that they have been too ready victims for advertising and salesmanship and easy credit). With very little hope of making work more meaningful, these people look to their leisure time and consumership for the satisfactions and pride previously denied them by the social order.

I am suggesting here that millions of Americans, coming suddenly upon the inheritance of abundance, are able like other nouveau riche people in the past to coast upon the goals set out for them by their social and economic pace-setters. "Coast" is perhaps not the right word for so energetic a movement, one which continues to power the economy, as millions are moved out of dire poverty and subsistence into the strata which have some discretionary spending power; while in better educated strata the absence of goals for leisure and consumption is beginning, or so I would contend, to make itself felt. In these latter groups, it is no longer so easy to regard progress simply in terms of "more": more money, more free time, more things. There is a search for something more real as the basis for life, a search reflected in the vogue of psychoanalysis, of self-help books (and, in a few circles, of theology), of the growth of adult education courses which are non-vocational, and in the more serious non-fiction reading which is reflected in many of the new series of paperbound books. Such Americans are not satisfied simply to attain material comfort far beyond what their parents possessed or beyond what obtains in most parts of the globe. In fact, the younger generation of reasonably well-off and well-educated Americans do not seem to me drivingly or basically materialistic; they have little ferocious desire for things for their own sake, let alone money or land for its own sake. At most it could be said that such Americans resent being deprived of those things they are supposed to have; consequently, they remain susceptible to advertising which tempts them with the halo of experience or associations surrounding goods—although not with the goods themselves as sheer objects. Hence in these strata there is a tendency for people, once accustomed to upper-middle-class norms, to lose eagerness for bounteous spending on consumer goods. Moreover, such Americans tend more and more to secure their children's future, not by large capital acquisitions and inheritances, but by giving them a good education and the motives for achievement that go with it; they will try to pass on their values as an insurance of continuing middle-class position, rather than their possessions and their specific place in the occupational scheme. It is in such relatively sophisticated Americans that we can see foreshadowed a decline of interest in material goods that may be a long time appearing in the working class and lower white-collar groups.

Indeed, the amenities which such educated people desire, once their own families are well provided for, are not those which can be bought by individuals acting in isolation from each other. They are rather such social goods as pleasant cities and sprawl-free countrysides; adequate public services, including transport; educational and cultural facilities which stimulate all ages and stages; freedom from crowding in the sites of leisure; and in general, wise and magnanimous use of the surplus which individuals at this level no longer need. But it is just at this point that the paucity of our individual goals, when amplified at the general social level, creates the most terrifying problems.

IX ABUNDANCE FOR WHAT?

Even the most confident economists cannot adequately picture a society which could readily stow away the goods likely to descend upon us in the next fifteen years (assuming only a modest rise in annual productivity), with any really sizable drop in defense expenditures. People who are forced by the recession or by fear of their neighbors' envy or by their own misgivings to postpone for a year the purchase of a new car may discover that a new car every three years instead of every two is quite satisfactory. And once they have two cars, a swimming pool and a boat, and summer and winter vacations, what then?

Increasingly, as we all know, the motivation researchers are being pressed to answer these questions, and to discover what the public does not yet know that it "wants." Just as we are lowering our water table by ever-deeper artesian wells and in general digging ever deeper for other treasures of the earth, so we are sinking deeper and deeper wells into people in the hope of coming upon "motives" which can power the economy or some particular sector of it. I am suggesting that such digging, such forcing emotions to externalize themselves, cannot continue much longer without man running dry.

Even now, some of the surplus whose existence presents us with such questions is being absorbed in the very process of its creation but by what I have termed the "conspicuous production" of our big corporations, acting as junior partners of the welfare state and absorbing all sorts of ancillary services for their own members and their own communities.[35]

Defense expenditures loom so large in our political as well as economic horizon because they do offer an easy and seemingly feasible way out by creating goods which do not themselves create other goods. (They are "multipliers" only in a Keynesian sense.) But of course the international consequences as well as the long-range domestic ones point the way only to lunacy and the alternatives of destruction or the garrison state. Indeed in a recent article, "Economic Implications of Disarmament," Gerard Colm argues that it would be difficult to deploy for public services our rising productivity even without reducing defense expenditures.[36] He sees education as potentially absorbing much the largest part of the surplus (education must be seen even now as the greatest leisure time-killer we have, keeping out of the labor force an increasingly large portion of the young). And Colm presents figures for highway and other transport, along with other public works, hospitals, and water conservation—yet these altogether hardly make up in ten years what we spend in one year for our armed forces. I would contend that expenditures which serve no real social imperative, other than propping up the economy or subduing the sibling rivalry of the armed services, will eventually produce wasteful byproducts to slow that economy down in a tangle of vested inefficiencies, excessively conspicuous production, lowered work morale, and lack of purpose and genuine inventiveness.[37] The word "to soldier" means "to loaf" and conscription gives training in soldiering to a large proportion of the future work-force (despite islands of ascetism in the Strategic Air Command or the air-borne "brushfire" infantry). For a time, men will go on producing because they have got the habit, but the habit is not contagious. Men will scarcely go on producing as mere items in a multiplier effect or conscripts in an endless Cold War, nor will they greatly extend themselves to earn more money which they are increasingly bored with spending. To be sure, many workers have little objection to getting paid without "earning" it by traditional standards of effortfulness. And while those standards are usually irrelevant in a society of advanced technology and high expenditures on research and development, there are certainly many parts of the economy, notably in the service trades, whose gross inefficiency we only conceal from ourselves by contrasting America with pre-industrial societies or with those possessing far less adequate resources of men and machines—if we compare ourselves with the West Germans, for instance, or with the Canadians, the advance in our economy since 1946, great as it is in absolute terms, is unimpressive. The pockets of efficiency in our society are visible and made more so by the myth that we are efficient; hence, the evidence of disintegration and incompetence that is all around us strikes us as temporary or aberrant.

X THE DISLOCATION OF DESIRE

Correspondingly, some of our desires have been made highly visible by advertising and market research and lead to equally visible results such as good cars and, intermittently, good roads to drive them over. But other desires, which require cooperation to be effective, are often lamely organized and all but invisible. Thus, while some of us have a missionary zeal for learning, which we regard as the basis of later leisure as well as later employment, we have not been helped even by the push of sputnik to get a bill for school construction past the same Congress which eagerly voted Federal money for highways (in part, no doubt, because the annual maintenance of schools falls upon a local tax base which grows constantly more inadequate while the maintenance of highways can be more easily financed from gasoline and registration taxes).[38] Other services, not so clearly "a good thing" as secondary and university education, are even more lacking in organized institutional forms which would permit the channeling of our surplus in ways which would improve the quality and texture of daily life. For example, even the great demand for scenic beauty (anemically reflected in the new highways) cannot make itself politically felt in preserving the countryside against roadside slums and metropolitan expansion, while men of wealth are missing who could buy up whole counties and give them to the nation as a national park. We see one consequence on summer weekends when millions pour onto the roads and breathe each other's fumes and crowd each other's resorts. And we see too that leisure is cut down by the time taken to get to and from work—commuting time increased by the desire to live in the suburbs in order to enjoy leisure! As our resources dwindle in comparison with population and as individual abundance creates social blight, we will increasingly find little solace in leisure without privacy. It is extraordinary how little we have anticipated the problems of the bountiful future, other than to fall back on remedies which did not work in the less bountiful past, such as individualism, thrift, hard work, and enterprise on the one side, or harmony, togetherness, and friendliness on the other. Meanwhile, we stave off the fear of satiation in part by scanning the technological horizon for new goods which we will all learn to want, in part by the delaying tactic of a semi-planned recession, and, as already indicated, in part by the endless race of armaments.

That race has its cultural as well as Keynesian dynamic: as poll data show, a majority or large plurality of Americans expect war, though perhaps in a rather abstract way—war is one of those extrapolations from the past; like technological progress, we find it hard to resist. And, on the one hand, the threat of war is one factor in discouraging long-term plans, while, on the other hand, the continuation of the Cold War provides a sort of alternative to planning. Thus, there tends to be a state of suspended animation in the discussion concerning the quality of life a rich society should strive for; social inventiveness tends to be channeled into the defense of past gains rather than into ideas for a better proportionality between leisure and work. Like soldiers off duty, "as you were," we subsist in default of more humane hopes.

But I should add that no society has ever been in the same position as ours, of coming close to fulfilling the age-old dream of freedom from want, the dream of plenty. And I want to repeat that millions of Americans, perhaps still the great majority, find sufficient vitality in pursuit of that dream: the trip to the end of the consumer rainbow retains its magic for the previously deprived. It is only the minority where, looking further ahead, we can see already the signs of a generation, prepared for Paradise Lost, which does not know what to do with Paradise Found. Regrettably, it will not be given a long time to come to a decision. For, by concentrating all energies on preserving freedom from want and pressing for consumer satiation at ever more opulent levels, we jeopardize this achievement in a world where there are many more poor nations than rich ones and in which there are many more desires, even among ourselves, for things other than abundance.

Notes

1. *Democracy in America,* Phillips Bradley edition (New York: Knopf, 1945), vol. 2, page 208. Tocqueville had in mind the contrast with the members of an aristocratic society who had a smaller portion of discontent because people knew their place and, whether resignedly or not, remained in it; his view anticipated that of Durkheim.

2. New York: Harper's, 1956.

3. Cf., e.g., Margaret Mead, *New Lives for Old* (New York: William Morrow, 1955); also Daniel Lerner, *The Passing of Traditional Society* (Glencoe, Ill.: The Free Press, 1958).

4. To be sure, something analogous to a reservation exists in our urban and rural slums to which migrants come and in which they seek, despite pressures and temptations, to preserve enclaves of traditionalism. Conversely, even in Africa, the reservation, though geographically more stable, proves fragile in the face of the inducements and pressures of industrialism and urbanization.

5. The consequences of this overexposure, in the short and in the long run, are complex and are the themes of passionate debate (cf. the contributions to *Mass Culture* and especially Clement Greenberg's article, "Work and Leisure under Industrialism" in this volume). While I agree with Lyman Bryson that it is not right to judge a culture by its peaks of art and artisanship alone but that one must also judge it in terms of the total quality of its life [cf. *The Next America* (New York: Harper's, 1950)], Bryson is readier than I to sacrifice the peaks of aristocratic attainment to the plateaus of popular contentment, in part because perhaps we differ on how long the latter can last without the former.

Certainly, the role of the artist changes when his patrons are no longer the few but the many. In a traditional society with a small elite, he is ancillary to the elite: they patronize him and he serves them, and may remain unaffected by the attitudes and desires of the mass of the people—save as these furnish folk themes for his music or imagery. Even if patronized, he moves among those who count, whereas today the successful artist may be rich and famous and still not feel he knows anybody who counts. Artists and intellectuals in our time have a choice of constituencies: they may try to serve the traditional elite of culture and taste or the mass of people who for the first time in history have money enough to become patrons. This dilemma has driven some artists towards willful efforts to stave off mass understanding, whether by obscurities, sadism, or serious attitudes which are unpopular. The results of this have not always been bad for art—on the contrary—but they do curtail some of the possibilities for the artist by making obscurities sometimes seem attractive per se. Conversely, such artists as, let us say, the typical jazz musician who plays popular, feel that they have sold out to the largest purse; the same with painters who go commercial. Sometimes artists are thrown back upon their fellow artists as the only ones who understand this dilemma, but this does not always save an artist from being caught in the enormous machinery for disseminating his work if it catches hold. Indeed, if popular taste were utterly debased, then what is "high" and "low" could be clearly differentiated; but we have a situation of an infinite series of minute gradations in which it is not easy to say what is high-brow and upper-middle-brow and so on; thus, the Book-of-the-Month Club may circulate a very good book at times. As a result, the climate for the most intensive achievements of art and intellect has a good deal of smog in it: the artist does not necessarily starve but may be all too well patronized without giving him any sense that he has a genuine audience. Moreover, in an age of plenty, it may require more conviction for an artist to remain poor than when all but a few were poor. (I have profited from the clarifying discussion of these issues in Nathan Glazer's, "Technology, Mass Culture, and High Culture," a paper delivered at the American Sociological Society meetings, August, 1958).

6. This situation in Britain has recently been described in Richard Hoggart's eloquent *The Uses of Literacy: Changing Patterns in English Mass Culture* (Fairlawn, New Jersey: Essential Books, 1957).

7. Since the writing of this paper, John Kenneth Galbraith's clarifying book, *The Affluent Society* (Boston: Houghton Mifflin Company, 1958) has appeared. With superb understanding, Professor Galbraith shows how the fear of economic insecurity which haunts Americans makes us the victims of our own productive processes—processes which create and then supply the "wants" as well as the leisure we choose because we don't want the wants that much. Galbraith

also shows that the very primacy given to full production and full employment in the United States robs the economy of the flexibility that would permit diverting some of the surplus to wiping out the residual but stubborn poverty in this country and to making a dent on the vast and apparently increasing poverty of the non-industrialized world. And Galbraith sketches some of the political and ideological reasons why "high production" has become a goal, not only for dairy cows, but for human beings—a goal which is now shared by liberals and conservatives and, almost by definition, by economists.

8. The space age is not a safety valve for the luxury economy and for our overflowing energies. Although the comparison is often made, I believe there is a real difference between our space age and the exploration of this continent in the fifteenth and sixteenth centuries; at that time Europe was cramped and bound in all kinds of traditional constraints, and could find in colonization an opening for its growing population, its growing energies, its growing rationalism; the "best" use of the space frontier today would be to deflect our weapons—we can bombard Venus rather than each other.

9. For a better grasp of some of these problems, I am indebted to the writings of John R. Platt, Harrison Brown, and Richard L. Meier.

10. Cf. for a fuller discussion, Riesman and Eric Larrabee, "Autos in America: Manifest and Latent Destiny," in Lincoln Clark, ed., *Consumer Behavior* (New York: Harper's, 1958), pp. 69-92.

11. "What's American about America?" *Harper's,* vol. 213, no. 1274 (July, 1956).

12. It is however a very different story when one views the rich, not in their individual capacity, but in their collective capacity, whether corporate or national. For a brief discussion of the two economies, that of luxury and that of subsistence, which exist side by side even in America see my article, "The Suburban Sadness" in William Dobriner, ed., *The Suburban Community* (New York: G. P. Putnam, 1958), pages 393 and *sec.* And for discussion of America's wealth as a barrier in our relations with other nations, see my Introduction to Daniel Lerner's book, *Op. Cit.,* and "Human Relations and National Boundaries," *Comprendre,* 1958.

13. This is not to say that the machine as such is bad for man. I don't share the imagery of *Brave New World;* it is rather that we need more *social* science fiction, more social science imagination as well as technological imagination in the design of our work routines. What I am opposed to is unidimensional so-called technological progress which is measured purely in the easily defined terms of output and fails to take account of the total constituency involved in that output. Thus, some automation serves to reassemble jobs and makes severe demands on intelligence, analogous to working or at the switchboard of a power grid or programing a computer. Such work is meaningful and much more demanding of course than routinized assembly-line work. What we must do is make just this sort of judgment about the consequences for the worker and not simply plow ahead in what is wrongly called "automation," namely, further specialization and not quite total elimination of human beings.

14. The extent of this companionship may be exaggerated at present by industrial sociologists. See the study by Robert Dubin, "Industrial Workers' Worlds," in *Social Problems,* vol. 3 (1956), pp. 131-140, and reprinted in this volume.

15. "The Function and Meaning of Work and the Job," *American Sociological Review,* vol. 20 (1955), pp. 191-98. I am indebted to Mr. Weiss for many helpful suggestions.

16. Spanish-American workers are reported as being different in this respect: their feeling of masculine purpose and dignity does not depend on holding a job. See "Spanish Americans of New Mexico, U.S.A.," in Margaret Mead, ed., *Cultural Patterns and Technical Change* (New York: Mentor Books, 1955), pp. 164-165.

17. Many of the workers in the Morse-Weiss study harbor the vague hope of some day having a small business of their own, such as a gas station or television repair shop. So too the practice of "moonlighting" or holding two jobs testifies not only to the continuing inflation of consumer wants and of the corresponding prices, but also to the fact that many factory workers are like the Russian peasants who were drafted into the collective farms: they give a minimum quantum of their work to the factory as the peasants did to the farms, and save up their real energies for the "private plots" of their work outside. Cf. Ely Chinoy, *Automobile Workers and the American Dream* (New York: Doubleday, 1955), and Charles R. Walker and Robert H. Guest, *The Man on the Assembly Line* (Cambridge, Mass.: Harvard University Press, 1952).

18. See Max Frankel, *New York Times,* September 21, 1957, p. 3, col. 1.

19. See, e.g., Peter Drucker, *Concept of the Corporation* (New York: Harper's, 1946), and the brilliant discussion by Daniel Bell, *Work and Its Discontents: The Cult of Efficiency in America* (Boston: Beacon Press, 1956).

To be sure, there would always be a question whether the work were being complicated only by the energy of the work force to create a plot for the daily drama of life or because the total configuration had been reorganized so that the work and the workers were seen as a "single" product. Assuredly, such reorganization, like anything else, could become a gimmick of management but it need not do so.

20. Nelson Foote tells me of a case in Detroit some years ago where workers through their union insisted on their right to sing at work against the objections of a Puritanical management. I am indebted to Mr. Foote, and particularly to his unpublished paper on "Stultification at Work,"

for much illumination concerning the themes discussed in this paper.

21. It may be asked (and was) whether we can reverse our technical impetus and the trend towards automation without losing the very source of our leisure and our high productivity. In my opinion, we are already far past the point where we must be bound by such alternatives. In the great world of impoverished people with a very low life expectancy and the annual income of, let us say, an Indonesian villager, the question would answer itself: many people would be willing to sacrifice much for the greater amenity and ease of life Americans have. But if in America the changes I am recommending would make industry less productive, which I doubt, I think many of us would be willing to pay the price of working harder and having less so that we might have a more meaningful life at work. In fact, however, we have no evidence it would lower our overall productivity to re-design our industrial pattern. Instead, I am convinced that ideology dominates factory and machine design to such an extent that we have a dream or myth of efficiency whose long-run cumulative costs are enormous in the sabotage and resentment of the work force, in boredom, in absenteeism, and so on. Engineers still act as if workers were as undisciplined and inefficient a group as they were before mass education and before industrialism—and by so doing they make our industry less productive than it might be even in its own terms.

22. *Communitas: Ways of Livelihood and Means of Life,* (Chicago: University of Chicago Press, 1946). Compare my discussion in "Some Observations on Community Plans and Utopia," *Yale Law Journal,* vol. 47 (1947), reprinted in *Individualism Reconsidered* (Glencoe, Illinois: The Free Press, 1954).

23. For an understanding of how to look for and interpret such symptoms in a whole society or subculture, I am indebted to the work of Erich Fromm. Compare especially *The Sane Society* (New York: Rinehart and Co., 1955).

24. Cf. Daniel Bell, *Work and Its Discontents, supra;* also "The Evasion of Work" in *Work and the Welfare Age,* L.P.E. Papers #4, July 1956, pages 23-30.

25. What is General Motors to make, for instance, of some of the UAW locals' demands which are being presented in the current negotiations as these pages go to press, e.g., that the scores of World Series and other baseball games be announced at the end of each inning over the public address system or that motor scooters be furnished for union committeemen, or that workers be allowed to buy GM products at 40% off! Another demand, that schedules be adjusted to allow employees wanting to go deer hunting to take time off (as in fact many do anyway), has a pre-industrial ring to it but hardly betokens a new rearrangement of work and leisure. See *Time,* June 9, 1958, page 84.

Lest I be misunderstood, let me make clear that I am not recommending arduousness per se nor do I object at all to the steps workers and unions have taken to make life pleasanter and less exhausting.

26. Regrettably, few women appear to read science-fiction and thus they fail to connect with a literature which at its best satirizes the additive and mechanistic quality of life; the world of technology remains a very "male" world and women rarely penetrate the technological fantasy to see the political fantasy which is on occasion at work underneath.

27. "The Midas Plague," in *The Case Against Tomorrow* (New York: Ballantine Books, 1957). I am indebted to Eric Larrabee for a reference to this story and for many stimulating conversations concerning matters touched on in this paper.

28. Cf. for a more general discussion of the attitudes towards work of college students today, "The Found Generation," *American Scholar,* vol. 25 (1956), pp. 421-436.

29. Eric Hoffer has written that people who remember the "real" pioneers describe them in terms which resemble our picture of the Okies. "The Role of the Undesirables," *Harper's,* December, 1952.

30. Even if proportionally there has been only a slight shift in the number of people who have no zest for work or shirk it, the social accent has shifted. It is clear from Leo Lowenthal's article on the change from heroes of production to heroes of consumption that even when men at work are pictured today in the mass media, what is emphasized is less their work than their golf score, their weekend behavior, their family life—and this emphasis must feed back to the men themselves and give them an image of how they ought to behave.

31. It would be interesting to know to what extent this change is a result of a general speeding up in the pace of life which seems to accompany urbanization and industrialization. I am told, for example, that the music of Bach and Mozart is played today some ten percent faster than the original tempo (the pitch is also higher). And it may be that the mass media, with their swift movement, help to expedite the rhythms of our contemporary life at work as well as at play. In this connection, Warner Bloomberg, Jr., has observed that factory workers in Gary sometimes have a hard time keeping their productivity down to the agreed-upon norms: they are apt to forget themselves and, without half trying, turn out too much (perhaps a little like the experience we may often have on a thruway of finding ourselves going faster than we had intended to). It would seem as if our society—in comparison with subsistence cultures—is geared to an interlacing of high-paced work and leisure; it gives that impression of speed-up still to visitors from abroad.

32. Pitirim A. Sorokin and Clarence Q. Berger, *Time-Budgets of Human Behavior* (Cambridge, Mass.: Harvard University Press, 1939).

33. Albert J. Reiss, Jr., "Rural-Urban and Social Status Differences in Interpersonal Contacts."

Paper delivered at the American Sociological Society meetings, August, 1958.

34. Alfred C. Clarke, "Leisure and Levels of Occupational Prestige," *American Sociological Review,* vol. 21 (1956), pp. 301-7; reprinted in this volume; see also Robert J. Havighurst, "The Leisure Activities of the Middle-Aged," *American Journal of Sociology,* vol. 63 (1957), pp. 152-162.

35. As Professor Galbraith makes abundantly clear in his book (*supra,* note 7), these corporations along with their employees are actually "senior partners," with the State and its subdivisions in contrast living shabbily as a very junior partner in a period of inflation. See *The Affluent Society,* ch. 14, 18, and elsewhere.

36. *Illinois Business Review,* 14 (July 1957), pp. 6-8.

37. Discussion period question: "Isn't there a good deal of cynicism or debunking among workers concerning the product they are making?" Answer: "You are right that the problem of meaning and work lies not only in its intellectual or physical gamesmanship but in its relevance to the total social context. Thus, one could make work in an aircraft plant or missile plant more intriguing without in all dimensions making it more meaningful. Of course it does not prove that something is a good product because it gets bought. Cynicism among advertising men comes out of the feeling that the work they do, although creative in many ways–artistic, imaginative, ingenious in terms of research methods–is not meaningful or is actually harmful so that they don't enjoy it. Surely this is the feeling of many intellectuals, whose work, although demanding and challenging, is not worthwhile. We must proceed on both fronts: to make the work more invigorating and pleasant in its own terms, that is, in terms of technical operations, and in terms of its bearing on what adds to human growth and development."

38. On this point, as on so many others of this paper, Professor Galbraith's discussion adds clarity and perspective. See *The Affluent Society,* chs. 11, 13, 22, 25, and passim.

Bibliography

A Comprehensive Bibliography on Leisure, 1900–1958

INCLUDING REFERENCES ON AMUSEMENT, BOREDOM, FREE TIME, PLAY, RECREATION, AND THE SHORTER WORKWEEK

By ROLF MEYERSOHN
With the Assistance of Marilyn Marc

THIS BIBLIOGRAPHY attempts to include all works on leisure written in the English language since 1900. However, as the essays in *Mass Leisure* make clear, the boundaries of leisure are vague and a bibliography rests largely on the compiler's definition: the area covered here includes scholarly and journalistic works on amusement, boredom, games, hobbies, play, recreation, free time, and problems of the shorter work week.

No attempt was made to cover the literature of mass culture or works on the mass media and mass communications. Other bibliographies exist here (notably Bruce L. Smith et al., *Propaganda, Communication and Public Opinion,* Princeton University Press, 1946) and selected references can be found in the companion volume, *Mass Culture.*

This bibliography grows out of an earlier publication of the Center for the Study of Leisure, a bibliography of 200 leading works on leisure collected and annotated by Reuel Denney and Mary Lea Meyersohn.[1] Its compilation was assisted greatly by Fred J. Schmidt, Jr., *Leisure Time Bibliography* (Ames, Iowa: Industrial Arts Department, Iowa State College, 1935, mimeographed) and by the catalogues of the University of Chicago Library; further assistance was rendered by the Chicago and New York Public Libraries, Columbia University Library, and Widener Library at Harvard University.

While this bibliography has arranged the entries according to decade, it seems appropriate to mention two classification systems which have been applied to this field. Reuel Denney composed a classification system of twenty categories, as follows:

- *I History of leisure
- *II The threat of leisure
- *III The ideals of leisure
- *IV Cultural norms of leisure and consumption
- *V The market for leisure

This is a publication of the Center for the Study of Leisure.

1. Reuel Denney and Mary Lea Meyersohn, "A Preliminary Bibliography on Leisure." In *The Uses of Leisure,* special issue of the *American Journal of Sociology,* volume 62, number 6 (May, 1957), pp. 602-15. Reprinted in Wayne R. Williams, *Recreation Places.* New York: Reinhold Publishing Corp., 1958.

*VI Individual physiology and psychology of play
*VII Recreation and leisure
*VIII Technology of leisure
*IX Sociology of leisure-time activities
*X American culture and character
*XI Philosophy and aesthetics of popular culture
*XII Popular culture: movies, music, sports, comics, pulps
*XIII Fads
XIV Hobbies and arts
XV Games
XVI Research in leisure of small groups
XVII Current methods of study
XVIII Leisure and public policy
XIX Criteria for leisure
*XX Bibliography of bibliographies

(*Categories included in Denney-Meyersohn, *op. cit.*)

Currently under way is a UNESCO project on the evolution of forms and needs of leisure in various European countries. As one part, an international bibliographical index for the sociology of leisure is being prepared. The categories suggested by Joffre Dumazedier are as follows:

I Problems and methods in the study of leisure
II Leisure and the evolution of civilization
III Leisure and culture (rest, distractions, artistic activities, education activities, cultural activities, social activities)
IV Leisure and personality
V Leisure and society (technological determinants; demographic determinants; socio-economic and occupational determinants; family, social, civic, political, philosophical, religious life; educational and cultural life; problems in lack of adaptation, social pathology)
VI The sociology of leisure and socio-cultural action.[2]

This bibliography is arranged according to decade. Publications of the Center for the Study of Leisure are starred; works included in MASS LEISURE are preceded by dagger.

2. Excerpted from a paper delivered by Joffre Dumazedier at the international meeting of the committee to study leisure sponsored by the UNESCO Institutes for Education and Social Sciences and the UNESCO Youth Institute. Gautung, Germany, December, 1957.

1900–1909

Battersea, Lady. "The Spirit of Amusement," *Sunday Magazine,* 29 (1900), 505.

Brackett, Anna Callender. *The Technique of Rest,* New York: Harper & Bros., 1892.

Dawson, P. M. "The Necessity of Leisure," *Charities and the Commons,* 20 (1908), 314-20.

"The Dread of Boredom," *Spectator,* 98 (1906), 938. Also *Living Age,* 250 (1906), 381-83.

Gorky, Maxim. "Boredom," *Independent,* 63 (1907), 309-17.

Groos, Karl. *The Play of Animals,* New York: D. Appleton & Co., 1901.

______. *The Play of Man,* New York: Appleton-Century Co., 1901.

Gulick, Luther H. "Play and Democracy," *Charities and the Commons,* 18 (1907).

Hartt, Rollin Lynde. *The People at Play,* Boston: Houghton Mifflin Co., 1909.

Huntington, Dwight W. "Our Prejudice Against English Game Preserves," *Independent,* 64 (1908), 292-99.

Johnson, G. C. *Education by Play and Games,* Boston: Ginn & Co., 1907.

"Laborious Leisure," *Living Age,* 255 (1907), 812-14.

"Leisure Class," *Spectator,* 96 (1906), 862-63. Also *Living Age,* 250 (1906), 120-22.

Mallock, W. H. "Leisure Class and Its Critics," *Independent,* 52 (1900), 2725.

Minchin, H. C. "Leisure's Miscellany," *Gentleman's Magazine,* 78 (1907), 602-9.

"Mistakes About Leisure," *Nation,* 88 (1909), 553.

Penn, William. *Some Fruits of Solitude,* Chicago: R. R. Donnelley & Sons Co., 1906.

Pitkin, W. B. "Leisure and the Leisure Class," *Nation,* 88 (1909), 553.

Repplier, Agnes. *Essays in Idleness,* Boston: Houghton Mifflin Co., 1893.

Schaeffer, N. C. "Education for Avocation," in *National Education Association Proceedings and Addresses,* 1908.

Simon, A. M. "Evolution of Leisure for the Many," *Craftsman,* 8 (1905), 777-80.

Wallis, Severn Teackle. *Leisure: Its Moral and Political Economy,* Baltimore: J. B. Rose & Co., 1859.

1910–1919

Appleton, Lilla E. *A Comparative Study of the Play Activities of Adult Savages and Civilized Children,* Chicago: University of Chicago Press, 1910.

Aronovici, Carol. "Organized Leisure as a Factor in Conservation," *American Journal of Sociology,* 24 (1919), 373-88.

Atkinson, Henry A. *Church and the People's Play,* Boston: Pilgrim Press, 1915.

Bangs, J. K. "Some Speculations as to Leisure," *Harper's Weekly,* 57 (1913), 5.

Basevi, V. "Curse of Regular Hours," *Canadian Magazine,* 48 (1916), 136-40.

Becht, J. G. "Training Children to a Wise Use of Their Leisure," *Annals of the American Academy,* 67 (1916), 115-22.

Bellamy, G. A. "Culture of the Family from the Standpoint of Recreation," in *National Conference of Charities and Correction Proceedings,* 1914, pp. 103-8.

Bennett, Arnold. *How to Live on Twenty-four Hours a Day,* Garden City, N. Y.: George H. Doran Co., 1910.

Bevans, George E. *How Working Men Spend Their Spare Time,* New York: Columbia University Press, 1913.

Bjorkman, E. "Leisure Class," *Century,* 92 (1916), 957-58.

Blunt, H. "Effects of Evil Recreation," *Indiana Bulletin of Charities and Correction,* 97 (1914), 188-94.

Bosanquet, B. "The Place of Leisure in Life," *International Journal of Ethics* (Jan., 1911), 153-65.

Collier, J. "Leisure Time, the Last Problem of Conservation," *Playground,* 6 (1912), 93-106.

______. "Lantern Bearers: Essays Exploring the People's Leisure," *Survey,* 34 (1915), 213-17, 315-17, 320, 423-27, 513-16.

Cox, L. H. "Value of the Woman of Leisure," *Journal of Home Economics,* 8 (1916), 407-13.

Crew, H. C. "This Matter of Idling," *Outlook,* 104 (1913), 381.

Curtis, Henry S. *Education Through Play,* New York: Macmillan Co., 1915.

______. *The Play Movement and Its Significance,* New York: Macmillan Co., 1917.

Davis, Michael M. *The Exploitation of Pleasure,* New York: Russell Sage Foundation, 1911.

Dewey, John. "Leisure and Labor," in his *Democracy and Education,* New York: Macmillan Co., 1916, pp. 293-305.

Edwards, Richard Henry. *Popular Amusements,* London: Association Press, 1915.

Finley, J. H. "Wisdom of Leisure," *Playground,* 9 (1916), 335-38.

Foster, W. T. *Vaudeville and Motion Picture Shows: a Study of the Theaters in Portland, Ore.,* Portland: Reed College Record (No. 16), 1914.

Gillin, J. L. "Wholesome Citizens and Spare Time," *Cleveland Recreation Survey,* 1918.

Howe, Frederic C. "Leisure for Millions," *Survey,* 31 (1914), 415-16.

______. "Recreation and the Problem of Leisure," in his *Modern City and Its Problems,* New York: Charles Scribner's Sons, 1915, pp. 305-21.

Jayne, I. W. "Leisure Time, the Municipality's Responsibility; with Discussion," in *1915 Proceedings of the League of American Municipalities,* 1916, pp. 19-30.

Kingsley, S. C. "Improper Recreations," in *Industrial Medicine:* Papers and discussion presented at the annual meeting of the American Academy of Medicine, 1914, pp. 87-97.

Lee, Joseph. *Play in Education,* New York: Macmillan Co., 1915.

______. "Standards for Children's Play," *Standards of Child Welfare,* U. S. Children's Bureau, 1919, pp. 54-70.

"Leisure and Aesthetics," *Nation,* 108 (1919), 187.

Library of Congress. *Select List of References on the Psychology of Play,* Washington, 1913.

McDowell, M. E. "Right to Leisure," *Playground,* 4 (1911), 328-31.

National Conference on the Leisure of the People. *Leisure of the People: a Handbook, Being the Report of the National Conference Held at Manchester, November 12-20, 1919,* Manchester, 1919.

"Neighborhood Play in Country and Village," *American City,* 13 (1915), 106-10.

Patrick, George T. W. *The Psychology of Relaxation,* Boston: Houghton Mifflin Co., 1916.

"Public Recreation Facilities," *Annals of the American Academy,* 35 (March, 1910).

Robinson, W. J. "A Plea for Leisure and Idleness," *Midland Drug and Pharmaceutical Review,* 44 (1915), 293-97.

Ross, Edward Alsworth. "Adult Recreation as a Social Problem," *American Journal of Sociology,* 23 (1918), 516-28.

Scott, Temple. "Right Use of Leisure," *Forum,* 46 (1911), 77-93.

______. *Use of Leisure,* New York: Viking Press, 1913.

______. "Wanted—Leisure," *Forum,* 45 (1911), 513-28.

Simkhovitch, Mary K. *The City Worker's World in America,* New York: Macmillan Co., 1917.

Sizer, James Peyton. *The Commercialization of Leisure,* Boston: Richard G. Badger, 1917.

Smith, Walter R. "Primary Social Groups: The Play Group," in his *Introduction to Educational Sociology,* Boston: Houghton Mifflin Co., 1917, pp. 78-96.

Stettzle, Charles. "How 1,000 Men Spend Their Leisure Time," *Outlook* (1910).

Stewart, Herbert L. "Ethics of Luxury and Leisure," *American Journal of Sociology,* 24 (1918), 241-59.

Tucker, W. J. "New Reservation of Time," *Atlantic Monthly,* 106 (1910), 190-97.

Weir, L. H. "Leisure of the Child," in *Standards of Child Welfare,* Washington: U. S. Children's Bureau, 1919, pp. 54-70.

Wood, Walter. *Children's Play and Its Place in Education,* London: Paul, French, Trubner & Co., Ltd., 1913.

1920—1929

Adams, F. A. "Manual Training and Education for the Use of Leisure," *Industrial Education Magazine,* 27 (1925), 50.

Alger, G. W. "Leisure for What?" *Atlantic Monthly,* 135 (1925), 483-92.

Arnquist, Inez F., and Evelyn H. Roberts. *The*

Present Use of Work Time for Farm Homemakers, Pullman, Wash.: State College of Washington Agricultural Experiment Station, 1929 (Bulletin 234).

Asbury, J. W. "Training for Leisure Time," *Platoon School,* 2 (1928), 26-30.

Atkinson, R. K. "Delinquency and Leisure," in *Seventeenth Annual Report of the New York State Probation Commission,* 1924, pp. 122-32.

Attwell, E. T. "Community Leisure Time Opportunities for Negroes," in *Proceedings of the National Conference of Social Work,* 1928, p. 310ff.

Bacheller, I. "My Greatest Possession," *American Magazine,* 98 (1924), 14-15.

Bailey, H. T. "Leisure Time," in *National Education Association Addresses and Proceedings,* 1923, pp. 925-28.

Barker, Ernest. "Uses of Leisure," *Journal of Adult Education,* 1 (1926), 27-35.

Bawden, W. T. "Education for the Proper Use of Leisure Hours," *Manual Training Magazine,* 22 (1920), 13.

Beard, Charles and Mary. *The Rise of American Civilization,* New York: Macmillan Co., 1927.

Beaufreton, Maurice. "Leisure Time Occupations in the Country," *International Review of Agricultural Economics,* 3 (1925), 3-27.

Bliss, E. H. "Planning Ahead for Leisure Time," *Child Study,* 7 (1929), 78-79.

Bok, Edward W. *Dollars Only,* New York: Charles Scribner's Sons, 1926.

Bowen, Wilbur P., and Elmer D. Mitchell. *The Theory of Organized Play,* New York: A. S. Barnes & Co., 1923.

Braucher, Howard S. "Play and Social Progress," *Playground,* 16 (1922), 103-4.

"Bryn Mawr Time Survey," *College News* (March 3, 1926).

Bukharin, Nikolai I. *Economic Theory of the Leisure Class,* New York: International Publishers, 1927.

Buranelli, Roger. "They Started the Crossword Puzzle Craze," *Collier's,* 75 (1925), 12ff.

Burnett, L. R. "A City's Responsibility for the Leisure Time of the Industrial Men," *American Physical Education Review,* 29 (1924), 1-4.

Butler, N. M. "Wants, Tastes and Leisure," *Playground,* 18 (1925), 691.

Campagnac, Ernest T. *Society and Solitude,* Cambridge: University Press, 1922.

Cannon, Cornelia J. "New Leisure," *North American Review* (Sept., 1926), 498-506.

Chapman, Maristan. "Education for Leisure," *Welfare Magazine,* 19 (1928), 224-32.

Chase, Stuart. *Men and Machines,* New York: Macmillan Co., 1929.

"City Worker's Spare Time in the United States," *International Labour Review,* 9 (1924), 896-916.

Collins, Frederick L. "I've Seen America," *Collier's,* 74 (1924), 7ff.

Comstock, Alzada. "Time and the College Girl," *School and Society* (March, 1925).

Condit, Abbie. "Comrades in Play: Leisure Time Activities Which the Young Men and Young Women of America Can Enjoy Together," *Playground,* 13 (1920), 463-75+.

Coyle, G. S. "Margins of Leisure," *Jewish Center,* 5 (1927), 20-24.

Crabtree, J. W. "Leisure; an Energizing Force," *Common Ground,* 9 (1929), 142-43. Also *Journal of Arkansas Education,* 8 (1929), 27.

Crawford, Ina Z. *The Use of Time by Farm Women,* Moscow, Idaho: University of Idaho Agricultural Experiment Station, 1927. (Bulletin 146.)

Cutten, George B. "Leisure and Education," *Playground,* 20 (1927), 601-5.

______. *The Threat of Leisure.* New Haven: Yale University Press, 1926.

Dark, Sidney. *After Working Hours: the Enjoyment of Leisure,* London: Hodder and Stoughton, 1929.

Davidson, I. "Training in the Right Use of Leisure," *Journal of Rural Education,* 3 (1924), 298-304.

Davidson, W. M. "Leisure and the School," *Playground,* 20 (1927), 607-11.

Davis, J. "Our Leisure Class at Play," *Christian Century,* 44 (1927), 897-99.

Dean, A. "Neither Vocationist nor Leisureite," *Industrial Education Magazine,* 26 (1925), 255-56.

Deering T. "Recreation a Necessity in Mental Adjustment," *Bulletin of the South California Society of Mental Hygiene,* 4 (1928), 10-13.

De Schweinitz, Karl. "New Tools of Leisure," *Family,* 8 (1927), 251-60.

Dewey, John. "The American Intellectual Frontier," *New Republic* (May 10, 1922), 303-5.

Dobbs, E. V. "Training for a Wise Use of Leisure," *Journal of the Florida Educational Association,* 1 (1924), 11-13.

Downs, R. E. "Education for Leisure," *Journal of Education,* 108 (1928), 437-39.

Edman, Irwin. "On American Leisure," *Harper's* (Jan., 1928), 220-25.

Essen, Raymond. "Less Money and More Life," *Harper's* (Jan., 1929), 158-67.

Fagan, B. J. "Safeguarding Children's Leisure," *Child Study Magazine,* 7 (1929), 69-71.

Faust, J. W. "Family Recreation the Most Fruitful Feature of Home Life," *School Life,* 14 (1929), 101-3.

Feld, R. C. "Now That They Have It," *Century,* 108 (1924), 747-56.

Forman, W. O. "The Use Made of Leisure Time by Junior High School Pupils," *Elementary School Journal,* 26 (1926), 771-74.

Fuller, R. G. "Play Needs and Work Needs of Children," *American Childhood,* 2 (1921), 345-58.

Gambrill, Merrydelle, *et al.* "Vassar College Time Survey," *Vassar Journal of Undergraduate Studies,* 1 (1926).

"Germany and Workers' Spare Time," *Industrial and Labour Information,* 19 (1926), 446-49.

Gibbons, M. E. "A Plea for Leisure," *Educational Times,* 5 (1923), 337.

Goetter, B. S. *A Study of the Recreational Activities of Employed Women.* Unpublished Master's Thesis, University of Pittsburgh, 1927.

Green, W. "Leisure for Labor—a New Force Alters Our Social Structure," *Magazine of Business,* 56 (1929), 136-37.

Grey, Edward Grey. *Recreation,* Boston: Houghton Mifflin Co., 1920.

Grimes, W. H. "The Curse of Leisure," *Atlantic Monthly,* 142 (1928), 355-60.

Gulick, Luther H. *A Philosophy of Play,* New York: Charles Scribner's Sons, 1920.

Hall, G. Stanley. "Notes on the Psychology of Recreation," *Pedagogical Seminary,* 29 (1922), 72-99.

Hammond, J. W. "The Challenge of Growing Leisure," *American Education,* 27 (1923), 166-67.

Harris, Constance. *The Use of Leisure in Bethnal Green,* London: Lindsey Press, 1927.

Hart, J. K. "Belonging to Too Many Groups," *Survey* (March 15, 1924), 718.

_____. "Place of Leisure in Life," *Annals of the American Academy,* 118 (1925), 111-15.

Hoyt, Elizabeth E. *The Consumption of Wealth,* New York: Macmillan Co., 1928.

Huxley, Aldous. "Work and Leisure," *Literary Review,* 5 (1924), 1-2.

International Labour Office. *International Labour Conference, Sixth Session, Geneva, June, 1924: Report on the Development of Facilities for the Utilization of Workers' Leisure,* Geneva: World Peace Foundation, 1924.

_____. *International Labour Conference, Sixth Session, Geneva, June, 1924: Supplementary Report on the Development of Facilities for the Utilization of Workers' Leisure,* Geneva: World Peace Foundation, 1924.

_____. *International Labour Conference, Sixth Session, Geneva, June, 1924: Second Supplementary Report on the Development of Facilities for the Use of Workers' Leisure,* Geneva: World Peace Foundation, 1924.

_____. *Report on the Use of Leisure Among the Working Classes,* Geneva: the Office, 1924.

Jacks, Lawrence. "Adult Education and the Arts," *Bulletin of American Association of University Professors,* 12 (1926), 521-24. Also *Educational Record,* 7 (1926), 3-10.

_____. "Education for Leisure," *American Federationist,* 36 (1929), 725-28.

_____. "The Ethics of Leisure," *Hibbert Journal,* 27 (1929), 270-81.

_____. *Responsibility and Culture,* New Haven: Yale University Press, 1924.

_____. "What's a Human Being For?" *Playground,* 23 (1929), 240.

Joad, Cyril E. M. *Diogenes; or the Future of Leisure,* New York: E. P. Dutton & Co., Inc., 1928.

Johnson, Alvin, *et al. Civilization and Enjoyment,* New York: D. Van Nostrand Co., Inc., 1929.

Johnson, W. H. "Education for Leisure," *Chicago Schools Journal,* 7 (1925), 204-7.

Jordan, D. S. "Go to the Bee; Contribution to the Permanence of Aristocracy," *Scientific Monthly,* 15 (1922), 448-54.

Jordon, H. W. "Spare Time," *Journal of Industrial and Engineering Chemistry,* 13 (1921), 253-4. *See also* criticism by Sprague, F. O., *Journal of Industrial and Engineering Chemistry,* 13 (1921), 474-6.

Kahn, O. H. "Leisure and Art," *Peabody Journal of Education,* 6 (1928), 131-44.

Kelly, F. C. "Our Need for Wasting More Time," *Harper's,* 150 (1925), 759-62.

Kelly, George A. *One Thousand Workers and Their Leisure.* Unpublished Master's Thesis, University of Kansas, 1926.

Kelso, R. W. "Significance of Educating for Leisure," *American Physical Education Review,* 32 (1927), 718-20.

Kennedy, H. A. S. "Tonic of Disaster." *Century,* 112 (1926), 478-84.

Keppel, Frederick P. "Leisure and Life," *Playground,* 21 (1927), 81-83.

_____. "Riding with a Purpose," *Journal of Adult Education,* 1 (1929), 246-53.

Kneeland, Hildegarde. "Is the Modern Housewife a Lady of Leisure?" *Survey Graphic* (June 1, 1929), 301-2.

Krout, John A. *Annals of American Sport,* New Haven: Yale University Press, 1929.

Lee, Joseph. "The Boy and His Leisure," *Child Welfare Magazine,* 24 (1929), 6-8.

Lehman, Harvey C., and Paul A. Witty. *The Psychology of Play Activities,* New York: A. S. Barnes & Co., 1927.

_____. "Training for the Profitable Use of Leisure," *Journal of Educational Method,* 6 (1927), 376-81.

"Leisure and Culture," *Saturday Review,* 4 (1927), 33.

Leisure: Being the Report Presented to the Conference on Christian Politics, Economics and Citizenship, at Birmingham [*Eng.*], *April 5-12, 1924,* London: Longmans, Green & Co., Ltd., 1924.

"Leisure of the People," *Spectator,* 124 (1920), 543-44.

Library of Congress. *Use of Spare Time: a Bibliographical List,* Washington, 1927.

Lies, Eugene T. "The Community's Responsibility Toward the Leisure Time Problem," *Proceedings of the National Conference of Social Work,* 1928, pp. 310-13.

_____. *The Leisure of a People,* Indianapolis: C. E. Cripper & Sons, 1929.

Lindeman, Eduard C. "Adult Education: a Creative Opportunity, *Library Journal,* 50 (1925), 445-47.

Liverpool Council of Voluntary Aid, Inc. *Report on the Uses of Leisure in Liverpool,* Liverpool: the Council, 1923.

Lloyd, Alfred H. "Ages of Leisure," *American Journal of Sociology,* 28 (1922), 160-78.

Loftus, J. J. "Training for Leisure," *Journal of Education,* 108 (1928), 35.

"Lordliness and Leisure," *Spectator,* 126 (1921), 707-8.

Lotka, A. J. "Our Growing Leisure; What Shall We Do with It?" *Outlook,* 152 (1929), 324-28.

Lynd, Robert S. and Helen M. *Middletown,* New York: Harcourt, Brace & Co., 1929.

McAfee, Helen. "Menace of Leisure; What to Do with the Sixteen-hour Day," *Century,* 114 (1927), 67-76.

Magnusson, Leifur. "The International Labor Office and the Leisure Movement," *Playground,* 20 (1927), 649ff.

Manning, B. "Leisure and Life," *Journal of Education,* 105 (1927), 94-95.

Maurer, J. H. "Leisure and Labor," *Playground,* 20 (1927), 649-55.

May, Herbert L., and Dorothy Petgen. *Leisure and Its Use: Some International Observations,* New York: A. S. Barnes & Co., 1928.

"The Menace of Leisure," in *Digest of the Proceedings of the American Association for Adult Education,* 1927, pp. 72-77.

Merz, Charles. *The Great American Bandwagon,* New York: John Day Co., 1928.

Mullenbach, J. "Industry and Leisure Time," *Playground,* 18 (1924), 333-34.

Nash, L. R. "Leisure," *Stone & Webster Journal,* 40 (1927), 152-56.

"National Organization of Workers' Spare Time," *International Review of Agricultural Economics,* 3 (1925), 704-8.

Nolen, John. "Leisure and Labor," *Playground,* 20 (1927), 659-60.

Noll, E. M. "How Pupils of the Lincoln Junior High School Spend Leisure Hours," *Educational Research Record,* 1 (1928), 16-18.

Nystrom, Paul H. "Leisure and Its Uses," Chapter 18 in his *Economic Principles of Consumption,* New York: The Ronald Press Co., 1929.

"On Finding Leisure," *Literary Review,* 4 (1923), 101.

"Our Vanishing Hours," *Bookman,* 62 (1925), 4.

Palmer, J. F. "Leisure Time of Junior High Pupils," *Journal of Education,* 102 (1925), 623-24.

Pangburn, Weaver W. "Challenge of Leisure," *Religious Education,* 23 (1928), 748-52.

______. "The Worker's Leisure and his Individuality," *American Journal of Sociology,* 27 (1922), 433-41.

Parker, W. A. "Challenge of Leisure to Intelligence," *Mind and Body,* 32 (1925), 677-78.

Patrick, George T. W. "The Play of a Nation," *Scientific Monthly* (Oct., 1921), 350-62.

Payne, A. A. "Education for Leisure as Well as for Vocation," *English Journal,* 10 (1921), 208-16.

Pearson, W. "Possibilities of Leisure Time," *Kansas Teacher,* 21 (1925), 14-16.

Phillips, Brucille. *Recreation in Industry.* Unpublished Master's Thesis, George Peabody College, 1926.

Platt, Charles. "Leisure and Crime," *Playground,* 21 (1927), 142ff.

Ponton, M. "Education for Leisure Time," *Virginia Journal of Education,* 17 (1923), 52-53.

Pound, A. "Education for Leisure," in Holmes, Henry W., and Burton P. Fowler, *The Path of Learning,* Boston: Little, Brown & Co., 1926, pp. 71-89.

______. "Iron Man," *Playground,* 16 (1923), 445-50.

______. "The Right Use of Leisure," *National Institute of Social Sciences Journal,* 9 (1924), 27ff.

Proctor, William M. "Guidance in the Worthy Use of Leisure Time," in his *Educational and Vocational Guidance,* Boston: Houghton Mifflin Co., 1925, pp. 196-215.

Pruette, Lorine. *Women and Leisure,* New York: E. P. Dutton & Co., 1924.

Rainwater, Clarence E. "Play as Collective Behavior," *Journal of Applied Sociology,* 8 (1924), 217-22.

______. *The Play Movement in the United States,* Chicago: University of Chicago Press, 1922.

______. "Socialized Leisure," *Journal of Applied Sociology,* 7 (1923), 255-59.

Rankin, J. O. *The Use of Time in Farm Homes,* Lincoln: University of Nebraska Agricultural Experiment Station, 1928. (Bulletin 230.)

Reed, E. M. "Training for Leisure Through Summer Activities," *Journal of Educational Method,* 7 (1928), 369-72.

Reeve, A. H. "Leisure and the Home," *Journal of Education,* 104 (1926), 568-70. Also *Playground,* 20 (1926), 494-6.

Reeves, W. R. "Leisure Time and Community Character," *City Planning,* 5 (1929), 222-27.

Renney, Jane. "The Recreational Needs of Adolescence," *Child-Study* (July, 1920), 1-5.

Rich, Margaret E. "New Tools of Leisure," in her *Family Life Today,* Boston: Houghton Mifflin Co., 1928, pp. 133-58.

Rodenwold, Zelta F. *The Use of Leisure by Homemakers in a College Community.*" Unpublished Master's Thesis, Iowa State College, 1929.

Ross, W. D. "Right Use of Leisure as an Objective of Education," *Educational Review,* 66 (1923), 71-74.

Rugg, Harold, and Ann Shumaker. *The Child Centered School,* Yonkers-on-Hudson, N. Y.: World Book Co., 1928.

Russell, Bertrand. "Leisure and Mechanism," *Dial,* 75 (1923), 105-22.

______. "The Sedentary Age," *Nation's Business,* 17 (1929), 35-37.

Russell, Dora W. *The Right to be Happy,* New York: Harper & Bros., 1927.

Russell, L. "Live While You Live," *Scribner's,* 78 (1925), 273-80.

Russell Sage Foundation. *Bibliography of Recreation.* Compiled by Marguerita P. Williams, New York, 1927. (Bulletin 156.)

______. *Bibliography on Amusements.* Compiled by H. R. Knight, New York, 1920. (Bulletin 151.)

Saxman, Ethel Julia. *Students' Use in Leisure Time of Activities Learned in Physical Education in State Teachers College.* Unpublished Ph. D. Dissertation, Teachers College, Columbia University, 1926.

Schalk, G. "The Worker's Spare Time in Industry," International Conference on Social Work, Paris, 1928.

Silver, R. "Leisure and Life," *Journal of Education,* 105 (1927), 39-41.

Skidelsky, B. C. "Effects of Recreation on the Nervous System," *Nation's Health,* 3 (1921), 331-33.

"South Australia and Workers' Spare Time," *Industrial and Labour Information,* 19 (1926), 37-40.

"Spare Time in the Country: II, Oversea Methods of Organisation," *International Labour Review,* 10 (1924), 121-35.

Stimson, H. A. "The Economic Value of Leisure," *Canadian Bankers' Association Journal,* 33 (1926), 462-67.

Street, Elwood. "Important Elements in a Comprehensive Leisure Time Program," in *Proceedings of the National Conference of Social Work,* 1928, pp. 313-16.

Sugg, R. *Crime and Leisure Time,* New York: Teachers College Contribution, Teachers College, Columbia University, 1929.

Sullenger, T. E. "One City's Program for Leisure Time," *Journal of Social Forces,* 2 (1924), 718-21.

Tagore, R. "Philosophy of Leisure," in Lang, S. E., ed. *Education and Leisure,* London: J. M. Dent & Sons, 1930. Also *British Columbia Teacher,* 8 (1929), 5-11.

Terhune, A. P. "You Can't Afford to Spare Your Spare Time," *American Magazine,* 107 (1929), 21.

Thompson, L. A., comp. "Workers' Leisure: a Selected List of References," *Monthly Labor Review,* 24 (1927), 637-47.

Thorndike, Edward L. "The Right Use of Leisure," *National Institute of Social Sciences Journal,* 9 (1924), 19.

Thrasher, Frederick. *The Gang,* Chicago: University of Chicago Press, 1927.

"Trend in Recreation in America Today," *Foundation Forum* (March, 1923), 1-7.

Trow, W. C. "Leisure Activities of Students and Their Instructors," *Pedagogical Seminary,* 34 (1927), 406-14.

Tunis, John R. "The Great God Football," *Harper's,* 157 (1928).

______. *Sports, Heroes, and Hysterics.* New York: John Day Co., 1928.

Unwin, Raymond. "The Influence of Housing Conditions on the Use of Leisure," *International Labour Review,* 9 (1924), 815-28.

"Utilization of Leisure in Austria," *International Labour Review,* 9 (1924), 227-41.

"Utilization of Leisure in Finland," *International Labour Review,* 9 (1924), 573-86.

"Utilization of Workers' Leisure in Various Countries," *Monthly Labour Review,* 19 (1924), 296-303.

"Utilization of Workers' Spare Time: Recommendation of International Labour Conference on This Subject Brought Before the Dominion Parliament and Provincial Governments," *Labour Gazette,* 26 (1926), 243-48.

Warriner, E. C. "Report of Committee on Best Use of Leisure Time," *Michigan Educational Journal,* 1 (1924), 347-49.

Watson, F. "Significance of Leisure," *Contemporary Review,* 118 (1920), 238-45.

Watson, Goodwin B. "The Education of Women for Leisure," *Journal of Home Economics,* 19 (1927), 491-95.

Wayman, A. R. "Leisure Time Programs," *South Dakota Educational Association Journal,* 2 (1927), 348-50.

Wegener, Albert B. *Church and Community Recreation,* New York: Macmillan Co., 1924.

West, S. F. "Education of Women for Leisure," *Journal of Home Economics,* 19 (1927), 491-95.

Whipple, L. "Freedom of Books," *Survey,* 49 (1922), 189-91.

White, E. W. "Leisure and Trained Leadership," *Playground,* 21 (1927), 142ff.

Wilcox, E. V. "High Cost of Leisure," *North American Review,* 224 (1927), 304-14.

Williams, J. B. "Progress in Community Recreation in the South," in *Proceedings of the National Conference of Social Work,* 1928, p. 310ff.

Wilson, Maud. *Use of Time by Oregon Farm Homemakers,* Corvallis, Ore.: Oregon Agricultural Experiment Station, 1929. (Bulletin 256.)

Winston, M. C. "The New Leisure," *Progressive Education,* 4 (1927), 315-17.

Witty, Paul A. *Deviates in Versatility and Sociability of Play Interests,* Contribution to Education, No. 470, New York: Teachers College, Columbia University, 1927.

Woll, Matthew. "Leisure and Labor," *Playground,* 19 (1925), 322-23.

Wood, M. T. "Crime Prevention Through Recreation," *National Municipal Review,* 13 (1924), 191-94.

______. "Education and the Larger Leisure," *National Education Association Journal,* 16 (1927), 173-74.

Woodford, K. L. "The Worthy Use of Leisure," *Hawaii Educational Review,* 14 (1926), 195-96.

Woods, G. H. "The Wider Use of Leisure," *Child Welfare Magazine,* 21 (1927), 564-66.

"Workers' Spare Time in Austria," *Industrial and Labour Information,* 17 (1926), 167-71.

"Workers' Spare Time in Canada," *Industrial and Labour Information,* 18 (1926), 143-46.

"Workers' Spare Time in Poland," *Industrial and Labour Information,* 18 (1926), 95-99.

Yarros, V. S. "Mechanism, Leisure and Beauty," *Open Court,* 37 (1923), 734-40.

Ziegler, L. H. "Some Observations on Recreations," *Archives of Occupational Therapy,* 3 (1924), 255-64.

1930–1939

"Activities for Unemployed and Unoccupied Young People: a Demonstration in County-wide Cooperation for the Unemployed," *Recreation,* 27 (1933), 9-15+.

Adam, T. R. *The Museum and Popular Culture,* New York: American Association for Adult Education, 1939.

Adkins, F. J. "The New Leisure," *Industrial Welfare* (Oct., 1934), 42-43.

Ahl, F. N. "Hobbies and the Leisure Time Problem," *High School Journal,* 20 (1937), 97-99.

Aiken, Ralph. "A Laborer's Leisure," *North American Review,* 232 (1931), 268-73.

Alexander, M. W. "Worker's Leisure," *Special Library,* 22 (1931), 450.

Allard, Lucille E. "A Study of the Leisure Activities of Certain Elementary School Teachers of Long Island," *Contributions to Education,* number 779, New York Teachers College (1939), 108-12.

Allen, Frederick Lewis. *Only Yesterday.* New York: Harper & Bros., 1931.

_____. "When America Learned to Dance," *Scribner's,* 102 (1937).

Allen, W. P. "America's Debt to Herself," *America,* 44 (1931), 599-600.

Allport, Floyd H. "This Coming Age of Leisure," *Harper's,* 163 (1931), 641-52.

Altaraz, I. M. "Recreation as a Factor in Handling Maladjusted Individuals," *Mental Hygiene,* 22 (1938), 276-85.

American Association of School Administrators. "References on Leisure Education," Washington, 1937. (Mimeographed.)

_____. "Youth Education Today," in *Sixteenth Yearbook,* Washington, 1938.

Anderson, Theresa W. "Girls' Recreation," *Research Quarterly* (Dec., 1934).

"Art and the Leisure Time of Workers," *Monthly Labor Review,* 41 (1935), 1235-40.

Artz, Frederick B. *Recreation and Revolution, 1814-1832,* New York: Harper & Bros., 1934.

Baker, Jacob. "Nation-wide Recreation," *Recreation,* 29 (1935), 249ff.

Baker, N. D. "Our Leisure Thinking; with Discussion," *Recreation,* 27 (1933), 418ff.

Barlow, Irene. *Leisure Time Activities of 200 High School Girls in Chicago.* Unpublished Master's Thesis, University of Chicago, 1934.

Barmack, Joseph E. "Boredom and Other Factors in the Physiology of Mental Effort," *Archives of Psychology,* 218 (1937), 1-83.

_____. "A Definition of Boredom," *American Journal of Psychology,* 52 (1939), 467-71.

_____. "Studies on the Psychophysiology of Boredom," *Journal of Experimental Psychology,* 25 (1939), 494-505, 634-42.

Batchelor, Wilbur Commodore. *Changing Conceptions of Leisure Education.* Unpublished Ed. D. Project, University of Pittsburgh, 1936.

Beinhart, F. "My Leisure Time; a Study of the Amusements of Forty-three Boys in the Training School at Vineland, N. Y.," *Training School Bulletin,* 27 (1931), 161-66.

Benjamin, P. L. "The New Leisure," *Recreation,* 29 (1935), 187-89+.

Benn, John. "The Economics of Leisure," *Nineteenth Century,* 113 (1933), 602-9.

_____. *Tradesman's Entrance,* London: P. Allan, 1935.

Berg, Jacob. "Educating Labor for Leisure," *Journal of Adult Education,* 3 (1931), 278-82.

Bergholz, M. C. *A Study of the Leisure Time of High School Girls.* Unpublished Master's Thesis, Oregon State Teachers College, 1935.

"Bibliography of Outstanding Books on Leisure Time Subjects," *Leisure,* 3 (1936), 60, and following issues.

Birkinshaw, M. "Leisure of the Adult Student: A Sample Investigation in London," *Journal of Adult Education* (March, 1937), 203-16.

Bizzell, W. B. "Learning and Leisure," *School and Society,* 39 (1934), 65-72.

Boeckel, Richard M. "The Thirty-Hour Week," *Editorial Research Reports,* 1 (1936).

Bogardus, Emory S. "Avocations and Personality," *Sociology and Social Research,* 18 (1934), 275-81.

"Boredom," *Literary Digest,* 115 (1933), 26.

Boyd, Neva. "Play as a Means of Social Adjustment," *Journal of Health and Physical Education* (Sept., 1936).

Boyd, William, and V. Ogilvie. *The Challenge of Leisure,* London: New Education Fellowship, 1936.

Braden, G. W. "National Trends in Planning for Wise Use of Leisure Time," *Western City* (July, 1934), 25.

Breckinridge, Sophonisba. *Women in the Twentieth Century,* New York: McGraw-Hill Book Co., 1933.

Breen, Mary J. *Partners in Play,* New York: A. S. Barnes & Co., 1936.

Brewer, John M. "Guidance for Leisure and Recreation," in his *Education as Guidance,* New York: Macmillan Co., 1932, pp. 382-415.

Briggs, E. S. "How Adults in Missouri Use Their Leisure Time," *School and Society,* 47 (1938), 805-8.

Brown, A. B. "Education for Leisure," *Hibbert Journal,* 31 (1933), 440-50.

_____. "The Leisure Problem," *Hibbert Journal,* 28 (1930), 455-64.

Brown, C. K. "Education in Machine Utopia," *American Review,* 3 (1934), 167-70.

Brown, V. K. "Is Recreation a Necessity?" *Parks & Recreation,* 15 (1932), 341-45.

_____. "Municipal Recreation Programs and Enforced Leisure," *Recreation,* 28 (1934), 245-46.

_____. "What Shall We Do with this New Leisure?" *Parks & Recreation,* 17 (1934), 361-64, 18 (1934), 26-29.

Brownell, C. L. "The Influence of School Training on Leisure Time Activities," *Journal of Health and Physical Education* (June, 1935).

Bruehl, C. P. "Education for Leisure," *Catholic School Journal*, 37 (1937), 31-34.

Brunner, Edmund de S., and J. H. Kolb. *Rural Social Trends*, New York: McGraw-Hill Book Co., 1933.

Buchan, John (Baron Tweedsmuir). "Leisure," *Canadian Chartered Accountant*, 28 (1936), 47-50.

______. "The Margins of Life," Birbeck College Foundation Oration, 1933.

Bunke, E. D. "My Hobby is Hobbies," *Survey*, 63 (1930), 580-81.

Burnham, William. *The Wholesome Personality*, New York: D. Appleton & Co., 1932.

Burns, Cecil Delisle. *Leisure in the Modern World*, New York: Century Co., 1932.

______. "Leisure of the Workless," *Spectator*, 150 (1933), 635.

Burt, C. "The Psychology of Leisure," *Listener*, 9 (1933), 295-96.

Butterheim, H. S. "Economic Significance of Voluntary Leisure," *Architectural Record*, 75 (1934), 224.

Butterworth, William. "New Leisure and a New Job for Management," *Factory Management and Maintenance*, 42 (1934), 167-69.

Buzzard, E. F. "Clinical Address on Rest, Work and Play in Health and Disease," *Canadian Medical Association Journal*, 24 (1931), 187-92.

Cahill, Marion Cotter. *Shorter Hours; a Study of the Movement Since the Civil War*, New York: Columbia University Press, 1932.

Calkins, E. E. "Lost Art of Play," *Atlantic Monthly*, 151 (1933), 438-46.

______. "The New Leisure: a Curse or a Blessing?" *Economic Forum*, 1 (1933), 371-82. Also *Recreation*, 28 (1934), 23-27+.

Carlton, F. T. "Employment and Leisure," *American Federationist*, 39 (1932), 1256-60.

Cassidy, Rosalind. "Youth Journeys and the Social Sciences," *Recreation* (April, 1938).

Castle, A. W. "What is Ahead for the Individual?" *National Education Association Proceedings*, June, 1932.

Castle, Edgar Bradshaw, A. K. C. Ottaway, and W. T. R. Rawson. *The Coming of Leisure*, London: New Education Fellowship, 1935.

"Chansons et Loisirs," *Spectator*, 158 (1937), 1145.

Chapin, F. Stuart. "Social Participation and Social Intelligence," *American Sociological Review*, 4 (April, 1939).

Chase, Stuart. "Leisure in a Machine Age," *Library Journal*, 56 (1931), 629-32.

Chin, Shu-Jung. *Relationship Between Certain High School Subjects and the Out-of-School Activities of the Students*. Published Ph. D. Dissertation, Columbia University, 1934.

Chubb, P. "Folk Culture and Leisure," *Recreation*, 28 (1934), 278-79.

"City Pleasures," *Economist*, 133 (1938), 210-11.

Clark, Ruth M., and Greta Gray. *The Routine and Seasonal Work of Nebraska Farm Women*, Lincoln, Nebraska: University of Nebraska Agricultural Experiment Station, 1930. (Bulletin 238.)

Cline, Dorothy I. *Training for Recreation Under the WPA (1935-37)*, Chicago: University of Chicago Press, 1939.

Coade, T. F. "Education for Leisure," in *Education of Today*, Young Public School Masters' Conference, New York: Macmillan Co., 1935, pp. 141-52.

Coffin, W. S. "Art and Leisure," *Art Digest*, 7 (1933), 10.

______. "Too Little Culture for Leisure," *American Magazine of Art*, 26 (1933), 299-300.

Coffman, L. D. "Youth Problem and Leisure," *Educational Record*, 20 (1939), 5-9.

Cohen, Felix S. "The Blessing of Unemployment," *American Scholar*, 2 (1933), 203-14.

Colcord, J. C. "Cooperation and the New Leisure," *Family*, 15 (1934), 35-38.

Cole, Stewart Grant. *Leisure in Our Time*, Prospect Park, Pa.: H. G. Smith, 1934.

Coleman, M. P. "Leisure and the Arts," *Library Journal*, 59 (1934), 60-61.

Collier, Dorothy. *A Psychological Analysis of the Leisure-Time Activities of Some Individuals of Normal and Some of Pre-Psychotic Personality*. Unpublished Ph.D. Dissertation, New York University, 1936.

Collier, John. "Fullness of Life Through Leisure," in Nash, Jay B., ed. *New York University School of Education: Interpretation of Physical Education*, New York: A. S. Barnes & Co., 1931.

Collis, J. S. "Poverty and Leisure," *Spectator*, 157 (1936), 452-53.

"Community Recreation: Leisure and its Significance," *Architectural Record*, 81 (1937), 148.

Corry, A. "Leisure and Culture," *Commonweal*, 19 (1934), 291-92.

Cotteral, Donnie. "A Study of the College Women's Physical Education Departments in its Relationship to the Communities' Adult Leisure-Time Activities," *Research Quarterly* (March, 1936).

Courter, C. V. "Education for Leisure," *Leisure*, 5 (1938), 31.

†Craven, Ida. "Leisure," in *Encyclopedia of the Social Sciences*, Vol. IX, New York: Macmillan Co., 1933, pp. 402-6.

Cressman, Elmer W. *The Out of School Activities of Junior High School in Relation to Intelligence and Socio-economic Status*. Unpublished Ph.D. Dissertation, School of Education, Pennsylvania State College, 1937.

Crews, Edwin H. *Some Possibilities for the Reconciliation of Competition and Cooperation in the Present Society Through the Medium of Recreation*. Unpublished Master's Thesis, Louisiana State University, 1939.

Cuber, J. F. "Patrons of Amusement Parks: Case Studies," *Sociology and Social Research,* 24 (1939), 63-68.

Cutten, George B. *Challenge of Leisure,* Columbus: American Education Press, 1933.

______. "Saving Power of Leisure," *National Education Association Proceedings,* 1932, pp. 579-84.

Dahlberg, Arthur O. *Jobs, Machines, and Capitalism,* New York: Macmillan Co., 1932.

Dale, E. "Diagnosis in Leisure Time Activities," *Yearbook of the National Society for the Study of Education,* 34 (1935), 477-86.

Daniels, A. "Responsibility of the College in Educating for Leisure," *School and Society,* 41 (1935), 706-7.

Dankert, C. E. "Work and Leisure," *Dalhousie Review* (July, 1931), 240.

Davis, Elmer. "Miniature Golf to the Rescue," *Harper's,* 162 (1930), 4-14.

Davis, George E. *The Prevalence of Hobbies and Their Educational Significance.* Unpublished Ph.D. Dissertation, University of Iowa, 1937.

Davis, John Eisele. *Play and Mental Health,* New York: A. S. Barnes & Co., 1938.

______. *Principles and Practice of Recreational Therapy,* New York: A. S. Barnes & Co., 1936.

Dawson, James W. *The Spirit of Leisure and the Spirit of Work,* Edinburgh: Oliver, 1935.

Debatin, F. M. "Leisure Time," in *National University Extension Association Proceedings,* 1934, pp. 72-75.

______. "Urban University and the New Leisure; with Discussion," in *Association of Urban Universities, Twentieth Annual Meeting,* 1933, pp. 66-79.

Destreé, J. "Popular Arts and Workers' Spare Time," *International Labour Review,* 27 (1933), 184-206.

Dimock, H. S. "Can We Educate for Leisure?" *Religious Education,* 29 (1934), 120-24.

______. "How Effective is our Education for Leisure?" *Recreation,* 30 (1936), 427-30.

Dodds, H. W. "The Problem of Leisure in an Industrial Age," *Official Register of Princeton University,* 29 (1938). Also *Vital Speeches,* 4 (1938), 619-21.

Douglass, H. R. "Our American Youth—Their Plight and a Program," *Journal of National Education Association* (April, 1937).

Downs, S. W. "Young Worker and his Spare Time," *Industrial Education Magazine,* 38 (1936), 256-58.

Dubbel, S. E. "Leisure at Horton," *South Atlantic Quarterly,* 36 (1937), 163-70.

Durost, W. N. *Children's Collecting Activities Related to Social Factors,* New York: Teachers College Contribution, Teachers College, Columbia University, 1932.

Edgren, Harry D. "The Interests and Participation of Boys and Girls in Out-of-School Recreation Activities," *Research Quarterly* (Oct., 1937).

Edmund, W. H. "Industrial Recreation," *Recreation* (Sept., 1936).

______. *The Trend of Industrial Recreation.* Unpublished Ph.D. Dissertation, Temple University, 1936.

"Education and Leisure in England," *School and Society,* 42 (1935), 222.

"Education and Leisure in Progressive Life," *Nature,* 136 (1935), 847-49.

"Education for Leisure," *Canadian Congress Journal,* 17 (1938), 41.

"Education for Leisure," *Times Educational Supplement,* 937 (1933), 113.

Eliot, Thomas D. "Revaluating Leisure in Our Civilization," *Christian Register,* 113 (1934), 758-59.

Elliott, Leo. *A Survey of Leisure Time Activities and Interests of L.S.U. Men.* Unpublished Master's Thesis, Louisiana State University, 1937.

Elvin, H. H. "Workers' Leisure," *Industrial Welfare,* 20 (1938), 413-16.

Enderis, D. C. "Dangers in the New Leisure Area," Official Report, *National Education Association, Department of Superintendents,* 1933, pp. 209-13.

Englehardt, N. L. "Leisure Education and Recreation, and the Educator's Responsibility," *Journal of Health and Physical Education* (June, 1937).

English, E. H. *The Recreational Preference of the Male Students of the Technical and Vocational School of San Antonio, Texas.* Unpublished Master's Thesis, University of Texas, Department of Education, 1936.

"Entertainment in Wartime," *Economist* (Dec. 30, 1939), 499-500.

Erroll, F. J., *et al.* "The Use of Leisure," *Spectator,* (May 13-June 17, 1938). Six articles.

Evjen, V. H. *Leisure-time Guidance and Delinquency,* Chicago: National Council on Education for Character and Citizenship, 1938.

Fairchild, Henry P. "Exit the Gospel of Work," *Harper's* (April, 1931), 566-73.

Faust, J. W. "Leisure and Living," *Playground,* 24 (1930), 323-29+.

Fennelly, E. "The Problem of Leisure," *Cooperative Review,* 11 (1937), 334-35+, 365-67.

Finley, J. H. "What Will We Do With Our Time?" *National Municipal Review,* 22 (1933), 416-17+.

Fisher, Dorothy Canfield. "The Bright Perilous Face of Leisure," *Journal of Adult Education,* 5 (1933), 237-43.

Flad, Marian. "Leisure Time Activities of Four Hundred Persons," *Sociology and Social Research,* 18 (1934), 265-74.

Flynn, F. J. "Leisure Culture as an Objective," *Nation's Schools,* 21 (1938), 28.

"Fortune Survey: Favorite Recreations," *Fortune,* 17 (1938), 88.

Fosdick, Raymond B. "The Public Hearings on the Use of Leisure," *Recreation,* 27 (1933), 418ff.

______. "Regimenting Leisure," *North American Review,* 238 (1934), 1-3.

Fox, J. F. "Leisure-time Social Backgrounds in a Suburban Community," *Journal of Educational Sociology,* 7 (1934), 493-503.

Frank, J. "Children and Their Leisure," *Childhood Education,* 15 (1939), 389-92+.

Frankl, Paul T. *Machine-Made Leisure,* New York: Harper & Bros., 1932.

Frayser, Mary E. *The Use of Leisure in Selected Rural Areas of South Carolina,* Clemson: South Carolina Agricultural Experiment Station, 1930. (Bulletin 263.)

Frazer, G. "The Day's Reward," *Millgate* (June, 1936), 509-10.

Gardner, Ella. *Development of a Leisure-Time Program in Small Cities and Towns,* Washington: U. S. Department of Labor, Bureau of Documents (no. 241), 1937.

______. "Leisure: a Community Resource," *Home Management* (1938), 83-87.

______. "Leisure and Small Town Youth," *Child Welfare,* 28 (1934), 513-17.

______. *Leisure Time Activities of Rural Children in West Virginia,* Washington: U. S. Children's Bureau, 1931. (Bulletin 208.)

Gardner, George, *et al.* "New Social Problem—Leisure Time," *School and Society,* 42 (1935), 294-96.

Geffen, B. "Use of Leisure Time," *American Childhood,* 23 (1938), 57+.

Gill, A. E. R. *Work and Leisure,* London: Faber, 1935.

Gleeson, J. D. "Leisure and Culture," *G K's Weekly,* 12 (1930), 250.

Gloss, G. M. "Ultimate Understanding For Recreational Planning," *Journal of Health and Physical Education* (Dec., 1938).

______. "What People Do in their Spare Time," *Research Quarterly,* 9 (1938), 141-42.

Glover, Katherine. *Youth: Leisure for Living,* Washington: Office of Education, U. S. Department of the Interior, 1936. (Bulletins 8-11.)

Graham, Rosalind. *Industrial Leisure.* Unpublished Master's Thesis, College of the City of Detroit, 1932.

______. "Problem of Industrial Leisure," *High School Teacher,* 9 (1933), 90+.

Greeley, Louisa M. *A Study of the Leisure Time Use of the Games Taught in the Physical Education Program to Fifth and Sixth Grade Children.* Unpublished Master's Thesis, New York University, 1931.

Green, Bernice C. *Recreation Hobbies of Business and Professional Women of Oklahoma.* Unpublished Master's Thesis, Oklahoma A. & M. College, 1936.

Green, Howard Whipple. *Persons Participating in Leisure-time Activities by Economic Status,* Cleveland: Cleveland Health Council, 1938.

Greenbie, Marjorie L. *The Arts of Leisure,* New York: Whittlesey House, 1935.

______. "The Meaning of Leisure," *Forum* (Dec., 1936), 290-92.

Greifer, J. L. "Time to Kill," *Recreation,* 31 (1937), 345-48.

Gruenberg, B. C. "Work and Leisure—a Changing Outlook," *Child Study,* 12 (1935), 163-66.

Hahn, Kurt. *Education for Leisure,* London: Oxford University Press, 1938.

______. "Education for Leisure," *Parents' Review* (Feb., 1939), 93-106.

Hall, Helen. "When Leisure Palls," *1932 Proceedings of the National Conference of Social Work,* 1933, pp. 309-14.

Hall, J. N. "State of Being Bored," *Atlantic,* 151 (1933), 318-21.

Hambidge, Gove. *Time to Live: Adventures in the Use of Leisure,* New York: McGraw-Hill Book Co., 1933.

Hamblen, Malinda. *A Study of the Leisure Time Activities of the Women Students of a Teachers College with Specific Reference to Activities Offered by WAA.* Unpublished Master's Thesis, New York University, 1930.

Hamilton, W. H. "Challenge of Leisure," *New Republic,* 74 (1933), 191-92.

Hammond, John L. "The Background of the Problem of Leisure," *Industrial Welfare,* 21 (1939), 333-36.

______. *The Growth of Common Enjoyment,* London: Oxford University Press, 1933. (Hobhouse Memorial Lecture.)

______. "Problem of Leisure," *New Statesman & Nation,* 4 (1932), 618-19.

Hansome, Marius. *World Workers' Educational Movements, Their Social Significance,* New York: Columbia University Press, 1931.

Harding, D. W. "The Place of Entertainment in Social Life," *Sociological Review,* 26 (1934), 393-406.

Harris, George A. *Recreational Preferences of the Men Students of the University of Texas.* Unpublished Master's Thesis, University of Texas, 1934.

Harrison, Randolph. "Italian National Leisure Time Society," *Monthly Labor Review,* 40 (1935), 266-78.

Heath, A. E., and W. E. Williams. "Leisure and the Adult," *New Era,* 16 (1935), 163-64.

Heaton, Kenneth L. *A Study of the Recreational Life of High School Students.* Unpublished Ph.D. Dissertation, University of Chicago, 1931.

Hermans, Mabel C., and Margaret M. Hannon. *Using Leisure Time,* New York: Harcourt, Brace & Co., 1938.

Hjelte, George. "Research in Recreation," *Research Quarterly,* 10 (March, 1939).

Hobbs, E. J. "Public Library and the Problem of Leisure, *Library World,* 35 (1933), 179-81.

Holbrook, E. A. "Leisure—a Fine Art," *Electrical Journal,* 30 (1933), 284-87.

Holroyd, George H. "Schoolmaster's Problems," *London Quarterly Review,* 162 (1937), 241-43.

Hood, Leon C. *The Pattern of a Good Time for the Dunbar Township High School Pupils.* Unpublished Master's Thesis, Columbia University, 1935.

Hoyt, Elizabeth E. "The Challenge of the New Leisure," *Journal of Home Economics* (Oct., 1933), 688.

Hupp, Carrie A. *An Analysis of the Leisure-Time Activities of the Graduates of a State Teachers College.* Unpublished Master's Thesis, Colorado State Teachers College, 1934.

Hutchinson, E. D. "Toward an Understanding of Leisure: What Preparations Are You Making for the Leisure Which Will Be Yours on Retirement?" *Recreation,* 32 (1939), 595-99+.

"In the Driftway; Spurious Leisure," *Nation,* 138 (1934), 73.

International Council of Religious Education. *Youth Action in the Use of Leisure Time,* The Council, 1935.

International Labour Office. *Recreation and Education,* London: P. S. King, 1936.

Jacks, Lawrence P. "The Coming Leisure," *New Era,* 13 (1932), 349-51.

_____. "Education and Training for Leisure," *Vocational Guidance Magazine,* 11 (1931), 28-31.

_____. *Education of the Whole Man; (a Plea for a New Spirit in Education),* New York: Harper & Bros., 1931.

_____. *Education Through Recreation,* New York: Harper & Bros., 1932.

_____. *Ethical Factors of the Present Crisis,* Baltimore: Williams & Wilkins Co., 1934.

_____. "Leisure; a New and Perplexing Problem," *World Wide* (July, 1931), 1091.

_____. "Leisure Time: a Modern Challenge," *Playground,* 24 (1930), 475-79+.

_____. "Outwitting the Machine," *Survey,* 67 (1931), 74ff.

_____. "Today's Unemployment and Tomorrow's Leisure," *Recreation,* 25 (1931), 478-82.

James, S. B. "Fallacy of the Leisure State," *Irish Monthly,* 61 (1933), 571-76.

Jameson, M. S. *The Soul of Man in the Age of Leisure,* London: S. Nott, 1935.

Jayne, L. H. *A Survey of the Leisure Activities of 360 Children.* Unpublished Master's Thesis, Teachers College, Columbia University, 1936.

Johnson, G. "Use of Leisure Time," *Catholic Action,* 14 (1932), 23-24.

Johnstone, J. *A Survey of the Voluntary Recreational Interests Among Students of the University of Michigan.* Unpublished Master's Thesis, Louisiana State University, 1937.

Jones, David C. *Social Factors in Secondary Education,* Liverpool: Daily Post Printers, 1932.

Jones, J. H. "Luxury and Leisure," *Accountant* (Jan. 8, 1938), 31-33.

Karsner, Milo G. *A Study of Leisure Time Interests, Needs, and Opportunities of University of Kentucky Men.* Unpublished Master's Thesis, Louisiana State University, 1937.

Katz, Daniel, and Floyd H. Allport. *Students' Attitudes,* Syracuse: Craftsman Press, Inc., 1931.

Keppel, Frederick P. "Mind Your Own Leisure," *Journal of Adult Education,* 6 (1934), 269-70.

_____. "Preparation for Leisure," *Journal of Adult Education,* 10 (1938), 23-6.

_____, and Robert L. Duffus. *The Arts in American Life,* New York: McGraw-Hill Book Co., 1933.

King, Beatrice. "Education for Leisure," *British-Russian Gazette,* 11 (1935), 147-48.+

_____, and Percy Ford. "Leisure in the USSR and Leisure in England," *Listener* (June 1, 1939), 1153-56.

Kingdon, Frank. "Leisure Time Recreation," *New Jersey Municipalities* (Dec., 1934), 21-24.

Kneeland, Hildegarde. "Homemaking in This Modern Age," *Journal of the American Association of University Women* (Jan., 1934).

Komarovsky, Mirra. "A Comparative Study of Voluntary Organizations of Two Suburban Communities," *Publication of the Sociological Society of America,* 27 (1933), 83-93.

Kress, A. J. "New Leisure," *Ave Maria,* 49 (1939), 193-96.

Lang, Sidney E. "The Philosophy of Leisure," in his *Education and Leisure,* London: J. M. Dent & Sons, 1930, pp. 33-40.

Langdon-Davies, John. "Children of the Future," *Delineator,* 122 (1933), 19ff.

Lawrence, Gladys C. *The History and Educational Uses of Some Leisure-Time Activities.* Unpublished Ed. D. Project, New York University, 1937.

Lazarsfeld, Paul F. "An Unemployed Village," *Character and Personality,* 1 (December, 1932), 147-51.

_____, and Philip Eisenberg. "The Psychological Effects of Unemployment," *Psychological Bulletin,* 35 (June, 1938), 358-90.

"Leisure-time Activities and Desires," *Monthly Labor Review,* 39 (1934), 344-45.

"Leisure Time Activities of C.C.C. Enrollees," *Monthly Labor Review,* 43 (1936), 61-62.

"Leisured Life," *New Statesman and Nation,* 8 (1934), 821-22.

Leslie, F. E. "Relation of Recreational Activities to Mental Health," *Maine Medical Journal,* 24 (1933), 195-201.

Lies, Eugene T. "Education for Leisure," *National Education Association Journal,* 21 (1932), 253-54.

_____. *The New Leisure Challenges the Schools,* Washington: National Education Association of the United States, 1933.

_____. "The New Leisure: Drafting a Program," *New York Times Magazine* (Dec. 3, 1933), 3.

_____. "The Problem of Leisure in Relation to Correctional Institutions," *Recreation,* 31 (1937), 209-11+.

Lindeman, Eduard C. "Conspicuous vs. Democratic Leisure," *Progressive Education,* 14 (1937), 430-33.

______. *Leisure—A National Issue.* New York: Association Press, 1939. (Pamphlet.)

______. "The Paradoxes of Modern Leisure," *Leisure,* 3 (1936), 31, 54.

______. "Problems of the New Leisure," *Leisure,* 3 (1936), 34-36.

______. "Recreation Reinterpreted," *Journal of Health and Physical Education* (Sept., 1937).

______. "Youth and Leisure," *Annals of the American Academy,* 194 (1937), 59-66. Issued as a mimeographed Bulletin by the Recreation Division of W. P. A., # 12623.

Lindsay, A. D. "Unemployment: The Meanwhile Problem," *Contemporary Review,* 143 (1933), 687-95.

Loeb, Harold. *Life in a Technocracy,* New York: Viking Press, 1933.

Loveman, A. "Clearing House," *Saturday Review,* 12 (1935), 20.

Lowenfeld, Margaret F. J. *Play in Childhood,* London: Victor Gollancz, Ltd., 1935.

Lundberg, George A. "Sociological Aspects of the New Leisure," *Sociology and Social Research,* 17 (1933), 416-25.

______. "Training for Leisure," *Teachers College Record,* 34 (1933), 569-79. Also *Recreation,* 27 (1933), 259-64.

______, Mirra Komarovsky, and Mary A. McInerny. *Leisure: A Suburban Study,* New York: Columbia University Press, 1934.

Lynd, Robert S. and Helen M. *Middletown in Transition.* New York: Harcourt, Brace & Co., 1937.

Lyons, E. "Menace of Leisure," *American Mercury,* 48 (1939), 477-79.

Lyttelton, E. "Personal Luxury and Public Need," *Spectator,* 154 (1935), 532. Discussion. *Spectator,* 154 (1935), 570+.

McClenahan, B. A. "Preparation for Leisure," *Sociology and Social Research,* 18 (1933), 140-49.

McColvin, L. R. "Library and Leisure," *Library Association Record,* 38 (1936), 329-34.

McDonald, Hovey C. *Recreation for Teachers.* Unpublished Master's Thesis, Stanford University, 1931.

MacDonald, J. "When Leisure Comes," *Truth,* 37 (1933), 16-17.

McPherson, Orpha Rebecca. *Summer Vacation Activities of One Hundred Farm Boys and Girls in a Selected Area.* Unpublished Ph.D. Dissertation, Columbia University, 1939.

"Machine and Leisure," *Industrial Arts and Vocational Education,* 26 (1937), 416-17.

Manchester, Herbert. *Four Centuries of Sport in America, 1490-1890,* New York: The Derrydale Press, 1931.

"Menace of Boredom," *Educational Forum,* 4 (1939), 101-2.

Menefee, Louis A., and M. M. Chambers. *American Youth,* Washington: American Youth Commission of the American Council on Education, 1938.

Mequet, G. "Possibilities of International Action in Regard to Workers' Spare Time," *International Labour Review,* 30 (1934), 582-600.

Miller, J. E. *Case Study of Murray College Men in Recreation After Graduation.* Unpublished Master's Thesis, George Peabody College, 1938.

Miller, Spencer, Jr. "Labor and the Challenge of the New Leisure," *Harvard Business Review,* 11 (1933), 462-67.

Missen, Leslie R. *The Employment of Leisure,* Exeter: A. Wheaton & Co., 1935.

______. "An Institute of Leisure for Youth," *Social Service Review* (1935), 199-206.

______. "Physical Recreation and Leisure," *Social Service Review,* 15 (1934), 1-8.

Mitchell, Claire. *Hobbies of a Few Professional Men and Women.* Unpublished Master's Thesis, George Peabody College, 1930.

Mitchell, Elmer, and Bernard Mason. *The Theory of Play,* New York: A. S. Barnes & Co., 1934.

Mongredien, Herbert. "Leisure," *New-Church Magazine* (April-June, 1934), 113-17.

Monroe, Day, *et al.* "Determination of Standards for the Establishment of Household Budgets for the Expenditure of Money, Time and Energy," *Journal of Home Economics,* 24 (1932), and 25 (1933).

Montgomery, Edward Wilkerson. *The Urbanization of Rural Recreation.* Unpublished Ph. D. Dissertation, University of Chicago, 1934.

Moorhead, W. G. "Two Committee Reports on Leisure Time," *Journal of Health and Physical Education,* 4 (1933), 34-36+.

Morgan, A. E. "Leisure Time in an Industrial Community," *Recreation,* 30 (1937), 571-76+.

Morrow, B. F. "Time Out for a Hobby: What Hobbies Can Do to Increase Anyone's Interest in his Daily Work," *Dun's Review* (March, 1939), 13-17.

Moulton, H. G., and M. Leven. *The Thirty Hour Week,* Washington: Brookings Institution, 1935.

Mullen, W. H. "Women's Leisure Time," *Printers' Ink,* 170 (1935), 45+.

Murdaugh, C. A. "Study of the Promotion and Organization of Leisure-time Interests and Activities in Small Towns and Rural Communities," *Research Quarterly,* 7 (1936), 129-39.

Murdock, E. *Co-Educational Leisure-Time Activities.* Unpublished Master's Thesis, Stanford University, 1936.

Nash, Jay B. "Leisure Time Recreation," *New Jersey Municipalities* (Jan., 1934), 11-14.

______. "The Problem of the Use of Leisure," *Leisure,* 5 (1938), 33-35.

______. *Spectatoritis,* New York: Sears Publishing Co., 1932.

"National Organizations Emphasizing Leisure," *Library Journal,* 58 (1933), 446-47.

National Recovery Administration. *Report of the New York Committee on the Use of Leisure Time,* New York, 1934.

National Recreation Association. "The Amusement Industry," *Recreation* (Feb., 1938).

______. *The Leisure Hours of 5000 People,* New York, 1934.

______. *National Recreation and Unemployment,* New York, 1933.

______. "Public Recreation in the United States," New York, 1935. (Mimeographed.)

Nelson, J. F. *Leisure-Time Interests and Activities of Business Girls: a Research Study,* New York: Woman's Press, 1933.

______. "What 5,000 People Do in Their Leisure Hours; the Leisure Hours of Young Business Women," *Recreation,* 27 (1934), 547-54.

Nestrick, W. Virgil. *Constructional Activities of Adult Males,* New York: Teachers College, Columbia University, 1939.

Neumeyer, Martin H. "The New Leisure and Social Objectives," *Sociology and Social Research,* 20 (1936), 347-51.

______, and Esther S. *Leisure and Recreation,* New York: A. S. Barnes and Co., 1936.

New York Committee on the Use of Leisure Time, *Report,* New York: Van Rees Press, 1934.

Newell, J. R. *Recreational Interests of College Alumni and Their Evaluation of College Physical Education.* Unpublished Master's Thesis, Springfield College, 1938.

"Norman Blood," *New Statesman and Nation,* 8 (1934), 41.

Ogburn, William F., ed. *Recent Social Trends in the United States,* New York: McGraw-Hill Book Co., 1933.

Okada, Miyo. *A Comparison of the Leisure-Time Activities of 200 Farm Women Living in Two Regions of the United States.* Unpublished Master's Thesis, University of Chicago, 1933.

Oliphant, J. D. *A Survey of the Leisure Time Activities and the Interests of the High School Boys of Webster Parish.* Unpublished Master's Thesis, Louisiana State University, 1939.

O'Neal, Harry E. *A Study of the Leisure Time Activities of Cincinnati Teachers.* Unpublished Master's Thesis, University of Cincinnati, 1934.

Orage, Alfred Richard. *The Art of Reading,* New York: Farrar & Rinehart, Inc., 1930.

______. *Social Credit; and the Fear of Leisure,* London: Nott, 1935. (Pamphlet on New Economy No. 5.)

"The Organization of Spare Time in Czechoslovakia," *International Labour Review,* 35 (1937), 78-82.

Orton, William Aylott. *America in Search of Culture,* Boston: Little, Brown & Co., 1933.

Ould, C. W. "Organization of Spare-Time Activities for Native Workers in Certain South African Towns," *International Labour Review,* 37 (1938), 25-43.

"Our New Interpretation of Leisure," *Forecast,* 47 (1934), 155-57.

Overstreet, Harry A. *A Guide to Civilized Loafing,* New York: W. W. Norton & Co., 1934.

______. "Leisure Time and Educational Opportunities and Needs," *Recreation,* 27 (1934), 499-500+.

Pack, Arthur N. *The Challenge of Leisure,* New York: Macmillan Co., 1934.

______. "Make Way for Leisure," *Leisure,* 3 (1936), 28-31, 42.

Palmer, C. "Teachers Experience the New Leisure," *Nation's Schools,* 15 (1935), 25-26.

Palmer, J. T. "New Leisure—Blessing or Curse?" *School Executives Magazine,* 54 (1935), 198-99+.

Pangburn, Weaver W. *Adventures in Recreation,* New York: A. S. Barnes & Co., 1936.

______. *Recreation a Major Community Problem,* New York: National Recreational Association, 1936.

______. "Vacation as a Creative Adventure," *New York State Education,* 21 (1934), 423-24+.

Parsons, A. H. "Challenge of Leisure," *Canadian Home Journal,* 34 (1938), 16, 67.

Patri, Angelo. "Leisure," *Recreation,* 26 (1933), 555-57.

Patterson, J. G. "Industry and Leisure," *Industrial Welfare* (June, 1934), 36-37+.

Patterson, M. *The Recreational Activities of Men Teachers in the State of Oklahoma.* Unpublished Master's Thesis, Oklahoma A. & M. College, 1936.

Payne, Roger. *Why Work? or The Coming Age of Leisure and Plenty,* Boston: Meador, 1939.

Pitkin, Walter B. *The Chance of a Lifetime,* New York: Simon & Schuster, 1934.

______. "Leisure," in his *The Consumer, His Nature and His Changing Habits,*" New York: McGraw-Hill Book Co., 1932, pp. 230-39.

______. *Life Begins at Forty,* New York: Whittlesey House, McGraw-Hill Book Co., 1932.

Plant, James S. "Recreation and the Social Integration of the Individual," *Recreation,* 31 (1937), 339.

"Pleasures of Dilatoriness," *New Statesman and Nation,* 9 (1935), 413-14.

"Portuguese National Leisure Time Foundation," *Monthly Labor Review,* 41 (1935), 1240-41.

"Problems of Increasing Leisure; Official Summary of Report of President's Research Committee on Social Trends," *Recreation,* 26 (1933), 511-13.

Punke, H. H. "Labor Laws and Leisure Hours," *Southern Economic Journal,* 6 (1939), 185-89.

______. "Leisure-time Attitudes and Activities of High-School Students," *School and Society,* 43 (1936), 884-88.

Raynor, Lois Willette. *Organized Recreation for Girls.* Unpublished Master's Thesis, Columbia University, 1932.

"The Recreational Dollar," *Business Week* (July 13, 1932).

Reed, Dorothy. *Leisure Time of Girls in a "Little Italy."* Unpublished Ph.D. Dissertation, Columbia University, 1932.

Reeves, W. R. "Ideals and Objectives of Public Recreation," *Playground,* 24 (1930), 15-20.

Reynolds, Flora P. *The Community Recreation Movement in the United States.* Unpublished Master's Thesis, University of Southern California, 1934.

Reynolds, Lucille W. *Leisure Time Activities of a Selected Group of Farm Women.* Published Ph.D. Dissertation, University of Chicago, 1935.

______. "Now That Farm Women Have Leisure," *Hygeia* (Feb., 1930), 136-39.

Rheinstein, A., and W. S. Brown. "Idle Time —What Shall We Do With It?" *American Machinist,* 77 (1933), 265-7. See also Discussion by Alexander, R. S., *American Machinist,* 77 (1933), 521.

Richardson, Jessie F. *The Use of Time by Rural Homemakers in Montana,* Montana State Agricultural Experiment Station, 1933. (Bulletin 271.)

Riley, John W., Jr. *Social Leisure: Dynamics of Non-Family Group Leisure.* Unpublished Ph.D. Dissertation, Harvard University, 1937.

Robinson, Reginald. "Leisure-time Activities of the Children of New York's Lower West Side," *Journal of Educational Sociology,* 9 (1936), 484-93.

Rockefeller, John D., Jr. "Leisure," *Recreation,* 32 (1938), 201.

Rogers, James E. "Avocational Education for the New Day," *School and Society,* 37 (1933), 793-99.

______. "Challenge of Leisure," *High School Teacher,* 11 (1935), 127.

______. *The Child and Play,* New York: Century Co., 1932.

Ruark, A. E. "The University and the Leisure of Tomorrow," *Pittsburgh Record* (Feb., 1932), 15-19.

Russell, Bertrand. *The Conquest of Happiness,* New York: Liveright Publishing Corporation, 1930.

______. "Reduction of Working Hours and the Advantages of Leisure," *Review of Reviews,* 82 (1932), 48-54.

Russell, W. F. "Leisure and National Security," *Teachers College Record,* 33 (1932), 569-75. Also *Recreation,* 26 (1932), 171-74. Also *National Education Association Proceedings,* 1932, pp. 575-84.

Russell Sage Foundation. *The New Leisure: Its Significance and Use; a Selected Bibliography.* Compiled by Grace P. Thornton, New York, 1933.

Rutledge, Leslie. *Jesus' Teachings and the Use of Leisure,* Kansas City, Kan.: University of Kansas Press, 1931.

Rutledge, R. H. "Planning the National Forests for Greater Recreational Use," *Recreation,* 29 (1935), 445.

Sailer, Randolph C. *Happiness Self-Estimates of Young Men,* New York: Teachers College, Columbia University, 1931.

Sanford, T. R. "Challenge of Leisure Time," *Virginia Journal of Education,* 28 (1935), 250-52.

Schmidt, Fred J., Jr. *Leisure Time Bibliography: A Guide to Books and Magazine Articles Pertaining to Leisure Time and to Avocational Interests Related to Industrial Arts Education,* Ames, Iowa: Iowa State College, Industrial Arts Department, 1935. (Pamphlet.)

Schwendener, Norma. *Games Preferences of 10,000 Fourth Grade Children.* Unpublished Ph.D. Dissertation, Columbia University, 1932.

Seebach, E. E. "List of Books on Leisure and Hobbies Recently Published," *Wisconsin Library Bulletin,* 33 (1937), 57-58.

Seman, P. L. "Leisure and Its Challenge," *Social Science,* 12 (1937), 72-77.

Shaffer, G. W. "Recreation as a Preventive and Therapy for Social Maladjustments," *Occupational Therapy,* 17 (1938), 97-106.

Slobodin, H. L. "Unemployment or Leisure—Which?" *American Federationist,* 37 (1930), 1205-208.

Smith, Elliott D. "Potent Leisure," *Survey Graphic,* 64 (1930), 134-37.

Smith, Mapheus, and W. C. Nystrom. "Study of Social Participation and of Leisure Time of Leaders and Non-leaders," *Journal of Applied Psychology,* 21 (1937), 251-59.

Snedden, David. "'Education for Leisure': Some Preliminary Considerations," *Teachers College Record,* 35 (1934), 387-95.

Snyder, L. L. "The World at Leisure; Observations in Many Countries," *Leisure,* 3 (1936), 26-29, and following issues.

"Social Aspects of Labour and Leisure," *Nature,* 134 (1934), 265-67.

Sommer, R. "Meaning of Recreation and Avocation in Mental Hygiene," *Proceedings of the First International Congress on Mental Health,* 2 (1932), 550-64.

Sorokin, Pitirim A., and Clarence Q. Berger. *Time-Budgets of Human Behavior,* Cambridge: Harvard University Press, 1939.

Spurr, Frederic C. *The Christian Use of Leisure,* London: Kingsgate Press, 1935.

Steiner, Jesse F. *Americans at Play; Recent Trends in Recreation and Leisure Time Activities,* New York: McGraw-Hill Book Co., 1933.

______. "Challenge of the New Leisure," *Recreation,* 27 (1934), 517-22+.

______. *Research Memorandum on Recreation in the Depression,* New York: Social Science Research Council, 1937.

Sternheim, Andries. "Leisure in the Totalitarian State," *Sociological Review,* 30 (1938), 29-48.

Stock, John Leofric. "Leisure," in his *Reason and Intuition,* New York: Oxford, 1939.

Stouffer, Samuel A., and Paul F. Lazarsfeld. *Research Memorandum on the Family in the Depression,* New York: Social Science Research Council, 1937.

"Survey Reveals How Employees Spend Extra Leisure Time," *System,* 63 (1934), 335-36.

Symons, A. J. "Housing and the Rights of Leisure," *Architectural Forum,* 70 (1939), 133-34.

______. "The Rights of Leisure," *Journal of the Royal Institute of British Architects* (Aug. 15, 1938), 918-22.

Taft, L. "Art and Leisure," in *National Education Association Proceedings,* 1933, pp. 699-701.

Talbot, P. D. *"A Survey of the Leisure Time Occupations, and Interests of Louisiana State University Women."* Unpublished Master's Thesis, Louisiana State University, 1937.

Tandy, W. Lou. *Economics of Leisure,* Urbana: University of Illinois Press, 1934.

Taylor, J. H., *et al.* "The Effects of Conditions of Work and Various Suggested Attitudes on Production and Reported Feelings of Tiredness and Boredness," *Journal of Applied Psychology,* 21 (1937), 431-50.

Teper, Lazare. *Hours of Labor.* Baltimore: John Hopkins Press, 1932.

Thorndike, Edward L. "How We Spend Our Time and What We Spend It For," *Scientific Monthly,* 44 (1937), 464-69.

______. "The Right Use of Leisure," *Journal of Adult Education,* 2 (1930), 42-46.

______. "Use of Leisure," *Playground,* 23 (1930), 713-14.

Thrasher, F. M. "Young Man and his Leisure: with Discussion," *Recreation,* 27 (1934), 452-56.

Tilgher, Adriano. *Work: What It Has Meant to Men Through the Ages.* Translated by Dorothy Canfield Fisher. New York: Harcourt, Brace & Co., 1930.

Timme, A. R. "The Significance of Play and Recreation in Civilized Life," *Mental Hygiene,* 18 (1934), 51-57.

Toogood, R. "A Survey of Recreational Interests and Pursuits of College Women," *Research Quarterly,* 10 (1939), 90-100.

Tunis, John R. "Changing Trends in Sports," *Harper's,* 170 (1934), 75-86.

______. "A Nation of Onlookers?" *Atlantic Monthly,* 160 (1937).

______. *Sports,* New York: John Day Co., 1938.

Turner, Grace. "The New Leisure of the New Deal," *Catholic World,* 138 (1933), 168-76.

U. S. Advisory Committee on Education. *The Education and Adjustment of Youth,* Washington, 1938.

U. S. Department of Agriculture, Forest Service. *Forest Recreation—A Bibliography,* Washington, 1938.

"Utilization of Leisure," *Nature,* 140 (1937), 229.

"Utilization of Workers' Leisure Time: Report of Director of International Labour Office," *Monthly Labor Review,* 31 (1930), 593-98.

"Utilization of Workers' Spare Time," *Monthly Labor Review,* 33 (1931), 581-84.

Vaile, Roland S. *Research Memorandum on Social Aspects of Consumption in the Depression,* New York: Social Science Research Council, 1937.

Varney, I. "Hobbies: a Bibliography," *Wisconsin Library Bulletin,* 33 (1937), 59-60.

Vernon, H. M. *The Shorter Working Week,* London: George Routledge & Sons, Ltd., 1934.

Vinson, R. E. "The Margin," *Clevelander* (May, 1933), 3+.

Walker, Louis C. *Distributed Leisure; an Approach to the Problems of Over-Production and Underemployment,* New York: Century Co., 1931.

Walker, Stanley. *The Night Club Era,* New York: Frederick A. Stokes Co., 1933.

Wallace, R. S. "Recreation and Unemployment," *Recreation,* 24 (1931), 650-56.

Warner, Kidd P. *A Study of Contemporary Physical Recreation for the Adolescent Girl in Russia, Italy, Germany, England, and the United States.* Unpublished Master's Thesis, Louisiana State University, 1939.

Watson, Goodwin B. "Educator Looks at Work and Leisure," *Recreation,* 27 (1934), 501-2.

______. "Families, Education, and the Use of Leisure in the Present Crisis," *Journal of Home Economics,* 25 (1933), 831-39.

Weaver, Robert Bartow. *Amusements and Sports in American Life,* Chicago: University of Chicago Press, 1939.

Webster, Doris. *How to Spend Your Husband's Leisure,* New York: Leisure League of America, 1934.

Weed, Thurlow. "Our Great American Sweepstakes," *Commonweal,* 28 (1938), 69-70.

Weedon, Vivian. *A Technique for Determining Interest in Leisure Time Activities.* Unpublished Master's Thesis, Ohio State University, 1933.

Weir, Lebert H. *Europe at Play,* New York: A. S. Barnes & Co., 1937.

______. "Parks and Recreation," Chapter 5 in *What the Depression Has Done to Cities,* Chicago: The International City Managers' Association, 1935.

Wells, H. G. "The Overflowing Energy of Mankind," in his *The Work, Wealth and Happiness of Mankind,* Vol. II, New York: Doubleday, Doran & Co., 1931, pp. 751-84.

"What is Leisure?" Annotated bibliography and report of National Recreation Association study. *Architectural Record,* 75 (1934), 194-223.

Whitehouse, J. H. "Problems of Leisure and the Mass Mind," in *Conference of Educational Associations Report,* 1934, pp. 69-80.

Willard, W. W. "Calamity or Opportunity?" *Leisure,* 4 (1937), 20-21.

Witcutt, W. P. "Drying Lands," *G. K.'s Weekly,* 25 (1937), 358-59.

Witherspoon, Edna. *A Study of Leisure Time of High School Girls.* Unpublished Master's Thesis, Indiana University, 1930.

Woll, Matthew. "Labor and the New Leisure," *Recreation,* 27 (1933), 418ff.

Woods, E. S. "Some Aspects of the Problem of Leisure," *Parents' Review* (June, 1937), 354-66.

Work Projects Administration. "Increasing America's Recreation Facilities," *Recreation* (Dec., 1936).

_____. *Planning Our Leisure,* Washington, 1938.

_____, Recreation Division. *Recreation: a Selected Bibliography with Annotations; References on Social and Economic Background, Philosophy of Leisure, Public Administration, Recreation Administration, Periodicals,* Washington, 1938.

World Congress for Leisure Time and Recreation. Prepared by the International Central Bureau Joy and Work, Hamburg: Hanseatische Verlagsanstalt, 1937.

Worman, E. C. "Trends in Public Recreation," *Recreation* (Aug., 1938).

Wright, E. A., comp. "Education for Leisure: Recent References," *Educational Method,* 14 (1935), 335-37.

Wright, W. R. *Recreational Education as an Integral Part of Twentieth Century American Living.* Unpublished Master's Thesis, Louisiana State University, 1938.

Wyne, Wilbert G. *Play as a Factor in the Foundation of Character.* Unpublished Master's Thesis, Notre Dame, 1933.

Yutang, Lin. "The Importance of Loafing," *Harper's* (July, 1937), 143-50.

Y.W.C.A. *Leisure-time Interests and Activities of Business Girls.* A Research Study Conducted during 1931-1933 by the Laboratory Division, National Board, Y.W.C.A., New York: Womans Press, 1934.

Zimmerman, Carle C. *Consumption and Standards of Living,* New York: D. Van Nostrand Co., Inc., 1936.

1940–1949

Alpenfels, Ethel J. "Work and Play as Seen by an Anthropologist," *Childhood Education,* 25 (1948), 149-52.

American Music Conference. *National Survey of Public Interest in Music,* New York: A. S. Bennett Associates, 1948.

Anderson, C. Arnold, and Bryce Ryan. "Social Participation Differences Among Tenure Classes," *Rural Sociology,* 8 (September, 1943).

Anderson, W. A. "The Family and Individual Social Participation," *American Sociological Review,* 8 (1943), 420-24.

_____. "Family Social Participation and Social Status Self-Ratings," *American Sociological Review,* 11 (1946), 253-57.

Axline, Virginia Mae. *Play Therapy,* Boston: Houghton Mifflin Co., 1947.

Bakke, E. Wight. *The Unemployed Worker: A Study of the Task of Making a Living Without a Job,* New Haven: Yale University Press, 1940.

Balint, E. "Play and Imagination," *New Era,* 28 (1947), 211-13.

Barton, W. E. "Leisure Time Activities and Mental Health," *Journal of Physical Education,* 45 (1947), 29ff.

Batten, E. M. "Spare Time in War-Time," *Industry Illustrated* (Feb., 1941), 30+.

Beach, G. B. "Liberal Education and Leisure in the Atomic Age," *Education,* 67 (1947), 595-602.

Bergler, Edmund. "On the Disease Entity Boredom ('Alysosis') and its Psychopathology," *Psychiatric Quarterly,* 19 (1945), 38-51.

Bermingham, C. E. "Leisure-time; a Two-edged Sword," *Catholic Action,* 27 (1945), 11.

Blanchard, B. E. "Recreation and Delinquency," *School Review,* 54 (1946), 360-63.

_____. "Recreation for Rural Areas," *School Executive,* 65 (1946), 52.

Bloch, Herbert A. "Alcohol and American Recreational Life," *American Scholar,* 49 (1948), 54-66.

Bogardus, Emory S. "Hobbies in War and Peace," *Sociology and Social Research,* 27 (1943), 215-22.

Boynton, P. L., and J. D. Wang. "Relation of the Play Interests of Children to their Socioeconomic Status," *Journal of Genetic Psychology,* 64 (1944), 129-38.

Brew, J. M. "What do Young People Do?" *Times Educational Supplement,* 1428 (1942), 450; 1429 (1942), 462.

Britt, Steuart H., and M. M. Balcom. "Jumping Rope Rhymes and the Social Psychology of Play," *Pedagogical Seminary,* 58 (1941), 304-6.

_____, and S. Q. Janus. "Toward a Social Psychology of Human Play," *Journal of Social Psychology,* 13 (1941), 378-84.

Brophil, G. R. "Recreation While Resting," *Occupational Therapy,* 21 (1942), 25-32.

Buchan, John (Baron Tweedsmuir). "Man and His Leisure," *Recreation,* 34 (1940), 407-9.

Burton, A. "Further Study of the Relation of Time Estimation to Monotony," *Journal of Applied Psychology,* 27 (1943), 350-59.

Bushee, Frederick A. "Social Organizations in a Small City," *American Journal of Sociology*, 51 (1945), 217-26.

Campion, H. A. "Youth's Leisure Time," *Nation's Schools*, 35 (1945), 23.

Canadian Youth Commission. *Youth and Recreation*, Toronto: Ryerson Press, 1946.

Catapusan, B. T. "Leisure-time Problems of Filipino Immigrants," *Sociology and Social Research*, 24 (1940), 541-49.

Cavanaugh, J. O. "Relation of Recreation to Personality Adjustment," *Journal of Social Psychology*, 15 (1942), 63-74.

Clarke, J. F. "We Make 'em Relax," *Management Review*, 31 (1942), 269-70.

Coffin, Thomas E. "Television's Effect on Leisure Time Activities," *Journal of Applied Psychology*, 32 (1948), 550-58.

Conant, W. H. "Less Leisure for Executives," *Barron's*, 20 (1940), 20.

Cook, K. M. "Recreation and Leisure Time Activities in the School Program," *School Life* (March, 1946), 29-31.

Creed, C. Edwin. "The Relationship of Recreational Participation to Industrial Efficiency," *Research Quarterly*, 17 (1946), 193-203.

Cureton, T. K. "Doctorate Theses Reported by Graduate Departments of Health, Physical Education, and Recreation 1930-1946, Enclusively," *Research Quarterly*, 20 (1949), 31-59.

Curtis, H. S. "Education for Leisure," *School and Society*, 61 (1945), 282-83.

Davis, John Eisele. "Psychiatric Concepts of Recreation," *Occupational Therapy*, 21 (1942), 1-16.

†Dulles, Foster Rhea. *America Learns to Play*, New York: Appleton-Century Co., 1940.

Durant, Henry. *The Problem of Leisure*, London: George Routledge & Sons, Ltd., 1948.

Eastwood, Floyd R. "Values and Problems in Industrial Recreation," *Occupational Therapy*, 2 (1946), 226-34.

Edgren, Harry D. "Contribution of Recreation to the Individual," *Journal of Health and Physical Education*, 15 (1944), 437-38+.

"Entertainment Favorites of High School Students," *Scholastic*, 54 (1949), 18-19.

Erikson, Erik H. "Clinical Studies in Childhood Play," in Barker, Roger G., *et al.*, eds. *Child Behavior and Development*, New York: McGraw-Hill Book Co., 1943, pp. 411-28.

______. "Studies in the Interpretation of Play. I: Clinical Observations of Play Disruption in Young Children," *Genetic Psychology Monographs*, 22 (1940), 557-671.

Faegre, M. E. L. "No Time on Their Hands," *National Parent-Teacher*, 35 (1941), 14-16.

Fisher, Dorothy Canfield. "The Djinn in the Bottle," *Journal of Adult Education*, 8 (1941), 349-52.

"Fortune Survey; Public Taste in Entertainment," *Fortune*, 39 (1949), 39-40+.

Friermood, A. T. "Educating for Leisure in Private Agencies," *Journal of Educational Sociology*, 21 (1948), 296-301.

Garrett, Sir Douglas T. "Out of School: a Layman's Thoughts on Leisure," *Parents' Review* (July-Aug., 1949), 161-8.

Garrett, John. "Art of Leisure," *Spectator*, 180 (1948), 42.

Garvin, Samuel. "Organization for Leisure," in Pendell, Elmer, ed. *Society Under Analysis*, Lancaster, Pa.: Jacques Cattell Press, 1942, pp. 449-69.

Giedion, Siegfried. *Mechanisation Takes Command*, London: Oxford University Press, 1948.

Gill, E. "Leisure State," *Clergy Review*, 18 (1940), 123-29.

Gillespie, James J. *Free Expression in Industry: A Social-psychological Study of Work and Leisure*, London: Pilot Press, 1948.

Glass, S. "Work and Play and the Need to Belong," *Childhood Education*, 25 (1948), 153-56.

Gloss, George M. *Recreational Research*, Baton Rouge, La.: J. E. Ortlieb Printing Co., 1940.

Goldhamer, Herbert. *Some Factors Affecting Participation in Voluntary Associations*. Unpublished Ph.D. Dissertation, University of Chicago, 1943.

Goodman, Paul and Percival. *Communitas*, Chicago: University of Chicago Press, 1949.

Graham, H. H. "It Pays to be Lazy," *Ave Maria*, 69 (1949), 215-16.

Greenbie, Sydney. *Leisure for Living*, New York: George W. Stewart, 1940.

Groves, Ernest Rutherford, Edna L. Skinner, and Sadie Johnetta Swenson, *The Family and Its Relationships*, Philadelphia: J. B. Lippincott Co., 1941.

Hall, G. B. "Are Amusements a Wartime Luxury?" *Domestic Commerce* (Oct. 22, 1942), 14-15.

Hamburger, Ernest. "Significance of the Nazi Leisure Time Program," *Social Research*, 12 (1945), 226-49.

Hammond, John L. and Barbara. *The Bleak Age*, Middlesex: Penguin, 1947.

Hammond, W. H. "An Analysis of Youth Centre Interests," *British Journal of Educational Psychology*, 15 (1945), 122-26.

Harford, Honoria. "The Use of Leisure in War-Time," *Social Work Journal*, 2 (1941), 73-78.

Harris, D. B. "Relationships Among Play Interests and Delinquency in Boys," *American Journal of Orthopsychiatry*, 13 (1943), 631-38.

Havighurst, Robert J., *et al.* "Leisure Activities and the Socio-economic Status of Children," *American Journal of Sociology*, 54 (1949), 505-19.

Hicks, J. "Brother, Can You Spare an Hour?" *Integrity*, 2 (1948), 26-31.

Hill, O. M. "Investing in Leisure," *Canadian Business* (Aug., 1949), 24-26+.

"Hobbies — Are We Emphasizing Them Enough?" *Industrial Arts and Vocational Education,* 36 (1947), 15.

Hollingshead, August Belmont. *Elmtown's Youth: The Impact of Social Classes on Adolescents,* New York: Wiley, 1949.

Holroyd, George H. *Education for Leisure,* Leeds: E. J. Arnold & Sons, Ltd., 1942.

Hoppock, M. E. "Guidance for Leisure: a Critical Review of Selected Literature," *Occupations,* 18 (1940), 588-92.

Horne, B. M., and C. C. Philleo. "Comparative Study of the Spontaneous Play Activities of Normal and Mentally Defective Children," *Pedagogical Seminary,* 61 (1942), 45-46.

Hughes, E. E. "Constructive Leisure-time Activities," *National Parent-Teacher,* 36 (1942), 32-34.

†Huizinga, Johan. *Homo Ludens.* Translated by R. F. C. Hull. London: Routledge & Kegan Paul, 1949.

Hunter, Guy. "Apathy, Energy and the Use of Leisure: Some Connections Between Work and Leisure," *Institute of Personnel Management Journal,* 31 (1949), 180-84.

Huxley, J. S. "War and Reconstruction," *Nature,* 145 (1940), 330-34.

Iams, J. P. "Leisure Time and Physical Education," *Recreation,* 35 (1941), 515-17+.

Industrial Recreation Association. *Odd Shift Recreation,* Chicago: the Association, 1944.

International Youth Conference. *Work and Leisure,* London, 1948.

Jaffe, A. D. "Technological Innovations and the Changing Socio-economic Structure," *Science Monthly,* 67 (1948), 93-102.

James, H. E. O. "Adolescent Leisure," *Lancet,* 244 (1943), 504.

______, and F. T. Moore. "Adolescent Leisure in a Working Class District," *Occupational Psychology,* 14 (1940), 132-45; *Part II,* 18 1944), 24-34.

Jones, Anna May. *Leisure Time Education,* New York: Harper & Bros., 1946.

Joyce, C. A. "The Use of Leisure," *Education* (Aug. 6, 1948), 218-19.

Keller, A. G. "Gratification Element," *Social Forces,* 21 (1942), 15-17.

Kerr, Chester Arthur. *Studies in the Free-Time Activities of Children,* New York: Association Press, 1947.

Keyser, C. P. "Our Leisure Time," *Parks & Recreation,* 24 (1941), 241-45.

Kingery, R. E. "Shall We Be Recreation Conscious?" *Library Journal,* 72 (1947), 149-51.

Kinzler, M., and B. S. Wortis. "Children's Leisure Time Activities," *Parents' Magazine,* 22 (1947), 10+.

Kirkpatrick, J. B. "Spectatoritis," *School* (Elementary Edition and Secondary Edition), 33 (1945), 850-51.

Knopf, R. C. "Educating for Leisure," *Ohio Schools,* 27 (1949), 10-11.

Komarovsky, Mirra. "The Voluntary Associations of Urban Dwellers," *American Sociological Review,* 11 (1946), 686-98.

Kouwenhoven, John. *Made in America,* Garden City, N. Y.: Doubleday & Co., 1948.

Lambert, Clara B. "After-school Hours: a Changing Pattern," *Child Study,* 22 (1945), 42-43+.

______. "Identification Through Play," *Childhood Education,* 25 (1949), 402-5.

Landis, J. T. "Hobbies and Happiness in Old Age," *Recreation,* 35 (1942), 607+.

"Leisure of the School Child," *Times Educational Supplement,* 1552 (1945), 42.

"Leisure-Time Activities," *Times Educational Supplement,* 1673 (1947), 247.

Leisure-Time Activities of Collier's Adult Readers, New York: Crowell-Collier Publishing Co., 1948.

Letton, Mildred Celia. *Your Child's Leisure Time,* New York: Teacher's College, 1949.

Lewinsky, Hilde. "Boredom," *British Journal of Educational Psychology* (Nov., 1943), 147-52.

Lindeman, Eduard C. "Dynamics of Recreational Theory," *Journal of Educational Sociology,* 21 (1948), 263-69.

Long, E. W. "A Survey of Pastimes and Hobbies of Secondary School Children," *University of Pittsburgh Bulletin,* 37 (1941), 186-94.

MacNeil, D. H. "Youth and Leisure in a New Jersey Town," *New Jersey Welfare Reporter* (1949), 13-14.

McColsky, M. A. "Importance of Recreation in a World at War," in *National Congress of Parents and Teachers Proceedings,* 1942, pp. 64-70.

McDermott, W. V. "Work and Leisure," *Parks & Recreation,* 23 (1940), 451-55.

McLaurine, W. M. "Recreation is a Vital Need," *Cotton* (Sept., 1943), 83.

Maddrell, Jane G. *Group of Descriptive Bibliographies of Miscellaneous Books, Languages, Home Economics, Entertainment, Sports, Travel,* Kansas City: Bibliography Publishing Co., 1949.

Mander, Alfred E. *Six P.M. til Midnight,* Melbourne: Rawson's, 1945.

Mannheim, Karl. "The Use of Leisure," Bibliography. In his *Man and Society in an Age of Reconstruction,* New York: Harcourt, Brace, 1940, pp. 437-38.

Mather, William G. "Income and Participation," *American Sociological Review,* 6 (1941), 380-83.

May, E. E. "Freshman Inventory of Leisure-time Skills," *Journal of the National Association of Deans of Women,* 9 (1946), 80-83.

______. "Guidance in Education for Leisure," *Journal of Health and Physical Education,* 17 (1946), 585+.

Mayo, Elton. *The Human Problems of an Industrial Civilization,* Cambridge, Mass.: Harvard University Press, 1946.

Menninger, Karl A., R. P. Knight, *et al.* "Recreation and Morale; a Subjective Symposium." Special issue. *Bulletin of the Menninger Clinic,* 6 (1942), pp. 65-102.

Menninger, William C. "Recreation and Mental Health," *Recreation*, 42 (1948), 340-46.

Meyer, Harold D., and Charles K. Brightbill. *Community Recreation: a Guide to Its Organization and Administration*, Boston: D. C. Heath & Co., 1948.

Miller, E. F. "Leisure-Time Activities," *Instructor*, 55 (1946), 17+.

Moffett, W. N. *Planning for Leisure*, Dublin, 1944. (Reconstruction Pamphlet.)

Monroe, E., and R. D. Lindquist. "Youth Attacks its Leisure Problem," in Arndt, Christian O., and L. J. Bowles, eds., *Parents, Teachers, and Youth Build Together*, New York: Hinds, Hayden & Eldredge, Inc., 1947, pp. 11-17.

Morgan, Charles. "A Leisured Civilization," in his *Reflections in a Mirror*, London: Macmillan & Co., Ltd., 1944.

Morgan, O. I. "The Effects of School Training on the Use of Leisure After Leaving School," *British Journal of Educational Psychology*, 14 (Feb., 1944), 51-53.

Mower, J. W. "A Comparative Study of Hobby Activities," *Bulletin of the Menninger Clinic*, 4 (1940), 82-87.

Nash, Jay B. *Leisure for What?* Iowa City, Iowa: The University, 1940.

______. "Philosophy of Recreation in America," *Journal of Educational Sociology*, 21 (1948), 257-63.

National Recreation Association. *A Bibliography for the Recreation Library*, New York: the Association, 1946.

______. *Bibliography for the Recreation Worker; Leisure and its Significance*, New York: the Association, 1945.

Newman, Robert G. "Leisure Interests [of Children: Statistics from Questionnaire]," *Library Journal* (Jan. 1, 1941), 24-25.

Olds, E. B. "How Do Young People Use Their Leisure Time?" *Recreation*, 42 (1949), 458-63.

"On Leisure," *Social Justice Review*, 38 (1945), 267.

"On the Creative Use of Leisure," *Labour*, 12 (1949), 434-35.

Partridge, Ernest D. "Should the Schools Train for Leisure: A Plan to Train High School Students for the Intelligent Use of Leisure; How One High School Trains for Leisure," *Recreation*, 34 (1941), 591-92+; 35 (1941), 24-26.

______, and Catherine Mooney. *Time Out for Living*, New York: American Book Co., 1941.

Patrick, C. "Relation of Childhood and Adult Leisure Activities," *Journal of Social Psychology*, 21 (1945), 65-79.

Peach, H. "Interest and Boredom in Repetitive Work: Some Observations on Egg Packing," *Bulletin of Industrial Psychology and Personnel Practice* (Melbourne), 2 (1946), 19-22.

Peters, C. C. "Education for Leisure," *Curriculum Journal*, 12 (1941), 246-49. Also *Education Digest*, 7 (1941), 39-41.

Pierce, D. J. "Leisure, Religion, and Culture," *Catholic Educational Review*, 44 (1946), 19-23.

Pittman, M. S. "After Retirement, What?" *Recreation*, 37 (1943), 222-23+.

Prewitt, Roy A. *The Economics of Public Recreation*, Washington: U. S. National Park Service, 1949.

Ranganathan, S. R. *Education for Leisure*, Delhi: Indian Adult Education Association, 1948.

Reaveley, C. "Renewal Through Leisure," *Spectator*, 173 (1944), 308-9.

"Recreation and Wartime Morale," *Parks & Recreation*, 25 (1942), 256-59.

Riecken, Henry W. *A Study of a Summer Shore Colony in a Rural Connecticut Town.* Unpublished Master's Thesis, University of Connecticut, 1941.

Rogers, J. E. "Leisure, Challenge to Education," *Journal of the American Association of Health, Physical Education, and Recreation*, 20 (1949), 316ff.

Samuel, Herbert L. S. *Leisure in a Democracy*, London: Cambridge University Press, 1949.

Schlosberg, Harold. "The Concept of Play," *Psychological Review*, 54 (1947), 229-31.

Schorsch, Robert Steven. *Psychology of Play*, South Bend, Ind.: Notre Dame Press, 1942.

Shaffer, G. W. "Some Comments on Recreation," *Occupational Therapy*, 20 (1941), 93-100.

Shanas, Ethel, and C. E. Dunning. *Recreation and Delinquency*, Chicago: Chicago Recreation Commission, 1942.

Shaw, John William. *The Social Phases of Industrial Recreation as They Affect Employee-Employer Relations in the Los Angeles Metropolitan Area.* Unpublished Ph.D. Dissertation, University of Southern California, 1948.

Simnett, William E. *Leisure: How to Enjoy It*, London: Allen & Unwin, Ltd., 1946.

Slavson, Samuel Richard. *Recreation and the Total Personality*, New York: Association Press, 1946.

Solomon, Ben. "Recreation and Delinquency," *Journal of Educational Sociology*, 21 (1948), 284-90.

"Space for Leisure," *Planning* (June 1, 1943), 2-13.

Starr, M. "Would Leisure be Just Awful?" *American Federationist*, 52 (1945), 29.

Staudinger, Hans. "Leisure-Time and Free-time Studies," *Synopsis*, Heidelberg: Lambert Schneider, 1948.

Steiner, Jesse F. *Recreation and Morale—Teaching American Youth How to Plan and Use Leisure Time*, Washington: National Council for Social Studies, National Association of Secondary-School Principals, Departments of National Association, 1942.

Stieglitz, Edward. "Wise Investment of Leisure," *Scientific Monthly* (Aug., 1940), 147-57.

Streit, W. K. "Approach to Leisure Time Activities," *American School Board Journal,* 119 (1949), 17-18.
Sullenger, T. E. "Leadership and Leisure-time Interest of Grade School Boys," *Sociology and Social Research,* 25 (1941), 351-55.
Sullivan, C. J. "Work Plans for Leisure," *Ave Maria,* 68 (1948), 595-97.
Super, Donald E. *Avocational Interest Patterns; a Study in the Psychology of Avocations,* Stanford, Calif.: Stanford University Press, 1940. Published also as Ph.D. Dissertation, Columbia University, 1940.
"Training for Leisure; Method and Results of an Inquiry," *Times Educational Supplement,* 1446 (1943), 34.
Tunis, John R. "Americans Need Play," *Harper's,* 183 (1941), 200-5.
U. S. Office of Education, Library Division. "Play and Recreation," in *Bibliography of Research Studies in Education, 1939-1940,* Washington, 1941, pp. 137-40. (Bulletin 6.)
U. S. Women's Bureau. *The Nonworking Time of Industrial Women Workers,* Washington, 1940. (Bulletin 181.)
Van Dalen, D. B. "A Differential Analysis of the Play of Adolescent Boys," *Journal of Educational Research,* 41 (1947), 204-13.
______. "Study of Certain Factors in Their Relation to the Play of Children," *Research Quarterly,* 18 (1947), 279-90.
Vivacecar, R. B. *Universalized Leisure with Life, Liberty and the Pursuit of Happiness,* New York: Freeland F. Penney, 1943. (Pamphlet.)
Volberding, Eleanor. "Out-of-school Behavior of Eleven-year-olds," *Elementary School Journal,* 48 (1948), 432-41.
______. "Out-of-School Living of Eleven-year-old Boys and Girls from Differing Socio-economic Groups," *Elementary School Journal,* 49 (1949), 348-53.
Wallace, I. K. "Women's Use of Leisure: Summary of the Replies to a Questionnaire Completed by College Women," *Journal of Higher Education,* 14 (1943), 301-6+.
Warner, W. Lloyd, and Paul S. Lunt. *The Social Life of a Modern Community,* ("Yankee City Series," Vol. I.) New Haven: Yale University Press, 1941.
Washington Public Opinion Laboratory. *Opinions and Attitudes of Adults Relating to Leisure Use in the State of Washington,* Pullman: State College of Washington, 1949.
Wendt, G. "Science and Leisure," *Science Digest,* 7 (1940), 1-7.
Wenger, P. N. "Living in a Dynamic World," *Industrial Arts and Vocational Education,* 38 (1949), 198-200.
Wesley, H. D. "Education for Leisure," *Texas Outlook,* 24 (1940), 29-30.
White, F. "Young Entry; Board of Education White Paper on Youth Registration," *New Statesman and Nation,* 25 (1943), 349-50.
White, H. C. "Leisure and the War Effort," *Journal of the National Association of Deans of Women,* 7 (1943), 17-20.
Whitman, Howard. "Play as You Go," *Reader's Digest* (March, 1948), 50-52.
Whyte, William F. *Street Corner Society,* Chicago: University of Chicago Press, 1943.
Wrenn, C. Gilbert, and D. L. Harley. *Time On Their Hands,* Washington: American Council on Education, 1941.
"Young People's Colleges and Leisure Time," *British Journal of Educational Psychology,* 14 (1944), 80-84.
Zirbes, L. "Work and Play," *Childhood Education,* 25 (1948), 147-48.

1950–1958

Adler, Mortimer J. "Labor, Leisure and Liberal Education," *Journal of General Education,* 6 (1951), 35-45.
AFL-CIO. *The Shorter Work Week,* Washington: Public Affairs Press, 1957.
Agnihotri, Vidyadhar. "Work, Leisure and Recreation," *Uttara Bharati,* 3 (1957), 48-60.
Allen, P. G. "Evening Activities in the Home," *Sociological Review,* 43 (1951), 127-41.
†Altick, Richard Daniel. *The English Common Reader; A Social History of the Mass Reading Public, 1800-1900,* Chicago: University of Chicago Press, 1957.
American Association for Health, Physical Education, and Recreation. *Recreation Bibliography,* Washington, 1953.
†Amory, Cleveland. *The Last Resorts,* New York: Harper & Bros., 1952.
Anderson, Harold H. "Self-Expression Through Creativity," in Donahue, Wilma, *et al.,* eds. *Free Time,* Ann Arbor: University of Michigan Press, 1958, pp. 141-50.
Anderson, Jackson M. *Industrial Recreation: A Guide to its Organization and Administration,* New York: McGraw-Hill Book Co., 1955.
Anderson, John E. "Psychological Aspects of the Use of Free Time," in Donahue, Wilma, *et al.,* eds. *Free Time,* Ann Arbor: University of Michigan Press, 1958, pp. 29-44.

Antoinette, Sister M. "Human Rights and the Child's Leisure Time," in *National Catholic Educational Association Proceedings,* 48 (1951), 403-7.

Astor, William and Charlotte. "Private Associations and Commercial Activities," *Annals of the American Academy,* 313 (1957), 92-98.

Axelrod, Morris. "Urban Structure and Social Participation," *American Sociological Review,* 21 (1956), 13-18.

Baley, J. A. "Recreation and the Aging Process," *Research Quarterly,* 26 (1955), 1-7.

Balsley, Gene. "The Hot Rod Culture," *American Quarterly,* 2 (1950), 353-59.

Baratta, A., *et al.* "Leisure Time; a Challenge to Education," *National Elementary Principal,* 37 (1957), 21-24.

Barber, Bernard. "Participation and Mass Apathy in Associations," in Alvin Gouldner, ed. *Studies in Leadership,* New York: Harper & Bros., 1950, pp. 477-504.

Barclay, Dorothy. "Emotional Stakes in Playing Games," *New York Times Magazine* (Aug. 7, 1955), 43.

Barkin, Solomon. "Discussion of the Shortening Work Week," *American Economic Review,* 46 (May, 1956), 223-26.

Bartlett, Sir Frederic. *The Mind at Work and Play,* London: Allen and Unwin, 1951.

"Beating Paths to New Luxury Market," *Business Week,* 37 (1952), 128-36.

Beaubien, R. "Nine Principles Deducible from a Definition of Leisure," *Franciscan Herald,* 37 (1958), 41-44.

Beirne, J. A. "The Shorter Working Week in the United States," *Free Labour World,* 71 (May, 1956), 32-37.

Bell, Daniel. *Work and Its Discontents,* Boston: Beacon Press, 1956.

Bendiner, Robert. "Could You Stand a Four-day Week?" *Reporter* (Aug. 8, 1957), 10-14.

Best, J. W. "Do We Educate for Leisure?" *Recreation,* 45 (1951), 201-2.

Betts, John Rickards. "The Technological Revolution and the Rise of Sport, 1850-1900," *Mississippi Valley Historical Review,* 40 (1953), 231-56.

Bieber, Irving. "Pathological Boredom and Inertia," *American Journal of Psychotherapy,* 5 (1951), 215-25.

Blakely, Robert J. "The Way of Liberal Education," in Donahue, Wilma, *et al,* eds. *Free Time,* Ann Arbor: University of Michigan Press, 1958, pp. 99-117.

Bossemeyer, James L. "Travel: American Mobility," *Annals of the American Academy,* 313 (1957), 113-16.

Boyce, Carroll W. "The Four-Day Week?" *Factory Management and Maintenance* (November, 1956).

Brandwein, Seymour. "Recent Accomplishments," in AFL-CIO, *The Shorter Work Week,* Washington: Public Affairs Press, 1957.

Bretsch, H. S. "Evaluation of the Objectives of Community Recreational Centers," *Journal of Educational Sociology,* 24 (1950), 177-84.

Brooks, George. "Historical Background," in AFL-CIO, *The Shorter Work Week,* Washington: Public Affairs Press, 1957.

Brouwer, Tony. *Limitations of the Work Week.* Unpublished Ph.D. Dissertation, University of Michigan, 1957.

Browne, Geoffrey. *Patterns of British Life,* London: Hulton Press, Ltd., 1950.

Bryson, Lyman. *The Next America,* New York: Harper & Bros., 1952.

Bucher, C. A. "Are Schools Developing Resources for Leisure?" *New York State Education,* 43 (1956), 611-13.

Buell, Bradley. *Community Planning for Human Services,* New York: Columbia University Press, 1952.

Burgess, Ernest W., ed. "Aging and Retirement." Special issue. *American Journal of Sociology,* 49, (January, 1954).

______."The Retired Person and Organizational Activities," in Donahue, Wilma, *et al,* eds. *Free Time,* Ann Arbor: University of Michigan Press, 1958, pp. 151-56.

______. "Social Relations, Activities, and Personal Adjustment," *American Journal of Sociology,* 59 (1954), 352-60.

Burtle, James. "Automation, the Guaranteed Wage and Hours of Work," *International Labour Review,* 75 (1957), 495-513.

Business Man's Leisure, Montreal: Royal Bank of Canada, 1952. (Pamphlet.)

Butler, George D. "The Structure of Public Leisure Agencies," *Annals of the American Academy,* 313 (1957), 119-25.

Butler, Rohan. "Beside the Point: Leisure," *World Review* (March, 1953), 6-10.

Calhoun, J. C. "Don't Be a Week-end Neurotic," *Catholic Digest,* 19 (1955), 19-22.

Campbell, M. E. "But Each for the Joy of the Working," *Occupations,* 30 (1952), 356-57.

Campbell, T. "Leisure Society," *Catholic Worker,* 18 (1952), 3+.

Cauter, T., and John S. Downham. *The Communication of Ideas: A Study of Contemporary Influences on Urban Life,* London: Chatto & Windus, 1954.

Chalfen, Leo. "Leisure Time Adjustment of the Aged: Activities and Interests and Some Factors Influencing Choice," *Journal of Genetic Psychology,* 88 (1956), 261-76.

Chapman, Dennis. *The Home and Social Status,* London: Routledge & Kegan Paul, Ltd., 1955.

Charlesworth, James C. "A Bold Program for Recreation," *Annals of the American Academy,* 313 (1957), 141-47.

Choate, Joseph E. "Recreational Boating: the Nation's Family Sport," *Annals of the American Academy,* 313 (1957), 109-12.

Clancy, W. P. "Leisure in a Bourgeois World," *Commonweal,* 56 (1952), 18-19.

Clark, T. C. "Leisure and a Happier and Better Life," *Education,* 71 (1950), 88-91.

†Clarke, Alfred C. "Use of Leisure and its Relation to Levels of Occupational Prestige," *American Sociological Review,* 21 (1956), 301-7.

______. *The Use of Leisure and Its Relation to Social Stratification.* Unpublished Ph.D. *Dissertation,* The Ohio State University, 1955.

Clawson, Marion. *Statistics on Outdoor Recreation,* Washington: Resources for the Future, Inc., 1958.

Clift, Virgil A. "Recreational and Leisure-Time Problems and Needs of Negro Children and Youth," *Journal of Negro Education,* 19 (1950), 333-40.

Climer, Fred W. "The Shorter Workweek Issue," in *Addresses on Industrial Relations, 1957 Series,* Ann Arbor: University of Michigan, 1957. (Bulletin 25.)

Coe, G. A. "Philosophy of Play," *Religious Education,* 51 (1956), 220-22.

Cohen, John. "Ideas of Work and Play," *British Journal of Sociology,* 4 (1953), 313-22.

†Collins, Herbert. "The Sedentary Society," *Scientific Monthly,* 79 (1954), 285-92.

Conn, Jacob H. "Children's Awareness of Sex Differences, II; Play Attitudes and Game Preferences," *Journal of Child Psychiatry,* 2 (1951), 82-99.

Connor, Ruth, T. B. Johannis, and James Walters. "Family Recreation in Relation to Role Conceptions of Family Members," *Marriage and Family Living,* 17 (1955), 306-9.

Cook, T. I. "Democracy, Leisure, and Communism," *Journal of Politics,* 12 (1950), 530-46.

Cooper, S. "Using the New Leisure," *National Elementary Principal,* 36 (1957), 9-12.

Corrie, Walter S., Jr. *Work as a Central Life Interest.* Unpublished Ph.D. Dissertation, State University of Iowa, 1957. (University Microfilms #23, 725.)

Cousins, Norman. "Science and Sense," *Saturday Review,* 39 (1956), 20.

Cozens, Frederick W., and F. S. Stumpf. *Sports in American Life,* Chicago: University of Chicago Press, 1953.

Cramer, M. W. "Leisure Time Activities of Economically Privileged Children," *Sociology and Social Research,* 34 (1950), 444-50.

Crespi, I. "Social Significance of Card Playing as a Leisure Time Activity," *American Sociological Review,* 21 (1956), 717-21. Correction. 23 (1958), 85ff.

Croft, F. E. "How Bored Can You Get?" *Catholic Digest,* 18 (1954), 60-63.

______. "Look What Utter Boredom Can Do," *Maclean's Magazine,* 67 (1954), 18-19, 88-90.

Dana, S. T. *Research in Forest Recreation,* Washington: U. S. Department of Agriculture, Forest Service, 1957.

Decicco, Ernest M. "The Four Day Week," *The New Leader* (July 29, 1957), 3-5.

Decker, Kenneth. "Can We Predict Recreation's Future?" *Journal of Health, Physical Education, and Recreation* (March, 1955).

Dempsey, David. "Myth of the New Leisure Class," *New York Times Magazine* (Jan. 26, 1958), 12ff.

Denney, Reuel. *The Astonished Muse,* Chicago: University of Chicago Press, 1957.

*______, and Mary Lea Meyersohn, comps. "Preliminary Bibliography on Leisure," *American Journal of Sociology,* 62 (1957), 602-15.

______, and David Riesman. "Leisure and Human Values in Industrial Civilization," in Staley, Eugene, ed. *Creating an Industrial Civilization,* New York: Harper & Bros., 1952, pp. 50-91.

______. "Leisure in Industrial America," in Staley, Eugene, ed. *Creating an Industrial Civilization,* New York: Harper & Bros., 1952, pp. 245-81.

______. "Until the Ball is Dead or Fairly So," *University of Chicago Magazine* (Nov., 1952).

______, *et al.* "The Tyranny of Leisure," University of Chicago Round Table, May 13, 1951, 1-11.

De Rosis, Louis E. "Leisure Time–Burden or Benefit?" New York: Auxiliary Council of the Association for the Advancement of Psychoanalysis, 1951.

Dewhurst, J. Frederic *et al.* "Recreation," Chapter 11 in *America's Needs and Resources, a New Survey,* New York: The Twentieth Century Fund, 1955, pp. 346-77.

DeWitt, N. J. "Education and Leisure," in Beck, Robert Holmes, ed. *Three R's Plus,* Minneapolis: University of Minnesota Press, 1956, pp. 360-69.

Dhingra, Baldoon. "The Spirit of Asian Leisure," *Way Forum,* 26 (1957), 6ff.

Dick, R. "Time and Space on our Hands," *National Elementary Principal,* 29 (1950), 30-31.

"Disappearance of the Leisured Class," *Social Justice Review,* 48 (1955), 88.

Dobbs, K. R. E. "Automation and Art," *Canadian Forum,* 36 (1956), 8-9.

Donahue, Wilma, *et al,* eds. *Free Time: Challenge to Later Maturity,* Ann Arbor: University of Michigan Press, 1958.

Dotson, Floyd. "Patterns of Voluntary Association Among Urban Working-Class Families," *American Sociological Review,* 16 (1951), 687-93.

Douglass, Paul F. "People, Power and Leisure," *Recreation,* 46A (1953), 210-12.

______, John L. Hutchinson, and Willard C. Sutherland, eds. "Recreation in the Age of Automation." Special issue. *Annals of the American Academy of Political and Social Sciences,* 313 (1957).

†Dubin, Robert. "Industrial Workers' Worlds: A Study of the 'Central Life Interests' of Industrial Workers," *Social Problems,* 3 (1956), 131-42.

Du Toit, J. B. *Youth, Work and Leisure* [A Summary Based on a Thesis submitted for the Ph.D. at the University of Stellenbosch,

Union of South Africa, November, 1956.] Chicago: University of Chicago, Center for the Study of Leisure. (Manuscript.)

Dutton, E. P. "Automation; Challenge to Recreation," *Recreation*, 49 (1956), 106-7.

†The Editors of *Fortune*. "$30 Billion for Fun," in *The Changing American Market*, Garden City, N. Y.: Hanover House, 1953, pp. 197-214.

Edman, Irving. "Qualities of Leisure," *Educational Record*, 33 (1952), 212-16.

Ennis, Philip H. "Leisure in the Suburbs: Research Prolegomenon," in Dobriner, William, ed. *The Suburban Community*, New York: G. P. Putnam's Sons, 1958, pp. 248-70.

Eppel, E. M. and J. "Young Workers at a County College: Part II," *British Journal of Educational Psychology*, 23 (1953), 87-96.

Eppley, G. G. "Recreation and the Schools," *Bulletin of the School of Education, Indiana University*, 33 (1957), 22-24.

Erwin, Ralph J. *Time Barriers*, New York: Greenwich Book Publishers, 1957.

Fadiman, Clifton. "The Decline of Attention," *Saturday Review Reader*, New York: Bantam Books, 1951.

Fellows, E. W. "Studies of Factors Related to a Feeling of Happiness," *Journal of Educational Research*, 50 (1956), 231-34.

Fenichel, Hanna. "Review of the Literature on Boredom," *Psychoanalytic Quarterly*, 20 (1951), 345-46.

Fenichel, Otto. "The Psychology of Boredom," in his *Collected Papers*, New York: W. W. Norton & Co., Inc., 1953.

Fitzgerald G. B. "Education for Leisure," *Review of Educational Research*, 20 (1950), 294-98.

Fogler, S. "Prometheus or Frankenstein," *Journal of Educational Sociology*, 24 (1950), 154-66.

Foote, Nelson N. "Discussion of Shortening Work Week," *American Economic Review*, 46 (May, 1956), 226-29.

______. "Family Living as Play," *Marriage and Family Living*, 17 (1955), 296-301.

†______. "Sex as Play," *Social Problems*, 1 (1953), 159-63.

Foskett, John M. "Social Structure and Social Participation," *American Sociological Review*, 20 (1955), 431-37.

Fox, Sherwood D. *Voluntary Associations and the Social Structure*. Unpublished Ph.D. Dissertation, Harvard University, 1953.

Frank, Lawrence K. "Play in Personality Development," *American Journal of Orthopsychiatry*, 25 (1955), 576-90.

Freeman, Howard E., Edwin Novak, and Leo G. Reeder. "Correlates of Membership in Voluntary Associations," *American Sociological Review*, 22 (1957), 528-33.

Friedmann, Eugene A. "The Work of Leisure," in Donahue, Wilma, *et al*, eds. *Free Time*, Ann Arbor: University of Michigan Press, 1958, pp. 119-32.

______, and Robert J. Havighurst, *et al. The Meaning of Work and Retirement*, Chicago: University of Chicago Press, 1954.

Frohlich, Philip E. *Sports and the Community: A Study of Social Change in Athens, Ohio*. Unpublished Ph.D. Dissertation, University of Wisconsin, 1952.

Ginsburg, Woodrow L., and Ralph Bergmann. "The Worker's Viewpoint, in AFL-CIO. *The Shorter Work Week*," Washington: Public Affairs Press, 1957.

Goldfinger, Nat. "Economic Considerations," in AFL-CIO. *The Shorter Work Week*, Washington, D. C.: Public Affairs Press, 1957.

Goldner, William. *Hours of Work*, Berkeley: Institute of Industrial Relations, University of California, 1952.

Grattan, C. Hartley. "Education for Understanding," in Donahue, Wilma, *et al*, eds. *Free Time*, Ann Arbor: University of Michigan Press, 1958, pp. 157-70.

Green, Arnold W. "Recreation in America," Chapter 24 in his *Sociology: An Analysis of Life in Modern Society*, New York: McGraw-Hill, 1956, pp. 478-502.

†Greenberg, Clement. "Plight of Our Culture; Work and Leisure Under Industrialism," *Commentary*, 16 (1953), 54-62.

Greenson, Ralph R. "Apathetic and Agitated Boredom," *Psychoanalytic Quarterly*, 20 (1951), 346-47.

Gregory, Paul M. *The Baseball Player: An Economic Study*, Washington: Public Affairs Press, 1956.

Grellinger, J. B. "Shorter Hours Need Longer Books," *Catholic Library World*, 27 (1955), 9-12.

Groombridge, B. "Watching Other People Working," *Journal of Education* (London), 90 (1958), 104-5.

Grygier, Tadeusz. "Leisure Pursuits of Juvenile Delinquents: a Study in Methodology," *British Journal of Delinquency*, 5 (1955), 210-28.

Gustavino, C. A. "Universal Ennui," *Américas*, 7 (1955), 38.

Haber, William. "The Shorter Workweek Issue," *Addresses on Industrial Relations, 1957 Series*, Ann Arbor: University of Michigan, 1957. (Bulletin 25.)

†Halmos, Paul. *Solitude and Privacy*, London: Routledge & Kegan Paul, Ltd., 1952.

Harlan, William H. *Isolation and Conduct in Later Life*. Unpublished Ph.D. Dissertation, University of Chicago, 1950.

Harmon, J. M. "The Psychology of Recreation," *Education*, 71 (1950), 99-104.

Hart, James David. *The Popular Book; a History of America's Literary Taste*, New York: Oxford University Press, 1950.

Hartley, Ruth E., Lawrence K. Frank, and Robert M. Goldenson. *Understanding Children's Play*, New York: Columbia University Press, 1952.

Havighurst, Robert J. "Flexibility and the Social Roles of the Retired," *American Journal of Sociology*, 59 (1954), 309-11.

______. "Leisure Activities of the Middle-aged," *American Journal of Sociology,* 63 (1957), 152-62.

______, and Ruth Albrecht. *Older People,* New York: Longmans, Green & Co., 1953.

Hawkins, Harold, and James Walters. "Family Recreation Activities," *Journal of Home Economics,* 44 (1952), 623-26.

Hay, Donald G. "The Social Participation of Households in Selected Rural Communities of the Northeast," *Rural Sociology,* 15 (1950), 146-47.

Hayner, Norman S. "Mexicans at Play—a Revolution," *Sociology and Social Research* (Nov., Dec., 1953).

Heckscher, August. "The Gift of Time," *Journal of the National Education Association,* 46 (1957), 326-29.

______. "Next Two Decades: Coming Changes in American Life," in National Conference on Higher Education, *Current Issues in Higher Education,* Chicago: Association for Higher Education, 1957, pp. 1-12.

Henle, Peter. "Proposals for Reducing the Workweek," *Monthly Labor Review* (Nov., 1956), 1267.

______. "Which Way to Greater Leisure?" In AFL-CIO. *The Shorter Work Week,* Washington, D. C.: Public Affairs Press, 1957.

Hepworth, A. L. "Meeting Workers' Leisure-time Needs," *Canadian Labour,* 3 (1958), 55-58.

Herbert, W. B. "Place of Leisure in Canadian Society," *Canadian Labour,* 3 (1958), 59, 67.

†Heron, Woodburn. "Pathology of Boredom," *Scientific American,* 196 (1957), 52-56.

Herrod, R. "Bigger and Better," *Spectator,* 196 (1956), 610-12.

Herrold, Z. C. "Community Recreation, a County Project," *Journal of Health, Physical Education, and Recreation,* 29 (1958), 24ff.

Highton, Frank. "The Issue of the Shorter Work Week," New York: General Electric Company, 1957. (Mimeographed)

Hill, L. F. "Why We Need to Play," *Journal of Health, Physical Education, and Recreation,* 28 (1957), 12ff.

Hillig, F. "Battle Against Present-day Restlessness," *Life of the Spirit,* 11 (1956), 263-70.

Houghton, A. A., Jr. "Leisure Time and the Liberal Arts," *Association of American Colleges Bulletin,* 39 (1953), 618-23.

Hoyt, G. C. "The Life of the Retired in a Trailer Park," *American Journal of Sociology,* 59 (1954), 361-70.

Hutchinson, John L. *Principles of Recreation,* New York: Ronald Press, 1951.

Hutchison, W. B. "Coming Revolt Against Leisure," *Maclean's Magazine,* 71 (1958), 18-19, 49-50+.

Huth, Hans. *Nature and the American,* Berkeley: University of California Press, 1957.

International Labour Office. "Recent Developments in the Reduction of Hours of Work in Europe," *International Labour Review,* 75 (1957), 468-78.

______. "Repercussions of a Reduction in Hours of Work," *International Labour Review,* 74 (1956), 23-45.

Jackson, Lydia, and Kathleen Todd. *Child Treatment and the Therapy of Play,* New York: Ronald Press, 1950.

*Jackson, Robin, and Rolf Meyersohn. "The Social Patterning of Leisure." Speech delivered to the 34th Annual Institute of the Society for Social Research, University of Chicago, 1957. Chicago: Center for the Study of Leisure, 1957.

Jones, M. L. "Those Family Hours and Business Men," *Dun's Review and Modern Industry,* 62 (1953), 48-50+.

Jordan, Millard L. "Leisure Time Activities of Sociologists and Attorneys," *Sociology and Social Research,* 40 (1956), 176-78.

Joussellin, J. "Leisure: Excerpts from Address at International Youth Conference, London," *Recreation,* 43 (1950), 464-5.

Juenger, F. G. "Leisure: Its Meaning and Its Worth," *Social Justice Review,* 46 (1953), 88.

†Kahn, Roger. "Money, Muscles—and Myths," *Nation* (July 6, 1957), 9-12.

Kaplan, Max. "Pressures of Leisure on the Older Individual," Conference of Gerontological Society, Inc., Cleveland, Ohio, November 1, 1957.

Katz, Elihu, and Paul F. Lazarsfeld. *Personal Influence.* Glencoe, Ill.: Free Press, 1956.

Kerr, Clark. "Discussion of the Shortening Work Week," *American Economic Review,* 46 (May 1956), 218-223.

Krasner, I. Bigford. "Factors Associated with Status in a Recreational Program for the Aged," *Jewish Social Service Quarterly,* 28 (1952), 290-301.

Kronenberger, Louis. *Company Manners,* Indianapolis: Bobbs-Merrill Co., 1954.

______. "Our Most Personal Possession: Leisure," *McCalls* (April, 1956).

"Labor's Drive for the Shorter Work Week," *Machinists,* 68 (1956), 268-70.

Lantos, Barbara. "Metapsychological Considerations on the Concept of Work," *International Journal of Psycho-Analysis,* 33 (1952), 439-43.

†Larrabee, Eric. "What's Happening to Hobbies," *New York Times Magazine* (Dec. 27, 1953), 10.

*______, and Rolf Meyersohn, eds. *Mass Leisure,* Glencoe, Ill.: Free Press, 1958.

Larson, Leonard A., and Rachael D. Yocom. *Measurement and Evaluation in Physical, Health and Recreation Education,* St. Louis: C. V. Mosby Co., 1951.

Lawrence, J. "Leisure: America's Coming Problem," *Ave Maria,* 85 (1957), 8-11.

Leevy, J. Roy. "Leisure Time of the American Housewife," *Sociology and Social Research,* 35 (1950), 97-105.

"Leisure and Culture." Special Issue. *Way Forum,* 26 (December 1957). [Published by the World Assembly of Youth, 25, rue d'Astorg, Paris.]

"Leisure Time," *Social Justice Review,* 50 (1957), 95.

"Leisure Time or Waste Time?" *Scholastic,* 64 (1954), 7-8.

"Leisured Masses," *Business Week* (Sept. 12, 1953), 142-46+.

Lerner, Daniel. "Comfort and Fun: Morality in a Nice Society," *American Scholar,* 27 (1958), 153-65.

Letton, Mildred C. *Your Child's Leisure Time,* New York: Columbia University Teachers College, 1952.

Leuchtenberg, William. *The Perils of Prosperity,* Chicago: University of Chicago Press, 1958.

Lewis, D. E. "Misty Flats," *Dalhousie Review,* 30 (1951), 413-16.

Lewis, H. Gregg. "Hours of Work and Hours of Leisure," *Proceedings,* 9th Annual Meeting, Industrial Relations Research Association, Madison, 1957.

Linden, Maurice E. "Preparation for the Leisure of Later Maturity," in Donahue, Wilma, *et al,* eds. *Free Time,* Ann Arbor: University of Michigan Press, 1958, pp. 77-98.

Lipscomb, Willis G. "Go Now—Pay Later: Time Payment for International Travel," *Annals of the American Academy,* 313 (1957), 117-18.

Lockwood, M. G. "Illusions of Leisure," *Civil Engineering,* 27 (1957), 316-17.

†Lynes, Russell. "Time on Our Hands," *Harper's,* 217 (July, 1958), 34-39.

†MacIver, Robert. "The Great Emptiness," in his *The Pursuit of Happiness,* New York: Simon & Schuster, Inc., 1955.

McEntire, Davis. *Leisure Activities of Youth in Berkeley, California,* Berkeley: Berkeley Council of Social Welfare and School of Social Welfare, University of California, 1952.

Mangels, William T. *The Outdoor Amusements Industry,* New York: Vantage Press, 1952.

Mannheim, Karl. "Work and Leisure," Chapter 11 in his *Freedom, Power, and Democratic Planning,* New York: Oxford University Press, 1950, pp. 266-74.

Martin, Alexander Reid. "Are You a Weekend Neurotic?" *This Week Magazine* (June 10, 1956).

______. "The Fear of Relaxation and Leisure," *The American Journal of Psychoanalysis,* 11 (1951), 42-50.

______. *A Philosophy of Recreation,* Chapel Hill: University of North Carolina, 1955.

______. "Using Leisure Time Agencies to Treat the Problems Confronting Adolescents," *American Journal of Psychiatry,* 109 (1952), 344-51.

Mattingly, C. Q. "Where Did the Time Go?" *Grail,* 38 (1956), 62-63.

Mayo, Selz C. "Social Participation Among the Older Population in Rural Areas of Wake County, North Carolina," *Social Forces,* 30 (1951), 53-59.

†Mead, Margaret. "The Pattern of Leisure in Contemporary American Culture," *Annals of the American Academy,* 313 (1957), 11-15.

Medical Department of the Equitable Life Assurance Society of the United States. *Leisure Time for Assurance of a Fuller Life,* New York: the Society, 1957. (Pamphlet.)

Menninger, William C. *Enjoying Leisure Time,* Chicago: Science Research Associates, Inc., 1950.

Methodist General Board of Education. "Bibliography of Leisure," *Leisure,* 12 (Fall, 1957). [P.O. Box 871, Nashville 2, Tennessee.]

Meyer, Harold D. "The Adult Cycle," *Annals of the American Academy,* 313 (1957), 58-67.

Meyer, Harold D. "Selected References on Education for Leisure Living," *High School Journal,* 37 (1954), 187-91.

*Meyersohn, Rolf B. "Americans Off Duty," in Donahue, Wilma, *et al,* eds. *Free Time,* Ann Arbor: University of Michigan Press, 1958, pp. 45-60.

*______. "Leisure in a Marginal Group," Speech delivered at the 33rd Annual Institute of the Society for Social Research, University of Chicago, 1956, Chicago: Center for the Study of Leisure, 1956.

*______. "The Leisure Revolution," Speech delivered to the Chicago Chapter of the American Marketing Association, November, 1956, Chicago: Center for the Study of Leisure, 1956.

*______. "*The Lonely Crowd* and Its Marketing Significance," in Bass, Frank M., ed. *The Frontiers of Marketing Thought and Science,* Chicago: American Marketing Association, 1958.

*______. "What Do We Know About Audiences?" *Journal of Broadcasting,* 1 (1957), 220-31.

*______. "Social Research in Television," in Bernard Rosenberg and D. M. White, eds., *Mass Culture,* Glencoe, Ill.: Free Press, 1957, pp. 345-57.

*______, and Robin Jackson. "Gardening in Suburbia," in Dobriner, William, ed. *The Suburban Community,* New York: G. P. Putnam & Sons, 1958, pp. 271-86.

*†______, and Elihu Katz. "Notes on a Natural History of Fads," *American Journal of Sociology,* 62 (1957), 594-601.

Michelon, L. C. "The New Leisure Class," *American Journal of Sociology,* 59 (1954), 371-78.

Mid-Continent Surveys. *Symphony Survey,* Minneapolis: The Minnesota Symphony Orchestra Association, 1956.

Miller, N. P. "Education for Leisure," *Journal of Health, Physical Education, and Recreation,* 27 (1956), 16ff.

Mills, C. W. "Unity of Work and Leisure," *Journal of the National Association of Deans of Women*, 17 (1954), 58-61.

Moran, Lawrence. "The Myth of Machine-made Leisure: Who Will Redefine Leisure?" *Social Order*, 6 (1956), 434-39.

"More and More Leisure," *America*, 90 (1954), 472.

"More Time to Consume," *Tide*, 30, 5-8 (March, April, 1956).

Morehead, Albert H. "Games: Who Plays What and Why," *New York Times Magazine* (Oct. 13, 1957), 54ff.

Morse, Nancy C., and Robert S. Weiss. "The Function and Meaning of Work and the Job," *American Sociological Review*, 20 (1955), 191-98.

Moyer, K. E., and B. Von H. Gilmer. "Experimental Study of Children's Preferences and Use of Blocks in Play," *Journal of Genetic Psychology*, 89 (1956), 3-10.

Muir, Kevin. "Freedom from the Machine," *Way Forum*, 26 (1957), 20ff.

Nash, Jay B. "Leisure, Then What?" *Education*, 78 (1958), 456-59.

______. *Philosophy of Recreation and Leisure*, St. Louis: C. V. Mosby Co., 1953.

National Conference on Education for Leisure. *Community Approach to the Leisure Problem*, Washington: American Association for Health, Physical Education, and Recreation, 1957.

National Recreation Association. *Proceedings of the International Recreation Congress*, New York, 1956.

______. *Supplementary Guide to Free and Inexpensive Publications on Recreation and Leisure*, New York, 1955.

National Social Welfare Assembly, Inc. "Leisure-Time Services: Trends and Developments, 1953-1955," 345 West 46th Street, New York 17, N.Y. (Mimeographed.)

______. "Leisure-Time Services Trends and Developments, 1955-1957," 345 East 46th Street, New York 17, N.Y. (Mimeographed.)

Neighborhood Activities Committee of the Character Building Division of the Related Activities Council, and the Division of Research of the Schenectady Public Schools. *Recreational Interests and Needs of Schenectady Teen-Age Youth*, Schenectady, 1952.

Nelson, Lloyd Palm. *Selected Factors Associated with High School Students' Original Interest and Subsequent Development in a Favorite Leisure-time Activity*. Unpublished Ph.D. Dissertation, University of Illinois, 1955. (University Microfilms, #15,250.)

Neubert, R. "Recreation and the Teenager," *Bulletin of the National Association of Secondary-School Principals*, 39 (1955), 135-40.

Neumeyer, Martin H. *Social Problems and the Changing Society*, Princeton: D. Van Nostrand Co., 1953.

______ and Esther S. *Leisure and Recreation*, Third ed., New York: Ronald Press, 1958.

"The New Do-It-Yourself Market," *Business Week*, 38 (1952), 60-79.

"The New Leisure Class," *Tide*, 31 (April 12, 1957), 38-42.

"A New Trend: Everybody's Going Out for Sports," *Business Week*, 37 (1952), 85-86.

Nicolson, Harold. *Good Behavior*, London: Constable & Co., Ltd., 1955.

Northrup, Herbert R., and Herbert R. Brinberg. *Economics of the Work Week*, New York: National Industrial Conference Board, Inc., 1950. (Studies in Business Economics, Number 24.)

O'Donoghue, D. "Leisure and the Life of the Mind," *Furrow*, 5 (1954), 566-70.

Ordway, Samuel. *Prosperity beyond Tomorrow*, New York: Ronald Press, 1955.

Orzack, Louis H., and L. W. Wager. "A Study of Mass Voluntary Behavior," *Public Opinion Quarterly*, 20 (Winter, 1956-57), 723-5.

Ostrow, Albert A. *How to Enjoy Yourself*, New York: E. P. Dutton & Co., Inc., 1954.

Overmann, H. A., S. F. Olson, and G. Mikan. "Leisure: Man's Key to Self-realization," *Minnesota Journal of Education*, 38 (1958), 12-14.

Overstreet, Harry A. "Family Recreation," *National Parent-Teacher*, 39 (1945), 13-15.

Paoletti, Henri. "Leisure Habits and Social Contacts from the International Point of View," *International Journal of Public Opinion and Attitude Research*, 4 (1950), 273-74.

Pennington, A. "An Enquiry into Leisure-time Interests," *British Journal of Educational Psychology*, 21 (1951), 154.

†Piaget, Jean. *Play, Dreams and Imitation of Childhood*. Translated by Margaret Cook. New York: W. W. Norton & Co., 1951.

Pieper, Josef. "Leisure and Human Life," *Way Forum*, 26 (1957), 3-5.

†______. *Leisure, the Basis of Culture*. Translated by Alexander Dru. London: Faber & Faber, 1952.

______. "Social Meaning of Leisure in the Modern World," *Review of Politics*, 12 (1950), 411-21.

"Plenty of Time," *Times Literary Supplement*, 2793 (1955), 525.

Polak, Fred L. "Television and Leisure," *Journal of Communication*, 2 (1952), 15-25.

Pope, Hallowell. *The Relationship of the Social Significance or Meaning of Leisure and Work in Middle-Aged Males*. Unpublished Master's Thesis, University of Chicago, 1957.

Potter, David M. *People of Plenty: Economic Abundance and the American Character*, Chicago: University of Chicago Press, 1954.

Prendergast, J. "Your Own Time," *American Federationist*, 58 (1951), 20-21+.

______, and J. B. Kessel. "Education for Creative and Recreative Leisure," *Journal of Adult Education*, 2 (1952), 205-7.

Pullias, E. V. "A Psychologist Looks at Recreation," *Journal of Health, Physical Education, and Recreation*, 28 (1957), 21-22.

Rabassiere, Henri. "The Right to be Lazy," *Dissent*, 3, 1 (Winter, 1956), 37-60.

______. "What Price Work?" *Dissent*, 4, 4 (Autumn, 1957), 421-27.

Rau, C. "Psychological Notes on the Theory of Art as Play," *Journal of Aesthetics*, 8 (1950), 229-38.

Reed, Bryan H. *Eighty Thousand Adolescents*, London: Allen and Unwin, Ltd., 1950.

Reissman, Leonard. "Class, Leisure, and Social Participation," *American Sociological Review*, 19 (1954), 76-84.

"Repercussions of a Reduction in Hours of Work; Benefits of Greater Leisure," *International Labour Review*, 74 (1956), 25-27.

Riemer, Svend. *The Modern City*, New York: Prentice-Hall, 1952.

*Riesman, David. "Abundance for What?" In *Problems of United States Economic Development*, Vol. I. New York: Committee for Economic Development, 1958, pp. 223-34. Also *Bulletin of the Atomic Scientist*, 14 (1958), 135-39.

_____. *Faces in the Crowd*, New Haven: Yale University Press, 1952.

*_____. "The Found Generation," *American Scholar*, 25 (Autumn, 1956).

_____. *Individualism Reconsidered*, Glencoe, Ill.: Free Press, 1954.

*_____. Introduction to *Crestwood Heights*, by John R. Seeley, R. Alexander Sims, and Elizabeth W. Loosely, New York: Basic Books, 1957.

_____. "A Lecture on Veblen," *The Journal of General Education* (April, 1952).

*†_____. "Leisure and Work in Post-Industrial Society," in Larrabee, Eric, and Rolf Meyersohn, eds. *Mass Leisure*, Glencoe, Ill.: Free Press, 1958.

*_____. *The Oral Tradition, the Written Word, and the Screen Image*, Antioch College Founders Day Lecture, Yellow Springs, Ohio: Antioch Press, 1956.

_____. "Recreation and the Recreationist," *Marriage and Family Living*, 14 (Feb., 1954).

_____. "Some Clinical and Cultural Aspects of Aging," *American Journal of Sociology*, 59 (1954), 379-83.

_____. "Some Observations on Changes in Leisure Attitudes," *Antioch Review*, 12 (1952), 417-36.

*_____. "Some Questions about the Mass Media," Speech delivered to the Radio and Television Research Council, New York, April, 1957.

*_____. "The Suburban Dislocation," *Annals of the American Academy*, 314 (1957), 123-46.

*_____. "The Suburban Sadness," in Dobriner, William, ed. *The Suburban Community*, New York: G. B. Putnam's Sons, 1958, pp. 375-408.

_____. "The Themes of Work and Play in the Structure of Freud's Thought," *Psychiatry*, 13 (1950), 1-16.

*_____. "Tocqueville and Associations: An Introduction," *Autonomous Groups' Bulletin*, 12 (1956), 1-3.

_____. "Veblen's System of Social Science," *Explorations*, 1 (Dec., 1953).

*_____, and Warner Bloomberg. "Work and Leisure: Fusion or Polarity?" In Arensberg, Conrad M., *et al*, eds. *Research in Industrial Human Relations: A Critical Appraisal*, New York: Harper & Bros., 1957, pp. 69-85. Revised version appeared in *Way Forum*, World Assembly of Youth, Paris, 1958.

_____, and Reuel Denney. "Football in America," *American Quarterly*, 3 (1951), 309-19.

_____. "Leisure in Urbanized America," in Hatt, Paul K., and Albert J. Reiss, Jr., eds. *Reader in Urban Sociology*, Glencoe, Ill.: Free Press, 1951.

_____, and Nathan Glazer. *The Lonely Crowd*, New Haven: Yale University Press, 1950.

*_____, and Eric Larrabee. "Autos in America: Manifest and Latent Destiny," *The Voice*, 22 (1957), 4-18 [published by Carleton College, Northfield, Minnesota]. Also Clark, Lincoln H., ed. *Consumer Behavior*, New York: Harper & Bros., 1958, pp. 69-92.

Rife, Stanley M. *The Public and Voluntary Recreation Services of a Medium-sized City*. Unpublished Ph.D. Dissertation, University of Chicago, 1951.

Robbins, Florence Greenhoe. *The Sociology of Play, Recreation and Leisure*, Dubuque, Iowa: Wm. C. Brown Co., 1955.

Robertson, Fyfe. "Would It Be a Curse or a Blessing to Have Leisure Unlimited?" *Picture Post* (April 2, 1955), 13-16.

Robertson, J. P. S. "Leisure Activities in Relation to Neuropsychiatric Diagnosis and Treatment," *Journal of Clinical Psychology*, 13 (1957), 56-58.

*Rolin, Babette, and Val Lorwin. "Changes in Consumer and Leisure Habits of the French Worker," Chicago: Center for the Study of Leisure, 1957. (Mimeographed.)

Rose, Alwin W. "Toward Understanding the Concept and Function of Play," *Educational Theory*, 6 (1956), 20-25+.

Rosenberg, Bernard, and David Manning White, eds., *Mass Culture*, Glencoe, Ill.: Free Press, 1957.

Rosenberger, H. T. "Wise Use of Leisure Time," *Bulletin of the National Association of Secondary-School Principals*, 40 (1957), 281-97.

Rottenberg, Simon. "Income and Leisure in an Underdeveloped Economy," *Journal of Political Economy*, 60 (1952), 95-101.

Rowntree, Benjamin Seebohm, and G. R. Lovers. *English Life and Leisure*, New York: Longmans, Green & Co., 1951.

†Russell, Bertrand. *In Praise of Idleness and Other Essays*, London: George Allen & Unwin, Ltd., 1954.

Russell Sage Foundation. *Five Hundred Over Sixty*, by Bernard Kutner *et al*. New York, 1956.

Seeley, John R., R. Alexander Sim, and Elizabeth W. Loosley. *Crestwood Heights*, New York: Basic Books, Inc., 1956.

Seligman, Daniel. "The Four-Day Week: How Soon?" *Fortune* (July, 1954), 81ff.
Shaffer, Helen B. "Four-Day Week," *Editorial Research Reports,* 1, 18 (May, 1957), 345-62.
Sheldon, M. "Leisure," *Food for Thought,* 15 (1954), 34-36.
Shock, Nathan. *A Classified Bibliography of Gerontology and Geriatrics,* Stanford: Stanford University Press, 1951. Supplement I, 1949-1955.
"The Shorter Workweek," *Management Record,* 19 (1957), 122-33.
Sieker, John H. "Recreation on the National Forest," *Annals of the American Academy,* 313 (1957), 126-31.
Sills, David. *The Volunteers,* Glencoe: Free Press, 1958.
Simmel, Georg. *The Sociology of Georg Simmel.* Translated by Kurt H. Wolff. Glencoe, Ill.: Free Press, 1950.
Singleton, James W. *Meanings of Work and Attitudes Toward Retirement among Steelworkers.* Unpublished Ph.D. Dissertation, University of Chicago, 1954.
"Sitting and Thinking," *Times Literary Supplement,* 2879 (1957), 273.
Smith, Patricia Cain. "The Curve of Output as a Criterion of Boredom," *Journal of Applied Psychology,* 37 (1953), 69-74.
______. "The Prediction of Individual Differences in Susceptibility to Industrial Monotony," *Journal of Applied Psychology,* 39 (1955), 322-29.
"Social Reform, Production and Leisure," *Social Justice Review,* 46 (1953), 90.
Soule, George. "The Economics of Leisure," *Annals of the American Academy,* 313 (1957), 16-24.
______. "Free Time—Man's New Resource," in Donahue, Wilma, *et al,* eds. *Free Time,* Ann Arbor: University of Michigan Press, 1958, pp. 61-76.
______. *Time for Living,* New York: Viking Press, Inc., 1955.
______. *What Automation Does to People,* London: Sidgwick & Jackson, Ltd., 1956.
Spiritual Statesmanship Conference on the New Leisure. "Problems and Challenges of the New Leisure," New York: The Jewish Theological Seminary of America, 1956. (Mimeographed.)
Staley, Eugene, ed. *Creating an Industrial Civilization,* New York: Harper & Bros., 1952.
Star, Shirley A. "Obtaining Household Opinion from a Single Respondent," *Public Opinion Quarterly,* 17 (1953), 386-91.
Starrak, J. A. "Leisure-time Activities of Iowa High School Students," *Midland Schools,* 64 (1950), 14-15.
Steere, Douglas Van. *Work and Contemplation,* New York: Harper & Bros., 1957.
Stevens, M. "Leisure: Hours of Labor," *Information,* 71 (1957), 55-60.
Stewart, Charles D. "The Shortening Work Week as a Component of Economic Growth," *American Economic Review,* 46 (May, 1956), 211-17.
______. "A Shorter Workweek as a Factor in Economic Growth," *Monthly Labor Review* (Feb., 1956), 157-60.
Stewart, Mary. "The Leisure Activities of Grammar School Children," *British Journal of Educational Psychology,* 20 (1950), 11-34.
†Stone, Gregory. "American Sports: Play and Dis-play," *Chicago Review,* 9 (1955), 83-100.
†______. "Research into the Human Element of Wilderness Use," in *Proceedings, Society of American Foresters, 1956,* Washington: the Society, 1956.
______. "Some Meanings of American Sports," *Proceedings,* 60th Annual Meeting, College Physical Education Association, Columbus, Ohio, 1957.
"Straw Vote Shows Members Prefer Fewer Work Days," *Oil, Chemical & Atomic Union News,* 12 (1957), 1.
Stuart, Margaret. "Boredom in a Case of Depression, *Psychoanalytic Quarterly,* 20 (1951), 346.
Sullenger, T. Earl, *et al.* "The Leisure Time Activities of Elementary School Children," *Journal of Educational Research,* 46 (1953), 551-54.
"Summer Problems of Children," *Ave Maria,* 83 (1956), 6.
Super, Donald E., and Jack W. Dunlap. "Interest in Work and Play," in Fryer, Douglas H., and Erwin R. Henry, *Handbook of Applied Psychology,* New York: Rinehart & Co., Inc., 1950.
Sussman, Marvin B. "Activity Patterns of Post-Parental Couples and Their Relationship to Family Continuity," *Marriage and Family Living,* 17 (1955), 338-41.
______. "Leisure: Bane or Blessing?" *Social Work,* 1 (1956), 11-18.
Sutherland, Willard C. "A Philosophy of Leisure," *Annals of the American Academy,* 313 (1957), 1-3.
†Swados, Harvey. "Less Work—Less Leisure," *Nation* (Feb. 22, 1958), 153-58.
Swensen, Jean, and Jessie Rhulman. "Leisure Activities of a University Sophomore Class," *Educational and Psychological Measurement,* 12 (1952), 452-66.
Sykes, Gresham. *Social Mobility and Social Participation.* Unpublished Ph.D. Dissertation, Northwestern University, 1954.
"Synthetic Recreation," *Today,* 8 (1953), 2.
"Taking People Way from Their Work," *Social Justice Review,* 49 (1956), 158.
Taylor, Gordon Rattray. "The Problem of Leisure," *World Review* (Aug., 1951), 33-36.
Thomas, Lawrence G. "Leisure Pursuits by Socio-economic Strata," *Journal of Educational Sociology,* 29 (1956), 367-77.
Tibbitts, Clark. "Aging as a Modern Social Achievement," in Donahue, Wilma, *et al,* eds. *Free Time,* Ann Arbor: University of Michigan Press, 1958, pp. 17-28.
Trow, William Clarke. *Recreation and Leisure,* New York: McGraw-Hill Book Co., 1951.
Tully, R. W. "Play and Recreation," in Lotz, Philip Henry, ed. *Orientation in Religious*

Education, New York: Abington-Cokesbury Press, 1950.

Tyson, R. "Work and Play," *Journal of Clinical Psychology,* 7 (1951), 74-78.

UAW-CIO Education Department. "Automation and the Short Workweek," in *Automation,* Detroit, 1955, pp. 25-27. (Publication Number 331.)

"Updates: Leisure," *Business Week* (Oct. 10, 1953), 54.

U. S. Department of Agriculture, Forest Service. *National Forest Recreation,* Washington, 1957. (Part 1 of *Operation Outdoors.*)

U. S. Department of Commerce, Bureau of the Census. *Preliminary Report on 1957 Travel Survey,* Washington, 1957.

†______, Small Business Administration. "The Do-It-Yourself Market," *Business Service Bulletin #84,* Washington, 1954.

U. S. Department of Labor, Bureau of Labor Standards. *They Work While You Play: A Study of Teen-age Boys and Girls Employed in Amusement Industries,* Washington, 1950. (Bulletin 124.)

U. S. Department of Labor, Bureau of Labor Statistics. *Automatic Technology and Its Implications. A Selected Annotated Bibliography,* Washington, 1956. (Bulletin 1198)

______. *Productivity: A Bibliography,* Washington, 1957. (Bulletin 1226)

______. "Shorter Hours of Work," Monthly Labor Review, 79 (November 1956). (Reprint 2211.)

U. S. Department of the Interior, Fish and Wild Life Service. *National Survey of Fishing and Hunting,* Washington, 1955. (Circular 44.) Also, *Sports Illustrated,* 5 (Sept. 17, 1956), 33-35.

*"The Uses of Leisure." Special issue. *American Journal of Sociology,* 62, 6 (1957).

Von Eckhardt, Ursula. *The Inalienable Right to the Pursuit of Happiness.* Unpublished Ph.D. Dissertation, New School for Social Research, 1953.

Walsh, V. C. "Leisure and International Trade," *Economica,* 23 (1956), 253-60.

Ward, J. C. "Children's Leisure," *Nature,* 168 (1951), 649-50.

Warden, William L. "The Cruiser Craze," *Holiday,* 16 (1954), 61-64.

Waterman, Leroy. "Religion and Religious Observance," in Donahue, Wilma, *et al,* eds. *Free Time,* Ann Arbor: University of Michigan Press, 1958, pp. 133-40.

Wattenberg, William W. "Family Recreation and Delinquency," *Focus,* 29 (1950), 6-9.

Wax, Rosalie H. "Free Time in Other Cultures," in Donahue, Wilma, *et al,* eds. *Free Time,* Ann Arbor: University of Michigan Press, 1958, pp. 3-16.

Webb, R. K. *The British Working Class Reader, 1790-1848.* London: George Allen & Unwin, Ltd., 1955.

Webber, Irving L., ed. *Aging: A Current Appraisal,* Gainesville: University of Florida, 1956.

______. "The Organized Social Life of the Retired: Two Florida Communities," *American Journal of Sociology,* 59 (1954), 340-46.

Welch, C. D. "Leisure Time Activities of Langston University Faculty Members," *Research Quarterly,* 24 (1953), 368-69.

Wendt, G. L. "More Time Tomorrow," *Journal of the National Education Association,* 46 (1957), 431-32.

West, S. L. *Have We Time for Reflection?* Gainesville, Fla.: University of Florida Bureau of Economic and Business Research, 1955. (Economic Leaflets, 14, Number 4.)

What's Happening to Leisure Time in Television Homes, New York: Batten, Barton, Durstine & Osborn, Inc., 1951. (Pamphlet.)

Wheatley, M. E., Jr. "All Work and No Play," *Journal of Health, Physical Education, and Recreation,* 28 (1957), 21-22.

"Where Leisure Time—and Money—Go . . ." *Business Week* (Sept. 12, 1953), 142-49.

†White, R. Clyde. "Social Class Differences in the Uses of Leisure," *American Journal of Sociology,* 61 (1955), 145-50.

White, Virginia Kann. *Measuring Leisure-Time Needs; a Report of the Group Work Council Research Project,* Cleveland: Welfare Federation of Cleveland, 1955.

Whyte, William H., Jr. *Is Anybody Listening?* New York: Simon & Schuster, 1952.

______. *The Organization Man,* New York: Simon & Schuster, 1956.

Williams, A. R. "Organized Leisure Among Secondary School Children, *Parents' Review* (June, 1951), 158-61.

Williams, Wayne R. *Recreation Places,* New York: Reinhold Publishing Corp., 1958.

Windholz, Emanuel. "Types of Boredom and Their Dynamics," *Psychoanalytic Quarterly,* 20 (1951), 345.

†Wolfenstein, Martha. "The Emergence of Fun Morality," *Journal of Social Issues,* 7 (1951), 3-16.

Wood, Margaret Mary. *Paths of Loneliness; the Individual Isolated in Modern Society,* New York: Columbia University Press, 1953.

Woody, Thomas. "Leisure in the Light of History," *Annals of the American Academy,* 313 (1957), 4-10.

†Wright, Charles, and Herbert Hyman. "Voluntary Association Membership," *American Sociological Review,* 23 (1958), 284-94.

Wylie, J. A., *ed.* "Education for Leisure." Special issue. *Education,* 71 (1950), 67-132.

______. "Survey of 504 Families to Determine the Relationships between Certain Factors and the Nature of the Family Recreation Program," *Research Quarterly,* 24 (1953), 229-43.

Yang, L. S. "Schedules of Work and Rest in Imperial China," *Harvard Journal of Asiatic Studies,* 18 (1955), 301-25.

---

*A publication of the Center for the Study of Leisure, the University of Chicago.
†Included in this volume.

Index

Index